CREDITS

Introductions Ronny Worsey
Researchers Alex Cameron, Jenny Carp,
Rehma Chandaria, Catherine Laurence,
Nadia Muscella, Nhatt Nichols,
Ronny Worsey
Design Irene Schneider studioloka.com.au
Photos Mike Bourke
michaelbourkephotography.com
Vicky Alhadeff happydogsandcats.co.uk
Maps Alexandra Boylan, Jenny Carp,
Mickaël Charbonnel, Jill Spence
Additional photos Tony Bishop Weston,
Alex Bourke, Alex Cameron, Jenny Carp,
Mickaël Charbonnel, Chava Eichner,
Clare Emery, Catherine Laurence, Nadia
Muscella, Ronny Worsey, the entries.
Veggie Guides logo Marion Gillet
mariongillet.com
Local contributors: Vicky Alhadeff, Aniel,
Barry Austin, Carole Backler, Jagtar Behal,
Emily Bennett, Johanna Best, Lukasz Birycki,
Vida Blackmoor, Jasmijn de Boo,
Sonia Burrows, Dawn Carr, Alison Coe,
Peter Despard, Lesley & Paul Dove,
Paul Gaynor, David Gore, Jonathan Grey,
Caitlin Galer-Unti, Hassan, Ona Helveti,
Brian Jacobs, Ayda Kay, Lily Khan,
Christine Klein, Laurence Klein,
Orna Klement, Andrew Knight, Robin Lane,
everyone at London Vegan Meetup and
London Vegans, London Vegan Campaigns,
Robb Masters, Caroline McAleese,
Nitin Mehta M.B.E., Åsa Melander,
Thomas Micklewright, Richard Molyneux,
Shivani Parikh, Amrit Patel, Rudy Penando,
Miriam Rice, Julie Rosenfield, Dawn Rowley,
Lia Saywhat, Bani Sethi,
Mahersh & Nishma Shah, Kim Shankar,
Kelly Slade, Paul Standeven, Hannah
Thrush, Maeve Tomlinson, Patricia Tricker,
Amran Vance, Jennifer Wharton,
Laura Wood, and everyone else **THANK
YOU**!

ABOUT THE EDITOR

Alex Bourke is the world's leading vegan
travel publisher, having produced 21 UK
and European Vegan Guides. He has
previously worked at one of Britain's highest
profile vegan outreach organisations Viva!,
is a former Chair and media spokesperson
for the Vegan Society, and from 2010 until
2018 was the monthly travel columnist at
the UK's biggest selling vegetarian lifestyle
magazine *Vegetarian Living*.

Alex makes it easy and fun to be vegan
anywhere, publishing comprehensive vegan
guides with local experts across Britain and
beyond. He wrote and co-produced the
documentary *Animal Rights*, which is used in
Citizenship classes in schools across Britain.
He has led vegan and publishing workshops
at vegan festivals on four continents. He has
been interviewed by *The Guardian* and *The
Times*, and appeared on many tv, national
and local radio programmes, including *The
Big Breakfast* with Johnny Vaughan, *Late
Night London* with Victoria Derbyshire, *The
Food Programme*, *Farming Today*, Excess
Baggage, and French tv channels *ARTE*,
EBN and *TF1*.

CONTENTS

Vegan London complete

EAST LONDON

Shoreditch & Hoxton

Brick Lane & Spitalfields

Bethnal Green

Canary Wharf

Dalston & Haggerston

Green Street & High Street North

Hackney

Homerton

Ilford

London Fields

Lower Clapton

Stratford

Walthamstow & beyond

NORTH LONDON

Brecknock Road

Camden

Crouch End

Edgware

Finchley

Finsbury Park & Stroud Green

Golders Green

Hampstead

Hendon & Brent Cross

Highgate

Holloway Road

Islington

Kentish Town

Kings Cross

Mill Hill Broadway

Muswell Hill

Stoke Newington & Newington Green

West Hampstead

Wood Green & Turnpike Lane

Rest of North London

SOUTH LONDON

Brixton

Clapham & Battersea

Croydon & Thornton Heath

Deptford & New Cross

Dulwich

Elephant & Castle

Greenwich

Kingston-upon-Thames

Peckham

Putney & Wandsworth

Richmond-on-Thames

Streatham

Tooting & Balham

Vauxhall

KEYS

Each entry is colour coded on the maps.
- Vegan
- Vegetarian
- Omnivorous
- Shop
- Other (accommodation, group)

Symbols for restaurant and shop details:
- Address
- Telephone number
- Opening hours M Tu W Th F Sa Su BH bank holiday
- Closest underground, station or bus
- Website or social media page

Wine: small glass 125ml, medium 175ml, large 250ml, carafe 500ml, bottle 750ml

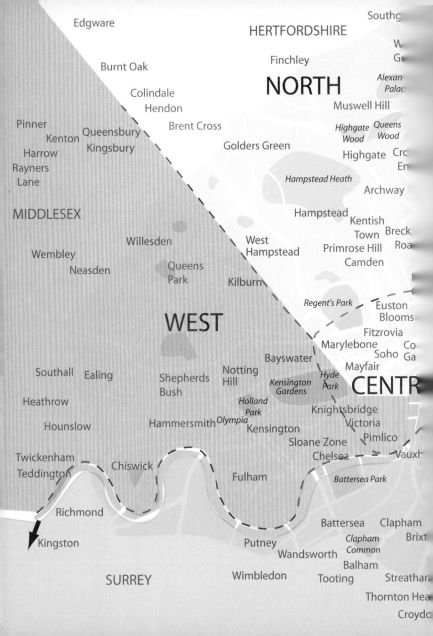

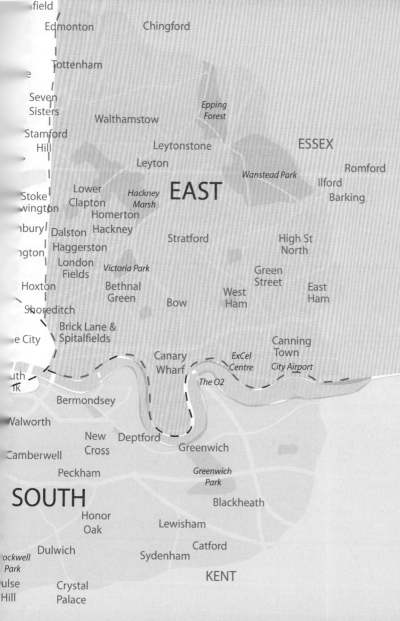

field

Edmonton   Chingford

Tottenham

Seven
Sisters
                    Epping
                    Forest
Stamford   Walthamstow
Hill
              Leytonstone   ESSEX

              Leyton   Romford
                        Wanstead Park
Stoke   Lower   EAST   Ilford
wington Clapton Hackney   Barking
         Marsh
         Homerton
bury Dalston Hackney
gton   Stratford   High St
     Haggerston   North
     London   Victoria Park
     Fields   Green
Hoxton Bethnal   Street East
        Green   Bow   West   Ham
Shoreditch   Ham
     Brick Lane &
e City Spitalfields
                          Canning
                Canary   ExCel Town
                Wharf   Centre City Airport
uth   The O2
k
     Bermondsey

Walworth
        New   Deptford
Camberwell Cross   Greenwich

     Peckham   Greenwich
                    Park
SOUTH   Blackheath

     Honor   Lewisham
     Oak
              Catford
ockwell Dulwich Sydenham
Park
ulse   Crystal   KENT
Hill   Palace

9

INTRO

Why I love London Town
Top areas to explore
Cheap days out
Getting around London with Oyster

WHY I LOVE LONDON TOWN

London is unique. If you ask a hundred people what it's like, you'll get a hundred different answers. It's a collection of villages, a sprawling metropolis, a blend of old and new, a thousand years of history and architecture, a seat of democracy, a public transport showcase, a traffic nightmare, and a melting pot of every culture in the world.

London is more than a city. It's one of the most important and famous places on the planet, and it's probably featured in more songs, films and stories than anywhere else. Every British person recalls their first childhood visit, and most of the world have it high on their list of dream destinations.

For me, London is quite simply the best place in Britain to get vegan food. Though Brighton, Edinburgh and Glasgow are contenders for the crown with their all-vegan pubs and tourist-pleasing restaurants, they don't even come close when it comes to providing a wide range of meat-free meals from around the world. In London, you'll find egg and dairy-free bakeries, raw food cafes and vegan buffets, not to mention all-vegan Indian, Mediterranean and Chinese restaurants. London's blend of ethnic communities means you won't struggle to find traditional vegan snacks like falafels, Jamaican patties, Ethiopian injera and kosher bagels. The choice and range of food is bewildering, and you can literally eat at a different vegan place every day for six months.

London covers 611 square miles (1,583 sq km), has eight million residents, and some districts are crowded with narrow streets, so it can be daunting trying to find your way around. We've included maps and descriptions of the different areas to help you out. As a general guide, the East End is full of markets and is the cheapest part of town, West London is grander and leafier, the North is the most diverse and the South has a strong community spirit. Central London is a patchwork of business and residential areas, where glittering high-rise offices and luxury flats stand beside Victorian terraced streets and post-war Council estates. Food and accommodation prices in the centre tend to be significantly higher than further out of town. It's well worth picking up an Oyster Card from any rail or tube station ticket window, as this makes travelling much cheaper and easier.

You'll find every cultural pursuit imaginable in London, from punk gigs to ballroom dancing, from gigantic West End 3D cinemas to activist films in squats. The range of eateries is similar, with everything from backstreet take-aways where you can fill up for a fiver, through great value buffets, to gourmet organic and raw food places that'll set you back £40 a head.

London has a much higher proportion of vegans than anywhere else in Britain, with plenty of social and campaigning groups to join if you want to meet like-minded people. There are vegan festivals each year: Vegan Life Live at Alexandra Palace early in the year, Vegfest at Olympia in October, Animal Aid Christmas Festival in Kensington in December, and Vegan Nights in Brick Lane several times each year. You'll also find loads of smaller events such as vegan markets, Vevolution, London Vegan Meetup's monthly Vegan Drinks and See You Last Tuesday (C.U.L.T.), food tastings, cookery demos and pot luck parties.

13

TOP AREAS TO EXPLORE

Bloomsbury

This has always been an arty, literary district full of small businesses that's got a community feel. It's just to the south of Euston and King's Cross and is dominated by university buildings, Great Ormond Sreet Children's Hospital and the British Museum, so its cafes and shops attract quite a mixed crowd.

Camden Town

One of the most visited parts of London, particularly on summer weekends, when the high street heaves with shoppers seeking urban fashion. The markets by the canal specialise in crafts, with everything from antique mirrors to hand-made soaps. Camden used to have no veggie cafes at all, but in recent years many excellent vegan market stalls and restaurants have opened. Regent's Park is a short walk along the canal.

Covent Garden

Covent Garden boasts talented street performers, classical musicians, opera and ballet. It also has some unusual shops, such as Neal's Yard Remedies, an astrology shop and some vegan cafes. The area has an exclusive feel, with prices to match.

The City (financial district)

A square mile of banks and high-rise offices with a very clinical feel, with ancient alleys and stone buildings tucked away in between. Names like Threadneedle Street give clues about the area's history. Few tourists venture here, except to visit St Paul's cathedral. Vegan food is most easily found north of Liverpool Street Station, and around the Barbican arts centre.

Finchley and Golders Green

The Jewish part of London, with lots of kosher, dairy-free food. Many visitors park here and get the tube into the centre of the city.

Hackney

Possibly the most multi-cultural part of London, Hackney is full of cheap cafes and gets better for vegan food each year.

Hammersmith and Fulham

A mostly residential, quite upmarket part of London, filled with gastropubs.

Hampstead

A quiet, posh place filled with pretty Edwardian terraces, small cafes and relaxed restaurants. Grab some picnic food and spend an afternoon roaming Hampstead Heath, or climb Primrose Hill for great views of the city, then head down to Camden and spoil yourself with a vegan feast.

Islington

A fashionable place for professionals to hang out. Densely-packed streets with few open spaces, but lots of small theatres, cafes and cocktail bars.

King's Cross

A public transport hub, with the Eurostar terminal, main line trains, tube and bus.

The area features a vegan Japanese restaurant, a branch of Mildreds, and the x boutique, which sells vegan cheese, akes and biscuits.

Shoreditch and Hoxton

Hoxton is the place to pose. Arty types, web designers, retro cyclists and cool kids abound. There has been a flurry of recent vegan openings, making Shoreditch the top area for vegan dining out, and you can also walk a few minutes to adjoining Brick Lane & Spitalfields or The City, or hop on a bus to Hackney or Islington.

Soho

A grid of narrow streets that run to the south of Oxford Street, Soho features cinemas, fabric shops, record shops and cafes, plus fruit and veg stalls staffed by traditional Cockney barrow boys. It's a buzzing, fun place both day and night. The far south end of Berwick St has a sleazy feel, with "adult" video shops. Covent Garden is to the east, Fitzrovia to the north, Mayfair to the west, Trafalgar Square and Chinatown to the south.

Spitalfields and Brick Lane

This area is fashionable and fun in a cheap kind of way. Spitalfields Market is best visited on a Sunday. It's full of clothes stalls, where you can kit yourself out with a totally individual new look, then grab some artisan bread, olives and fresh juice. If you fancy a huge box of raw salad, head for the Mel Tropical stall. Around the edge are some veggie-friendly cafes with a relaxed, sociable atmosphere. The south end of Brick Lane has a large Bangladeshi community, with lots of vegan curry options, and two vegan cafes, while the middle has a dozen vegan food stalls at weekends more vegan cafes. Or you can head off to eat and drink in Shoreditch.

CHEAP DAYS OUT

Follow the canal to Camden Lock and Regent's Park

Spend a relaxing morning browsing stalls in Camden Market, with breakfast at Nectar Cafe or one of the vegan stalls, then stock up on picnic food at Whole Foods Market or Holland & Barrett and take a stroll along the canal to Regent's Park. The West End (Soho) is then a short hop away, or you can continue along the canal to Paddington.

Roam the Heath

Hampstead Heath is so wild and attractive that it's hard to believe you're in the heart of London. It's the perfect place to let kids and dogs run around, while you relax under a tree. Get the overground train to Hampstead Heath station and load up on picnic food at House of Mistry Wholefoods or Friendly Falafels, then it's less than five minutes walk to the heath itself. For the evening, both Hampstead and Camden have some friendly, lively pubs with outdoor seating, or you could try Primrose Hill. If you'd prefer to carry on walking, take the Northern Line southwards and head over to Regent's Park. If you're tired of fresh air and crave the city lights, stay on a few more stops to reach Leicester Square.

Hang out in Hackney

On a warm Saturday morning, go for a swim at the London Fields Lido (a huge, heated outdoor swimming pool), then take a stroll through the food stalls of bustling Broadway Market and its separate vegan market, and relax for a while in London Fields park. Walk north up Mare Street to Temple of Hackney for vegan fried chick'n or Black Cat Cafe for a huge slice of vegan cake, or head south toward Bethnal Green to check out one of its vegan restaurants.

Shop 'til you drop, then take in art

Walk the full length of Oxford Street for every chain store you could wish for, then just before Tottenham Court Road. At the Selfridges end you can grab a bite at Mae Deli (behind Bond Street tube), while towards the Tottenham Court Road end turn south down the narrow streets of Soho to get some sit-down grub at Govinda's or Mildreds or Vantra Loungevity, or grab and go at Whole Foods Market. The bookshops of Charing Cross Road are then a short walk away.

At the bottom of Charing Cross Road you'll reach Trafalgar Square, with the National Gallery and National Portrait Gallery, which are both free. The cinemas and theatres of Leicester Square are also nearby. Another good food option is Tibits in Mayfair, a vegetarian buffet with loads of choice, which is midway between Oxford Circus and Piccadilly Circus.

Get your fill of Museums

The Science Museum, Victoria & Albert Museum and Natural History Museum are right next to each other in South Kensington and all are free to enter (through there are also special exhibitions that charge admission). You can then do the tourist thing and walk along Brompton

PLANT POWERED
INDIAN FOOD

BUILD A SPICEBOX

	BABY SPICE	BIG SPICE
1 Main	£5	£8
2 Mains	£6	£9
(SASSY SPICE)		

MAIN :
JACKFRUIT TIKKA MASALA
TANDOORI CAULIFLOWER STEAK
SEASONAL SPECIAL

BASE :
BROWN BASMATI RICE
QUINOA PILAU

SIDES (all inc.) :
INDIAN SLAW, RAITA, CHUTNEY
PICKLES, CASHEWS + CRISPY ONIONS

100% PLANT BASED. ASK ABOUT ALLERGENS

spicebox

JACKFRUIT
TIKKA MASALA   SEASONAL SPECIAL   TANDOORI
CAULI STEAK

oad to Harrods, or head north up xhibition Road into Hyde Park. There are several raw food cafes around here, and Wulf & Lamb vegan restaurant at Sloane Square. Otherwise take the Piccadilly Line from Knightsbridge or Hyde Park Corner to Leicester Square or Covent Garden.

From the North side of Hyde Park, you can walk into Notting Hill, or take the Central Line from Marble Arch to Oxford Circus or Tottenham Court Road. Alternatively, walk up Edgware Road and check out one of the many Lebanese cafes, where you can get lovely falafel, stuffed vine leaves and fresh juices such as pineapple and melon, or one block away is The Gate in Marylebone. On the south side of Hyde Park are Lebanese restaurants around Kensington, though beware that some of them are quite a bit pricier than others.

Walk the South Bank

If you set off from Westminster tube station and cross the Thames via Westminster Bridge, you can do an excellent two-mile walk. The embankment footpath takes you past the London Eye ferris wheel, the National Film Theatre and the Oxo Tower, with stunning views north across the river. After passing Blackfriars Bridge, you reach the Tate Modern gallery and the Globe Theatre, a reconstruction of an Elizabethan theatre that hosts Shakespeare plays. You then have to turn right and head inland along Southwark Bridge Road, then left along Southwark Street through the excellent Borough Market, which is a great place to get food. Carry on past Southwark Cathedral, Borough Market and London Bridge Station to cross the river again via Tower Bridge, or finish your walk at the station.

You can get great veggie food at Tibits Bankside swish Swiss vegetarian buffet restaurant, behind the Tate Modern, at various places around London Bridge, and By Chloe vegan restaurant at the south end of Tower Bridge. Alternatively, do the walk in reverse and book a meal at Bonnington Cafe in Vauxhall (open lunchtimes and evenings, but not afternoons), or head north towards Charing Cross and Trafalgar Square for Soho.

Go Womble-spotting

Get the train or District Line tube to Wimbledon, then 10 minutes' walk along Wimbledon Hill Road brings you to the famous common, which is a lovely, wild place to stroll. If you want even more exercise, cross the road bordering the north-west of the common to enter Richmond Park, which is even bigger and has herds of red and fallow deer, along with ancient trees, birds and unusual beetles. You can get a decent meal in Richmond from The Retreat Cafe, Tide Tables, Hollyhock or Bhuti, or take the District Line or a bus back into London.

Plan your trip with the official Visit London travel guide, covering attractions, sightseeing, getting around and what's on.

www.visitlondon.com

UNDERGROUND

GETTING AROUND - THE WORLD'S YOUR OYSTER

The underground train network in London is referred to as both "the London Underground" and "the Tube." This is our equivalent to the Paris Metro or the New York Subway. Tube stations are very close together in the centre of the city (Zone 1) and grow much further apart as you reach the outskirts (Zone 6). Tube trains are fast and frequent, though some lines are more reliable than others. You'll rarely have to wait more than three or four minutes for a train on the Northern, Victoria, Piccadilly or Central Lines, whereas the District and the Hammersmith and City Lines in particular can have much longer gaps between trains.

In addition to the Tube, you can get Overground trains, which link up with some Tube stations and cost the same, so they can just be thought of as an extension of the Tube. There is also a very cheap network of buses which run until late and often 24 hours.

The first thing to do in London is collect a free tube map and buy an Oyster Card from a ticket window at any mainline train or main tube station, ticket machines (especially when there is no ticket office open) or many local newsagent shops. Alternatively, you can buy a card online from almost anywhere in the world and have it posted to you, which means you won't have to risk standing in a queue. The card costs £5, but this is a returnable deposit that you can get back if you leave London for good.

The Oyster card works by storing credit to use on public transport anywhere in London. Instead of having to buy tickets from machines, you simply touch your card to a sensor at ticket barriers or when getting on a bus, which deducts the cost of travel. Not only is this really quick and easy, but you pay significantly less. If you end up making loads of journeys in one day, the card caps your spend at the daily Travelcard rate, so you don't have to worry about spending more money if your plans change.

You can register your card to your name and address. Then top it up and check the balance online, and cancel your card if it is lost or stolen. You can also get the card anonymously with no personal data linked to it.

How much can you save?
Here are some examples, (correct prices as at Novemberr 2019):

Single, peak-time tube journey between zones 1 and 2 :

» £4.90 without Oystercard,
» £2.90 with Oystercard

Single, off-peak tube journey between zones 1 and 2:

» £4.90 without Oystercard,
» £2.40 with Oystercard

So ... to give an example: I want to make a return journey from Victoria Station (zone 1) to Camden Town (zone 2), after 9.30am. If I buy two tube tickets, it will cost £9.80. If I use an Oystercard, it will cost only £4.80.

A full day's travel in zones 1 and 2 with an Oystercard is capped at £7. This is much less than buying a £13.10 Travelcard (all-day ticket).

Single, peak-time tube journey between zones 1 and 6 :

» £6 without Oystercard,
» £5.10 with Oystercard

Single, off-peak tube journey between zones 1 and 6 :

» £6 without Oystercard,
» £3.10 with Oystercard

Bus journey (any distance and any time of day):

» £1.50 with Oystercard
» £4.50 daily price cap with Oystercard if making multiple journeys

You cannot pay cash on buses.

You can change buses within one hour and swipe your card again and the second bus is free, this is called a Hopper fare.

www.tfl.gov.uk

oyster®

Transport for London

Issued subject to conditions - see over

CENTRAL LONDON

Soho
Bloomsbury
Covent Garden
Euston
Fitzrovia
Marylebone
Mayfair
South Bank
The City

* OUR TOP 5 - BEST OF CENTRAL LONDON *

Buffets
Diwana, Euston
Ravi Shankar, Euston
Tibits, Mayfair & South Bank
Vantra Eden lunch, Fitzrovia
Vantra Loungevity, Soho

Cosmetics
Alara, Bloomsbury
Health Food Centre, Fitzrovia
Lush, Oxford Street
Planet Organic, Bloomsbury
Whole Foods Market, Soho

Food Shopping & Snacks
Alara, Bloomsbury
Health Food Centre, Fitzrovia
Holland & Barrett
Planet Organic, Fitzrovia
Whole Foods Market, Soho

Juices & Raw Food
CPress, Fitzrovia
Raw Press, Mayfair
Redemption, Covent Garden
Vantra Loungevity, Soho
Wild Food Cafe, Covent Garden

Late night Soho
Wagamama, 23.30
Fiori Corner, 01.30, F/Sa 3am
Leggero, 23.00
Yorica , Th-Sa 01.00am

Lunch with friends
By Chloe, Covent Garden
Drummond Street Indian, Euston
Ethos, Fitzrovia
Sagar, Fitzrovia
Tibits, Mayfair

Picnic Spots
Golden Square, Soho
Gordon Sqare, Bloomsbury
Regents Park, Euston
Soho Square, Soho
St James's Park, Mayfair

Vegan Cake/Dessert
Mae Deli, Mayfair
Tibits vegan Tuesdays, Mayfair
Vantra Loungevity, SOho
Wild Food Cafe, Covent Garden
Yorica vegan ice-cream, Soho

West End Cafe
Govinda's, Soho
Kin Cafe, Fitzrovia
Mary Ward, Bloomsbury
Vantra Lougevity, Soho
Wild Food Cafe, Covent Garden

West End Dinner
By Chloe, Covent Garden
Coach & Horses, Soho
Ethos, Fitzrovia
Mildred's, Soho
Tibits, Mayfair

Neal's Yard

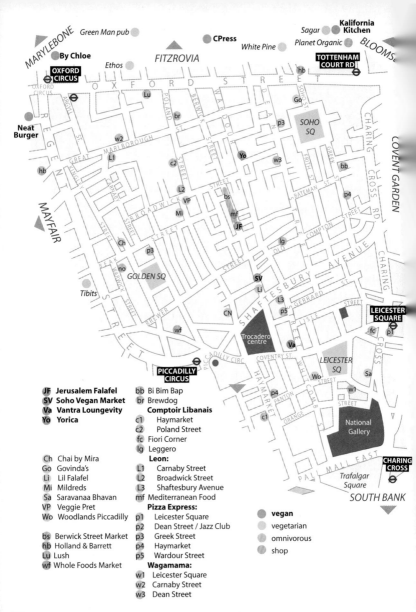

MARYLEBONE

Green Man pub

CPress

Sagar · Kalifornia Kitchen

White Pine · Planet Organic

BLOOMS

FITZROVIA

By Chloe

Ethos

OXFORD CIRCUS

OXFORD CIRCUS

TOTTENHAM COURT RD

hb

O X F O R D   S T R E E T

Lu

Go

SOHO ST

SOHO SQ

CHARING

br

p3

Neat Burger

w2

MARLBOROUGH STREET

L1

c2

Yo

w3

BERWICK STREET

FRITH STREET

GREEK STREET

bb

COVENT GARDEN

hb

MAYFAIR

L2

VP

Mi

bs

mf

BATEMAN STREET

p4

JF

lg

COMPTON STREET

Ch

p3

no

OLD

GOLDEN SQ

S H A F T E S B U R Y   A V E N U E

CHARING

Tibits

SV

Li

L3

GERRARD

p5

CARNABY STREET

WARDOUR STREET

BREWER STREET

CN

LEICESTER SQUARE

fc

p1

wf

Trocadero centre

Va

LEICESTER SQ

Sa

PICCADILLY CIRCUS

PICCADILLY CIRC

Coventry st.

Wo

w1

PANTON STREET

CHARING CROSS

HAYMARKET

c1

National Gallery

Trafalgar Square

SOUTH BANK

PALL MALL EAST

JF	Jerusalem Falafel	**bb**	Bi Bim Bap
SV	Soho Vegan Market	**br**	Brewdog
Va	Vantra Loungevity		**Comptoir Libanais**
Yo	Yorica	c1	Haymarket
		c2	Poland Street
		fc	Fiori Corner
		lg	Leggero
			Leon:
Ch	Chai by Mira	L1	Carnaby Street
Go	Govinda's	L2	Broadwick Street
Li	Lil Falafel	L3	Shaftesbury Avenue
Mi	Mildreds	mf	Mediterranean Food
Sa	Saravanaa Bhavan		**Pizza Express:**
VP	Veggie Pret	p1	Leicester Square
Wo	Woodlands Piccadilly	p2	Dean Street / Jazz Club
		p3	Greek Street
bs	Berwick Street Market	p4	Haymarket
hb	Holland & Barrett	p5	Wardour Street
Lu	Lush		**Wagamama:**
wf	Whole Foods Market	w1	Leicester Square
		w2	Carnaby Street
		w3	Dean Street

● **vegan**

● vegetarian

● omnivorous

● shop

SOHO

Central London

oho, the area to the south of Oxford treet, is the place for meeting friends in entral London. There are theatres, inemas, fashion shops, Trafalgar Square, he National Gallery, and some terrific vegetarian cafes and restaurants.

The map shows vegan places in pink, vegetarian in green, omnivorous in blue, and shops in orange, many new in the last few years. Most offer take-away at lunch time, perfect for a warm day in one of the parks or squares.

We can hardly contain our excitement at the opening of **Soho Vegan Market**, every Monday lunchtime, with around a dozen food stalls.

Vantra, in Chinatown at the south end of Wardour Street by Leicester Square, is Soho's only 100% vegan restaurant. It's also our favourite vegan restaurant in London, and the healthiest, with a sumptuous self-serve Asian and raw buffet for a reasonable £1.80 per 100 grams. And they have wine and raw vegan cakes.

Trailblazing **Yorica** on Wardour Street is the UK's first vegan ice cream parlour, and they also do pancakes.

Govinda's Hare Krsna restaurant does a great-value vegan Indian platter.

Top veggie cafes: Veggie Pret was the first 100% vegetarian branch of Pret A Manger, great for grab and go food or a coffee meet with a friend. For a leisurely latte try **Chai by Mira**, perhaps after a drop-in yoga class next door at Triyoga.

Vegetarian sit-down restaurants are **Mildreds** with international food and at night a party atmosphere, Indians **Woodlands** and **Saravanaa Bhavan**, and upmarket buffet restaurant **Tibits** (see Mayfair) which has an all vegan buffet on Tuesdays. Also check out **Neat Burger** vegan fast food at Oxford Circus (see Mayfair). Along the north side of Oxford Street (see Fitzrovia) are lots more vegan and vegetarian places to explore.

If you're with carnivorous mates who veto a veggie venue, there's plenty of vegan choice at Korean **Bi Bim Bap**, **Comptoir Libanais**, gluten-free Italian **Leggero**, **Leon, Pizza Express** which has vegan cheese, and Japanese **Wagamama**.

Whole Foods Market (previously Fresh & Wild) has moved from Brewer Street to Glasshouse Street. It's a wholefoods supermarket with fridges all along the back wall and several take-away counters at one end. The Oxford Street branch of budget health food chain **Holland & Barrett** has some real bargains for snacks and home cooking. For unpackaged soaps and other cosmetics, and just the aromas as you walk in, visit the **Lush** flagship store on Oxford Street.

...antra Loungevity
...gan restaurant

5 Wardour Street W1D 6PB
020 7287 5222
Tu-Sa 12.00-23.00, Su-M 13.00-20.00

Piccadilly Circus, Leicester Square

vantra.co.uk
facebook.com/VantraLondon

London's healthiest restaurant, combining their previous branches Vitao that was in Wardour Street and Vantra in Soho Square, continues their ever popular and unique slow food Asian fusion and living foods buffet from India, China, Japan, Korea, Malaysia and Thailand. It's perfect if you are into raw, macrobiotic or avoiding gluten, sugar or nuts. The guilt-free desserts are heavenly.

The all-day buffet of Asian and organic raw dishes is £1.80 per 100 grams. Dishes include Thai green and Malaysian yellow curies, chili non carne. mushroom stroganoff, moussaka, dim sum, chickpea curry, kimchi, korma, sweet and sour veg, noodles and salads.

Until 5pm you can get a great-value box of food to eat in for £7 small or £8 large. Take-away boxes available all day for 50p less.

Soup of the day £2.50 such as white bean with coriander.

Exquisite raw desserts £3.50-£5.50 taste divine and rich, a natural high demanding to be eaten slowly, such as chocolate brownie, creamy lemon cake, apple pie, blueberry fudge cake, chocolate ganache, raspberry chocolate tart, mango or strawberry cheesecake.

Fresh green coconut £5, take-away £4.50. Juices £3.30-£5.90 (take-away £3.10-£4.80).

Teas and coffee from £2.20, plus caffeine free alternatives such as lucuma or maca hot drinks, add superfoods 80p each. Also enzymatic drinks such as water kefir and kombucha.

Alcohol is all vegan organic with no sulphites. Wines £4.80 small glass, £21-£33 bottle. Sam Smith and other beers £4.80.

Children welcome, high chairs. Events, see website for what's coming. Another branch Vantra Eden in Fitzrovia open M-F 12.00-13.00.

Mildreds, Soho

Vegetarian restaurant

- ☛ 45 Lexington Street W1F 9AN
- ☎ 020 7494 1634
- 🕐 M-Sa 12.00-23.00, Su closed
- ⊖ Piccadilly Circus, Oxford Circus
- ↖ mildreds.co.uk
  facebook.com/mildredsrestaurant

Stylish vegetarian café-restaurant and take-away on two floors. with hip young clientele to match, crowded and enthusiastic. This is the top place in Soho for veggies going out for dinner and a bottle of wine. It can get quite noisy but is lots of fun.

The food is modern European with some Asian influences. Lots of healthy Mediterranean or stir-fry, but you can also have a burger and fries. Nowadays most of the food is vegan or vegan-option.

Mon-Fri lunchtime there is a daily changing self-serve salad bar, large £6.50, medium £5.25, small £4; also hot dishes which change daily such as bakes, stuffed aubergine, sweet potato curry, sitr-fry, and burgers, £4.50-7.50. Most of the menu is available as take-away.

Eat in starters £5-£7 such as soup, gyoza dumplings with dipping sauce, or tostada grilled courgettes and aubergine, lettuce, pico de gallo salsa and guacamole.

Many of the main courses £7-£11 are vegan, such as mixed mushroom, porcini and ale pie with mushy peas and fries; stir-fried Asian veg in sesame oil and teriyaki sauce with ginger and fresh chili on organic brown rice, organic marinated tofu and toasted cashews; organic detox salad; fennel and chickpea tagine with date and pistachio couscous.

Desserts £6.50 include banana to coconut cheesecake with maple syrup; w raspberry and dark chocolate truffle; fr crumble with (vegan) custard (soya) cream.

Organic smoothies and fresh organic juice £3.75.

Vegan organic wines from £4.75 glass £17.50 bottle. Vegan organic lagers an ciders. Cocktails.

Optional 12.5% service charge added to bill. No reservations but you can have drink at the front while you wait. Also take away. Children welcome, 4 high chairs. Private dining room for 8-14 people upstairs.

Also in Camden, Kings Cross (both North London) and Dalston (East London).

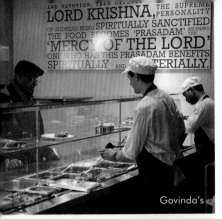
Govinda's

Yorica

Woodlands Picadilly

Govinda's
Vegetarian Indian restaurant

- 9/10 Soho Street W1V 5DA
- 020 7440 5229
- M-Sa 12.00-21.00, Su 12.00-16.00
- Tottenham Court Road
- iskcon-london.org

Popular, great value vegetarian India
restaurant and café on the ground floor of
the Hare Krishna temple at the eastern end
of the Oxford Street fashion mile.

They offer four thalis from £6.95 with five
items up to a belt-buster for £13.95 with
rice, bean pot, lentil soup, two curries,
bread roll, popadom, green salad, pakora
and chapati. You can also have individual
items 60p-£3.95 such as burger, dal, bean
pot, curry, rice, pakora veg fritter, samosa,
spring roll, salads (large £5.95) and Indian
breads.

Two of the cakes are vegan.

Hot drinks £1.50, they have soya milk.
Juices and smoothies £2.25-£2.75.

No eggs, garlic or onion. No alcohol.
Children welcome. 15% student discount
excluding special offers.

oodlands Piccadilly
getarian S. Indian restaurant

37 Panton St, London SW1Y 4EA
(between Haymarket and south-west
corner of Leicester Square)
020-7839 7258

M-Su 12.00-22.30

Piccadilly Circus, Leicester Square

woodlandsrestaurant.co.uk

One of three branches in London. Lunch
all dishes £5.95, all thalis £7.75.

There is a separate vegan menu featuring
14 starters and snacks £2.25-£5.75 from
papadum, lemon or dal soup, to mini
uttapam, samosas or cashew nut pakora,
or have a platter for two £12.95. 10 main
course dosas £4.95-7.25. Three kinds of
utthappam lentil pizza £6.75. Thalis £18.50.
Side curries £6.75-7.50. Steamed rice £4.25,
lemon rice £4.95, roti or two chappatis
around £3.

With such an extensive vegan menu, it's a
shame there's only one vegan dessert, but
then that is one more than in 90% of Indian
restaurants, even the vegetarian ones. It's
jaggary dosa £5.95, a golden "butter"
crepe but made with oil, smothered with
warm sugar cone (without ice-cream for
vegans).

House wine £1.95-£6.25 glass, £16.25-
£25 bottle. Small beer £2.95, large £5.50.

Children welcome, no high chair.

Yorica
Vegan ice-cream & pancakes parlour

130 Wardour Street W1F 8ZN
020 7434 4370

M-W 13.00-22.00, Th 11.00-23.00,
F-Sa 11.00-24.00, Su 12.00-22.00

Leicester Square

yorica.com

Opened in 2016, Britain's first vegan
ice-cream parlour also serves frozen yogurt
and shakes and is open till midnight on
weekends. Come for a decadent treat, or
finish up here after a regular restaurant that
doesn't do dairy-free desserts.

Ice-cream here is made with rice milk and
comes in gluten-free cones £2.15 and three
sizes of tub: classic £4.25, big £5.25, and
epic £6.25 which they say is great for
sharing. You can mix and match flavours
such as chocolate, vanilla, strawberry,
mango, blackcurrant, melon, moringa,
violet, bubblegum, cookies & cream,
beetroot & chocolate, chocolate & orange,
matcha, or caramel. Then top it off with
sprinkles, sauces such as chocolate or
raspberry coulis, fruits like blueberries, or
dry toppings such as chocolate, soy
marshmallows or cookies. Frozen yogurt
works the same way except the flavours are
vanilla, chocolate, raspberry or matcha.

Design your own shake £6.65 with up to
three flavours of ice-cream, topped off with
chocolate or coconut whipped cream plus
sprinkles, sauce, fruits or drop toppings.

Waffles and crepes £8.95 comes with
ice-cream, fruit, cookie crunch, sauces,
marshmallow. Waffle or crepe solo £4.50.

Everything is free from wheat, gluten, dairy,
eggs and nuts. They have a fridge full of
cold drinks in cartons, bottles and cans.

Veggie Pret
Vegetarian cafe & take-away

- 35 Broadwick Strreet W1F 0DH
  (north-east corner of Lexington Street)
- 020 7932 5274
- M-F 06.30-21.00, Sa 08.00-20.00,
  Su 09.30-19.00
- Piccadilly Circus
- pret.co.uk

In June 2016 Pret A Manger sandwich shops opened a one month popup vegetarian one in the middle of Soho. It was such a success, with 20,000 customer feedbacks, that they made it permanent and plan to open more. Staff from the nearby Lush flagship store come here to pick up lunch. Vegan food is clearly labelled and there is plenty of it.

Pots and packs £2.25-£4.50 take-away (£2.70-£5.40 eat in), such as Rainbow veggie pot, Asian greens, tapenade and avocado salad with lentils and quinoa, hummus and cucumber on rye, mushroom and avo salad, falafel mezze, Asian tofu salad.

Wraps, sandwiches and subs £2.99-£3.50 (£3.75-£4.50) include African chakalaka beans wrap with coconut yogurt, red pepper, spinach and roasted squash.

Breakfast pots £2.25 (£2.70) like Bircher, cacao orange.

Cakes and croissants are not vegan, but the raw fruits seed bar and chocolatey coconut bite are £1.55 (£1.89).

Cold drinks £99p-£2.79, cold pressed juices £3.49. Teas and coffes £1.49-£2.75 such as coconut milk latte or hot chocolate.

Second branch opened in Shoreditch in 2017, and a third in Exmouth Market.

Soho Vegan Market
Vegan street food market

- Rupert Street W1D 7PQ
- Every Monday 11.30-14.30
- Piccadilly Circus
- facebook.com/sohoveganmarket
  instagram.com/SohoVeganMarket

From April 2018, the regular (very meaty) Rupert Street food market went 100% vegan on Saturdays, then relaunched in July 201? on Mondays. A typical lineup could include Greedy Khao (Thai), Eat Chay (Vietnamese), Young Vegans pies, Pig Out hot dogs, Jake's Vegan Steaks, Lime Hut (Caribbean), Little Leaf pizza, Dough Society donuts, Lele's Vegan Patisserie, Flip 80/20 crepes, Fruity Fresh Smoothies.

V for Vegan Greek food, The Nooch bratwurst hot dogs, Garden of Afruika Caribbean, The Hogless Roast,

Lil'Falafel
Vegetarian street food stall

- Street Food Union Market, Rupert
  Street W1D 7PQ
- M-F 11.00-15.00
- Piccadilly Circus
- streetfoodunion.com/traders/
  lils-falafel
  instagram.com/lil_falafel_

The only vegetarian stall at this otherwise very meaty weekday street food market. Vegan falafel and salad in tortilla wrap £6, or in a box. On Mondays the stall goes all vegan as part of Soho Vegan Market.

Jerusalem Falafel
vegan falafel stall

- In Berwick Street Market W1
- 07411 128 115
- M-F 11.00-16.00, Sa-Su closed
- Piccadilly Circus, Leicester Square
- jerusalemfalafel.com
  twitter.com/JerusalemFalafe

Falafel stall in the fruit & veg street market in the middle of Soho. Falafel wrap (3 pieces) £4, rocket falafel wrap (5 pieces) £5.

Mediterranean Food

Mediterranean Food
Omnivorous salad bar take-away

- In Berwick Street Market W1
- M-F 11.30-14.30, Sa-Su closed
- Leicester Square, Piccadilly Circus

Beatroot Cafe may have been lost after 18 years to a new hotel development, but at weekday lunchtimes the Berwick Street market still has a falafel stand and this big salad bar, where you can assemble a mix and match take-away box for £4.80 from 20 dishes.

Berwick Street Market
Fruit and veg market

- South end of Berwick Street W1
- M-Sa 09.00-18.00
- Leicester Square, Piccadilly Circuss
- thisissoho.co.uk/the-market

Fruit and veg market with bargains in £1 bowls. Also a flower stall and a dried fruit and nuts stall. Combine your shopping with a falafel or salad box lunch.

Soho Vegan Market

Saravanaa Bhavan, Leicester Sq

Vegetarian South Indian chain restaurant

- 🖝 17 Charing Cross Road WC2H 0EP
- ☏ 020 7839 8797
- 🕔 M-Sa 12.00-22.30, Su 12.00-22.00
- ⊖ Leicester Square
- ➤ facebook.com/
  SaravanaBhavanLeicesterSq

Big new Indian vegetarian restaurant opened 2018 on Charing Cross Road, part of a worldwide chain. Same huge menu as their branches in outer London, but this is central London so prices are higher.

The menu marks if dishes are gluten-free, vegan option, or contain nuts. Unfortunately none of the desserts are vegan, which they confirmed to us in writing.

Dosas and uttapam £6.90-£9. Curries and stir-fries £7-£8.90. Rice, noodles and biryanis £3.50-£9.90. Thalis £9, £15.90, £17.90.

Chai by Mira

Vegetarian Ayurvedic cafet & juice bar

- 🖝 2nd floor Kingly Court. Kingly Street
  W1B 5PW
- ☏ Cafe 07479 700604
  Yoga 020 3362 3355
- 🕔 M-F 10.00-18.30, Sa-Su 10.00-
  16.30
- ⊖ Oxford Circus, Piccadilly Circus
- ➤ triyoga.co.uk
  chaibymira.com
  facebook.com/chaibymira
  instagram.com/chaibymira

Mira Manek's veggie oasis is next to the Triyoga centre on the second (top) top floor of Kingly Court, a foodie mall between the south end of Carnaby Street and Kingly Street. Take-away food, smoothies, juices, hot drinks.

Savoury bowl £7.50 with quinoa, chickpeas, tamarind tahini, courgetti, beet patties, chickpea crips, sauerkraut. Lentil coconut soup bowl £6.50 with seeded gluten-free toast. Salted caramel porridge bowl £5.50 with miso caramel, chia berry jam, peanut butter, granola dust. Avocado or beet patties on toast £6.50.

Plant milk of your choice smoothies £6.

Treats like spiced banana bread made with organic spelt flour, chia seeds and coconut oil, try it for breakfast with peanut butter and their homemade chia jam. Saffron key lime and other energy balls.

Lots of chais £3.80 including latte, masala coffee, spicy turmeric, rose, matcha, matcha peppermint, cocoa, rooibos. Peppermint or orange ssential oil infusion £3.80. Coffees £1.80-£3.20. Easy tummy tea £2.20 is made of cumin, fennel and carom (Indian herb) seeds.

ey sell Ayurvedic and other supplements.
onthly Chai Stories early evening events
th a speaker.

Bim Bap

mnivorous Korean restaurant

- 11 Greek Street W1D 4DJ (behind Foyles bookstore)
- 020 7287 3434
- M-Sa 12.00-15.00, 18.00-23.00, Su closed
- Tottenham Court Road
- bibimbapsoho.com
  facebook.com/bibimbap.soho

Bibimbap means mixed rice, a traditional Korean bowl of warm white rice topped with namul (sautéed and seasoned vegetables) and gochujang (chili pepper paste). The ingredients are stirred together thoroughly just before eating. It can be served either cold or in a very hot stone bowl with sesame oil at the bottom that turns some of the rice golden brown and crispy.

Mixed mushroom bi bim bap £8 comes in a hot stone bowl with shitake, white, oyster and black mushrooms and veg. Nutritious has ginseng, ginko, dates, chestnut and veg on brown rice. Tofu comes with mixed veg £7.50. Miso soup £1.95. Vegetable noodles £7.

Korean hot and cold teas £1-£2.50. Hite Korean beers £3.60.

Bi Bim Bap

Chai by Mira

Saravana Bhavan

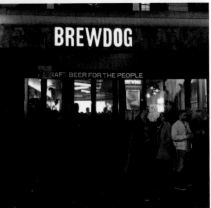

Brewdog, Soho
Omnivorous food pub with vegan beers

- 21 Poland Street W1F 8QG
- 020 7287 8029
- M-Th 12.00-23.30, F-Sa 12.00-24.00, Su 12.00-22.30
- Oxford Circus
- brewdog.com/bars/uk/soho
  facebook.com/brewdogsoho

Craft beer pub on two floors, each with twenty craft beer taps. Most beers are vegan and clearly labelled.

The only pub in Soho with a vegan bbq Hail Seitan burger £8, which comes with crispy kale, hummus and sunkissed tomato chutney. Soy Division tofu dog £8 in brioche bun, with avocado hummus, tenderstem broccoli, carrot and scallion. Add fries £2.

Standalone hopped up fries £3.50

Superfood salad £8 with quinoa, sweet potato, brown rice, pumpkin seeds.

Leggero pasta

omptoir Libanais, Soho
mnivorous Lebanese chain restaurant

52 **Poland Street** W1F 7NQ

020 7434 4335

M-Sa 08.00-23.00, Su 09.00-22.00

Oxford Circus, Tottenham Court Rd, Piccadilly Circus

57-60 **Haymarket** SW1Y 4QX

020 3355 2779

M-Th 12.00-23.00, F-Sa 12.00-24.00, Su 09.00-21.00

Piccadilly Circus

comptoirlibanais.com (menus)

Handy if Mildreds is full. Vegan dishes marked on the menu, and we love that you can filter the online menu for vegan and allergies. Mezze platter for one £9.95, for two £19.95, with baba ghanoush, hummus, tabouleh, falafel, lentil salad, pita etc.

Fiori Corner & Espresso Bar
Very late night omnivorous cafes

North-east corner of Leicester Square, opposite Warner West End cinema and Hippodrome

Every day till 01.30, F-Sa 05.00

Leicester Square

At 1am get falafels, hummus with salad in pitta, chips, coffee, beer or wine.

Leggero
Omnivorous Italian gluten-free restaurant

64 Old Compton Street W1D 4UQ

020 7434 3617

M-W 12.00-22.00, Th-F 12.00-23.00, Sa-Su 11.00-22.30

Leicester Square, Piccadilly Circus

leggero-london.com
facebook.com/LEGGEROlondon

Hooray, a mainstream restaurant that proudly promotes its vegan dishes on the menus and in the window. Previously called La Polenteria and still clearly labelling its vegan dishes. Leggero in Italian means of little weight, not heavy, the feeling of bodily light and wellbeing.

Salads and small plates £6-£6.50 include spinach, avocado and vegan cheese; courgetti spaghetti with hummus and tomatoes; green pesto polenta gnocchi with tomato and basil sauce topped with veg; courgette burger with mixed veg. Main course handmade sorghum and hemp tagliatelle with baba ganoush and grilled courgettes £12.50. Mango and raspberry cheesecake £6.

Vegan prosecco £6 small glass, £26 bottle. Other wines from £6.90 medium glass, £21 bottle. Beers from £4.50, cocktails £7.50, soft drinks from £2.50.

Also in Mercato Metropolitano at Elephant & Castle (South London).

Leon, Soho
Omnivorous chain cafe & take-away

- 35 Great Marlborough Street (north corner of **Carnaby St**) W1F 7JE
- (020 7734 8057
- ● M-Th 07.00-22.00, F 07.00-23.00, Sa 08.30-23.00, Su 09.30-20.00
- ⊖ Oxford Circus

- 42-44 **Broadwick Street** W1F 7AE
- (020 3238 0111
- ● M-Th 07.30-21.00, F 07.30-21.30, Sa 09.00-21.30, Su 12.00-21.00
- ⊖ Oxford Circus, Tottenham Court Rd, Piccadilly Circus

- 62 **Shaftesbury Avenue** W1D 6LT
- (020 7287 8477
- ● M-Th 07.30-23.00, F 07.30-24.00, Sa 11.00-24.00, Su 11.00-20.00
- ⊖ Piccadillly Circus
- ✦ leon.co

Laid back healthy cafe with lots of vegan options such as jack wings, burgers, lentil masala, Brazilian black beans, hummus, flatbreak, baked fries, crushed pea salad, slaw, sauces.

Pizza Express, Soho
Omnivorous Italian restaurant

- **Leicester Square** branch: 43 Charing Cross Road WC2H 0AP
- (020 7287 3322
- ● M-Sa 11.30-24.00, Su 11.30-23.30

- PizzaExpress **Jazz Club**, 10 **Dean Street** W1D 3RW
- (020 7437 9595
  Jazz 020 7439 4962
- ● M-Sa 11.30-24.00, Su 11.30-23.30
- ⊖ Tottenham Court Road
- ✦ pizzaexpresslive.com

Live jazz downstairs seven nights a week.

- 20 **Greek Stree**t W1D 4DU
- (020 7734 7430
- ● Tu-Sa 11.30-24.00, Su-M 11.30-23.00
- ⊖ Leicester Square

- 26 Panton House, **Haymarket** SW1Y 4EN
- (020 7930 8044
- ● M-Tu 11.30-23.00, W-Th 11.30-23.30, F-Sa 11.30-24.00, Su 11.30-22.30
- ⊖ Piccadilly Circus

- 29 **Wardour Stree**t W1D 6PS
- (020 7437 7215
- ● M-Tu 11.30-23.30, W-Sa 11.30-24.00, Su 11.30-23.00
- ⊖ Piccadilly Circus, Leicester Square
- ✦ pizzaexpress.com

Now offering vegan cheese. See Chains. Open every day till around 11pm.

Wagamama
Omnivorous Japanese chain restaurants

☛ **Leicester Square** branch: 14 Irving Street WC2H 7AF

☏ 020 7839 2323

🕐 M-F 11.30-23.00, Sa 11.30-23.00, Su 11.30-22.00

⊖ Leicester Square, Charing Cross

☛ **Carnaby Street** branch: 42 Great Marlborough Street W1F 7JL

☏ 020 3794 4338

🕐 M-F 11.00-23.00, Sa 11.30-23.00, Su 11.30-22.00

⊖ Piccadilly Circus

☛ 81 **Dean Street** W1D 3SW

☏ 020 3198 2984

🕐 M-Su 11.00-23.00

⊖ Tottenham Court Road

↖ wagamama.com

Omnivorous fast food Japanese noodle restaurant with a separate vegan menu. Very busy, totally authentic, heaps of fun. Dishes include miso soup with pickles, raw salad, yasai yaki soba with rice or udon noodles, yasai pad Thai, tofu glass noodle salad, steamed gyoza, yasai kamla curry, kare burosu tofu and udon noodles with veggies in curried veg broth, katsu curry. For dessert mango and matcha layer cake, unusual ice creams, pink guava and passion fruit sorbet.

Wagamama

Whole Foods Market, Soho
Omnivorous wholefood cafe & supermarket

- 20 Glasshouse Street W1B 5AR
- (020 7406 3100
- M-F 07.30-22.00, Sa 09.00-22.00, Su 12.00-18.00, Bank hols may vary
- Piccadilly Circus
- wholefoodsmarket.co.uk/

Organic wholefood supermarket. Organic fruit and veg, heaps of take-aways, deli, salad bar and juice bar/cafe with seating outside and upstairs.

You will see quite a bit of dairy and meat, but there is an astonishing range of vegan delights to stock your kitchen or create a picnic. On the left side of the shop are lots of take-away food counters including pizzeria, sushi, Mexican, smoothies, hot drinks, and a huge self-serve hot and cold buffet. Also fridges with grab and go wraps, salads, desserts and cakes.

Futher fridges along the back wall have Bute Island Sheese, Redwood vegan cheeses and meat replacers, dips, Sojade and Provamel yogurts and many variations of tofu. To the right of the deli are organic veg, then several grocery aisles with all your favourite wholefoods and many you've never seen before. Non-dairy ice-creams include Bessant & Drury, Booja Booja, Swedish Glace and Rookbeare sorbets.

The meat and cheese sections are tucked away at the back on the right, along with the fresh olives bar, a huge chocolate section, and lots of beer and wine.

Upstairs are some cafe tables and a section for health, body and skincare which includes Dr Hauschka, Ren, Weleda, Faith in Nature, Jason, Urtekram, Green People.

Holland & Barrett, Oxford St
Health food shop

- 52 Oxford Street W1D 1BG (corner of Rathbone Place)
- (020 7580 2768
- M-F 08.00-21.30, Sa 09.00-21.30, Su 10.00-20.30
- Tottenham Court Road

Fridge and freezer.

ush, Oxford Street
ruelty-free cosmetics

- 175-179 Oxford Street W1D 2JS
- 020 7789 0001
- M-Sa 10.00-21.00, Th 22.00, Su 11.30-18.00
- Oxford Circus
- lush.co.uk/shop/london-oxford-st

The huge new Lush flagship store on three floors opened 2015, replacing the Covent Garden and Regent Street branches. There are 200 exclusive products which are not in their other shops including perfumes, new bath bombs, a new makeup range, and there is a spa for treatments.

Lovely cosmetics, all vegetarian and most vegan and clearly labelled with the Vegan Society logo, and ingredients listed in both English and Latin. Worth going in just for the fantastic smells. Solid shampoo such as shower sheets and body wash powder are perfect for travellers and foaming bath balls make luxurious gifts.

A lot of the staff are vegetarian or vegan women and are very helpful. It's perfect for scared blokes who don't know what to buy their girlfriends. They say they get a lot of them, and they'll help you choose. She can always change it later if necessary if you keep the receipt.

Treatments available on the lower floor include full body massage and facials.

The top floor has a fun area where children can play plus lots of giftwrap ideas.

Whole Foods

Lush

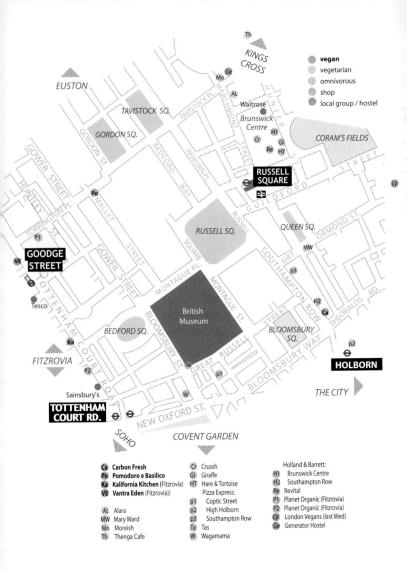

vegan
vegetarian
omnivorous
shop
local group / hostel

KINGS CROSS

Th
Mo Ge
AL
Waitrose
Brunswick Centre
EUSTON
TAVISTOCK SQ.
GORDON SQ.
Cr H1
Gi
Re HT
CORAM'S FIELDS

RUSSELL SQUARE

GOWER STREET
GORDON ST.
HUNTLEY ST.
TORRINGTON PL.
Po
P1
VE
GOODGE STREET
Tesco
TOTTENHAM COURT ROAD
BEDFORD WAY
WOBURN PL.
MARCHMONT
TAVISTOCK PL.
HUNTER

GUILDFORD

LV

RUSSELL SQ.
QUEEN SQ.
MW
p3
ORMOND ST.
SOUTHAMPTON ROW

MONTAGUE PL.
MONTAGUE ST.
RUSSELL SQUARE

British Museum
BEDFORD SQ.
Ka
FITZROVIA
P2
Sainsbury's
TOTTENHAM COURT RD.

Ta
p1
W
BLOOMSBURY SQ.
GREAT RUSSELL
BLOOMSBURY WAY
H2
Ca
THEOBALDS RD.
p2
HOLBORN
THE CITY

SOHO
NEW OXFORD ST.
COVENT GARDEN

Ca **Carbon Fresh**
Po **Pomodoro e Basilico**
Ka **Kalifornia Kitchen** (Fitzrovia)
VE **Vantra Eden** (Fitzrovia))

AL Alara
MW Mary Ward
Mo Moreish
Th Thenga Cafe

Cr Crussh
Gi Giraffe
HT Hare & Tortoise
Pizza Express:
p1 Coptic Street
p2 High Holborn
p3 Southampton Row
Ta Tas
W Wagamama

Holland & Barrett:
H1 Brunswick Centre
H2 Southampton Row
Re Revital
P1 Planet Organic (Fitzrovia)
P2 Planet Organic (Fitzrovia)
LV London Vegans (last Wed)
Ge Generator Hostel

44

BLOOMSBURY

Central London tranquil hotspot

This residential and university area, to the east of Tottenham Court Road and north of Covent Garden, has many midrange and budget hotels. University College London and the 800-bed Generator backpacker hostel ensure that the streets are thronged with young people from all over the world.

The top attraction here is the **British Museum**, the largest of London's 150 museums, featuring Egyptian mummies, Greek and Roman antiquities, the Rosetta Stone, and other British Empire loot. It was the location for the Ben Stiller movie *Night At The Museum 3* and there is a digital centre to keep the kids amused.

Our favourite road is **Marchmont Street** with cafes, take-aways, a cinema nearby in the Brunswick Centre, and a real community feel. The superb **Alara** wholefoods store has a veggie café, take-aways and extremely charming staff. A little further up the street, **Moreish** cafe has recently gone vegetarian and is constantly creating new flavours of their own vegan gelato. It is very close to the Generator backpacker hostel.

Bloomsbury's best kept veggie secret is the **Mary Ward Centre** cafe, an Italian run veggie cafe open term times in an adult education centre. Just go there, you won't regret it!

Thenga Cafe is a new vegetarian Indian cafe on the way to Kings Cross. They have vegan cakes!

For a completely vegan offering, try **Carbon Fresh**, or **Pomodoro e Basilico** vegan food stall on Tuesdays at the Farmers Market.

The vegan-friendly chain restaurants are well represented in the area, particularly in the Brunswick Centre.

Picnic tip: Fancy a day off lounging on the grass reading a novel? On a warm day load up with picnic munchies at **Alara** or a mix and match buffet box at **Planet Organic** or **Vantra Eden** (see Fitzrovia) and head for tranquil Russell Square, Bloomsbury Square, Gordon Square (week days only, full of students revising) or Queen Square. Or pay your respects by placing a candle in a jar at the base of the statue of Gandhi in Tavistock Square.

Top attractions:
» British Museum
» Several little parks

www.britishmuseum.org

45

Thenga Cafe

Carbon Fresh

Alara
Wholefood store and vegetarian cafe

- 📞 58-60 Marchmont Street WC1N 1AE
- ☎ 020 7837 1172
- 🕐 M-F 9.00-20.00, Sa 10.00-19.00, Su 11.00-18.00
- ⊖ Russell Square
- ⌁ alarashop.com, Facebook: Alara Health Store & Organic Café

Big family run vegetarian healthfood shop in a lovely street that is very popular with locals, opposite an Indian vegetarian restaurant. It's near Russell Square and the British Museum. There are 12 cafe tables outside under an awning, and a large take-away section - one of the best places to grab lunch to go. Popular with local residents and office workers, students from the nearby universities, tourists and backpackers from the many hotels and the Generator hostel around the corner. Bustling at lunchtime and chilled out rest of the day.

Help yourself to 100% organic salads and hot food, £1.15/100g, such as gluten-free veg curries, Dhansak, Moroccan bean stew, chickpea casserole, coconut rice, Japanese rice with arame.

Gigantic range of desserts (£1.99-2.99), many vegan, such as organic, gluten-free and sugar-free cakes like cheesecake, hazelnut and chocolate chip blondie cake; strawberry delight yogurt with granola on top; vegan rice pudding; Wot No Dairy desserts in peach, raspberry and black cherry; inSpiral brownies; apricot and pumpkin seed flapjack.Hot drinks are all organic such as herbal teas £1.09, moccaccino £1.75, soya latte £1.49, with ginger +20p.

Freshly made organic juices £2.09 small,

edium £2.29, £2.89 large, such as range, apple, carrot with ginger. Cockails 2.79-3.69 such as apple, beetroot and arrot. Smoothies with yogurt £3.29-4.19, an be with rice or soya milk.

tacks of vegan and organic produce, read, Swedish Glace and Booja Booja egan ice-cream, frozen foods. Organic uices and fruit smoothies.

Supplements include Viridian, Solgar, Terra Nova, Pukka, A.Vogel.

Bodycare by Dr Hauschka, Weleda, Antipodes, Jason, Weleda Baby, Natracare. Essential oils.

They have experienced and charming staff to give advice about nutrition. Every week qualified nutritionist and herbalist in store. 10% student discount.

Children welcome. Covered outside seating, dogs welcome. MC, Visa.

Thenga Cafe
Vegetarian Indian cafe

- 120 Cromer Street WC1H 8BS (entrance on Judd Street)
- 020 3817 9919 office
- M-F 10.00-16.00, Sa Su closed
- Kings Cross
- thengacafe.com
  facebook.com/thengacafe

Great value new cafe in the back streets towards Kings Cross. Thali £4.95. Menu changes every day, most dishes are vegan including cakes £1.80, biscuits. Tea £1.50, organic coffee £2, large £2.40, they have almond milk.

To get there from Alara, walk north up Hunter Street across Tavistock Place into Judd Street. Cromer Street is the next on the right.

Carbon Fresh
Vegan organic juice bar and tea house

- Inside Hello Love, 62-64 Southampton Row WC1B 4AR
- 020
- M-F 9.00-18.00, Sa 9.00-17.00, Su closed
- Holborn, Russell Square
- carbonfresh.org
  instagram.com/carbonfresh
  hellolove.org
  facebook.com/hellolovehome

Vegan cafe inside Hello Love, which offers yoga, massage and various New Age treatments.

Cold pressed juices £4-£7.50 range from carrot or orange to the unusual watercress, green pepper, green leaves and apple.

All day brunch muesli or fruit bowl £4.50, avocado on sourdough rye toast £5.50 (add red onion, pistachios or tomatoes 50p-£1 each). Build your own salad obowl £7.50, add £1.50 for toast.

Loose leaf teas, matcha, cacao chai, coffees, turmeric or ginger latte £2.50-£4. 300ml almond, cashew or hazelnut milk with figs £3.50. Add ginger shot £1, CBD oil £3.50.

Mary Ward
Vegetarian café

- 🏠 42 Queen Square WC1N 3AQ
- ☎ 020 7269 6085
- 🕐 M-Th 9.30-20.45, F 9.30-20.00, Sa 9.30-16.00, Su closed
- ⊖ Russell Square, Holborn
- ↖ marywardcentre.ac.uk

Completely vegetarian cafe in an adult education centre by green Queens Square. Modern and bright with monthly changing art exhibits. Friendly Italian owners so expect a Mediterranean flavour on the menu which changes daily. It's great value.

Breakfast options are vegetarian, but you could have something savoury like bhajias.

The lunch menu includes daily changing salads with four choices which are vegan and wheat-free, £2.95 small, £3.95 large, with Italian, French or olive oil dressing. Lots of small things such as bhajia, crostini, polenta or croquettes. They bake bread on the premises such as herby garlic.

Light meals vary such as stuffed baguettes, such as red lentil and olive pate with lettuce; soup (always vegan); tortilla stuffed with roast butternut squash, olives and aubergine. Main dishes £4.80 such as roast veg with couscous; pasta bake; potato pie; roast onion stuffed with veg; stews such as lentil or bean especially in winter. £5.40 with mixed green salad or £5.90 with selection of 3-4 salads.

Cakes £2.60-£2.70, always something gluten-free and vegan from a repertoire of 30, such as orange and almond, avocado and banana, polenta and orange, spicy pear and chocolate.

Plenty of cold drinks such as fresh juices,

Rebel coconut milk with chocolate, "this water. Herbal teas, Yogi tea, Sassett coffee, soyacinno, almondcinno, latte chocolate, Barleycup, from 75p-90p for tea to £2 for cappuccino, £2.25 mocha.

Near London Vegans' last Wednesday evening venue (see Local Groups) so a great place to unwind beforehand.

Kids welcome, small portions. Not licensed. No dogs except guide dogs. MC, Visa £6 minimum.

Moreish
Vegetarian cafe

- 🏠 76 Marchmont Street WC1N 1AG (corner Tavistock Place)
- ☎ 020 7388 0084
- 🕐 M-Su 08.00-18.00
- ⊖ Russell Square, Kings Cross
- ↖ moreishcafedeli.co.uk
  facebook.com/moreishcafedeli

A few minutes walk south of Kings Cross station and the British Library. Owner Jenny, who previously worked on The Great British Bakeoff, has recently turned her cafe vegetarian, and they can veganize more things.

Breakfasts for a fiver or less include hot banana bread, porridge topped with apple and banana or agave and almonds, muesli.

Sandwiches £5.50 such as asparagus and avocado. Plate of three salads for £5.80 such as pasta, mixed beans, and carrot salad, comes with a dollop of hummus. Savouries include vegan spanokopita and pies. Soups and chilli Sept-March, lentil soup with paprika £5.20, with bread, gluten-free add 50p. Veg chilli and rice £6.50.

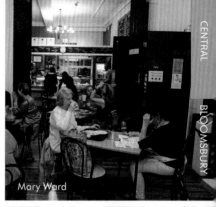

Mary Ward

Vegan Sacher torte £4.50 with gelato. Lots of vegan gelato ice-cream flavours made here with coconut milk. 1 scoop £3, 2 £4, 3 £5. Flavours include strawberry prosecco, chocolate, matcha green tea, pistachio, rum and raisin, coffee, mango, rhubarb and ginger, and they are constantly coming up with new ones. At Christmas time they have vegan truffles.

Juices around £3. Soft drinks £1.50. Teas £2.10-£3.10. Coffees from £1.60 for a small espresso to £2.90 for a large latte or cappuccino. Soya milk +20p, almond or oat 30p.

Spanish wholefoods for sale at the back such as Pardinia lentils, chocolate or pickled figs, fig balsamic and sherry vinegars.

Seating inside and out. Children welcome. Dogs welcome. Discount for students, senior citizens, NHS and military.

Moreish

Crussh, Russell Square
Omnivorous chain cafe

- ☛ Unit 28, Brunswick Centre WC1N 1AW (opposite Holland & Barrett)
- ☎ 020 7837 6848
- 🕐 M-F 08.00-19.00, Sa 10.00-19.00, Su 11.00-18.00
- ⊖ Russell Square

See Chains for details.

Crussh

Pomodoro e Basilico
Vegan Italian street slow food stall

☞ **Bloomsbury Farmers Market**,
Torrington Square / Byng Place
WC1E 7HY (near Planet Organic)

☎ 07866 194 403

◔ Thursday only 9.00-14.00

⊖ Euston Square, Goodge Street

↖ facebook.com/PomoBasilico
instagram.com/pomodoro_e_basilico
lfm.org.uk

Italian chef Sara worked for several vegan
restaurants and bakeries before starting
her own food business out of a passion for
made-from-scratch slow vegan food with
seasonal ingredients.

Sara brings burgers, pizzas and vegan cakes
to the market with bags of enthusiasm

Also at South Kensington Farmers Market
Tuesday (West London), Alexandra Palace
Sunday (Wood Green, North London), and
usually at Portobello Vegan Night Market
in Notting Hill (West).

Also private catering.

Giraffe

Giraffe, Brunswick Ctr
Omnivorous chain restaurant

🍽 19-23 Brunswick Shopping Centre, Brunswick Square WC1N 1AF (East side of precinct by cinema)

☎ 020 7812 1336

🕐 M-F 08.00-22.30, Sa 09.00-22.30, Su 09.00-22.15

⊖ Russell Square

🔗 giraffe.net

Bright, lively, fun, very friendly and packed with young people. Global menu that is great for veggies and vegans, and breakfasts too, and a children's menu. Licensed.

Pizza Express, Bloomsbury
Omnivorous Italian chain restaurant

🍽 30 Coptic Street WC1A 1NS

☎ 020 7636 3232

🕐 Su-W 11.30-23.00, Th-Sa 11.30-24.00

⊖ Tottenham Court Road

🍽 99 High Holborn WC1V 6LF

☎ 020 7831 5305

🕐 M-Sa 11.30-23.30, Su 11.30-22.00

⊖ Holborn

🍽 114 Southampton Row WC1B 5AA

☎ 020 7430 1011

🕐 Su-Th 11.30-23.00, F-Sa 11.30-23.30

⊖ Holborn, Russell Square

Now with vegan cheese.

Tas, Bloomsbury
Omnivorous Turkish chain restaurant

🍽 22 Bloomsbury St, WC1B 3QJ

☎ 020 7637 4555/1333

🕐 M-Sa 12.00-23.30, Su 12.00-22.30

⊖ Tottenham Court Rd

🔗 tasrestaurants.com

Similar menu to the Waterloo branch (see South Bank section) with stacks of veggie and vegan Turkish dishes. Licensed.

Wagamama, Bloomsbury
Omnivorous Japanese chain restaurant

🍽 4A Streatham Street, off Bloomsbury St WC1A 1JB

☎ 020 7323 9223

🕐 M-Sa 12.00-23.00 (last order), Su 12.30-22.00

⊖ Tottenham Court Rd

🔗 wagamama.com

This was the first branch of many Japanese noodle restaurants listed in this book, with over nine veggie and vegan dishes and huge portions. Licensed. See Chains for details.

Revital, Russell Square
Health food chain store

- The Brunswick Centre WC1N 1BS
- 020 7837 0185
- M-F 9.00-19.00, Sa 9.00-18.00, Su 11.00-16.00
- Russell Square
- revital.co.uk

This store does not do so much take-away as there is so much else available nearby, but has a huge range of bodycare, supplements and protein powders.

Vegan cheeses by Violife, Taifun tofu, vegan kefir. Chegworth Valley juices.

Protein powders by Hero, Macacha, Garden of Life, Nuzest, Sun Warrior, Plantfone, Revital, Pulsin, Nutristrength. Superfoods. Supplements by Higher Nature, Nature's Plus, Solgar, Wild Nutrition, Life Extension, NHP, Revital, Lamberts, Biocare, Nutri Advanced, Biotics Research, Allergy Research Group.

Bodycare by Noah, Green People, Weleda, Andalou, Dr Bronner, Barefoot SOS, Fushi, Salcura, Dr Hauschka, Pacifica, Nourish. Incognito insect repellant. Vogel remedies. Tisserand and Absolute Aromas aromatherapy.

Holland & Barrett
Health food store

- Unit 29, Brunswick Shopping Ctr WC1N 1AE
- 020 7278 4392
- M-Sa 08.3-20.30, Su 11.00-19.00
- Russell Square

Fridge and freezer.

- 72 Southampton Row WC1B 4AR
- 020 3490 4555
- M-F 08.00-20.0, Sa 10.00-18.00, Su 11.30-17.30
- Holborn, Russell Square

Fridge.

For the two Planet Organic stores, see Fitzrovia chapter.

ondon Vegans
egan social group

- 50 Millman Street Community Rooms
  from, press Community Centre bell
- Last Wednesday of the month (not
  December) 19.00
- Chancery Lane, Holborn
  Bus: 19, 38, 55, 243
- londonvegans.org
  meetup.com/londonvegan
  shambhus.co.uk/lv

Monthly vegan social meeting from 7pm, a talk at 7.30pm, then more socialising and some people go on to the pub. Vegan food by Shambhu's Kitchen, pre-order by 3pm Tuesday from their website. Vegan information stall. A great place for vegans and vegan-friendly types to make new friends.

These meetings may also be at Thenga Cafe.

London Vegans

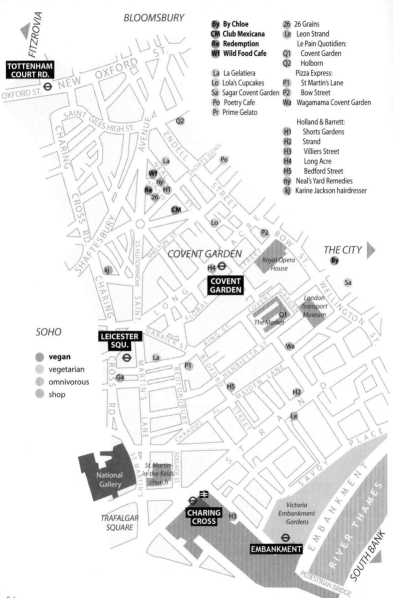

By By Chloe
CM Club Mexicana
Re Redemption
Wf Wild Food Cafe

La La Gelatiera
Lo Lola's Cupcakes
Sa Sagar Covent Garden
Po Poetry Cafe
Pr Prime Gelato

26 26 Grains
Le Leon Strand
Le Pain Quotidien:
Q1 Covent Garden
Q2 Holborn
Pizza Express:
P1 St Martin's Lane
P2 Bow Street
Wa Wagamama Covent Garden

Holland & Barrett:
H1 Shorts Gardens
H2 Strand
H3 Villiers Street
H4 Long Acre
H5 Bedford Street
ny Neal's Yard Remedies
kj Karine Jackson hairdresser

FITZROVIA

TOTTENHAM
COURT RD.

OXFORD ST.
NEW OXFORD ST.

BLOOMSBURY

SAINT GILES HIGH ST.

CHARING CROSS RD.

ENDELL ST.

SHORTS GDNS

Q2

La

Po

Wf
ny
Re 26
H1

CM

Lo

P2

SHAFTESBURY

NEAL ST.

SHELTON ST.

kj

COVENT GARDEN

H4
COVENT
GARDEN

Royal Opera
House

THE CITY
By

London
Transport
Museum

Sa

SOHO

● vegan
● vegetarian
● omnivorous
● shop

LEICESTER
SQU.

La

Ga

P1

LONG ACRE

FLORAL ST.

GARRICK ST.

KING ST.

COVENT GARDEN
The Market

Q1

BEDFORD ST.

HENRIETTA ST.

MAIDEN LANE

H5

Wa

H2

Le

WELLINGTON ST.

CHARING CROSS RD.

ST. MARTIN'S LANE

BEDFORDBURY

CHANDOS PL.

ADELAIDE ST.

National
Gallery

St. Martin-
in-the-fields
church

TRAFALGAR
SQUARE

ST. MARTIN'S

CHARING
CROSS

H3

EMBANKMENT

STRAND

SAVOY PLACE

Victoria
Embankment
Gardens

EMBANKMENT

RIVER THAMES

SOUTH BANK

PEDESTRIAN BRIDGE

COVENT GARDEN

Central London

Covent Garden is a big tourist attraction for its multitude of cute little shops. The **covered market**, south of the tube station, is Covent Garden 'proper' with street theatre in the Piazza on the west side, cafes, craft stalls and a complex of trendy shops. Here you will also find the Royal Opera House, London Transport Museum, and behind that **Sagar**, a great value south Indian vegetarian restaurant.

North of the tube station, around Long Acre and Neal Street, the streets are packed with unique and enchanting shops from astrology to all sorts of designer gear. There are veggie and vegan cafes off Shorts Gardens. Turn right after Holland & Barrett, down a narrow alley into **Neal's Yard**, a flowery courtyard with shared outside tables. **Wild Food Cafe**, upstairs to the right, is run by raw food fans - enjoy an afternoon tea and slice of raw cheesecake gazing over the world below. Ahead of you is vegan restaurant and mocktails specialist **Redemption**. To your left is **26 Grains**, the go-to place for all-day porridge with superfoods. **Neal's Yard Remedies** is a typically fun Covent Garden shop and has adjoining therapy rooms for a massage or other treat.

In 2018 New York's vegan cafe chain **By Chloe** arrived in Drury Lane. It's big and bright with fast food such as burgers, healthy salad bowls, and lots of cakes.

Just before we went to print, east London vegan taco meisters **Club Mexicana** opened up in the new food court on Earlham Street.

After renovations, the vegetarian **Poetry Cafe** is back.

Also in the area are ice cream parlours with vegan options, chains such as Leon, Pizza Express, Wagamama and Le Pain Quotidien, several branches of health food store Holland & Barrett which is brilliant for picking up snacks, and top end vegan hairdresser **Karine Jackson**.

Wild Food Cafe

Vegan and raw restaurant

- ☛ First floor, 14 Neal's Yard WC2H 9DP
- ☎ 020 7419 2014
- ◕ Su-M 12.00-17.00, Tu-Sa 12.00-22.00 (last food orders 21.30)
- ⊖ Covent Garden, Tottenham Court Rd, Leicester Square
- ↖ wildfoodcafe.com
  facebook.com/WildFoodCafe

Raw food masters Joel and Aiste Gazdar are the force of nature behing this bright, fun, sophisticated and elegant vegetarian café with a central open kitchen, trailblazing raw options and amazing juices. There's an open plan kitchen in the centre so you can see all the food being prepared.

Raw purists will love the pure plant versions of living chickpea hummus £6.50 with beetroot and carrot salad on sourdough bread; raw pistachio and olive falafel with kale and parsley tabouleh on sourdough pitta £12; olive and shitake burger with baba ganoush on sprouted organic wheatbread £12.50; wild pizza on an almond and squash base with purslane pesto and toppings £12.50.

Salads with foraged wild leaves and seasonal ingredients £9.70. Ayurvedic salad £9.80, large £15.60,with amaranth, courgetti spaghetti, hiziki seaweed, artichoke hearts, avocado, marinated shitake, mango salsa,

Fill up with sides £2-£3.50 such as guacamole, coconut cheeze or baked sweet potato wedges.

Raw desserts £3.50-£6.70 include chocolate and berry tart, cake special, lemon tart on a soft crust of organic almonds, dates and coconut, chocolate ar almond mousse, chocolate pralines, waln banana bread, and oven baked season tart.

Sensational 12oz juices and smoothie £4.50–£6 made to order, like Incredibl Green, or Superberry mixture with organi rum. Fentimans ginger beer or botanica coke £2. Coconut water £2.80. Teas, cha coffee £2-2.50. Wines from £4.25 glass £18 bottle.

Children welcome. They run evening talks, two day immersion raw food chef courses for beginners to seasoned enthusiasts, and raw food and yoga retreats. A new, bigger branch opened 2019 in Islington, North London.

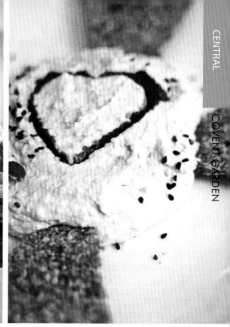

WILD FOOD CAFE

REMEDIES

By Chloe, Covent Garden
Vegan restaurant

- 📣 Drury House, 34-43 Russell Street WC2B 5HA
- 📞 020 3883 3273
- 🕐 Su-W 10.00-22.00, Th-Sa 10.00-23.00
- ⊖ Holborn, Covent Garden
- ⭮ eatbychloe.com
  facebook.com/eatbychloeuk

This American chain landed early 2018 here in Covent Garden, then added three more branches. Big salad bowls, soups, burgers, pasta, sandwiches and lots of cakes.

Most **main dishes** are just under £10. Salads such as Kale Caesar, spicy Thai, quinoa taco with spicy seitan chorizo and black beans, Greek. Burgers come in tempeh-lentil-chia-walnut, black bean-quinoa-sweet potato, pesto meatball. Tofish n' chips with mushy peas and tartar sauce. Royal Roast celery root with veggies, thyme potatoes, Yorkshire pudding and rosemary gravy. Ground seitan shepherd's pie with mash and veggies.

Mac n' cheese or avocado-cashew pesto pasta £4.80. Air baked original or sweet potato fries £4. Daily soup £3.60, large £7.20. BLT or chickpea tuna sandwich takeout around £5.

Brunch Sa-Su till 4pm (Oxford Circu₁ branch weekdays too from 7am), dishe₁ £4.80-£9 include morning oats with quino₁ and flaxseed and fresh berries; granola an₁ berries smoothie bowl; raw almond butte₁ and banana toast; various forms of Fu₁ English such as with scrambled tofu₁ spinach, maple sausage, walnuts, greens₁ 7-grain toast; quinoa hash browns with tof₁ sour cream; daily pancake with coconu₁ whipped cream.

Desserts include sticky toffee pudding with coconut whipped cream, banana walnut bread, muffins, cookies, cupcakes.

Lots of **cakes** such as banana walnut, cupcakes, chocolate chip pecan cookies £2-£3.90.

Smoothies, juices, lemonade, kombucha, coffees and iced coffees, teas. Almond, oat or soy milk. Wine £7 glass, £22 bottle.

Deliveries by Deliveroo, To-go by Chloe, corporate delivery.

Children welcome. Dogs welcome, water bowls, bag of peanut butter dog bones £5, whole oat K9 cupcake £1.95.

Also at Oxford Circus (Fitzrovia), Tower Bridge (South Bank), North Greenwich.

lub Mexicana, Seven Dials
egan Mexican fast food take-away

- Seven Dials Market, Earlham Street, Covent Garden WC2H 9LX
- hello@clubmexicana.com
- M-Sa 11.00-22.00, Su 12.00-21.00
- London Fields BR
- clubmexicana.com
  instagram.com/clubmexicana

The maestros of corn tortilla vegan tacos opened up here in September 2019 in this swish new indoor food and drink market by Kerb Food.

Old classics from their kitchens at Shoreditch Dinerama and the Spread Eagle vegan pub in Homerton (both in East London) are jonied by some newbies. Cheezeburger tacos, annato glazed short rib burritos, loaded nachos. Chipotle mushrooms and smoked tofu taco with pink onions, tahini salsa, and sour cream. Shawarma style pork taco with charred pineapple and pickled cauliflower.

Vegan wine, beer and frozen margaritas.

Also at the Spread Eagle pub in Homerton and Dinerama in Shoreditch.

Redemption, Covent Garden
Vegan restaurant

- 2 Neal's Yard/15 Shorts Gardens WC2H 9AT
- 020 7379 5955
- M-F 12.00-22.00, Sa 10.00-22.00, Su 10.00-21.00
- Covent Gaden, Tottenham Court Road
- redemptionbar.co.uk

New, healthy, vegan restaurant in Neal's Yard. They specialise in raw food and mocktails. As well as lunch and dinner, it is great for a quiet afternoon tea with a cake or cheesecake. See Notting Hill, West London or Shoreditch, East London for the type of food they serve.

59

Sagar Covent Garden
Vegetarian South Indian restaurant

- 📍 31 Catherine Street WC2B 5JS (near Aldwych)
- ☎ 020 7836 6377
- 🕐 M-Sa 12.00-23.00, Su 12.00-22.00
- ⊖ Covent Garden, Holborn
- ↖ sagarveg.co.uk

Great value south Indian food, with a similar menu and prices as their branch in Fitzrovia (see there for menu).

Look out for the separate vegan menu, £5.95 weekday lunch platter, £3.50 lunch boxes, dosas and thalis. Licensed.

Sagar

Poetry Cafe
Vegetarian cafe

- 📍 22 Betterton Street WC2H 9BX
- ☎ 020 7420 9888
- 🕐 M-F 11.00-23.00, Sa open for events (check their calendar), Su closed
- ⊖ Covent Garden
- ↖ facebook.com/thepoetrycafe poetrysociety.org.uk

After extensive renovations, the Poetry Society's cafe reopened bigger and better in summer 2017. Soups and stews, cakes and flapjacks, loose leaf tea, Fairtrade coffee, artisanal soft drinks.

Lost of events such as book launches. Poetry Unplugged on Tuesdays is open mic night from 8.30pm, sign up by email or arrive 6.45-7.15pm, £5 admission, E4 for readers. People who have never read a poem in public can do so for the first time, or experienced poets can try out something new.

6 Grains
mnivorous cafe

- 1 Neal's Yard WC2H 9DP

- M-F 08.00-16.00, Sa 09.00-16.00,
  Su 10.00-16.00
- Covent Garden
- 26grains.com
  instagram.com/26grains

Cafe that majors in wholesome grain based bowls £5.40-£6.50. Almost everything is vegetarian or vegan, though vegans should check ingredient lists before ordering.

The recipe begins with oats, quinoa, buckwheat, barley, millet, amaranth, spelt, flaxseed and rye, cooked with nut milk, coconut milk, water or juices. Then add spices such as cardamon, ginger, cinnamon, nutmeg and star anise, plus for sweetness maple syrup, fresh fruit and coconut. Finish off with toppings like nuts, fruit, compotes and granolas.

Breakfast-style porridge bowls lead the menu, such as almond milk oats with coconut yogurt, cacao nibs, banana and date syrup; or rhubarb buckwheat cardamon granola. Savoury dishes contain more vegetables. Cold bowls include Bircher muesli, or a smoothie bowl with coconut milk, berrries, fruits, cinnamon, cardamon granola, coconut flakes and goji berries. Buckwheat, millet and banana waffles come with chia, lemon, banana and maple.

Sweet treats £2.50 include superfood energy bites. Vegans note the banana bread contains eggs and honey.

Smoothies £4.50., the usual hot drinks, iced tea and coffees.

La Gelatiera
Vegetarian ice-cream parlour

- 🖝 27 New Row WC2N 4LA
- (020 7836 9559
- 🕐 Su-Th 13.00-23.00, F-Sa 12.00-23.30, Su 12.00-23.00
- ⊖ Covent Garden
- 🕯 lagelatiera.co.uk

Vegan sorbets here include dark chocolate, almond, peach and Prosecco bellini, pineapple and fresh mint, mojito rum with lime and fresh mint, mango, coconut and choc chips. Four sizes from £1 to £5. Coffee.

Prime Gelato
Vegetarian ice-cream parlour

- 🖝 216 Shaftesbury Avenue WC2H 8EB
- (07840 803338
- 🕐 M-Sa 11.00-23.00, Su 12.00-22.00
- ⊖ Covent Garden
- 🕯 facebook.com/PrimeGelatoLondon

Vegan gluten-free gelatos include hazelnut.

Leon, Strand
Omnivorous cafe & take-away

- 🖝 73-76 The Strand, WC2R 0DE
- (020 7240 3070
- 🕐 M-F 07.00-22.00, Sa 09.00-22.00, Su 11.00-19.00
- ⊖ Charing Cross
- 🕯 leonrestaurants.co.uk

See Chains.

Lola's Cupcakes, Covent Garden
Vegetarian take-away

- 🖝 14-18 Neal Street WC2H 9LY
- (020 7240 4249
- 🕐 M-W 08.00-20.00, Th-F 08.00-21.00, Sa 09.00-21.00, Su/BH 11.00-19.30
- ⊖ Covent Garden
- 🕯 lolascupcakes.co.uk

Cupcakes, cakes, shakes, coffee. Vegan chocolate brownie £2.75, cupcake £3.25, cherry pistachio mini cupcake £1.75.

Pain Quotidien, Covent Garden
Omnivorous Belgian cafe and bakery

- 48 & 49 The Market, Covent Garden Piazza WC2E 8RF
- 020 3657 6928
- M-Th 08.00-22.00, F-Sa 08.00-23.00, Su/BH 09.00-21.00. No bookings M-F 12.00-1500, Sa-Su/BH, or for the outside terrace.
- Covent Garden
- lepainquotidien.com

Veggie/vegan-friendly Belgian cafe chain that has some great vegan items such as tofu salad with sauces and bread, soups, mint tea and vegan blueberry muffins. Free wifi. See Chains section for more details.

Le Pain Quotidien, Holborn
Omnivorous Belgian cafe in a spa

- 174 High Holborn WC1V 7AA (in the Aveda Institute) (near Endell St)
- 020 3657 6947
- M-W 08.30-18.30, Th-F 08.00-19.30, Sa 09.00-18.00, Su/BH 11.00-16.30
- Holborn, Tottenham Court Road
- lepainquotidien.com, aveda.co.uk

This branch is in an upmarket hairdresser and beauty salon that uses and sells products, some of which are vegan. Free wifi.

Pizza Express
Omnivorous Italian restaurant

- 80-81 St Martin's Lane WC2N 4AA
- 020 7836 8001
- Su-Tu 11.30-23.00, W-Sa 11.30-23.30
- Leicester Square

- 9-12 Bow Street WC2E 7AH
- 020 7240 3443
- Su-Tu 11.30-23.00, W-Sa 11.30-23.30
- Covent Garden
- pizzaexpress.com

See Chains for menu. Both have baby facilities, disabled toilet, venue hire.

Wagamama Covent Garden
Japanese omnivorous restaurant

- 1 Tavistock Street WC2E 7PE
- 020 7836 3330
- M-Sa 11.00-23.00, Su 11.00-22.00
- Covent Garden
- wagamama.com

Omnivorous fast food Japanese noodle bar with some extremely filling veggie and vegan dishes. See Chains section for menu. Free wifi. Braille menus. Baby facilities. Disabled toilet and lift.

Holland & Barrett
Health food shop

- 21 Shorts Gardens WC2H 9AS
- 020 7836 5151
- M-Sa 08.30-20.00, Su 11.00-19.00
- Covent Garden

- 390/391 Strand WC2R 0LT
- 020 7836 5192
- M-F 08.00-20.00, Sa 10.00-19.00, Su 11.00-18.00

- Unit 16, Embankment Shopping Centre, Villiers St WC2N 6NN
- 020 7839 4988
- M-F 08.00-19.00, Sa 10.00-19.00, Su 11.30-19.00
- Embankment, Charing Cross

- 39 Long Acre WC2E 9LG
- 020 7836 0639
- M-F 07.30-21.00, Sa 9.00-19.00, Su 11.30-18.30
- Covent Garden

- 37 Bedford Street WC2E 9EN
- 020 7836 9363
- M-F 09.00-20.00, Sa 9.00-19.00, Su 12.00-18.00
- Leicester Square

Neal's Yard Remedies
Herbs and complementary health

- 2 & 15 Neal's Yard, WC2 9DP
- Shop 020 7379 7222
  Therapies: 020-7379 7662
- Shop M-F 10.30-19.00 (Th 19.30), Sa 10.30-19.00, Su 11.00-18.00. Therapies M-Th 9.00-21.00, F 9.00-19.00, Sa 10.00-18.30, Sun 9.45-18.30
- Covent Garden
- nealsyardremedies.com

200 herbs and spices by weight, organic toiletries, natural remedies, cottonwool, soaps, books on homeopathy and remedies.

Consultations available with multi-lingual staff. Therapy rooms upstairs at number 2 offering dozens of healing treatments from acupuncture to zero balancing and a drop-in herbal medicine clinic on certain days.

Karine Jackson
vegan hairdresser

- 24 Litchfield St WC2H 9NJ
- 020 7836 0300
- M 10.15-20.00, Tu 10.00-21.00,
  W-Th 08.00-21.00, F 10.30-19.00,
  Sa 9.15-18.00, Su closed
- Leicester Square
- karinejackson.co.uk

Karine, a former London Hairdresser of the Year, uses vegan Organic Colour Systems and Unite products and you can have vegan cookies and almond milk in tea and coffee.

Vegan cut and colour £90-£257. Vegan colour £62-£167. Cut and finish from £27 men, £35 women, with a graduate stylist, with prices increasing with a stylist, senior stylist or specialist, up to £120/£150 with the direector. Wash and blow dry from £25 up to £75.

They also do braids, pleats, volume, perming, straightening, facials, nails, body treatments, lashes and brows, hair removal, makeup, spray tans, and a wedding service for women and men. Full price list on the website.

Neal's Yard Rememdies

Karine Jackson Hair and Beauty

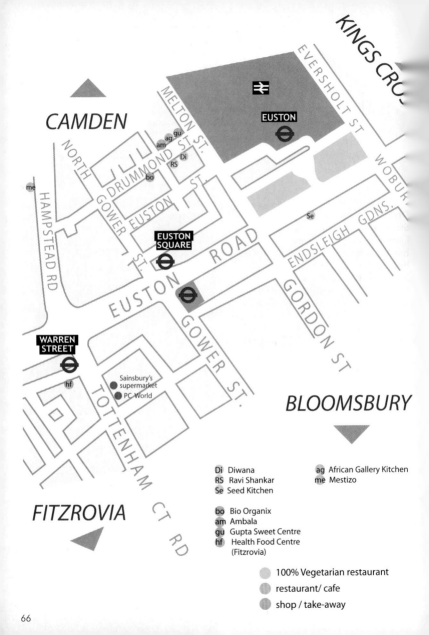

KINGS CRO...

CAMDEN

EVERSHOLT ST

MELTON ST

EUSTON

ag gu
am
Di
RS
bo

DRUMMOND ST

EUSTON ST

NORTH GOWER ST

HAMPSTEAD RD

me

WOBUR...

Se

EUSTON SQUARE

EUSTON ROAD

ENDSLEIGH GDNS.

GORDON ST

GOWER ST

WARREN STREET

hf

Sainsbury's supermarket
PC World

BLOOMSBURY

TOTTENHAM CT RD

FITZROVIA

Di Diwana
RS Ravi Shankar
Se Seed Kitchen

ag African Gallery Kitchen
me Mestizo

bo Bio Organix
am Ambala
gu Gupta Sweet Centre
hf Health Food Centre
   (Fitzrovia)

100% Vegetarian restaurant

restaurant/ cafe

shop / take-away

EUSTON

Central London

Drummond Street runs between Euston Station and Hampstead Road, and it's an institution. Despite being slap bang in the business hub of London and a mere hundred yards from hectic Euston Road, it has the feel of a village high street, with friendly shopkeepers and cafe owners who are happy to chat, cheap food and hardly any traffic. You could while away hours here at a relaxed pace, before heading off to get a train. The best thing about Drummond Street is the abundance of great vegetarian food.

Drummond Street is legendary in the vegan community for two terrific value south Indian vegetarian restaurants. **Diwana** has a buffet every lunchtime and does not sell alcohol, but you can bring your own and there is an off licence next door. **Ravi Shankar** is a la carte only and sells alcohol. (Another Indian restaurant Chutneys used to be vegetarian but has now started serving meat, so we have taken them out of this book.)

African Gallery Kitchen offers a completely unique gourmet menu. Around the corner in Hampstead Road, **Mestizo** Mexican restaurant has a separate vegan menu.

Bio-Organix, the new health food store, sells vegan ice cream and vegan cheesecake by Shambhu's. **Gupta Sweet Centre** has take-away samosas and for a sweet treat, vegan ladhu.

Seed Kitchen vegetarian restaurant will open at the end of 2019 opposite Euston station.

Euston rail station is the gateway to the north and north-west. Train food can be grim, so fill up or load up first in **Drummond Street or at Health Food Centre** (Fitzrovia).

Diwana
Vegetarian South Indian restaurant

☞ 121-123 Drummond Street NW1 2H
☏ 020 7387 5556
🕐 M-Sa 12.00-23.30, Su 12.00-22.30
⊖ Euston, Euston Square
↖ diwanabph.com

One of the larger vegetarian Indian restaurants on Drummond Street established over twenty five years. Light wood décor and lots of potted palms give a relaxed and informal feel. The food is inexpensive and tasty. They offer an eat as much as you like lunch buffet M-F 12.00-14.30, weekends 12.00-16.00, for £6.95 which has different dishes daily, and also a full a la carte menu all day.

Starters such as dahi vada chick pea fritters £3.60, mixed starters £3.80, platter £4.50.

Thalis £6.05-£8.95. Daily chef special £6.60 such as on Wednesday pumpkin curry with chapatis or special rice.

Dosas £5-£8 and vegetable side dishes like bombay aloo and aloo gobi around £4-£5.

Lots of desserts but vegans may have to settle for fruit salad. However you already be too full to care.

Diwana are not licensed but you can bring your own with no corkage charge. There is an off licence next door. No cheques.

Ravi Shankar

Friends House

avi Shankar
Vegetarian South Indian restaurant

- 133-135 Drummond Street NW1 2HL
- 020 7388 6458
- M-Su 12.00-22.45; buffet: M-F 12.00-15.00, Sat 12.00-17.00, Sun all day
- Euston, Euston Square
- ravishankaruk.com

One of three great value vegetarian South Indian restaurants in this street. Daily specials throughout the week. This place has a more informal, cafe atmosphere compared to the others. There's always plenty for vegans.

Buffet £6.95. Daily special £6.50 such as vegetable biryani with fried onions and cashew nuts, served with vegetable kofta, sauce and a dessert.

Usual starters all under £4, or have a platter £4.10. Curries £5-£7. Rice £2.70. Plain dosas £5.95, with fillings £7.05.

Set menu £15.95 for snacks, starter, main with three Keralan style curries, lemon or coconut rice and dessert. Lots of thalis £6.50-£11.95.

Desserts £1.95-2.50, but none vegan, however you can always pop into Gupta Sweet Centre opposite

Wine from £11.95 bottle, £2.75 small glass. Organic vegan wine £14.95 bottle. Beer £3.95 500ml bottle. Children welcome, no high chairs.

Seed Kitchen
Vegetarian restaurant

- In Friends House, 173 Euston Road NW1 2BJ (opposite Euston station)
- 020 7663 1000
- M-F 12.00-14.00 lunch, 14.00-16.00 coffee hub. Sa-Su closed.
- Euston, Euston Square
- friendshouse.co.uk/restaurant

The old restaurant in this Quaker centre has been refurbished and reopened autumn 2019 with one very important improvement, it is now vegetarian. They' say they are doing it because of climate change, so we are hopeful it will be mostly vegan. They aim to source organic ingredients from within 100 miles. Dishes will be made to order from a seasonal menu.

Meanwhile the omnivorous Quaker Centre Cafe in the building is open M-F 08.00-18.00, Sa 08.30-15.30, Su closed. Prices are low and they serve mainly vegetarian food, though last time we visited it was not great for vegans. You might find soup, baked potato with vegan chilli, salad pot, or dish of the day such as pie with potatoes. Sustainably sourced and locally produced cold drinks such as Dalstons and Chegworth Valley. Fairtade organic coffee and teas. **Fairtrade vegan snacks such as crisps, raw chocolate and flapjacks.** Around 40 seats. Children welcome, no high chairs. Toilets are up a flight of stairs.

Friends Meeting House is a great place to organise business or charity meetings.

African Gallery Kitchen
Omnivorous Afro-Carib restaurant

- 102 Drummond St NW1 2HN
- 020 7383 0918
- M 17.30-22.30, Tu-Su 12-15.30, 17.30-22.30
- Euston, Euston Square

Cosy restaurant, dairy-free and 50% vegan, with five tables, African wood carvings on the walls and big carved giraffes in the window.

Ten starters £3.50 mains £6.25. Different dishes every day such as blended beans with spices and tomatoes; fried plantain or cassava fritters; chick pea, butter beans, yam and sweet potato porridge; and black beans in bonnet chilli sauce.

They use only olive oil for cooking, no dairy or animal fats, wheat or additives, apart from condensed milk in one of the desserts.

Choose from mango, pumpkin or banana flan for dessert £3.50, or coconut, mango and blackberry balls.

Freshly squeezed juices £3.50. Herb teas. Litre bottles of beer £4.50; wine £3.50 a glass.

Mestizo
Omnivorous Mexican restaurant

- 103 Hampstead Road NW1 3EL (corner of Netley Rd, two streets north of Drummond Street)
- 020 7387 4064
- M-Sa 12.00-23.00, Su 12.00-16.00, 17.00-22.30
- Warren Street, Euston, Euston Square; bus 24,29,253
- mestizomx.com
  facebook.com/mestizolondon

Mexican restaurant and tequila bar 100 yards from Drummond St, with separate wheat-free, nut-free and even a substantial vegan menu, which are also on the website. From the outside, the place doesn't look promising for veggie options, but ignore the pared-down display menu in the window and venture in. The 20 vegan options include light meals and fuller meals, rather than starters and mains, so combine them according to your appetite.

Avocado tortilla £4.50; flautas de papa (potato tortillas) £7.20; guacamole £6.50. Vegetable tacos £5.60. Roast veg in banana leaf £10.50. Enchiladas de papa (potato, tomatoes and chocolate in an enchilada, served with rice and beans) £10.50. Sharing platter £9.80 or £14 per person with various dishes or tacos.

Vegan desserts include sorbets £4.80; mixed fruits in agave syrup £4.20; tamales de dulces £5.80, 2 corn-based dough tamales steamed in a leaf wrapper with sweet fillings.

Range of cocktails £4.50. Corona and similar beers £2.50. Wine from £10 bottle.Outside Congestion Charge zone, free street parking from 18.30.

io Organix
ealth food shop

- 141-153 Drummond St NW1 2PB
- 020 7383 3993
- M-F 9.30-19.30, Sa 12.00-18.30, Su closed
- Warren Street, Euston, Euston Square
- bio-organixhealth.com

New health food shop selling the kind of things nobody else in the area stocks, such as seaweed pasta. chia seeds, kale chips and raw chocolate. Organic Indian spices. Herb teas, organic drinks and superjuices. Gluten-free and spelt noodles. Lots of Japanese products, like nori. Good range of supplements, essential oils and eco-friendly household products.

Fridge with vegan cheeses and sausages, yogurt and soya milk. Freezer with ready meals, veggie sausages etc. Small range of books that they plan to expand.

10% discount to Vegetarian and Vegan Society members, and also members of the National Candida Society and National Autistic Society.

Mestizo

Ambala
Indian vegetarian sweet shop

- 🖝 141-153 Drummond St NW1 2HN
- ☎ 020 7387 7886, 7387 3521
- 🕐 M-F 9.30-20.00, Sa 10.00-19.00, Su 11.00-17.00
- ⊖ Euston, Euston Square
- ↖ ambala.co.uk

The oldest branch of this chain of takeaways and sweet shops, opposite Ravi Shankar and Diwana, for when you need to eat on the run. Very chunky and filling samosas 75p; pakoras £5/kilo, Bombay mix, pickles, chutney. Boxes of authentic Turkish delight with no nasty gelatine. The Indian sweets all contain dairy.

Gupta Sweet Centre
Indian vegetarian sweet shop

- 🖝 120 Drummond Street NW1 2HN
- ☎ 020 7380 1590
- 🕐 M-Sa 11.00-20.00, Su 12.00-20.0C
- ⊖ Euston, Euston Square
- ↖ facebook.com/GuptasUK

Small, friendly shop selling samosas, bhajias, veg cutlets, kachoris and Indian sweets, several of which are vegan including laddu and jelabi. Outside catering.

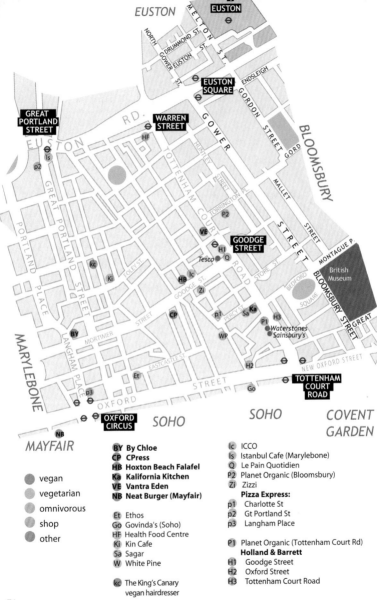

EUSTON

EUSTON

EUSTON SQUARE

GREAT PORTLAND STREET

WARREN STREET

GOODGE STREET

British Museum

BLOOMSBURY

TOTTENHAM COURT ROAD

OXFORD CIRCUS

MAYFAIR

SOHO

SOHO

COVENT GARDEN

Waterstones
Sainsbury's

vegan
vegetarian
omnivorous
shop
other

BY By Chloe
CP CPress
HB Hoxton Beach Falafel
Ka Kalifornia Kitchen
VE Vantra Eden
NB Neat Burger (Mayfair)

Et Ethos
Go Govinda's (Soho)
HF Health Food Centre
Ki Kin Cafe
Sa Sagar
W White Pine

kc The King's Canary
vegan hairdresser

Ic ICCO
Is Istanbul Cafe (Marylebone)
Q Le Pain Quotidien
P2 Planet Organic (Bloomsbury)
Zi Zizzi
Pizza Express:
p1 Charlotte St
p2 Gt Portland St
p3 Langham Place

P1 Planet Organic (Tottenham Court Rd)
Holland & Barrett
H1 Goodge Street
H2 Oxford Street
H3 Tottenham Court Road

74

FITZROVIA

Central London

zrovia, the area to the west of ttenham Court Road, is a mainly sidential area with some great places eat vegan that you could easily overlook hout this book. Its backstreets are full new vegan and vegetarian eateries, for quieter experience than in Soho.

alking north from Tottenham Court ad station, past a new branch of **Planet rganic** that has stacks of hot and cold ffet take-away food, brings you to rcy Street. **Kalifornia Kitchen** is the ettiest vegan restaurant in central ndon. Next door is the terrific value **gar** Indian vegetarian. At the end of rcy Street and left a bit is **White Pines**, Scandinavian style vegetarian cafe.

ound **Goodge Street** are **Vantra en**, the weekday lunchtime outpost of bulous Soho vegan buffet restaurant ntra, and **CPress** vegan cafe for juices, lads and cake, plus **Hoxton Beach** afel stall. Explore north into the ckstreets for **Kin** vegetarian cafe which big on healthy light meals and coffees, d just around the corner is vegan irdresser **The King's Canary**.

ose to **Oxford Circus** are two big taurants: **By Chloe** American vegan er with stacks of fun food and even vegan g treats, or the very elegant **Ethos** getarian buffet restaurant.

Omnivorous places with decent vegan choices include **Le Pain Quotidien** for soups, salads and muffins; **Zizzi**, **ICCO** and three branches of **Pizza Express** for Italian food with vegan cheese; and the fridges at three branches of health food chain store **Holland & Barrett**.

The new branch of **Planet Organic**, near Sainsbury's supermarket and Waterstones bookstore on Tottenham Court Road, is mainly a huge take-away for picking up a filling and cheap lunch. To eat in, head to their original wholefood supermarket in Torrington Place (down the side of Barclays Bank) which has a food counter where you can get a buffet box of food and some treats to enjoy at the tables inside or take to one of the nearby little parks in Bloomsbury.

At the north end of Tottenham Court Road is central London's biggest computer store PC World, where you can try out laptops, compare printers and televisions, and discover every accessory. For an awesome take-away selection, cross the street to **Health Food Centre** in Warren Street, so much more than a health food store, with generously filled vegan sandwiches and fabulous hot food take-aways and cakes. Load up here for an afternoon in Regent's Park.

DON'T KALE MY VIBE

alifornia Kitchen
egan American restaurant

- 19 Percy Street W1T 1DY
- 020 7504 4444
- Tu-Sa 11.00-22.00, Su 11.00-19.00, M closed
- Goodge Street, Tottenham Court Rd
- kaliforniakitchen.co.uk
  Facebook Kalifornia Kitchen Percy Street
  instagram.com/KaliforniaKitchen

Malibu Barbie would be right at home in this beautiful pink vegan restaurant with modern vegan dishes such as pancakes, burgers and salads. There's even a CBD (cannabis oil) menu.

Breakfast till 6pm £7.50-£10 includes chia pot; smoothie bowl; stacked banana pancakes with coconut yogurt and almond brittle; avo on toast with smoked pickled carrots and cashew cheese; scrambled turmeric tofu on sourdough with tomatoes, onions and spinach. The vegan full English £12.50 comes with sausage, scrambled tofu, spicy lentil dal and garlic field mushrooms.

Tapas £7-£13 feature pulled banana skin tacos in hickory smoked bbq sauce with rainbow slaw; jackfruit tacos; patatas bravas; blackbean and rice croquettes with beetroot aioli and pickled cabbage.

Mains and large plates £10-£15.50 star tempeh caesar salad; rainbow bowl; Moving Mountains B12 burger with guac or smoked Gouda; battered banana blossom fish & chips with chips and mushy peas; chickpea and date tagine; sweet potato and truffle mash with cherry wine tomato and oyster mushrooms; Mexican smokey black beans with avo and mango salad; Lebanese mezze platter.

Sides £5-£6 include paprika and thyme or sweet potato fries, (spicy) kale chips, guacamole, Asian slaw.

Desserts £7.50-£10 are matcha cheesecake, sticky toffee pudding, or pecan pie, all served with ice cream.

CBD menu £28 per person gets you a selection of items all containing 5% CBD drops including a latte or smoothie (or a glass of Moet champagne), banana cupcake with strawberry icing, hazelnut truffles rolled in desiccated coconut, turmeric and ginger gummies, raspberry Madeleines, granola. Add a bottle of prosecco for £20.

Smoothies £6, juices £3-£4.50, Karma cola £3, Jarr kombucha £4. Beers £5 include Freedom organic. Wines from £5 medium glass, £24 bottle. Coktails and mocktails.

Teas, coffees, fancy lattes £2.50-£4. CBD latte £5.50.

Deliveroo, Uber Eats..

Vantra Eden
Vegan restaurant & take-away

- 📢 79a Tottenham Court Road W1T 4TB
- 📞 Call Soho branch for information
- 🕐 M-F 12.00-15.00, Sa-Su closed
- ⊖ Goodge Street
- ➤ vantra.co.uk
  facebook.com/vantraeden

Smaler weekday lunchtime branch of the legendary Soho Vantra vegan restaurant, this one is between Goodge Street tube and the American church, opposite Habitat. Their mission is "making nutritious vegan food affordable, accessible and enjoyable."

Soups £2. Self-service south-east Asian and raw buffet, box of food £6 or £7, meal deal add £1 for a hot drink or soup. See the Soho branch for more about the food.

Freshly pressed juices £3-£3.90, with superfoods £4.70 . Organic Fairtrade coffees £1.40-£2.20 with almond, coconut or soy milk, also teas, matcha, chai, hot chocolate, add superfood shots 80p. Covered outside seating.

CPress, Fitzrovia
99% vegan healthy cafe & take-away

- 📢 31 Berners Street W1T 3LR
- 📞 020 3927 4306
- 🕐 M-F 07.00-20.00, Sa-Su/BH 9.00-17.00 #website has 08.00-18.00
- ⊖ Goodge Street
- ➤ cpressjuice.com
  facebook.com/cpressjuice

All vegan except cow's milk. 100% organic and gluten-free. No refined sugar, they use dates, coconut sugar or maple syrup.

Organic smoothies £6.75-£7.95, some with an impressive 20g of plant protein. Cold drinks and stacks of cold pressed juices £3.50-£7.95.

Gluten-free oat porridge before 11am £5.95 made with coconut milk and topped with berries. Chia pots £2.75-£3. Açai or pitaya (cactus fruit) bowls £8.95, with hemp protein £10.95, lots of toppings.

Gluten-free toasts £5.99-£6.95 take-away, £7.20-£8.34 eat-in, include two slices with toppings such as almond butter with banana, cacao nibs, cinnamon; or turmeric hummus with sundried tomatoes, olives, chilli flakes.

Salads such as Thai black rice noodles with edamame £5.99 take-away, £7.20 eat-in.

Sweet treats £1.40-£3.25 include dark chocolate truffle, cacao or coconut protein ball, vanilla cashew cookie, CBD brownie, raw Snickers or Matcha Bounty, blueberryor banana muffin.

Organic coffees £2.50-£3.90 include espresso, macchiato, flat white, latte, drip, bulletproof with MCT oil, cold brew, iced, ice latte. Homemade almond milk add 75p,

at and coconut 45p, decaf 60p, CBD £1.
Hot choc £3.90. Also teas, matcha latte.

Deliveroo. Also in Chelsea (West London)
and Brick Lane (East London).

Hoxton Beach Falafel, Goodge
Vegan falafel stall

- Goodge Place Market, off Goodge
  Street W1T 2NR
- 07931 375632
- M-F 11.30-14.30, Sa-Su closed
- Goodge Street
- hoxtonbeach.com

Falafel wrap in Arab khubz bread with
tahini, chilli sauce, their homemade turnip
pickle, cucumber and chilli pickles, salad
and hummus. Regular £3.50, large £4.50,
add a cooked vegetable for 50p such as
aubergine, sweet potato, cauliflower or fuul
fava bean stew. Also loose falafel balls or
fuul with salads. Drinks £1 include lemon,
elderflower, hibiscus.

By Cloe, Oxford Circus
Vegan restaurant

- 4-5 Langham Place W1B 3DG
- 020
- M-W 07.00-22.00, Th-F 07.00-23.00,
  Sa 10.00-23.00, Su 10.00-23.00
- Oxford Circus
- eatbychloe.com
  facebook.com/eatbychloe

Opened June 2019. For menu see Covent
Garden branch. This is the only branch that
opens really early on weekdays so the
brunch menu is available here every day.

Also at Tower Bridge (South Bank) and North
Greenwich.

White Pine
Vegetarian organic boutique cafe & juice bar

- 35-36 Rathbone Place W1T 1JN
- 07388 412 486
- M-F 06.30-20.00, Sa 08.30-19.00, Su 9.00-18.00
- Tottenham Court Road, Goodge St
- white-pine.co.uk
  facebook.com/whitepinelifestyle
  instagram.com/whitepinelifestyle

Scandinavian boutique vegetarian cafe and coffee bar opened October 2018.

For breakfast try matcha-pistachio overnight oats. Filled bagels or muffins £5.45 such as creamy cheese with mozzarella, pesto and salad; or vegan chicken, asparagus, sriracha, pea shoots, mayo and salad. Caesar salad £8.95 with vegan chicken and parmesan.

Treats include red velvet cake, carrot cake, triple chocolate hazelnut muffin or cookie, salted peanut fudge doughnut, chocolate avocado mousse with berries, brownies, energy balls, Raw Halo and Vivani chocolate bars.

Cold drinks include 450ml juices and smoothies £5.55; lucuma or maca or açai shot 85p, CBD £2. Espresso ginger beer, iced vanilla or hazelnut latte, kombucha, Not Botanicals herb water.

Organic teas and coffees £2.60-£4.40 include herbals, black, chai latte,

All packaging is made from plants not plastic, such as trees, corn and sugar cane, including lids and cutlery. It is all recycled along with food waste. They also sell designer home wares, gifts and plants.

TOFU
CHILI
MASALA

BABY
MUSHROOMS
IN
TOMATO +
GARLIC
SAUCE

CUM
POTA
CO

...AVE IT YOUR WAY...

...URRIES, 1 RICE, 3 FRITTERS
£5.99

...NAN BREAD £6.99

THE WAY TO GOOD HEALTH

VITAMINS, SPORTS NUTRITION, NATURAL SKINCARE, HEALTHY GROCERY

Facials
Threading
Waxing
Massage

NOW OPEN
Vitamins
Natural Skincare
Sports Nutrition
Energy Rooms
Health Grocery
Detox
Herbal
Viagras

Health Food Centre
Health food shop & vegetarian take-away

- 10 Warren Street W1T 5LG
- 7387 9289
- M-F 9.00-18.00, Sa 10.00-17.00, Su closed
- Warren Street
- ukhealthfoodcentre.co.uk

Well-stocked health food shop and take-away tucked away down the side of Warren Street tube. The owner Raj is very friendly and a committed veggie. Also a smoothies, juice and coffee bar with a table outside, weather permitting. Handy for Euston or Regent's Park.

Vegan sandwiches £2.75, such as fake chicken and salad; lentil burger and hummus with salad; date, walnut and banana; burger and hummus; veggie BLT. Plus filled topedos, baps and baguettes. Panini £3.50. Pastries and Indian snacks from 90p.

3 or 4 hot curries each day, like saag aloo, or tofu veg masala. Brown rice or cumin jeera rice ice and two curries with naan £6.99. Also some Italian dishes for those who don't like spicy food.

Cakes on the counter from 80p, including vegan choc brownies, date slice, apricot slice and chocolate tiffin.

Good range of fresh squeezed juices £3 including melon and kiwi, or pineapple, apple and ginger. Their speciality is smoothies £3.50 that are more like a meal, with dates, banana, cacao, lucuma etc. Optional spirulina, algae and other superfood shots £1. Organic canned drinks £1.

The shop packs a lot of wholefoods into a small space. Extensive range of cruelty-free toiletries, herbal and Ayurvedic supplements and remedies, vitamins.

Therapy room for pre-booked full body massage, one hour £50.

Ethos
Vegetarian restaurant

- ☛ 48 Eastcastle Street W1W 8DX
  (behind Top Shop)
- ☎ 020 3581 1538
- ◑ M-F breakfast 08.00-11.00; M-Sa
  lunch 11.30-15.00, afternoon tea
  15.00-17.30, dinner 17.30-22.00; Su
  closed
- ⊖ Oxford Circus
- ↖ ethosfoods.com
  facebook.com/ethosfoods

Opened September 2014, this is a big, gorgeous, elegant restaurant with floor to ceiling windows, white, blue and gold interior, and even indoor silver birch trees.

Choose exactly what you want from the buffet, £2.30 per 100 grams breakfast, £2.50 lunch, £2.70 dinner. Vegan and gluten-free and clearly labelled and they have vegan wine.

Breakfast options (£3.25-£4.50 eat in, cheaper to take-away) include smoothies, avocado on toast, gluten-free oat porridge made with almond milk and toppings such as raspberry with maple and almond, or banana with chocolate chips and walnuts.

Just over half the dozen each of hot and cold lunch and dinner buffet items are vegan, probably reflecting that "our target market are not actually vegetarians, it's just people who like good, interesting food." But if it is healthy vegan food you're after, you can feast on salads, couscous with pesto, hummus, guacamole, roast cauliflower with tahini and cranberries, Asia stir-fry with tofu, Japanese miso aubergine, puy lentil with coconut cream, Lebanese roasted green beans, feijoada, sweet potato fries.

Desserts £1.80-£3 change daily such a black bean brownie, choc peanut butte bomb, carrot cake.

Wine from £5 mediium glass, £14 half litre, £18 bottle. Camden Brewery beers and Ashridge organic cider £4.50. Cocktails £7.50.

Kin Cafe
Vegetarian cafe

- ☛ 22 Foley Street W1W 6DF
- ☎ 020-7998 4720
- ◑ M-F 07.30-17.00, Sa-Su closed
- ⊖ Goodge Street
- ↖ kincafe.co.uk
  facebook.com/kincafelondon
  instagram.com/kin_cafe

Lovely veggie café with savouries served with salads, fresh juices, and their big speciality is coffees which rotate between some of the country's top roasters large and small.

Lots of breakfast options £4.50 to £8.50 such as porridge with fruit toppings, chia pudding, granola bowl, avocado on sourdough toast, tofu and spinach vegan shakshuka with toasted sourdough, or sweet potato and kale hash with smashed avo and asparagus.

Lunch salads £4.50 small box, £6.50 large, with quiche £7. Soup £3.90 such as roasted beetroot with squash, ginger and coconut. Savoury items £4.50 such as stuffed squash with watercress peso, sunflower seeds, parsley and flaked amonds; soy roasted oyster mushrooms with roasted peppers, spinach and peanut sauce.

Cakes £3.10 include vegan options such as orange and almond polenta.

Organic juices to order £3.50 such as broccoli, kale, celery and apple, and 50p back if you bring back your bottle.

Sagar
Vegetarian South Indian restaurant

- 🖝 17A Percy Street W1T 1DU (off Tottenham Court Rd)
- ☎ 763 1 3319
- 🕐 M-F 12.00-14.45, 17.30-22.45, Sa 12.00-23.30, Su 12.00-22.00, Bank Hols 13.00-22.00
- ⊖ Tottenham Court Rd, Goodge St
- ↖ sagarveg.co.uk

This third branch of Sagar opened in 2007, offering South Indian vegetarian and vegan cuisine at excellent value, especially the £5.95 lunch platter (M-F) and £3.50 lunch box (every day). Warm interior with wood panelled walls and wooden tables. Special vegan menu and helpful staff.

M-F three course lunch platter £5.95 changes daily with starters, special rice, curry, dosa, dessert (not vegan). Lunch box £3.50 every day with 2 curries, rice, chappati, salad and raita.

Starters £2-£4.75 include samosas, bhajias and veg kebab, but why not try something unusual such as Kancheepuram rice and lentil dumplings with green chili, pepper and cashew nuts; Medu vada fried lentil doughnuts; or special upma cream of wheat with fresh tomato, peas and cashews.

12 kinds of dosa stuffed pancakes, 8 variations of uthappam lentil pizzas, 15 curries £3.95-6.25. Curries include suki bhajee dry vegetable tossed in karahi with coconut, or onion and tomato sambar with fresh coconut and lentil.

Ethos

Sagar thalis £14.25, Rajdani or Udupi tha £16.95, the latter can be vegan with lentils pappadam, palaya, sukhi bhaji, kootu, veg sambar, dal, rasam, basmati rice, poori an dessert. Rice £2.95-4.45 including with garlic and spices, or lemon and peas Vegetable biryani £5.95.

Desserts £2.75-3.45, no vegan ones on the main menu but they do have mango sorbet on the vegan menu.

House wine £13.95 bottle, £3.45 glass. Coffee £1.95. Children welcome, high chairs.

Children welcome, high chairs.

Planet Organic, Tottenham Court Rd
Natural and organic supermarket and mainly vegetarian take-away

- ☛ 23-24 Tottenham Court Road W1T 1BJ
- ☏ 020 7436 1929
- ◐ M-Sa 07.30-21.00, Su 12.00-18.00
- ⊖ Tottenham Court Road, Goodge St
- ↖ planetorganic.com

New branch opened 2016 at the south end of Tottenham Court Road. Here the focus on take-away food including porridge £2.95-4.95, organic hot soup £3.50-£5.50, organic stew and brown rice £5.50; mix and match veggie box £5.50 small, £7.50 medium, £8.50 large. Vegan tuna on rye £4.95. Seating upstairs.

Planet Organic, Torrington Place

Natural and organic supermarket and mainly vegetarian café

- 22 Torrington Place WC1A 7JE
- 020 7436 1929
- M-F 08.00-21.00, Sa 09.00-20.00, Su 12-18.00
- Goodge Street
- planetorganic.com

Organic wholefood supermarket off Tottenham Court Road, with a juice bar and café. Most dishes, snacks and cakes are labelled with symbols to show if they're gluten- / sugar-free, vegetarian or vegan. Ingredients displayed for some cafe dishes; available for others on request.

There is a deli/cafe at the front and in this branch they have made the entire hot food section vegan. Hot and cold dishes and salads, for take-away or eat in at the tables inside or out. Bowl of food £5.50, £7.50 or £8.50. Gluten-free vegan porridge £2.95 or £4.95. Everything is cooked fresh each day. Cakes, cookies, muffins and brownies, some vegan or dairy-, wheat- or gluten-free. Lots of juices and smoothies £4.95-£5.95, teas and coffees £1.65-£2.95, with different kinds of plant milk at no extra cost. Speciality lattes £3.15-£4. Fridges also have take-away food such as wraps, falafel meals, salads and calzone.

The shop sells just about everything for veggies including organic fruit and veg, stacks of tofu and tempeh, fake meat, pastas including spelt, quinoa and amaranth, macrobiotic Japanese foods, raw foods including chocolate and brownies, Inspiral raw cakes and Living Food Kitchen cheesecakes. Vegan wines and beers. Some bread baked daily on the premises. Lots of dairy-free ice cream including indulgent Bessant & Drury and Booja Booja.

Huge section devoted to health and body care, including vitamins, herbs, tinctures, homeopathy, aromatherapy oils, suncream, makeup (Organic Bloom, Desert Essence, Antipodes, Dr Hauschka, Lavera), shampoos and conditioners, sun cream including Weleda, Green People, Barefoot Botanicals, Jason, Ren, Akin, Neals Yard, John Masters. Staff are very friendly and knowledgeable to deal with queries, several being practitioners or in training.

A great place for presents like pretty candles and incense. Chocolate and other treats. Fitness, pilates, yoga products and DVDs, even razors, body and toothbrushes made from recycled materials.

Children welcome.

ICCO
Omnivorous Italian pizza restaurant

- 46 Goodge Street W1T 4LU (corner Charlotte Street)
- 020 7580 9688
- M-Th 07.00-23.00, F 07.00-24.00, Sa 08.00-23.30, Su 08.00-23.00
- Goodge Street
- icco.co.uk

Recommended to us by a vegan Italian for their 12-inch (30cm) vegan pizza £7.20 made before your eyes with vegan cheese, caramelised onions, roasted aubergine, courgette and pepper. Extra veg 80p each. Large black coffee £2.

Le Pain Quotidien
Omnivorous Belgian cafe

- 64 Tottenham Court Rd W1T 2ET (corner Goodge St)
- 0207486 6154
- M-F 07.00-22.00, Sa 09.00-22.00, Su & holidays 09.00-21.00
- Goodge Street
- lepainquotidien.co.uk

See Chains section. Free wifi.

Pizza Express, Charlotte Street
Omnivorous pizza restaurant

- 7-9 Charlotte Street W1T 1RB
- 020 7580 1110
- M-Su 11.30-23.00
- Goodge Street
- pizzaexpress.com/charlotte-street

3 floors plus garden dining and private room hire. Baby facilities. Disabled toilet.

Also branches at Langham Place and Great Portland Street, see Marylebone chapter.

Zizzi, Charlotte Street
Omnivorous pizza restaurant

- 33-41 Charlotte Street W1T 1RR
- 020 3802 6110
- M-Th 11.30-23.00, F-Sa 11.30-23.30, Su 12.00-22.30
- Goodge Street
- zizzi.co.uk

They use vegan Mozzarisella cheese in original, smoked, cheddar and blue. And they have vegan desserts!.

The King's Canary
Vegan hair salon

- 81 Great TItchfield Street W1W 6RQ
- 020 7637 7322
- Tu-F 10.00-20.00, Sa 10.00-18.00, Su-M closed
- Great Portland Street, Oxford Street Goodge Street, Regent's Park
- thekingscanary.com facebook.com/TheKingsCanary

Eco-friendly hair salon aiming to minimise their footprint for guilt-free pampering. They use organic vegan Evo products (accredited by PETA) and ammonia-free dyes. Ladies cut & dry £63, men's cut & style £50, wash and blowdry £50. Tints, highlights, balayage, creative colour, T-line, bleach with toner £75-£150.

Free drinks with appointment. Book through the website.

eir other branch is called the Canary in thnal Green, East London, and includes vegetarian cafe.

Holland & Barrett
health food shop

- **Goodge Street**: 65 Tottenham Court Road W1T 2EU
- ☎ 020 7580 5389
- 🕐 M-F 07.30-20.00, Sa 10.00-19.00, Su 11.00-19.00
- ⊖ Goodge Street

Fridge but no freezer.

- 52 **Oxford Street** W1D 1BG (corner of Rathbone Place)
- ☎ 020 7580 2768
- 🕐 M-F 08.00-21.30, Sa 9.00-21.30, Su 10.00-20.30
- ⊖ Tottenham Court Road

Fridges and freezer.

Pizza Express

- 254 **Tottenham Court Road** W1T 7RB (opposite Sainsbury's)
- ☎ 020 7580 3219
- 🕐 M-F 08.30-21.00, Sa 9.30-20.00, Su 10.00-20.00
- ⊖ Tottenham Court Road

New branch. Fridge and freezer.

CAMDEN

REGENT'S PARK

GREAT PORTLAND ST.

EUSTON

FITZROVIA

REGENT'S PARK

BAKER STREET
Madam Tussaud's & Planetarium

MARYLEBONE

EDGWARE ROAD

EDGWARE ROAD

Daunt Books (travel)

Waitrose supermarket

Chess & Bridge

Selfridges

MARBLE ARCH

BOND STREET

OXFORD CIRCUS

Tesco 24/24

SOHO

PADDINGTON

HYDE PARK

MAYFAIR

- **vegan**
- **vegetarian**
- **omnivorous**
- **shop**

Cr Vegan Crosstown
By By Chloe (Fitzrovia)
De Deliciously Ella (Mayfair)
Ne Neat Burger (Mayfair)
Ga The Gate 3
Ma Mayfair Juicery
Wo Woodlands
Et Ethos (Fitzrovia)
Ki Kin (Fitzrovia)
As As Nature Intended
fg The Fruit Garden
re Revital Health Shop
ny Neal's Yard Remedies
Gi Giellly Green hairdresser
Holland & Barrett:
H1 Baker Street
H2 Marble Arch
H3 Marylebone
H4 Edgware Road
H5 West One (Mayfair)
H6 Maddox St (Mayfair)

co Comptoir Libanais
Is Istanbul Cafe
JL John Lewis Place to Eat
LC Lebanese Cafes, Edgware Rd
Le Leon, Regent Street
Q Le Pain Quotidien
ph Phoenix Palace

Pizza Express:
P1 Baker Street
P2 Great Portland Street
P3 Langham Place
P4 St Christopher's Place
P5 Thayer Street

so Sofra
W Wagamama

MARYLEBONE

Oxford Street to Regent's Park

's W1, but not as you know it. Unlike the party furore of Soho, this residential area between Regent's Park in the north and Oxford Street in the south, Edgware Road on the west and Great Portland Street on the east, has wide streets and ample pavement space.

The Gate 3 opened December 2016 near Marble Arch, with a similar menu to Islington and Hammersmith, except that this one also serves breakfast. When you're ready for a retox, head for **Vegan Crosstown** donuts and coffee cafe behind Selfridges. **Woodlands** vegetarian restaurant offers elegant and classic South Indian dining. Behind Bond Street station is **Deliciously Ella**'s gorgeous healthy vegan cafe (see Mayfair). Near Oxford Circus is **Neat Burger** (see Mayfair).

Meanwhile just over in Fitzrovia are the new **By Chloe** American vegan restaurant, **Ethos** vegetarian buffet restaurant and **Kin** vegetarian cafe (see Fitzrovia section)

Marylebone High Street, home of the wonderful Daunt travel bookshop, has a branch of Le Pain Quotidien, a French-style (actually Belgian) cafe chain offering tofu salads, vegan soup and blueberry muffins.

For a fast lunch whilst fashion shopping on Oxford Street, try Sofra Turkish, a pastie from Holland & Barrett in the Bond Street underground station (see Mayfair), or grab a falafel from one of the Lebanese take-aways on Edgware Road. **As Nature Intended** is a gorgeous new wholefoods supermarket on Edgware Road. While down the other end of Oxford Street, **Revital** is the place to shop. And don't miss **The Fruit Garden** if you're around Baker Street or Marylebone.

Meet your heroes, with absolutely no risk of clamming up, at **Madame Tussauds**. The legendary London attraction houses 300 unbelievably lifelike and constantly updated waxworks of the hip and famous, or notorious, across 14 interactive zones. Snap selfies with the kids' favourites like Spiderman, Yoda and Darth Vader, musicians from Marley to Miley, and sports superstars Usain Bolt, Sir Mo Farah and Dame Jessica Ennis-Hill. There are Hollywood hunks and heroines galore from Hepburn to The Hunger Games, and even Simon Cowell and The Donald. Book in advance for best prices and to minimise queuing.

For a real treat, **Gielly Green** is a top end hairdresser with their own range of vegan products.

Top tourist attraction: Madam Tussauds waxworks and Planetarium, next to Baker Street underground.

Top attraction for locals: Selfridges department store.

The Gate, Marble Arch
Vegetarian restaurant

- 22-24 Seymour Place W1H 7N
- 020 7724 6656
- M-Th 08.00-22.30, F 08.00-23.00, Sa 09.00-23.00, Su 09.00-21.00
- Marble Arch
- thegaterestaurants.com

The third branch of the Gate opened December 2016

The main menu includes dishes such as aubergine teriyaki, green banana fritters, plantain chips and green dragon tofu salad, three-way filled globe artichoke, aubergine schnitzel, and wild mushroom rotolo. See the branches in Hammersmith and Islington for more dishes.

This is the first branch to serve breakfast, such as scrambled tofu with smoky shiitake mushroom.

Crosstown Marylebone
Vegan donuts cafe

- 5-6 Picton Place W1U 1BL (behind Selfridges)
- 020 7487 3733
- M-F 9.00-18.00, Sa-Su 10.00-18.30 or until sold out
- Bond Street
- crosstowndoughnuts.com

Crosstown Vegan, the first fully vegan branch of this doughnut and coffee shop chain, opened here in March 2018.

Wacky flavours include pink beetroot with crumbed pistachios, or spirulina with coconut custard and a lime glaze.

Coffee and other vegan hot and soft drinks.

Three bar seats and two outdoor tables with two seats.

Mayfair Juicery
vegan juice take-away

- north-west corner of Vere St and Oxford Street W1 (to the right of Debenhams)
- M-Su 10.00-19.00, sometimes earlier or later
- Bond Street, Oxford Circus

Cold-pressed solo juices, combos and smoothies with almond milk or coconut water. £4 small, £5 large, £6 bottle. Add-ons £1 include almond butter, avocado, cacao nibs, chia seeds, flax, maca, oats, peanut butter, turmeric, vegan protein powder. Cash only.

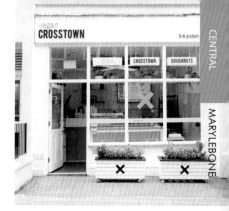

The Gate

Mayfair Juicery

Woodlands Marylebone
Vegetarian Indian restaurant

- ☛ 77 Marylebone Lane WIU 2PS
  (off Marylebone High St.)
- ☏ 020 7486 3862
- ◷ M-F 12.00-15.00, 18.00-23.00
  Sa-Su 12.00-23.00 (last orders
  14.45, 22.30)
- ⊖ Bond Street, Baker Street
- ↖ woodlandsrestaurant.co.uk

Perhaps the largest vegetarian Indian chain in the world, with 3 London branches and over 30 in India, from where the chefs come. This branch is smart with walnut flooing, cream linen and granite bar. Ideal for large parties, couples and business meetings. 75 dishes on the menu with many different flavours, textures and colours.

Lots of starters £4.95-6.50 from idli rice balls to banana, potato and dry fruit kebab, or a mixed tandoori platter for two £12.50. Soups £3.95.

Ten varieties of dosa (vegetable stuffed pancake, made from rice and wheat) £4.95-7.25. Their specialty is uthappam or lentil pizza, with coconut, tomato, green chilli £6.75. Traditional village vegetable curries £6.25-7.50 include Kootu (daily changing vegetables cooked in coconut milk).

Rice £3.25-4.95 such as pilau or lemon. Indian hot £2.75-3.25 such as poori, bathura, paratha, naan.

Thalis or set meals £18.50 with dessert.

Unfortunately for vegans, all 9 desserts appear to be made with dairy, but they say that Jaggary dosa can be made vegan, an Indian crepe filled with pure sugar cane and cardamom at £3.95.

Glass of house wine £4.95, bottle £16.2 Beer £2.75 small, £4.95 large. Spiri £2.75-£2.95.

This branch has a two course lunch men £10.50, three £13.50. They cater fc parties. MC, Visa, Amex

If you like this you'll probably like their othe branches in Panton Street off Leiceste Square (Soho), and Hampstead.

Istanbul Café
Omnivorous Turkish bistro

- ☛ 305 Great Portland Street W1W
  5PW
- ☏ 020 7580 9142
- ◷ M-F 07.00-24.00, Sa-Su 08.00-
  24.00
- ⊖ Great Portland Street
- ↖ bistroistanbul.com/

Handy for Regent's Park, this is a big all-day Turkish omnivorous café next to Great Portland Street underground station and opposite International House student hostel. Tables inside and out. Previously called Meze Cafe.

Open for breakfast, lunch and dinner, and chilling out at any time. Cooked breakfast £4.95 7am-3pm , you can swap out any items.

Most of the cold and several hot meze are veggie or vegan, £5.50 eat in (£4.95 take-away). Meze combination £12 per person, minimum two people, for around ten meze bowls to share. Two course special £8.90 lunch, £11.90 evening, with coffee or tea. For main course have iman bayildi stuffed aubergine or falafel with hummus, salad and rice. Turkish wraps £5.50 take-away, £6.95 eat in with chips.

ouse wine £12.90 bottle, £3.60 glass.
er £3.25. Freshly squeezed orange juice
2.80. Pure fruit smoothies £3.25. Coffee
1.80 in (£1.70 take away), tea £1.50
1.30).

hildren welcome, no high chair. Dogs
elcome. MC, Visa, 50p charge under £10.
Opposite a Pret, 24 hour grocers Tesco
xpress and Portland Food & Wine, and
wo pubs Green Man and The Albany.

Comptoir Libanais, Wigmore St
Omnivorous Lebanese restaurant

- 🍴 63 Wigmore Street W1U 1JT
- ☎ 020 7935 1110
- 🕐 M-Sa 08.00-23.00, Su 09.00-22.00
- ⊖ Bond Street
- ↖ comptoirlibanais.com

Comptoir Libanais, John Lewis
Omnivorous Lebanese restaurant

- 🍴 4th floor John Lewis, 300 Oxford Street W1C 1DX
- ☎ 020 3355 5558
- 🕐 M-Sa 9.30-19.30 (Th 20.30), Su 11.30-17.30
- ⊖ Oxford Circus, Bond Street
- ↖ comptoirlibanais.com

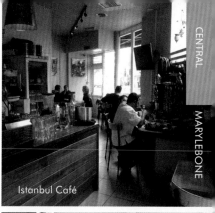

Istanbul Café

Lebanese Cafes, Edgware Rd
Omnivorous cafes & grocers

- ☛ South end of Edgware Road
- ◕ Mon-Sun very late
- ⊖ Marble Arch, Edgware Rd

There are lots of Lebanese grocers and cafes on Edgware Road. Look out for falafels, juice bars, and lovely things to take home including big tubs of tahini sesame spread for making your own hummus.

Leon, Regent Street
Omnivorous cafe & take-away

- ☛ 275 Regent Street W1B 2HB
- ☎ 020 7495 1514
- ◕ M-F 07.30-21.00, Sa 11.00-20.00, Su 11.00-19.00
- ⊖ Oxford Circus
- ↖ leonrestaurants.co.uk

Fast food cafe with great value veggie food. Check their website for the full menu.

Le Pain Quotidien, Marylebone
Omnivorous restaurant

- ☛ 72-75 Marylebone High St W1U 5JW
- ☎ 020 7486 6154
- ◕ M-F 07.00-21.00, Sa 08.00-21.00, Su and bank holiday 08.00-19.00
- ⊖ Baker Street
- ↖ lepainquotidien.com

There is a French enclave at the north end of Marylebone High Street. Unfortunately the French are not noted for their vegetarian sympathies , but this cafe-style restaurant with olde worlde wooden tables is marvellous exception. See Chains sectio for menu. At lunchtime it gets busy so wo just a few minutes to be seated in th patisserie at the front, which also sells ja of olives, capers, olive tapenade sprea and aubergine paté.

Phoenix Palace
Chinese omnivorous restaurant

- ☛ 5-9 Glentworth Street NW1 5PG
- ☎ 020 7486 3515
- ◕ M-Sa 12.00-23.30, Su 11.00-22.30
- ⊖ Marylebone, Baker Street
- ↖ phoenixpalace.co.uk

Big, very elegant, high class Chinese restaurant with a set vegan menu around £26 each for minimum two persons with vegan platter, rainbow bean curd soup, quick fried three vegetables, crispy beancurd in black pepper sauce, Szechuan aubergine hot pot in spicy sauce, mixed veg fried rice. It's absolutely huge, enough for 2 meals, but you can take half of it home to have the next day.

The a la carte menu has two pages of veg and bean curd dishes £7-13.80 such as monk's vegetables. Rice or noodles from £3. Vegans can enjoy mango tofu dessert £4.20, lychees £3, mango or ginger and lime sorbet £3.50.

Wine from £4.50 medium glass, £17 bottle, up to £888. Beer £3.20-4.40. Cocktails £8-9, mocktails £4.50-£6. Spirits around £3-4 up to £3,800 for a bottle of 50 year old Mou Tai liquor. Chinese tea £1.80.

Children welcome, high chairs. MC, Visa, Amex. 280 seats, good for weddings,

...rties and events. Note they do have a fish ...nk.

...zza Express, Marylebone
...mnivorous Italian restaurant

- 133 Baker Street W1U 6SF
- 020 7486 0888
- Su-W 11.30-23.00, Th-Sa 11.30-24.00
- Baker Street

- 215-217 Great Portland St W1W 5PN
- 020 7580 2272
- Su-Tu 11.30-23.00, W-Sa 11.30-23.30
- Great Portland Street

- 4-5 Langham Place W1B 3DG
- 020 7580 3700
- M-Sa 11.30-23.30, Su 11.30-23.00
- Bond Street

- 21-22 Barrett Street, St Christopher's Place W1U 1BD
- 020 7629 1001
- Su-W 11.30-23.30, Th-Sa 11.30-24.00
- Bond Street

- 13-14 Thayer Street W1U 3JS
- 020 7935 2167
- M-Th 11.30-23.00, F-Sa 11.30-23.30, Su 11.30-22.00
- Bond Street
- pizzaexpress.com

They have vegan cheese.

Sofra, St Christopher's Place
Omnivorous Turkish restaurant

- 1 St Christopher's Place W1U 1LT
- 020 7224 4080
- M-Su 08.00-23.00 or later
- Bond Street
- sofra.co.uk

Healthy menu £11.95 per person, after 6pm £14.95, gets you 8 meze dishes in individual bowls such as tabouleh, falafel, lentil patties, broad beans, ratatouille, hummus, baba ganoush, salad.

Wagamama, Wigmore Street
Omnivorous Japanese restaurant

- 101A Wigmore St W1H 9AB (behind Selfridges)
- 020 7409 0111
- M-Sa 11.30-23.00, Su 12.00-22.00
- Bond Street
- wagamama.com

Large Japanese fast food noodle restaurant. See Chains section. Baby facilities. Free wifi. Disabled full access.

Gielly Green
Vegan hairdresser

- 42-44 George Street W1U 7ES
- (020 7034 3060
- M 10.00-17.00, Tu-Sa 9.00-18.00, Su closed
- giellygreen.co.uk

Luxury hair salon with 70 seats and their own brand of vegan haircare products.

Neal's Yard Remedies
Organic health and beauty

- 112 Marylebone High Street W1U 4SA
- (020 7935 0656
- M-Sa 10.00-19.00, W-Th till 20.00, Su 11.00-18.00
- Bond St, Baker St, Regent's Park
- nealsyardremedies.com

Organic skin and bodycare, natural remedies, therapies and treatments - walk-ins available.

The Fruit Garden
Health food shop, grocer and greengrocer

- 21-23 Melcombe St, NW1 6AG
- (020 7935 5161
- M-F 08.00-21.00, Sa 09.00-21.00, Su 11.00-19.00
- Baker Street, Marylebone

Now expanded to two shops with a bigger range. The left shop is a grocer, the right one a health and organic food store. Wholefoods, fruit and veg. Vegan chocolate by Vivani, Conscious, Organica, Nakd, Plamil, Organica, Montezuma. Ella's Kitchen baby food. Swedish Glace ice-cream.

As Nature Intended, Marble Arc
Omnivorous wholefood supermarket

- 36 Edgware Road W2 2EH
- (020 7723 6750
- M-F 09.00-21.00, Sa 08.00-20.00, Su/BH 12.00-18.00
- Marble Arch

Big new wholefoods store. For the kind of things they sell see Chiswick branch (West)

evital Health Shop
Health food shop

- 22 Wigmore St W1U 2RG (between Wimpole Street and Harley Street)
- 020 7631 3731
- M-F 9.00-19.00, Sa 9.00-18.30, Su 11.00-16.00
- Bond Street, Oxford Circus
- revital.co.uk

The flagship central London branch of this chain of health food stores, not just for locals but also the nearby Harley Street healthcare practitioners and their patients.

Health foods including gluten and wheat-free and organic. Fridge with tofu, Sojade yogurts, Covo coconut milk yogurt, drinks.

Bodycare and natural beauty products including Dr Hauschka, Weleda, Green People, Lavera, Natracare.

Supplements include Solgar, Lamberts, Nature's Plus, Biocare, Higher Nature, Viridian, sports nutrition. All staff are qualified in health care such as naturopathy, food science or personal trainer and some are veggie too. They can dispense "practitioner only" supplements. Nutrition books.

Cleaning products by Ecover, Attitude.

Revital Education Centre downstairs offers seminars, classes and workshops with a discount on anything you buy that day. Seminar and clinic rooms for hire. Regular hynotherapist and nutritionist by appointment.

Holland & Barrett
Health food shop

- 78 Baker St W1U 6TD
- 020 7935 3544
- M-F 8.30-18.30, Sa 9.30-17.30, Su 11.00-17.00
- Baker Street

- 526 Oxford Street W1C 1LW
- 020 7499 6773
- M-F 08.00-22.00, Sa 09.00-22.00, Su 09.00-18.00
- Marble Arch

- 104 Marylebone High Street W1U 4RR
- 020 7935 8412
- M-F 08.00- 19.00, Sa 9.00- 18.30, Su 11.00-18.00
- Baker Street

- Unit 1, 159-163 Edgware Rd W2 2HR
- 020 7706 4377
- M-F 09.00-21.000, Su 10.00-20.30
- Edgware Road

Tibits

MAYFAIR

Central London

Mayfair, the poshest of posh between Oxford Street and Piccadilly, has a sprinkling of vegan-friendly eateries that won't deliver you a three-figure bill (and plenty of not so vegan-friendly ones that will). Once a vegan desert, exemplifying the rule that the richer the establishment, the worse the food, we now have a decent number of options, all close to Oxford Street, Regent Street and Piccadilly.

Swish Swiss vegetarian chain **Tibits** has opened a fabulous gourmet buffet restaurant just off Regent Street. It's the perfect place to meet friends and the basement is popular for groups small or huge. We love Tuesdays, when everything on the huge buffet is vegan. If you want to meet local and international vegans, come to London Vegan Meetup's See You Last Tuesday (C.U.L.T. - they say it's because everyone else thinks we vegans are a cult), when from 6pm on the last Tuesday of the month we fill the basement. There are plenty of vegan wines and beers to keep the party going.

Fans of superstar vegan cookbook author **Deliciously Ella** head to her healthy cafe behind Bond Street tube.

Raw Press cafe is part of the raw-volution that has stormed in from America and is sweeping across London with cold-pressed vegetable juices and healthy salads.

On the other hand for something with a little more olive oil, head for **Sofra** for a platter of Turkish meze, either the Mayfair branch, or cross Oxford Street to the one in Marylebone. Alternatively, **Chor Bizarre** is a very elegant and upmarket North Indian.

For a swift lunch, **Crussh** has vegan soups, wraps and smoothies.

Whilst fashion shopping on Oxford Street, you can sit down at **Le Pain Quotidien**, or grab something from the fridges in the **Holland & Barrett** store in the Bond Street underground station.

Stella McCartney is the top vegetarian fashion store in the world, and nearby Bond Street is Vogue heaven.

Neat Burger has just opened a fast food restaurant off Oxford Circus. If you're into burgers and loaded fries, it's heaven. Just bring plenty of money, this is Mayfair.

> **Tourist tips:**
>
> Check out the water birds in St James's Park, wander down The Mall to **Buckingham Palace**, take in an art exhibition at the **Royal Academy**, picnic in **Green Park**, and roam the gigantic **Selfridges** department store.

ibits, Mayfair

ternational vegetarian restaurant

- 2-14 Heddon Street, W1B 4DA (off Regent Street)
- 020 7758 4112
- M-W 09.00-22.30, Th-F 09.00-24.00, Sa 11.30-24.00, Su/BH 11.30-22.30. Food served till 30 minutes before closing.
- Oxford Circus, Piccadilly Circus
- tibits.co.uk

Big and beautiful new gourmet vegetarian buffet restaurant close to where the much loved Country Life used to be, operated by the owners of a chain of vegetarian restaurants in Switzerland. Country Life fans will enjoy the big buffet with over 50 items and that it's open longer hours and has wine. For such an elegant restaurant, the prices are very reasonable, so we have listed them in full as you will probably want to come here a lot to meet friends and choose exactly what and how much you want to go on your plate.

Gourmet buffet with over 40 items. Breakfast £1.80 per 100gr includes vegan Swiss Birchermuesli, fresh fruit, breads, cereals and dried cranberries. Lunch £2.50, dinner £2.80. The buffet has lots of salds, hot dishes such as polenta, and six desserts of which at least two are vegan and all of them on Tuesdays, when the entire buffet is vegan, such as sticky toffee pudding, chocolate mousse, strawberry muesli, and fresh mango.

Sandwiches to order £3.30. Soup and bread £3.80. Pastries and cakes from the counter too though these tend not to be vegan.

Extensive vegan wine list, from £4.80 medium glass, £6.30 large, £17.50 bottle. Freedom organic vegan lager and pale ale £2.50 half, £4.40 pint. Partizan Brewing IPA 5.7% £4.70 (330ml). Orpens Craft Cider £3.60 (330ml). Spritis and liqueurs £2.90-£4, doubles £5-£7.10.

Freshly squeezed juices £2.60-3.70. Coffee, cappuccino, latte £1.70-£2.80. Teas, chai £2.20-£3.10. They have soya milk. Soft drinks and water £1-£2.50, kombucha £3.70. Help yourself to free filtered water.

Some outside tables. No reservations (except downstairs party area). Children welcome, kids area downstairs. Gift vouchers.

London Vegan Meetup fill the downstairs every last Tuesday of the month, but you don't have to be vegan to join in, just eat vegan for the evening, which is very easy here.

A second branch opened on the South Bank summer 2017, near the Tate Modern.

Mae Deli
Vegan cafe

- 18-20 Weighouse Street W1K 5LU
- M-F 7.30- 21.00 Sa-Su/BH 9.00-21.00
- Bond Street
- themaedeli.com

Cosy, new plant based, organic cafe opened late 2016 by top food writer "Deliciously Ella" Mills and her husband Mathew, hence MAE (Matthew and Ella). It has a warm feel with a lot of space and daylight. Big table at the back and many other seats by the windows. Wifi.

Breakfast served till 11am on weekdays and midday on weekends. Breakfast bowl £5.50, you choose your base such as coconut or red berry chia pudding, porridge, açai and Coyo coconut yoghurt. You can also add 3 of the following toppings: almond or peanut butter, maple syrup, coconut chips, spiced apple and cranberry compote, strawberry chia seeds jam, granola, and mixed seeds.

Rye or gluten-free toast topped with jam £2, nut butter £2.50, peanut butter and jam £4.50, smashed avocado £4.50.

Lunch and dinner served from 11 on weekdays and midday on weekends. The food changes every two months and the salads and vegetables are seasonal.

Mae bowl eat in or take out £9.75 for 4 items from: black rice with squash, beetroot and Brussels sprouts, roasted pumpkin with chickpeas and chilli, charred broccoli with kohlrabi, chilli and black beans, broad bean and cauliflower falafel, Christmas cabbage salad, pea and avocado hummus, apricot and cauliflower dhal with brown rice (served warm), 5 bean chilli with brown rice (served warm). Soup with bread £4.50

Puddings £3/£3.50 include fudge browni giant banana and peanut butter cup orange Mae cake , red berry cheesecake Energy balls £1.50.

Organic pressed fruit and vegetables juice £6.95 such as Greens, Roots, Deep Greer Lemonade £3.50. Smoothies £5.50-£6.5! including peanut butter protein , tropica berry, green glow, blueberry breakfast.

Hot drinks £2.50-£3.50 including matche latte, turmeric latte, organic tea , ho chocolate , mocha, espresso, Mae coffee Americano. All coffees are organic. 25p of hot drinks when you take your own cup. Selection of plant milks.

Raw Press
Vegetarian cold pressed juice & salad cafe

- 32 Dover Street W1S 4NE (down-stairs)
- 020 3627 3190
- M-F 08.00-18.00, Sa-Su closed
- Green Park
- rawpress.co
  facebook.com/rawpressco

New salad and juice bar, all vegan apart from milk in coffee, and bee pollen.

Superfood breakfast bar till 11.00, fill your own bowl with a selection of grains, fruit and coconut yogurt with nut butter. All day breakfast açai bowl £7.50/£9 with greens, blackberry, strawberry and coconut yogurt. Homemade granola £6.60. Porridge with superfood toppings £5.50/£6.60. Toasters on the table to make your own artisan toast with nut butters for breakfast with your laptop or a breakfast meeting.

Raw/vegan and gluten-free salads small £7.50/£9, large £10.50/£12.50 such as kale with spiced almonds, cherries and figs; Thai papaya; apple, red cabbage and kohlrabi slaw with rawnnola crumble. Daily soup £5.50/£6.50 such as corn chowder. Baked sweet potato £4.50/£5.50 with coconut yogurt.Gluten-free cakes and energy balls.

Cold pressed mixed vegetable and fruit juices (250ml/500ml) £5.50/£7.50. Tonics (100 ml) £3.50. Almond milk with coconut milk and coffee or raw cacao. Teas £3-£5, cofffees £2.20-£3, mocha hot choc £3.50. Matcha £3, kombucha (250ml) £5.50, tumeric latte and soon medicinal mushrooms.

They have some interesting products on the shelves like Pana raw chocolate, Aduna baobab and moringa powder, preserves from Bermondsey, Argan oil, raw apple cider vinegar, Primrose's Kitchen raw/gluten-free muesli, Punch Foods organic, gluten-free superseed bars, Quinola gluten-free/organic granola.

Huge table at the back with lots of people with their laptops. Wifi. Newspapers and magazines available.

Mae Deli

Raw Press

Neat Burger
Vegan fast food cafe

- ☛ 4 Princes' Street W1B 2LQ (west side of Regent Street just below Oxford Circus)
- ☏ 020 7355 1551
- 🕐 M-Th 11.30-23.00, F-Sa 11.30-24.00, Su 12.00-22.00
- ⊖ Oxford Circus
- ↖ neat-burger.com
  facebook.com/neat.burger
  instagram.com/neat.burger

For the last year vegan junk food junkies have been flocking to the vegan burger bars and dawg dens of Camden, Shoreditch, Brick Lane and Hackney for a filthy fix of mouthwatering magic. From summer 2019 central London joins the party. Neat Burger, opening midway between Oxford Circus and Hanover Square soon after this book goes to print, specialises in vegan burgers, hot dogs and other guilty delights you thought you'd never enjoy again when you made the choice to put animals, planet and health first.

The Neat Burger teaser campaign has been running for months on social media with previews of what will be on offer. All patties are to be supplied by Beyond Meat, including the Beyond Burger and the new Beyond Sausage, both apparently so realistic they fool carnivores. Making this the perfect place to invite reluctant veggies since they won't even notice their meal is vegan.

Also meatball sliders, fries, loaded dirty fries, milkshakes too tasty to want to share, and ice cream.

ChikP
Falafel stall

- Outside St James's Church, Piccadilly W1J 9LL (right of Waterstones books)
- Monday only 11.30-14.30
- Piccadilly Circus
- Twitter @FalafelCo

Falafel wrap with hummus, salad and pickles, optional aubergine. Falafel salad box. When we say salad, we don't mean the usual lettuce and tomato, but also red cabbage, pickled turnips and gherkins. Around £5.

Chor Bizarre
Omnivorous North Indian restaurant

- 16 Albemarle St London W1S 4HW
- 020 7629 9802
- M-Su 12.00-15.00, 18.00-23.30 (Su 22.30)
- Green park
- chorbizarre.com/lon

Big, very upmarket Indian with quite a bit of vegetarian food and a separate menu. Thali £30. Wine from £28 bottle. You can book the whole restaurant for 30-50 people. 12.5% discretionary service charge.

Crussh, Mayfair
Omnivorous cafe

- 1 Curzon Street W1J 5HD
- 020 7629 2554
- M-F 07.00-18.00, Sa 09.30-16.30, Su/BH closed
- Green Park
- crussh.com

Great for a fast breakfast or lunch with plenty of vegan options such as acai strawberry breakfast bowl, organic cinammon porridge with soya milk and two toppings, butternut and spinach coconut curry, aubergine ratatouille, quinoa and vegetable spiced pot, sweet potato falafel wrap and lots of juices. Wifi.

Le Pain Quotidien
Omnivorous Belgian restaurant

- 16 North Audley Street W1K 6WL
- 020 3657 6943
- M-F 07.00-20.30, Sa 08.00-20.30, Su and bank holidays 09.00-20.00
- Bond Street, Marble Arch
- lepainquotidien.co.uk

See Chains for menu. Free wifi.

Pizza Express, Bruton Place
Omnivorous Italian restaurant

- 23 Bruton Place W1J 6ND
- 020 7495 1411
- M-F 11.30-23.00, Sa 11.30-22.00, Su 11.30-21.00
- Green Park
- pizzaexpress.co.uk

Three storeys which are good for parties, functions and private rooms. See Chains for menu.

Sofra Mayfair
Omnivorous Turkish restaurant

- 18 Shepherd Street W1Y 7HU
- 020 7493 3320
- M-Su 12.00-24.00
- Green Park
- sofra.co.uk

Excellent Mediterranean food. The Healthy Menu gets you 8 meze dishes in individual bowls. Children welcome, high chairs. Another branch at 1 St Christopher's Place in Marylebone, opposite Bond Street tube.

Lush, Mayfair
Cruelty-free cosmetics shop

- 44 South Molton Street W1K 5RT
- 020 7629 4493
- M-Sa 10.00-20.00, Su 11.00-19.00
- Bond Street
- lush.co.uk

Lovely cosmetics, all vegetarian and most of it vegan and clearly labelled. See Soho branch for more details.

NAK No Animal Killed
Vegan shoe shop

- Bond Street W1 (by appointment)
- 020 7112 9249
- M-F 9.00-17.00
- nakfashion.com
- facebook.com/nakfashionltd

NAK (No Animal Killed) is a new luxury vegan shoe company based in Bond Street, very expensive, elegant, handmade and waterproof. Women's and men's Italian shoes and boots £265-£395.

Email info@nakfashion.com to book an appointment to come try on some shoes.

Stella McCartney
Non-leather shoes & accessories

- 23 Old Bond Street, Mayfair W1S 4PZ (south end of New Bond St)
- 020 7518 3100
- M-Sa 10.00-18.30, Su closed
- Piccadilly Circus, Green Park, Oxford Circus
- stellamccartney.com

The highest of vegetarian high fashion with no leather or fur, though vegans beware of silk and wool. Allow £300-£500 for shoes or boots.

Holland & Barrett, West One

Health food shop

- Unit C12, West One Shopping Centre, corner of Davis St & Oxford St, W1C 2JS
- 020 7493 7988
- M-F 07.00-22.00, Sa 0.00-22.00, Su 10.00-21.00
- Bond Street

Big shop with many fridges, amongst the basement shops of Bond Street underground station.

Holland & Barrett, Maddox Street

Health food shop

- 6-8 Maddox Street W1S 1NR
- 020 3205 1038
- M-Sa 08.00-20.00, Su 10.00-19.00
- Oxford Circus

Fridge and freezer.

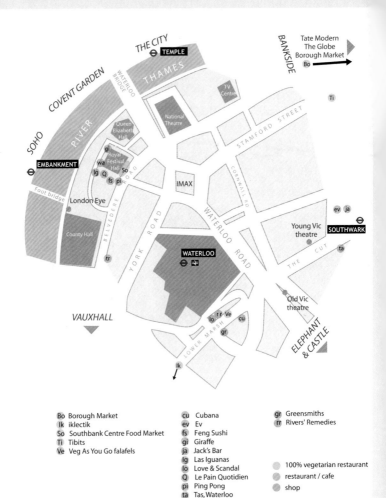

Bo Borough Market
Ik iklectik
So Southbank Centre Food Market
Ti Tibits
Ve Veg As You Go falafels

cu Cubana
ev Ev
fs Feng Sushi
gi Giraffe
ja Jack's Bar
lg Las Iguanas
lo Love & Scandal
Q Le Pain Quotidien
pi Ping Pong
ta Tas, Waterloo
tr Troia
wa Wagamama

gr Greensmiths
rr Rivers' Remedies

○ 100% vegetarian restaurant
○ restaurant / cafe
○ shop

SOUTH BANK

London Eye to Tower Bridge Bridge

The South Bank is a fabulous place to wander by the river, packed with landmark sightseeing, the arts, and many new places to grab some plant based food or have a drink.

Around Waterloo station are the National Theatre, National Film Theatre, Royal Festival Hall, Gabriel's Wharf (an interesting place by the river to meander if you like craft shops and bars), and IMAX cinema. County Hall contains the London Dungeon museum of horrors, a 5 star Mariott Hotel, a budget Premier Inn, and the visitor centre for the London Eye giant ferris wheel.

On Fridays and weekends, grab lunch or a bargain early dinner at **Southbank Centre food market** behind the Royal Festival Hall, open Fri-Sat till 8pm and Sun till 6pm. There are street food stalls including vegetarian Indian by Horn OK Please, Italian bruschetta, juices by Turnips, coffee and even a cider stall.

When the market is closed, along two sides of the **Royal Festival Hall** are chain restaurants with great vegan choices including Giraffe, Wagamama, Le Pain Quotidien, Los Iguanas, Ping Pong and Feng Sushi.

Tucked away behind Waterloo Station lies a street called **Lower Marsh**. There is a street market with various ethnic hot food stalls including one dedicated to falafels. At night you can try Cubana restaurant.

Crossing Waterloo Road, Lower Marsh becomes **the Cut**, with the New and Old Vic theatres, restaurants and supermarkets.

Heading south a few minutes' walk is **iklectic** vegetarian cafe and bar in a backstreet arts centre, on the way to Vauxhall. For an amazing value two or three course meal, end your day at **Bonnington Cafe**, as long as you've booked (see Vauxhall chapter). You can walk there south along the river, opposite Big Ben and Parliament, until you get to the M.I.6 building.

Strolling east along the river, past the Tate Modern art gallery, Shakespeare's Globe theatre, Clink prison museum and full-sized reconstruction of Sir Francis Drake's 16th century galleon the Golden Hinde (first ship to circumnavigate the world), you reach Southwark Cathedral, next to London Bridge and **Borough Market** where there are vegetarian food stalls, and some veggie-friendly restaurants in the vicinity. But best of all is the new Bankside branch of **Tibits** vegetarian buffet restaurant, behind Tate Modern.

On the way from London Bridge to **Tower Bridge** you can eat at **Arancini Brothers**, or right next to London's most famous landmark at **By Chloe** vegan restaurant.

iklektik Art-lab & Cafe
Vegetarian cafe-bar in arts space

- Old Paradise Yard, 20 Carlisle Lane SE1 7LG (Royal St corner, next to Archbishiop's Park)
- 07809 727 199
- M-Su 10.00-19.00, events until 22.30, kitchen 10.00-15.00
- Waterloo, Vauxhall
- iklectikartlab.com, Facebook i'klectic

New vegetarian cafe in a brand new creative arts space between Waterloo and Vauxhall.

Vegan soup with bread £3.50. Quiche of the day, may be vegan, £4, with salad £5. Sourdough open sandwich £4, such as crushed avocado, tomatoes and cucumber, or hummus with roasted veg. Sourdough toasties £5. Burgers £6.50 come in three innovative varieties: beetroot, millet, carrot and mixed seeds; red lentil, red pepper and nigella seeds; spinach, millet, mushroom and mixed seeds; all served with salad, roasted veggies and hummus or vegan aioli sauce.

Cakes £2.50-£3 such as vegan organic chocolate.

Water, soft drinks and juices £1-£1.50. Teas, coffee, cappuccino etc £1.80-£2.40.

Beer £3.50, cider £4, ales and craft beers £4.50. Wine £4 small glass, £4.50 medium, such as Rioja or Shiraz red or Pinot Grigio or Chardonnay white. Caipirinha and mojito cocktails £5.

Children welcome, high chairs. Dogs welcome inside and out.

iklektik

iklektik

Southbank Centre Food Market
artisan street food market

- Southbank Centre Square, behind Royal Festival Hall SE1 8XX
- F 12.00-20.00 (summer 21.00), Sa 11.00-20.00 (summer 21.00), Su and bank holiday M12.00-18.00
- Waterloo
- southbankcentre.co.uk /whatson/festivals-series/markets and /whats-on/124134-finnish-rooftop-sauna-201

Originally launched in 2010 as Real Food Market, with stalls including some vegetarian businesses, cider, coffee, bread. Below are some of the regulars.

Queen Elizabeth Hall is renovating, due to reopen in 2018, however the **Roof Garden** is open spring and summer 10.00-22.00, free admission, and you can bring your own food. Relax among wild flowers, fruit trees and allotments with views over the Thames and London. Bar with soft drinks, alcohol, tea, coffee. In winter there is a rooftop **Finnish sauna**, up to 90C, £15-£25 for 70 minutes including towels and lockers for small bags, then cool down in the open and enjoy the views. Cold water buckets, if you're brave enough. Book online.

Arabica
Omnivorous street food from the Levant

- 020 7708 5577
- arabicafoodandspice.com

Falafel wrap with salad £4, add pickles £5. Meze lunch box £7. Also at Borough Market (London Bridge) Th-Sa.

Bruschetta
Omnivorous Italian market stall

- 0845 47 47 142
- breadtree.co.uk

The bruschetta £3 and most other items are vegan, just check the labels. Also pestos, colourful pasta, bags of seasoning, cold pressed unblended olive oil, Sicilian semolina bread. Also at Croydon Boxpark.

Ethiopiques
Vegan Ethiopian food stall

- 07963 550171
- instagram.com/ethiopiques

Big plate of everything on the stall, salads and veggies £8, plus olives, lentils, chickpeas, sorghum seeds, with injera (Ethiopia flatbread like a pancake), rice or couscous. You can also have injera with any of: Mesir Wet tomato puree, garlic and green lentils; Gomet Wet: spinach and carrots sautée with garlic, onion, ginger and jalapeño pepper; Mittin Shuro soya beans roasted in a traditional sizzling clay pot with veg. Kids' meals £5. Also weekends at Brick Lane.

Horn OK Please
Vegetarian Indian street food stall

- 07900 648 499
- hop.st   facebook.com/hornplease

Street food from all over India such as dosas £5, bhel poori chaat £3, samosa chaat with chickpeas £5, pani poori, aloo tikki chaat. Everything can be made vegan except yogurt chutney. The name comes from the sign on the backs of trucks in India. Also at Borough Market.

Turnips
Vegetarian juices, fruit & veg stall

☎ 020 7357 8358

🖊 turnipsboroughmarket.com

Juices and smoothies £2.50-£3, plus soups in winter. Also beautiful fruit and veg. Also at Borough Market W-Sa and Greenwich Market.

Fitaly
Omnivorous Italian food stall

☎ facebook.com/fitalyfood

Food from Abruzzo, including vegan wrap £6 with chickpeas, rocket and rosemary; gluten-free sweet potato wrap with avocado, rocket, chives and chilli.

Veg As You Go
Jordanian vegan falafel stall

☎ In front of Boots, 98 Lower Marsh SE1 7AB

🕐 M-F 11.30-15.00, Sa-Su closed

🖊 twitter.com/falafellwrmarsh

Falafel in a wrap with salad, hummus and pickles £3, large £4. Salad box £4.

The Pure Body Company
Vegan smoothie stall

☎ opposite Rivers Remedies

🕐 Tu-Sa 09.30-14.30

⊖ Waterloo

🖊 facebook.com/Se1Therapies

Two therapists from Rivers Remedies' shop serve up freshly squeezed juices and smoothies £3.50. Nut milks, some with turmeric or chocolate, and unusual drinks such as cranberry juice with chia seeds. Raw organc kombucha £3. All sugar--free. Return the bottle for 10% discount. Bottles are recyclable plant-based plastic.

Damascus Kitchen
Omnivorous salad bar

☎ opposite 103 Lower Marsh SE1 7RG

📞 07482 591617

🕐 M-F 11.00-14.30, Sa-Su closed

⊖ Waterloo

🖊 facebook.com/Damascusfood

Mix your own salad, large box £5, regular £4, all with bread. Salads include lentil, mushroom, mixed olives, red and white cabbage, potato, sundried tomatoes, hummus, stuffed vine leaves, carrots etc.

Extra stuffed vine leaves 30p. Hummus or olives pot £3. Soup £2, with bread £3.

Raffo & Ridgeway
Cake and savouries stall

- 🏃 opposite La Barca restaurant
- ☎ 07955 588603
- 🕐 Tu-Sa 09.30-16.00, Su-M closed
- ⊖ Waterloo
- ↖ Facebook Raffo & Ridgweay

Set up by former forensic scientist Amanda Raffo, specialising in vegan. Cupcakes and brownies £2, cheaper if you buy a mixed box. Biscuits £1. Some savouries such as summer pie and pizza slice. Bespoke vegan cakes for all occasions.

Cubana
Omnivorous Cuban/Creole

- 🏃 48 Lower Marsh, SE1 7RG
- ☎ 020 7928 8778
- 🕐 M-Tu 12.00-24.00, W-Th 12.00-01.00, F 12.00-03.00, Sa 13.00-03.00 (kitchen closes 02.00), Su 14.00-23.00. Closed Xmas New Year. Open bank holiday M, F and New Year's Eve. Last food service seating M-Th 22.00, F-Sa 21.45, Su 20.30. Street food 11.30-14.30.
- ⊖ Waterloo
- ↖ cubana.co.uk menus
  facebook.com/Cubana.London

Right at the beginning of Lower Marsh you think you are in a different country. Cubana takes over the little square with its vibrant colours, music, tables outside, food, and street stalls. Inside with its decor, yellow and blue colours, a lot of Cuban art on the

Cubana

walls. It's a party restaurant with live music and DJs that becomes a salsa club late night F-Sa.

Cuban tapas falafel £4.50 with garbanzo bean, coriander, plantain, sweet potato, tomato salsa; Cuban black beans £3; sharing tapas £7.

Mains £8: black and white bean feijoada ; slow cooked okra with sweet potato and veg; served with chilli rice and plantain. Salads £4-£5. Plantain or sweet potato chips £3.50.

Some dishes served at the street food stand 11.30-14.30 weekdays, eat in or take away.

Cantina lunch menu 12.00-15.30, mains £7, two courses £9, three £11.Pre-theatre menu daily 15.30-18.30, two courses £11, three £12.

Smoothies and juices £3 large, £6 jug. Lots of cocktails £5-£7, jug £12-19, two for one 4-7pm, made with freshly squeezed juices. Sangria £5, jug £12. House wine £15 bottle, £4.20 medium glass, £5.20 large. Beer £4.

Service can be slow sometimes - but this is a young, lively place and gets crowded Wed-Sat, popular with large groups. Salsa and Latin live music every evening 11pm till close. Children welcome till 7pm. 12.5% discretionary service charge for food and drink served at tables. Outside seating. Dogs welcome. Private parties. Another branch in Smithfield.

Ev
Omnivorous Turkish restaurant, bar and delicatessen

- The Arches, 97-99 Isabella St SE1 8DA
- 020 7620 6191
- Cafe M-Sa 12.00-23.30, Su 12.00-22.30
  Deli: M-F 07.30-22.00, Sa 08.00-21.00, Su 08.00-22.00
- Southwark
- tasrestaurants.co.uk

Three arches, the first with a bakery and delicateseen with Mediterranean organic foods, meze and vegan dishes; second a fish and meze restaurant in the style of Tas Pide with lots of vegan dishes; the third a wine bar that seats 100. Outside tables in summer. Part of the Tas chain. House wine £16.45 bottle, £4.55 medium glass. Children welcome, high chairs.

Feng Sushi, South Bank
Omnivorous Japanese restaurant

- Unit 9, Festival Terrace, Southbank Centre, Belvedere Road SE1 8XX
- 020 7261 0001
- Su-W 12.00-22.00, Th-Sa 12.00-23.00
- Waterloo
- fengsushi.co.uk

Part of a chain of filling Japanese restaurants. Good vegan dishes to look out for £3-£8 are tempura, Nippon duck (tofu mock duck rolls), salads and sushi.

Giraffe, Southbank Centre
Omnivorous restaurant

- Riverside Level 1 SE1 8XX (behind Royal Festival Hall)
- 020 7928 200
- M-Th 08.00-23.00, F 08.00-23.30, Sa 09.00-23.30, Su 09.00-22.30
- Waterloo
- giraffe.net/classic

Good selection of vegan dishes. See Chains section for menu. Some outside seating. Children welcome, kids' menu. Free wifi. No reservations at weekends 11.45-17.00.

Jack's Bar
Omnivorous food pub

- 96 Isabella Street SE1 8DD
- 020 7928 0678
- M-Sa 12.00-23.30, Su closed; kitchen closes 22.30
- Southwark, Waterloo
- jacksbarlondon.co.uk

Cosy bar tucked under the converted railway arch, with a separate vegan menu. Gluten free options.

Tacos 2 for £7.50, 3 for £9 include jerk quinoa broccoli wings with mango salsa, pea shoots, sesame seeds, slaw and guacamole; Thai bbq seitan ribs with bean sprouts, pickled cucumber, carrot, chilli nuts and Sriracha hot sauce. Burgers £7.95-£9 include quinoa with broccoli, smashed chickpeas, in-house vegan halloumi, smoked tomato hummus, olives and red onion; seitan chilli dog.

Pizza £7-£9 can come with marinara sauce, cheese, sausage, wild broccoli. crispy bacon, red chilli, pumpkin, pumpkin seed crust, spicy almond.

Extras £3.50 oregano or sweet potato fries, smashed cucumber with chilli and sesame oil, Jack's slaw with sesame seeds. Corn chips and dips £6.

Discretionary 12.5% service charge. Wifi. Outside tables.

Las Iguanas, Royal Festival Hall
Omnivorous South American restaurant

- Festival Terrace, Southbank Centre SE1 8XX
- 020 7620 1328
- M-Tu 10.00-23.00, W-Th 10.00-01.00, F-Sa 10.00-02.00 Su 10.00-22.30
- Waterloo
- iguanas.co.uk/locations/london-roy-al-festival-hall

Stacks of vegan small dishes and mains, see Chains. Cocktail bar open till late most nights. Deliveries.

Le Pain Quotidien
Omnivorous restaurant

- Upper Level Festival Terrace, Royal Festival Hall, Belvedere Road SE1 8XX
- 020 3657 6925
- M-F 07.30-23.00, Sa 08.00-23.00, Su/BH 09.00-22.00
- Waterloo
- lepainquotidien.com

Vegan-friendly Belgian cafe chain. We love their soup, salad, mezze and blueberry muffins. See Chains for details. No bookings Sa-Su 09.30-17.00. Free wifi.

Tas, The Cut

Turkish/Anatolian omnivorous restaurant

- 33 The Cut, Waterloo SE1 8LF
- 020 7928 1444
- M-Sa 12.00-23.30, Su 12.00-22.30
- Waterloo, Southwark
- tasrestaurants.co.uk

This chain that is really welcoming to veggies and vegans. See Chains.

Troia

Omnivorous Turkish/Anatolian restaurant

- 3F Belvedere Road, County Hall SE1 7GQ
- 020 7633 9309
- M-Sa 12.00-23.30, Su 12.00-22.30
- Waterloo
- www.troia-restaurant.co.uk

Lots of vegan options in this restaurant near the London Eye. A separate vegetarian set mixed mezze for £9.95 or £13.95 per person for 8 to 11 dishes, a couple need substituting for vegan. Hot and cold starters £5.45-£5.95, mains £10.45-£12.95. Lunch special M-F 12.00-17.00 two courses £9.95, dessert add £2.95.

Wine from £19.95 bottle, £4.95 medium glass. Children welcome, high chairs.

Wagamama, Royal Festival Ha

Omnivorous Japanese restaurant

- Riverside level, Royal Festival Hall SE1 8XX
- 020 7021 0877
- M-Sa 11.00-23.00, Su 11.00-22.00
- Waterloo
- wagamama.com

Large Japanese fast food noodle restaurant. See Chains section.

Greensmiths

Wholefood store and omnivorous cafe

- 27 Lower Marsh SE1 7RG
- 020 7921 2970
- M-F 08.00-20.00, Sa 08.00-18.00, Su closed
- Waterloo, Lambeth North
- greensmithsfood.co.uk

More like a supermarket with several shops in one and lots of rooms, most welcome after the closure of Coopers wholefood store and cafe nearby. Ignore the butcher at the front, use the side door and head for the artisan bakery, greengrocer, or basement wholefoods and wines.

Highlights include baby food, vegan ice-cream, VBites sausages, burgers and falafels, Booja Booja truffles, and chocolate bars by Divine, Montezuma and Doisy & Dam.

The cafe does coffees, smoothies, vegan pasties and sausage rolls £1.90, and there are salad boxes in the fridge. Vegan flapjacks £1.50. Seating outside and in.

Rivers' Remedies
Health food shop & therapy rooms

- 42-43 Lower Marsh SE1 7RU
- 020 7202 9000
- Shop M-Sa 09.30-20.00, Sa 10.00-18.00, Su closed. Treatments M-F 08.00-21.00, Sa 10.00-18.30, Su closed.
- Waterloo, Lambeth North, Southwark
- rivers-remedies.co.uk
  waterloobodystation.co.uk

Rebecca Rivers' beautiful shop specialises in organic beauty products and body treats with only British brands including Absolute Aroma, Akamuti, Barefaced Beauty, BWC, Essential Care, Faith in Nature, Green People, Organic Surge, Ren, Skin Blossom and lots more. Makeup by Barefaced Beauty, Beauty Without Cruelty, Lily Lolo, Green People, Essential Care. The owner is very knowledgeable about natural health and the products.

Raw chocolate and healthy snacks. Supplements. Yoga stuff. Baby products by Beaming Baby, Little Violets, Green Baby, Bentley Organic.

Therapy rooms open late for all kinds of massage, facials, hair removal, manicure, pedicure, acupuncture, osteopathy.

Troia

Borough Market
Huge covered food market

- 8 Southwark Street SE1 1TL (between Stoney Street and Bedale Street; by Southwark Cathedral)
- 020 7407 1002
- M-Th 10.00-17.00, F 10.00-18.00, Sa 08.00-17.00, Su closed
- London Bridge (Jubilee & Northern)
- boroughmarket.org.uk

This food market is the Daddy, featuring an astounding array of stalls with exotic foods from around the the world. For a great foodie day out or something like truffles to impress your dinner guests, no other market comes close. Plenty of organic normal fruit and veg too. Th-Sat are the best days.

The top places (listed below) for a veggie lunch are Turkish Meze vegetarian cafe by the railway bridge, and the row of vegetarian stalls along the cathedral wall which on any one day includes at least three of the following: Horn OK Please or Gujarati Rasoi Indian street food, Koshari Street Egyptian street food, Arabica Lebanese falafel, and a juice stall. Turkish Meze has tables, and there are shared tables in other areas.

Along the edge of the market, sushi restaurant Feng Sushi and Tapas Brindisa are a good bet for an evening meal.

Gujarati Rasoi
Vegetarian Indian street food stall

- Borough Market, next to the cathedral
- 020 7394 1187
- M-Sa
- gujaratirasoi.com

Long established at Broadway Market since 2004, mother and son team Lalita and Urvesh Patel now also have a stall at Borough Market in the area at the bottom of the steps down from London Bridge, by the cathedral. Box of rice, curry and chaat £6 or £4.50. Samosas and bhajias £1.50 each or £4 for 3.

If you like this then try their restaurant in Dalston. Take the 149 bus from London Bridge due north to Dalston Kingsland station. They also do outside catering for parties, festivals and corporate events from their Tower Bridge base.

Horn OK Please
Vegetarian Indian street food stall

- Borough Market next to the cathedral,
- 07900 648 499
- Th-Sa every week, M-W alternate weeks
- hop.st   facebook.com/hornplease

Street food from all over India freshly made such as dosa, aloo tikki with chickpea curry. Everything can be made vegan except yogurt chutney. Also at Southbank market behind the Royal Festival Hall F-Su.

The Turkish Deli
Vegetarian Turkish cafe & take-away

- Borough Market, Stoney St SE1 9AA
- 020 7476 6639, 07949 411 194
- Tu-Th 08.30-17.00 (later in summer), F -18.00, Sa 08.00-17.30, Su closed
- theturkishdeli.com
  Facebook The Turkish Deli

Permanent cafe with tables and take-away owned by an Anglo-Turkish couple, very popular with workers from the local Turkish bank. Lunch box £5 for a choice of at least 10 daily dishes from a repertoire of 35. Most dishes are vegan and clearly labelled including some you've never seen in the UK like saksuka aubergine and tomato, piyas bean meze with various veg cooked with their own olive oil, patlican ezme aubergine paste, yesil biber dolma stuffed green pepper, borulce blackeye bean salad, mercimek lentil kofte, yer el masi Jerusalem artichoke, bikla broad beans and artichoke.

Also olives from the family farm, at least 20 kinds of Turkish delight of which all but one are vegan, and pure olive oil soap. Covered tables. Dogs welcome.

Koshari Street
Vegan Egyptian street food stall

- Borough Market, next to the cathedral
- 020 3667 8781
- Th-Sa
- kosharistreet.com
  facebook.com/KoshariStreetLondon

A unique street food koshari pot £4.95 (classic) and £6.95 (king) filled with rice, lentils, vermicelli pasta, spicy tomato sauce, caramelised onions, chickpeas and chilli oil, sprinkled with doqqa (crushed peanuts, coriander seeds, sesame seeds, dry mint and chickpeas). Baladi salad £4.95. Combo koshari baladi £5.95. Also omnivorous cafes in Covent Garden and South Kensington.

Mini Magoo
Organic cereals and granola

- Borough Market, near the cathedral
- 020 8691 3331
- Th 11.00-17.00, F 12.00-18.00, Sa 08.00-17.00, Su-W closed
- minimagoo.com

Award-winning brand of handmade organic cereals that are also free from gluten, wheat, additives, oil and salt. Various granola, cornflakes, porridge, muesli, granuesli and funstuff (seeds & nut mix), all packed with different spices and dried fruits.

The Free from Bakehouse
Vegetarian bakery

- In the Green Market (behind Mini Magoo)
- 020 3601 6199
- W-Sa market trading hours
- thefreefrombakehouse.com

Award winning independent bakery which specialises in gluten-, wheat-, dairy- and sometimes sugar-free cakes. They are increasing the number of products without eggs, £1.80-£4, such as cupcakes £2.50 such as cupcakes in lemon meringue (made from chickpea aqua faba instead of egg, salted caramel, banana & choc chip loaf, pear and stem ginger muffin, rosemary and raisin cookie gift bag, tahini and apricot almond flapjack, rocky road. Also seasonal cakes like boozy fruit & nut Xmas cake £9.50. You can also order online and they supply cafes and delis throughout London.

Turkish Deli

Borough Olives
Mediterranean vegetarian antipasti

- ☛ Borough Market south side, near Stoney Street
- ☎ 01376 322225
- 🕐 Tu-Th 10.00-17.00, F 10.00-18.00, Sa 08.00-17.00
- ↟ borougholives.co.uk

Olives fan heaven, 17 kinds and many other things such as tapenade, Moroccan chermoula, sundried tomatoes, vine leaves, artichokes, pickled garlic, sweet and spicy peppers, sweet chilli paste, cornichons with pickled onions, hummus, harissa, olive oil, vinegar. Delivery free over £28. Also in Broadway Market (Sa) and Columbia Road flower market (Su).

Total Organics
Juice bar

- ☛ Middle Market, Borough Market
- ☎ 01745 826195
- 🕐 M-W 07.30-15.00, Th & Sa 07.30-16.00, F 07.30-17.00
- ↟ facebook.com/totalorganics1

Deep inside the market, previously a salad bar, now they are focused on organic juices, £3-£4. Wheatgrass shot £2.50. Mulled wine in winter £3.50-£4.

Also try **Ted's Veg**, **Sweet Roots** liquorice stall, **Spice Mountain** and **Tea2you**.

Feng Sushi, Borough Market
Vegetarian & fish Japanese restaurant

- ☛ 13 Stoney Street SE1 9AD
- ☎ 020 7407 8744
- 🕐 M-W 11.30-22.00, Th-Sa 11.30-23.00, Su 12.00-22.00
- ⊖ London Bridge
- ↟ fengsushi.co.uk

The only place we know that does brown rice sushi £4 in cucumber or avocado with sesame. Miso soup £1.50. Edamame soya beans £3-£4. Salads £6-7 such as udon or soba noodle, or Japanese bean with organic tofu, edamame and French beans. Shiitake mushroom tempura £6.25. Glass of wine £5, bottle £18, sake £5.75.

Wok It
Omnivourus noodles & rice bar

- ☛ 3 Stoney Street SE1 9AA
- ☎ 020 7403 2111
- 🕐 M-Tu 11.30-20.00,W 11.00-20.30,Th11.30-20.30, F11.30-22.00, Sa 11.00-21.00
- ↟ wokit.co.uk.

Healthy vegan-friendly restaurant with a vast selection of noodles and rice cocked in front of you after you pick the ingredients. Eat in or take away. Veggies from Ted's Veg stall. Pick your base £4-£4.50 from udon, rice or black bean or sweet potato and buckwheat noodles, spiralised courgette, or rice (Jasmine white, wholegrain or cauliflower). Add soya protein shot £2.50. All meals include cabbage, carrots, bean sprouts, spring onions, garlic and ginger. Extra veg £1.50. Sauces are free.

Water £1, juices £1.50. Other places worth trying in Borough Market are **Wasabi** and **Pret a Manger**.

Tapas Brindisa, London Bridge
Omnivorous Spanish tapas restaurant

- 🖝 18-20 Southwark Street SE1 1TJ((next to Borough Market)
- ☎ 020 7357 8880
- 🕐 M-F 08.30-23.00, Sa 9.00-23.00, Su 11.00-22.00
- ⊖ London Bridge
- ➤ tbrindisa.com

A few vegan dishes £4-£5.95 such as patatas bravas, spinach with pinenuts and raisins, various toasts with dips, salads. Hot food from 12.00, except M-Sa 16.00-17.30 cold tapas only. No bookings, bar area for snacks and drinks while waiting when busy. Discretionary service charge 12.5%.

Falafel House
Vegetarian street stall

- 🖝 In front of post office, 19A Borough High St SE1 9SF (opposite Borough Market)
- 🕐 M-F 11.00-16.00
- ⊖ London Bridge
- ➤ instagram.com/humansoffalafel

Falafel wrap £4, with canned drink £5.

Hing Loong
Omnivorous Chinese restaurant

- 🖝 159 Borough High Street, SE1 1HR
- ☎ 020 7378 8100
- 🕐 M-F 12.00-23.30, Sa-Su 12.00-15.00, 17.00-23.30
- ⊖ Borough, London Bridge

Recommended by staff at the PETA office that used to be nearby. Fab gluten fake meat dishes like sweet and sour 'pork' and stir fried 'duck' £6.50, plus the usual Chinese veg and bean curd dishes. Multi-course set dinner £14.50 per person for two or more. Licensed. Children welcome, high chairs.

Tas Cafe/Deli
Omnivorous Turkish cafe & take-away

- 🖝 76 Borough High Street SE1 1QF
- ☎ 020 7403 8557
- 🕐 M-F 07.00-18.00, Sa 08.00-16.00, Su 9.00-16.00
- ⊖ Borough, London Bridge
- ➤ tasrestaurants.co.uk

Meze take-away and eat in, point to what you want and pay by the spoonful. Soya milk for coffee. 50% off one hour before closing.

Tas Restaurant, Borough
Omnivorous Turkish restaurant

- 🖝 72 Borough High Street SE1 1XF
- ☎ 020 7403 7200
- 🕐 M-Sa 12.00-23.30, Su 12.00-22.30
- ⊖ London Bridge, Borough
- ➤ tasrestaurant.com

Similar menu to the Waterloo branch with stacks of vegan Turkish dishes. Licensed.

Holland & Barrett, London Bridge
Health food shop

- 📍 43 Borough High Street SE1 1LZ
- 📞 020 3620 7791
- 🕐 M-F 07.30-19.00, Sa 9.00-19.00, Su 11.00-17.00

Neal's Yard Remedies
Herbs and organic bodycare

- 📍 4 Bedale St, Borough Market SE1 9AA
- 📞 020 7940 1414 therapy rooms
  020 7407 4877 shop
- 🕐 M-Th 10.00-19.00, F-Sa 9.00-19.00, Su closed
- 🚇 London Bridge
- 🔗 nealsyardremedies.com

Also therapy rooms. On Monday they run graduate clinics, £25 for 1 hour. See also Covent Garden.

Hoxton Beach Falafel
Vegan falafel market stall

- 📍 Ropewalk Market, Maltby St SE1 3PA
- 🕐 Market open Sa 9.00-16.00, Su 10.00-16.00
- 🚇 Bermondsey, London Bridge
- 🔗 hoxtonbeach.com

South of Tower Bridge by the railway line. Falafel wrap in Arab khubz bread with pickles, salad and hummus, regular £3.50, large £4.50, add a cooked vegetable for 50p such as aubergine, sweet potato, cauliflower, or fava bean stew. Also loose falafel balls or fava with salads. Drinks £1. Also weekdays at Whitecross Street (City) and Fitzrovia.

Snowsfields Wellness
Health food shop & complementary clinic

- 📍 41 Snowsfields SE1 3SU
- 📞 020 7407 9910,
- 🕐 M, F 9.30-18.30, Tu, Th 9.30-19.30, W 9.30-20.30, Sa 10.00-17.30, Su closed.
  Clinic from 12.00, Sa 10.30.
- 🚇 London Bridge
- 🔗 snowsfields.co.uk

Small boutique health food store and natural clinic. A few wholefoods such as rice, quinoa, rice noodles, millet, gluten-free pasta, herbal teas, nuts and seeds, but butters, olives, snacks, but not beans. Raw chocolate and Nakd bars. Fridge with organic tofu, oils, coconut water, aloe vera juice, apple cider vinegar drink, omega oils. Hemp, soya and Sproutein powders.

Skin care by Ila, Wuchi, Yoah and Miessence.Natracare and baby wipes. Supplements by Higher Nature, Teranova, Nutri. Cleaning by Earth Friendly, Ecos. Books.

Workshops and talks. Nutritional therapy, sports massage, naturopathy, osteopathy, craniosacral, reflexology, counselling psychology, medical herbalism, eating disorder support group. MC, Visa. The cafe next door has some vegan food.

Finally, here are some evening places between Borough Market and Shakespeare's Globe Theatre and Tate Modern.

Tibits, Bankside
Vegetarian restaurant

- 📞 124 Southwark Street SE1 0SW
- ☎ 020 7202 8370
- 🕐 M-W 07.30-22.00, Th-F 07.30-24.00, Sa 10.30-23.00, Su/BH 10.30-22.00. Food served until 30 mins before closing.
- ⊖ Southwark
- ↖ tibits.co.uk
  facebook.com/tibitsbankside

Big new buffet vegetarian restaurant opened summer 2017, just minutes from the Thames, Take Modern and Shakespeare's Globe Theatre. The centrepiece is the "food boat" buffet with over 40 hot and cold dishes, salads and desserts, most vegan, and all of them on Vegan Tuesdays. Per 100gr breakfast £1.80, lunch £2.50 from 11.30am, dinner £2.80 from 6pm. Juices, craft beers, vegan wines and cocktails.

120 seats. Inside/outside garden room at the back. See Mayfair branch for more details.

Flat Iron Square
Omnivorous food court

- 📞 Flat Iron Square, 68 Union St SE1 1TD
- ☎ 020 3179 9800
- 🕐 M-Su 10.00-late
- ⊖ Borough, Southwark
- ↖ flatironsquare.co.uk

Opened 2016, indoor foodie take-away market under the railway arches on the south side of Southwark Street, north side of Union Square, between Southwark Bridge Road and O-Meara Street. Places with great vegan options include **Ekacha** (Oriental) and **Savage Salads**. Indoor seating at wooden tables, like eating in a nice restaurant at market prices.

Leon, Bankside
Omnivorous cafe & take-away

- 📞 7 Canvey Street, The Blue Fin Building SE1 9AN (behind the Tate Modern)
- ☎ 020 7620 0035
- 🕐 M-F 08.00-22.00, Sat 12.00-22.00, Su 12.00-19.00
- ⊖ London Bridge, Southwark
- ↖ leonrestaurants.co.uk

Fast food cafe with great value veggie food. See Chains section or website for the full menu.

By Cloe, One Tower Bridge
Vegan restaurant

- One Tower Bridge, 6 Duchess Walk SE1 2SD
- 020
- Su-W 10.00-22.00, Th-Sa 10.00-23.00
- London Bridge, Tower Hill
- eatbychloe.com

Opened summer 2019. For menu see Covent Garden branch. Also at North Greenwich (South London) and Oxford Circus (Fitzrovia), opens 7am weekdays.

Deliveroo, Corporate delivery, To-go by Chloe.

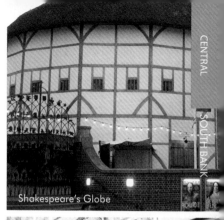
Shakespeare's Globe

Arancini Brothers
Vegan cafe

- Arch 34, Maltby Street SE1 3PA
- 020 7207 1618
- M-Su 9.30-20.30, bank holidays 10.30-33.20
- Bermondsey
- www.arancinibrothers.com

The fourth branch of the vegan risotto balls and burgers cafe and take-away. At weekends there is a street market outside.

Also in the City (Old Street), Dalston (East London) and Kentish Town (North London).

Flat Iron Square

Tas Pide (South Bank)
Omnivorous Turkish restaurant

- 20-22 New Globe Walk SE1 9DR (near The Globe theatre)
- 020 7928 3300
- M-Sa 12.00-23.30, Su 12.00-22.30
- London Bridge
- tasrestaurants.co.uk/pide.html

Pide is a traditional Anatolian dish made from dough in the shape of a boat, baked in a wood fired oven, producing a crispy outer crust, with a variety of highly flavoured, aromatic fillings, best eaten by hand. Ask for Pirasali vegetarian pide, around £7, without the cheese topping, made with leek, green lentils, potatoes, raisins, tomatoes, sesame seeds, red basil.

Tas has three more similar places around here plus Ev, and more restaurants in the City and Bloomsbury.

Wagamama
Japanese omnivorous restaurant

- 1 Clink Street SE1 9BU (opposite Vinopolis)
- 020 7403 3659
- M-Sa 11.30-23.00, Su 11.30-22.00
- London Bridge
- wagamama.com

Londis, Union Street
Supermarket with vegan Indian take-away

- 77-79 Union Street SE1 1SG (corne Ayres Street)
- 020 7407 2652
- M-F 06.00-20.30, Sa 07.00-20.00, Su 07.00-19.30
- Borough, London Bridge, Southwark

This used to be Union Newsagents and fu of vegan sandwiches, to the delight of th workers in the nearby offices of PETA and League Against Cruel Sports. LACS and PETA have moved away, M&S has opened up nearby, and there is no longer sufficien demand to meet the wholesaler's minimum vegan sandwich order, but the vegetarian owner still has take-away samosas, pakoras, spring rolls, vegan biryani and stir-fry, and salads - plenty for a picnic on the South Bank. He recently rescued a cat who lives in the shop.

Try it

There's more than you think at

Leather Lane
market

Monday to Friday

hot food, fruit, drinks,
clothes, bags, flowers,
vegetables, jewellery,
and lots more.

 Camden

THE CITY

Central London

The Square Mile of the financial capital still has a few pinstriped suits and brollies, though these days you're more likely to see smartly dressed young and not so young men and women heading for the gym or a healthy lunch, as fitness clubs and multicultural food continue to expand and thrive in London.

New in Farringdon in 2019 are two vegan restaurants, **Flipside** for fast food and **Stem & Glory** for more leisurely dining.

Vanilla Black is the original veggie posh restaurant in the heart of the City, at the top of Chancery Lane. Always popular with meat-eaters, it originally had lean pickings for vegans, but today has plenty.

The other long-standing vegetarian restaurant is **Carnevale** in Whitecross Street, in the thick of the best weekday street **market** for take-away vegan food.

Other top end places bordering The City are **The Gate** (see under Islington) and **Itadaki Zen** (Kings Cross).

For a fast weekday sit-down lunch, head to newly veganized cafe **Arancini Bros**. There are falafel cafes galore around the City, and branches of all the major chains. City branches of **Holland & Barrett** have fridges full of take-away pasties, pies and slices.

Veggie Pret opened its third branch in October 2017. It's in Exmouth Market,

and as in Shoreditch and Soho branches, around half the food is vegan.

For sit-down salad buffet cafes, you can't beat **Leather Lane Market**.

Around Liverpool Street, try the new branch of **Planet Organic**, or refer to our East London chapter for **Spitalfields Market** which has an Ethiopian vegan and Asian food stalls and two branches of **Pilpel Falafel**.

For a night out dining, drinking and clubbing in London's new Vegan Village, hop on a bus or walk up to **Shoreditch** (see East London) and any of seven new vegan eateries, plus another Veggie Pret. For convenience these are also shown on the map on the next page, top right.

This chapter is arranged by postcode:

EC1 north-west City

FC1 north-central

EC2 & E1 east

EC3 south-east

EC4 south

Top attractions:

The Tower of London, Tower Bridge, St Pauls Cathedral, Barbican Arts Centre, Spitalfields and Brick Lane Sunday markets, Shoreditch Boxpark.

133

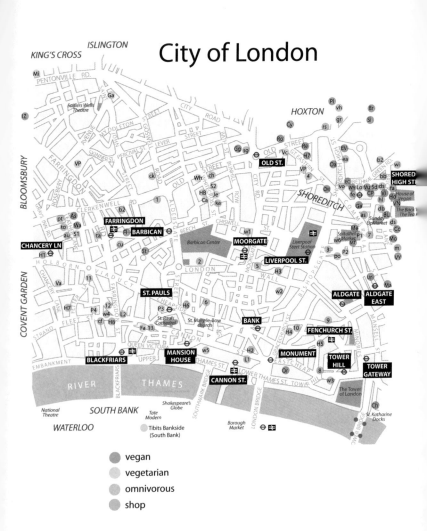

City of London

KING'S CROSS
ISLINGTON
HOXTON
BLOOMSBURY
SHOREDITCH
CHANCERY LN
COVENT GARDEN
SOUTH BANK
WATERLOO

OLD ST.
FARRINGDON
BARBICAN
MOORGATE
LIVERPOOL ST.
SHORED HIGH ST
ST. PAULS
ALDGATE
ALDGATE EAST
BANK
FENCHURCH ST.
BLACKFRIARS
MANSION HOUSE
MONUMENT
TOWER HILL
TOWER GATEWAY
CANNON ST.

Sadlers Wells Theatre
Barbican Centre
Liverpool Street Station
Spitalfields Market
St. Pauls Cathedral
St. Mary-le-Bow church
The Tower of London
St. Katharine Docks
Shakespeare's Globe
Tate Modern
National Theatre
Borough Market
Tibits Bankside (South Bank)
House of Vegan
The Back
The Tea

RIVER THAMES
BLACKFRIARS

- vegan
- vegetarian
- omnivorous
- shop

134

EC1 Exmouth Market, Farringdon, Leather Lane

Fl Flipside
St Stem & Glory (Nov 2018)
IZ Itadaki Zen (Kings Cross)
As Astro Vegan
Wa Warung Tempeh
Mi Mildreds (Kings Cross)

Ga The Gate (Islington)
VP Veggie Pret, Exmouth
S1 Sunny's Leather Lane
ta Tas Farringdon
pt Ptooch
to Tony's Cafe

au Cafe l'Auberge
b1 Brewdog, Clerkenwell
ck Counter Kitchen
cu Cubana, Smithfield

H1 Holland & Barrett, High Holborn

EC1 Whitecross Street, Old Street, Clerkenwell

Ca Carnevale
HB Hoxton Beach Falafel
S2 Sunny's Whitecross
Je Jevi Sweet
Wh Wholefood Heaven

ka Karuna
ck Counter Kitchen
gr Grind
ch Chao
1 Pizza Express Clerkenwell Rd

gr The Grocery
rs Raw Store

EC2 Liverpool Street (City) & E1 Shoreditch/Brick Lane (East)

CM Club Mexicana
EV Essential Vegan
Gg Good To Go Ro Roadtrip
Br Bright Store Si Site
Oa Oasi H7 Hoxton 7
Ge Genesis
EC Eat Chay
Wh What the Pitta
BL Brick Lane stalls
VN Vegan Nights
Cc Canvas Cafe
Ma Maree's Mo Mooshies
Vi Vida Bakery
VY Vegan Yes CP CPress
Vu Vurger fa Fauxmagerie
Me Merkamo
MT Mel's Tropical Creations

Pl Plates Re Redemption
Cy Cyclelab Un Unity Diner
Lo Lokma Tasty Bite
Vc Veggie Curry Box
VP Veggie Pret
P1 Pilpel Spitalfields
P2 Pilpel Brushfield
po Planet Organic
ea East London Juice Co.
fe Felafelicious
vo Voodoo Ray's
ds Dark Sugars x 2
b2 Brewdog, Brick Lane
wi Wedge Issue pizza
db Damascu Bite
hl Hookah Lounge
sg Shoreditch Grind
vg Viet Hoa

Pizza Express:
2 Alban Gate
3 Bishopsgate
4 Curtain Road
5 Finsbury Circus
6 Russia Row
7 Spitalfields
Wagamama EC2:
w1 Moorgate/Barbican
w2 Old Broad St/Bank
w6 Spitalfields
as As Nature Intended
5d Fifth Dimension tattoos
m Monster House hair
H3 Holland & Barrett, Old Broad St
gr The Grocery
rs Raw Store

EC3 Fenchurch Street, inc Tower of London

Ch ChikP
Or Organic Chickpeas

Pizza Express:
8 Byward Street
9 Fenchurch St
10 Leadenhall Market

w3 Wagamama Tower Hill

Holland & Barrett:
H4 Leadenhall
H5 Fenchurch

EC4 St Pauls, along the river

Va Vanilla Black
Fa Falafel
P3 Pilpel St Pauls
P4 Pilpel Fleet Street

cf Chilango Fleet Street

Leon:
L1 Cannon Street
L2 Ludgate Circus

Pizza Express:
11 New Fetter Lane
12 St Bride Street
13 St Pauls

Wagamama:
w4 Fleet St
w5 Mansion House

Holland & Barrett:
H2 Cannon Street
H6 Cheapside
H7 Fetter Lane
H8 Ludgate

em & Glory
vegan restaurant & bar

60 Bartholomew Close (Barts Square), Farringdon EC1A 7BF

020 3969 9392

M-F 11.30-23.00, Sa 11.30-23.30, Su 11.30-17.00

Barbican, Farringdon, Moorgate, St Pauls

stemandglory.uk
facebook.com/stemandglory

Farringdon's first 100% vegan restaurant. They already have two vegan restaurants in Cambridge and raised an astonishing £600,000 on Crowdcube to open in another in London. High quality, healthy vegan gourmet food, with a similar but different menu to Cambridge.

Nibbles £3-£4 are nori tapenade with multiseed crackers, steamed edamame beans, roasted almonds with rosemary.

Small plates £7-£11 such as patatas bravas, kimchi pancakes, aubergine chermoula, turmeric hummus with grilled chilli peppers and multiseed crackers.

Larger plates £10.50-£15 such as Roinbow Bowl with courgetti spaghetti, watercress salad, avo, nori, seaweed tapenade, olives, baked squash; vegan shakshuka with chickpeas in tomato sauce, roasted eggplant and scrambled tofu, leaves, polenta chips; aubergine and zucchini lasagne with cashew béchamel sauce; marinated pulled jackfruit blue corn tacos with pineapple kimchi; pulled bbq jackfruit in a bao bun; Thai green curry with cauliflower rice; quinoa paella.

Weekends till 4pm full English £12.50 with scramboled tofu, tempeh bacon, mushrooms, spinach, avo, beans and toasted sourdough. Sunday roast £15 of slow roasted veg in puff pastry with celeriac steak, roast potatoes, brussels, purple carrots, broccoli, and rich onion and mushroom gravy.

Desserts £6-£7 include ice-cream aiwth coulis and fruit, chocolate almond cake, raspberry cashew cheesecake.

Weekend all day vegan full English cooked breakfast and a Sunday roast.

Kids menu: mini bites £3.95, choose from hummus with crudites and multiseed crackers, or kimchi pancakes, or roasted potato chips with ketchup. Mains £5.95: pasta with tomato sauce, hot dog with potatoes and salad, or paella. Dessert £1.50 ice cream or fruit salad. Meal deal £9.50 for hummus with crudites, choice of main and dessert plus juice.

Juices and smoothies £4.50-£6. Soft drinks £3-£4.50 include Eager juices, Square Root sodas, kombucha mocktails.

Craft beers, cider, even 0.5% kombucha beer, £4.50-£5.50. Vegan wines are mostly organic from £7 medium glass, £9 large, £22 bottle. Cocktails from £8.50. Mocktails £5. Spirits from £3.50.

Set lunch M-F till 15.30 two courses for £15.95, add dessert for £6. Deliveroo. Chef's table with view of the kitchen. Groups up to 40. Private functions up to 56.

FlipSide
99% vegan American fast food restaurant

- 88 Cowcross Street, Farringdon EC1W 6BP
- 020 7250 1103
- M-W 07.00-20.00, Th-F 07.00-21.00 Sa 11.00-21.00, Su closed
- Farringdon
- flipsidefood.com
  instagram.com/flipside_food

Created by Jen Pardoe and Claudia Tarry, whose experience includes working at PETA and Meat Free Mondays before starting their own catering company. It's all vegan apart honey in certain items. The online menu is huge, you'll need your biggest computer screen. No cash. Deliveroo.

Weekdays they target the office breakfast crowd with grab and go items under £3 like all day breakfast sandwich, fruit and granola pots, and oat pots with chia or flax. Also made to order pots like scramble with rashers and hot beans. Organic protein pancake £3.50 (weekend £5.50) with blueberries and banana. Bigger breakfast bowls £4.50 (weekend £6.50) include Protein Feast with sausage, rashers, scramble, quinoa and beans; Easy Flip with scramble, avo, tomato, quinoa, beans, almond feta; Sunrise with scramble, rashers, tomato, chestnut mushrooms.

Weekend brunch grills £8.50 in sandwich such as chicken burger with crispy rashers; sausage and scramble with sticky and crispy rashers, tomato, red onion, Hollandaise sauce; portobello mushroom and peppers with baby spinach, onions, Hollandaise. Add for £1 avocado, almond feta or Gouda style cheese, £2 air-baked fries. Whole 9 Yards (full English) £10 with 2 sausages, 2 rashers, scramble, roasted tomato, fries,

:th sourdough doughnut , toast or 20stack ancake with maple butter and maple syrup.

.unch burritos £5.50 weekdays (£6.49 veekend), with chicken or mince and pinto eans. Superbowls £5.49 (£6.49) are the ealthy option with ingredients such as roast quash, broccoli, beet, slaw, quinoa, leaves, almond feta, pinto and black beans, rice, oaked sweet potato, curry chickpeas, kale. Extra protein £1.50 such as chicken or mince. Lunch chicken or quarter pounder burgers £9.50. Mac and cheese regular £3, large £5, comes with either baked shiitake, onions, rashers, broccoli & peas, or tomatoes.

Grab and go lunches under £4 such as several hot soups, sandwiches, baguettes, wraps, melts, with such goodies as roasted chicken and apple slaw, ploughman's with smoked ham and cheese, buffalo chicken and red slaw, butternut and beets. Salads £5.50. Mac and cheese £4.75.

Stacks of sweet treats £1.20-£2.25 such as popcorn, pink iced brioche doughnut, muffins, cinnamon rolls, spelt croissant, oat bars, chocolate or lemon iced loaf cake.

Evenings from 4pm they specialise in burgers £9.50-£11 such as quarter pounder, Beyond Burger with cheese and Baconnaise, chicken patty, or any of these New York style with blue cheese dressing. Also superbowls, and sides £1.50-£4.50 such as buffalo tenders, slaw, air-baked fries, sweet potato fries, rashers, soup, meatballs marinara, loaded nachos, mac and cheese. Evening desserts £3.99 such as baked Alaska, warm caramel brownie or sticky toffee pudding with ice cream. Coconut rum cocktail £6.50.

Organic coffees, bulletproof, hot choc, mocha £1.65-£2.45 (£2.50-£3.50 evening), extra shot 35p, own cup 25p off. Tea £1.90. Fancy teas £2.90 like turmeric chai, spiced blueberry. Almond, coconut, oat or soya milk. No plastic bottles in their fridge. Fresh juices £2.99. Smoothies £4.50. Shakes £5.50.

Leon, EC1 Farringdon
Omnivorous cafe & take-away

- ☞ 20 Cowcross Street EC1M 6DH
- ☎ 020 7250 3670
- ◖ M-F 07.00-22.00, Sa 10.00-19.00, Su 11.00-17.00
- ⊖ Farringdon
- ↖ leonrestaurants.co.uk

Fast food cafe. See Chains for details.

Tas Farringdon
Omnivorous Turkish cafe & take-away

- ☞ 37 Farringdon Rd EC1M 3JB
- ☎ 020 7430 9721
- ◖ M-Sa 12.00-23.30, Su 12.00-22.30
- ⊖ Farringdon
- ↖ tasrestaurant.co.uk

Similar menu to the South Bank branch with stacks of vegan Turkish dishes. Licensed.

Around the northern edges of the City are some excellent eateries. Firstly in Shoreditch, just up from Liverpool Street or to the east of Old Street, are:

Redemption, Shoreditch
Vegan restaurant

- ☛ 320 Old Street EC1V 9DR
- ☏ 020 7613 0720
- ◕ M-F 12.00-22.30, Sa 10.00-22.30, Su 10.00-17.00
- ⊖ Old Street
- ↖ redemptionbar.co.uk/

New, healthy, vegan restaurant opened 2016, close to where Saf used to be, specialising in raw food and mocktails. As well as lunch and dinner, it is great for a quiet afternoon tea with a cake or cheesecake. See Shoreditch chapter (East London).

Other vegan places in the Shoreditch section of East London are **Essential Vegan** (Brazilian) on Calvert Avenue off Shoreditch High Street, **Genesis** at the top of Commercial Street, **Club Mexicana** on Great Eastern Street, **Eat Chay** (Vietnamese) and **What the Pitta** (kebabs) in Shoreditch Boxpark, **Site** on Columbia Road, and **Bright Store** on Hackney Road.

Near the bottom of Brick Lane you'll find **Mooshies** vegan burger cafe and **Vegan Yes** Korean-Italian fusion cafe. On Whitechapel Road between the bottom of Brick Lane and Aldgate East tube is the great value **Maree's** Caribbean vegan fast food cafe and take-away.

On the north-west edge of the City:

The Gate, Islington
Vegetarian international restaurant

- ☛ 370 St John Street EC1V 4NN
  Opposite Saddlers Wells theatre. Turn left out of Angel tube, walk south across the big junction towards Rosebery Ave.
- ☏ 020 7278 5483
- ◕ M-Su 12.00-23.00; lunch 12.00-14.30 last orders. Dinner 18.00-22.30 last orders. Weekend brunch 10.00-15.00
- ⊖ Angel
- ↖ thegaterestaurants.com

Big, elegant new branch of the top class international vegetarian restaurant that started out in Hammersmith, opened here in June 2012, a stone's throw from Sadler's Wells theatre.

See Islington for full details (North London).

Itadaki Zen
Vegan organic Japanese restaurant

- ☛ 139 Kings Cross Road WC1X 9BJ
- ☏ 020 7278 3573
- ◕ M-Sa 12.30-15.00, 18.00–22.00 (last orders 15 minutes before closing); Su, bank holidays closed
- ⊖ Kings Cross
- ↖ itadakizen-uk.com
  Facebook Itadakizen London

Beautiful, authentic Japanese vegan restaurant. See Islington for full details (North London).

little further north is a branch of Mildreds vegetarian restaurant, on Pentonville Road, with a similar menu to the Soho branch.

Veggie Pret, Exmouth Market
Vegetarian cafe & take-away

- 🖝 19-21a Exmouth Market EC1R 4QD
- ☎ 020 7837 7189
- 🕐 M-F 06.30-19.00, Sa 08.00-18.00, Su 08.00-18.00
- ⊖ Bus 19, 38
- ↖ pret.co.uk/en-gb/veggie-pret

Following the success of converting two existing stores from Pret a Manger to Veggie Pret in Soho and then Shoreditch, this third branch was the first to open from scratch as a Veggie Pret in October 2017.

They sell the same sandwiches and wraps as the other two branches, around half of them vegan. Look out for vegan mac & cheese, artichoke and tapenade wholegrain stone baked baguette.

It's a shame they use heaps of dairy, and how come avocado and beans toasted tortilla isn't vegan, or even the falafel in flatbread, so they've still got a way to go to catch up with the rest of Shoreditch and Brick Lane. Also in Shoreditch and Soho.

Gulshan
Omnivorous Indian market stall

- 🖝 Stall in Exmouth market
- 🕐 M-F 11.00-14.30

Veggies with pilau rice and salad £5. Choose from mixed veg, dal, dal/chickpeas, spinach dal, aubergine, samosa, mint sauce.

The Gate

Itadaki Zen

Charcoal Grill
Omnivorous Middle Eastern market stall

☛ Exmouth Market
🕐 M-F 12.00-15.00

Mixed mezze £5 with falafel, hummus, tabouleh, nut salad, aubergine, baby broad beans, lentil paté with rice, salad and bread.

Cinnamon Tree
Vegetarian stall in front of their omnivorous restaurant

☛ 14 Exmouth Market EC1R 4QE
📞 07505 141621
🕐 Stall M-F 12.30-14.30

Box of food £5 with rice, dal, chickpeas, mixed veg, aubergine pakora, samosa and a free bottle of water.

Freebird Burritos
Omnivorous Mexican street food

☛ 22 Exmouth Market EC1R 4QE
  (outside William Hill betting shop)
📞 020 7621 1882
🕐 M-F 11.30-14.30
🏹 freebirdburritos.com

£6.20-£6.50 for the veg option. First choose from burrito with rice and beans, fajita which adds sautéed peppers and onions instead of beans, tacos, or naked served in a box. Secondly select a vegan filling of guacamole with a choice of beans and peppers. Thirdly pick your salsa, for exam-ple mild with tomato, lime, coriander, onion and seasoning. Finally add a drink.

Also at 24 Liverpool Street EC2M 7PD.

Cielo Blanco
Omnivorous Mexican restaurant

☛ 55-57 Exmouth Market EC1R 4QL
📞 020 3034 0066
🕐 M-Su 11.30-23.00
🏹 cieloblanco.co.uk

Snacks to share £4.50-£5.95 include fresh guacamole, chilango sweet corn come with corn chips and house salsa.

Street food £4.95-£5.95 such as superfood tacos with quinoa, hearts of palm and mint, served in lettuce leaf cups; mushroom enchilada; black bean tostatads with tomato and avocado. Wild rice salad £4.50 with corn, beans, cucumber and cumin; or quinoa and black bean salad with pomegranate, heart of palm and mint.

Vegetable meze sharing board £12.95 each for at least two people, with salsas, guacamole, rice, warm tortillas, mushroom enchiladas, stuffed jalapenos, potato and herb flautas, corn on the cob, black bean tostadas, quinoa superfood tacos. Sides and dips £2.50-£3.95 like sweet potato fries, herby green rice with pepitas.

Superjuices £4.25-£4.50such as Amarillo with yelllow pepper, pineapple, fresh turmeric and lime. Agave cocktail bar downstairs with hundreds of cocktails, tequila. Wine £4.50 glass, £10.70 carafe, £16 bottle. Beers £4.20-£4.70.

Astro Vegan
Vegan Italian street stall

- 20-22 Leather Lane Market EC1N 7SU
- 07969 162733
- M-F 12.00-14.30
- Barbican, Old Street
- www.facebook.com/AstroVegan

They started out vegetarian in Camden then went vegan and came here. Ten dishes such as salads, polenta with bean stew, wraps, gnocchi £6.50-£6.95. Generous portions. Sometimes cakes £2.50 or drinks.

Astro Vegan

Warung Tempeh
Vegetarian Indonesian street stall

- Leather Lane Market EC1N 7NJ (north end, opposite the Craft Beer Co pub)
- info@warungtempeh.com
- Th-F 12.00-14.00
- Barbican, Old Street
- warungtempeh.com
  Facebook The Tempeh Man

Two "meaty" tempeh main dishes £5.50, with organic tempeh made by the owner from soya beans, water, rice wine vinegar and Rizopous Oligosporus culture.

Lodeh tempeh curry contains coconut milk, traditional spices such as lemongrass and kaffir lime leaves, julienne carrots and fine green beans, topped with fresh coriander and served with rice and Indonesian chili sambal. Tempeh Jinten cumin tempeh slowly cooked with red peppers, cherry plumb tomatoes and a range of spices creating a

drier dish, served with flatbread, lime, fresh coriander and Indonesian chili sambal (ask for dairy-free yogurt). Or have a mixed box with a bit of both dishes.

They supply tempeh to restaurants, shops and individuals, and you can buy it here but come early!

Leather Lane Market
Street market

- 🐾 Leather Lane, EC1
- 🕐 M-F 10.30-14.30
- ⊖ Farringdon, Chancery Lane

Fruit and veg, clothing and household goods. The market has two juice bars and a stall selling fruit, nuts and olives. The Oasis Mediterranean cafe sells falafels.

Leather Lane is full of sit down weekday lunch cafes with big self-serve salad bars where most dishes are vegetarian, vegan even. Starting at the north end you will find King of Falafel, Moroccan, fruit and veg, jacket potatoes, luggage, flowers, Ptooch Café, Tony's Café, plants, Thai, El Jugo juice bar trailer, Sunny's vegetarian Turkish salads stall, more fruit and veg, Mexican, Oasis Salad Bar, Prufrock Coffee Bar, clothes.

Sunny's Olive Tree, Leather Ln
Vegetarian Turkish salad stall

- 🐾 Opposite Café l'Auberge, 43 Leather
- 🕐 Lane EC1N 7TJ M-F 08.00-15.00
- ⊖ Chancery Lane, Farringdon
- ↖ Sunnyolivetree.com

A franchise of the original Whitecross Street stall, with a mouthwatering 25 bowls of salads to make your box of food £3.50, £4.50. Olives box £2.50, £3.50.

144

Ptooch
Omnivorous salad buffet café

- 🐾 63 Leather Lane EC1N 7TS
- ☎ 07804 975935
- 🕐 M-F 11.00-14.30
- ⊖ Farringdon, Chancery Lane

Awesome salad bar with around 30 vegan self-serve dishes. Eat-in plate £5, take-away box £3 small, £4 large, £5 extra large. Water and soft drinks 80p. They also own Café l'Auberge further down the street.

Tony's Café
Omnivorous buffet cafe

- 🐾 61 Leather Lane EC1N 7TJ
- ☎ 074122 63039
- 🕐 M-F 11.30-16.00
- ⊖ Chancery Lane, Farringdon
- ↖

Fantastic value gigantic buffet where 34 of the 36 dishes are vegetarian. Salads and hot dishes such as stir-fry, spinach and potato, pasta. Take-away boxes £3, £3.50, £4. Eat-in plate £4.95. Cans 60p.

Café l'Auberge
Omnivorous buffet cafe

- 🐾 43 Leather Lane EC1N 7TJ
- ☎ 020 7404 9466
- 🕐 M-F 11.00-15.00
- ⊖ Chancery Lane, Farringdon

Another big buffet café with lots of seating. Here is more meaty than the others but still most dishes are veggie. Take-away boxes in four sizes £3, £3.50, £4, £5. Eat-in plate £4.70 salads only, £5.20 with hot food. Drinks 80p.

El Jugo
Juice bar

📣 Pitch 38, Leather Lane Market

☏ 0749 141 532

🕐 M-F 08.00-15.00

🔗 eljugo4you.wordpress.com

Fresh smoothies and juices small £2.20, medium £2.70, large £3.70. Supersmoothies with vegetable juice 50p extra. Booster shots £1.50 such as wheatgrass, chlorella, hemp, spirulina, morenga, macca, chia, açai. Ginger lime shot £1.

Free delivery before midday. Also at Russell Square, Euston, Torrington Square.

Daddy Donkey
Omnivorous Mexican take-away

📣 50 Leather Lane EC1N 7TP

☏ 020 7404 4173

🕐 M-Th 11.00-16.00, F 11.00-16.00

🔗 daddydonkey.co.uk

Everything here can be made vegan. Daddy D burrito £5.95 is a "Big-Ass flour tortilla" with coriander-lime rice, black beans, guacamole, salsa, lettuce; mini version £4.95. Fajita burrito adds sauté coriander-lime peppers and onions instead of black beans. Kick-Ass burrito combines the two. Naked burrito puts one of these three into a box instead of a tortilla. Also tacos, tostadas. Tortilla chips with salsa and/or guacamole £2.25-£2.95. Also jalapenos, pots of salsa or guacamole, extra tortilla. Soft drinks £3-£1.50, Corona beer £3.50.

Chick
Omnivorous Middle Eastern restaurant

🍴 90a Leather Lane EC1N 7TE

🕐 M-F 11.30-15.30

Falafel in wholewheat pitta with salad £4.80. Falafel salad £5.80. Juices £3.25-£3.75 such as Gringo Goddess, Immune Booster, Skin Glow, Rockin' Beet. Soft drinks £1.

In front of the restaurant is a falafel stand (pitch 17-19) open the same times, serving the same options, and also accepting cards.

Curry Zone
Vegetarian Indian

📣 In the market next opposite Daddy Donkey, next to El Jugo

New vegetarian stall (January 2017) that does not use ghee. Mix and match veg box with rice £3-£4. Dishes include chana masala chickpea, sag aloo potato, veg curry, veg Madras, vindaloo, dopiaza, jalfrezi, balti, rogan, biryana, tikka masala.

Holland & Barrett, High Holborn
Health food shop

📣 8 High Holborn WC1V 6DR

☏ 020 7430 9346

🕐 M-F 07.30-20.00., Sa 10.00-17.00, Su 11.00-17.00

⊖ Chancery Lane

Fridge and freezer.

Carnevale
Mediterranean vegetarian restaurant

- 135 Whitecross Street EC1Y 8JL
- ℃ 020 7250 3452
- ● M-F 12.30-15.30, 17.00-23.00, Sa 17.00-23.00, Su closed
- ⊖ Old Street, Barbican, Moorgate
- ↖ carnevalerestaurant.co.uk

Lovely little restaurant, snack bar and take-away with a glass roofed area out back. Near Barbican Centre and Museum of London. They have a few vegan options.

Set menu £13.50 (3 courses, or 2 courses and a drink): for example soup of the day; risotto with giroles, mascarpone and herbs; plum and almond tart.

Lots of lunchtime hot and cold sandwiches £2.25-4.50 such as baba ghanoush with roasted peppers, artichoke hearts with olive relish and leaves, aubergines and peppers with pesto or sun-dried tomatoes. 25p extra for ciabatta, walnut or organic sourdough bread. Extra fillings form 25p. Hot take-away £5.75 such as spring veg casserole with broad beans, artichokes and chilli polenta fritters. Eat in deli plate £5.95. Lots of salads £2.25-£4.25.

A la carte starters include vegan soup of the day £5.50; young artichoke stuffed with walnut, lemon parsley, breadcrumbs, on a bed or caramelised red onion £7.25.

Main courses £13.50 such as falafel, pepper, harissa casserole served with homemade hummus; potato cakes with fennel, lemon, basil with provençale veg casserole and mixed rocket salad; saffron risotto with baked squash; homemade sausage with mashed potato in a red wine rosemary sauce.

Side dishes £2.5-£4.50 include salads, lemon and rosemary roast potatoes, roasted artichokes, olives.

The only vegan dessert £6.25 is chocolate roulade filled with raspberries, Earl Grey truffles and vanilla soya cream.

Wines from £4.50 glass; organic wines from £5.75 glass, £20 bottle, half litre £16.50. Cocktails £5.50-£6.50. Juices £2.50 are mostly organic. Soft drinks £2-£2.50. Coffee £1.75-£2.25, they have soya milk. Herbal teas £1.50.

Whitecross Street Market
Street market

- Whitecross Street EC1 (off Old Street) M-F 11.30-15.00
- ↖ bitecross.co.uk

Whitecross Street Market is fantastic for a weekday lunch. You can sit down at Carnevale restaurant, or choose from four vegetarian take-away stalls plus others with soup, artisan bread, coffee and fruit and veg, Mexican, Thai and more, which you can eat at tables next to the big playground in Fortune Street park.

Carnevale stall
Vegetarian falafel & salad stall

- In front of Carnevale restaurant, 135 Whitecross Street EC1Y 8JL
- ℃ 020 7250 3452
- ● Stall M-F 12.00-14.30; restaurant M-F 11.30-23.00, Sa 17.30-23.00
- ↖ carnevalerestaurant.co.uk

Falafel £4.50 with hummus, £5 with baba ghanoush. Vegan salad boxes £4.50, £5, add 50p for hummus. Salads include bulghur tabouleh; new potatoes with olives, capers, parsley; broccoli with chillies; pasta with baked tomatoes, capers, pine nuts and oregano; carrot with toasted mustard seeds, mint and lemon dressing; beans; mixed green leaf and herb. Cold drinks 80p-£1.50.

Hoxton Beach Falafel
Vegan falafel & salad stall

- ☛ Pitch 36, in front of 135 Whitecross Street EC1Y
- ☏ 07931 375632
- ◐ M-F 11.30-15.00
- ⊖ Barbican, Old Street
- ↖ hoxtonbeach.com

Falafel wrap in Arab khubz bread with tahini, chilli sauce, their homemade turnip pickle, cucumber and chilli pickles, salad and hummus. Regular £4, large £5, you can add a cooked vegetable such as sweet potato, cauliflower or fuul fava bean stew. Also loose falafel balls with salads. Drinks £1 include lemon, elderflower, hibiscus.

Sunny's Olive Tree, Whitecross
Vegetarian Turkish salad bar

☛ Whitecross Street Market EC1Y 8JL, Pitch 38-40, next to Hoxton Beach Falafel, in the middle of the market, just look for the one with big bowls of olives

📞 07956 938 194

🕐 M-F 10.00-14.00

↖ sunnysolivetree.com

The biggest street stall salad bar you've ever seen with 25 bowls including iceberg, red cabbage, potatoes, couscous, kidney beans, sundried tomatoes, roasted red pepper, stuffed vine leaves, mixed veg, green beans and carrots, courgette, quinoa, beetroot, olives.

Box of food £3.40, £4.40. Olives box £2.50, £3.50.

Jevi Sweet
Vegetarian Indian street food stall

☛ Opposite 131 Whitecross Street (Carnevale)

🕐 M-F 10.00-15.00

Fabulous value basic food such as bhel puri or sev pui. Savouries are two for £3 such as crunchy pani puri, or big kachori pastry balls stuffed with potato and peas or lentils, or aloo tikki potato patties, all served with salad, chutney and tamarind sauce. Desserts include vegan jelabi (looks like an orange Curly Wurly) and ladhu balls. Masala tea £1 with mint, ginger and cardamon, can be made without milk.

Wholefood Heaven
Vegetarian food stall

- Pitch 12, In front of 191 Whitecross Street (corner Garrett St)
- M-F 11.30-15.30
- wholefoodheaven.co.uk

Unique healthy take-away in a converted Citroen H van run by husband and wife team Charlotte, a life vegetarian and homeopath, and David, a restaurant chef who went vegetarian in 2005 and was a founding head chef at gourmet vegan restaurant Saf and has worked at other vegetarian restaurants in London. Their speciality is Buddha Bowl, a hearty meal in a round box for £4.50 or £5, with a whole grain as the base such as organic brown rice, a hearty stew or curry such as massaman with new potato, pineapple and soya chunks, plus steamed greens, something fermented such as kimchee Chinese cabbage with chilli, garlic and ginger with carrot pickle and omega mixed seeds. Wheat and gluten-free. Organic cans £1. Vegetarian, vegan, raw and special diet catering for events, meetings, dinner parties and personal chef, tuition and workshops.

Winner of Best British Street Food Award.

Karuna
Omnivorous Indian food stall

- Almost opposite Carnevale EC1Y 8QJ
- 020 7527 1761
- M-F 11.30-14.30
- twitter.com/Karunacatering

Three vegan curries each day in a box, small £4, medium £4.50, large £5, such as chana masala chickpea, sag spinach, aloo gobi potato, moong dal, tarka dal, veg coconut curry, veg biryani rice. Samosas, onion bajia, 2 for 50p.

At the top of the street, CHAO Vietnamese Café does tofu and veg rice £5.20.

Arancini Bros
Vegan cafe & take-away

- 42 Old Street EC1V 9AE (between Aldersgate and Whitecross Street)
- 020 7253 5718
- M-F 9.30-16.00, Sa-Su/BH closed
- Old Street
- arancinibrothers.com

Fast take-away lunches are the specialty, but there are plenty of seats too and filter coffee. Risotto balls are the speciality, plus burgers, chickn, salad boxes.

For menu see Dalston (East London). Also at Kentish Town (North London).

Counter Kitchen

Omnivorous healthy cafe

- 63 Goswell Road EC1V 7EN (corner Northburgh Street)
- 020 3441 9562
- M-F 08.00-18.00, Sa-Su closed
- Barbican
- counterkitchen.com
  facebook.com/counterkitchen

New cafe where you order at the counter and collect from the kitchen. Around half the menu is vegan. Tomato soup £4. Salad and warm bowls £6.50-£8 contain some combination of veggies, salad, pulses, soba noodles, quinoa, brown rice, seaweed, crushed peanuts, sesame seeds.

Wedge Issue

Omnivorous pizza restaurant & take-away

- 91-95 Clerkenwell Road EC1R 5BX (opposite Laystall Street)
- 020 7242 3246
- M-W 12.00-22.00, Th-F 12.00-23.00, Sa 17.00-22.00, Su closed
- Chancery Lane, Farringdon
- wedgeissuepizza.com

Serves pizzas with vegan cheese, and craft beer. Table service. Event space. Friday is open mic night. See Brick Lane (East London) for menu.

Brewdog, Clerkenwell

Omnivorous restaurant-bar

- 45-47 Clerkenwell Rd EC1M 5RS
- 020 7608 2989
- Sa, M-W 12.00-23.00, Th-F 12.00-24.00, Su closed
- Farringdon
- brewdog.com/bars/uk/clerkenwell
  facebook.com/brewdogclerkenwell

Vegan craft beers and a food menu that includes Hail Seitan bbq steak or southern fried seitan burger, tofu hot dog, all £9, superfood salad £8, fries and sweet potato fries £3.50-£4.

Cubana Smithfield

Omnivorous Cuban restaurant & coffee shop

- 59 Charterhouse Street EC1M 6HA
- 020 7490 1209
- M-Th 08.00-23.00, F 08.00-24.00, Sa 18.00-24.00, Su closed
- Farringdon
- cubana.co.uk
  facebook.com/Cubana.Smithfield

Restaurant, bakery, cafe, mojito bar and coffee roastery in Smithfield. See original South Bank branch for menu.

Planet Organic, Liverpool Street
Wholefood store & omnivorous take-away

- 10 Devonshire Square EC2M 4AE
- 020 7220 9060
- M-F 07.30-21.00, Sa-Su closed
- Liverpool Street
- planetorganic.com

The newest branch of Planet Organic has a big organic take-away section with a few seats inside and tables and chairs outside in the traffic-free courtyard. Much more here is actually organic than other big wholefood stores, amazing quality, and they use sustainable packaging where possible.

Most of the hot and cold take-away counter is vegan, with the animal stuff down one end. Hot soups £2.99 small, £4.99 large. Buffet deli counter £5.50 small box, £7.50 medium, £8.50 large. Big range of dishes that varies every day and changes completely monthly, for example one day could be steamed brown rice, quinoa, roast potatoes, hot stews, lentil dal, steamed broccoli, tofu stir-fry, several seasonal salads.

Smoothies and juices to order £4.50-5.95. Hot drinks £1.65-2.95. Speciality lattes £3.15-£4. Choice of several plant milks at no extra charge. Cbd oil can be added to any drink.

Lots of fridges with grab and go salads, sandwiches, breakfast pots, vegan desserts, ready meals, soups, exotic tofu, vegan yogurts. Huge range of Laura's Idea vegan salads, wraps, granola breakfast pots, cheescake, calzone, tortilla, desserts including raw ones.

This is the only wholefood store in the area to have a freezer, with ready meals, berries and vegan ice-creams such as Booja Booja

and lollies.

Fruit and veg produce section is 100% organic. Paul's bread. inSpiral kale chips. Clearspring Japanese foods. Gluten-free pasta. Vegan organic wines and beers.

Huge bodycare section with Jason, Weleda, Green People, Nourish, Avalon, Laidbare, Lavera, Sukin, Pukka, Pai, Neal's Yard, Ren, Dr Hauschka, Jurlique, Antipodes, Desert Essence, Roots & Wings, John Masters, Dr Bronner, Natracare. Aromatherapy and candles.

Vegan protein powders in various flavours such as Sun Warrior, Vega and Form. Chia, cocoa nibs, acai powder, spirulina, chlorella, hemp protein, barley grass, maca, lucuma, baobab.

Supplements by Solgar, Viridian, BioCare, Higher Nature, New Chapter, Terra Nova. Vogel remedies.

Wagamama, EC2
Japanese omnivorous restaurant

- Moorgate/Barbican, 1a Ropemaker Street EC2Y 9AW
- 020 7588 2688
- M-F 11.30-22.00, Sa-Su closed
- Moorgate

Now with a separate vegan menu such as Vegatsu vegan katsu curry. Street level access. Free wifi. Disabled toilet. See Chains for details.

Holland & Barrett, Old Broad St
Health food shop

- 85-86 Old Broad St EC2M 1PR
- 020 7256 8499
- M-F 07.30-19.30, Sa 10.00-18.00, Su 11.00-18.00
- St Pauls

Fridge and freezer.

ChikP
Falafel stall

- St Katherine's Docks, 1 Marble Quay E1W 1UH (between the Thames and the Guoman Hotel, by Tower Bridge and Tower of London)
-
- Friday only 11.30-14.30
- Tower Gate, Tower Hill
- Twitter @FalafelCo

Falafel wrap with hummus, salad and pickles, optional aubergine. Falafel salad box. When we say salad, we don't mean the usual lettuce and tomato, but also red cabbage, pickled turnips and gherkins. Around £5.

Organic Chickpeas
Vegan Mediterranean organic take-away

- 8 Botolph Alley EC3R 8DR
- 020 7283 8313
- M-F 11.00-14.30, Sa-Su closed
- Monument

New take-away in the space that was previously Futures! They use organic veg, pita, herbs, spices, even oil.

Falafel wrap £5.15, falafel salad bowl £5.25, hummus plate £5.15. Extra pitta 50p, aubergine 75p. Falafel portion £2.50.

Lemonade £1.50, San Pellegrino mineral water £1.25.

Wagamama EC3, Tower Hill
Japanese omnivorous restaurant

- 2b Tower Place EC3N 4EE (big glass building next to Tower of London)
- 020 7283 5897
- M-Sa 11.00-22.00, Su 11.00-21.00
- Tower Hill
- wagamama.com

Baby facilities. Lift. Disabled toilet. Free wifi.

Also on Cheapside are Marks & Spencer (salad pots and a couple of vegan sandwiches), Itsu and Pure. On Bow Lane are Pret, Eat and Paul's. On Cannon Street are Pod, Itsu, Pret, Eat, M&S, Vital Ingredient and Leon.

At the other end of London Bridge, to the right and down the steps, is Borough Market, which always has some vegetarian and vegan food stalls along the south side of Southwark Cathedral. See the South Bank section.

Holland & Barrett, Leadenhall
Health food shop

- 87 Gracechurch Street EC3V 0AA
- 020 7929 5833
- M-F 07.30-20.00, Sa-Su closed
- Bank, Monument

Fridge with take-away food. No freezer.

Holland & Barrett, Fenchurch
Health food shop

- 16-18 London Street EC3R 7JP
- 020 3632 2455
- M-F 07.00-20.00, Sa-Su closed
- Fenchurch Street BR, Monument, Tower Hill, Tower Gateway, Aldgate

Fridge with take-away food. No freezer.

Pilpel, Lime Street
Vegan food pub

- 21 Lime Street EC3V 1PL
- 020 7199 2969
- M-F 10.00-20.00, Sa-Su closed
- Monument, Bank, Fenchurch St BR
- pilpel.co.uk

Same menu as St Pauls EC4 branch.

Vanilla Black
Vegetarian restaurant

🖝 17-18 Tooks Court, The City, EC4A
   1LB (off Chancery Lane)

☏ 020-7242 2622

🕐 M-Sa 12.00-14.30 (last orders),
   18.00-22.00 (last orders), Su closed

⊖ Chancery Lane

🔖 vanillablack.co.uk

"Pretentious vegetarian restaurant which tries too hard. Want burrito and wedges? Fancy a big bowl of veggie curry? Go elsewhere." Say Vanilla Black at the top of their own Twitter page @vanillablack1.

This is a top class restaurant, one of the rare places you can have a quiet, classy veggie lunch in London. Good for business lunches and taking people to who don't normally do veggie but are into gourmet. The decor is impressive, service immaculate, and Michelin has given them a star. Fans praise Heston Blumenthal style innovation ar foodie journalists love the unique dishe Our readers report good food though tir portions, a sort of nouvelle cuisin végétarienne, food as art. You'll eat thing it would be hard to make yourself even you are into cooking BUT don't come her hungry and expect to leave full - the portion are bijou!

When it opened there were almost no vegar options for walk-ins, but there is now separate vegan menu and. Some vegans say it is the best vegetarian restauran they've ever been to, others say it is the worst. Here are a few readers' views to help you make up your mind. "The taste of everything was exquisite. I would certainly go there again." "Enjoyed it. It's a bit overpriced (small portion sizes) but there aren't many upmarket vegetarian restaurants in London, so it's definitely filling a gap. Emphasis very much on vegetarian rather than vegan, but all the food was tasty and immaculately presented." "Loved the

space and the service - more upmarket than anything else in London. Whereas the food was good, but not noteworthy. And I was still hungry afterwards, so popped into Maoz on the way home!" "I can't remember them using dairy alternatives at all which can limit dessert options." "Worst meal I have ever had, over priced, awful food - I felt I had been swindled. It was highly recommended by veggie (not vegan) friends. We split up and are close to being divorced. OK, I can't blame it entirely on that restaurant but I reckon it tipped the balance!"

A la carte two courses for £31, three for £41.50. Five course set menu £55, to be taken by the entire table, wine pairing £39. Lunch set menu two courses £21.50, three £26.50. Optional 12.5% service charge will be added to your bill and goes to your waiting staff. Here is a sample vegan menu:

Starters such as sweet potato and puy lentil dal; pickled cucumber, sticky rice and ginger purée; watermelon, red pepper and tomato with shallot cream.

Mains such as fried porridge with spring greens and edamame soya beans; fried shiitake, pine nuts purée and crispy couscous; smoked vegan cheese, black sesame and fried gram (chickpea) flour.

Desserts such as kahlua coffee cake with coconut and toasted rice mousse; peanut butter cheesecake and cracked cocoa beans; poached rhubarb and pomegranate.

Amazing wine list, almost all vegan, from £6.50 medium glass, £23.95 bottle.

Inform them when booking of any intolerances or allergies. Allow a little extra time to find as it is tucked away. It's not far from the Inns of Court with their nice quiet gardens (handy for a picnic another time).

Falafel House
Vegetarian cafe & take-away

- 116 Cannon Street EC4N 64S
- (020 7626 6570
- M-F 08.00-16.00, Sa-Su closed
- Monument

- 48 Carter Lane EC4V 5EA (south side of St Paul's cathedral)
- (020 7248 3228
- M-F 11.00-15.00, Sa-Su closed
- City Thameslink, Blackfriars, St Pauls
- falafel-house.co.uk

Breakfast from 8am to 11am such as porridge with two toppings £1.99, muesli with two toppings £1.75, bloomer with jam £1.50.

All day coffee £1.30-£2.50. They have soya milk. Soft drinks £1, water 95p.

Falafel £4.75 in white or brown pita with salad. Add £1 for guacamole, extra hummus, stuffed vine leaves, grilled veg, grilled aubergine or olives. Salad box £6.50 with falafel, hummus, brown or white pita and one of the extras. Salad without falafel but one topping £5.50. Five falafel balls £2.20, with hummus £3.50. Piri piri hummus £1. Pitta £1. A few seats inside or go sit by the cathedral or down by the river. They do platters for several people to share.

Pilpel St Pauls
Vegetarian cafe & take-away

- Unit 5, Queens Head Passage, Paternoster Square EC4M 7DZ
- 020 7248 9281
- M-F 10.00-21.00, Sa-Su closed
- St Pauls
- pilpel.co.uk

The Spitalfields falafel and hummus bar has new branches at St Pauls and Fleet Street and this is the biggest of the four.

Falafel with salad and hummus £4.80 in white or wholemeal pita, £5.80 in a box. Choose salad from carrots, chickpeas, green salad, jalapenos, onions, tabouleh, pickled cucumbers, red and white cabbage. Extra toppings 60p such as aubergine or guacamole, or sun-dried tomato £1.

Hummus and salad with pita in a box £4.25, toppings 60p, add 4 falafels £1.

Cold drinks 95p-£1.50.

It gets very busy with a queue 12.00-14.00. To save time you can order lunch online by 11.30 and collect by 12.00.

Pilpel Fleet Street
Vegetarian cafe & take-away

- 146 Fleet Street, 1a Wine Office Court EC2A 3BY (through an ancient covered narrow alley)
- 020 7952 1205
- M-F 11.00-16.00, Sa-Su closed
- City Thameslink BR
- pilpel.co.uk

Same menu as St Pauls branch.

Chilango, Fleet Street
Omnivorous Mexican cafe

- 142 Fleet Stree EC4A 2BP
- 020 7353 6761
- M-F 11.00-21.00, Sa-Su closed
- City Thameslink
- chilango.co.uk

See Islington (North) for details.

Also at Chancery Lane, London Wall, Brushfield (Spitalfields).

Crussh, Ludgate Circus
Omnivorous cafe

- 6 Farringdon Street EC4M 7LH
- 020 7489 5916
- M-F 07.00-18.00, Sa-Su closed
- City Thameslink, Blackfriars
- crussh.com

Juices, wraps and soups. See Chains.

Leon, EC4
Omnivorous cafe & take-away

- 28 Watling Street EC4M 9BR
- 020 7236 3375
- M-F 07.00-17.00, Sa-Su closed
- St Paul's,
- leonrestaurants.co.uk

Fast food cafe. See Chains for details.

- 86 Cannon Street EC4N 6HT
- 020 7623 9699
- M-F 07.00-21.00, Sa-Su closed
- St Paul's, Blackfriars
- leonrestaurants.co.uk

Fast food cafe. See Chains for details.

- 12 Ludgate Circus EC4M 7LQ
- 020 7489 1580
- M-F 07.30-22.00, Sa-Su closed
- St Paul's, Blackfriars
- leonrestaurants.co.uk

Fast food cafe. See Chains for details.

Wagamama
Japanese omnivorous restaurant

- 1 Ludgate Hill EC4M 7AA
- 020 3771 3421
- M-Th 11.00-22.30, F-Sa 11.00-23.00, Su 11.00-22.00
- City Thameslink BR, St Paul's
  Near St Pauls. Baby facilities. Free wifi.
- Mansion House: 4 Great St Thomas Apostle, between Garlick Hill and Queen Street, EC4V 2BH
- 020 7248 5766
- M-Sa 11.00-22.00, Su closed
- Mansion House
- wagamama.com

Restaurant is at street level. Baby facilities. Free wifi.

Fleet Street also has Eat, Vital Ingredient, Aboka and Tesco Express.

For a really good licensed vegetarian buffet restaurant, cross Blackfriars Bridge or Southwark Bridge and head for Tibits Bankside. Tuesdays is vegan day. See the South Bank section for location, or Mayfair for menu.

Holland & Barrett, EC4
Health food shop

- 📍 130-131 Cheapside EC2V 6BT
- 📞 020 7726 6069
- 🕐 M-F 07.30-19.00, Sa 10.00-18.00, Su 11.00-17.00
- ⊖ St Pauls

Fridge and freezer.

- 📍 119 Cannon Street EC4N 5AT
- 📞 020 7929 6252
- 🕐 M-F 07.00-20.00, Sa 9.00-18.00, Su 10.00-18.00
- ⊖ Cannon Street BR, Monument

Fridge and freezer.

- 📍 144-146 Fetter Lane EC4 1BT
- 📞 020 3638 6430
- 🕐 M-F 08.30-18.30, Sa-Su closed
- ⊖ Temple, Chancery Lane

Fridge.

- 📍 5 Ludgate Circus EC4M 7LF
- 📞 020 7353 9380
- 🕐 M-F 08.00-19.30, Sa 10.00-17.00, -Su closed
- ⊖ Blackfriars, St Pauls

Fridge full of Scheese, Violife, jumbo sausage rolls, porkless pies etc. Freezer.

VEGAN EAST
LONDON

1st edition

The complete insider guide to the best vegan food in London

Alex Bourke
Vegetarian Guides

EAST
LONDON

* OUR TOP 5 - BEST OF EAST LONDON *

Breakfast
Black Cat (Sunday)
Buhler & Co
Feel Good Cafe
Gallery Cafe
The Larder

Lunch with Friends
House of Vegan, Brick Lane
Broadway Vegan Market
Mel Tropical (Sunday)
Unity Diner
Young Vegans Pizza Shop

Community Spirit
Black Cat
Gallery Cafe
Hornbeam
Temple of Hackney
Unity Diner

Tea and Vegan Cake
Black Cat
Buhler & Co
Essential Vegan
Feel Good Cafe
Vida Bakery

Dinner
Cook Daily
Essential Vegan
Genesis
Mildreds Dalston
Spice Box

Food Shopping
As Nature Intended
Green Street
The Grocery
High Street North
Plant Based Supermarket

Hackney Cafes
Black Cat
Lele's
Palm Greens
Smashing Kitchen
WAVE

Drinking
The Birds pub, Leytonstone
Brewdog Dalston
Brewdog Shoreditch
The Hive, Bethnal Green
The Spread Eagle, Homerton

HOXTON

OLD ST.

SHOREDITCH HIGH STREET

House of Vegan

SHOREDITCH

The Back Yard (inc The Tea Rooms)

Sunday UpMarket

MOORGATE

Liverpool Street Station

Spitalfields Market

LIVERPOOL ST.

ALDGATE   ALDGATE EAST

- ● vegan
- ● vegetarian
- ● omnivorous
- ● shop

EC2 Liverpool Street (City) & E1 Shoreditch/Brick Lane (East)

CM Club Mexicana	Pl Plates Re Redemption	Pizza Express:
EV Essential Vegan	Cy Cyclelab Un Unity Diner	2 Alban Gate
Gg Good To Go Ro Roadtrip	Lo Lokma Tasty Bite	3 Bishopsgate
Br Bright Store Si Site	Vc Veggie Curry Box	4 Curtain Road
Oa Oasi H7 Hoxton 7	VP Veggie Pret	5 Finsbury Circus
Ge Genesis	P1 Pilpel Spitalfields	6 Russia Row
EC Eat Chay	P2 Pilpel Brushfield	7 Spitalfields
Wh What the Pitta	po Planet Organic	Wagamama EC2:
BL Brick Lane stalls	ea East London Juice Co.	w1 Moorgate/Barbican
Ho House of Vegan	fe Felafelicious	w2 Old Broad St/Bank
VN Vegan Nights	vo Voodoo Ray's	w6 Spitalfields
Cc Canvas Cafe	ds Dark Sugars x 2	as As Nature Intended
Ma Maree's Mo Mooshies	b2 Brewdog, Brick Lane	5d Fifth Dimension tattoos
Vi Vida Bakery	wi Wedge Issue pizza	m Monster House hair
VY Vegan Yes CP CPress	db Damascu Bite	H3 Holland & Barrett, Old Broad St
Vu Vurger fa Fauxmagerie	hl Hookah Lounge	gr The Grocery
Me Merkamo	sg Shoreditch Grind	rs Raw Store
164 MT Mel's Tropical Creations	vg Viet Hoa	

SHOREDITCH

& Hoxton, East London's Vegan Valley

Move over Soho, the capital's hippest young women and bearded guys are flocking to Shoreditch. Stretching east from the Google building at Old Street's Silicon Roundabout to Brick Lane, through the clubs and pubs of Old Street and Curtain Road, this is the mecca for social media jobs, independent cinemas, cutting edge vegan diners from raw to kebabs, fashion boutiques from vintage to indie designers, and gigantic weekend clothes and food markets around nearby Brick Lane and Spitalfields.

No need for a taxi home at 3a.m. after the club. On Friday and Saturday, overground trains run all night between Highbury & Islington and New Cross Gate.

While Soho has just three vegan eateries, East London's hipster heaven Shoreditch has, well, countless, all distinct and brilliant.

SHOREDITCH BOXPARK is at the centre of the vegan fun fast food and drinking action, a late night fashion and feasting mall in black shipping containers. Exit the overground and follow round to the left, up the metal steps and through the covered seating and bar area to two adjacent fabulous vegan places. **What the Pitta** create massive vegan kebabs, while **Eat Chay** do Vietnamese wraps. There's also **Falafelicious** salad bar nearby, Açaí Berry downstairs for healthy Brazilian bowls, and downstairs right at the other end **Voodoo Ray's** serve vegan pizzas and slices.

SHOREDITCH HIGH STREET: Essential Vegan Brazilian restaurant is a gorgeous oasis of calm, with fabulous cakes. Or grab a burger at Oasi inside Phoenix Bar.

HOXTON: The area along Old Street is home to some pubs with all-vegan food: **Roadtrip & The Workshop** with catering by **Black Cat Cafe**, and **Hoxton 7** with food by **Greenbox**. **Cyclelab** is a chilled out veggie cafe in a bicycle shop. Closest to Hoxton overground is **Plates**, offering exclusive Saturday night vegan fine dining, by reservation only.

Redemption is an alcohol-free, sugar-free and wheat-free vegan restaurant-bar with lots of raw food. Off Old Street roundabout is **Good to Go**, a modern weekday vegan cafe in a shopping and office complex. Between these two is **Veggie Curry Box** Indian take-away, at the junction of Old Street and Great Eastern Street, while further along the latter are **Veggie Pret** and **Club Mexicana**.

Continue on down Commercial Street (towards Spitalfields Market) for **Genesis**, a handsome new vegan organic restaurant on two floors.

Late night wholefood supermarkets for stocking up before heading home include **As Nature Intended** (till 8pm), **The Grocery** (10pm), and **Raw Store** (till midnight, or weekends 4am).

Away from the party zone, along Hackney Road or Columbia Road, relax with coffee and cakes at arty vegan cafes **Bright Store** and **Site**.

What The Pitta, Shoreditch
Vegan kebab take-away

🖝 52 Boxpark, 2-10 Bethnal Green Rd
   E1 6GY (upstairs)
📞 07912 860293
🕐 Su-W 11.30-22.00, Th-Sa 11.30-
   22.30
⊖ Shoreditch High Street, Liverpool St
🖢 whatthepitta.com
   facebook.com/whatthepitta

Fantastic, London's first vegan doner kebab take-away started on Shoreditch High Street and moved in June 2017 to permanent premises in the Boxpark.

Huge doner £7.95 comes either in a wrap, or in a box with chips or couscous, packed with soya chunks, hummus, tzatziki, salads and chilli. Here you can see Woollybum, the co-organiser of Hackney Vegan Meetup, enjoying a monster kebab.

Vegan lahmacun Turkish pizza £7.95 on thin dough topped with minced soya and veg plus herbs, tomato, onions, spices. Cold meze £7.95 comes with olives, hummus, tzatziki and two lots of homemade Turkish zaatar flatbread.

What the Pitta

op up with extra bread £3, chips £3.50, olives £2.50, hummus or tzatziki £3.

or dessert £2.50 you can have vegan baklava made with layers of filo pastry, crushed almonds and syrup. Beer £3.50, soft drinks £2.

Meal Deal 1 with kebab or lahmacun, baklava dessert and soft drink £10. Meal Deal 2 £12 replaces the baklava by chips.

Deliveroo, UberEats. Also at Croydon Boxpark and Camden.

Eat Chay
Vegan Vietnamese & Korean take-away

- 🍴 48 Boxpark, 2 Bethnal Green Road E1 6GY (upstairs)
- ☎ 020 3287 8597
- 🕐 Su-W 12.00-21.00, Th-Sa 12.00-22.00
- ⊖ Shoreditch High Street
- ➤ eatchay.com
  facebook.com/eatchayclub
  instagram.com/eatchayclub

Chay is Vietnamese for vegan, featuring banh mi filled baguettes, bao buns, bento box, bowls, even f'sh & chips.

Banh mi £7.50-£8 filled with chilli lemongrass grilled soya chick'n, mushroom and walnut paté and pickled carrots; or Korean bbq crispy smoky seitan with kimchi and sriracha mayo. Two steamed bao buns £7.50, three £10, filled with bbq seitan or Korean fried tofu with gachujang Korean red chilli sauce or fried f'sh. Bento box £9 with two baos of your choice plus noodle salad or chips.

Bowls £7.50-£8.50 include noodle salad with grilled soya chick'n; or bibimbap mixed rice with bbq seitan, kimchi, shiitake msuhroom, pickled daikon, beansrpouts, sesame, seaweed, gachugang.

Top up with kimchi or chips £2, fried tofu £6, f'sh & chips £8.

Acai Berry, Shoreditch Boxpark
95% Vegetarian Brazilian cafe & take-away

- ☛ 32 Boxpark, 2 Bethnal Green Road E1 6GY (downstairs)
- ☎ 020 7729 4930
- 🕐 M-Sa 08.00-20.00, Su 10.00-19.00
- ⊖ Shoreditch High Street
- ⚲ acaiberryfoods.com
  instagram.com/acaiberryfoods

Opened summer 2019 on the ground floor of Shoreditch Boxpark, serving açai bowls, juices, smoothies and organic coffees. Açai is a Brazilian fruit and its pulp looks and tastes like chocolate milkshake, to which has been added guarana extract. Most items are vegan, apart from the sandwiches, Barebells protein bars, cakes on the counter, and yogurt or bee products in some items.

Six kinds of Auperfood Açai Bowls £7.50 (12oz/340g) or £8.50 (16oz/450g) have an açai base topped with granola and fresh fruits with add ons such as peanut butter, seeds, coconut flakes. Extras £1.50 include nuts, paçoquinha (Brazilian peanut candy).

High protein (24g) waffle pancakes £7.50-£9.50 are topped with sliced fruits, fresh berries.

Superfood Açai Smoothies £6.50 are made with almond milk and fruits, or kale and banana, or peanut butter and protein powder.

Organic cold pressed juices £4.50, Super Juices £5.80 with fruit, green veg, matcha, ginger. Ginger/turmeric shot £2. Innocent Bubbles soft drinks £2. Kombucha £3.90. Vita coconut water £2.20.

Superfood lattes £3.95 with maca, turmeric or matcha. Coffees, frothy coffees, mocca, hot choc, chai latte, teas £1.50-£3.20.

Dogs welcome. Also at Oxford Circus (Argyll Street), Carnaby Street (Kingly Court) and Chelsea (247 King's Road).

Falafelicious
Omnivorous Israeli falafel and salad bar cafe

- ☛ 59 Box Park, 2 Bethnal Green Road E1 6GY (upper floor entrance, over-ground station end)
- ☎ 020 7729 3888
- 🕐 M-Sa 11.00-23.00, Su 11.00-22.00
- ⊖ Shoreditch High Street
- ⚲ falafelicious.co.uk
  Facebook myFalafelicious

The falafels are made from chickpeas, lava beans, herbs and some secret healthy ingredients. Serve yourself from the big salad bar. The counter at the back has the basics like tomato, hummus and lettuce. In the middle are olives etc. Closest to the entrance is a changing selection of the fun stuff like sweet potato, roasted veggies, smoked aubergine, quinoa salad. Falafel

Voodoo Ray's, Boxpark
Omnivorous pizza restaurant

- 01-03 Box Park, 2 Bethnal Green Road E1 6GY (ground floor, corner with Shoreditch High Street)
- 020 7033 4100
- M-Sa 12.00-23.00, Su 12.00-22.00
- Shoreditch High Street
- voodoorays.com

They make 22-inch (58cm) pizzas here, and two generous slices are equivalent to a normal 11" pizza (28cm). Queen vegan pizza slice £3.70, with artichoke hearts, green olives, sunblush tomatoes, tomato sauce and green pesto sauce. Earl of Portobello £3.90 with Portobello mushrooms, red onion, courgettes, tomatoes, and soya yogurt dressing. Or have a monster 18" (45cm) pizza £17.50 delivered by deliveroo.co.uk. They sell beer. Seating inside and out.

Lokma Tasty Bite
Vegetarian falafel stall

- Outside Shoreditch High Street overground on Bethnal Green Road
- M-F 10.00-15.00, Sa-Su closed
- Shoreditch High Street

Hummus & salad falafel wrap medium £4, large £5. Falafel salad box £5. Drinks £1.

Essential Vegan

Vegan Brazilian restaurant

- 6 Calvert Avenue E2 7JP
- 020 7739 3628
- Tu-F 12.00-21.00, Sa 11.00-21.00, Su 11.00-19.00 M closed
- Shoreditch High Street, Old Street
- essentialvegan.uk
  facebook.com/EssentialVegan

Opened October 2017 just off Shoreditch High Street by Vanessa and Neni Almeida, who had been running popular vegan food stalls at events and popups for years.

The irresistible menu includes juicy burgers £8-£9 such as BBQ slow cooked jackfruit or Cluckin' Good deep-fried breaded seitan chicken with grilled almond cheese and sweet chilli sauce; mouthwatering Brazilian cuisine such as Moqueca Bahiana casserole £12 with plantain, palm hearts and veg with coconut spiced sauce and basmati rice; Brazilian baked cheese balls, potato rissoles with sweetcorn cream, or Coxinha crunchy deep-fried potato dough with chicken jackfruit, all £4.50; six seitan chicken style nuggets with two dips £4.50.

Specials of the day £8.50 such as spinach ricotta lasagne with salad; cheesy quiche with roast potatoes and salad.

Sa-Su brunch until 15.00 £8.50 features chickpea pancake with scramble tofu and kale, avocado, mushrooms and roasted tomatoes. Garlic and nooch roast potatoes £3.50.

Decadent cakes £3.50 include chocolate options such as "Bounty" or crunchy almond and baked cheescakes such as passion fruit. Cinnamon roll £2.50.

Artisan nut cheeses platter £9 includes aged smoked, ricotta, garlic & chives, sourdough bread, walnuts, grapes.

Cold drinks £1.50-£3 include passion fruit lemonade, ChariTea mate, ginger kombucha. Hot drinks £2-£2.80 with oat, soya or almond milk. Bring your own wine.

Dogs welcome. You can make reservations on the website or call them. Deliveroo. Buy their gorgeous cookbook too. Whole akes to order from their website.

Oasi Burger at Phoenix Bar
Vegan fast food in pub

- 138-139 Shoreditch High Street E1
  6JE (corner Rivington Street)
- 07828 496 923
- Food: M closed, Tu-Su 12.00-22.00
  Bar: M 13.00-24.00 (no food),
  Tu 12.00-24.00, W 12.00-01.00,
  Th 12.00-01.30, F-Sa 12.00-02.00,
  Su 12.00-01.00
- Shoreditch High Street (closest), Old
  Street, Liverpool Street
- oasiburger.com
  facebook, instagram oasiburger
  phoenixbarlondon.com

Independent pub with all-vegan kitchen. Two kinds of patty, grilled made with spelt or battered made with quinoa, plus chickpeas, veg and spices. Basic grilled burger or cheeseburger £6 with tomato, onion, ketchup and mustard. Double £9. Classic battered burger with cream cheese, Special with beetroot cream plus baby spinach and feta, or Phoenix with cheddar and stewed onion, all £8. The Big One £12 double grilled patty with double cheddar, onion rings, bacon, salad, garlic mayo.

Tofu based hot dogs £5. Sides of French or sweet potato fries or onion rings £3-£4. Spelt or quinoa bowl £7 with veggies and walnuts or black olives. New items planned include cauli wingz, mac n cheese, desserts.

Sharing platter £30 for 6 to 8 people, with all the sides and battered hot dogs, or a combo of their sandwiches with vodka cocktail sauce.

Vegan draught beers from £5/pint include Grolsch, Guinness, Chieftain IPA and Redordlig dray cider. Cocktails £9.50.

Deliveroo, Uber Eats, Just Eat, Karma.

East London Juice Company
95% vegetarian raw take-away

- At front of Ace Hotel, 100 Shoreditch
  High Street E1 6JQ
- 07482 244218
- M-Su 08.00-20.00, Su 12.00-21.00
- Shoreditch High Street
- eastlondonjuice.com
  facebook.com/eastlondonjuice

Handy to grab something on the run if pubbing and clubbing in Shoreditch. All vegan apart from some bee products and the bone broth soup. They major in cold pressed organic juices £5-£8, plus some food such as acai bowl with guarana £8.50, chia parfait £4.50, raw pad Thai £8.50 with cashews, avocado and seeds. Snacky things £5 such as mango jerky, shroom nuts, cakes. Cold brew coffee £4. Hot cacao ceremony £6 with maca, matcha, greens, dates and house nut mylk.

The BRIGHT Store
Vegan coffee shop and ethical lifestyle store

- 268 Hackney Road E2 7SJ (opposite Queensbridge Road)
- no
- M-F 08.00-18.00, Sa-Su 9.00-18.00
- Hoxton overground, Cambridge Heath BR
- brightzine.co/the-bright-store
  facebook.com/thebrightstoreldn
  instagram.com/thebrightstoreldn
  thebrightclub.co

Laura Callan's trailblazing vegan magazine BRIGHT opened a vegan cafe in 2019, with a retail store to showcase their line of Vegan Queen clothing and other ethical lifestyle products from independent vegan-owned businesses.

Savoury food includes filled croissants, avocado on toast. Cakes by Brick Lane's Vida Bakery. Drinks, kombucha and coffees.

10% discount for BRIGHT magazine subscribers.

Also at the same address is The BRIGHT Club, the UK's first vegan private members' club with businesss networking events, talks, panels, yoga clubs and co-working space for 20 people at once.

Another vegan cafe called Unripe Banana used to be in the same premises.

Site

Vegan coffee shop & design space

- 112 Columbia Road E2
- no
- M-Su 08.00-16.00
- Shoreditch High Street, Old Street
- instagram.com/site_london

Vegan coffee shop opened summer 2018. Owner Elly Ward, an architect, has created an immersive installation artspace with evening events. Rich Havardi, formerly of pioreering raw food restaurant NAMA, brings expertise in the kitchen.

All kinds of coffee, iced, hot choc, mocha, matcha latte £2.50-£3.50. Oat, almond, soya milk, and one blended from coconut cream, cashew, brown rice, Himalayan salt and nutritional yeast.Cold pressed juices £2.80.

Cakes and croissants around £2.80-£3 such as spiced raw carrot cake, vanilla choc chip cookie, blueberry muffin, almond or chocolate croissant.

They are trying out breakfast pots, toasts, and savoury items such as pizza slices.

BLUEBERRY MUFFIN

Greenbox at Hoxton 7
Vegetarian food residency in cocktail bar

- at Hoxton 7 bar, 66-68 Great Eastern Street EC2A 3JT
- Food 07590 071 242
  Bar 020 7739 3440
- **Food** Tu-Th 12.00-15.00, 17.00-22.00; F-Sa -23.00; Su-M closed.
  Pub M-W 12.00-24.00, Th-Sa 12.00-01.00, Su 12.00-23.30
- Old Street
- greenboxfoodco.com
  facebook.com/greenboxfoodco
  instagram.com/greenboxfoodco
  hoxtonseven.com
  facebook.com/Hoxtonseven

Co-director Ross Milne grew up eating his Granny Jill's nut roast burgers. Now teamed up with Tom Smith and Charles Howe, their burgers ££8.50 also include bbq pulled jackfruit, or black bean, mushroom and jackfruit, pimped up with slaw, coconut cheese, aioli, crispy onions and gherkins.

There are also subs £9 filled with pulled sticky bbq jackfruit, Philly "steak", or Viet Sup Lo chilli and garlic caramelised cauli, plus all the usual extras. And regular £7.50 and large £9 salad boxes with a daily selection of salads. Side salad £3.50.

Chips or sweet potato fries £4. For £7 skin-on fries come topped with either slaw, bbq pulled jackfruit, crispy onions, bbq sauce and mayo; or vegan "steak" mix, slwaw, onions, chimichurri and special sauce.

Hoxton Dippers Southern fried oyster mushrooms served with a selection of dips, 6 for £4, 9 £6, 12 £7. Loaded nachos £8-£12 toped with crispy onions, siracha, dips and/or bbq jackfruit.

Wines from£4.50 small glass, £6.50 large, £15 bottle. Cocktails £8.50-£13.50. "Fish bowl" giant cocktails £35. Vegan bottled beers £4.50 include Pistonhead, Coors Light, Corona, also Goose Island IPA £6. Draught £5.50 Grolsh, Coors Light; Bulmers pear cider £5, Blind Pig cider £6.

Soft drinks and juices £2-£2.50.

Happy Hour 12.00-20.30 two cocktails £10, 4 house beers £10. Cocktail bar on two floors, resident DJs Fri-Sat. Groups can book a table.

Shoreditch lunch deliveries 10.30-13.30, preorder for big orders and custom lunch packages. Deliveroo, Uber Eats. Corporate events catering.

Club Mexicana @Dinerama
Vegan food stall in food court

- 19 Great Easter Street EC2A 3EJ
- hello@clubmexicana.com
- Th-Sa 12.00-23.00, Su-W closed
- Shoreditch High Street, Old Street
- clubmexicana.com
  streetfeast.com/visit-us/dinerama

Dinerama is a big food court with a bar, and seating plus tables in the middle. It's great for socialising, though very noisy, especially if you are right under a speaker.

Tacos 2 for £7, 3 for £10, are tofish, carne asada, or pulled jackfruit tinga. Chick'n wings £6 with hot sauce and sour cream, beer battered cheeze fries or tortilla chips and guacamole £5.

Also in Camden Market every day and doing the food at the Spread Eagle pub in Homerton.

Veggie Pret, Shoreditch
Vegetarian cafe & take-away

- 57 Great Eastern Street EC2A 3QD
- 020 7932 5393
- M-F 06.30-20.30, Sa 07.30-20.30, Su 08.00-20.00. Bank holiday weekends Su-M close 17.30.
- Old Street, Shoreditch High Street
- pret.co.uk/en-gb/veggie-pret

Following the success of the first Veggie Pret in Soho in summer 2016, this second Veggie Pret opened in April 2017. Big seating area downstairs. Wifi. See Soho for menu. Boxes include sweet potato falafel mezze £4.50; artichoke, tapenade and olive baguette £3.45; hummus and crunchy veg wrap; beans, veg, brown rice and quinoa box £4.50; chilli and avocado flat bread. £3.99; super greens pot £2.49.

Add 50p-90p for eat in.

Curry Box
Omnivorous Gujarati Indian take-away

- 101 Great Eastern St EC2A 3JD (Old Street end)
- 07956 399592
- M-F 9.00-21.00, Sa-Su closed
- Old Street
- facebook.com/ theveggiecurryboxlondon

Weekday Indian take-away counter at the front of an off-licence, with many items vegan and clearly marked on the giant menu on the wall. They used to be all vegetarian during the day but we've kept them in here for now for when you're skint but still fancy a very cheap take-away.

Bowl of curry £3.99, curry with basmati jeera or onion masala rice £4.50, add salad for £1. Five vegan curries include chickpeas with tomato and onion sauce, mixed veg in spicy spinach cashew sauce, potatoes in tomato cashew curry sauce Kashmiri style, veg and banana balls in mild Rajsthani curry sauce. Chana masala or subzi kofta paratha wrap £4.50.

Salad box £3. Samosa or Bombay bhel chaat £3. Samosa £1.25, three £3. Coffee £1.50. Samosa and coffee breakfast £2.25.

EAST

SHOREDITCH • GREAT EASTERN STREET

179

Good To Go
Vegan cafe & take-away

☛ Unit E + F, The Bower shopping centre, 207-211 Old Street EC1V 9NR (go along the right side of Shoreditch Grind, then turn right and down the steps)

🕐 M-F 08.30-16.30, Sa-Su closed

⊖ Old Street exit 4

↖ goodtogo.london
instagram.com/goodtogohq
theboweroldst.com

New vegan cafe well away from the busy main road, in the Bower office and retail complex, which includes a boutique hotel Z Hotels. Plenty to grab and go.

Breakfast till 11.00, lunch 11.30-15.00, such as granola; spicy tofu sandwich; mixed potato hash, crispy kale and cherry tomato salad; breakfast muffin £3.50 with scrambled tofu, roasted tomato, cashew spread and leafy salad; spiced tofu omelette and roasted veg in a bap.

Dishes include soups; toasties; bean chilli with tortillas and brown rice, guacamole and oat cream; tofu poke bowl; cauliflower bake; chestnut mushroom curry; smoky sweet potato ciabatta; green curry; chilli; baguettes like marinated Portobello mushroom with pak choi salad, or smoky sweet potato with sriracha mayo and salad, or charred red pepper with mashed chickpea and miso spread; wraps, sandwiches £5.25 such as pea fritter with spicy sweet corn relist and steamed greens.

Treats £1.50-£2.95 include cookies, croissants, pain aux raisins, brownies, banan loaf, lemon drizzle, cinnamon muffins.

Coffee. Plant milks. Packaging and cutlery are compostable.

Roadtrip & The Workshop

Roadtrip & The Workshop
Vegan food residency in bar/night club

- 243 Old Street EC1V 9EY (opposite the top of Great Eastern Street, look out for their terrace)
- 020 7253 6787
- **Bar:** M 16.00-01.00, Tu 02.00, W-Th 04.00, F 05.00, Sa 12.00-05.00, Su 12.00-01.00.
  Food: M-Th 16.00-21.00, F 22.00, Sa 12.00-22.00, Su 12.00-21.00.
- Old Street exit 2
- roadtripbar.com
  facebook.com/roadtripworkshop
  (events)

We've waited years for this, a **vegan night club** in Shoreditch. Hackney legends Black Cat Cafe are doing the "tapas without borders" food menu in this late night bar by Old Street station. Relaxed rock 'n' roll vibe, some live music, DJs, or pick a tune from the juke box. South facing garden, basement space for gigs and club nights.

Burgers £7.50-£8.50, choose from smoked tofu with cheddar and bacon, or cashew buttermilk corn crusted seitan burger, or seitan club sandwich, or tempeh BLT.

Small plates £5.50-£7 include sausage meatballs in white wine gravy, leek and mushroom croquettes, Portuguese style battered cod and potato cakes, arancini cheesy risotto balls, buttermilk fried cauliflower with garlic tahini sauce, chickpea and cod-style pieces fisherman's stew.

Skin on fries with herby parmesan dust £3. Patatas bravas £4. Warm marinated olives £3. P&T grilled sourdough smothered in tomato, garlic and olive oil £3. Buttered sourdough £2.50.

Sofot drinks from £1.90. Teas £1.60. Coffees £1.80-£2.40.

Draught beers and cider £4.40-£6, bottles from £4. Wine from £3.80 small glass, £7.20 large, £19 bottle. Cocktails £8.50, jug £25.. Mocktails £3.50, some with Red Bull (well they are open till 5am). Happy hour 4pm-7pm and 11pm-1am, all day Sunday, two cocktails £10, bottle of house wine £16, two bottles of Sol beer £6.

Sky Sport and BT Sports. You can book some space with a £50 deposit which is a minimum spend for food and drinks on the night, but you still have to queue. Children welcome with adult, 18+ after 9pm, ID check and search policies. Disabled toilet, but narrow stairs to The Workshop hireable space downstairs. They can call you a licensed minicab. No flip-flops late Fri-Sat night when the clubby vibe kicks in, they don't want your toes to get hurt on the dance floor..

Shoreditch Grind
Omnivorous cafe

- 213 Old Street EC1V 9NR (north-west corner of the roundabout)
- 020 7490 7490
- M-Th 12.00-22.00, F-Sa 12.00-24.00, Su 12.00-22.00
- Shoreditch High Street
- facebook.com/pg/Thefalafelqueen

Basically a noisy cocktail bar, with some vegan cocktails and food including vegan pizzas. Vegan croissant, pain au chocolat, cinnamon bun, flapjack, £2.30-£2.90. Snacks such as Brave roasted peas, bars by Clif, Beond, Pulsin, Pip & Nut peanut butter squeeze pack. Emily veg crisps; lentil, quinoa, hummus or kale and spinach tortilla chips, hummus chips. Kookie Cat cookies. Raw snacks. Energy balls. Conscious chocolate. Booja Booja mini packs. Whole Earth cans, kombucha.

Redemption, Shoreditch
Vegan restaurant, tea room & no alcohol bar

- 320 Old St. EC1V 9DR (south side)
- 020 7613 0720
- M-F 12.00-22.30, Sa 10.00-23.30, Su 10.00-17.00. Kitchen closes 1 hour before.q
- Old Street
- redemptionbar.co.uk

One of London's healthiest restaurants, all vegan, no alcohol or wheat, organic where possible, some raw. The menu changes every few months.

Daytime menus starts with soup of the day £5.95 served with sunflower and flaxseed bread. Chunky guacamole or spicy black bean chimichurri on toast £7.50. At weekends there are smoothie bowls £6.95.

Mains are mostly under £10 such as brown rice penne pasta with shitake mushroom bolognese and roasted pecan parmesan; Californication roasted sweet potato and red onion hash with m; or ushrooms, kale, spinach, rosemary and lemon; buckwheat pancakes with coconut oil, coconut yogurt, seasonal fruit and maple syrup; sweetcorn and red pepper pancakes with guacamole. Kale Caesar salad; raw courgette spaghetti in basil and pumpkin seed pesto with Brazil nut parmesan; and a different Buddha bowl each day of the week.pulled bbq jack or protein packed buff burger, add chunky sweet potato fries for £2.95.

The evening menu adds nibblles £3.50 such as kale crisps, long soaked slow roasted activated nuts. Corn chips with turmeric hummus and guacamole £7.95. More starters around £8-£9 are Thai watermelon and cucumber salad; or grilled aubergine and tahini with white miso and sesame glaze, toasted pine nuts, pomegranate seeds and micro basil. Main course asparagus and pea black rice risotto £14.75.

Desserts £5.75-£7.50 include raw dark chocolate and date truffles rolled in coconut, cashew cream lime cheesecake on coconut almond crust, seasonal berries and crème Chantilly, Ruby Forest gateau..

Smoothies and fruities £4.75-£5.96. Knees sparkling non-wine £4 glass, £18.50 bottle. Fitbeer £4. Mocktails £4.95-£6.50 from pina colada to Moscow mule. All kinds of Union coffee or pot of tea £2.95. Turmeric, matcha or guarana cacao latte £4.95.

Also in Covent Garden (Central London) and Notting Hill (West London).

Plates
Vegan English restaurant & food studio

- 93a Kingsland Rd, Hoxton E2 8AG
- 07786 636432
- Saturdays only 18.45-23.00
- Hoxton overground
- plates-london.com
  facebook.com/platesfood
  instagram.com/plates_london/

Siblings Kirk, a former Michelin starred chef who went vegan, and Keeley, who has a background in art and design, Haworth's exclusive Saturday night vegan restaurant is by reservation only. Many customers are huge fans and return every month.

5 seasonal courses for £45 such as caramelised onion broth, wild thyme, kombu and sea vegetables; or carrot and yuzu curry. Optional paired wines £35.

During the week their food studio works with brands and clients on collatorations and catering.

Cyclelab & Juicebar
Vegan cafe and bicycle shop

- 16b-18a Pitfield St, Hoxton N1 6EY
- 020 3222 0016
- M-F 08.00-19.00, Sa 11.00-18.00, Su closed
- Old Street
- cyclelabuk.wordpress.com
  facebook.com/CycleLabUK

Bike repairs and parts on the left, open long hours for everything from a puncture fix to building a custom bike. Vegan (since April 2018) cafe on the right. While you wait, have a tea, coffee, mocha, hot choc, turmeric or matcha mint or beetroot & cocoa latte £2-£3, smoothie or juice £4.50-£6 made with organic fruit and veg.. Try a chocolate almond milkshake with dates. Also salads, breakfast pots, acai bowls made to order, vegan cakes from Manna Cakes, and they make their own gluten-free banana bread. Also salads to eat in or take-away. Acai balls and granola balls. Weekday lunch 12-3 offers a soup £5.50 such as carrot and ginger wtih cashew cream, a stew £6.50, or a box of salads £6.90 from the salad bar. Pizza slices, jackfruit chili wrap all under £5.

Redemption

EAST

SHOREDITCH - OLD STREET

Viet Hoa
Omnivorous Vietnamese restaurant

- 70-72 Kingsland Road E2 8DP
- 020 7729 8293
- M-Su 12.00-15.30 last order, 17.30-23.30
- Shoreditch High Street

Of the Vietnamese cafes and restaurants clustered at the bottom of Kingsland Road, this is our favourite for its amazing tofu dishes £4.95.

TZATZIKI

OYSTER
MUSHROOMS

COCONUT
CHEESE

CUCUMBER
RIBBONS

GENESIS

Genesis

vegan organic international restaurant

144 Commercial Street E1 6NU

020 7059 0138

M 11.30-21.30, Tu 11.30-22.00, W-Th 11.30-22.30, F-Sa 09.00-22.30, Su 09.00-21.00

Shoreditch High Street, Liverpool St

eatgenesis.com
facebook.com/EatGenesis
instagram.com/eatgenesis

Fully organic vegan restaurant on two floors, opened September 2018. Look out for the marble, pastel pink tiles, copper detailing and neon sign. 70 seats. The menu features both health foods and fun foods, a fusion of Mexican, American, Middle Eastern and South-East Asian.

Breakfast/brunch £9.50-£10.75, Fri-Sun till 11.45am, includes waffles with berries, coconut yogurt, banana and maple syrup; scrambled ackee on sourdough toast with smoked chorizo, salsa, pico de gallo and avo; huevos rancheros tacos with smoky chipotle beans, ackee scramble, cashew cheese sauce; carrot salmon tostadas; chilaquiles nachos with ackee, avo, chipotle mayo, steamed kale; kimchi pancakes; açai bowl; Colombian patacones bowl with crispy plantain, quinoa, kale, smoky black bean, spicy chickpeas, cashew cheese sauce. Smoothies £9. Juices £6. Shakes £7.

Burgers and hot dogs £9.50-£11.95 feature the Genesis Burger with gherkins, garlic mayo, cheddar and red onion; American Woman burger with creamy coleslaw and whisky bbq saucfe; seitan fried 'chicken' sandwich; Korean street sandwich with panko aubergine, kimchi, sticky bbq sauce, sriracha; seitan doner shawarma with Persian salad and green tahini sauce;

banh mi dog; Mayan dog with guacamole, sour cream, salsa, nachos, jalapeños, pico de gallo; seitan pastrami Reuben dog with sauerkraut, Swiss cheese, Russian dressing, mustard, jalapeños.

Tacos £5-£5.50 filled with smoked chorizo, panko avocado and smoky chipotle beans, crispy jackfruit 'duck' hoisin, seitan doner and pineapple salsa, or New York seitan pastrami Reuben style.

Street dishes £7.75-£9.75 include nachos with sour cream, guac, and all the spicy usuals; Aztec chilaquiles tortillas with smoky chipotle beans, sour cream, mango and guac; Korean bbq sticky seitan wings; Tandoori charred broccoli with Makhani gravy, mango chutney and coconut yogurt.

Noodles, soups and salads £8.95-£11.95 feature Caesar salad, Thai Som Tam salad with papaya and candied cashews, jackfruit 'duck' hoisin salad, Middle Eastern salad with roasted cauli and spicy chickpeas, Yucatan street bowl of veggies with quinoa and smoky chipotle beans plus cashew nacho cheese, Malaysian char kway teow brown rice noodles with stir-fry veg and spicy black bean sauce, Vietnamese pho soup.

Sldes £4.75-£7.50 such as kimchi or sweet potato fries, cheese sticks, kamut mac & cheese.

For decadent **dessert** £7.95-£11 enjoy chocolate hazelnut cheesecake, blueberry bread and butter pudding, sticky toffee pudding with cashew and coconut ice cream, chocolate brownie with ice cream, ice cream sundae with sauces and chocolate buttons. Soft serve ice cream £4.95.

Kombucha £4.95. Soft drinks £3.95. Beers from £5. Wine £6.50 glass, £35 bottle. Cocktails £10.95. Mocktails £6. Kombucha £4.95. Teas, coffess, fancy lattes £2.50-£6.

The Grocery
Organic wholefood supermarket & cafe

- ☛ 54-56 Kingsland Road E2 8DP
  (south end by railway bridge)
- ☏ shop 020 7729 6855
  wine, cafe 020 7739 0105
  therapies 020 7739 6545
- ◑ M-Su 08.00-22.00
- ⊖ Hoxton, Shoreditch High Street;
  Bus 48, 55, 67, 149, 242, 243
- ⬈ thegroceryshop.co.uk
  therapiesatthegrocery.co.uk

Big, independent, mostly organic shop. They source stock from a range of local producers and wholesalers. Bread, veg, fruit, wholefoods, Clearspring Japanese foods, household, natural remedies. Big fridges at the back left full of vegan goodies.

There is a separate drinks department at the back right with organic wines and Freedom organic vegan-certified lager.

You can email or phone in your shopping list (minimum order £20, you can specify a maximum spend) before 3pm and the order will be ready to collect from 6pm onwards.

The cafe used to do food, but now they just do drinks, and you can bring in food from the shop to eat.

Therapy rooms downstairs 11am-8pm (Sun 7pm), offering many types of massage.

Raw Store
Omnivorous wholefood store and off-licence

- ☛ 343 Old Street EC1V 9LL
  (by railway bridge)
- ☏ 020 7033 2975
- ◑ Su-W 07.00-24.00, Th 07.00-03.00,
  F-Sa 07.00-04.00 (not a misprint!)
- ⊖ Shoreditch High Street, Old Street
- ⬈ facebook.com/rawstore.organics

London's most late night wholefood store opened May 2017. Do your shopping after a night out in Shoreditch, or pick up munchies and booze to continue the party at home.

11am-5pm self-serve salad bar at the front on the right, £4.99 for a box. Take-away coffees £2.20-£2.70 with soya or almond milk, 10% off if you buy an ecoffee cup.

There are fridges all along the inside walls. The left wall is all drinks. On the right wall by the coffee and salad bar are 350gr take-away lunch boxes £7.99 by Pollen & Grace such as Detox, probiotic, Endurance, with ingredients such as crispy millet falafels, sweet potato hummus, quinoa, kelp noodles, veggies, salad. 170gr pots £3.99. Thrive On Five spicy Mexican falafel £5.99. Ginger's Kitchen salad pots £3.29. Biona miniburgers, spring rolls, Delphi dips.

Nuuk vegan bakery supplies donuts, brownies, energy bombs, raw tarts and cakes. Huge range of wholefoods, health drinks. Los of Taifun tofu, Tofurky, Sojade burgers, Cauldron. Ready meals by Amy's Kitchen, Linda McCartney. Sheese, Violife vegan cheese. Follow Your Heart vegan dressings. Alpro ice-cream. Energy balls and bars. Vegan chocolate by Pana, Ombar. Herbs.

Bodycare by Faith In Nature. Cleaning by Method, Ecover.

The Grocery

Ginger's Kitchen Salads

◇ Indian Spiced

Pasta, Pea & Pesto

Chargrilled Couscous

Raw Store

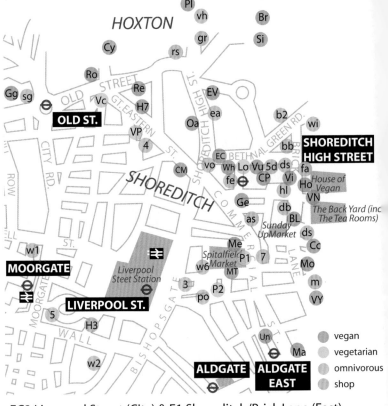

EC2 Liverpool Street (City) & E1 Shoreditch/Brick Lane (East)

CM	Club Mexicana	Pl	Plates Re Redemption
EV	Essential Vegan	Cy	Cyclelab Un Unity Diner
Gg	Good To Go Ro Roadtrip	Lo	Lokma Tasty Bite
Br	Bright Store Si Site	Vc	Veggie Curry Box
Oa	Oasi H7 Hoxton 7	VP	Veggie Pret
Ge	Genesis	P1	Pilpel Spitalfields
EC	Eat Chay	P2	Pilpel Brushfield
Wh	What the Pitta	po	Planet Organic
BL	**Brick Lane** stalls	ea	East London Juice Co.
Ho	House of Vegan	fe	Felafelicious
VN	Vegan Nights	vo	Voodoo Ray's
Cc	Canvas Cafe	ds	Dark Sugars x 2
Ma	Maree's Mo Mooshies	b2	Brewdog, Brick Lane
Vi	Vida Bakery	wi	Wedge Issue pizza
VY	Vegan Yes CP CPress	db	Damascu Bite
Vu	Vurger fa Fauxmagerie	hl	Hookah Lounge
Me	Merkamo	sg	Shoreditch Grind
MT	Mel's Tropical Creations	vg	Viet Hoa

	Pizza Express:
2	Alban Gate
3	Bishopsgate
4	Curtain Road
5	Finsbury Circus
6	Russia Row
7	Spitalfields
	Wagamama EC2:
w1	Moorgate/Barbican
w2	Old Broad St/Bank
w6	Spitalfields
as	As Nature Intended
5d	Fifth Dimension tattoos
m	Monster House hair
H3	Holland & Barrett, Old Broad St
gr	The Grocery
rs	Raw Store

Legend:
- vegan
- vegetarian
- omnivorous
- shop

BRICK LANE

& Spitalfields Market

Brick Lane is London's Vegan Mile with a sumptuous seven vegan cafes, from **Vurger** and **CPress** at the northern Shoreditch end down to **Marees** Caribbean at the southern Aldgate end. In between are **Vida Bakery** cake cafe, **Canvas Cafe**, **Mooshies** burger restaurant open every night, and **Vegan Yes** Korean Italian fusion. There's also **La Fauxmagerie** vegan cheese shop.

But that's not all. At weekends there are several fashion and food markets, and nowhere else in London will you find so much vegan street food. Sunday is the best day, though Saturdays are also pretty good, while during the week the permanent cafes and shops are much less crowded. Look out for **Osu Coconuts** on the street, which serves sweet and savoury vegan pancakes.

The indoor **Sunday Upmarket** (open Sun 10.00-17.00), around the middle of Brick Lane where it meets Hanbury Street, is a huge fashion market with over 200 stalls and a large indoor food area on Sundays. It's located all around and inside the Old Truman Brewery building, Elys Yard, Hanbury Street and Brick Lane. For food, enter from Brick Lane just above Hanbury Street, and start with the astoundingly good **Ethiopiques** vegan salads stall.

Further north up Brick Lane on the opposite (east) side are the **Backyard Market** and adjacent **Tea Rooms** at 146 (both open Sat 11.00-18.00, Su 10.00-17.00), the former home to younger designers and artists, full of clothes, prints and jewellery, the latter full of antiques, homeware and a coffee shop. bricklane-tearooms.co.uk

Best of all at weekends, at 152 is the **House of Vegan** food market, open 11.00-18.00, with at least a dozen international food stalls, a bar and shared seating. This is also part of the venue for **Vegan Nights**, a monthly huge vegan party on a Thursday 5pm-11pm with 40 food stalls, live music and DJs.

Nearby are two branches of **Dark Sugars** chocolate shops.

At the southern Aldgate end are Bangladeshi restaurants and food shops. City Spice at 138 has a separate vegan menu. city-spice. london

Heading west down Hanbury Street, you come to **Spitalfields Market**. This is *the* place for independent fashion on Sunday morning and afternoon, packed with small designers and their clothes, hand-made jewellery, a secondhand record stall, and plenty of vegan food. Look out for **Mel Tropical Kitchen** (Sunday only) with luxurious and great value salad boxes and luscious raw cakes, **Merkamo** Ethiopian food stall (every day), and two **Pilpel** falafel cafes. There are also chain restaurants open late that know how to cater for vegans.

Near the top of the main road Commercial Street is wholefood supermarket **As Nature Intended**, plus **Genesis** vegan restaurant (see Shoreditch chapter). Vegan super-activist Earthling Ed Winter's impressive new vegan restaurant and bar **Unity Diner** has just relocated from Hoxton to larger premises between Spitalfields and Aldgate.

Canvas Cafe
Vegan cafe

- 📞 42 Hanbury Street E1 5JL
- 📞 020 7018 1020
- 🕐 Open Tu-F 08.30-21.00, Sa-Su 10.00-20.00. Kitchen M-Tu 11.00-19.30, W-F 11.00-21.30, Sa-Su 10.00-19.30q;;
- ⊖ Shoreditch High Street, Aldate East
- ↖ thecanvascafe.org
  facebook.com/TheCanvasCafeE1
  instagram.com/TheCanvasCafeE1

Not-for-profit community cafe upstairs and and creative space downstairs, just off the middle of Brick Lane. In January 2018 Ruth the manager turned it 100% vegan. Even before then Canvas Cafe were the pioneers of vegan freakshakes, a totally bonkers dessert of ice-cream blended with almond milk, topped with whipped cream and a cake on top. These are still available for £8.

Breakfasts £4-£9.50, served all day, include full English with sausages, tofu scramble, pan-fried potatoes, herbed beans, greens, sourdough toast. Cinnamon French toast. Avo on sourdough toast with lime and chilli flakes. Tofu scamble on toast. Peanut butter and banana on sourdought toast.

Today's special £5 such as carrot soup or creamy pea, mushroom and bacon pasta, add a hearty salad £7.50. Not-chicken escalope sourdough sandwich and handcut fries £9.50. Other mains £10.50 such as tofish and chips with peas and chips, not-meatball marinara sourdough sandwich with fries, pulled jackfruit sandwich and sweet potato fries.

Lots of cakes £2.50-£3.50 such as choco coffee walnutty slice, choco peanut butter, fruity seedy flapjack, lemon drizzle, Oreo cupcake, salted caramel cheesecake.

Banana bread and butter pudding £5.

Square Mile Coffee, We Are Tea loose lea matcha, chai, turmeric latte, £2.50-£3.3 with almond, oat or soya milk.

Beers £4 such as Freedom, Meantime Caden Hells. Wine from £5 per glass. Gi or vodka and tonic £4.50, double £6.50 Non-alcoholic wine £17.50 bottle. Happ hour 5pm-7pm, 2 cocktails for £10.

You can hire the basement space for events meetings, workshops, away days, such as theatre, comedy, poetry, live music, yoga and dance classes, vegan popups. Free space for community groups wanting to improve the lives of others.

Cards only, no cash.

Mooshies Vegan Burgers
Vegan burger cafe

- 104 Brick Lane (corner Princelet Street, just below Hanbury Street)
- 07931 842458
- Su-W 12.00-21.30, Th 12.00-22.30, F-Sa 12.00-23.00
- Aldgate East, Shoreditch High Street, Liverpool Street
- facebook.com/mooshieslondon mooshieslondon.com

Brick Lane's first vegan restaurant opened in 2016, specialising in burgers plus cakes, ice-cream, beers and wines.

Four kinds of burgers: battered aubergine phish, black bean and quinoa beef, pulled jackfruit, all £7.50, and spciy onion bhajia guacamole £8.50. Extra toppings £1-£1.50 include aubergine, avocado, extra cheese, sauces. Sides £3-£4.50 such as (cheezy) sweet potato fries, chick 'P' bites, guacamole with plantain crisps, coleslaw.

Desserts £4.50, created by Dani and Vane from vegan Vida Bakery, include peanut, Oreo and matcha brownies. Mini vegan Magnum style vanilla choc ice £2, also Swedish Glace.

Soft drinks £2.50 include Dalston's cream solda, ginger beer, lemonade, fizzy apple; Karma Cola; coconut water; mango juice. Water £1.50. Teas £2.

Vegan bottled pale ale and sour ale beers by Moncada Brewery Notting Hill £4.50, large rubye rye dark ale £6.50. Wine £6 glass, £16 bottle. Prosecco bottle £20. Spirits with mixer £6, double £11.

Vegan Burger Menu

Vegan Burgers
'Vegan Street Food'   'Vegan Supper Clubs'
100% Plant Based Street Food
appear here
veganburger.org

Vegan Yes
Vegan Korean-Italian cafe & take-away

- 64 Brick Lane E1 6RF (corner Heneage Street)
- 020 7247 0044
- M-Su 12.00-21.00
- Aldgate East
- veganyes.uk
  facebook.com/Vegan.Yes
  MiaMammaFoundation.org

Opened August 2017 towards the south end of Brick Lane by Italian chef Mauro and Korean Dr. Min, who together already had a successful stall in Nag's Head Market (see Holloway Road, North London). They use only aw extra virgin olive oil and don't fry.

Main dishes £6.50-£15.50 include four kinds of kimchi bibimbap with baby spinach and steamed rice; kimchi lasagne; bolognese lasage; healthy sweet potato with rice, seaweed, extra virgin olive oil and roasted sesame seeds. Smaller dishes £4-£6 such as kimchi, seaweed side salad.

Dark mochi dessert £3.50, a chewy rice ball with red bean paste centre, covered with dark chocolate and sesame seeds. Chocolate mousse £4.50.

Teas, coffees, moringa, miso hot drink, £2, can be with soya or almond milk, moringa, turmeric, ginger. Canned drinks and bottled water.

Vegan wines £4.50-£8.50 small glass. Vegan beers.

Cooking and self-healing classes, see their website Mia Mamma Foundation.

Vida Bakery
Vegan cake cafe

- 139 Brick Lane E1 6SB (north end)
- 020
- M 13.00-19.00, Tu-Su 11.00-19.00
- Shoreditch High Street
- vidabakery.co.uk
  facebook.com/vidabakery
  instagram.com/vidabakery

100% vegan, 100% fun, 100% delicious. East London's cake shop got a permanent bakery and cafe home in June 2018, baking the world a better place, one cake at a time. Check out their instagram to see just how pretty their cakes are. They also do soft serve ice-cream with crunchy bits, and coming soon are breakfasts, brunch and afternoon high tea.

Cupcakes £3 include banoffee, vanilla caramel, double chocolate, peanut chocolate, pb and jelly, lemon curd, Oreo. Cake slices £4.50 such as Notella, rainbow, marble, Oreo, Victoria sponge. Brownies £3.80. Oat raisin cookie £2.50.

Soft-serve vanilla ice-cream £3.50 can be topped with pieces of cake, cookie, brownie, chocolate and strawberry syrup, sprinkles. Or try their ice-cream cookie sandwich with peanut butter on top.

Tea, coffee, latte, hot choc, iced coffee £2-£3 with Oatly and soy milk.

Also at events such as Vegan Nights.

Vurger, Shoreditch
vegan burger restaurant & take-away

- Unit 9 Avant Garde Building, 6 Richmix Square, Ctnet Street, Shoreditch E1 6LD (opposite Rich Mix cinema)
- feedme@thevurgerco.com
- Su-Th 12.00-21.00, F-Sa 12.00-22.00
- Shoreditch High Street
- thevurgerco.com
  facebook.com/thevurgerco

After a couple of years building a fanbase with market stalls and popups, then one of the most successful vegan crowdfundings ever seen in London, Vurger opened up their swish new restaurant in March 2018 right in the heart of London's Vegan Valley, between Shoreditch High Street overground and the top of Brick Lane. It's high class fast food like luscious burgers and salad boxes, mac n cheese, ice-cream and wine. It's plastic-free, they use compostable Vegware containers, cups and cutlery. Tables inside and out.

Four kinds of burgers £8.45 are served on a vegan brioche bun, which can be gluten-free. The Classic is made from black beans, chargrilled pepper and corn, topped with tomato, red onion and their own burger sauce. The Auburger is made from aubergine, caramelised red onion and tabasco chipotle chickpea, served with pickled red cabbage, gherkins and cumin mayo. MLT is roasted mushrooms, borlotti beans and parsley, topped with tomato, rocket, ketchup and their sundried tomato and walnut pesto. Holy Habanero corn fritter burger comes with crunchy slaw, topped with spiced almonds, crispy tortillas and habanero mayo. Or go bun free in a bowl for £7.95

Sides £2.95-£5.75 include skin on fries, sweet potato fries, house slaw, mac n cheese (which can be gluten-free) with optional pesto, Kentucky dunkers.

Ice-cream £3.95, a different flavour each day, with sauce and toppings. Chocolate hazelnut or salted caramel MiiRo lolly £2.95. Shakes £4.85 comes in berry, vanilla, mocha or banana caramel. Add a shot of whisky or rum for £2.

Lemonade, cola, juice £2.50. Beers £4.50-£4.75 include Camden Hells and Pale Ale, Hawkes cider. House wine £4.75 medium glass, £16.95 bottle. Tea, coffees, hot choc £1.95-£2.45.

Meal deal M-Th 12.00-16.00 any burger, skin on fries and soft drink £10.

No cash, only cards, Apple and Android pay. No reservations, walk ins only. High chairs. Another branch in Canary Wharf.

La Fauxmagerie
Vegan cheese shop

- 20 Cheshire Street E2 6EH
- 07552 953509
- M-Tu closed, W-F 12.00-19.00, Sa 11.00-19.00, Su 11.00-18.00
- Shoreditch High Street
- lafauxmagerie.com
  Facebook La Fauxmagerie
  instagram.com/lafauxmagerie

The UK's first plant-based cheesemonger was opened by vegan sisters Charlotte and Rachel Stevens in a tiny unit in Brixton Market in February 2019, and promptly sold out on the first day. By summer their range had doubled to 120 cheeses from 17 artisanal suppliers and so in July 2019 they moved to these much larger premises just off the top of Brick Lane.

Delicious, decadent and inspired plant-based cheeses include varieties for every purpose such as melting, grating, spreading, relishing and devouring.

Suppliers include: Black Arts Vegan, Good Food by Sumear, I Am Nut Ok (chipotle & goji, black truffle & turmeric), Kinda Co, Naturally Vegan Food Company, New Roots, Nush, The Nutcrafter Creamery, Raw Food Rose, Tyne Chease, and many more.

They also offer plant-based preserves, breads, and accoutrements to add the perfect final touches to your cheese board or banquet.

Also available online.

CPress @ Triyoga Shoreditch
vegan healthy cafe

- 10 Cygnet St E1 6GW) (between Shoreditch High Street overground and the top of Brick Lane)
- 07799 881 002
- Cafe M-F 07.30-20.00, Sa-Su 07.30-19.00.
  Classes M-F 06.00-21.00, Sa 08.45-18.45, Su 07.30-18.30.
- Shoreditch High Street (3mins walk), Liverpool Street (13m), Old Street 14m)
- cpressjuice.com/pages/triyoga-shoreditch
  facebook.com/cpressjuice
  triyoga.co.uk

Brick Lane's best kept vegan secret is this healthy cafe located on the bend in Cygnet Street, next to Vurger. Come here for breakfast from 7.30a.m., organic juices, smoothies, artisan coffee, bowls, toasts, cookies, brownies, muffins, energy balls.

Organic bowls include porridge with almond milk and toppings £5.95 (before 11am), açaí banana or pitaya £8.95 which come with lots of toppings, hemp protein açaí banana £10.95. Gluten-free toasts £5.99 topped with almond butter, avocado or turmeric hummus, and extras to spice it up such as cacao nibs, cinnamon, pink salt, chilli flakes. Chia pots £2.75-£3.

Sweet treats £1.40-£3.25 include dark chocolate truffle, cacao or coconut protein ball, vanilla cashew cookie, CBD brownie, raw Snickers or Matcha Bounty, blueberry or banana muffin.

Organic smoothies £6.75-£7.95, some with an impressive 20g of plant protein. Cold drinks and cold pressed juices £3.50-£7.95.

Hot drinks £2.30-£3.90 with almond, oat or coconut milk, include teas, drip coffee, cold brew, iced, MCT bulletproof, chai or turmeric or matcha latte, flat white, macchiato, hot choc.

Drop in for many kinds of yoga including hot, pilates, barre, or treat yourself to a massage, acupuncture, physiotherapy, osteopathy, or something from their yoga lifestyle shop. Drop-in classes cost £17, or buy a 5-class pass (£15 each), 10 (£13.50) or 20 (£12) (each valid for 3 months), or the popular unlimited monthly pass for £108, ideal if you live or work in the area. New students can get the monthly pass for a bargain £54, valid across all Triyoga centres including Shoreditch, Camden, Soho, Chelsea, and Ealing. Gift cards.

CPress are also in Fitzrovia and Fulham Road. Deliveroo.

Osu Coconuts
Vegan coconut pancake and roti stall

- ☛ M-F Sclater Street close to the overground station just to the right of Boxpark. Su further down Brick Lane.
- ☛ M-F 11.30-16.00, Su 10.00-16.30
- ⊖ Shoreditch High Street
- ↖ instagram.com/osucoconuts

By Shoreditch High Street overground on weekdays, on Brick Lane on Sundays. Gluten-free savoury organic pancakes £6 or stack of sweet pancakes, such as Caribbean chickpea and pumpkin curry with plantain, South American black beans, apple cinnamon crumble, berries, or banana and peanut butter with strawberries and raw choc sauce. Made fresh in front of you with coconut water, coconut meat and coconut flour.

Also Caribbean dal roti wraps filled with pumpkin and channa with the option of adding avocado and plantain, £5 or £6. Cooked in coconut oil. Fresh coconut water £3.50.

On Saturdays they are at Broadway Market. Check instagram to confirm times.

Marees Sauces and Food
Vegan organic international restaurant and take-away

- ☛ 91 Whitechapel High St E1 7RA
- ☎ 020 7247 0900
- ◐ M-Sa 12.00-22.00 (last order), Su closed
- ⊖ Aldgate East
- ↖ facebook.com/mareesauce
  instagram.com/msandfood

Opened April 2018 near the bottom of Brick Lane, but with noticeably lower prices. It's counter service, with seating inside, outside and upstairs. Choose from burgers, wraps, rotis, Oriental bowls, fries, wedges, and finish off with pancakes and ice-cream or Southern buttermilk biscuits, vegan style. It's bring your own alcohol with no corkage charge, or pick some up at the Costcutter shop next door.

Burgers £5 are made on site and come in ultimate veggie with vegan Red Leicester cheese, chickpea falafel, sweet potato chickpea, special jerk made with chickpea falafel, spiced lentil. Black bean burger £6. Quinoa pizza burger £6.50 with melted mozzarella.

Wraps £5 are Caribbean, Chinese tofu, sweet potato falafel, or special jerk.

Choose a BBQ sauce such as peach, sweet & sticky, citrus, wild berry.

All day meal deal £7 adds a full portion of wedges, sweet potato fries or mixed avocado salad. Lunchtime meal deal £5 till 2.30pm for any burger or wrap with small portion of wedges.

Rotis £5.50 are veg curry or spinach and chickpea.

Bowls £8 feature Thai butternut squash, or sweet and sour chickpea, both served with either soba noodles or quinoa with wild rice.

Sweet potato fries £3. Peanut punch £2.

Blueberry, strawberry, banana or cinnamon swirl pancakes with ice-cream and agave syrup, £3.50 for 2, £5 for 3.

Southern buttermilk biscuits £1.50 for 3, £2.50 for 6.

Cold drinks £1-£2.25 include Whole Earth cans, beetroot punch, peanut punch, ginger beer, James White apple & ginger, chocolate Koko, bottled water.

Kid's box £2.99 for small burger, wedges, biscuit and drink.

20% student discount. Loyalty card, buy 9, get 1 free. Dogs welcome outside. Deliveroo, Ubereats.

EAST

BRICK LANE

Brewdog, Shoreditch
Pub with mainly vegan craft beers

- ☛ 51 Bethnal Green Rd E1 6LA
  (opposite the top of Brick Lane)
- ☎ 020 7729 8476
- 🕐 M-Th 12.00-24.00, F 12.00-02.00,
  Sa 11.00-02.00, Su 11.00-24.00
- ⊖ Shoreditch High Street
- ⬆ brewdog.com
  facebook.com/BrewDogBarShoreditch

Most beers here are labelled vegan.

The food menu includes BBQ Hail Seitan steak £8 in a wholemeal bun with crispy kale, tomato chutney and hummus. Add fries £2.

Children welcome until 8pm. Disabled access. If you want vegan burgers and dawgs with your beer, head up to Brewdog Dalston which is 100% vegan, all beers, all the food!

Damascu Bite
Omnivorous Syrian restaurant

- ☛ 119-21 Brick Lane E1 6SE
- ☎ 020 7033 0400
- 🕐 Su-Th 11.00-24.00, F-Sa 11.00-
  02.00
- ⊖ Shoreditch High Street
- ⬆ Facebook Damascu Bite

Stacks of vegan dishes at this great value open fronted restaurant. Cold starters are under £4 such as hummus, baba ganoush, vine leaves, falafel, tabouleh, salads. Hot dishes such as mixed fried veg, lentil rice, chips. Mixed mezze £7.95. Also falafel wraps, vegetarian platters .

Hookah Lounge

Dark Sugars
Two vegetarian chocolate shops

- big shop: 124-126 Brick Lane E1 6RU (opposite Upmarket)
  small shop: 141 Brick Lane E1 6SB (south-west corner Cygnet Street, next to Vida Bakery)
- 07429 472606
- M-Su 10.00-22.00
- Shoreditch High Street, Aldgate East
- www.darksugars.co.uk
  facebook.com/darksugarschocolates

Fatou Mendy studied chocolate making in Belgium and Switzerland before opening stalls in Spitalfields and Borough Market and eventually this upmarket chocolate boutique. She has also spent years visiting cocoa farms in South America and Africa.

At least 15 of the treats are vegan, high in chocolate and low in sugar, including truffles, chocolates, and fruits dipped in chocolate. Warming hot chocolate drink £3 in chilli, cardamon, cinnamon, nutmeg or ginger.

The big shop has an ice-cream counter at the front with 11 vegan flavours, tubs for £4.50 or £5.50 with one or two flavours. Cones are not vegan.

Hookah Lounge
Omnivorous Moroccan style cafe

- 133 Brick Lane (near the top) E1 6SB
- 020 7033 9072
- M-Th 11.00-23.00, F-Sa 11.00-02.00, Su 11.00-22.30
- Shoreditch High Street
- hookah-lounge.co.uk

This place is something quite unusual, just south of the bagel shops at the top of Brick Lane, with comfy chairs you can collapse into with a cup of mint tea, or a plate of Sultan's or veg cold mezze £4.50-6.95. Vegan almond and apricot energy balls £1.50. Lots of teas, coffees, juices, wine and cocktails. Free wifi.

Monster House London
Vegan hair salon

- ☛ 2 Heneage Street E1 5LJ (next to Vegan Yes)
- ✆ 020 7377 6486
- ◔ M-Sa 12.00-20.00, Su closed
- ⊖ Aldgate East, Shoreditch High St
- ↖ facebook.com/monsterhouselondon
  instagram.com
      /monsterhouselondon

Think of the funkiest, punkiest hair you've seen around Camden, double it, and that's just a normal day here. You can sit in stylist Enric's cozy, witchy living room enjoying a nice cup of tea, having a chat or reading occult books, stroking Bruja the black cat, and getting that crazy haircut you always dreamed of. It's an incredible experience for those who prefer chilling with a friend rather than sitting in a regular brightly lit and sterile salon. Goth, dreads, grunge, extensions, Mohican, rainbow colours, wigs, all genders. Olaplex treatment available to protect your hair from chemical damage.

Fifth Dimension
Vegan tattoo & piercing shop

- 🖝 16 Bacon Street E1 6LF (top of Brick Lane)
- ☎ 020 7613 2736
- 🕐 W-Sa 11.00-19.00, Su 13.00-19.00, M-Tu closed, by appointment
- ⊖ Shoreditch High Street
- 🖐 fifthdimensiontattoo.co.uk
  facebook.com/fifthdimensiontattoo
  instagram.com/fifthdimensiontattoo

Fifth Dimension is London's haven for fully vegan piercings and tattoo art. From the ink to the aftercare to the soaps, sprays and stencil paper, the entire range of supplies are animal-free.

Fifth-D is a leader in contemporary tattooing, featuring geometric patterns, illustrative and graphic-style art, all made from scratch. The interior carries a "spiritual vibe" which they've picked up over the years, as they believe the environment helps their clients relax. They are artists through and through!

ethiopique

vegi

THE
HREE SAUSE
WRAPP

CHICKPEAS
WITH MIX
VEGETABLES

COURGETTE
AUBERGINE &
PEPPERS

END OF DAY
3.50

END OF DAY
3.50

END OF DAY
3.50

END OF DAY
3.50

FALAFEL WRAP MENU
AVOCADO £6.00
VEGAN HALLOUMI 6.50
VEGAN MEATBALL 6.50

GÖ

FALA
EN

AVOCADO
FALAFEL
WRAP
£6

FALAFEL
SALAD
WRAP
£5

VEGAN
HALLOUMI
BOX
£6.50

Tikka
Sala

Lamb
Curry

Surimi Prawn
Masala

Stir Fried
Lamb Doner

Fresh TURKISH FOOD
VEGAN & VEGETARIAN

BAKLAVA

FALAFEL
WRAP

DOLMA

FRESH

HOUSE OF VEGAN

Vegan food market every weekend at 152 Brick Lane E1 5EQ

House of Vegan
Vegan food market

🐾 Brick Lane Food Hall (The Boiler House), 152 Brick Lane E1 5EG

📞 020 7770 6028

🕐 Sa-Su 10.00-18.00

⊖ Shoreditch High Street

↖ trumanbrewery.com/markets

At the end of 2018 the Boilerhouse Food Market, which had several vegan and vegetarian stalls, went completely vegan.

Now there are at least a dozen international vegan food stalls, a bar, beer garden, and a shared seating area upstairs.

Typical stallholders are Ethiopiques, The Portobello Attic, Club Cultured, High Grade coffee, Fishout, We Are Planted, Vegan Rudeboy, PBJN Society, V Dawg, Vegalicious, Kalifornia Kitchen, Dutch Pancakes, Jake's Vegan Steaks, Omkara Indian food.

Free entry. Dog friendly. This building is also part of Vegan Nights, see next page.

Check out the Youtube videos *House of Vegan London Brick Lane* by Shiran De Silva (3 minutes), and *Brick Lane vegan food* by Vegan Franzi (5 minutes).

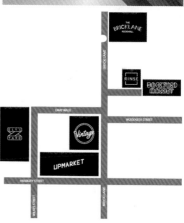

Vegan Nights
Vegan food party and bar at the Boilerhouse

- 93 Feet East, 150 Brick Lane E1 6QL
- 020 7770 6028
- One Thursday of the month 17.00-23.00 (not every month)
- Shoreditch High Street
- vegannights.uk
  facebook.com/vegannightsldn
  instagram vegannightsldn

London's monthly giant vegan food fayre and party. The first Thursday night time vegan market in September 2017 was packed out with massive queues, and it's been like that ever since. Each event now has up to 40 insanely nom food vendors, Djs, live acts and warm vibes.

The September 2019 event featured the following food stalls: Jake's Vegan Steaks, Phung Kay, Kind Burger, Unity Diner, Vegan Vice, Vausages, Little Leaf, The Green Grill, Pig Out, Nulla Mors, Club Cultured, Wholesome Junkies, Renee's Kitchen, Picky Wops, Omkara, Vegan Rudeboy, The Hogless Roast, Dappa, Yo Dough, Cupcakes & Shhht, Humble Dough, Lovely Buns, Myshrooms, Juice Junkiez, Re+CBD, City Juice, Lucky Pineapple Bar, Fizzi Rascal, Jim & Tonic.

Entrance on the door (limited) £10-£15 depending on the event, in advance £5-£10. The final event of 2019 was Halloween fancy dress / World Vegan Day. Please don't bring in any liquids or foods. All ages welcome, kids under 12 go free, pets welcome. The event is both indoors and outdoors.

In August 2019 they ran a Vegan Days event all weekend.

VEGAN
NIGHTS

Sunday UpMarket

91 Brick Lane E1 6QL indoor market, Su 10.00-17.00

Sunday UpMarket starts in the Old Truman Brewery at 91 Brick Lane E1 6QL, where it meets Hanbury Street, with food stalls at the front and a huge fashion market with over 200 stalls in the building and beyond along Hanbury Street. Most food stalls have a vegan dish or cake, but some are exclusively vegan. Open Sunday 10.00-17.00.

- sundayupmarket.co.uk
  facebook.com/UpmarketE1

Ethiopiques, UpMarket
Vegan Ethiopean food stall

- 07963 550 171

For many people this is the best food stall in all of London. A fantastic plate of food for £7 with salads, grains, grilled aubergine and courgette, lentils, soya, chickpeas, spinach, mixed vegetables and sauces.

If you catch them at closing time, the price is halved.

Cold drinks £1. They have another stall in the Boiler House Food Hall a little further up Brick Lane on the opposite side. Also at South Bank Fri-Sun.

Planet Falafel
Vegetarian falafel stall

- 07985 541 786
- planetfalafel.weebly.com
  facebook.com/PlanetFalafel

Falafel and hummus wrap £5.50. Cold drinks £1.30.

SPITALFIELDS MARKET

and nearby

From the middle of Brick Lane, walk west along Hanbury Street to this huge covered market with food stalls on weekdays, but Sunday is the mega day with a maze of independent designers selling their clothes, hand-made jewellery, even a secondhard record stall. For map see Brick Lane or Spitalfields.

For years vegans from all over London started their Sunday market tour with a luscious big box of raw food and raw cakes from Rainforest Creations. They are long gone but their former staffer Mel runs a very similar stall **Mel Tropical Kitchen**. **Merkamo** Ethiopian joined him in 2016 and are here every day.

There are two vegetarian **Pilpel** falafel cafes, and Asian food stalls along the north side, where there are shared wooden tables in the style of a pub garden. Also in or next to Spitalfields are branches of chain restaurants open late, such as Chilango, Giraffe, Las Iguanas, Leon, Wagamama, and the Montezuma chocolate shop.

On Commercial Street are a Pizza Express, a new branch of wholefood supermarket **As Nature Intended**, and near the top (see Shoreditch) is new vegan restaurant Genesis. Down the bottom end, **Unity Diner** vegan restaurant has just moved into bigger premises after starting out in Hoxton.

- fspitalfields.co.uk
  oldspitalsmarket.com

Merkamo
Vegan Ethiopian take-away stall

- Spitalfields Market E1 6EW (north side)
- 07432 600625
- M-F 11.00-17.30, Sa-Su 10.00-18.30
- facebook.com/merkamolondon

Since starting in 2016, at Merkamo they say a colourful meal is a good meal. Zinash and her crew serve up a huge plate of food for £6 or £6.50 which can be mostly salads, traditional with lentils and veggies, or half and half, accompanied by injera bread to mop it all up. You can also go gluten-free or mostly green veggies. They bake with a mixture of rice, maize, sorghum seed and wheat flour, and sometimes teff. Dumplings, made with coconut water, and lentil samosas 50p. Coconut water £1. There is a juice stall next door and benches and tables nearby to eat at.

Mel Tropical Kitchen
Vegan Caribbean raw food stall

- Spitalfields Market
- Sunday 10.00-17.00
- meltropical.com
  facebook.com/meltropical

Colourful, super-healthy raw food boxes with a mix of salads. Each salad can itself contain as many as ten ingredients.

Merkamo

Mel Tropical Kitchen

EAST

SPITALFIELDS

The Little Tibet

Box £6 or roti wrap £5 comes with three salads and a savoury item such as falafel, quiche, flan or lentil burger, the latter made with lentil and chickpea sprouts, veg, sunflower seeds, pumpkin, sweet potato, paprika, turmeric, and herb salt. The spinach flan contains courgette, sweet potato, plantain, red onion, hot pepper and herbs. Hummus is made with chickpea sprouts. Tropical salad pot £4.50.

Raw cakes £4 are made with an almond and cashew base, such as lemon cheesecake, mango and coconut, or chocolate berry. Chocolate balls and pumpkin coconut cubes £1.

Pilpel Falafel
Vegetarian falafel cafes

☛ Unit E, Pavillion Building, Old Spitalfields Market E1 6EW
☏ 020 7375 2282
🕐 M-F 11.00-18.00, Sa-Su 11.00-19.00
⊖ Liverpool Street, Shoreditch High St, Aldgate East
➤ pilpel.co.uk

In a row of food vendors on the north side of the market, with lots of trestle tables to eat at. Falafel with salad and hummus £4.80 in white or wholemeal pita, £5.80 in a box.Extra toppings 60p or £1. For full menu see The City (central London).

☛ 38 Brushfield Street E1 6AT
☏ 020 7952 5768
🕐 M-F 10.00-21.00, Sa closed, Su 12.00-18.00
⊖ Liverpool Street
➤ pilpel.co.uk

In the street running along the south side of Spitalfields Market.

☛ 60 Alie Street E1 8PX (2 blocks south of tube)
☏ 020 7952 2139
🕐 M-F 10.00-16.00, Sa-Su closed
⊖ Aldgate East
➤ facebook.com/pilpel.co.uk

Two blocks south of Aldgate East tube.

As Nature Intended, Spitalfields
Omnivorous wholefood supermarket

- The Exchange Building, 132 Commercial Street E1 6NG
- 020 7247 9596
- M-F 9.00-20.00, Sa-Su/BH 10.00-20.00 (closed Xmas, New Year)
- Shoreditch High Street, Liverpool St
- asnatureintended.uk.com

Big new wholefood supermarket with lots of organic and free-from foods. Organic fruit and veg. Lots of fridges and freezers with all the brands. Laura's Idea wraps and pots. Self-serve grains, beans, nuts, even coffee-beans. Fresh olives £1.69 per 100g. Bread. Ella's baby food.

Supplements by BioCare, Higher Nature, Lamberts, Nature's Plus, Solgar, Terra, Viridian, Wild Nutrition. Herbal remedies by Vogel and Pukka.

Bodycare by Akin, Antipodes, Argiletz, Dr Dr Bronner's, Faith In Nature, Hauschka, Green People, Jason, Lavera, Pai, Ren, Sukin, Weleda. Natracare. Aromatherapy. Cleaning by Method and Ecover. Ecover refills. Salt crystal lamps.

Also in Balham, Chiswick, Ealing, Marble Arch, Stratford.

iFalafel
Vegan falafel stall

- Goulston Street Market E1 7TP
- 07447 046608
- M-F 10.00-15.00, Sa-Su closed
- Aldgate, Aldgate East
- Facebook: I Falafel

Incredibly fast falafel made in 20 seconds

with Jordanian flatbread, chilli sauce (options), pickled gherkin, pickled turnip, tomato, cucumber, lettuce, tahini. Medium £3, large £4.

10 Cable Street
Plant based events venue

- 10 Cable Street E1 8JG (City end)
- info@tencablestreet.com
- Mainly evenings
- Aldgate East, Tower Hill, Shadwell
- tencablestreet.com facebook.com/tencablestreet

New venue for hire in London E1, hosting vegan supperclubs, classes, talks and workshop events based around sustainability and wellbeing. Events have included talks on zero waste, yoga classes, and vegan popup afternoon tea or tapas dinner. If you are a chef or event organiser, get in touch with Moko.

Holland & Barrett, Whitechapel
Health food shop

- Unit 4, 75 Whitechapel Road E1 1DU
- 020 7377 8476
- M-F 08.00-18.30, Sa 9.00-18.00, Su 10.30-18.00
- Whitechapel, Aldgate East

Fridge and freezer.

Unity Diner
Vegan restaurant & bar

- 60 Wentworth St, Spitalfields E1 7AL)
- 020 7033 3753
- Tu-F 12.00-22.00, last order 21.30;
  Sa 12.00-23.30, last order 22.30;
  Su 12.00-19.00, last order 18.30;
  M closed
- Aldgate East 4 mins walk),
  Liverpool Street 8 mins
- unitydiner.co.uk
  instagram.com/unitydiner
  facebook.com/unitydiner
  facebook.com/earthlingedpage

Brand new non-profit restaurant opened end September 2018 in Hoxton by vegan activist Earthling Ed and his Surge animal rights organisation. A year later they moved to this bigger venue. They aim to funnel profits into large scale vegan advertisement campaigns in London, mini-documentaries, and the development of Surge Sanctuary, opening late 2019. "Eat, drink and make a difference." How's this for an awesome menu....

Weekend breakfasts till 3pm. Savoury choices £6-£7 include toast topped with beans, mushrooms, scrambled tofu or smashed avo; chikken waffle or pancake stack with breaded seitan and maple syrup, add bakon £1; full English £12 starring sausages, scrambled tofu, beans, mushrooms, tomato, bakon, wedges, toast and salad garnish. Sweet breakfasts £4.95-£7.95 include seasonal fruit salad with coconut yogurt and mint; porridge with coconut milk, banana, berries and toasted seeds; chocolate waffle stack; fruit pancake stack.

Weekdays till 5pm, toasted sandwiches served with coleslaw £6.50-£7, such as BLT,

pesto grilled veg, or seitan steak with roasted mushrooms and melted cheeze.

Starters £5-£6: tofish bites in nori seaweed with tartar sauce; crispy fried cauliflower wings with coleslaw and ranch mayo; raw tacos with jalapeño nut cheese; seitan fried chikken wings.

Burgers £8-£12, choose from cashew and mushroom patty, ale battered tofish fillet, breaded seitan chikken with hot buffalo sauce, or juicy b12 patty in a pretzel bun with melted cheeze, fried onion, grilled peppers, sundried tomato pesto, basil mayo.

Mixed leaf salad £5, Epic veggies salad £8.95. Sharing plates for two, around £9, such as loaded fries with melted cheeze, onions, grilled veg, goji berry sauce and mixed seeds; or tofish bites, onion rings, cauliflower fried wings, seitan chikken wings.

Three evening only mains from 6pm: mac & cheese £8; raw zucchini spaghetti with sundried tomato pesto, plum toatoes, caRAWmalised red onions, sprouts and seed

parmesan, on rocket £9.50; chickpea and seitan grilled steakk with wedges, garlicky curly kale and cherry tomatoes with red wine and lentil gravy £10.95.

Desserts £5-£6.50 feature ice-cream sundae in chocolate or strawberry; cherry and apple pie with vanilla ice-cream or soya crea; warm chocolate and walnut brownie with ice-cream and chocolate sauce; baked cheesecake with raspberry coulis.

Wine from £5.50 glass, £21 bottle. Lager, ales, cider £4-£4.70. Soft drinks £2.50-£2.90. Juices. Kombucha £4.50. You can add a short of spirit. Coffee and tea with oat, soya or coconut milk.

Children welcome. Dogs welcome.

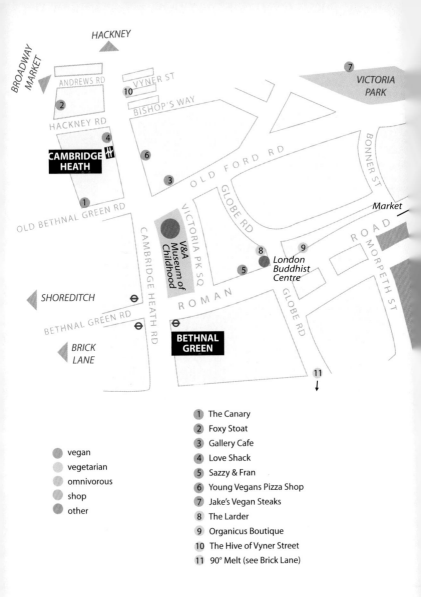

1. The Canary
2. Foxy Stoat
3. Gallery Cafe
4. Love Shack
5. Sazzy & Fran
6. Young Vegans Pizza Shop
7. Jake's Vegan Steaks
8. The Larder
9. Organicus Boutique
10. The Hive of Vyner Street
11. 90° Melt (see Brick Lane)

○ vegan
○ vegetarian
○ omnivorous
○ shop
○ other

BETHNAL GREEN

including Cambridge Heath

Bethnal Green saw a flurry of new vegan openings in 2018 and 2019. It is a much more laid back experience than the hectic Shoreditch or Brick Lane, and there is the London Buddhist Centre (www.lbc.org.uk) which offers meditation classes.

Victoria Park is popular with runners and has a lovely lake. Bring a picnic and something to read.

The Gallery Cafe has gone fully vegan and runs events such as music or poetry evenings. It's part of the St Margaret's House charity centre building with rooms and halls available for community events

The other old-timer is **The Larder**, handy for a cuppa and vegan cake after a daytime class at the Buddhist Centre next door.

The new vegan eateries are:

Foxy Stoat vegan cafe has a nineties Britpop theme and specialises in baked goods.

Round the corner is **Love Shack**, also open late and offering the chance to lounge in a hammock or do Saturday morning yoga before breakfast.

Sazzy & Fran is perfect for light meals and cakes.

The area's best kept secret could be **The Canary**, a top end hairdresser with all vegan products and a cafe.

For fun fast food, head to **Jake's Vegan Steaks** in Victoria Park on Sundays.

Opening after we go to press is new restaurant **Young Vegans Pizza Shop**.

The Hive opened vegan, but as vegan pioneers here they weren't getting enough footfall - hopefully we can help change that. It's the best place if you love wine.

Organicus Boutique is open the longest hours of all, with almost all vegan food.

TIP: **V&A Museum of Childhood** at 230 Cambridge Heath Rd, E2 9PA is open every day **10am - 5.45pm**

* Admission is free.

Foxy Stoat
Vegan coffee shop

- 19 Containerville, Emma Street, Hackney Road E2 9FP. Entrance on the corner of where Emma Street meets Hackney Road.
- 07493 701272
- M-W, F 9.30-17.30, Th 10.00-22.00, Sa closed, Su 11.00-16.00
- Cambridge Heath BR, Bethnal Green
- facebook.com/foxystoatofhackney instagram.com/foxystoatofhackney

Opened autumn 2019, a vegan-friendly vinyl lovers' cafe with a Britpop theme. Britpop being mid-1990s alternative rock bands such as Blur, Oasis, Pulp and Suede, who were later joined by Cast, Elastica, Sleeper, Supergrass and The Verve. Chef Kirsty is also an expert vegan baker.

They say the menu is fun, not healthy and damned tasty! As well as a daily special, there are homemade cakes and pastries, such as lusciously moist double chocolate cupcakes and apple and pear chimichangas coated in cinammon sugar (photo). You can generally get lunch for £2.80, such as a small take-away chilli or stew with bread. Cakes start at £1.20. Teas are £1.20 and coffee starts at £1.50.

Organicus Boutique
Vegetarian cafe and events venue

- 65 Roman Road E 0QN
- 07581 55 08 48
- M-Th 07.00-24.00, F 07.00-02.00, Sa 07.00-03.00, Su 10.00-22.00
- Bethnal Green
- facebook.com/organicus.boutique

Opened late 2019 by Tariq, who makes everything vegan apart from milk, butter and tzatziki. There is a courtyard, and downstairs lounge for live music and events.

Food includes falafel wrap, aubergine pakora, spiced potato spiral, sweet potato fries. Specials such as lentil soup £3. Organic salad picked from Cranbrook Community garden.

Cakes £3-£3.50 such as beetroot brownies, sweet potato blondies, banana crumble muffin.

Seasonal juices. Non-alcoholic cocktails. Organic tea and coffee.

ST. MARGARET'S HOUSE SETTLEMENT

A unique community charity providing space, opportunities and art events all under one roof

THE GALLERY CAFÉ

Vegetarian / vegan café and
popular arts venue
thegallerycafe.wordpress.com

AYOKA

Charity shop with new stock on
the rails every day
ayokacharityshop.wordpress.com

THE CREATE PLACE

Workshop space for activities,
classes and events
thecreateplace.co.uk

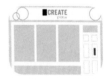

OFFICE SPACE

Discounted office space for charities
and voluntary/non-profit organisations
stmargaretshouse.org.uk

21 Old Ford Road | Bethnal Green | London E2 9PL | 020 8980 2092

The Gallery Cafe
Vegan restaurant & cafe

- St Margarets House, 21 Old Ford Road E2 9PL
- 020 8980 2092
- M-F 08.00-20.00, Sa 09.00-20.00, Su 09.00-19.00, kitchen closed an hour before. Open till late for events. May close briefly for event set-up.
- Bethnal Green
- stmargaretshouse.org.uk/gallerycafe facebook.com/thegallerycafelondon

Cosmopolitan cafe where all food is vegan since late 2017, with an international menu, and just around the corner from the Museum of Childhood. The cafe is a not-for-profit enterprise, part of The St. Margaret's House Charity, so the prices are always very reasonable, with all dishes under £10. The menu is varied and in the evenings they often host events; these include art, poetry, music and cinema. Since 2011 they have been using biodegradable packaging, more local, seasonal and organic produce and continue to look for ways in which to maximise the benefits for animals and the environment. There are gluten-free options.

They use local suppliers wherever possible and source coffee roasted by Allpress in Dalston, bread from the E5 Bakery, and local Five Points beer and Urban Orchard cider made from apples donated from people's gardens.

Outside seating all year round on the flower-filled, south-facing terrace and comfy sofas inside; on special occasions the beautiful garden at the rear is open to the public.

Breakfast served until 12pm on weekdays and 1pm at the weekends. A variety of options including avocado on rustic sourdough toast; potato rostis with whole baked Portobello mushroom, spinach and smoky homemade ketchup; superfood bowl; American style pancakes; the always popular Full English which is a vegan alternative to the traditional fry-up.

The main menu includes the homemade vegan burger, the Southern fried seitan burger, jackfruit tacos, falafel wrap. Loaded fries are topped with puy lentil chili, green pea guacamole, coconut sour cream, jalapeños and coriander. Also sandwiches and wraps. There are three specials every day which reflect seasonal ingredients and dishes from around the world. These include pasta dishes, curries, soup and salads, and can sell out fast so it's worth getting there early!

They are proud of their wide range of vegan desserts which change every week, from morning croissants to iced cupcakes, brownies, oatmeal cookies, carrot cake and banana bread, plus other specials that vary and include flapjacks, gingerbread and of course mince pies at Christmas.

The specialist Teapigs tea starts at £1.50 per mug or cup and £2.60 for a pot for two.

Wines from £4 medium glass, £5 large, £14.95 a bottle. Lagers, local ales and ciders.

No bookings. 2 high chairs, baby changing table. Dogs welcome inside and out. Free wifi. Visa, MC over £5.

Organic Porridge £3

Toasties £3

Coffee &
Walnut Cake
£2.80

The Love Shack

vegan cafe, bar and events space

Arch 298-299 Cambridge Heath Road E2 9HA

07794 192901

M-Tu 12.00-23.00, W-Th 12.00-23.30, F 12.00-01.00 or 03.00 if late licence event, Sa 10.00-01.00 or 03.00, Su 10.00-23.00

Cambridge Heath BR (next door), Bethnal Green

loveshackldn.com
facebook.com/loveshackldn
instagram.com/LoveShack_LDN

Opened May 2018 by an Englishman, an Irishman and a Mylkman, a plastic-free patch of vegan paradise at the southern edge of Hackney. It's around the corner from Just Fab and Sazzy & Fran, right next to Cambridge Heath station. If you like a New Age vibe or yoga before breakfast, or you have a dog, you may just fall in love with this place.

Raw juices £4.50 such as orange, apple, carrot and ginger; or pineapple, pear, kiwi, apple and ginger.

Smoothies £4.50 are made with Mylkman coconut or almond mylks. Top Banana has frozen banana, peanut butter, oats, cacao, date, agave. Club Tropicana features pineapple, mango, apple, ginger. Acai bowl £5.50 has granola, buckwheat, dried coconut, fresh fruits, agave, coconut mylk.

Breakfast till midday such as a stack of gluten-free banana and buckwheat pancakes £6.50 with fresh fruits, maple syrup and nut butter; fruit salad or blueberry and raspberry porridge £4.50; full English £9 featuring scrambled tofu, chargrilled plum tomatoes, sausages, baked beans, hash browns, wilted spinach and toast, add

£1 for smoke on the water cheese.

Plates £5-£7.50 such as Med roasted veg with hummus sourdough sandwich; pear, avocado and walnut salad; kim-cheese toastie; smashed guacamole with red onion and green chilli on sourdough with watercress salad; sourdough bruschetta; smoked tofu sandwich with Black Arts Aphrodite vegan cheese, mustard, mayo and pickles.

Evening starters £4-£5 such as dumplings and kimchi; or tempura courgettes with oyster mushroom and sweet chilli. Evening mains £8-£9 such as Sichuan cauliflower; smoked tofu and oyster mushrooms in a kelp broth; both served with terderstem broccoli, grilled baby corn and your choice of rice or salt and chilli chips; hummus Beiruti, quinoa, roasted Med veg and zhough on toasted sourdough; poached pear, avo and toasted walnut salad on quinoa, leaves, pomegranate, with maple and mustard dressing. Salt and chilli chips £2.50. Desserts of the day.

Cocktails such as pina colada, watermelon daquiri, mojito, Long Island ice tea, espresso martini, Bye My Chai (Cointreau, Aura Chai mix, termeric, ginger, oat milk). London Fields Brewery beer. Kombucha on tap. Hot drinks such as Yellow Bourbon coffee, matcha latte, mushroom tea.

What else? Sometimes there is morning yoga. Film nights. Drumming chanting get up and move shamanic full moon celebtration spiral love vibes type events. You can put on your own event. Dogs are welcome, doggie discount 10%, they want you to bring yours to play with theirs. And they have hammocks!

The Larder
vegetarian restaurant and cafe

241-24 Globe Road E2 0JD

020 3490 1404

M-F 08.00-19.00, Sa-Su 9.00-17.00. Kitchen closes 3pm.

Bethnal Green

larderlondon.co.uk
facebook.com/thelarderBG

Next door to the London Buddhist Centre, which runs evening classes and lunchtime drop-in meditation sessions. There's a secluded covered garden at the back, dogs welcome there, and bike racks at the front.

Breakfasts, till midday weekdays and 3pm weekends, include granola or muesli with fresh fruit and soya yogurt £5.10, smashed avocado on toast £6.40. On weekends there are also big cooked breakfasts £8.70 such as Mexican with avocado mash and homemade baked beans on sourdough toast served with fresh spinach and tomato salsa.

Soup £4.90 with bread is almost always vegan. The light lunch items on the counter such as quiche, pizza and tortilla are not vegan, but the veg strudel parcels are. Main courses £8.70 such as homemade crunchy mushroom and chickpea burger, red cabbage coleslaw and hand-cut chips; lentil hotpot with pita bread and couscous; baked aubergine with roasted Mediterranean style veg and side salad; superfood salad.

Always 2 or 3 vegan cakes such as carrot cake, mango sorbet-style cheesecake.

Cold drinks include Whole Earth cans, lots of Fentimans, Innocent smoothies, Purdeys. Teas, pots of tea, coffees, they have soya milk.

Children welcome, 5 high chairs, baby changing, Play Cube. Kids' parties and evening functions. Outside catering and cakes.

There is a small wholefood shop section with granola, muesli, spreads, teas, Vegideli sausages and falafels, Sojade yogurts, Indian and Thai curry paste, Chegworth Valley apple juices, Belvoir cordials, Ella's Kitchen baby food.

The Hive of Vyner St
Vegetarian organic restaurant (90% vegan)

☛ 286-290 Cambridge Heath Rd E2 9DA (by the canal)

☎ 020 8981 9245

🌑 M-F 08.00-22.00, Sa 09.00-22.00, Su 10.00-22.00

⊖ Bethnal Green, Cambridge Heath BR

➤ thehivewellbeing.com
facebook.com/thehivewellbeing
thehiveskincare.com

Opened August 2015 by young Italian couple Ilaria Giovannini and Marco Tassone, who had started out with nearby vegan micro-cafe G&T before finding these bigger premises by the bridge over the canal, between Broadway Market and Bethnal Green. Elegant cafe and juice bar atmosphere by day, more of a tapas cocktail bar by night. Desserts are all vegan.

Exquisite breakfast £4-£7.50 ranges from sourdough toast with almond butter; açai bowl with sprouted buckwheat granola, hemp and pumpkin seeds, coconut, banana, berries, macadamia, hazelnuts; Bircher musli with coconut yogurt; banana nut overnight oats with cacao nibs and cinnamon.

Weekday lunches £5-£8 such as miso soup, hummus and tempeh sandwich with sundried tomatoes, grilled peppers and courgette on toasted local sourdough bread from the E5 Bakery; baked tofu sandwich with olive tapenade, tomato and baby leaves; quinoa and avocado salad with roasted whole shallots and leaves.

Hive burger £7 day, £9 evening, made from mushroom, courgette and pumpkin seed, with plum chutney on sprouted wheat bun.

Tapas from 5pm £3-£5.50 include activated almonds, bread and oil, olives, toasted potatoes with thyme and cayenne tomato sauce, farinata, hummus dip, artichoke heart with stalk.

Desserts £2-£6 are all vegan: raw cashew and pistachio brownie with coconut ice-cream; affogato (ice-cream with double shot of espresso) lemon coconut cheesecake with raspberry coulis; energy balls, flapjacks; muffins; almond biscotti; apple, pinenuts and cardamon cake.

Cold pressed mixed veg juices £4.60 , large £8.50. Smoothies £7.50 such as Stracciatella with banana, cacao butter and nibs, dates, chia, coconut oil, almond milk. Cans £2.

French house wine £4.50 small glass, £9 large. Other Italian wines focus on Marco and Ilaria's home regions of Piemonte and Trentino, such as Barolo, Manzoni Bianco, Teroldego, from £5.50 for a small glass. Bottled beers from £3.50. Cocktails £5-£8.

They sell wines by the bottle to take home. Friday 5pm-9pm you can buy a bottle at the shop price and sit there and drink it. Sat-Sun from 5pm wine tastings. They can advise you on vegan food and wine pairing.

Coffee beans come from local Square Mile Coffee Roaster. Try a matcha or latte with a choice of milks including almond. Teas and coffees, hot choc, matcha latte, £2-£3.

They sell organic vegan skincare products by Suti and other hard to find brands. Also green juices to take take home.

Free wifi. Outside tables.

The Canary

Vegetarian cafe, hair salon & event space

☛ 61-63 Old Bethnal Green Rd E2 6QA (corner Canrobert St)

☎ 020 8257 8170

🕐 W-F 08.30-20.00, Sa 09.30-20.00, Su 9.30-18.00. and about to open 7 days.

⊖ Bethnal Green, BR Cambridge Heath

↖ thecanary.co.uk
instagram.com/thecanarye2

Opened February 2016, the cafe and hair salon are on the ground floor, with an events space downstairs. It's great for a fast lunch, or bring your laptop in the afternoon for cake and latte. Owner Victoria's fashion design background shows in the range of colours and textures in the food with original dishes debuting each month. Everything is homemade. Art on the walls is for sale.

Big salads £4.80 such as tofu satay glass noodles with veggies; Keralan bhel salad with turmeric puffed rice; cavolo nero with coconut bacon, satsuma and kidney beans; black rice, sweet potato, pumpkin seeds, pickled lemon, and hot chilli dressing.

Cakes £2.80, vegan ones include plum and stem ginger; cherry, chilli and coconut; gluten-free banana bread with summer fruits; coconut cheesecake on cashew and almond base with blackberry and cherry topping; chocolate espresso lemon cheesecake; persimmon and pecan; and there are dozens more recipes.

Freshly squeezed juices £2.90-£3.50. Unusual locally bottled cold drinks £2.20-£2.50. Teas and all the classic coffees including long and even longer black £2.30-£2.70. Rainbow latte, pick a colour, such as RED rooibos and raspberry. They carry soya, coconut and oat milk, plus a homemade milk of the week such as almond-cashew.

Hairdresser uses organic vegan Evo products (accredited by PETA) and ammonia-free dyes. Ladies cut & dry £56, Men's cut & style £45, wash and dry £30, men's express cut £20, children £15, beard trim from £15, colour £60-£130, free drinks with appointment.

Children's corner with crayons and kids' books to keep them occupied while you get your hair done, and some local grown-up books too. Popup events like art launches, birthday parties. Dogs welcome, water bowl. Outside seating in summer.

Nail, facial and beauty treatments coming using vegan "Lashes 10 Free" products.

Another branch called The King's Canary in Fitzrovia, Central London.

Sazzy & Fran
Vegan Italian cafe

📍 33 Roman Road E2 0HU

🕐 M-F 07.30-17.00, Sa 08.00-17.00, Su 9.00-17.00

☎ 07428 717579

⊖ Bethnal Green, Cambridge Heath BR

↖ facebook.com/sazzyandfrancafe
instagram.com/sazzyandfrancafe

Opened in 2018, vegan breakfast and lunch cafe by young Italian couple Sarah (Sazzy) Harrison and Francesco Stornaiuoloin 2018.

Breakfast £4-£5 such as avocado on sourdough toss with Sicilian olive oil, oregano and a squeeze of lemon; porridge with cinnamon, peanut butter and berries; overnight oats layered with fruit, agave syrup and topped with peanut butter.

Lunch dish of the day £5-£6, served 12.00-15.00, such as sandwiches with curried chickpeas, lettuce and mango chutney (salad add £1); mushroom risotto; marinated tofu with avocado, green veg, brown rice and peanut dressing; pesto and roast tomato pasta salad; pizza (book ahead if possible); pancakes with lots of toppings. Check Instagram for the menu for this week.

Often they bake fresh bread and focaccia and they make fresh hummus.

Cheesecake or carrot cake £3, matcha brownie £2.50, protein balls £1.80.

Fresh mixed fruits or veggies juices £4. Teas and coffee. Outside communal tables. Wifi. Almost everything they use is biodegradeble and recyclable. They also sell Love Matcha tea from Japan and cold pressed Sicilian olive oil from the owner's father's olive tree.

The Canary

EAST

BETHNAL GREEN

Sazzy & Fran Cafe

90° Melt
Vegetarian Modern American restaurant

☛ 235 Mile End Road E1 4AA
☎ 020 3754 5711
🕐 M-F 10.00-22.00, Sa 11.00-22.00, Su 11.00-16.00
⊖ Stepney Green
↖ 90degreemelt.co.uk

Americans style comfort food, near Queen Mary University, where almost everything can be made vegan. When they opened in early 2017 the speciality was melted cheese sandwiches, and now the menu could be straight out of an American diner.

Lentil superfood or beetroot salad £4. Tomato basil soup, bean stew..

A melt is a tapas sized gourmet grilled cheese sandwich for £4.50. Melt varieties feature Waldorf with green apples and nuts, Spa artichoke with spinach and chilli sauce, Margarita with pizza sauce and olives, Mush-Blush with pesto and mushrooms, Harissa, and the very popular Donald Trump Mexican with smoked chipotle sauce, roasted peppers and baby corn. Weekday lunch deal 12-4pm two melts £6.99.

Weekday and Saturday night "Something Meaty" menu has typical American diner dishes £4.95-£6.95 including stir-fried soya chicken lettuce wraps, corn-battered deep-fried hot dogs, burger with guacamole and cheese, cauliflower "buffalo chicken" wings, Tex-Mex wedges, chili cheese wedge fries.

Top up with sides £4.50 such as mac n cheese, jalapeno cornbread, onion rings with sauce, potato wedges, vegan gravy n mash. Sauces/dips 75p and £1 include green chilli, smoky chipotle, guacamole, coriander chutney, buffalo wings sauce, yogurt. Pickles £2.

Weekend brunch till 4pm: small plates £4-£4.50 include fried grilled cheese balls, mini breakfast melt, avocado on toast, potato wedges and dip, smoothie bowl, and cinnamon, banana and nut porridge. Big plates £7-£8.50 such as tofu scramble with toast and guacamole, or pancake stack with mascarpone, banana and berries.

Glass of wine £5, carafe £14, bottle £19. Beer £3-£5. Champagne and cocktails £7.50. Soft drinks £2.50-£4.

Disabled toilet.

Jake's Vegan Steaks
Vegan modern British food stall

- ☛ Victoria Park Market, The Nightwalk E2 9JW (enter at 55 Gore Rd E9 7HN)
- ℂ
- ◑ Sunday 11.00-16.00
- ↖ jakesvegansteaks.com
  instagram.com/jakesvegansteaks

Philadelphia style cheezesteaks, which are shredded seitan steak with melted cheeze in a baguette, with various toppings and thyme fries.

Other stalls include a juice bar, coffee, wines, spirits, craft beer, herbs and spices, olives, Ted's Veg, olives, pickles, and some very non-vegan ones. Also live jazz and children's drawing gallery.

Jakes have a take-away shop in Holloway Road, and you can sit down with your food at the pub next door. (North London). Also at Vegan Nights (Brick Lane).

Young Vegans Pizza Shop
Vegan Italian restaurant

- ☛ 393 Cambridge Heath Road E2 2AR
- ℂ deathbypizza@youngvegans.co.uk
- ◑ M-Tu closed, W-F 17.00-22.00, Sa-Su 12.00-22.00
- ⊖ Cambridge Heath BR, Bethnal Green
- ↖ youngvegans.co.uk
  facebook.com/youngveganspizzashop

Opening at the end of 2019 after we go to print. See London Fields Death By Pizza for the kind of food, and they will add starters and desserts here in their first restaurant.

Deliveroo..

CANARY WHARF

Docklands

Vurger, Canary Wharf
Vegan burger restaurant & take-away

- ☛ Unit 1 The Wharf Kitchen, Jubilee Place Lower Mall -2, Canary Wharf E14 5NY
- ☏ feedme@thevurgerco.com
- 🕐 M-F 11.30-21.00, Sa 12.00-21.00, Su 12.00-19.00
- ⊖ Canary Wharf
- ↖ thevurgerco.com
  facebook.com/thevurgerco

Classy fast food like luscious burgers and salad boxes, mac n cheese, ice-cream and wine. It's plastic-free, they use compostable Vegware containers, cups and cutlery.

Four kinds of burgers £8.45 are served on a vegan brioche bun, which can be gluten-free. The Classic is made from black beans, chargrilled pepper and corn, topped with tomato, red onion, gherkins and their own burger sauce. The Auburger is made from aubergine, caramelised red onion and tabasco chipotle chickpea, served with pickled red cabbage, gherkins and cumin mayo. MLT is roasted mushrooms, borlotti beans and parsley, topped with tomato, rocket, ketchup and their sundried tomato and walnut pesto. Holy Habanero corn fritter burger comes with crunchy slaw, topped with spiced almonds, crispy tortillas, habanero mayo. Or bunless in bowl £7.95.

Sides £2.95-£5.75 include skin on fries, sweet potato fries, house slaw, mac n cheese (which can be gluten-free) with optional pesto.

Ice-cream £3.95, a different flavour each day, with sauce and toppings. Chocolate hazelnut or salted caramel MiiRo lolly £2.95. Shakes £4.85 comes in berry, vanilla, mocha or banana caramel. Add a shot of whisky or rum for £2.

Lemonade, cola, juice £2.50. Beers £4.50-£4.75 include Camden Hells, and Pale Ale, Hawkes cider. House wine £4.75 medium glass, £16.95 bottle. Tea, coffees, hot choc £1.95-£2.45.

No cash, only cards, Apple and Android pay. No reservations, walk ins only. High chairs. Another branch in Shoreditch.

Garbanzos
Vegetarian falafel stall

- ☛ Reuters Plaza E14 5AJ
- ☏ 3 Reuters Plaza E14 5AJ
- 🕐 M-F 09.00-24.00, Sa 10.00-19.00, Su 12.00-18.00
- ⊖ Canary Wharf
- ↖ canarywharf.com/eating-drinking/directory/garbanzos-reuters-plaza

Falafel and pitta £5.20; salad bowl £5.70; hummus plate £5.20 with 5 falafels and pitta, falafel portion £2.50. Extras 60-75p such as aubergine, guacamole and pitta. Fruit salad £2.50. Soft drinks £1.25.

Birleys

Birleys
Omnivorous salad bar

- ☞ Promenade Level, Cabot Place West E14 4QT
  020 7513 0040, 020 7512 8112
- ◕ M-F 06.00-18.00, Sa 10-00-19.00, Su closed
- ⊖ Canary Wharf
- ↖ birleysandwiches.co.uk

Salad bar serving made-to-order salads, fresh made to order baguettees, and hot and cold drinks. Choose your base from baby greens, rice noodles, herbed couscous and fusilli for £2.95; add deli roasted veg, marinated olives, sun blushed tomato, spiced mixed beans, avocado, tomatoes, sweetcorn, cucumber, carrot and onion, each 40p-£1. Also croutons, chilli, sultanas, parsley and coriander, dressing free of charge.

Also at Unit 23, Canada Place Mall E14 5AX.

Hazev

Hazev Restaurant
Omnivorous Turkish restaurant

- Discovery Dock West, 2 South Quay Square, Canary Wharf E14 9RT (by Hilton Canary Wharf)
- 020 7515 9467 / 8
- M-Sa 12.00-23.30, Su 12.00-22.30 Cafe M- Su 08.00-22.00
- South Quay, Canary Wharf (across footbridge)
- hazev.com

Spacious restaurant, part of the Tas chain (see Bloomsbury or South Bank), in a beautiful location on the quay.

A la carte cold and hot starters and soup £5.95-£6.25 include red lentil soup, chilli tomato soup with mint and croutons, grilled aubergine and peppers, bulgur wheat with crushed walnuts and hazelnuts, salad with cracked wheat, stuffed vine leaves with rice and pine kernels, ground chickpeas and broad beans falafel with hummus;

Mains £12.95 feature sautéed kidney beans with potato and veg; vegetable stew served with couscous; sundried aubergine stuffed with couscous; chickpeas onion and garlic; stuffed cabbage with bulgur wheat, tomato, onion, mint, paprika and cumin seds; grilled aubergine, tomato, sweet peppers and onion served on bread with tomato sauce.

Wine small glass £4.95, bottle £18.45. Cocktails £6.95-£7.95, non alcoholic cocktails £4.25-£4.75.

Private parties up to 100 people. High chair.

Velo
Omnivorous Vietnamese street food kiosk

- Kiosk 4, Reuters Plaza E14 5AJ
- 020 7519 1026
- M-F 9.00-21.00, Sat 10.00-19.00, Su 12.00-18.00
- Canary Wharf
- velorestaurant.com

Tofu summer roll £2.40. Pho noodle soup or green papaya salad with lemongrass tofu £6.20 (gluten-free on request).

No cash cards only. They deliver group orders or office catering.

Crussh, Canary Wharf
Omnivorous juice bar and cafe

- Tabot Place, Tower Concourse Level E14 5AB
- 020 7513 0076
- M-F 07.00-19.00, Sa/BH 10.00-18.00, Su closed
- Canary Wharf

- Unit 21 Jubilee Place E14 5AB
- 020 7519 6427
- M-F 07.00-21.00, Sa 09.00-19.00, Su 10.00-19.00
- Canary Wharf
- crussh.com

Juices made in front of you, soups, salads and sandwiches to eat in or take away.

Leon, Canary Wharf
Omnivorous cafe & take-away

- Promenade Level, Cabot Place West, Canary Wharf E14 4QS
- 020 7719 6200
- M-Th 07.00-21.30, F 07.00-21.00, Sa 10.00-19.00, Su 11.00-18.00
- Canary Wharf

- Unit 62 Lower Mall, Canary Wharf E14 5NY
- 020 7512 9419
- M-F 09.00-21.00, Sa-Su 09.00-19.00
- Canary Wharf
- leonrestaurants.co.uk

Lebanese style chain with lots of vegan food.

Le Pain Quotidien, Canary Wharf
Omnivorous Belgian cafe chain

- Unit 84 Lower Mall, Canary Wharf E14 5NY
- 020 3617 6631
- M-F 07.00-21.00, Sa 09.00-19.00, Su-BH 09.00-18.00
- Canary Wharf
- lepainquotidien.co.uk/store/canary-wharf

Try the soups, tofu salad and blueberry muffins.

Soups & Salads
Omnivorous salad bar

- Promenade Level, Cabot Place West E14 4QT
- 020 7513 0040, 020 7512 8112
- M-F 10.30-15.00, Sa-Su closed
- Canary Wharf
- birleysandwiches.co.uk

A lot of vegetarian and probably vegan menu items. including a lovely veggie chilli. Certainly the salads are mostly vegan. Friendly staff and cheap too!

Wagamama, Canary Wharf
Omnivorous Japanese restaurant

- Jubilee Place, 45 Bank St, E14 5NY (by Canary Wharf tube)
- 020 7516 9009
  M-Sa 11.30-22.00, Sun 12.00-21.00
- Canary Wharf
- wagamama.com

Big restaurant with several vegan noodle based dishes. See Chains or website.

There is also a Wahaca, and inside the shopping complex there is Lola's cupcakes.

Holland & Barrett, Canary Wharf
Health food store

- Cabot Place, Unit RP470, Canada Square E14 5AX
- 020 7715 9241
- M 07.00-21.00, Tu-W 07.00-20.30, Th-F 07.00-20.00, Sa 09.00-19.00, Su 10.30-19.00
- DLR Canary Wharf

Freezer.

Holland & Barrett, Jubilee
Health food store

- Unit 18, Jubilee Place, Canary Wharf E14 5NY
- 020 7512 9826
- M-F 07.00-21.00, Sa 09.00-19.00, Su 10.30-19.00
- Canary Wharf tube

Neal's Yard Remedies
Herbalist

- Unit 2 Canary Wharf underground Station E14 4HJ
- 020 7519 6896
- M-F 08.00-20.00, Sa 10.00-18.00, Su 12.00-18.00
- Canary Wharf
- nealsyardremedies.com

Lola's Cupcakes
Cupcakes stand

- ☛ Unit 5, 16-19 (opposite Waitrose)
  Canada Square E14 5EQ
- ☏ 020 7516 0534
- ◐ M-Th 07.00-20.00, F 07.00-21.00,
  Sa 10.00-20.00, Su-BH 11.00-18.30
- ⊖ Canary Wharf
- ↖ lolacupcakes.co.uk

Lots of vegan cupcakes.

Zizzi, Canary Wharf
Omnivorous chain restaurant

- ☛ 33 Westferry Circus E14 8RR
- ☏ 020 7512 9257
- ◐ M-Sa 11.30-23.00, Su 12.00-22.30
- ⊖ Westferry DLR
- ↖ zizzi.co.uk

See Chains section.

HC: Serves meat, vegan options available. Italian chain restaurant with a separate vegan menu offering starters like bruschetta and garlic bread, plus pasta and pizza with vegan mozzarella, and sorbet for dessert.

There are also plenty of places to get sushi which they assure us can be vegan.

Crossrail Place by the canal has a fantastic 4,160sq m roof garden designed by Foster & Partner. On the ground floor there is Everyman Cinema, Poncho 8 Mexican food, Chai K Indian.

Sticks 'n' Sushi
Omnivorous Japanese restaurant

- ☛ Crossrail Place E14 5AR
- ☎ M-W 11.30-22.00, Th-Sa 11.30-23-00, Su 12.00-21.00
- ☏ 020 3141 8230
- ⊖ Canary Wharf, Poplar
- ↖ sticksnsushi.com

Although the menu is predominantly non-veggie, their vegan offerings are excellent. Classy Japanese decor with Scandinavian twist: lanterns, high ceilings, exposed brick wall, shared tables and central bar.

Sides £2-£6 include seaweed salad, fried cauliflower, Jerusalem atichoke, grilled corn, edamame beans and rice. Sushi uramaki or hosomaki £6.50 for 8 pieces such as mamma mia roll with avocado and cucumber, rolled in chives and soy sesame. Nigiri £2.20 with asparagus or grilled king oyster mushroom;

The Green Keeper meal £22 consists of salad, nigiri, maki, hosomaki, spicy edamame beans, grilled corn and seaweed salad. Also good is the Greengate salad £15 with grilled king oyster mushroom, sweet potato and tender stem broccoli, on a salad of gem leaves, cabbage, tomato, edamame, avocado, radish, cauliflower, onion, ginger, chives, quinoa topped with pine nuts. Veggie salad £9.50 with crunchy veg, edamame beans, avocado, soy sesame, red onion, ginger, chives, tofu, and grilled vegetables in teriyaki and wafu dressing. Yuzu sorbet.

Wine from £3.10/£4.10 glass, £16.50 bottle. Soya milk available for hot drinks with no extra charge.

Kids welcome. High chirs available. Wifi.

DALSTON

and Haggerston

Biff's Jack Shack at BrewDog Dalston

100% Vegan food pub

- 33-35 Stoke Newington Road N16 8BJ (north of Rio cinema, same side)
- 020 3026 0790
  dalstonbar@brewdog.com
- M-W 16.00-24.00, Th 12.00-24.00, F 12.00-02.00, Sa 11.00-02.00, Su 11.00-24.00. Food until 22.00.
- Dalston Kingsland (closest, turn left out of station), Dalston Junction
- brewdog.com/bars/uk/ brewdog-dalston
  facebook/Instagram BrewDogDalston
  biffsjackshack.com

Dalston is the first branch of the **Brewdog** bars chain to make *all* their drink and food vegan, with food by **Biff's Jack Shack** (lately of Shoreditch Boxpark). It's two floors of Scottish-brewed draught craft beer haven plus Biff's bangin' filthy fast food heaven.

Ten types of huge, luscious **burgers** £8.50-£10.50 feature the Biff's signature crispy fried jackfruit patty in a toasted bun, with cheeze, red onion, lettuce, tomato. Sam Hell Jackson adds hot sauce and chipotle slaw. Father Jack has smoky bacun jam and bourbon bbq sauce. Jack Bauer Tower of Power is a double burger with hash brown, bacun, deep fried cheeze slice, garlic mayo.

Crispy fried jackfruit **wingz** come on a sugarcane "bone" with toppings and various sauces such as blue cheeze Buffalo hot or Bourbon sticky bbq or Ranch with bacun bits and maple chipotle.

Filthy fries £3.50-£6 include Cajun Dusted skin-on fries; Poutine AF with cheeze curds, porcini mushroom gravy, gnarly seitan bacon and toasted seeds; Bang Bang cinnamon sweet chilli, miso mayo, toasted nuts, shallots and coriander; Bacunator with garlic mayo; Dirtbag Melt with Punk IPA cheeze, bacun, sweet pickle sprinkes; Italia 90 parmasan shavings with truffle oil and bacun; or Chilli Cheeze fries with jackfruit brisket chilli, spooned over Cajun dusted fries and smothered with Punk IPA cheeze sauce and coriander, also in large size £8.

Plates and sides £2-£6 such as mustard mayo slaw, southern smoky meatloaf with bourbon bbq dipping sauce, loaded nachos, corn ribs, watermelon salad (which might be the only non-filthy AF menu item).

For **dessert** £5.50 they offer sweet jackfruit pie with ice cream and salted caramel, or three scoops of assorted ice creams with matcha caramel sauce and toasted nuts.

Sharing board £30 with double meatloaf, corn ribs, filthy fries, wings.

100% vegan beers, wines, spirits and soft drinks. Great for groups or parties. Children welcome. Outdoor seating. Biff's is also at Walthamstow Eat 17 Spar.

Mildreds Dalston
Vegetarian restaurant

- Dalston Square, Dalston Lane E8 3GU (behind the overground station)
- 020 8017 1815
- M-F 12.00-23.00, Sa 10.00-23.00, Su 10.00-22.00
- Dalston Junction overground
- mildreds.co.uk
  facebook.com/mildredsdalston

The fourth branch of Mildreds opened August 2017. Almost everything is or can be vegan and most dishes are gluten-free.

Brunch Sa-Su 10.00-15.00.

Starters and small plates £3-£6 such as gyoza dumplings, roasted miso aubergine with ginger and spring onions, smashed avocado with corn chips, Asian watermelon salad with shiso leaf and yuzu dressing.

Smoked tofu burgers £8 with lentil, piquillo pepper in a focaccia bun, add cheese £1, fries or sweet potato fries £3-£4 with basil mayo or chipotle ketchup .

Large plates £12 such as Soul bowl with quinoa, veg, cashew cheese and seeds; Detox salad with marinated tofu; mushroom and ale pie with minted mushy peas and fries; Vietnamese mock duck and rice noodle bowl; Sri Lankan sweet potato and green bean curry; stir-fried veg with peanuts, organic tofu, brown jasmine rice and kimchi.

Puddings menu £6.50 features passion fruit meringue tartlet with coconut yogurt; chocolate and hazelnut brownie with salted caramel sauce and ice-cream; pannacotta with hibiscus scented lychees; lemon mascarpone cheesecake. Ice-cream with chocolate and pomegranate sauce £5. Truffles or raw balls £3.

Organic fresh juices £4.50, soft drinks £2.50-£3. Vegan wines medium glass £5.50-£6.50, bottle £20-£31. Organic beer and cider £4.20-£4.90. Cocktails, mocktails, £4-£7.50. Teas, coffees £2-£2.70.

12.5% optional service charge. Some outside tables. Take-away. Deliveries by Deliveroo.

All Nations Caribbean Vegan House
Vegan Jamaican cafe-restaurant & take-away

🖝 8 Sandringham Road E8 2LP
   (opposite Argos, near Harvest)

📞 020 7254 0023

🕒 M-F 12.00-20.00, F-Sa 12.00-22.00, Su 12.00-18.30

⊖ Dalston Kingsland overground
   facebook

🖊 facebook.com/allnationsveganhouse
   instagram.com/allnationsveganhouse

Chef Atreka Cameron went vegan for health 8 years ago and noticed an increase in energy and better skin. In December 2017 she opened All Nations, Dalston's most chilled out and relaxing cafe, with healthy cooked wholefood dishes at great prices.

Each day the special is a main and a grain £8 with salad and magic sauce. Side dishes £2-£4 include coleslaw, calaloo, cabbage with okra, fried plantain, yam chips with sweet and sour dip, pholourie (deep fried spicy split pea dough).

Start with the house speciality spicy, smoky sweet potatoes £3 which just melt in your mouth, served with crispy nori seaweed and tomato pieces. Main and grain with salad £8.50, such as pinto bean stew for main, with bulgur and quinoa grain which comes with gunga peas, and you might add a side of ackee and mushroom, or plantain with cucumber and sweet chilli sauce.

Banana blueberry or chocolate plantain cake £3, with custard £4.

Soft drinks £2, water £1. Kombucha £3.50 bottle, £2.50 can. They brew their own alcohol-free wine, £5 large glass.

Children welcome, high chair. 14 seats

inside, big table outside where dogs are welcome. It gets busy Friday and Saturday night so best to reserve. Free wifi.

Eat in £1 service charge. Big take-away box £7 for main, grain, salad and smoky potatoes. Or have bigger portions served in a big box plus two smaller ones for £10.

There is a fascinating selection of books around the cafe enticing you to linger here and return, including How Not to Die by vegan M.D. Michael Greger, London's East End Then & Now, Rich Dad Poor Dad, The Power of Now, Dalston in the 80s, Yardie, The Secret, The Concise Oxford Companion to English Literature, 101 Amazing Women, Girls Who Changed the World, Natural Remedies, and lots more.

As the sun streams in through the back window, you could be in a beachside cafe on a Caribbean island, an oasis of calm away from the bustle of Kingsland High Street. "Hey sistaa!" "How are you, my brother?" A little girl asks if they have cake today. "Auntie has to put the cake in the oven. Next time we'll have some, princess." Customers wave hello or goodbye to you with a smile. Vegan reggae legend Macka B sang about a 4 minute vacation. This was a 4 hour vacation from London. I loved it.

Rogue Vegan

Rogue Vegan
Vegan Mauritian & Caribbean wholefood restaurant

- ☎ 584 Kingsland Road, Dalston E8 4AH
- ✆ 07852 973 778
- 🕐 Sa-Su 12.30-21.30 M 17.00-21.30, Tu-F closed
- ⊖ Dalston Junction
- ➤ eatrogue.com
  facebook.com/rogueveganrestaurant
  instagram.com/rogue.vegan

Healthy, tasty and great value vegan food

Starters £5-£8 such as smokey veg salad with seeds and apple cider vinaigrette; rich creamy coconut sweet potato and plantain soup with cinnamon and nutmeg; hoisin plum jack salad with crispy jackfruit pieces.

Mains £10 such as Waffle Burger with battered oyster mushroom, pineapple slice, fried plantain, cheese and salad served with fries; Mountain Bowl with baked plantain, chickpea special, fried breadfruit, sweet potato mash, griddles pineapple, quinoa and slaw; Tamarin Bay Bowl with spiced mashed pumpkin, mushroom stew, Mauritian slaw, fried green banana, quinoa, chickpeas and green beans; Highbryd Bowl.

Top up with crispy breaded jackfruit nugget balls and tamarind sauce £5, spelt pasta mac no cheese £5, fries £2, beet slaw £3.

Desserts £5 include Mauritian chilli pineapple; peach, banana and apple pie topped with spelt crumble; both served with homemade vanilla ice cream. Or three scoops of mint choc coco vanilla ice cream.

Freshly pressed juice , coconut water, ginger beer £2.50-£4.50. Bring your own alcohol, no corkage. Children welcome. Patio at the back when not raining, dogs welcome there.

Andu
Vegan Ethiopian cafe

- 528 Kingsland Road E8 4AH
- 020 7254 1780
- M-Su 12.00-21.00
- Dalston Junction
- facebook.com/Andu-Cafe-1653247514905380
  Facebook Andu Cafe

Spicy, filling food at a fraction of the price you would pay in other Ethiopian restaurants. If you can't get into Mildreds, head down here, lots of other people do and love it! Lentil and veg dishes come with injera bread, like a big pancake, which you break into pieces and use to pick up the food.

Have a plate of spicy lentils, yellow split peas, potatoes with spinach and carrot, and green bean salad, around £7, or for two people £12.

Finish off with some strong Ethiopian coffee.

If you've come to Mildreds and can't get in, Rogue Vegan and Andu are just around the corner.

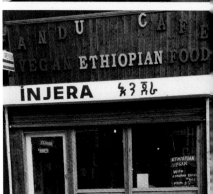

Arancini Bros

Stunt Dolly

Kaffa Coffee

Arancini Brothers, Dalston
Vegan Italian cafe & take-away

🖝 592 Kingsland Road E8 4AH

☎ 020 3583 7303

🕐 M-Su 10.00-22.00

⊖ Dalston Junction

↖ arancinibrothers.com
facebook.com/ArancinibrothersLdn
instagram.com/arancinibrothers

Vegan wraps, burgers, stews, salad boxes, and their speciality is risotto balls. Most items are gluten-free.

Originally omnivorous, owner David Arkin turned the Old Street branch vegan as a test for Veganuary 2018. Sales rose 30%, so in February he turned this branch and the Kentish Town one vegan too.

Golfball size risotto balls, which are or can be served with pretty much everything, come in original or mushroom. Prices range from £5.20 for 5 to £10.20 for 12.

Breakfasts include three kinds of wraps £6.70-£7.20 filled with mushroom and roast tomato, or spicy chorizo and roast tomato, all served with risotto balls and salad. Breakfast baps £4.70-£6.20 filled with ingredients such as roast mushroom or tomato, spicy sausage, chimichurri, cheese, special mayo.

Risotto burgers £7.20-£9.70 come in six versions, the most popular are smoky chorizo and cheese, or the FGV burger with double cheese, pickles, crispy onion, ketchup and mustard.

Wraps in regular or large £5.70-£7.70 all include risotto balls and salad plus for example chick'n and citrus dressing.

Lentil and spinach stews £6.70-£7.20,

hoose from butternut or chick'n.

salad boxes £6.20-£7.70 can include chick'n, roast mushrooms, chutney, mayo, eggplant sauce.

Top up with fries £2.40 small, £4.20 large. Side salad £2. Extra chutney or eggplant sauce 50p.

Cake of the day £4.70.

Tea and all kinds of coffee, mocha £1.50-£2.60. Cans £1.70, Moju juices £3.70.

Deliveroo. Branches in the City (Old Street) and Kentish Town, and they are at markets such as Kings Cross or Vegan Nights.

Stunt Dolly
Vegan hairdresser

- 582 Kingsland Road E8 4AH (next to Rogue Vegan)
- 020 7018 2191
- M 12.00-20.00, Tu-F 10.00-20.00, Sa 10.00-18.00, Su closed
- Dalston Junction
- stuntdolly.com
  facebook.com/stuntdolly
  instagram.com/stuntdolly

Hair salon for all genders. They use vegan, non-toxic, organic, sustainable products.

Cut, complex or simple undercut, colouring, roots, blowdry, Olaplex, plant based keratin treatment, beard shaping, balayage, wedding and bridal hair, and more, can all be booked on the website with the team member of your choice, prices from £23 to £97.

See Facebook and Instagram for hundreds of stunning examples of their styles.

Kaffa Coffee
Ethiopian coffee cafe

- 1 Gillett Square N16 8AZ
- 07506 513267
- M-Su 09.00-23.00
- Dalston Kingsland
- kaffacoffee.co.uk
  facebook.com/kaffacoffeeuk

Want to escape the traffic and bustle of Kingsland High Street? Come to Markos's coffee shop and juice bar in pedestrianised Gillette Square for a juice or an Ethiopian coffee, chill out with some Ethiopian jazz, reggae and blues, and soak up the atmosphere. Kaffa is the south-west region of Ethiopia, and Markos roasts beans from there. Also teas, smoothies, juices.

Ethiopian vegetarian lunch on Thursdays and Fridays, served with injera bread baked by Kaffa. They make a variety of stews such as lentil, black and green beans, quinoa salads with croutons.

Healthy Stuff
Omnivorous cafe & wholefood shop

- 168 Dalston Lane E8 2EQ
- 020 7812 9604
- M-F 08.00-18.00, Sa-Su 10.00-18.00
- Hackney Downs
- healthystuff.london
  Facebook Healthy Stuff E8

On the way from Dalston to Black Cat Cafe is this super little cafe and shop with seating inside and out. Co-owner Marina trained as a nutritional therapist at the Institute for Optimum Nutrition and previously managed a busy central London health shop, while Benny has worked in various cafes, bars and restaurants around Hackney, and they really know how to make a cafe and shop both welcoming and super-healthy.

Cafe mains £5-£6.50 such as falafel salad, basil tofu avocado sandwich on sourdough bread from E5 Bakehouse. Soup. Homemade granola with berries and soya yogurt £4. Vegan cakes £3-£3.30 such as carrot and walnut, choc chip sandwich, berry and lime drizzle.

Fruit and veg juices £3.75 made to order. Smoothies. Tea and coffees £1.70-£2.70, they have almond and coconut milks.

Children welcome. Outside seating, dogs welcome.

The shop sells organic fruit & veg, rye and gluten-free bread, and staples you don't find in regular shops such as mueslis, nut butters, plant milks, Japanese foods, lots of teas, raw chocs and energy bars. In the fridge are fresh saeurkraut, sausages, tofu, tempeh, sprouts, soya yogurts. Raw and superfoods. Booja Booja and raw chocolates.

Bodycare by Faith in Nature., Green People Urtekram, Dr Bronner, Weleda. Baby stuff Supplements including some Biocare/Vogel Herbal remedies. Aromatherapy.

Cleaning by Ecover and Bio-D and refills, Libby Chan probiotic cleaner, soap nuts. Brita cartridges and recycling.

For vegan Sunday roast in a pub, try **The Railway Tavern** at 2 St Jude Street N16 8JT, or **Farr's School of Dancing** (yes that is a pub!) at 17-19 Dalston Lane E8 3DF.

Dalston Curve Garden, opposite Dalston Junction overground, is the area's best kept secret. and free to enter, the perfect oasis for a quiet meetup with friends or catch up on your reading or writing. There are trees, outdoor and covered tables, some with floppy sofas, a cafe inside the entrance selling vegan soup and soft drinks, and right down the end a playground. Open every day 11.00-19.00, F-Sa till 22.00.

- dalstongarden.org

For take-away vegan pizza, **Voodoo Ray's** at 95 Kingsland High Street E8 2PB.

Holland & Barrett Dalston
Health food shop

- Unit 2B, Kingsland Shopping Centre, Dalston E8 2LX
- 020 7923 9113
- M-Sa 9.00-19.00, Su 11.00-17.00
- Dalston Kingland, Dalston Junction

Health food store near Ridley Road market. Take-away Jamaican, veg and Cornish pasties. Soya cheese and ice-cream. Frozen pasties, soysage rolls, porkless pies.

Harvest E8
Omnivorous cafe & wholefood shop

- 130-132 Kingsland High St E8 2NS
- 020 7254 9711
- M-Sa 07.00-22.00, Su 09.00-21.00
- Dalston Kingsland
- facebook.com/Harvest.E8

Big wholefood store opened 2013 with a cafe at the front with juices, cappuccino, sandwiches and at least 10 vegan cakes. Lots of organic and Fairtrade products.

Another branch in Stoke Newington.

Haggerston Grocer
Omnivorous wholefoods shop and grocer

- 197-199 Haggerston Road E8 4HU (go past overground station to end of Lee Street and turn right, follow round past the chemist)
- 07725 889 574
- M-Th 07.30-22.00, F-Sa 07.30-23.00, Su 08.00-22.30
- Haggerston overground

New shop north of the canal, open long hours, with a good range of wholefoods, including Sojade yogurts, tofu, Taifun sausages, plus bread, fruit and veg. We love the Italian antipasti in jars for £2 such as garlic cloves, garlic pieces (great for making bruschetta) and artichoke hearts. Vegan chocolate bars including Vego, Blackfriars flapjacks. They also sell mainstream household products and all kinds of beer and other alcohol.

Ridley Road Market
Fruit & veg market

- Ridley Rd, E8, off Kingsland High St
- M-Sa 9.00-17.00, Su closed
- Dalston Kingsland (opposite)
- hackney.gov.uk/ridley-road-market. htm

This is yer genuine great value East End street market with bustling fruit and veg stalls, some Caribbean food and household goods. Lots of bowls of fruit for a quid.

There is sometimes a falafel stall.

TFC Dalston
Omnivorous Mediterranean supermarket

- 89 Ridley Road E8 2NP
- 020 7254 6754
- M-Sa 08.00-21.00, Su 08.30-21.00
- Dalston Kingsland, Hackney Downs
- tfcsupermarkets.com/

Right at the back end of Ridley Road market, we like this place for bargain huge bags of dry beans and lentils, olives and tubs of tahini.

Queen's Deli
Omnivorous deli and coffee shop

- 349 Queensbridge Road E8 3LG (between Richmond Rd and Mapledene Rd)
- 020 7254 0056
- M-Su 07.00-20.00
- Haggerston
- facebook.com/queensdeli349

Coffee shop that sells some wholefoods.

GREEN STREET

and High Street North

Green Street E7, where the tube station is Upton Park, is like a more multicultural Southall or Brick Lane, full of Asian shops run by Sikhs, Muslims, Hindus, Buddhists, even Hare Krishnas, selling henna, incense, clothes and with some veggie restaurants.

Vijay's Chawalla
Vegetaria south Indian restaurant

- 268-270 Green Street E7 8LF
- 020 8470 3535
- M-Su 11.00-21.00
- Upton Park
- vijayschawalla.co.uk

South Indian, Gujarati and Punjabi food. Really good and vegan-friendly, with vegan items marked on the menu and unlike many Indian places they have vegan desserts. It's the favourite restaurant of vegan tv presenter and poet Benjamin Zephaniah. Eat for around £10 a head.

Starters £2.50-£4.50 include unusual ones such as spicy masala potato chips garnished with lime juice, cassava chips with tamarind chutney. Dish of the day £5-£7. Uthapam and dosas £5.50-£6.50. Curries £4-£5.50, rice £3-£4.50, breads £2.50-£3. Thalis £7.50-£9.50. Vegan desserts made from gram flour and sugar such as jelabi, gulab jamun. Soft drinks £1.5, juices £3, tea and coffee £1.50. No alcohol. Visa, MC over £5. Children welcome, high chairs.

Shinde's
Vegetarian Indian restaurant

- 302 Green Street E7 8LF (near Plashet Road, next to Barclays Bank)
- 020 3598 5474
- M-Su 10.00-22.00
- shindes.com
  Facebook Shinde's Pure Veg

New restaurant that opened just before we went to press. Punjabi, South Indian chaat, Indo-Chinese and Tandoori cuisine. It didn't look too vegan-friendly with lots of paneer cheese dishes, even in the £8 thali. Masala dosa £5.

City Sweet Centre
Vegetarian Indian cafe, take-away & sweets

- 510-512 Romford Rd E7 8AF
- 020 8472 5459
- W-M 10.00-19.00, Tu closed
- Bus 25, 86 Stratford 10mins
- citysweetcentre.com/

The best sweet shop in the area for vegans, with ladhu, jelabi, bundi, all made on the premises. Mostly take-away with a few seats.

Savouries, chaats, bhel puri, bhajias. Samosas 50p. At weekends curries for £3.50 with pooris. Take-away box of curry £3.80.

Ambala
Vegetarian Indian sweet shop

- 104 Green Street, E7 8JG
- 020 8586 9186
- M-Su 09.00-21.00
- ambalafoods.com

Indian sweets and savouries to take away.

Green Village
Vegetarian greengrocer & Indian grocer

- 10 Carlton Terrace, Green St E7 8LH
- 020 8503 4809
- M-Su 08.00-20.00

Freezers with jumbo boxes of samosas, breads and exotic veg.

Patco
Vegetarian grocer & greengrocer

- 374 Romford Road E7 8BS
- 020-8552 7314
- M-Sa 10.00-19.45, Su 10.30-16.00
- Woodgrange Park or Forest Gate BR

First Asian shop in east London, since 1962. Lots of frozen Indian foods, savouries, papaya, plantain, concentrated papaya juice, pulses, spices, curry paste, pickles.

Holland & Barrett, Upton Park
Health food shop

- 354/356 Green Street E13 9AP
- 020 3659 6879
- M-Sa 9.00-19.00 Su 11.00-18.00

Fridge and freezer.

Chawalla

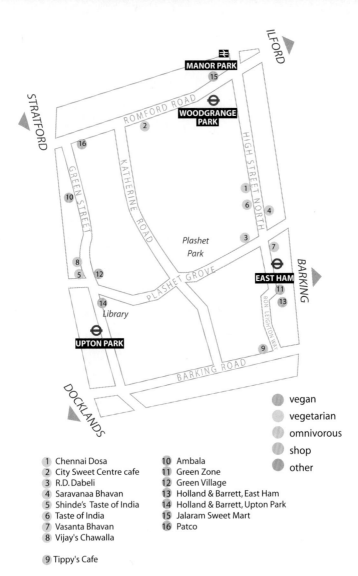

ILFORD

MANOR PARK

STRATFORD

ROMFORD ROAD

WOODGRANGE PARK

HIGH STREET NORTH

GREEN STREET

KATHERINE ROAD

Plashet Park

BARKING

EAST HAM

PLASHET GROVE

RON LEIGHTON WAY

Library

UPTON PARK

BARKING ROAD

DOCKLANDS

- vegan
- vegetarian
- omnivorous
- shop
- other

1 Chennai Dosa
2 City Sweet Centre cafe
3 R.D. Dabeli
4 Saravanaa Bhavan
5 Shinde's Taste of India
6 Taste of India
7 Vasanta Bhavan
8 Vijay's Chawalla

9 Tippy's Cafe

10 Ambala
11 Green Zone
12 Green Village
13 Holland & Barrett, East Ham
14 Holland & Barrett, Upton Park
15 Jalaram Sweet Mart
16 Patco

HIGH ST NORTH

High Street North E12 is packed with south Indian and Sri Lankan restaurants and shops, many of them vegetarian.

Taste of India
Vegetarian south Indian restaurant

- 293-295 High Street North E12 6SL (corner Byron Road)
- 020 8472 9779
- M-Su 08.30-22.30
- East Ham
- tasteofindia.asia

Big restaurant (170 seats) opposite Saravanaa Bhavan and the Sai Baba centre. South Indian and some north Indian food, over 130 main menu items and 20 desserts including vegan. Glass topped tables and some American diner style booths. Relaxed, calm ambience.

Mon-Fri (not bank holidays) till 10.30am breakfast buffet £5.25 includes idli, medu vada, poori/bhajia, pongal, semiya kichadi, dosas, uttappam, chutney, tea or coffee.

Over 30 starters, salads, soups £1.90-3.80 include Manchurian mushrooms.

20 gravies (curries) £3.80-3.95. 25 kinds of dosa and uttapam lentil pancake £2.30-3.70. Tandoori dishes £4.75. Over 30 varieties of rice, noodles and breads £1.20-3.95.

Taste of India special meal £7.50 with chappatis, poori, rice, curries and dessert. Punjabi thali: £7.90 with chappatis, curries and dessert.

Most desserts £2-3.95 all with ice-cream, vegan options are fruit salad or halva made with almonds, wheat or asoha (mung dhal) or dry fruits.

Soft drinks 80p-£1. Shakes and freshly squeezed juices (no ice added) £2.50-£3. Coffee £1-2. Teas £1-£2.25. Kumbakonam filter coffee. No soya milk.

Party area for 30 people. Free delivery over £30 within 2 miles. Catering up to 1,000 people.

Children welcome welcome, high chairs. No alcohol. Free parking after 6.30pm & Sun. MC, Visa over £10.

Chennai Dosa
Vegetarian South Indian restaurant

- 339 High Street North E12 6PQ
- 020 7998 0370
- M-Su 09.00-22.30
- East Ham
- chennaidosa.com

The all day buffet here is fantastic value. Breakfast buffet until 11.30am £3.99 with dosa, mini uttapams, porri, potato masala, idli, vada, other savouries and a sweet. Lunch and dinner buffet all day from 12.00 £4.99 with chappati, rice, dal, mixed vega korma, salad, sweet and more.

The a la carte menu has over 100 items with prices as low as anywhere in London, for example rasam tamarind soup 95p; starters 45p-£3.65; dosas, uttapam and curries £1.99-3.25; plain rice £1.60; tomato, lemon, tamarind or coconut rice £2.60; veg biryani £3.99; cashew nut pilau £3.45.

Desserts 80p-£1.60 but not vegan. Juices £1.60. Tea and coffee 90p-£1.25. No alcohol. Children welcome, high chairs. Cash only.

R.D. Dabeli
Vegetarian Gujarati fast food cafe & take-away

- 239 Plashet Road E13 0QU
- 07956 550 004
- M-Su 11.00-21.30
- East Ham
- facebook.com/pg/R.D.Dabeli

Vinod and his wife, from Bhuj in the Kutch district of Gujarat, serve up street food snacks £1.50-£2 each like bhelpuri, pani puri, vada pav, and dabeli which is a burge bun filled with chutney, mashed potato anc chaat served warm.

Vasanta Bhavan
Indian Vegetarian restaurant

- 206 High Street North E6 2JA (junction Sibley Grove)
- 020 8475 8986
- M-Su 09.00-22.30
- East Ham (right next to it)
- thevasantabhavan.com

Fantastic value south Indian restaurant with young staff from Chennai. Over 100 items on the menu. Starters, dosas, utthappam, curries and Chinese dishes £1.40-£3.40. Fri-Sun lunch buffet 12.30-16.30 £5.50. Mini meal set lunch every day 11.00-17.00 £4.50. Butter ghee used in some dishes, can substitute oil for vegans, but no vegan desserts.

Tea 70p, coffee £1, no soya milk. No alcohol. Children welcome, high chairs. Party hall for functions.

Saravanaa Bhavan East Ham
Vegetarian South Indian restaurant

- 300 High Street North E12 6SA (corner Byron Avenue)
- 020 8552 4677
- M-Su 09.00-23.00
- East Ham
- saravanabhavan.co.uk
  menu at saravanabhavan.com

Very good vegetarian restaurant with a sweet shop at the front, part of a UK and international chain, with branches in Ilford,

Wembley, Southall. It's next door to the UK headquarters of the Sai Baba organisation.

Starters £2.45-3.95 including Chinese items such as chili mushroom.

Main courses include of course dosas £2.45 to £4.25 for a tailor made one with your choice of three fillings. South Indian meal £6.95 with curries, rice, salad, side dish, chappathi or poori and sweet. North Indian thali £7.95 with soup, salad, pulao, 3 side dishes, dal, kattol, fried papad, 3 chappathis and sweet. Business meal £4.25.

Vegans will be pleased that desserts £1.50-£3.95 as well as fruit salad include two not on the menu, halva or ladu.

Juices £2.75. Fizzy drinks 95p. Tea or coffee £1, no soya milk. No alcohol and you can't bring it in. Children welcome, high chairs.

Tippy's Cafe
Omnivorous Thai/English cafe and take-away

- 291 Barking Road E6 1LB (between Ron Leighton Way and Hartley Ave, opposite Bartle Ave)
- 020 8552 4227
- M-Sa 11.00-22.00, Sun/BH closed
- East Ham
- tippyscafe.co.uk

For a change from Indian food, there is a separate Thai vegetarian menu. Starters £3.50 such as tempura veg, spring rolls, spicy corn fritters, to fu tod fried beancurd with ground peanuts and sweet chili sauce, soups £3.95. 13 mains £4.95 including red, green (the most popular), yellow or jungle curry with veg or tofu, Thai spicy rice or noodles with lots of veg, stir-fried aubergine, salt and chili cauliflower, stir-fry tofu with cashew nuts. Rice and noodles £1.80-£3.

Desserts £2-3.50 such as banana cooked in coconut milk, lychees, banana fritters. Hot and cold drinks 70p-£1. Bring your own wine £1.50 bottle, off-licence two doors down.

Children welcome, high chairs.

Green Zone
Grocer and greengrocer

- 156 High Street North E6 2HT
- 020 8471 0616
- M-Su 08.00-20.00
- East Ham

Old fashioned greengrocer plus lots of spcies and dried pulses.

Jalaram Sweet Mart
Vegetarian Gujarati Indian take-away & sweets

- 649 Romford Road, E12 5AD
- 020 8553 0894
- Tu-Su 9.00-20.00, M closed
- Woodgrange Park

Good value take-away curries, savouries and sweets.w

Holland & Barrett, East Ham
Health food shop

- 133a High Street North E6 1HZ
- 020 8552 6090
  M-Sa 9.00-19.00 Su 11.00-18.00

Big shop with fridge and freezer.

HACKNEY

Hackney, a pleasant bike ride or walk along the canal from Islington, is an ethnically diverse area, with a beautiful mix of cultures. It's also the best value place in inner London, and easy to get to by tube since the opening of an overground line from Highbury & Islington down to Whitechapel and beyond. Several vegan cafes have recently opened, and a (roughly) monthly **vegan market** in HackneyCentral.

In Hackney Central, alternative types flock to **Black Cat** vegan cafe for Sunday brunch and one of London's best displays of vegan cake and cheesecake.

Temple of Hackney was the UK's first vegan "fried chick'n" shop.

WAVE (We Are Vegan Everything) is a gorgeous new tucked-away cafe.

Between these three trailblazing iconic vegan venues lies **Palm Vaults**, London's prettiest vegetarian cafe.

Hackney Fresh is one of the best stocked independent wholefood stores with lots of unusual and hard to find items. While at **Bulk Market** you can fill your own bags then head to **Saint Pizza**..

This chapter got so huge with all the new openings, we split it into five. For the east side of Hackney see Homerton & Hackney Wick. North side is Lower Clapton. West side is Dalston & Haggerston. South side is London Fields & Broadway Market. Decide for yourself which side is da best side.

Hackney Vegan Village
Vegan street market

- Bohemia Place Market E8 1DU
- Monthly Sa-Su 11.00-18.00
- Hackney Central overground (opposite)
- Facebook Hackney Vegan Village
  bohemiaplacemarket.com
  plantbasedeventsco.com/events
  instagram.com/plantbasedeventsco

In summer 2019 vegan entrepreneur JP McCarmack, aka Portobello Vegan (see West London), launched a big monthly vegan street market in Bohemia Place, home to Bulk Market and Saint Pizza, with up to 50 vegan stalls. We wait to see how often the event will run in the colder months.

The best of all things vegan, with food from naughty stacked burgers and loaded fries to raw, healthy wraps and summer salads. Drinks from tipples to healthy, and specialist traders like kombucha or CBD cold pressed juices.

Entertainment, artisanal traders and carbon positive products such as reusable toiletries, beauty, sustainable clothing, eco-jewellery.

Free entry. Check Facebook for latest details. See website for other weekend markets.

Black Cat

Vegan cafe-restaurant

🖝 76a Clarence Road E5 8HB (top of Mare Street)

☎ 020 8985 7091

🕐 M, W-F 10.00-21.00, Tu closed, Sa 11.00-21.00, Su 11.00-20.00

⊖ Hackney Central, Hackney Downs

🖈 blackcatcafe.co.uk
facebook.com/blackcathackney
twitter instagram @blackcathackney

Pogo vegan cafe transformed in 2013 into Black Cat co-op, beautifully redecorated with new wooden tables and a big picture window, a more professional restaurant feel, but still the same fantastic value. Tasty food with lots of new and healthy and fun options, and cakes people cross London for. Local art on the walls for sale. Favourite dishes are on every day, plus daily specials.

Weekday breakfasts till midday such as scramble on sourdough toast, crispy tempeh bacon and silken tofu omelette sandwich, croissants, Danish, sausage rolls. Weekend fry-up till 4pm £8.50 features beans, sausage, mushrooms, tofu scramble, wedges, toast, bacon.

Regular dishes £7.75-£9.50 include beef style seitan and soya mince burger with mayo, gherkins, tomato, served with chips and salad. BBQ tofu ciabatta sandwich with herby mayo and pickled onions. Chickpea flour pancake with roasted veg and fresh herbs, like a Spanish omelette. Veg curry with steamed rice, yogurt and a crunchy onion bhajia. Soya mince lasagne with red wine slow cooked. Lots of salads such as giant couscous with roasted veg, quinoa with pickled veg, Mexican bean salad.

Sourdough ciabatta sandwiches such as chickpea tuna, seitan steak with chimichurri sauce, corn crusted battered Chickun filled made from tofu and seitan. Also NY bagel with miso umeboshi cream cheese, salt roasted beetroot and carrots, capers, nori, dill on a hoagie roll.

Specials such as daily sandwiches, soups, salads, jerk tofu stew with rice, golden coconut tofu Thai curry, lentil shepherd's pie, sweet potato tagine, chickpea patties, seitan steaks, moussaka, 5-spice mince stew, pasta bake, burrito, chicken pot pie, Caribbean fishless stew with fried plantain.

Soups on rotation such as butternut squash with sweet potato and coconut, roasted red pepper and tomato, cheezy broccoli, rustic minestrone with butter beans, leek and potato, Turkish style red lentil.

Desserts dazzle including croissants and cakes such as Rocky Road with chocolate, marshmallows and digestive biscuits, cheesecake, cinnamon buns. Special guest cakes from Manna such as almond orange polenta cake. Ice-cream and squirty cream. You can order a whole cake. Sweet crêpe with ice cream £5.50.

Milkshakes £3.75. Vegan ice-cream. Hot drinks £1.50-£3 including teas, pot of tea, coffees, cappuccino, latte, hot choc (add marshmallows 50p). Kombucha. Soft drinks.

Bring your own alcohol, off-license a few doors down, free corkage. Lots of gluten-free. Child-friendly, high chair, baby changing table. Dogs welcome. Free WiFi.

Look out for special Tuesday events, fundraisers and benefits or organise your own. Shop section with chocolate bars, Vego bars ("cheapest in London") and spread, Black Cat bags and T-shirts. Black Cat also run the kitchen at Roadtrip & The Workshop pub at 243 Old Street EC1V 9EY, see Shoreditch chapter.

WAVE (We Are Vegan Everything)
Vegan cafe

- 📍 11 Dispensary Lane E8 1FT (down the side of Santander, at the top of Mare Street, near Holland & Barrett)
- ☎ 07734 253 401
- 🕐 M-F 9.00-17.00, Sa 9.00-18.00, Su 10.00-16.00
- ⊖ Hackney Central overground
- ▸ wearevaganeverything.com
  facebook.com/wearevaganeverything
  instagram we_are_vegan_everything

Gorgeous vegan cafe down a lane off the pedestrian bit at the top of Mare Street, with a softer feel than others and lots of outdoor seating in summer.

Bircher or chia bowl £5. Three plump gluten-free pancakes stack £9 such as blueberry topped with coulis, banana, Oatly cream or ice cream, cinnamon, coconut sugar and syrup. Or try coconut bak'n pancakes. Bowls £7.80 such as Blue Spirulina with banana, kale, almond milk, pineapple, coconut, almonds, pumpkin seeds, chia, flax, banana chips, blueberries, kiwi.

Brekkie bowl £12.50 starring organic turmeric scrambled tofu with chives and black salt, basil roasted plum tomatoes, walnuts, smoky aubergine, avocado, chilli flakes, mixed seeds and rocket.

On the counter £4-£7.20 baked mushroom sausage roll; toastie of the day such as mushrooms with cream cheese, cashew pesto, mixed seeds; carrot "salmon" bagel with cream cheese and watercress;

Sourdough open sandwiches £7.20-£10.20 such as avo and Marmite; tomato basil and hummus; tofu chive scramble with smoked aubergine rashers; mushrooms and walnuts

Top up anything for £1-£2 with turmeric, chia, flax, protein powder, lucuma, spirulina, cacao, ginseng, goji, matcha, hemp, maca, reishi, wheatgrass.

Specials such as stuffed croissant £6. filled with cheese, roasted tomato, toasted and topped with rocket and mixed seeds; mac & cheese £9 with broccoli, roasted tomatoes, crispy onions, crispy kale, coconut bak'n; spiralised courgetti £9 with cashew pesto, sundried tomatoes, walnuts, mixed seeds; coconation cauliflower and chickpea toastie £7.20.

Shakes and smoothies £6. Freakshakes £9.60.

Lots of cakes and pastries £3.50-£5 such as plain, almond or chocolate croissant, cupcakes, gluten-free brownies, cookies such as peanut butter with pb buttercream or raspberry jam filling, cheesecakes, raw slices and brownies. Energy balls £2.

Juices £6, superfood shots £3. Booch kombucha on tap £3..

Hot drinks £1.50-£4.50 include teas, coffees, Himalayan salted cofffee, turmerica and cacao, matcha latte, chai, peanut butter coffee, bulletproof coffee, any of them iced for 50p more.

Take-away items around £1 less. Children welcome, high chairs. Dogs welcome.

Stuffed Croissant
£6

Temple of Hackney
Vegan fried chick'n cafe & take-away

- 🐓 5 Morning Lane E9 6NA (just off Mare Street)
- 📞 Way too busy to chat
- 🕐 M-Sa 12.00-21.00, Su 12.00-18.00
- ⊖ Hackney Central overground
- ⬆ templeofseitan.co.uk
  facebook.com/templeofseitan

This runaway success of a vegan startup opened in January 2017, serving seitan burgers, chick'n wingz and fries. Selling out by 4pm in the early days, the original four staff rapidly expanded to 13 and they added another kitchen to handle overwhelming demand as salivating vegans from across London flocked in for a fun fast food fix of fake fried fowl.

£6 gets you a main such as Temple Burger with bacon, cheese, pickles and ranch mayo; Spicy Burger with jalapeños, hot sauce, cheese, coleslaw and chipotle mayo. Two chunky wingz or two fillet pieces £5. Add fries or coleslaw for £2-£3, gravy £1. Or try mac n' cheez £5, popcorn bites £4. Standalone temple fries or coleslaw £3.

Desserts £3 from the Peanut Butter Bakery such as vanilla maple and chai donuts or chocolate tart.

Canned drinks include Karma cola, Lemony lemonade, Gingerella ginger ale, and bottled water.It gets busy so be prepared to queue for a few minutes, like at any other fast food place. There are tables out front. They have been so fun-omenally successful that another bigger branch with indoor seating opened by the canal between Kings Cross and Camden

Saint Pizza at ABQ
Vegan pizzeria in cocktail bar

- 18 Bohemia Place (in the garden behind ABQ cocktail bar) E8 1DU)
- 020 3488 1678
- M-Tu closed, W-F 17.00-23.30, Sa 15.00-23.30, Su 15.00-21.30
- Hackney Central overground
- abqlondon.com/saint-pizza
  facebook.com/abqlondon

Wacky mad scientist style molecular cocktail bar decked out as a colourful chemistry lab, part of it in an RV bus themed on *Breaking Bad*. There are two floors, three bars and a vegan pizzeria. Don a bright Hazmat boiler suit to create cocktails using huge syringes and the menu instructions. You need not be a chemist or mixologist, just have a sense of fun. Bbook the full cocktail chemistry experience for £36 per person which gets you 1 hour 45 minutes in the RV, welcome drinks, and cooking two cocktails. Or just drop in and pay as you go.

Or simply chill at the back with vegan pizza made to order in a proper pizza oven, probably a good idea to book though. Sourdough bases, gluten-free options. Soya or coconut cheeses. 10 kinds of pizzas £7-£11 include marga, mushroom, spicy, Calabria with bean Nduja salami, Carne with sausage and salami, Los Pollos with vegan chicken, Allo palak with spinach and cumin, Regi no cheese with roast potatoes and rosemary. Side and full meal salads £3.50-£8.50, the big one has vegan sausage and chicken. Dips £1.50, roasted nuts or olives £3.50.

Beers £5, bar cocktails £9.50. Natural wines £5 glass, £22 bottle. Soft drinks £2.50-£4. No bookings Saturday, walk ins only. Deliveroo, Uber Eats.

Palm Vaults
Vegetarian cafe

- 411 Mare St E8 1HY (right at the top)
- (07511 445 104
- W-F 08.30-16.30, Sa 10.00-17.30, Su 10.00-17.00
- Hackney Central, Hackney Downs
- palmvaults.com
  facebook.com/palmvaults
  instagram.com/palmvaults

New healthy cafe opened 2016. Called "London's most Instagrammable cafe", they are big on pastels interior decor, house plants and brightly coloured smoothies.

Juices £4.20 such as Green Goddess with kale, spinach, apple, cucumber, ginger and lime. Smoothies £6 are all vegan, using cashew, oat, coconut, soya, rice or almond milk.

Breakfast smoothie bowls £6.50 are all vegan such as raw cacao, or acai berry. Chia pudding £5.50.

Toasties £5.50 such as peanut butter jelly. Smashed avocado on sourdough toast £6.50 with chilli omega seeds and herbs, add toppings for £1-£1.50 such as turmeric sauerkraut, smokey coconut, sundried tomatoes, pomegranate with mint. Toasted banana bread £4.50.

Rose button cakes £3.50. Vegan banana bread with Coyo coconut yogurt £4.50.

Dogs welcome.

Sutton & Sons, Hackney
Omnivorous fish n chip shop

- 218 Grahjam Road E8 1BP
- 020 3645 1801
- Su-Th 12.00-22.00, F-Sa 12.00-22.30
- Hackney Central
- instagram.com/suttonandsonsvegan
  suttonandsons.co.uk

After the success of the vegan menu at their Stoke Newington branch, owner Danny Sutton expanded it to the Hackney Central and Islington branches. The fish fillet is made from tofu or banana blossom flour, popular in Asian cooking, marinated overnight in seaweed and samphire, then spiced with cumin and garlic powder, and fried in egg-free batter and groundnut oil.

For starters: Classic prawn cocktail £5.95, fish cake £3.95, onion rings £3.50, battered calamari strips £5.95.

Mains £8.50-£8.95: Vish and chips; fish or no bull or no chicken burger and chips; scampi and chips; seitan steak and ale pie and mash with onion gravy; and this is the only branch of their three to do seitan doner kebab. Battered or grilled sausage and chips £6.95.

Sides 85p-£3.95 include chips, fries, sweet potato fries, onion gravy, curry sauce; pickled onion, gherkin, mushy or garden peas, seasonal salad, pickles.

Black Milq ice cream £2.95, two scoops £5. Soft drinks £2.25-£2.95 include cola, ginger beer, lemonade, Fentimans. Bottled beers from £3.95, pint of Guiness £4.95. Wine £4.75 medium glass, £16.50 bottle. Teas £1.95, coffee £2.25.

Service charge not included. Cash only.

Hackney Fresh
Wholefood shop & vegetarian take-away

🚋 334 Mare Street E8 1HA (in front of Tesco, opposite Graham Road)

📞 020 8510 0110

🕐 M-F 07.00-21.00, Sa 08.00-21.00, Su 10.00-20.00

⊖ Hackney Central

↖ hackneyfresh.co.uk
facebook.com/hackneyfresh

One of the best stocked wholefood stores in London, with lots of unusual brands, right in the heart of Hackney by the railway bridge and bus station.

As well as all the usual wholefood store goodies, they have fruit and veg, daily bread deliveries by the nearby E5 Bakehouse, lots of fridges and freezers, drinks and hot food to take away, wines including vegan ones, bodycare, cleaning products. They are pecialists in Oriental organic foods. Lots of local suppliers including bakeries, cosmetics, kobucha.

Hot food such as brown rice and korma £5.99, soups £2.99. Vegan croissants in plain £1.50, almond, and au chocolat £2. Artisan coffees £1.60-£2 with Oatly or almond milk.

Fridges contain vegan cheeses including Sheese and Violife, vegpots, chia pots, yogurts. Terra Vegane bacon, ham, chorizo, beef, black bean burgers. Tofurky, Taifun, vegan feta, spreads, tempeh, mayo, eggless fresh pasta, Clive's Pies, Amy's Kitchen, Fry's. Lots of brands of kombucha including their own brew, coffee cartons to go and other drinks

A whole upright freezer packed with London's best choice of vegan ice-cream by Almond Dream, Booja Booja, Coyo, Coconuts, Coconut Collatorative, Jollyum, Lily & Hanna, Swedish Glace, Yee Kwan matcha green tea sorbet, Frill frozen smoothies, and frozen fruit including acai for making smoothies at home.

Many unusual types of pasta made from hemp, flax, green pea, brown bean, black bean spaghetti, and Really Healthy Pasta sprouted spelt lasagne.

The baking section has some unusual flours like quinoa, almond, coconut, sesame, peanut. Egg-free omelette mix. Unusual nut butters such as almond with maca. Many types of granola, crackers, energy bars, vegan and raw chocolate. Stacks of teas, even for babies. Superfood powders. Bragg apple cider vinegar.

Supplements by Viridian, Sogar, Biocare. Vogel remedies. Aromatherapy. Ainsworth tinctures and Weleda homeopathy. Bach flower remedies. Nature's Answer alcohol-free plant tinctures.

All organic bodycare by Akin, Avalon Organics, Faith in Nature, Green People, Jason, Sukin, Weleda, and a whole cabinet of Lavera with testers. Feminine hygiene by Natracare and Organic. Everything for babies.

Vegan T-shirts and soy wax candles made by the owner. Ecover refills. Half price hargains area at the back.

HOW IT WORKS

BYO
BYO (Bring Your Own) containers to the shop or purchase a reusable one

TARE
Weigh your containers and take a note of the weight, so it can be deducted at the till

REFILL
Fill your container with any bulk item

PAY
Take your shopping to the till to pay. The weight of your containers will be deducted and you will pay only for the refills.

FOR LIQUIDS

BYO
BYO (Bring Your Own) bottles to the store or purchase a reusable one to refill.

CHECK THE SIZE
We do liquids by volume (ml) and not by weight, so no need to tare it on the scale! Just check the size of your bottle first

REFILL
Refill your bottle with any bulk liquid. You can refill full or half bottle

PAY
Just take your refilled bottles to the till to pay

Bulk Market
Vegetarian zero waste wholefood shop

- 🐀 6 Bohemia Pl, E8 1DU
- 🕐 M closed, Tu-Sa 10.00-19.00, Su 11.00-17.00
- ⊖ Hackney Central overground
- ➤ bulkmarket.uk
  facebook.com/bulkmarketuk

Ingrid Caldironi launched Hackney's first plastic-free shop as a popup in Dalston in 2017, then here as a crowdfunded permanent shop in December 2018 in a railway arch., benefiting from the "Attenborough Effect" inspiring consumers to cut back on plastic after watching *Blue Planet*.

Bring your own jars, bags and boxes, or use the ones donated by customers and shops. 97% organic. Refill everything! Refuse, reduce, reuse, recycle, rot (compost), using the principles of the Circular Economy.

Whole grains, flours, oils and vinegars, pasta, nuts and seeds, herbs and spices, loose leaf teas, specialty coffees, dried fruits, breakfast cereals, bakery goods, fruit and vegetables, nutritional yeast, frozen goods, chocolate. There's even a nut grinder to make peanut butter. Bread from Better Health Bakery in Hackney. Plant mylks by the MylkMan, with no Tetrapaks!

Beer and wine, gin, kombucha.

Natural beauty ingredients, essential oils

Soap, shampoo, bamboo toothbrushes. Cleaning products. Recycled toilet paper.

Free tap water. They sell stainless steel water bottles, travel cutlery and cotton bags.

Full product list on their website.

Holland & Barrett, Hackney
Health food shop

- 🐀 376 Mare Street, Hackney E8 1HR (near Palm Vaults
- 📞 020 8985 2906
- 🕐 M-Sa 9.00-17.30. Su 11.00-17.00
- ⊖ Hackney Central overground

Freezer and fridge.

HOMERTON

and Hackney Wick

The eastern part of Hackney, on the north side of Victoria Park, has some terrific new vegan venues.

The Spread Eagle pub has been taken over by street food heroes **Club Mexicana**, who have made the food, all the booze and even the furniture vegan.

It's well worth a stroll across the river Lea to the very pretty waterside **Mother** vegan cafe-restaurant. There are free shuttle buses to and from **Stratford** shopping centre.

In Hackney Wick, easily reached from Hackney Central by bus 236, **The Old Baths Cafe** is London's only Greek vegan cafe, with a garden out back.

Vivid Reality is London's first virtual reality gaming centre with a vegan cafe.

At the top end of Well Street are **The Grand Howl** daytime vegetarian cafe and two wholefood stores. Except that one of them was taken over in 2019 and turned into **Plant Based Supermarket**. Nearby **I Will Kill Again** is a biker coffee cafe that specialises in vegan food.

Kingfisher chip shop, opposite the Spread Eagle, has an impressive vegan menu.

For more vegan cafes, Lower Clapton is at the western end of Homerton High Street, London Fields at the south end of Well Street, and Hackney Central between these.

The Spread Eagle
Vegan food pub

- 224 Homerton High Street E9 6AS
- 020 8985 0400
- Pub open M-Th 16.00-23.00, F 16.00-02.00, Sa 12.00-02.00, Su 12.00-23.00.
  Food W-F 17.00-22.00, Sa 12.00-22.00, Su 12.00-21.00, kitchen closed M-Tu
- Homerton
- thespreadeaglelondon.co.uk
  facebook.com/thespreadeaglelondon
  clubmexicana.com
  facebook.com/clubmexicana

In January 2018 a traditional East End food pub, founded in 1752, was 100% veganized by friends Sherri-Lee Estabrook and Luke McLaughlin, together with chef Meriel Armitage of vegan street food taco maestros Club Mexicana. And by 100% vegan they mean not just the food, but all the drinks, and any leather (animal skin) fixtures and fittings like seats have been replaced with plant-based and sourced sustainably where possible.

You can eat at wooden tables all around the main pub, which has the bar in the middle, or in the comfy sofas section at the back with low tables, or out back in their beer garden.

The menu is built tapas style from small

plates and includes what looks and tastes like a fried chicken burger £9, beer battered tofish and chips £9, tacos (two for £7, three £10) filled with tofish or jackfruit or marinated fake pork, popcorn chick'n salad £9.50. Pan seared scallops £6 (made from oyster mushrooms poached in garlic oil), triple fried potatoes £4, tortilla chips with salsa and guacamole £5.

There are even beer pairing suggestions £6-£7: deep fried cheeze with Pacifico beer, chick'n wings with Five Point Pale, chorizo quesadilla with Camden Hells.

For dessert £5 there is vegan ice-cream rolled in cornflakes and deep fried, served with chilli-chocolate sauce.

Rotating cask ales are specially brewed vegan for them without the addition of finings, meaning this is the only pub where you can get vegan versions of some. 14 draught lines include cult brands such as Beavertown Gamma Ray and Old Blue Last lager.

Small batch wines £4.90-£7.60 medium glass, £6.50-£9.70 large. Bottle of house wine £19.

Classic cocktails with a vegan twist, using aqua faba (chickpea water) to replace egg white in sours.

DJs Friday and Saturday 11pm-2am

Families and dogs welcome, they even have water bowls and vegan dog treats. They can host parties of all sizes. Occasional events such as quizzes.

You can also enjoy Club Mexicana food at Shoreditch Dinerama Th-Su from noon till late.

The Old Baths Café
Vegetarian Greek organic cafe and food company

☞ 80 Eastway, Hackney Wick E9 5JH

☏ 07429 099 888

🕒 M-Th 08.00-15.00, F 08.00-16.00, Sa-Su 9.00-16.00

⊖ Hackney Wick overground 7min walk. Bus 236, 276, 388 (all stop outside), 26, 30, 488.

🖉 theoldbaths.co.uk
gaiapulses.com
instagram.com/gaiapulses
facebook.com/gaiapulses

Greek entrepreneur Yolanda Antonopoulou and her team create healthy feel-good dishes inspired by traditional vegan Greek cooking, with many ingredients from the family farm in Greece. As we write, they are about to transition to all vegan.

The theme of the place is pulses, and Gaia Pulses ("Earth is alive") is the in-house food company that supplies old-school Greek dishes with beans and lentils, packed with protein and fibre, distributed in compostable packaging to some independent retailers across London.

Breakfast/brunch £6-£8.50 till 12.30 includes Gaia granola with almond milk; brown tahini on sourdough with banana, grape molasses and seeds; Vegan Brunch with roasted homemade butterbeans, red pepper, zesty mushrooms, Greek olives, sauerkraut, avocado, spinach, sourdough.

All day lunch starters £3-£6 such as Greek olives and homemade pickles, hummus and pitta, Cretan Dakos artisanal crispy barley bread with tomato, avocado and vegan feta.

Greek stew of the day £6.50, which could be butter beans with veggies, zesty yellow lentil mash with caramelised onion, smoky giant beans with red pepper and sundried tomato, or Green lentil and quinoa with veg. Extra toppings £2.50 such as avocado, vegan feta, or olives and pickles.

Warm falafel wrap £7 made with lentil and chickpea keftedes balls, with side salad £8.50. Greek salad £8 with lots of veggies, barley rusk and vegan feta.

Gaia Mezze £10 features stew of the day, salad, keftedes, pita, hummus, olives and pickles; also daily specials.

Cakes £2.80-£3.50, more vegan ones are being introduced. Also traditional Greek fruit preserve made by Yolanda's mum in Greece.

Pots of Greek medicinal wild herbal teas, Greek coffees cold and hot, turmeric latte, unsweetened real cacao. Organic fruit smoothies £5. Locally made kombucha and soft drinks, all in recyclable materials.

Organic grape molasses as a sweetener, also available for sale.

Greek wines £5 medium glass. Volkan Greek beer from Santorini. Non-alcoholic local beer.

They sell wholefoods, homemade organic jams, organic olive oil, organic Greek lentils in bulk to cook at home.

Gluten-free options. Children welcome, high chairs. Dogs welcome. Private events and parties. Outside catering.

Large community garden at the back with seating. In the building are yoga classes, cinema evenings with dinner, photo and film studios for hire, gallery and meeting spaces.

MOTHER - Juice Works
Vegan cafe

☛ Unit 1, Canalside Here East, Hackney
Wick E20 3BS (between Victoria Park
& Stratford)

☏ kitchen@mother.works

🕐 M-Su 08.30-17.00 all year,
summer Th-Sa -20.00

⊖ Hackney Wick (8 mins walk)

↖ mother.works
facebook.com/motherjuiceworks

Gorgeous vegan cafe in the row of cafes
and bars in the 2012 Olympic press building
running alongside the River Lea. 10 minutes
walk from Victoria Park, 15 mins from the
Olympic Pool. 20 minutes walk from
Stratford Westfield shopping centre or take
the free shuttle bus.

All day breakfast £5.50-£12 such as
granola with fruits and goji, frozen açai
bowl, sourdough toast wtih avocado and
chilli flakes or peanut butter and banana,
smoked carrot salmon bagel with cashew
cream cheese, poached eggless eggs royale
with carrot salmon, eggless Benedict with
coconut bacon.

Lunch from 12pm £8-£10 adds Caesar
salad, juice pulp burger with nacho cheese,
BLT with coconut bacon on toasted
sourdough, loaded nachos with homemade
beans, burrito bowl with herb quinoa and
pineapple salsa; Mother Bowl with roast
sweet potato, quinoa tabouleh, purple slaw,
super green salad, beetroot hummus,
turmeric sauerkraut, mayo, seeds and
sprouts.

The counter is covered in cakes, flapjacks,
bars and pastries such as peach and
blackcurrant flapjack, sausage roll, banana
and peanut butter granola bar, caramel
slice, chocolate cake with fig, walnut and
carrot cake, energy balls.

Organic cold pressed raw juices £4.50, £8
for half litre, £14 litre, in glass bottle.
Smoothies £8 such as green, detox, berry,
peanut butter with maca, cookie dough.
Add protein £1. Hot drinks include matcha
or turmeric latte. Bottled beers in the
evening.

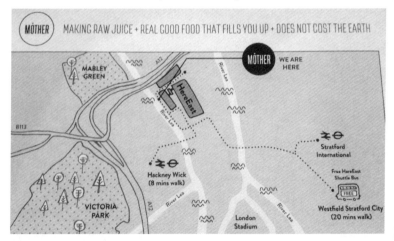

JUICE WORKS+PLANT BASED CAFE

REFUEL WITH
MOTHER
FRESH SMOOTHIES
JUICE
ENERGY

Vivid Reality
VR gaming lounge & vegan dessert bar

- 174 Homerton High Street E9 6AG
  (corner Mackintosh Lane)
- 020 8533 3811
- W-Th 15.00-23.00, F 13.00-23.00,
  Sa 11.00-23.00, 1.00-21.00, M-Tu
  closed
- Homerton overground (1 min walk)
- vividreality.london
  facebook.com/vividreality.london
  instagram vividreality.london

Welcome to London's virtual reality gaming lounge and vegan dessert bar. Play with six VR stations backed by super-charged gaming computers, with a choice of thrilling games and experiences available with every session you book including VR racing simulators.

Choose your time slot of 15, 30 or 60 minutes, prices start from £9.50 per person. Play solo or multiplayer with friends and switch between games and experiences as much as you like. You can also chill out on beanbags or sofas whilst playing on their 100 inch (250cm) gaming screen. This all happens in their cosy lounge, if you book a station in ther Lounge package then you gain access to their Playstation 4 with 4 controllers and over 4,000 retro games on their Old Skool Arcade System with consoles such as SNES, N64, Sega Mega Drive, Gameboy and more.

Love gaming? Grab a Gamers Club monthly unlimited pass which gives you access to play whenever you like, every weekend and after work. Also monthly offers and Gamers Club only content and events. Gift options for VR slots and Gamers Club subs too.

Blood sugar dropping or need an adrenaline rush? Refuel and chill out in their vegan cafe space upstairs. Waffles £5.50 such as biscoff madness, strawberry bliss or salted banoffee, extra toppings £1.50. Enjoy their best selling red velvet and white chocolate chip cookies £1.50 each. Four mini donuts for £5 in salted caramel, chocolate, or sugar and cinnamon.

Milkshakes from £4 in flavours including Biscoff Madness and Oreo.

You can hire the lounge for private events, such as a VR birthday gaming tournament with up to 6 people. FIFA, Mortal Kombat, Mario Kart, whatever your style, bring your competitors and they'll do the rest. More than 6 of you? Why not hire out the whole venue and have exclusive use of Vivid Reality? Book online and get ready to step into a reality more vivid than ever.

The Grand Howl
Vegetarian cafe

- 📞 214 Well St E9 6QT (Homerton end)
- ☎ 020 3659 9631
- 🕐 M-F 08.30-16.30 (16.00 in school holidays), Sa-Su 9.00-17.00
- 🚇 Homerton overground
- ➤ facebook.com/thegrandhowl

This regular cafe went vegetarian in October 2016. A combination of wood and bricks with a twist of industrial elements makes the space quite unique. Food served till 3pm.

Savoury items £4-£8.50 include granola with fruit compote, soy yoghurt, agave; Bircher muesli with soy yoghurt and fruit compote; pancakes with caramelised apple and strawberries; avocado and tofu scramble with toast; jalapeño, sweetcorn and mint yogurt fritters. Vegan toasties come in Mexican bean and cheddar; Vegemite and cheese; or aubergine, sundried tomato and cheese.

Vegan banana bread £2.50, more vegan cakes are planned.

Coffees £2-£2.80; Joe's organic tea £2; Redbush/Rooibos latte £2.80; Redbush apple cooler £3.50; iced coffee £2.90, Karma cola drinks £2 and grapefruit juice £2.80. Almond and soy milk.

High chairs. Wifi. Dogs welcome.

Tables inside and just seats outside.

I Will Kill Again
Omnivorous cafe

- 📞 Arch 216, 27a Ponsford Street, Homerton E9 6JU
- ☎ 020 3774 0131
- 🕐 Th-Su 10.00-16.30 or later, M-W closed
- 🚇 Homerton
- ➤ facebook.com/Iwillkillagain
  instagram.com/iwillkillagain

Next door to VDeli, the Dark Arts Coffee Roastery transforms on Thursdays into a brunch cafe with a biker, metal and occult feel. It attracts lots of vegans with its fabulous brunches, pastries, cakes and coffee. Most of the food is vegan, with maximum choice at the weekend. Tables inside and out and plenty of parking for motorcycles.

Big brunches £8.50-£9.50 such as muffin with za'tar (herbs), vegan cream cheese, rosti, avocado, smoked tempeh, oven blush tomatoes and kasundi (mustard sauce); or Canadian baked beans with avocado on toast and a side of vegan chorizo; or Keralan donut with black beluga dal, black rice and chutneys; or burrito with refried beans, black rice, chipotle ratatouille, guacamole, cream cheese and spinach. Extras £1-£2 such as ratatouille, beans, cream cheese, pancetta, tempeh, chorizo, avocado. They can do gluten-free bread.

Pastries and cakes £2-£4 such as plain, almond and/or chocolate croissant, fruit Danish, tahini chocolate brownie, gin and lemon drizzle loaf, carrot and ginger cake with nutmeg icing.

Coffees come in three sizes £2-£3.50. Also sodas £2, orange juice £2.50, iced coffee £3.

Kingfisher

Omnivorous fish & chip shop with vegan menu

- 147 Homerton High Street E9 6AS
- 020 8985 4444
- M-F 11.30-22.00, Sa 12.00-21.00, Su closed
- Homerton

Proprietor Emina Mustafa, whose parents opened the shop in 1971, never realised there were so many vegans until the Spread Eagle pub opposite went 100% vegan. Then in June 2019 she launched a big vegan menu, proudly displayed in the windows.

All vegan main means are £7.90. Vegan fish and chips in tempura batter, served with mushy peas and tartare sauce. Pie and chips, contains minced beef and onion in gravy pie, served with mushy peas and gravy. Burgers come in beef, fish or chicken style, Jackfruit, halloumi cheeze, Portobello mushroom, or spinach and falafel. Seitan doner kebab or BBQ pulled jackfruit wrap, add £1 as loaded chips.

Corn dog, popcorn bites, fishless fingers all £5.50. Standalone pie £4.50. Sweet treats £3.90.

I Will Kill Again

Grand Howl

Wholemeal Shop

The Wholemeal Shop
Health food shop

☛ 190 Well St, E9 6QT (NW side of Victoria Park, a few minutes' walk east of London Fields)

☎ 020 8985 1822

🕐 M-Sa 9.00-18.00, Su closed

⊖ Homerton overground

In the fridge are VegiDeli, Taifun, Clearspring tofu, spreads, Tofutti, Provamel, Sojade and Coyo.

Wholefoods. Loose herbs and spices. Patés by Granovita and Tartex. Zest pesto and pasta sauce. Meridian spreads. Lots of teas.

Supplements including Solgar, Lamberts, Higher Nature, Floradix and Vogel.

Bodycare by Green People, Weleda, Faith in Nature, Avalon, Mistry, Dr Bronner's and Jason.

Cleaning products by Ecover, BioD, Ecoleaf, Ecozone and Earth Friendly.

No credit cards, but free cashpoint outside.

Plant Based Supermarket
Vegan supermarket

🖝 187 Well Street E9 6QU

📞 020 3952 2191

🕐 M-Sa 09.00-20.00, Su 10.00-19.00

⊖ Homerton overground

↖ Facebook plant based
supermarket ltd
instagram plant_based_supermarket

East London's first fully vegan supermarket as of summer 2018, specialising in ethical and locally sourced products. And they've added a coffee bar to what was previously Well Organics. Seating inside and out.

Fridge and freezer with sandwiches, wraps, salads, cheeses, sausages, vegan bacon, burgers, ravioli, ready meals, pizza, tempeh,yogurt, berries ice-cream such as Coyo and Booja Booja.

Lots of plant milks including almond, cashew, coconut, Good Hemp, Oatly, soya

OK, now for the hard to find good stuff: Go Vegan chocolate croissants, Vegan Bakery cookies, banana blossom, for making vegan phish n chips, Alpha Bites Bear cereal, Stubb's BBQ sauce and liquid smoke, several brands of chocolate chip cookies, Anandas blackcurrant and liquorice marshmallows, I Am Nut OK cheeses, Norah's brownies, fermented and smoked lupin beans, Vego bars and spread (the crack of vegan chocolate, one bite and you're addicted for life), vegan Wagon Wheels, black pudding.

Free wifi. Community board.

ILFORD

East London

Saravanaa Bhavan, Ilford
Vegetarian south Indian restaurant

- ☛ 115-127 Cranbrook Road IG1 4PU
- ☏ 020 8911 8718
- ◷ M-Su 09.30-23.00
- ⊖ Ilford BR
- ➘ saravanabhavan.com

Very big vegetarian Indian restaurant, seating 250 people on two floors, near Ilford station, part of a worldwide chain with branches in East Ham, Tooting, Southall and Wembley. This branch is the poshest with slightly higher prices but still excellent value and a gigantic menu.

Starters £2.95-£5.25 such as vada, idli, samosa, chilli mushroom, spring rolls, fried corn and parotta.

Main courses £3.45-£5.45 include curries, a dozen kinds of dosas, even a tailor made one with your fillings of your choice, uthappam lentil pizzas, Chinese noodle and fried rice dishes such as Manchurian vegetables.

South Indian meal £7.25 with 2 curries, chapati or poori, rice, sambar, rasam, special kuzhambu (dal), appalam (papad) and pickle. North Indian thali £7.95 with soup, salad, 3 side dishes, dal biryani, spring rolls, fried papad, pickles and 2 chapati. Business meal £5.45 with rice, vegetable biryani, poriyal, appalam and pickle.

Fruit salad £1.75. Wine from £5 glass bottle £14-£20. Beer £1.95-£3.75, Juices £2.95, fizzy drinks £1. Tea or coffee £1.25-£1.50, no non-dairy milk.

Children welcome, high chairs. Party room.

Mr Singh's
Vegetarian pizza and fast food restaurant

- ☛ 387 Eastern Ave, Gants Hill IG2 6LR
- ☏ 020 8270 1234
- ◷ M-Th 12.00-23.00, F-Su 11.00-23.00
- ⊖ Gants Hill (exit 3)
- ➘ mrsinghspizza.co.uk (menu)

New vegetarian fast food restaurant with lots of vegan options including vegan cheese. They have amazing pizza, especially the awesome Meat Feast, also hotdogs, burgers and lots of sides, and great prices.

Starters ££3.75-£3.99 such as salad, garlic or chilli tortilla. 10 types of pizza £3.99-£14.99 from small, medium, large and extra large, with toppings including sausage, meat feast, and classic calzone with tomato sauce, cheese, mushroom, red onions, pepper and sweetcorn. Extra toppings 50p-£1.10.

Burgers £3.25-£4.75 include chilli chicken style, spicy soya, double decker cheeseburger, and the Mega burger with

EAST

ILFORD

Karamsar Gurdwala Sikh temple

bacon rashers, triple cheese, BBQ sauce and mayo.

Wraps £4,75, choose from naan or tortilla filled with spicy soya sticks and kebab plus fries, salad, ketchup and mint sauce. Or Thai sweet chilli wrap.

Side dishes £1.25-£3.50 include crispy garlic mushrooms, potato wedges, cheesy fries and salad, hotdog, chicken style nuggets, chilli cheese nuggets, curried beans, spicy soya sticks.

Their most popular dish is Mr Singh's Sizzler £8.99 with mixed grill of soya chunks, green pepper, mushroom, onion in BBQ sauce.

At present the only vegan desserts on a whole page of desserts are cookie dough and churros £4.95, but they tell us more vegan desserts are on the way.

Soft drinks £1.75-£2.50. They have soy milk for shakes £3.50.

High chairs. Free delivery within 3 miles, beyond that £2 to £4.

Dosa Rani & Royal Sweets
Vegetarian Indian restaurant & shop

- 56-58 Goodmayes Road, Ilford IG3 9UR
- 020 8598 8333
- M-Su 11.00-23.00
- Goodmayes BR
- Facebook Dosa Rani & Royal Sweets

Vegetarian Indian and Singaporean restaurant and sweet shop by the bridge over the railway, with some outside tables at the front.

Lunch special £4.99 with rice, veg, curry of the day and dal. Lunch thali £6.99, dinner £8.99, with two curries, rice, salad, dal, two rotis.

Starters £1.70-£6.50. Dosas and uttapam £3.99-£4.99. Curries £5.75-£6.50.

Chinese starters £4.25-£4.75, noodles £6.75-£7.20, rice £5.95-£7.20, special £6.95-£7.50.

Take-away tiffin service £5.50-£7.70, 10% off if you order in advance.

No vegan desserts.

Soft drinks, juices, tea, coffee £1.50-£2.40. No alcohol.

Cards minimum £15 or 50p extra. Children welcome, high chairs. Dogs welcome.

Barfia Deli
Vegetarian Indian take-away

- 693 High Road, Seven Kings IG3 8RH
- 020 3730 2236
- M-F 11.00-20.00, Sa 9.30-21.00, Su 10.00-20.00
- Seven Kings BR
- barfia.com

Hot food tiffins £4 cooked daily with rice, vegetable curry and dal. None of the sweets are vegan. Soft drinks £1.20. Coffee £2.

Free delivery on orders over £15 within 2 miles radius. You can also eat in.

Wazir
Omnivorous Turkish and Persian restaurant

- 55-57 Cranbrook Road, Ilford IG1 4PG
- 020 8478 0500
- M-Su 11.00-23.00
- Ilford
- wazirrestaurant.co.uk

Vegan dishes £3.90-£4.90 include chickpea soup, hummus, quisir (cracked wheat mixed with tomatoes, celery, parsley, spices, olive oil and pomegranate sauce), dolma, shakshuka (sautéed aubergine, red and green peppers, carrots. garlic and tomato sauce), falafel. Falafel platter £8.90 with hummus, various vegetables and chargrilled veg cubes, with bread, salad, sauces, rice or couscous, or swap for chips for £1.50. Couscous, rice, chips £2.

Soft drinks £1.90-£3.90, juices £1.90, fresh orange juice £3.45. Tea and coffee £2.50.

Take away. High chairs. Special events.

Wok Wala
Omnivorous Street Asian Kitchen

- 733 High Road, Ilford IG3 8RL
- (020 8598 9656
- M-Su 11.30-23.00
- ⊖ Ilford BR
- ↖ wokwala.com

Modern and colourful restaurant which prepares a meal in front of you. Adults £7.99, kids £4.49.

First choose your base such as thin rice vermicelli, soba noodles, ho fun noodles, basmati rice, brown or biryani rice. Second add your filling starting with tofu, and any five vegetables from aubergine, baby corn, bamboo shoot, broccoli, chickpeas, coriander, edamame beans, fresh chillies, mangetout, mixed peppers, mushroom, pak choi, peas, pineapple, potatoes, red onions, spring onions, and Thai chillies. Extra veg 30p each. Finally pick your sauce from Beijing black bean, Saigon ginger and spring onions, Hong Kong sweet and sour, Szechuan , Mongolian BBQ, dhal, coconut and almond korma, mild masala, medium Madras, or fiery hot vindaloo.

Top up with samosas £1. Mango, lemon and raspberry sorbet £2.99. Cold drinks £1, orange juice £1.50.

Satsang Sweet Mart
Vegetarian Indian delicatessen

- 149 Ley Street, Ilford IG1 4BL (tow centre)
- (020 8514 8288, 07960 724 912
- M-Sa 10-45-19.00 , Su 10.45-16.00
- ⊖ Ilford BR
- ↖ Facebook Satsang sweet mart

Gujarati Indian take-away with sweet shop Samosa, spring rolls, Punjabi potato rice, pakora, kebab, bhajia 40p-£1. Thali £5 with a curry, dal, rice, roti; medium £7, large £10. Box of just rice and curry £2 small, £3 medium, £5 large.

Health Mantra
Health food shop

- 75 Cranbrook Road, Ilford IG1 4PG
- (020 8514 4443
- M-Sa 9.30-18.30, Su 11.30-15.30
- ⊖ Ilford BR
- ↖ healthmantra.co.uk

No fridge but orders can be placed on customer request. Wholefoods such as grains, pulses, nuts, seeds, pasta, pasta sauce and pesto. Biona bread. Meridian and Biona spreads. Plant milks and oils. Organic superfoods such as Naturya and Go Life protein powder.

Vast variety of tea including Dr Stuart, Pukka, Heath and Heather, Higher Living, Yogi, Cotsworld, Clipper, Organic India.

Bodycare includes Jason, Faith In Nature, Weleda, Avalon and Dr Bronner. Natracare oganic women's personal care and hair colours. Weleda, Earth Friendly babycare. Ecover and BioD cleaning products.

Supplements include Solgar, Nature's Plus, Viridian, Biocare. Pukka herbal remedies. Weleda, Nelson's and Ainsworth homeopathy. Some books on health, vegan and gluten-free cooking.

Holland & Barrett, Ilford
Health food shop

- 52 Cranbrook Road, Ilford IG1 4PG
- 020 8553 2808
- M-Sa 9.00-19.00, Su 10.30-17.00
- Ilford BR

Fridge with Sheese, Violife, Provamel, Cheatin, Dragonfly, Vegout , VegiDeli, Tofurky, Dee's. Freezer wotj Fry's, VegiDeli, Tofurky, Clive's Pies, Secret Sausage; Booja Booja and Jollyum non-dairy ice-cream.

- 162 High Road, Ilford IG1 1LL
- 020 8514 5786
- M-Sa 9.00-18.00, Su 10.00-17.00
- Ilford BR

New branch. No fridge or freezer.

Holland & Barrett, Barking
Health food shop

- Unit 1, The Vicarage Centre, Ripple Walk, Barking IG11 7NR
- 020 8617 0797
- M-Sa 9.00-17.30, Su 10.00-16.00
- Barking

Freezer and fridge.

Holland & Barrett, Barkingside
Health food shop

- 65 High Street, Barkingside IG6 2AF
- 020 8551 7573
- M-Sa 9.00-17.30, Su 10.00-16.00
- Barkingside

Freezer and fridge.

Holland & Barrett, Loughton
Health food shop

- 212 High Road, Loughton IG10 1DZ
- 020 8532 1163
- M-Sa 9.00-17.30, Su 10.00-16.00
- Loughton

Freezer and fridge.

Holland & Barrett, Romford
Health food shop

- Unit 16, Laurie Walk, Romford RM1 3RT
- 01708 747 192
- M-Sa 09.00-18.00, Su 10.30-16.30
- Romford BR
  No freezer or fridge.
- Unit N4/5, Liberty Centre, Romford RM1 3RT
- 01708 721 932
- M-Sa 09.00-18.00, Su 10.30-17.00
- Romford BR

Fridge and freezer.

LONDON FIELDS

and Broadway Market

London Fields park is perfect for picnics, and barbecues are allowed on the west side. At the north end is London's only heated open air swimming pool. There are seven vegan eateries along the east (Mare Street) and south (Westgate Street) sides. For a pint try *The Pub On The Park*.

Broadway Market is a street running from the south end of London Fields park down to the canal. There are cafes including vegetarian **Baba Souks**, two wholefood stores, pubs, lots of cute shops and three independent bookshops. On Saturdays there is a superb street market with several vegan stalls.

Westgate Street runs east from the top of Broadway Market to Mare Street. On the right in *Netil Market* are vegan take-away junk stars **Death By Pizza** and healthy take-away **Planted,** with a few outdoor tables. Further along on the left in railway arches is awesome vegan restaurant **Cook Daily**. Just past the railway bridge, at the end of the alley on the right, upstairs in *Netil House* is healthy vegan cafe **Palm Greens**.

On or just off **Mare Street**, on the east side of London Fields, are three new vegan eateries. **Smashing Kitchen** is a lovely healthy cafe. **Mao Chow** serves Chinese food in the evenings. **Plant Hub** is an evening restaurant and weekend cafe, with a huge second kitchen housing **Plant Academy** vegan cookery school.

Broadway Market Saturday
Amazing Saturday street market

☛ Length of Broadway Market, a street running due south from London Fields Park to the canal, Hackney E8

🕐 Sa 9.00-17.00

⊖ London Fields BR, Bethnal Green. Buses 26,48,55,106,388,D6.

↖ broadwaymarket.co.uk

On Saturdays the street called *Broadway Market* is pedestrianised to host perhaps the classiest street market in London, with 120 stalls. There are stacks of artisan food stalls such as juices, bread, and many vegan and vegetarian street food stalls.

Starting from the park end, look out for **Gujarati Rasoi** selling curry boxes with crunch, **Urban Falafel**, and **Chegworth Valley** apple and pear juice in big bottles. Further along are **Osu Coconuts** doing all-vegan pancakes and roti wraps, **Artisan Vegan Cheese**, **Zakuski** salads, **Ted's Veg** fruit 'n' veg stall, and **Kompassion Kombucha** on tap. Towards the south end is a fabulous olives stall.

If you need cash, head to the post office, open Saturdays until 5pm.

Cookdaily
Vegan restaurant

- Arch 358, Westgate Street E8 3RN (between Broadway Market and Mare Street, under the railway line)
- 07498 563 168
- Tu-Su 12.00-22.00, M closed
- London Fields BR
- cookdaily.co.uk
  instagram.com/kingcookdaily

Chef King Cook and his pioneering vegan restaurant Cookdaily are east London vegan legends, with 43,000 and 20,000 instagram followers respectively. King was first to open a vegan restaurant in Shoreditch Boxpark. Now he's expanded into this dedicated location on the south side of London Fields, next to Broadway Market. The range of dishes is impressive, some reflecting his Laotian heritage and from around south-east Asia, plus French, chickn and mushroom pie, and a full English. With all dishes priced at just £8.50-£9.50, it's terrific value. No wonder this is many people's favourite place for meeting friends.

Choose from: **Chickn and mushroom pie** with chickpeas, potato, veggies and cream of truffle. **Le Garden** sautéed veggies and greens French style with garlic, herbes de Provence and white truffle oil served with brown rice plus tofu or chickn.

Yoga Fire sweet pululo veggie curry, spiced chickpeas and dal simmered in golden coconut milk. **High Grade** stir-fry veggies with hemp oil in smoky sweet n sour BBQ sauce on brown rice with tofu or chickn or chickpeas. **The Hard Bowl** veggies with yam, dumplings, plantain and ackee. **Full English** tofu "egg" scramble, sausages, mushrooms, tomatoes, greens, crispy baecon, brown rice and brown sauce. **Da**

Infamous, King's mum's green curry recipe with brown rice and a choice of just veggies, tofu and veg, chickn and veg, or chickpeas and veg. **Coco Soup Bowl** coconut broth with brown rice plus veggies with optional tofu or chickn. **Coco Ginger** and coconut nectar stir-fried with just veggies, puff tofu and veg, or chickn and veg. Udon **noodle bowl** with stir-fry veggies, tofu or chickn. **3S Spicy Sweet n Sour** with choice of tofu, chickn, prawn or mini spring rolls. **Pad Thai** flat rice noodles stir-fried with "egg" tofu, crushed peanuts and vegan fish sauce plus tofu or chickn or prawns. **Jungle Curry**. **The Jerk** chickn or puff tofu stir-fry with high grade colesalw over brown rice.

Drinks: Water and pop cans £1.50. Hot teas £2.50. Pea flower iced tea £3. Daily smoothie £4. Hemp mylk £6.

Extras: Chickn bites with sticky teriyaki glaze £5.

Meal deals add: 4 mini spring rolls £1.50, 8 for £3 with HG sauce, daily smoothie £2

No reservations, but there is ample seating both inside and out.

They also sell Bright magazine and some funky vegan T-shirts.

90% gluten-free. New branch opened summer 2019 in Victoria.

Palm Greens
Vegan healthy cafe

- ☛ at NT's Bar in Netil House, 1 Westgate Street E8 3RL
- ☎ 07841 581 060
- 🕐 M-F 9.00-16.00, Sa-Su 10.00-16.00
- ⊖ London Fields BR
- ↖ palmgreens.co.uk, kalicooking.com
  instagram.com/palmgreens
  Facebook palmgreens, kalicooking

Salad bar and workspace with sunny rooftop terrace, opened here April 2019. Kali travelled the world as a chef for over ten years and trained in vegetarian healthy food at the Natural Gourmet Institute in New York. Memby has worked in the music industry for 20 years and loves bringing people together through food and music. The menu changes with the seasons, weekly specials on instagram. Everything made from scratch.

Organic granola bowl £4.50. Avo and salsa, or rhubarb and tahini, or peanut butter and banana,on toasted sourdough £5.50-£6.50.

Mains £7.50-£8 such as scallion pancake with ginger toasted tempeh and tamari seeds, soft on the inside and crunchy on the out; Mexican red rice and black beans with black bean hummus, red cabbages, pickled onions, leaves, tamari seeds; Mexican black bean toastada with UK grown quinoa, veggies, chipotle crema; Kale Caesar salad.

Square Root soft drinks made in Hackney £2.85. Hackney Moju cold pressed juices £3. Real Kombucha £3.75.

Wine £6.50 glass, £25 bottle. Beers £4.50. Spritz cocktails £7-£8.

Teas, Allpress coffees, iced latte, chai or matcha or turmeric latte £2.20-£3.20.

Children welcome. Card payments only. Dogs welcome. Compostable packaging, discounts for bringing your own lunchbox, or buy a Black & Blum leakproof lunchbox here. Workspace with fast wifi. Yoga Sundays 10-11am. Also at Broadway Market Saturdays 10.00-16.00. Catering.

To enter: by the railway bridge over Westgate Street, walk to the end of Netil Lane, where there is a white door on the left. Ring the buzzer and walk up two floors. Lift access on Westgate Street via reception.

Glasshouse Salon
Vegan hairdresser

- ☛ Netil House, 1 Westgate St E8 3RL
- ☎ 020 3095 9783
- 🕐 Tu 10.00-20.00, W-Th 11.00-20.00, F 9.00-18.00, Sa-Su 10.00-18.00
- ⊖ London Fields BR
- ↖ glasshousesalon.co.uk

Men's and women's hairdresser where all but two (beeswax) of their Organic Colour Systems products are vegan. Appointment essential.

Ladies cut and blow dry £58-£75, gents cut and style £50-£55. Tints, highlights, full head lightening or balayage £60-£140.

No cash. MC, Visa, Amex, Apple Pay. Organic makeup and skincare for sale by Honest Skincare, RMS Beauty, ILIA Beauty, Jane Iredale, Guy Morgan.

Entrance is on the main road next to the railway bridge, take the left staircase to the first floor.

Planted
Vegan wholefood take-away

- Netil Market, Westgate Street E8 3RL
- 07792 842 560
- M-F 12.00-15.00, Sa 10.00-18.00, Su 11.00-17.00
- London Fields BR
- instagram.com/plantedhut (here) weareplanted.com (catering)

Gabriella and Molly started out doing vegan catering in Brighton in 2016 and in 2019 relocated to London and opened up in what used to be Club Mexicana's Netil Market popup, now repainted dark blue.

The menu changes weekly and is posted on instagram.

Hot box £9 such as mac & leek cheese with salads. Cold box £8 with a selection of what's on the counter such as arancini with mozzarella, crispy smoked tofu and two salads. The salads can be pretty amazing such as squash, sweet potato, charred corn, sage and pickled onion - that's one salad.

Weekend monster brunch bap £6.50 with sausage patty, hash brown, fried vegg (a vegan Scotch egg), ketchup.

Pizza slice £3. Sausage roll £3. Scotch vegg £5.

Dessert treats such as biscoff brownie £2.50, cinnamon roll or apricot Danish £3.

There are a couple of tables in front and a coffee place opposite open Wed-Sun.

Death By Pizza
Vegan pizzeria take-away

- Netil Market, 13-23 Westgate Street (between Broadway Market and Mare Street)
- 07494 333639
- W-Su 12.00-22.00, M-Tu closed
- London Fields BR
- deathbypizza.co.uk facebook.com/DeathByPizza666 facebook.com/NetilMarket

Young Vegans, who opened London's first vegan pie shop in Camden Market, followed up with this wood fired pizza palace. All mock meats, cheeses, sauces and dough are made from scratch at their prep kitchen in Camden.

Butt Nakes pizza £8 has mozzarella, marinara sauce and basil. Blood Drive £8 adds kalamata olives, samphire and capers. For £10 get a Filthy Weekend, Holy Ghost, Devil's Coglioni, Dead Barbie or Smoke House, with ingredients such as seitan ham, pepperoni, chicken, ricotta, red or green smoked mushrooms, pine nut purée, onions, spinach, bbq sauce. Dips £1.

Peanut butter chocolate mud pie £3.

Beer £3, soft drinks £2, water £1. Pizza plus beer deal £12.

Click and collect on the website. Just Eat, Deliveroo.

At the end of 2019 they are opening Young Vegans Pizza Shop nearby in Bethnal Green, their first sit-down restaurant, at which time they may reduce the hours at this branch to just Saturdays or even close it. But it's not far to walk to the new place, which has 30 seats indoors!

Plant Hub & Academy
Vegan organic, gluten-free cafe, restaurant and culinary academy

- 217 Mare Street E8 3QE
- 020 8510 0948
- Tu-Th 18.00-22.00,
  F-Su 12.00-22.00, M closed
- London Fields BR
- planthub.net
  facebook.com/planthubuk
  facebook.com/plantacademyuk
  instagram.com/planthubuk

Italian David Bez started with a little healthy vegan cafe called Salad Pride in Neal's Yard. Now he has joined forces with chef trainer Lauren Lovatt, who used to run vegan pop-ups and restaurant Asparagasm, plus Sicilian baker and classically trained chef Antonio Alderuccio, to open this gorgeous daytime cafe and evening restaurant on Mare Street. Dishes here are original and very colourful and you won't find them anywhere else. Menus change frequently, below are some examples of dishes.

A second huge kitchen houses **The Plant Hub** vegan culinary academy, which can train up to 16 people at a time, offering one to one tuition with course leaders and assistants. There are classes for new cooks, budding entrepreneurs, specialist classes for business and advanced programmes for classically trained chefs, all helping to grow the plant based movement and vegan scene.

Lunch: Focaccia toasts £8 with Portobello mushroom, cashew truffle cheeze and kale; or roasted pepper, aubergine, tomatoes, olives and cheeze sauce. Three kinds of focaccia burgers £9 with mushroom, farinata chickpea omelette, greens, cashew faux gras; Italian cheeze and roasted veg;

salt beet, beetroot butter beans hummus, smoked saeurkraut, green leaves, tahini. Superfood salads £10.

Stacks of cakes £3.50 such as carrot, apple and cinnamon, chocolate, courgette and coffee, brownie. Sweet berry burger £7 filled with black pea brownie, banana, coconut ice cream, rose and raspberry jam.

Smoothies and acai ice cream bowls £5. Kombucha mocktails £5. Teas £3. Coffees £2-£3.50 include bulletproof with coconut oil, all available iced. Super lattes £3.50-£6 such as turmeric, chai, cbd, matcha kujji, reishi mushroom kuji.

Restaurant: Small plates £6.50-£8 such as cheeze with pickles and focaccia; white asparagus with elderflower and toasted almonds; baby courgette gremolata. Mains £9.50-£11.50 such as gnocchi wiwth cashew pesto and tomato sauce; aubergine parmigiana with almond, cashew pesto and salad; bulgogi (Korean fire meat) lion's mane mushroom steak with buckwehat, courgette, aubergine; oyster mushroom, Sichuan squash purée, bitter cress and umeboshi.

Sweet burger £9, brownie with vanilla ice cream £7, cake of the day £5. Wines.

Dogs welcome. Uber Eats.

KITCHEN + ACADEMY

planthub

Smashing Kitchen
Vegan cafe

- 🖝 1a Bayford Street E8 3SE
- ☎ 020 8525 1118
- 🕐 M-Th 08.30-16.30, 17:30-21.00; F 08.30-16.30,17.30-22.00; Sa 9.00-17.00; Su closed / private events.
- ⊖ London Fields BR
- 🗲 smashingkitchen.co.uk
  facebook.com/smashingkitchen

Vegan healthy cafe, open for lunch and dinner, opened in May 2018 by Asia (pronounced Asha) on the east side of London Fields, just off Mare Street.

Little snacks and sharing plates for one or two £4-£9.50 such as homemaked nachos or raw veggies with hummus or guacamole, butter bean cheezy hummus, nuts and seeds buckwheat bread with vegan butter. Soups £5 such as beetroot with chunky veg and butter beans, or creamy pumpkin/squash and sweet potato with coconut and Thai spices; add two slices of home baked bread £2, vegan butter 50p.

Salads and bowls £4.50 small or £6.50 large are assembled from chickpeas, kidney beans, tomatoes, leaves, quinoa, beetroot, broccoli, white buckwheat, green beans; or create your own.

Main dishes, burgers and wraps £7.50: chickpea curry with spicy brown rice; pesto gluten-free fusilli and veg; lentil bolognese gluten-free spaghetti; Thai spiced sweet potato burger with sweet chilli sauce in gluten-free bun; wraps such as Mexican spiced kidney beans, buckwheat, sweet chilli sauce and guac; or falafel, butterbean hummus, pickled red cabbage, coconut tzatziki. Specials £8-£8.50 such as pesto sourdough pizza packed with veggies; Rainbow stir-fry; hearty Bigos sauerkraut stew with mushrooms, chickpeas and crushed baby potatoes.

Desserts such as cheesecake £4.50. Cakes £2.50 such as peanut butter and chocolate slice, or pumpkin spice almond and coconut cake with dried fruit, add custard 70p.

Smoothies £4.50 such as green, berries, protein.

Cold drinks £1.50-£3.50 include their homemade orange or berry soda with a generous amount of real berries, Wild Fizz ginger turmeric kombucha, freshly squeezed watermelon juice. Hot drinks £1.80-£2.50 feature raspberry or ginger mint tea, herbal teas, nut or oat milk coffee. Bring your own booze, £1.50 per person corkage.

Discretionary 12.5% service charge. Groups of 6+ people should book at least a day in advance by phone or email.

Mao Chao
Vegan Chinese restaurant and take-away

- 159a Mare Street E8 5RH (corner Bayford Street, opposite Well Street)
- julian@mao-chow.com
- Tu-Sa 18.00-23.00, Su-M closed
- Hackney Central, Hackney Downs
- mao-chow.com
  facebook.com/maochowuk
  instagram.com/mao_chow

Vegan chef Julian from L.A. trained under New York chef Jonathan Wu to create Chinese regional food from Szechuan, Yunan, Shaanxi and Xinjiang. Following residencies at Bar Pamela in Dalston, downstairs from Palm Vaults in Hackney, and Love Shack in Bethnal Green, he now has his own place amongst the cluster of new vegan restaurants on the east side of London Fields. Come with friends and share a selection of dishes.

Dishes £4-£9 vary. A typical menu is smacked cucumber with black vinegar, sesame oil and crushed garlic; Gong Bao asparagus with purple sprouting broccoli and peanuts; meaty veg dumplings; oyster mushroom bao; ginger-scallion jackfruit with jasmine rice; dan dan spicy sesame noodles with mince.

Youtiao Chinese doughnut with ice cream £4.50.

Tsingtao beer £3. Baijiu liqueur shot £2.50. Casa Belfi prosecco £6 glass, £34 bottle. Or bring your own alcohol. Malted soy milk, or chrysanthemum tea, £2.

No reservations. Cash only. 12 seats.

Baba Souks Cafe & Kitchen
Vegetarian Middle Eastern cafe

- 62 Broadway Market E8
- 020 7687 0236
- Tu-Th 08.00-17.00, F-Sa 10.00-22.30, Su 10.00-17.00, M closed
- London Fields BR
- babasouks.co.uk
  instagram.com/babasouks

Feasts in the East with mezze and sharing plates.

Weekday breakfast white beans in smoky tomato and red pepper sauce on sourdough toast £6. Gluten-free oat muesli £5 with pistachios, almonds, coconut, dates, fresh berries, oat milk. Toast and jam £4. At the weekend there is also a sharing platter for two £20 with beans, roasted cauliflower, falafel, hummus, veggies, quinoa tabouleh, sourdough flatbread.

Mezze and dips £3-£5 include marinated olives, falafel, chargrilled padron peppers, roasted cauliflower with tahini and pomegranate seeds, hummus, moutabal (baba ghanoush smoked aubergine purée), muhammara roasted red pepper, pomegranate and walnut purée. Falafel, hummus and toasted quinoa tabouleh salad £8.

Cakes and pastries such as date cake £3.

Loose leaf teas and artisanal coffees, raw cacao hot choc, matcha latte £2.20-£3. Almond and Oatly oat milk. Natural wines and craft beers, glass bottles, metal straws.

Organic O
Wholefood shop and greengrocer

- 25 Broadway Market E8 4PH
- 020 7254 6664
- M-Su 08.00-21.00
- facebook.com/ OrganicoBroadwayMarket

All the usual wholefoods, plus deli counter for bread, olives, vegan cakes such as banana and walnut loaf, organic mixed juices and smoothies £3.50-£5, coffees from £1.80, granola or porridge £5.50., freshly made sandwiches £around £5, vegan sesame burger £6.50 with coconut vegan cheese and avocado. Seitan, dips, Booja Booja ice cream, vegan chocolate. Bodycare by Faith In Nature.

Green Island Whole Foods
Greengrocer & wholefood shop

- 47 Broadway Market E8 4PH
- M-Su 07.00-21.00

Veg at the front and wholefoods at the back.

Mao Chow

Lele's
Vegan cafe & bakery

- 50 Lower Clapton Road E5 0RN
- 07807 740049
  info@leleslondon.com
- M-F 08.00-18.00, Sa-Su 9.00-17.00.
- Hackney Downs, Hackney Central, Homerton
- leleslondon.com
  facebook.com/lelesclapton
  instagram.com/leles_london

Having opened Lele's as a vegetarian cafe, the owners went vegan when they found out what happens to dairy cows and calves, and from December 2017 made their cafe vegan too. The seasonal menu is updated every couple of months and there is a daily special. They specialise in breakfast pancakes and patisserie such as plain and filled croissants, pain au raisin and cinnamon buns.

Buckwheat pancakes £8.75 come with fresh strawberries, sliced banana, toasted almond flakes and chia seeds. They use maple and agave syrup or coconut sugar. French toast £7 topped with summer fruit compote, coconut cream, peanut butter, toasted almond flakes and chia seeds. Sweet porridge £5.50 with hot maple syrup butter, sliced bananas, blueberries, crunchy almond flakes and chia. Coconut, banana and granola yogurt pot with maple syrup £4.20. Avo on toast £7.50 with roast aubergine, coriander, pomegranate seeds.

Cooked brekkie £7.50 with scrambled tofu, sourdough toast, garlic mushrooms and pea shoots. Full English £9.50 has sausage, baked beans with red pepper, sourdough toast, roast oregano tomato, butter spring greens with crunchy paprika flax seeds and spicy balsamic ketchup.

Soup of the day £5.50 with sourdough bread. Superfood bowl £8.50 made to order with quinoa, spinach, tomato, garden peas, grilled courgette, red cabbage, carrot, flax seeds and cashew nuts toasted in turmeric and olive oil, seasoned with fresh mint sauce, lemon and olive oil. Sabih spiced chickpeas £8.50 with hummus, Israeli salad, roast aubergine, flatbread. Special of the day £8. Various salads. Sandwiches £5.50 made with local E5 Bakehouse bread. Cheesy sourdough toasties £5.50.

Homemade cakes. Raspberry and peanut butter balls, brownies.

Fruit and veg juices and smoothies £3.50. Hot drinks £1.80-£3.20, babyccino free. Soya, almond and coconut milk.

One Sunday afternoon per month afternoon tea 2pm-5pm features their Lele's Vegan Patisserie delights. You need to book.

Dogs welcome. Wifi. Private catering, wholesale made to order vegan cakes and spectacular wedding cakes, can be gluten-free. Also at Soho Vegan Market, Rupert Street, Saturdays 11.00-15.00.

Organic & Natural

Organic & Natural
95% veggie cafe & wholefood shop

- 191 Lower Clapton Road, E5 8EG
- 020 8986 1785
- M-F 10.00-20.00, Sa 09.00-20.00, Su 10.00-18.00
- Hackney Central, Hackney Downs, Clapton (all approx 1km)
  Bus 38,48,55,106,253,254, 425,488
- palm2.co.uk/cafe/organic-and-natural

Mediterranean cafe at the back of a wholefood store, with Arab, Greek, Turkish and Moroccan dishes and salads. 80% vegan. Point to what you want in the deli style counter. £6.50 for a plate of food, take-away £5.50. Seating at the back and in the covered garden behind.

Wraps £2.50 such as potato, tomato, bean.

Cakes £2.75 such as polenta, vegan mango cheesecake with coconut topping.

Bring your own booze or buy in the shop, no corkage. Organic and vegan wines. Vegan German beer. Freshly squeezed orange juice £2.50. Coffee, cappuccino £1.80, soya milk +20p. Tea £1.40. Smothies such as orange and ginger, or acai berry with cacao nibs, and plenty more drinks in the shop fridge.

The shop specialises in organic food and has very well stocked fridges with tofu, meat substitutes, Swedish Glace vegan ice-cream. Fresh daily bread. Body care. Cleaning products. They also own Palm 2 grocers on the other side of the road.

Hoxton Beach

Palm 2
Omnivorous grocer, wholefoods & off-licence

- 152-156 Lower Clapton Rd E5 0QJ
- (020 8533 1787
- (M-Sa 07.00-24.00, Su 07.00-23.00
- ⊖ Bus:
  38,48,55,106,253,254,425,488
- ⬧ palm2.co.uk

Locals call this the best corner shop in London, with things that are hard to find in north Hackney such as their fresh olives counter which also has artichoke hearts, grilled aubergine and peppers. Salad greens. Fresh bread from E5 Bakehouse and Spence Bakery in Church Street, including rye and spelt. Soya, rice, almond and hazelnut milk, soya dessert. Delphi take-away meze salads. Innocent smoothies. Copella aplle juice. Indian spices, Turkish herbs. Lots of Italian pasta. A few wholefoods, the rest you can get from their other shop Organic & Natural diagonally opposite. Lindt dark chocolate.

Vegan beer monster heaven: German beers (in Germany by law beer is vegan), Sam Smiths and local beers.

Tables outside. In the morning they serve fresh orange juice and coffee, and have soya milk.

Hoxton Beach Falafel
Vegan falafel stall

- Chatsworth Road market E5 0LH
- 🕐 Sundays 11.00-16.00
- ⊖ Homerton
- ⬧ hoxtonbeach.com

Falafel wrap in Arab khubz bread with tahini, chilli sauce, their homemade turnip pickle, cucumber and chilli pickles, salad and hummus. Regular £3.50, large £4.50, add a cooked vegetable for 50p such as aubergine, sweet potato, cauliflower or fava bean stew.

The Green Basket
Organic food shop

- 155 Lower Clapton Road E5 8EQ
  (opposite Laura Place)
- (07817 914753
- (M-Sa 07.30-21.30, Su 08.00-21.30
- ⊖ Bus:
  38,48,55,106,253,254,425,488
- ⬧ the-green-basket.business.site

Opened February 2019. Fresh fruit and veg. Wholefood vegan and organic products. Coffee. Ecover refills.

STRATFORD

Rosa's
Omnivourus Thai cafe

- 212 The Balcony, Westfield Stratford City E20 1GN
- 020 3582 2528
- M-W 11.00-21.00, Th-Sa 11.00-22.00, Su 12.00-18.00
- Stratford
- rosasthaicafe.com
  facebook.com/RosasThaiCafe

They have a separate vegan menu. Noodles and rice £7.99 including Pad Thai with rice noodles, or tofu stir-fried flat noodles, both with veggies and tofu. All rice dishes are served with jasmine and brown rice. Stir fried red curry; stir fried tofu and veggies with chilli and basil; stir fried in Rosa's homemade sayce with veggies and tofu. Veggies and tofu rice noodle in coconut soup, with mushroom, tomato, lemongrass and lime leaves.

Sides and salads £4.99-£7.99 spring rolls, papaya salads etc.

Wine 187 ml £4.99; Chang beer and London craft beer £3.99, Pils £4.50 and IPA £5. Tea £2.99. Soft drinks £2.25-£2.49; juices £2.75 and coconut water £3.50.

Branches at Spitalfields, Angel, Soho, Carnaby Street, Chelsea, Pimlico, Brixton, West Hampstead.

Applejacks
Health food store & take-away

- Unit 28, The Mall, The Stratford Centre E15 1XD
- 020 8519 5809
- M-Sa 9.00-18.00, Th-F 08.30-19.000, Su 10.30-16.30
- Stratford
- applejacks.co.uk

Excellent funky general health food shop. If they don't have it they'll get it within a week.

Full range of vegan, gluten-free, organic food. Fridge with Taifun, Clive's Pies, VegiDeli, tofu, tempeh, vegan cheeses by Violife, Tofutti and Vegusto. Di Fatti gnocchi in plain, spinach or tomato. Follow Your Heart salad dressing, Plamil mayo. Rhythm Health vegan kefir. Provamel, Coyo and Soyade yogurts.

Bodycare by Lavera, Jäson, Dr Bronner's, Avalon, Weleda, Earth Friendly Baby.

Supplements including Solgar, Viridian and FSC. Lots of bodybuilding stuff such as Met-Rx, EAS, U.S.N., Maximuscle.

Aromatherapy, homeopathy, herbal. Cleaning products include Ecover, Greenscent, Enviroclean.

As Nature Intended, Stratford
Organic & health food shop

- Green Eastern Market, Lower Ground Floor, Westfield Stratford City E20 1EH
- 020 8534 8807
- M-F 10.00-21.00, Sa 09.00-21.00, Su/BH 12.00-18.00
- Stratford
- asnatureintended.uk.com

95% organic store that aims to combine the variety of a supermarket (over 5,000 products) with the product range found in traditional health food shops. Not completely vegetarian but many veggie and vegan items, including Japanese and tofu-based foods and tempeh.

Many items are suitable for those with food allergies such as sugar-, gluten-, salt- or yeast-free. Bread and gluten-free muffins. Raw foods and superfoods. Plenty of chocolate.

Beauty and skincare products including Tisserand, Jason, Sukin, Pai, Avalon, Ren, Green People, Faith in Nature, Earth Friendly Baby. Inika (100% vegan) and Lavera (vegan items labelled) makeup.

Vitamins and minerals include Viridian, Pukka, Terranova and Biocare. Herbal and homeopathic remedies, aromatherapy oils.

There is a qualified nutritionist in the remedies section, and an experienced advisor with in-house training. Lots of information on recommended treatments for various conditions on their website. Magazines.

Other branches in Ealing, Chiswick, Marylebone, Spitafields and Balham.

Holland & Barrett Stratford
Health food shop

- 110-12 The Mall, Stratford Centre E15 1XA
- 020 8519 5182
- M-Sa 08.00-20.00, Su 10.00-18.00
- Stratford

Fridge and freezer.

- Unit SU0051, Westfield Shopping Centre E20 1HG
- 020 8522 1998
- M-F 10.00-21.00, Sat 09.00-21.00, Su 12.00-18.00
- Stratford

Fridge and freezer.

Also In Westfield there are the following chain restaurants: Comptoir Libanais, Tossed, Franco Manca, Giraffe, Las Iguanas, Ping Pong, Wagamamma, Wahaca.

Hornbeam Cafe
Vegan cafe in eco centre

- ☛ Hornbeam Environmental Centre, 458 Hoe Street E17 9AH (1 min from Baker's Arms)
- ☏ 020 8558 6880
- 🕐 Cafe: Tu-W 9.00-17.00, Th-F 10.00-17.00, Sa-Su 10.00-17.00, M closed. Stall: Sa 10.00-15.00.
- ⊖ Walthamstow Central (Victoria line); Walthamstow Queens Road, Leyton Midland Road (Barking to Gospel Oak line)
  Buses on Hoe Street include 20,48,69,230,257,357,W15,W19. 55,56 from central London run nearby.
- ⊖ hornbeam.org.uk
  facebook.com/HornbeamCafe
  Twitter @Hornbeamcafe

The menu uses local produce from Organiclea and market stalls and changes daily with growing conditions in north-east London and East Anglia, with a focus on seasonal, local, organic produce.

Breakfast £2-£4.50, served till 4.30pm, includes two sourdough toast with jam; homemade beans or tofu scramble on toast; sausage sandwich; sausage with tofu scramble and pickles; homemade granola with coconut yogurt.

Lunch from 11am £3-£6 could be soup of the day and sourdough toast; dahl and rice with onion pickle; seasonal salad plate; quiche on its own or with salad; hot daily main such as beetroot curry, vegetable pakora and rice; lentil, mushroom and chard lasagne with green salad; kidney beans, mushroom and nut burger with flatbread and seasonal salad

Weekend brunch £4.50-£6.90 features 2 sausages, homemade beans, fried potato, steamed greens and mushroom tofu scramble with sourdough bread; fried potato with herby green and tofu; chickpea flour vegetable fritter with tofu, greens, tomato and tamarind chutney. Extra items £1.

Cakes 80p-£2 are organic and baked in-house: banana, coconut, chocolate chip; carrot and walnut; chocolate and date brownie; peanut butter chocolate chip cookie.

Organic juices £2, homemade cordial £1. Organic herbal teas £2.60. Climpsons coffees £1.50 to £2.40. Almond, oat and soy milk. House wine large glass £4.80, £18 bottle. Cocktails £4.90. Locally brewed beers £3.80 and cider £4.

Children very welcome, two high chairs, toys. Table for two outside at the front, weather permitting.Dog friendly. Cash only (cashpoints at Bakers Arms crossroads 2 mins away). Wifi. Community board. Catering.

The centre enables practical sustainable

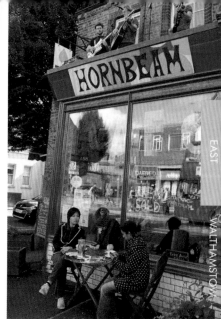

EAST

WALTHAMSTOW

Biff's

Bühler & Co

environmental activity at a local level. They hold community events, run school programmes and offer meeting space, office space and a mail collection service for groups."

The cafe is also an eco-centre selling homemade organic bread, eco-friendly household cleaning refills, homemade vegan butter, peanut butter, Coyo yogurt, tempeh and tofu. On Wednesdays they have homemade organic sourdough bread. On Saturdays 10.00-15.00 there is an organic fruit & veg stall outside selling locally grown produce.

The centre is organised and run by its users and volunteers and is the base for local food, environmental and volunteer projects. Hornbeam operates as not-for-profit business with all the surplus income being reinvested into the centre to fund community projects. All staff receive the same wage including the manager. Zero waste kitchen and cafe with recycling managed by Forest Recycling Project. Knitting and crafts every Thursday 2-4pm Catering for meetings, birthdays, weddings and events.

Hornbeam Nights
Evening events with vegan food

- ☛ Hornbeam Centre
- ☏ 020 8558 6880
- ◔ Th-Sa 19.00-23.00
- ⚓ hornbeam.org.uk/events/hornbeam-activities/hornbeam-nights

On Thursday nights at Hornbeam there are educational, social and environmental talks.

On Friday night it's Open Decks with DJs, bring vinyl, spin some tunes, buy records, mingle, dance. bands, jams and film night.

Saturday nights there are popup supper clubs, supporting aspiring cooks, such as East Meets East with Chinese and Indian food for £15, two sittings at 7pm and 9pm with light entertainment.

You can also hire the cafe during closing hours. On the first floor there is a meeting room for up to 12 people, £15 per hour per community group. Bookings include access to tea and coffee facilities by donation. Also 3 desks for hire Monday to Friday for £2 an hour.

Biff's Jack Shack, Walthamstow
Vegan fast food take-away

- inside Spar supermarket (Eat 17), 24-28 Orford Road E17 9NJ
- Biff's 07881 555 788 (& Whatsapp) Spar 020 8521 8187
- **Biff's** M closed, Tu-Th 17.00-21.30, F 17.00-22.00, Sa 12.00-22.00, Su 12.00-20.00.
  Spar: M-Sa 08.00-22.00, Su/BH 09.00-21.00.
- Walthamstow Central
- biffsjackshack.com/walthamstow (menu)
  instagram.com/biffsjackshack
  eat17.co.uk

"The world's filthiest and most indulgent vegan junk, in person and via Deliveroo and Uber Eats." For menu see Shoreditch Boxpark branch. Online orders closes 15 mins before shop.

Also in Brewdog Dalston.

Bühler & Co
Vegetarian cafe

- 8 Chingford Road (A112) E17 4PJ (continuation of top end of Hoe St)
- 020 8527 3652
- M-W 08.00-17.00, Th-F 08.00-22.30, Sa 09.00-22.30, Su 09.00-17.00. Kitchen closes 3pm M-Sa, 4pm Su; open evenings 5pm-10pm.
- Walthamstow Central
- buhlerandco.com
  instagram.com/buhler_and_co

In the Bell Corner end of Walthamstow, and owned by kiwi sisters Meg and Rosie Bühler, the specialities here include all day brunch and baked sweet treats. During the day there are only three vegan options, but in the evening 8 out of 12 dishes are vegan or can be, though sometimes "vegan by omission" as they don't appear to do scrambled tofu or vegan cheese. Menus change with the seasons.

They say bring your book , your babies, or your best friends. There is a beautiful, bright, airy interior, with art on the wall by local artists, and a covered back garden. Also a private room at the back for hire with 14 seats for parties and workshops.

Daytime menu £8.50-£11 includes avocado on toast with dukkah, pickled red onion and leaves; vegan fry-up; and we like the sound of their automaticallly vegan Indonesian gado gado with sweet potato, marinated tempeh, spring onion, mange-tout, spinach, peanut sauce, crispy onions. Gelato £2 per scoop.

Evening small plates £3.50-£8 from 5pm are designed to share, such as spicy nuts; sweet potato, orange and ginger croquettes with ginger and orange dip; bao buns with mixed mushrooms and leaf salad;

yellow curry with bulgar; fried seitan goujans with maple mustard mayo and slaw; to-fish tacos with sweetcorn and mango salsa; purple potatoes, dukkah, penang sauce, pickled kohlrabi, sesame seeds and greens.

Evening desserts £4.50-£6.50, as well as gelato, coconut cheesecake, limoncello.

Vegetable and fruit Moji cold pressed juice £3.50, smoothies £4. Tea, coffee, iced coffee and chai £2.20-£3, soy and oat milk 50p.

Vegan wines small glass £4.50, medium £5.50, carafe £14.70, bottle £21.50. Beer £4. Cocktails £6.50-£8.

Discretionary 10% service charge. High chairs. Wifi. Communal board.

Spice Box
Vegan Indian restaurant

- 58 Hoe St, Walthamstow E17 4PG
- 020 8521 0906
- Tu-Th 17.30-21.30, F-Sa 17.30-22.30, Su 10.00-16.00, 17.30-20.30. Last orders 30 minutes before closing. Brunch Sa-Su 10.00-15.00. M closed.
- Blackhorse Road then 1km north
- eatspicebox.co.uk
  facebook.com/eatspicebox
  instagram.com/eatspicebox t

How great is this, a vegan Indian curry house in Walthamstow. After trading at markets and festivals for three years, then a test kitchen at The Hornbeam in September 2018, in January 2019 Spice Box opened their own curry restaurant. They've already won best take-away in east London at the London Curry Awards. Most dishes can be made gluten-free.

PRESENTS THE DOSA WAFFLE POP UP!

Weekend brunch features dosa waffles, Keralan fried chick'n, South Indian brunch thali, or go for the Full Indian waffle stack with spicy jackfruit beans, crispy Bombay potatoes and coconut sambol.

The dinner menu features bajias, samosa, chick'n tikka, pani puri, staters sharing platter, jackfruit jalfrezi curry, shroom keema with walnut and soya, cashew and coconut chick'n korma, chick'n tikka masala, chickpea curry, lentil dansak, rice, paratha, roti, naan, garlic naan, aloo gobi, saag aloo, Bombay potatoes, raita.

For dessert coconut ice cream, mango sorbet, bana chai dosa waffle stack, biscoff and cardamon paratha with ice cream and Biscoff crumb.

Soft drinks, beer, wine, spicy cocktails, msala chai, organic drip coffee, with oat milk, Indian cola.

The Green Grill
Vegan fast food restaurant

- ☛ at Crate container village, 35 St James Street E17 7HN
- ☏ 07575 767 579
- ◔ M-F 12.00-21.00, Sa 11.30-21.00, Su 11.30-20.30
- ⊖ St James Street BR
- ↖ thegreengrill.com
  facebook.com/TheGreenGrill
  stjamesstreet.crateuk.com

Specialists in bangin' chewy seitan-based vegan junk food like burgers, hot dogs, popcorn chkn and chargrilled chkn shish wrap, with plenty of mustard and toppings.

Bad Boy Burgers £8-£9 include Red Devil made from sweet potato and red kidney beans, Mighty Meaty soy based, Surfs Up

battered deep fried nori wrapped tofu, Green Monster from peas, broccoli, red pepper and sundried tomato garlic and basil aioli. Each has a different coloured bun.

The Main Event alternatives £7.50-£8.50 feature Vdawg seitan sausage with kimchi, Chkn Shish wrap, Chkn Caesar salad, Chkn waffle with maple and peanut butter dips.

Snacks £3 or £5 include chkn bitez, cheez bitez, Cajun chipz, cheesetastic vegan cheez board. PB waffle or cheezcake £7-£7.50.

Naughty weekend brunch menu includes Breakfast Boat with vdawg sausage in a turmeric bun with splashes of sautéed spinach, garlic mushrooms and a sea of beans. Dunk in a couple of hasbrowns and Ahoy!

Just Eat, Deliveroo. Pillars vegan craft beer brewery are their neighbour, handy for an accompanying pint on sun trap dining terrace.

battered deep fried nori wrapped tofu, Green Monster from peas, broccoli, red pepper and sundried tomato garlic and basil aioli. Each has a different coloured bun.

The Main Event alternatives £7.50-£8.50 feature Vdawg seitan sausage with kimchi, Chkn Shish wrap, Chkn Caesar salad, Chkn waffle with maple and peanut butter dips.

Snacks £3 or £5 include chkn bitez, cheez bitez, Cajun chipz, cheesetastic vegan cheez board. PB waffle or cheezcake £7-£7.50.

Naughty weekend brunch menu includes Breakfast Boat with vdawg sausage in a turmeric bun with splashes of sautéed spinach, garlic mushrooms and a sea of beans. Dunk in a couple of hasbrowns and Ahoy!

Just Eat, Deliveroo. Pillars vegan craft beer brewery are their neighbour, handy for an accompanying pint on sun trap dining terrace.

Veg Hut
Health food shop

- 2b Chingford Road E17 4PJ
- 020 8527 5030
- M-Su 10.00-19.00
- Walthamstow Central
- veghut.net

About 95% of their products are organic. All the usual wholefoods, Suma, Amy's, Geo organic and Free & Easy soup. Organic pizza bases. Big range of Zest sauces, Suma pesto and Mr Organic sauce. Leonessa sun dried tomato or olive tapenade. Big range of spices and herbs from Steenbergs and Hatton Hills. Protein and chocolate bars,

Eat Real chips. Big fruit and veg secttion at the back.

Fridge with Violife, spreads, Taifun, Clearspring, Tyford soup, Sojade, Booja Booja truffles. Freezer with Booja Booja ice-cream, organic tempeh, frozen veg and fruit. One vegan wine and a vegan prosecco.

Organic loose pasta 28p for 100 gr. Organic refill extra virgin olive oil 96p for 100 ml. Aspall organic cider vinegar refill 34p for 100 ml. Bredi's flaxseed bread sour and cabbage; courgette; onion and garlic; sunflower; beetroot; Biona and Natural Era bread.

Kids and baby foods.

Faith in Nature plus some baby/kids body products. Ecover and Ecoleaf refills and Ecover, Ecozone, Ecoleaf and Ecoegg for washing.

Follow Your Heart vegan eggs, original and soya-free vegenaise. Provamel and Oatly cooking creams. Meridian, Clearspring, Whole Earth, Sunita, Sun & Seed spreads and jams, carob spread. Zest and Mr Organic sauces. The Cornish Seaweed Company sea salad, kombu and spaghetti. Big range of tea. Chocolate, Veggiebear organic jellies and Hippeas vegetable cheese puffs.

Bodycare by Lavera, Faith in Nature, Mistry's and Urtekram. Nature's Own and essential oils.

Cleaning products by Ecover (and refills), Simply Gentle, Essentials and Ecoleaf

They only deliver within 7 miles radius of the store, to keep food miles to a minimum and ensure the freshest produce. Delivery/ service charge is £1.75 whatever size, and 90p if there is one more delivery in the same street.

Second Nature
Organic wholefood store & deliveries

- 78 Wood Street E17 3HX
- 020 8520 7995, fax too
- M-Sa 8.00-17.30 (F 18.00), Su closed
- Wood Street BR

Wholofoods, mostly UK grown produce and only certified organic fruit and vegetables. Big discount if you buy fruit, vegetables and anything else in bulk. Around 50 products are Fairtrade and they don't stock anything with artificial additives.

Fridge: VBites, Taifun, Cheatin, Violife, Vegusto, Cheezly, Follow Your Heart, Tofutti. Povamel, Koko, Sojade, spreads. Frozen: Amy's, Fry's and Clive's pies.

Vita Health
Wholefoods shop

- 565 Lea Bridge Rd, **Leyton** E10 7EQ
- 020 8539 3245
- M-Sa 9.00-18.00, Su closed
- Leyton

Usual range of wholefoods and chilled and frozen veggie foods including veggie sausages and burgers, but no fresh take-away. Small toiletries section with cruelty-free shampoos and soaps and a few books. Vitamins and supplements including Solgar.

The Birds

KeraSpice

Holland & Barrett, Walthamstow
Health food shop

- Unit 34/35 The Mall, 45 Selborne Road, Walthamstow E17 7JR
- 020 8521 5281
- M-Sa 9.00-19.00, Su 10.30-17.00
- Walthamstow Central

Fridge and freezer.

- 174 High St, Walthamstow E17 7JS
- 020 8617 9489
- M-Sa 9.30-18.00, Su 11.00-17.00
- Walthamstow Central

No fridge or freezer.

Walthamstow Market
Street market

- The entire length of Walthamstow High Street (which appears as just a thin blue line on google maps)
- Tu-F 08.00-17.00, Sa 08.00-17.30, Su closed
- Walthamstow Central
- walthamforest.gov.uk/content/walthamstow-market

Starting just north of the tube and bus station and running west for 1km along the pedestrianised high street as far as St James Street. Dating from 1885, this is the longest outdoor market in Europe, with 500 stalls, plus supermarkets, shops and cafes including English, Indian, Turkish, Chinese, Portuguese, and a couple of pubs. While the area is 41% black and ethnic minority, especially Pakistani and Afro-Caribbean, the market still has a traditional cockney feel.

Walthamstow Farmers' Market
Street market

- Town Square by Selbourne Walk
  Shopping Centre, off the High
  Street, Walthamstow E17 7JN
- Su 10.00-14.00
- Walthamstow Central
- lfm.org.uk/markets/walthamstow
  facebook.com/
  WalthamtowFarmersMarket

Look out for Global Fusion Foods vegan
cakes and pastries (see Stoke Newington),
and locally grown Organiclea veg.

LEYTONSTONE

The Birds
Omnivorous food pub

- 692 High Rd **Leytonstone** E11 3AA
  (corner Aylmer Road)
- 020 8556 1131
- Food M-Su 11.00-22.00. Open M
  09.00-23.00, Tu-Th 09.00-24.00,
  F-Sa 09.00-01.00, Su 12.00-23.00.
- Leytonstone
- thebirds.pub
  facebook.com/thebirdsleytonstone
  instagram.com/thebirdsleytonstone

As in the iconic film by local boy Alfred
Hitchcock.

From summer 2018 half the menu at this
pub is vegan fast food (like Temple of Seitan
or The Full Nelson pub in Deptford). Mains
£6.50-£7.50. Seitan chicken burger, mac
n cheese, buffalo wrap, dirty fries, tempura
cauliflower in sticky Asian sauce. Seitan
Sunday roast £13 with all the trimmings.
American pancakes £6, vegan snickers
£2.50. Vegan beers are labelled, craft

beers, ciders, fruit ciders on tap.

Beer garden. Children welcome until 8pm.
Dogs welcome, water bowls. Party Fri, DJ
Sat 21.00-01.00, quiz Wed.

Also a hostel upstairs in 6 or 9 bed mixed
or female dorm £12-£15.

KeraSpice
Omnivorous south Indian restaurant

- 715 High Road, Leytonstone E11 4RD
- 020 8539 1700, 079 1835 8587
- Sa-Su 12.00-14.30, 17.30-22.30; M,
  W-F 17.30-22.30; Tu closed
- Leytonstone
- keraspice.com
  facebook.com/keraspice

Recommended by Feel Good Cafe for
interesting vegan dishes with coconuts, and
traditional Keralan masala dosa.

Yat Sing
Chinese & Thai take-away

- 316 Grove Green Road, Leytonstone
  E11 4EA
- 020 8539 4957
- M-Sa 12.00-14.30, 17.00-24.00,
  Sun 14.00-24.00
- Leytonstone
- yatsing.co.uk

A dozen vegetable, veg duck and beancurd
dishes £3.50-£4.50. Meal for 2 with 5
dishes £17.50. Banana or pineapple fritter
£2.50.

Nature's Choice
Health food shop

- ☛ 47 Church Lane, Leytonstone E11 1HE
- ☏ 020 8539 4196
- 🕐 M-Sa 9.00-18.30, Su 11.00-16.30
- ⊖ Leytonstone

Health food shop with organic bread, vegan cheese and ice-cream, magazines and books, body care and a small savoury and sweet take-away selection. Ecover and refills.

Natural remedies, supplements. Chinese medical centre, nutritionist, Reiki, food allergy testing, hypnotherapy, every day by appointment.

Feel Good Cafe
Vegan organic cafe & shop

- ☛ The Village Arcade, 49 Station Road, **Chingford** E4 7DA
- ☏ 07799 965611
- 🕐 M-Sa 10.00-15.00, Su closed
- ⊖ Chingford BR
- ➤ thefeelgoodcafe.com
  facebook.com/TheFeelGoodCafe

Healthy, cosy cafe for eat in or take away, with four seats inside and lots more outside in the arcade.

Smoothies and cold-pressed juices £5. Smoothie bowls £6, porridge £5, topped with fruit, nuts and seeds. Choice of almond milk or apple juice.

Lentil burger meal £8.50 in a sourdough bun with salad. Veggie stew £5. Hummus and roasted vegetable on rye; avocado on rye and peanut butter and topping on rye; all £5.

Treats and cakes subject to availability including carrot cake, matcha brownie, raspberry and almond brownie, flapjack £2.50-£3. Ice-cream cup small £2, large £4, chocolate, raspberry ripple, vanilla, add toppings 50p.

Coffee £2.20-£2.70, tea £1.80, golden milk £3; summer special iced tea, iced latte, add ice cream for 50p. Soya and almond milk.

In the fridge: Violife, Soyade, Booja Booja truffle, Ombar chocolate and Aduna; Whole Earth drinks, Rude Health milk and quinoa baby food.

On the shelves: Chicla organic chewing, Rock and Raw cacao nibs, Ombar buttons, Suma peanut butter, Kirkland maple syrup, Pukka teas, Profusion red lenti pasta, Engevita, Organic vegetable bouillon, Rw Garcia sweet potato crackers.

Organic cotton and Fairtrade T-shirts, hoodies, fabric shoppers, aprons £10-£40.

Seating in courtyard. Wifi. High chairs. All packaging is compostable. Catering. Workshops and nutrition courses.

Village Health
Health food store

- ☛ 36 Station Road, **North Chingford** E4 7BE
- ☏ 020 8524 5484
- 🕐 M-Sa 9.00-17.30, Su closed
- ⊖ Chingford BR

Previously Food & Fitness health food store, and run by two of its staff, the nutritionist and allergy tester.

Wholefoods. Gluten-free. Organic baby foods. Bodycare, vitamins, herbs, aromatherapy, flower remedies, sports nutrition.

Waltham Forest Vegans
Local groups

- ➤ Facebook Waltham Forest Vegans

Facebook group for vegans in or around the London Borough of Waltham Forest to share about local places to get vegan food. Includes Chingford, Leyton, Leytonstone, Walthamstow. Over 700 members.

VEGAN EAST LONDON © Copyright

1st edition by Alex Bourke
EAN 978-1-902259-15-4
Published January 2020
by Vegetarian Guides Ltd
www.veganlondon.guide

2 Hilborough Court, Livermere Road, London E8 4LG, UK
Tel: 020-3239 8433 (24 hrs)
International: +44-20-3239 8433

Distributed in UK by Bertrams, Gardners, Marigold
In USA/Canada by Book Publishing Company, TN. www.bookpubco.com
Updates to this guide at: vegetarianguides.co.uk/updates
Link and earn 10% commisssion: vegetarianguides.co.uk/affiliate

In the same series:
VEGAN CENTRAL LONDON
VEGAN NORTH LONDON
VEGAN SOUTH LONDON
VEGAN WEST LONDON
VEGAN LONDON comprehensive edition

Printed by Buxton Press

VEGAN NORTH
LONDON

1st edition

The complete insider guide to the best vegan food in London

Alex Bourke
Vegetarian Guides

AWARD WINNI
GOSH BROWN

GTA Awarded So
Moist and Choco
Brownie — bet y
can't tell it's vega

NORTH LONDON

* OUR TOP 5 - BEST OF NORTH LONDON *

Dining Out
The Gate, Islington
Loving Hut, Holloway Road
Mildreds, Camden
Mildreds, Kings Cross
Rasa, Stoke Newington

Indian
Healthy Wealthy, Brecknock Rd
Jai Krishna, Finsbury Park
Rani, Finchley
Rasa, Stoke Newington
Woodlands, Hampstead

Oriental
Dou Dou, Camden
Itadaki Zen, Kings Cross
Loving Hut, Archway
Lemongrass, Camden
Zen Buddha, Edgware

All you can eat
Dou Dou, Camden
Indian Veg, Islington
Loving Hut, Archway

Vegan Cake/Dessert
Bodega 50, Stoke Newington
Cookies & Scream, Holloway Rd
Healthy Wealthy, Brecknock Rd
Nora & Nama, Camden
Vx, Kings Cross

Camden Cafes
Fields Beneath
Hawraman Cafe
Highstone Brew
Nectar Cafe
Amorino

Camden Fast Food
Magic Falafel
Rudy's DIrty Vegan Diner
VBurger
What the Pitta
Young Vegans Pie Shop

Wholefood Shopping
Bumblebee, Brecknock Rd
Earth Natural, Kentish Town
Haelan Centre, Crouch End
Mother Earth, Stoke Newington
Planet Organic, Essex Road

Vegan Clothing
The Third Estate, Brecknock Rd
Vx, Kings Cross
Thamon, Camden
Camden Markets

Night Out
Green Note, Camden
Karamel, Wood Green
Mildreds, Camden or Kings Cross
Purezza, Camden
Rasa, Stoke Newington

Healthy Wealthy
101% Vegan Indian restaurant

🖝 10 Brecknock Road N7 0DD
📞 020 77000 777, 07466 838943
🕐 M-Sa12.00-21.00, Su closed
⊖ Kentish Town, Camden Road
🡥 hwrestaurant.com

London's only VEGAN Indian restaurant opened in 2017 just up the road from Camden and opposite The Third Estate vegan clothing shop. It is an airy, luminous, spotless family restaurant - and there are stacks of vegan desserts! Everything is made in-house, even the vegan ice-cream, which is why they say it is 101% vegan as there is no outside production.

Medium thali £6.99 varies each day, with rice, soup, dal, curry, salad and poppadom. They always have 2 rice, 2 soups and 4 curries to choose from. The menu changes often, such as cumin rice, lemon yellow rice, blackeyed bean soup and toor dahl for £2.50, spinach and tofu curry, tofu jalfrezi, aloo gobi, soya chunk curry and pumpkin and banana squab for £3, and salad for £2.50. Smal thali £5 with rice, dal and curry. Queen £8.99 and King thali £9.99 include extra curries.

Snacks 50p-£1 includw samosa, kachori, roti, chapati, pakora, naan and poppadom.

Indian restaurants, even vegetarian ones, are almost always utterly hopeless for vegan desserts. But not here. There's a whole glass cabinet chock full of them. Desserts and snacks £1-£3 include pannacotta with strawberry or passion fruit sauce, energy balls, halva, and all these cakes: carob, mango , ginger, mango and ginger, vanilla and carob, raisin.

Soft drinks £2. Vegan mango lassi and rose

milk £3. Smoothies £2.50. Teas £1.50. No alcohol or bring your own - they are Krishna devotees and do not believe it is healthy.

The walls display local paintings which are for sale. They will have tables outside ready for summer. Wifi and highchairs. Minimum card payment £5.

Bumblebee
Wholefoods store, organic greengrocer, bakery, take-away and natural remedies

---

☛ 32, 33, 35 Brecknock Road N7 6AA

(020 7607-1936

◑ M-Sa 9.00-18.30, Su closed

⊖ Kentish Town, Camden Road BR
Bus 393, 390, 29, 253

↘ bumblebeenaturalfoods.co.uk

Independent wholefoods heaven! Three shops close together: a bakery/deli, a dry/sauces and natural remedies shop, and a greengrocer/dairy shop. Lots of unusual hard-to-find items.

Massive selection of wholefoods, health foods, organic fruit and veg, macrobiotic foods and the bakery has organic bread delivered daily from organic bakers. Big range of south European foods and olive oils.

Takeaway foods and lunches 11.30-15.00 £2.95-£3.95. Always at least two vegan hot dishes based around rice. Tofu quesadillas, tofu pasties, burritos, samosas. Salads made in house. Soup £1.75.

Box scheme (different sizes) for organic fruit and veg. Trade delivery service for other produce.

Nice things in the fridge include tofu, fake meats by Tivall; Sojade, Koko and Provamel yogurts; Sheese, Violife, Tofutti; Vegenaise Cesar and Ranch sauce, spreads, Fry's. Swedish Glace, Booja Booja soya-free ice-cream.

Enormous selection of vegan and organic wines and beers, probably the biggest in London.

Vegan and organic wines and beers.

Household products such as Ecover, Ecoleaf, BioD, Earth Friendly, Method.

Natural Remedies include herbal, homeopathy and flower essences. Vitamins and minerals including Solgar, Viridian, Biocare, Nature's Own. Lots of bodycare, creams, shampoos and cosmetics by Dr Hauschka, Green People, Jäson, Lavera, Dr Bronner's, Urtekram, Weleda. Mother and baby things.

Large selection of herbs and spices that you can weight out yourself 90p-£2.95 per 100 gr. Loose Nuts and seeds 38p-£2.40.

Magazines.

Pay and display parking on street.

The Third Estate
Vegan clothing and shoes shop

- 27 Brecknock Road N7 0BT
- 020 3620 2361
- Tu 11.00-19.30, W-Sa 10.00-18.00, Su-M closed
- Kentish Town, Camden Road BR Bus 29, 253, 390, 393
- TheThirdEstate.co.uk
  shop@TheThirdEstate.co.uk
  facebook.com/thirdestatelondon
  Facebook The Third Estate

The Third Estate have been selling men's and women's clothing and footwear since 2005.

All the footwear is vegan. Brands for women and men include Vegetarian Shoes, Nae, Workers Playtime, Veja, Walsh, Jonnys Vegan, Wills, Inkkas and Fair. Nikwax footwear cleaning gel and spray waterproofing.

Also a range of independent clothing made from organic or reclaimed materials and clothing which is fairly/ethically traded.

Clothing brands include Monkee Genes, Fred Perry, Mud jeans, Dedicated Komodo, People Tree, Workers Playtime, Armed Angels and Sketch.

Big range of bags from Matt & Natt.

To get here from Camden: from Sainsbury's, take a bus 29 or 253 a mile north-east along Camden Road towards Palmers Green and get off at Brecknock Road.

THE THIRD ESTATE

HAMPSTEAD

KENTISH TOWN

BRECKNOCK ROAD

CHALK FARM

HAWLEY RD

ROYAL COLLEGE STREET

CAMDEN ROAD

Ma

Stables Market

Mu
Ha

Ru
MF
Do
MF
Camden Lock Market
No
VB
YV

Te

Morrison's Supermarket

PRIMROSE HILL

CAMDEN RD

KENTISH TOWN RD

JAMESTOWN ST

Wa
Mi
Ne
Am

DD
Wo

CAMDEN ROAD

CAMDEN ROAD

INVERNESS ST

HB

CAMDEN TOWN

Br
Wh

Fi

CAMDEN STREET

PARKWAY

Pu
WF
Gr
Ro

HIGH STREET

BAYHAM ST

PRATT ST

Se

PLENDER ST

ARLINGTON RD

DELANCEY ST

EUSTON

CAMDEN LOCK MARKET
No Nora & Nama
VB VBurger
YV Young Vegans

STABLES MARKET
Do The Green Dough
MF Magic Falafel (x2)
Ru Rudy's Dirty Vegan

SHOPS
HB Holland & Barrett
WF Whole Foods Maret

PRIMROSE HILL
Ma Manna

CAMDEN TOWN
DD Dou Dou
Fi Fields Beneath, Camden
Pu Purezza
Te Temple of Camden
Wh What the Pitta

Am Amorino ices
Gr Green Note
Ha Hawraman
Mi Mildreds Camden
Ne Nectar Cafe
Br Brewdog Bar
Le Lemongrass
Mu Muang Thai
Ro Round Falafel
Se Seto (Japanese)
Wa Wagamama (Japanese)
Wo Woody / Hummus (Turkish)

⬤ vegan
⬤ vegetarian
⬤ omnivorous
⬤ shop

CAMDEN

Camden Town, Markets, Primrose Hill

Camden, on the north-east edge of Regent's Park, features some of the best bars, clubs and pubs in London which are the basis of a lively music scene. The various huge and unique covered markets attract an eclectic mix, who flock there at the weekend in their thousands. It's a magnet for all ages, especially the alternative crowd and vegans.

Near the tube: Right outside **Camden Town** tube is **Dou Dou** with a big all-you-can-eat vegan Chinese buffet (probably moving south to Plender Street). Down Bayham Street are **What the Pitta** vegan kebabs and **Brewdog** bar, full of vegan craft beers, and around the corner a new branch of **The Fields Beneath** vegan cafe that started in Kentish Town. Walk down to the canal and along it towards Kings Cross to reach **Temple of Camden** vegan fried chick'n restaurant.

Heading north up Camden High Street past a large Holland & Barrett, the last street on the left before the canal, Jamestown Road, features **Mildreds** proper sit-down vegetarian restaurant, and furher along is Triyoga Centre (previously in Primrose Hill) with its **Nectar Cafe** that specialises in salads.

Camden Lock Market: On the left of Camden High Street, after the bridge over Regents Park Canal, is the beginning of the main attraction, Camden Market, giving you the best choice of hip new and secondhand clothes in town, jewellery, crafts, hippy and Goth stuff galore. A little way in are **VBurger**, behind them **Nora & Nama** cakes, then **Young Vegans** pie and mash shop.

Stables Market: Deep inside this market, past the newest branch of **Magic Falafel**, along the path next to the main road, you'll find **The Green Dough**, then the original **Magic Falafel**. Down the end, past the statue of local hero Amy Winehouse, is **Rudy's Dirty Vegan Diner**, sit-down fast food heaven.

Chalk Farm Road: Opposite the bustle of Camden Stables market, Kurdish run veggie cafe **Hawraman** is an oasis of tranquility, offering huge plates of food for under a tenner. We had a relaxing time sipping lentil soup, smoothies and chai.

Up the hill on the left after Chalk Farm tube station is **Primrose Hill**, with a magnificent view over London and top end vegan restaurant **Manna**. (closed for renovations as this book goes to print)

Parkway, running west from the tube station towards Regents Park, stars new vegan Italian restaurant **Purezza**, **Whole Foods Market** for picnic supplies for the park, and at the far end is **Green Note**, a basement live music venue pub, with paying events most nights and light vegetarian meals.

Non-vegan places that vegans love include Cambodian, Japanese, Thai or Turkish.

When you've had your fill of Camden, head north to the food stores and Ethiopian restaurants of **Kentish Town**, or north-east to **Brecknock Road** for vegan clothing at The Third Estate and London's first 100% vegan Indian restaurant Healthy Wealthy. Or a gentle ramble on **Hampstead Heath**.

Dou Dou

Dou Dou
99% Vegan Chinese buffet restaurant

- 6 Kentish Town Road NW1 9NX (by the tube)
- 07850 663328
- Su-Th 12.00-22.30, F-Sa 12.00-23.00
- Camden Town

Chinese vegan buffet and take-away with lots of fake meat. Open every day for lunch and dinner. All you can eat £5.90, £6.90 after 5pm and Sunday, plus 10% service charge, so it's actually £6.49 and £7.59. Take-away box £3.50 or £4.50 large.

Fritters (banana, apple, pineapple) three pieces £2, six £3. Vegans should note that the banana ship dessert £3.80 contains dairy ice cream.

Soft drinks or tea £1.50. Fresh juice £2.50. Wine glass £3.50, bottle £14, beer £2.60-£3. Cash only.

As of October 2019 there was a notice in the window saying that they are moving to Plender Street, which is at the bottom of our Camden map.

Purezza

#plantpione

Purezza

Purezza
Vegan Italian restaurant

- 43 Parkway NW1 7PN
- 020 3884 0078
- Su-Th 12.00-22.00, F-Sa 12.00-23.00
- Camden Town
- purezza.co.uk/london-restaurant
  instagram purezzauk

After the phenomenal success of Purezzas's first branch near the seaside in Brighton, this second branch opened March 2018 close to Camden Town tube and Whole Foods Market. Unlike pizza chain restaurants, here all the cheese is vegan, made in house, such as silken tofu ricotta, cashew and almond nut cheeses, melty coconut, and brown rice mozzarella. It's classy with lots of wood, even a wood fired oven. Soya, nut or gluten-free no problem. Kids get a free mini pizza when adults order from the main menu, one child per adult.

Starters £3.50 include garlic bread, marinated olives, or crunchy giant fried corn with peanuts and harissa spice.

Mains £10-£16.50 include seitan calzone, gluten-free ragu mince lasagna, Pure Bowl (chickpeas, quinoa, squash, veggies, fermented onion, cashew cream cheese), even a raw pizza. Regular pizzas come on wholegrain, hemp or gluten-free sourdough, with toppings that can include smoked mozzarella, ricotta, marinated artichoke, smoked beetroot carpaccio, olives, fried aubergine, seitan, tofu sausage, smoked tofu, pine nuts, portobello and chestnut mushrooms, sundried tomato, garlic mayo, BBQ sauce, oven roasted potato, veggies.

Mon-Fri lunch menu with smaller version of their classic main dishes, all £5 or less till 4pm, and a £10 set menu gets you a 7-inch pizza or mac n cheese (add £1 per extra topping), garden bowl, cheesy dough balls. courgetti spaghetti or coleslaw (all of which can also be served as sides), plus some nibbles and a drink.

Desserts £4.50-£5.85 feature chocolate brownie with dark chocolate sauce, raw tiramisu, crème brûlée, Oreo pizza with hazelnut chocolate spread and mascarpone style sauce, banana baked gelato. Cashew cheese board £12.

Superfood smoothies or chocolate Oreo milkshake £5.50-£6. Soft drinks, fresh coconut, ginger kombucha £3-£4.85. Tea, espresso £1.50, latte or cappuccino £3.50, cacao and maca hot chocolate £3.95, almond Baileys latte £5.50.

House wine £4.50 medium glass, £5.50 large, £16.50 bottle. Beers, cider from £3.95. Cocktails £6.

10% discount on eat in or take-away food for students, NHS and Amex staff from their local HQ (not Deliveroo).

The Fields Beneath, Camden
Vegan cafe

- 29a Pratt Street, Camden NW1 0BG
- 020 7879 9164
- M-F 07.00-16.00, Sa 08.00-16.00, Su 9.00-16.00
- Camden Town
- thefieldsbeneath.com
  facebook.com/fieldsbeneath

After turning their original cafe in Kentish Town fully vegan in March 2017, this second branch opened in 2019 just south of Camden Town tube. For menu see Kentish Town.

Temple of Camden
Vegan fast food restaurant

- 103a Camley Street N1C 4PF
- no phone
- M-Sa 11.00-21.00, Su 11.00-18.00. Also breakfast M-F 9.00-11.45.
- Camden Town, Mornington Crescent, Camden Road BR
- templeofseitan.co.uk

Following the phenomenal success of their first vegan fried chick'n shop in Hackney Central in 2017, in 2018 Temple of Seitan opened another at Hackney Downs, and here by the canal between Camden and Kings Cross. This is their flagship, a sit-down diner with tables inside and out. Access it from the street, or walk along the canal from either Kings Cross or Camden Town.

Main dishes £5-£7 include various flavours of fried chick'n burger with extras that include bacon, cheese, chipotle mayo, coleslaw, jalapenos, sriracha, pickles; a quarterpounder cheeseburger with bacon; or hot dipped, buffalo or BBQ wings; .Add fries or coleslaw and a drink for £2.50, large portion £3.50. Mac 'n cheese £3.50, large £5. Top up with an extra burger, popcorn bites, coleslaw, gravy, extra bacon or cheese, pot of mayo (chipotle, ranch, classic, or lemon pepper).

Lots of desserts £2-£3 on display in a glass cabinet such as choc brownies, peanut butter cookie sandwich, marshmallow chocolate cookie, carrot cake, cinnabuns, summer berry slice, croissant, pain au chocolat, pain au raisin.

Dark Arts coffee, latte, cappuccino, flat white, cortado £2-£2.60. Teapigs tea £1.50. 30p discount if you bring your own cup. With Oatly or Bonsoy. Cans £1.50.

What The Pitta, Camden
Vegan kebab restaurant

- 89-91Bayham Street, NW1 0AG
- 07857 576 177
- Su-W 11.30-21.00, Th-Sa 11.30-23.00
- Camden Town
- whatthepitta.com
  facebook.com/whatthepitta

Opened March 2018, the third branch of London's vegan kebab shop chain. It's south of the tube station, just past Brewdog.

Huge doner £7.95 comes either in a wrap, or in a box with chips or couscous, packed with soya chunks, hummus, tzatziki, salads and chilli.

Top up with fries £3.50, hummus £2.50, or mixed olives £2.50. Vegan lahmacun Turkish pizza £4 on thin dough topped with minced soya and veg plus herbs, tomato, onions, spices.

For dessert £2.50 you can have vegan baklava

Beer £3.50, soft drinks £2.

Meal Deal 1 £10 gets you a main, soft drink, and baklava dessert, made with layers of filo pastry, crushed almonds and syrup. Meal Deal 2 £12 for main, drink and fries.

Seats inside. Ice-cream coming soon. Deliveroo, UberEats. Also in Shoreditch Boxpark, Croydon Boxpark and Brighton.

To avoid queuing, you can place your order using the At Hand app and it will be waiting for you:

- athand.co.uk
  athand.co.uk/brands/what-the-pitta

Manna
Vegan restaurant

- ☛ 4 Erskine Road, Primrose Hill NW3 3AJ
- ☏ 020 7722 8028
- ◑ Tu-F 12.00-15.00 (last orders), 18.30-22.00; Sat 12.00-15.00,18.00-22.00; Su 12.00-20.30; M closed
- ⊖ Chalk Farm
- ↖ mannalondon.co.uk

Very classy international gourmet vegan restaurant with very reasonable prices for the high standard and location, set in a picturesque street near Primrose Hill, still going strong since 1966, with incredibly friendly and efficient service by staff from all over the world. The menu is constantly changing with the seasons.

Lunch dishes £7-£8 include soup of the day, falafel burger with fries, Italian baguette sandwich with veatballs and salad veg, courgette and corn fritters with cashew sour cream, polenta tart with roasted garlic and basil cashew ricotta, raw tacos, raw maki rolls, or baked potato filled with black beans, jalapeno cheese, guacamole and salsa. For a bit more you can have organic spaghetti and veatballs or a chef salad. Soup and main £12. Lunch desserts £6 or less such as cheesecake with vice-cream, raw carrot cake, fruit and berry salad with ice-cream or sorbet, or a plate of truffles with chcolate and small biscuits.

Sensational evening starters £7-£8 include wild mushroom and walnut paté ravioli with fennel cream sauce; cashew spiced jerk tofu with plantain and sweet potato kebab; or share a starters mezze selection £22.

Evening mains £11-£14 feature a huge black bean and cashew nut cheese enchilada casserole, root veg tagine with quinoa and pistachio tabouleh, organic bangers and mash. Or build your own meal from any four sides for £14.

Desserts £5-£8 are astounding, like liqueur vice-cream, cranberry orange cheesecake, banoffee trifle, and chocolate almond torte.

5-course chef's menu with aperitif and glass of house wine is £40 each for four people, designed for you and needs pre-booking. Wine matching available.

Organic vegan wine from £5 glass, £22 bottle. Cocktails, mocktails and aperitifs £4-£9.

On Saturday there are some extra surprise specials, while Sunday they add a roast that changes from week to week.

Service charge 12.5%. Children's portions. Booking advised. High chairs. MC, Visa.

Available Tu-F for parties of 20+, set menu with minimum charge. Gift vouchers. Cookery classes in London and Los Angeles. Private tuition and consultation. They supply organic cakes, muffins, brownies and flapjacks to restaurants and street markets.

During 2019 Manna has been "closed for ongoing refurbishment" but they have assured us that they are intending to reopen.

Mildreds Camden
Vegetarian restaurant

- 9 Jamestown Road NW1 7BW
- 020 7482 4200
- M-Sa 12.00-23.00, Su 12.00-22.00
- Camden Town
- mildreds.co.uk/camden
  facebook.com/mildredsrestaurant

The second branch of Mildreds has the classic a la carte dishes from the original Soho restaurant, and a weekday lunchtime salad bar. Following the 2016-17 trend in vegetarian food, most dishes are now vegan and 95% of the drinks.

Starters £4-£7 include gyoza dumpling, hummus with rose harissa and flat bread, chargrilled Roman artichokes with crostini, Egyptian spiced spinach with raisins and pistachios, chickpeas and roasted red pepper with paprika, tenderstem broccoli with confit garlic and chilli, roasted miso aubergine with ginger and spring onions, smashed avocado with lime and chilli and corn chips, Iceberg wedge with smoked pecan and salad cream.

Burgers £8, made with smoked tofu and lentils or Polish style with beetroot and white beans. Add vegan cheese £1. Other main courses £12 such as Sri Lankan sweet potato and bean curry with roasted lime cashew, pea basmati rice and coconut tomato sambal; stir-fried veg with tofu brown jasmine rice, kimchi and peanuts; Mexican spicy black beans with quinoa, raw corn salsa, corn chips, grilled pineapple and smashed avocado; superfood soul salads bowl; detox salad; wood roasted mushroom with ale pie with minted mushy peas.

Desserts £3-£6.50 include passionfruit meringue tartlet with coconut yogurt; chocolate and hazelnut brownie with salted caramel sauce and ice cream; panna cotta with hibiscus scented lychees; peach, strawberry and bramley apple polenta crumble with ice-cream; vanilla ice-cream with dark chocolate and pomegranate sauce; Pedro Ximenez truffles; fuzzy green raw balls.

Wine glass £5.50, bottle £20, beer and cider £4.20-£4.90, cocktails £6.50-£7.50, mocktails £4.80, after dinner liqueurs £3.65-7.50. Fresh organic juices £4.50, soft drinks £2.50-£3.

Organic coffee £2.10-£2.50, tea £2, Bonsoy 30p extra.

High chairs. Advance reservations for up to 12 people by email to camden@mildreds. co.uk. They do not take on-the-day bookings, just come along as they keep half the restaurant available for walk-ins.

Also in Dalston, Kings Cross and Soho.

Amorino, Camden
Vegetarian ice-cream parlour & cafe

- ☛ 237 Camden High St, London NW1 7BU
- ☏ 020 7482 5416
- 🕐 M-Th 11.00-24.00, Sa 10.30-24.00, Su 10.30-23.00
- ⊖ Camden Town
- ⬉ amorino.com

Many of the sorbets here are vegan and labelled with the Vegan Society trademark, including the very creamy chocolate, and you can mix flavours in a but.

Also coffees and herb teas.

Note that extras like cornets etc are not vegan, though in one branch they told us they are working on that.

Hawraman Cafe
Almost vegan Mediterranean restaurant

- 38 Chalk Farm Road NW1 8AJ
- 07737 892812
  Su-Th 10.30-21.30, F-Sa 10.30-22.30, last order one hour before closing
- Chalk Farm, Camden Town
- hawramancamdencafe.com
  Facebook Hawraman Cafe

A gem just opposite the Stables market, run by two Kurdish brothers Salar and Kawa Hamarash. From 2007 until 2017 they ran My Village vegetarian restaurant next door, but were forced to close by a huge rent increase. Beautiful, eclectic, ethnic interior with objects from Iraq, Bangladesh, India, Morocco, Italy etc. If you are looking for something original and special, this is the place. The owners always have time for a friendly chat. There is a cute room at the back, Berber style with rugs, seating on the floor, comfy cushions and a fireplace, that that can also be hired for private events. Also a garden at the back.

For breakfast try nutty or berry granola £6.50, add 40p for almond milk, £1.50 for a coffee, £2.50 for a smoothie.

All soups £5.50 are vegan, such as brown and yellow lentil with tomato, served with toasted brown Greek bread. Appetizers and plates £5-£10.45 include green hummus with dill, aubergine with tomato sauce, babaganoush aubergine dip, green hummus falafel, Hawraman salad. The Hawraman Plate which includes rice with yellow split peas and a separate clay hotpot of aubergine, chickpeas and tomato sauce, plus babaganoush, and tons of mixed salad with olive oil pesto.

Gluten-free chocolate brownie and raw orange brownie, gluten-free flapjack £2.50. Pulsin bar £1.79, buy five get one free.

Smoothies, juices and shakes £3-£4. Soft drinks 99p-£1.50.

Wine medium glass £4.50, large £5.75, bottle £17.50. Beers £4-£4.50, one is gluten-free. Organic cider ££4.50. Ouzo glass £6.50, 20cl bottle £14 comes with hummus and sliced cucumber.

Hot drinks £1.95-£4 include (iced) coffee or mocha, Greek frappe coffee, chai or matcha latte, hot chocolate, with added orange, mint or cinnamon. Almond milk 30p extra. Teas include Japanese organic green, soba buckwheat, gobo-cha detox, matcha.

For take out most of the prices are cheaper. Cash only. Tables outside and cosy garden at the back. Table games: dominos, chess, backgammon. No wifi.

Green Note

Nectar

Green Note
Vegetarian bar with live music

- 106 Parkway NW1 7AN
- 020 7485 9899
- Su-Th 19.00-23.00, F-Sa 19.00-24.00, also Su 14.00-17.30 when events
- Camden Town
- greennote.co.uk (events listings)

Founders Immy and Risa have created a place where you can enjoy quality live music and good veggie food, in a laid-back, friendly atmosphere. Live music most nights includes blues, jazz, folk, roots, world, alt-country, jazz and singer-songwriters. It's one of London's top venues for the very best roots, world and acoustic music and a great night out. Performers since they opened in 2005 have included Amy Winehouse and Leonard Cohen. Advance prices are normally £5 to £10, or up to £15 for big names like Hank Wangford or Tir na nOg, and £2 for open mic nights.

You can read about upcoming acts on the website, buy tickets, listen to tracks and watch video clips. You can also buy tickets at the venue during opening hours. The door price is usually slightly higher than the advance price and many events sell out, but certain events have tickets on the night only so check first. If you'd like a seat, best to arrive early, especially if you want a table, it's first come first served.

Bar food and simple tapas £2.50-3.50 come from local, independent artisan bakers and chefs and includes samosas, bhajias, quiches (not vegan), hummus and pitta, olives, filo wraps filled with Bombay potato or Moroccan spinach. Cakes £3.50 are not vegan but the Happy Kitchen brownies £3 are also gluten-free.

House wine £3.95 glass, £14.50 bottle. Beer £4 bottle, £4.10 pint. Cocktails. Coffee £2.35.

You can hire the Green Note for events, parties for children and adults, film screenings. They have a full PA system, projector, bar and catering facilities and can provide entertainment if required.

Nectar Cafe at Triyoga Camden
Vegetarian cafe in holistic centre

- 57 Jamestown Road NW1 7DB
- (020 7483 3344
- Cafe M-Su 08.00-20.00 (Sat 19.00)
  Centre M-Su 06.00-21.30
- Camden Town
- www.triyoga.co.uk/camden
  facebook.com/triyogauk
  Cafe website or Facebook?

The Triyoga Centre and cafe relocated Dec 2014 from Primrose Hill to a beautiful old Victorian piano factory in Camden with high ceilings and plenty of natural light. The tranquil cafe was set up by Katia Narain Philips, a pioneer of the raw food movement, and offers a nutrient-rich menu including bio-dynamically grown ingredients. You can even pre-order food and juices before class.

Breakfast includes organic raw oat and chia seed porridge sprinkled with rose, lime and toasted pumpkin seeds.

For lunch and dinner there are soups, curries and stews during cold season, and in summer raw vegan sushi, salads and platters. Also wraps. Beetroot paté with cucumber and carrot sticks, or organic mashed avocado on sourdough toast £5.50. Salad bowl £7.50 changes daily,

with ingredients such as quinoa with wild green dressing, beetroot salad with orange and red vinegar dressing, toasted pumpkin seeds.

Cakes and snacks £1.50-£2.50 such as almond tahini and cacao nibs, which they say are a popular post yoga treat. Raw coco chocolate energy balls.

Organic fresh juices £4.75; smoothies £5.50; shots 2. Fairtrade coffee and teas, energising wheatgrass blends. Special hot drinks including trikatu latte (with ginger, turmeric and pepper,), macaccino, matcha, beetroot latte, chai latte. Almond or oat milk 30p extra.

The centre has studios for yoga, hot yoga, pilates, Barre and Gyrotonic, a meditation room and far infrared sauna. Treatments include acupressure, acupuncture, aromatherapy, Ayurveda, CBT, chakra balancing, craniosacral, facials, homeopathy, hypnotherapy, various massages, Metamorphic Technique, naturopathy, NLP, nutrition, osteopathy, physiotherapy, qi gong, reiki and others.

There is a shop with books, cds, dvds, yoga clothes and equipment, flipflops, massage oil massage, candles, aroma diffusers, Himalayan salt, teas, breathable nail varnish

Brewdog Bar Camden
Omnivorous food pub with vegan beers

- ☛ 113 Bayham Street NW1 0AG (walk south from tube down Camden High Street, turn first left into Greenland Street and walk to the end)
- ☎ 020 7485 6145
- ◑ M-Th 12.00-23.30, F-Sa 12.00-24.00, Su 12.00-22.30
- ⊖ Camden Town
- ↖ brewdog.com/bars/camden
  Facebook BrewDog Bar Camden

Chain of pubs with craft beers that are clearly labelled if vegan. A great place to end your evening.

Vegan dishes £8 include Hail Seitan bbq steak with crispy kale, sun kissed tomato chutney and hummus in a bun; Soy Vision tofu dog with avocado hummus, broccoli, carrot and scallion in a bun; superfood salad with quinoa, sweet potato, brown rice, pumpkin seeds. Add fries or sweet potato fries £2-£2.50. Snack on hopped up fries £3.50, sweet potato fries £4.

Dogs welcome. Wifi. Also in Clapham Junction, Clerkenwell, Shepherds Bush, Shoreditch, and Soho.

Wagamama, Camden
Omnivorous Japanese restaurant

- ☛ 11 Jamestown Road NW1 7BW
- ☎ 020 7428 0800
- ◑ M-Sa 12.00-23.00, Su 11.00-22.00
- ⊖ Camden Town
- ↖ wagamama.com

Omnivorous Japanese noodle restaurant with a separate vegan menu.

Lemongrass
Omnivorous Cambodian/SE Asian restaurant

- ☛ 243 Royal College Street NW1 9LT
- ☎ 020 7284 1116
- ◑ Tu-Sa 17.30-23.00, last orders 22.30, Su-M closed
- ⊖ Camden Road, Camden Town
- ↖ lemongrass-restaurant.co.uk
  facebook.com/
  lemongrass1stcambodianrestaurant

Behind Camden Road overground station, London's only Cambodian restaurant has been serving contemporary Cambodian food since 1987. It's small and brightly-lit, with a small menu of mostly stir-fry dishes. The owner is also a chef.

Starters £4.20-£5.50 include veg spring rolls; garlic lemon mushrooms; fried leek cake with chilli sauce; sharing platter for 2 peopl £15, 3 £22.50, 4 30.

Mains £6.70-£7.70 such as Buddhist cabbage with peppers, rainbow stir-fry, pak choy ginger, spicy veg, fresh asparagus. Mango salad £5.50. Steamed rice £2.60. Set vegetarian feast £16.70 a head gets you five treats with dips, mango salad, Buddhist cabbage, fresh asparagus or spiced veg, steamed rice.

Wine from £3.90 glass, £14.60 bottle. Sake half bottle £6.60. Beer £3.30. Spirits £3.30, double £4.60. Soft drinks and juices £2. Coffee £2.50, pot of herbal tea £2.20.

Children welcome, high chairs. Parties up to 25 people.

Muang Thai
Omnivorous Thai restaurant

- ☛ 71 Chalk Farm Road NW1 8AN (between Belmont and Ferdinand Street, opposite the Roundhouse)
- ☏ 020 7916 0653
- ◑ M-F 17.30-23.00, Sa-Su 12.00-23.00
- ⊖ Chalk Farm
- ↖ muang-thai.co.uk

Thai restaurant with lots of veggie options. Coconut rice and garlic rice (ask for no butter) £3.50-£3.65 plus over a dozen veggie dishes £7.95-£8.95 including Pad Thai veg and noodles, red or green curry, stir-fry tofu and ginger, or massaman mild curry with tofu in creamy coconut milk cooked with peanut, potato and onion. Thai soups £4.95. Spring rolls £4.95.

Desserts £5.95 include banana fritter, steamed banana with sweet coconut milk, lychees, sweet sticky rice and bananas, rambutan.

House wine £3.90 medium glass, £4.95 large, £15 bottle. Thai beer £3.65. Spirits and liqueurs £2.80-£3.50. Warm saké £4.50 quarter bottle, very popular in winter.

Children welcome, high chair.

Round Falafel, Parkway
Omnivorous Lebanese falafel take-away

- ☛ 79B Parkway NW1 7PP (between Green Note & Mooboo, opposite side)
- ◑ M-F 10.00-16.00, Sa-Su closed
- ⊖ Camden Town
- ↖ facebook.com/snapsoon instagram.com/round_falafel

Falafels £3-£4.50, small or large, with hummus or aubergine. Also lentil samosas, Lebanese bread. Cans 70p. Tea or mint tea £1.20. Coffee £1.50.

Seto
Omnivorous Japanese restaurant

- ☛ 6 Plender Street NW1 0JT
- ◑ M--Sa 12.00-14.30, 18.00-21.30 Su closed
- ⊖ Camden Town
- ↖ facebook.com/japaneserestaurantseto

Authentic Japanese restaurant with Japanese staff. Vegan options can be arranged on almost everything because it is all made from scratch.

Appetiser £3.80-£4.80 vegetable gyoza (3 or 6 pieces), fried tofu, cold tofu, vegetable tempura, cucumber roll (6 pcs). Mains £7.50-£9 such as vegetable ramen. vegetarian fried noodles, vegetable tempura set, vegetable gyoza set, stir-fried vegetables (with tofu) set. Set menu for £10 includes rice and miso soup. Fully licensed bar, hot sake 220ml bottle £4.25, 720-750ml £18-£25. Sho-chu barley or sweet potato bottle £35-£40. Wine £4 glass, £15 bottle. Beer £2.80-£4. Soft drinks £1.50-£2.50. Minimum order £10. Take-away.

Woody Grill / Hummus
Omnivorous Turkish cafe

- 🖝 1a Camden Road NW1 9LG
- (020 8616 9587
- 🕑 M-Su 11.00-23.00
- ⊖ Camden Town
- ↖ thewoodygrill.co.uk

On the left is a kebab shop that does falafels, on the right a sit-down place with mostly veggie food. You can buy a falafel on the left and eat it sor outside or take it into the sit-down place on the right.

Start with warm pide Turkish bread base which is free, then choose hummus, olives, chips £2.50-£3.90. Hummus wrap, falafel wrap and salad wrap, all with salads and sauce, £3.90-££7.90.

Desserts such as baklava are not vegan.

Freshly squeezed juices £2.40-£3.60 include orange, apple, OJ with carrot and ginger, or apple and celery. Cans £1.50. Tea and herb tea £1-£1.60, coffees £1.90-£2.60, they have soya milk.

Kids welcome, no high chair. Cash only. Note that people might bring in food if their kebab shop next door gets very busy.

Whole Foods Market Camden
Mostly organic supermarket, omnivorous café & take-away

- 🖝 49 Parkway NW1 7PN
- (020 7428 7575
- 🕑 M-F 08.00-21.00, Sa 08.00-21.00, Su 08.00-21.00
- ⊖ Camden Town
- ↖ wholefoods.com

Big wholefoods supermarket with cafe tables outside. They sell everything from tea to toothpaste and have a big take-away food and juice bar. Load up here for a picnic day in Regents Park. 60-80% of fresh produce is organic with lots of local suppliers.

Buffet take-away food bar with salads, baked tofu and savouries (and quite a lot of meat). up to £1.99 per 100gr, though veggies and beans £1.60. Muffins, cakes include gluten-free, vegan carrot and chocolate.

Great choice of organic fruit and vegetables. Lots of fresh breads including gluten-free. Big range of own brand value foods such as rice and oat cakes. Artesan chocolates. Lots of mueslis and everything you need to make your own.

Lots of refrigerated and frozen vegan products such as ice-creams, fake meats and pies. Vegan wines, Weston's cider and beers, vegan Baileys Almande.

Bodycare, makeup and hair dyes. Aromatherapy, natural remedies and supplements with staff on hand to give advice.

Holland & Barrett, Camden
Health food shop

- 189-191 Camden High St NW1 0LT
- 020 7485 9477
- M-F 08.30-20.00, Sa 09.00-20.00, Su 11.00-20.00
- Camden Town

One of the largest London branches of this national chain. Lots of take-away items such as pies, pastries, Mexican slices, cakes, sprouts. A whole aisle of nuts, seeds and dried fruit. Oat cakes, patés, vegan chocolate.

Large range of soya milks, dried goods, frozen ready meals, nut roasts, toiletries, non-dairy cheeses, soya yogurt and ice-creams. Bodycare, aromatherapy. Supplements, hardcore bodybuilding.

Things to look out for in the fridges: VegOut, Cheatin, Tofurky, Dragonfly, Violife, Sheese, Provamel, Pudology, The Chia Company, VBites raspberry and black cherry dessert.

CAMDEN LOCK MARKET WEST YARD

Coming from Camden Town tube station up Camden High Street, just after the bridge over the canal, turn left into Camden Lock Market. Straight ahead on Camden Lock Place is VBurger, with Nora & Nama vegan cake shop just beyond. At the back left of that street is Young Vegans.

To your right, behind VBurger, is the Stables Market, with two long aisles of shops and take-aways running parallel with Chalk Farm Road.

To your left, behind Young Vegans, are more stalls and shops right up to the canal. There are some omnivorous places with good vegan options.

If you're having trouble finding a particular stall, each has a page with a map at

☛ camdenmarket.com/food-drink

VBurger
Vegan fast food burger shop

☛ Camden Lock Place NW1 8AF (next to Gilgamesh restaurant)
● M-Su 10.00-19.00
↖ burger.co.uk (story and menu)
facebook.com/VBurgerCamden

Opened summer 2017 by Amir and Reuven with chef Yossi Edri, serving three kinds of burger for £8 made from beetroot and quinoa, green falafel, or deep fried and breaded seitan schnitzel. That last burger can be doubled up for £3. Also Moving Mountains burger £9.

The Up-beet also comes with with smoked tomato relish, lettuce, tomato, dill gherkins,

sliced red onion topped, and garlic and chive aioli. Feisty Falafel adds fried aubergine, spiced harissa mayo and tahini. Seitan has chipotle mayo and dill gherkins.

For £1-£1.50 you can add vegan sliced cheddar cheese, or smashed avocado with lime and coriander. Sides £2.50 such as skin-on chips made from rustic potato or sweet potato, onion rings, or coleslaw.

Desserts £2.50-£3 are chocolate brownie or date and cacao energy ball. Cold drinks £1-£2.50.

Young Vegans Pie Shop
Vegan pie and mash shop

☛ 60 Camden Lock Place NW1 (past VBurger at the end on the left)
(07949 059049
● M-Su 11.00-19.00
↖ youngvegans.co.uk
facebook.com/youngvegans

London's first vegan pie and mash shop opened October 2017 by Marco the Lord of the Pies and his chef wife Carla. There are always four pies, plus limited edition specials such as Christmas. Choose from seitan ale, curry, all day breakfast, sweet potato, all served with mash, crispy onions and gravy.

Gluten-free mud pie dessert £3 made with peanut butter and cacao. Bottomless coffee with any meal, Pukka teas, ethical soft drinks all £2. Water £1. Frozen pies to cook at home £3.50.

Meal deal £10 for pie and mash, dessert and any drink. Bar seating. They have just opened a vegan pizza restaurant in Bethnal Green, East London.

Nora & Nama
Vegan cake shop & deli

- Unit 596-598 Camden Lock NW1 8AF (to the left of VBurger)
- 07583 233 459 07939 234657
- M-Su 10.00-19.00
- noraandnama.com
  facebook.com/NoraAndNama
  instagram.com/nora.and.nama

Nora and Nama opened their artisan vegan bakery here in December 2018, a much welcome addition after Cookies & Scream (see Holloway Road) closed their Camden branch after a terrible fire gutted their building.

We are talking vegan artisan cakes, cheesecakes, banoffee pie, cookies, brownies, baklava, chocolate truffles, rocher, croissants.

Also toasted bagels and sandwiches such as eggless egg tofu salad with aubergine and rocket, pastrami with coleslaw, or chease' with red pesto, spinach and olives.

Organic coffee.

Some non-vegan stalls around the canal side of the market have good vegan options:

Maize Blaise (Bogota Bandejas), Colombian street food, does a Lean Mean Vegan Machine £7, large £9, with sautéed mini potatoes, garlic rice, slow-cooked red beans, guacamole, sweet fried plantain, balsamic red cabbage, on a bed of salad with toasted pumpkin seeds.

Arepa Venezuelan cornflour wraps, gluten-free with black beans, avocado, and pico de gallo (salsa).

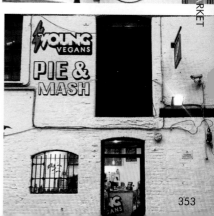

353

Makatcha Indonesian rendang curry £5 with chickpeas, mushrooms, veg, rice, peanut sauce and achar pickles).

Sonita's Kitchen Indian veg curry box £7 or £9 with rice, and pickle.

Crêpes à la Carte French gluten-free buckwheat savoury pancake with raw mushroom, spinach and tahini £5.50. Sweet with sugar and lemon or strawberry jam £3-£3.50, extras 50p such as banana and mixed nuts.

maizeblaze.com
facebook.com/ArepazoBros
makatcha.co.uk
sonitas.co.uk
Facebook Crêpes à la carte

CAMDEN STABLES MARKET

Rudy's Dirty Vegan Diner
Vegan fast food cafe

- Unit 729-731 Camden Stables Market NW1 8AH
- Rudy@rudysdirtyvegandiner.com
- M-Su 11.00-21.00
- rudysdirtyvegandiner.com
  facebook.com/rudysDVD
  instagram.com/rudysdvd
  twitter.com/rudysDVD

Not a food stall, this is a proper sit-down fast food vegan cafe that opened March 2018 in the Stables Market, after the Amy Winehouse statue, almost at the end on a corner near the main road. And it is fast food heaven. Tables inside and outside and stools at the bar. After a year they moved to a bigger unit nearby.

Mains are near all £8 such as Dirty burger with cheeze, pickles, baycon, fried onions, lettuce, ketchup and mayo. Also buffalo chick'n or saboteur's chick'n burger, loaded seitan hot dog, seitan pastrami Reuben classic New York sandwich, chick'n Caesar salad. Extra Dirty more toppings £1.

Pimp up your feast with dirty sides and sharers like mac and cheeze, chilli bowl, Southern-fried chick'n wings, slaw, or loaded or skin-on or cheezy fries, £2.50-£6.50. Dirty Fries £7 are loaded with soya mince chill-non-carne, cashew nut cheeze sauce, jalapenos, coiander and a bit of slaw and corn chips.

Meal deal of burger, fries and drink £10.

Occasional specials, sometimes to test out new dishes, such as club sandwich, meat loaf, buffalo wings with blue cheeze sauce, or spicy chick'n burger.

Sweet treats £4 such as giant cookie cream sandwich. Bottomless cup of coffee £2. Sodas £1.50. Filty shakes. Brewdog beers£4.

Magic Falafel
Vegan falafel cafe and stall

- North Yard, Stables Market NW1 8AH
- 07482 646 499, 07490 466 662
- M-Su 11.00-20.00 or later
- facebook.com/MagicFalafel
  instagram.com/magic_falafel

Their original stall is in the middle of the Stables market, near the entrance on Chalk Farm Road. This was joined in 2018 by a second unit with some seats inside, at the beginning of the Stables Market, behind VBurger.

Falafel in pitta bread £6, Magic box £6.50, plate £7, all include gluten-free falafel, salad, hummus and sauces.

Pitta, salad and hummus £4. Salad box and hummus £5. 6 or 10 falafel balls with tahini £3 or £4.50.

Extra aubergine or pitta 50p. Box of hummus or spicy sauce £1.50, big £2.50. Also brownies.

Rudy's

The Green Dough
Vegan cookie dough stall

☞ Near Cyberdog, moves around
☎ 07521 625 618
🕐 M-Su 10.00-19.00
🔗 thegreendough.webs.com

Friendly French-run outdoor stall with a Cookie Dough sign, on the path from Cafe Loren to Cyberdog. Mix and match a pot of 1. cookie dough, 2. crunchy toppings, 3. fruits garnish. Regular £3.50, large £5. Cookies £2. Donate £1 to plant a tree.

Amy Winehouse statue, Camden Stables

Supplant Foods
Vegan bistro and bar

- 23 Park Road, Crouch End N8 8TE
- 07540 155 343
- M closed; Tu-F 12.00-16.00, 17.00-22.00; Sa 11.00-17.00, 18.00-22.00; Su 11.00-17.00
- Crouch End BR
- www.supplantfoods.co.uk
  facebook.com/mirandacafeuk
  instagram.com/supplantfoods

After a popup in Finsbury Park, Jeremy and Jo have opened Crouch End's first vegan restaurant. Everything is vegan down to the furniture, cleaning products and compostable, chemical-free packaging. Daytime it's light meals, evenings a licensed restaurant.

Daytime menu offers brunch, burgers, sandwiches, toasties and salads £6.50-£10.50.

The full English breakfast inludes sausage, garlic mushrooms, tomato, hash brown, sourdough. Or go lighter with mushrooms or avo on toas, or blueberries and nuts on soya yogurt. Sourdough toasties come in cheese and tomato or seitan ham, chick'n and mayo, or thick seitan with hot pepperjack cheese and fruity chutney. There's a Beyond Meat cheeseburger, a NYC style Vienna hot dog with sauerkraut and mustard, and a crispy coconut bacon butty with hot banana. Salads can be seitan and mushroom, chick'n and capers, or Greek with vegan halloumi. Fill any corners with some plain or rosemary fries or a small salad, both £3.95.

Daytime sweets and treats are all under a fiver such as choc brownie or banana bread or fruit salad with ice cream, banana and peanut sundae, or Oreo-style shake.

Juices, Dalston's fizzy drinks, cola, coffees £2.25-£2.95. Pot of tea £3.25. Same prices in the evening.

Dinner starters £5.50 and under include a mini cheeseboard, mini kebabs, pitta and hummus plate, or tomatoes with pesto.

Dinner mains £10.50-£11.85 include mushroom curry or chili sin carne with rice, lasagne, Beyond Meat cheeseburger with rosemary fries, spicy soy kebabs with rice and salad. Extra veg £3.95. Also specials such as cheezeburger pie with mash, peas and gravy or chips and beans.

Desserts £4.95 or £5.95 feature lime cheesecake with raspberry and pistachio; iced banana bites; hot choc brownie and ice cream; banana and peanut sundae; fruit salad and ice cream.

Wines from £5.75 medium glass, £19.95 bottle. Small glasses also available. Cocktails £7.95. Beers and ciders.

Miranda
Vegetarian cafe-restaurant

- 28 Broadway Parade N8 9DB (at Elder Avenue)
- hello@mirandacafe.co.uk
- Su-W 10.00-17.00, Th-Sa 10.00-21.00
- Crouch End BR, Hornsey BR
- mirandacafe.co.uk
  facebook.com/mirandacafeuk
  instagram.com/mirandacafe

Crouch End's original veggie cafe has most items vegan and they look mouthwatering on their Facebook menu page. Now open evenings too, and they run vegan supper clubs such as One Night In Bangladesh.

Brunch until 3pm includes banana bread with peanut butter, banana and cacao nibs £5.95; pancakes and berries £9.85, and you can add vegan bacon for £1.85; vegan eggs rancheros with black beans, guac, salsa, cheese £9.95; full English cooked £10.95 or go Latin American with cornbread arepas and fried plantain.

Nibbles and starters £3.25-£8.45 include roasted corn, lentil tomato soup with sourdough, edamame, chargrilled artichoke with hummus and garlic crostini, gyoza dumplings, guac and chips, hummus platter.

Burgers around £10.65 are served with roasted potatoes and come in BBQ jackfruit, kimchi bean, or mock chicken. Reuben New York seitan beef sandwich £9.75 with sauerkraut, cheese, slaw, guac. Hot dog and roasted potatoes £9.75.

Mains £11.95 feature Spanish omelette, chili con carne, Buddha bowl, lasagna, katsu curry with seitan, or Caribbean jackfruit in tomato sauce with black beans, guac, plantain and coconut rice.

Desserts are all vegan, mostly under £5 such as cakes, cheesecakes, tiramisu, chocolate hazelnut mousse with ice cream.

Wine from £5.95 medium glass, £21.95 bottle. Cocktails all under £7.50. BrewDog beers £5.50.

Smoothies £4.25. Soft drinks from £2.65. Many types of latte, even açai, £3.95. Teas from £2.95.

Kids' menu £3.45-£6.65 such as scrambled vegan eggs on sourdough, pancakes, full English, cheese open sandwich, seitan hot dog, soup, rice and black beans, penne pasta with pesto.

VEGAN

SUNDAY ROAST

Banner's
Omnivorous restaurant

- 21 Park Rd N8 8TE
- 020 8348 2930
- M-Th 09.00-23.30, F 09.00-24.00, Sa 10.00-24.00, Su 10.00-23.00
- Finsbury Park then W7 bus, Archway or Turnpike Lane then 41 bus
- bannersrestaurant.com

Jamaican influenced really rad little restaurant. Unusual vegan dishes £11.75-£12.25 feature black bean chilli with coconut rice and guacamole; apple and sage veggie sausages with bubble n' squeak, port and Madeira gravy; 10 veg and bean burger in an onion bap with bbq sauce. Also roast red pepper, hummus and falafel sandwich £6.80. Soup with bread £5.25. Sides £1.50-£3.95 such as coconut basmati rice, rice and peas, refried beans, fried plantain, garlic chips, sweet potato fry, avocado and mixed vegetables.

Wifi. High chairs. Community board.

Ginger & Mint
Omnivorus Juice bar and food cafe'

- 11 Park Road N8 8TE
- 020 8341 9181
- Mo-Sa 7.00-18.00, Su 08.00-18.00
- Crouch Hill, Hornsey BR
- gingerandmint.co.uk
  facebook.com/gingerandmint
  instagram.com/gingerandmintuk

A vibrant and colourful cafe with a huge list, around 90 in between juices, pure greens, fruity greens, milkshakes, fruit smoothies, breakfast smoothies, superfood smoothies, protein shakes. All can be made with almond, brown rice and coconut milk. Small £3.50-£4, medium £4-£5 and large £4.50-£5.50. Shots and boosters ££1-£4.

For breakfast you can also have porridge or granola or acai bowl with optional fruit £3-£5.

Various salad boxes £6.50, extra toppings £2 extra. Sandwiches and wraps £5 made with brown bread, gluten-free, brown wrap or ciabatta, all served with salad. Falafel, grilled vegetable and spinach; veggie ball and grilled vegetables and some of them can be made as vegan option.

Coffes and teas £1.50-£2.20.

They also sell fruit and veg, almond and olive oil, teas, plant milk, Ella's Kitchen drinks, Nakd, Meridian and Trek bars, Ombar chocolate, agave syrup and peanut butter.

Cards accepted over £4. Wifi. High chairs. Seats inside and out.

The Haberdashery
Omnivorous cafe

- 22 Middle Lane N8 8PL
- 020 8342 8098
- M-Su 9.00-17.30.
- Crouch Hill, Hornsey BR
- the-haberdashery.com
  facebook.com/groups/
  thehaberdashery

The Haberdashery is a really cool and cute cafe/art gallery with vintage decor.

Vegan breakfast £9.25 with scrambled spiced tofu, plenta, avocado, confit tomato, spinacy, mushroom and sourdough. Before 10a.m. with any hot or soft drink £9.95. Also countryside porridge or muesli jar poached pear, banana, cinnamon with soy, almond or oat millk.

Weekday lunch special deal of any salad or sandwich, teacup of soup plus hot drink or soda jar for £11.95. They have a few vegan options including falafel burger £8.95 and a large grilled polenta salad £8.75 with baby spinach, minted chickpeas, avocado and tomato in a poppy seed dressing.

Mains include sautéed caramel falafel with bread and 2 sides £13.95. Vegan cake available.

Tea, infusions, coffees £2.50-£2.95. Soya, almond or oat milk 30p extra. Fresh juices £3.75-£4.25, soda jars £2.75, seasonal spiced apple juice £2.95. Wine from £4.60 glass, £16.50 bottle. Beers £3.50-£4.50. Cocktails £7.95.

They host a vintage 'barboot sale' every month which brings a buzz to Crouch End!

Below £5 on debit or credit card there is a charge of 50p. Private parties. Kids' menu, high chairs. Wifi.

Hot Pepper Jelly Cafe
Omnivorus cafe & take-away

- 11 Broadway Parade N8 9DE
- 020 8340 4318
- M-Sa 08.30-17.30, Su 10.00-17.00
- Crouch Hill, Hornsey BR
- facebook.com/Hotpepperjellycafe

Very bright, family-run business. Plenty of vegan and gluten-free, their motto is if we can do it we will, so if you don't see what you like just ask.

Vegan breakfast £7.25 with two sausages, hash brown, mixed beans, grilled tomato, mushrooms and granary toast with spread. Falafel and hummus with salad £6.95. Mediterranean sandwich £5.95 with artichoke hearts, red peppers, sundried tomatoes, black olives and coriander. Mediterranean pasta with side salad £5.50 comes with artichoke hearts, red peppers, sundried tomatoes, black olives and coriander. Jacked potato served with salad and 1 topping £4.50, 2 £5, add £1 for sweet potato; toppings include homemade baked beans, hummus, sunblushed tomato.

Vegan and gluten-free cakes £2.50-£3.95.

Soft drinks and juices, milkshakes, frappé, smoothies, teas, coffees and iced coffee, mocha, matcha chai £1.5-£4.

They sell their very popular jars of hot pepper jelly for £4.50 to use at home or have your sandwich made there with peanut butter and other ingredients. Wifi, highchairs, toys for kids.

NORTH

CROUCH END

Clock Tower Store
Greengrocer

- 52 The Broadway N8 9TP
- ☎ 020 8348 7845
- 🕐 M-F 08.30-19.00, Sa-Su 10.00-18.00

Traditional greengrocer with a Greek grocery store at the back selling wholefoods and olives.

Broadway Fruiterers
Greengrocer

- 15 The Broadway N8 8DU
- ☎ 020 8340 8593
- 🕐 M-Sa 08.00-19.00, Su 9.00-17.00

Has some organic produce and also sells olives, hummus, muesli, pasta, pulses, grains.

Haelan Centre
Wholefood shop

- 41 The Broadway, Crouch End N8 8DT
- ☎ shop 020 8340 4258
  clinic 020 8340 4258
- 🕐 M-Sa 9.00-18.00, Su 11.00-16.00
- ⊖ Crouch Hill, Hornsey BR
- ⬥ haelan.co.uk
  organic2yourdoor.co.uk (deliveries)

Large independent wholefood shop located in hip Crouch End since 1971, one of the oldest wholefood centres in London. Complementary health clinic upstairs. A great place to buy presents or just little cruelty-free luxuries to pamper yourself.

Ground floor is food, including organic fruit & veg, large fridge/ freezer section with several types of vegan cheese, ice-creams and selection of veggie foods. Pies and cakes for take away. Herbs, teas, amazing amount of dry wholefoods and pulses and a good selection of Japanese seaweeds and oriental sauces. Vegan wines.

The second floor is an Aladdin's cave of non-food items which always smells lovely thanks to the fab toiletries. Great variety of cruelty-free toiletries, soap, moisturisers, shampoo from Green People, Noah, Urtekram, Dr Bronnes, Weleda, Avalon, Sukin, Nourish and Antipodes. Inika make-up. Oils, incense and perfumes. Many household products like environmentally friendly cleaning stuff, vegetable wash and Ecover refills.

Supplements such as Viridian, Terranova, Nature's Plus, Lambeth and Pukka. Loose herbs.

Kids' section, books, yoga and pilates accessories, weights, mats, bags etc.

There are four clinic rooms plus a studio for yoga, pilates and meditation, with a counter for those wanting to make appointments Homeopath, herbalist, acupuncturist, osteopath, all types of massage therapy, nutritionist, Chinese herbalist, relexology, Reiki.

Haelan Centre, Park Road
Organic shop

- 304 Park Road, Crouch End N8 8LA
- 020 8340 1720
- M-Sa 9.00-18.00, Su 11.00-16.00
- Finsbury Park, W7/W3 bus
  Alexandra Palace BR
- haelan.co.uk

Organic food shop, although not veggie. On the hill not far from Alexandra Palace, so good for picnic supplies. They have a selection of Laura's Idea sandwiches, wraps and salads and Gobblins.

Organic foodstuffs including pastas, noodles, breads, fruit and veg. Soya yogurts, Booja Booja organic ice-cream and Swedish Glace ice-cream. Organic baby foods.

Organic bodycare including Weleda, Lavera, Jason, Barefoot Botanicals, Urtekram, Yaoh hemp moisturiser, Dr Bronner soaps.

Homeopathic remedies. Vegan wines. Local deliveries.

Previously called Just Natural, now part of Haelan Centre.

EDGWARE

Zen Buddha
Vegetarian/vegan Chinese restaurant

- 236 Station Road HA8 7AU
- 020 8905 3033
- M-F 12.00-14.30, 18.00-22.30 (F 22.50), Sa-Su 12.00-15.00, 18.00-22.50
- Edgware
- zen-buddha.co.uk

The ideal night out for both reluctant and avid vegetarians, with 90 items on the almost entirely vegan menu. They specialize in an astonishing range of fake meats and other dishes from China, India, Thailand and Britain. Hot dishes are labelled with 1, 2, and one with 3 red warning chillis.

Lunch buffet M-Sa £7.99, Su/BH £10.99. Evening buffet M-Tu only (not bank holiday) £10.99. A la carte menu all you can eat £18.95 eat in only, child £8.85 (under 120 cm). You can also order and pay for individual dishes.

The buffet changes often and includes rice steamed and with veg, two soups (sweetcorn or spicy yum), spring rolls, fries, potato wedges, onion rings, crispy bhajia, mixed veg tempura, stir-fried noodles with veggies, veg curry, sweet and sour veggie meat, chilli tofu, stir-fried veg and mushrooms, meat in black bean sauce etc. Salad bar with mixed leaves, sweetcorn, tomato, cucumber, pickles, olives, nuts and sultanas. Fruit salad, jelly and toffee banana.

A la carte appetizers include 8 soups, tempura deep fried veg, satay veg chicken or prawns on skewers, crispy seaweed or tofu, dumplings, spring rolls, veg sesame prawn toast, dim sum, crispy veggie fish, smoked shredded veggie chicken, chicken drumsticks, fried wontons. Mixed hors d'oeuvres platter with spring rolls, crispy seaweed, sesame toast, Mandarin mushrooms, satay veggie chicken on skewers.

Over 40 main courses. Meat substitutes include crispy duck or lamb; veg lamb with veggies in hot pot; veg fish and veg chicken dishes; veg steak; Cantonese barbecue veg pork. Vegetables include monk's veg in clay pot; spicy aubergine hotpot. Tofu dishes include black bean with pepper in spicy Szechuan sauce; sweet and sour sauce with pepper and pineapple and crispy golden tofu in batter. Indian hot masala mushrooms or tofu and crispy mogo chips. Thai dishes such as green or red curry with chicken, lamb, prawns, fish or mixed vegetables, Thai style fish cake, Thai style vegetables or aubergine.

Barbecue combo £12.80 includes seaweed, BBQ veg duck and pork, soya veg chicken, homemade soya ham.

Several kinds of noodles can come with chicken, lamb, seafood (veggie, fish and prawns), tofu and veggies in black bean or soya sauce. Rice or organic brown rice dishes.

British favourites feature fish and chips; fish, beef and chicken burger; chicken nuggets (8 pcs); club sandwich.

Set meals for two or more people, with mixed hors d'oeuvres or soup, then three or four mains, special fried rice or noodles with beansprouts, finish with toffee banana or lychees.

Desserts feature pan fried red bean pancake, deep fried toffee apple or banana or pineapple, cheesecake, carrot cake, lychees, vanilla, raspberry ice cream, banana boat and ice cream.

Drinks £1 include soft drinks, freshly made fruit and vegetable and bottled juices, mocktails, lemonade, milkshakes, alcohol free beers. Tea by the cup or pot, hot choc.

10% service charge. Credit card minimum £10, though at the time of printing they were accepting only cash. No alcohol. Children welcome, one high chair. Deliveroo, Just Eat. Previously called Loving Hut, and before that Mr Man.

EDGWARE

Falafel Cafe
Omnivorous cafe

- 222 Station Road HA8 7AU
- 07940 104092
- M- Sa 08.30-23.00, Su 11.00-23.00
- Edgware

Cold starter £4-5 hummus; spicy hummus with hot peppers, parsley, garlic, lemon juice topped with broad beans, tabbouleh salad; fattoush salad; mixed salad and falafel box (5 pcs) plus salad.

Hot Starter £1.50-4.50 falafel (5 pcs) with Lebanese bread; foul madamas boiled broad beans, chickpeas seasoned with garlic, olive oil and lemon juice; batata spicy potato with coriander, pepper and garlic; chips.

Sandwiches served with pitta or wrap £3-5 including classic falafel served with hummus, tomato, pickled turnips and cucumber, lettuce and parsley; falafel served with hummus all the classic fillings and salad plus florets of cauliflower; falafel and spicy potatoes again with all the classic fillings and salad plus cubes of fried potatoes with coriander; falafel with avocado plus the classic fillings and salads; vegetable cocktail served with florets of cauliflower and fried potatoes and aubergines, garlic sauce, lemon juice and pickles; batata cubes of potato with coriander, peppers and garlic; hummus served with salad.

Fresh juices £3 any mixed juices £3.50, soft drinks 80p, coffee £1.60-2.50, tea £1.80.

Many seats inside. High chairs.Wifi. Cash only.

Falafel
Omnivorous cafe

- 33 Station Road, Edgware HA8 7HX
- 020 3643 6926
- M-Sa 11.00-20.00, Su closed
- Edgware
- Facebook Falafel Edgware

Everything but one item is vegetarian or vegan. Falafels £4-£5 with hummus, pickled turnips and salad, can add fried cauliflower, spicy potato cubes, fried aubergine. Hummus, tabouleh, mixed salad, box of falafel with salad, broad beans with chickpeas, batata spicy potato cubes, all £4-£5. Chips £1.50.

Soft drinks 80p. Mint, green or English tea £1.50. Deliveroo.

Hadar
Kosher supermarket

- 301 Hale Lane HA8 7AX
- 020 8958 1119
- Su-W 07.00-22.00, Th 07.00-24.00, F 07.00-1.5 hours before Sabbat, Sa from 1.5 hours after Sabbath
- Edgware
- hadaredgware.com

Just 4 weeks of life, this supermarket offers a vast range of vegan food.

As soon as you walk in on your right hand side there is a sushi bar with a variety of vegetables and fruit rolls including cucumber, avocado and cherry tomatoes, cucumber, avocado, mango ad lettuce; avocado, mango and cashew nuts; passion fruit and mango with crunch; kiwi, mango, avocado with kiwi outside; carrot and avocado; spinach and cucumber;

asparagus, avocado and cucumber; Portobello mushroom and cucumber; some of the classical ones: cucumber; carrot; avocado; pepper (red, green and yellow) and mixed vegetable roll with 3 choices of veggies. All 8 pieces £4.95, vegetarian snack 2 rolls 4 pcs of each and a vegetarian hand roll £6.99.

Take away fridge: Yarden babaganoush, hummus, hummus with zaatar, tahini, hummus and garlic, pepper and paprika, hummus chilli sauce, grilled aubergine, aubergine salad, guacamole and matbucha. Mee Too: aubergine with red pepper, original hummus, hummus and red pepper, tahini, aubergine babaganoush and harissa.

Also tabouleh salad, roasted vegetable cous cous, eggplant paste, date spread and date syrup.

Fridge: Tofutti, Sheese, Alpro yoghurt, drinks and dessert. Frezeer: Fry's, Tivall, Me Too falafel, original, sweet potato and spinach. Swedish Glace, Tofutti cuties chocolate, Food Heaven ice cream.

Fruit and vegetables.

Olives, oils, pulses, Dove's farm maize and rice pasta, Goldbaum's brown rice pasta, Israeli cous cous, sauces, vegan pesto such as classic, Sicilian and arrabbiata, grilled pepper and artichoke spread. Wheat free pretzel, rice snacks, gluten free and organic Matzo, fresh bread. Dried fruits and nuts. Ella's kitchen.

Made Good musli chic and chip, apple and cinnamon and chocolate and banana.; Nakd posh bits cocoa with mandarin or sea salt or raspberry ; Homefree biscuits double chop chip, chic chip and banana; Doves Farm biscuits and flapjack such as apple and sultana; chic chip; apricot and chia. Vegan halva and sugar free. Protein bars. Pukka's tea.

Mendy's Kosher Supermarket
Omnivorous supermarket

- 17 Edgwarebury Lane HA8 8LH (near south end)
- 020 8958 3444
- M-W 07.30-21.00, Th 07.30-23.00, F 06.30-17.00 (summer), -2 hours before shabbat (winter), Sa closed summer, 18.00-22.00 winter, Su 08.00-21.00
- Edgware
- mendys.co.uk
  facebook.com/mendyskosher

Lots of vegan products including the entire Swedish Glace ice-cream range, Fry's, Alpro, Tofutti, and lots of parve biscuits which just need to be checked for eggs.

Food to go fridge with a lot of salads £2.45-£4; Israeli olives; roasted vegetable; roasted potato; fried aubergine. Half a dozen kinds of hummus. Tahini, aubergine and many other different spreads and dips.

Pulses, grains, dried fruits, seeds, nuts and olives. Big section of fruit and vegetables.

FINCHLEY

North London

Rani
Vegetarian Gujarati & South Indian restaurant

- 7 Long Lane, Finchley N3 2PR
- 020 8349 4386
- M-F 11.00-15.00, 18.00-23.00);
  Sa-Su 12.00-16.00, 18.00-23.00
- Finchley Central
- rani.uk.com

Home-style Gujarati cooking at the top of Long Lane, run by a Gujarati family since 1984. Vegan friendly as they don't use egg at all and only vegetable ghee. Items containing dairy, sugar, peanuts, wheat, onions and garlic are marked.

Daily buffet £8.95 from 12.00 to 15.00, Saturday and Sunday lunch buffet £12.50 from 12.00 to 15.00 and evening buffet £15 from 18.30 to 22.00. Children under 10 half price. The buffet contains eight hot and cold starters, nine main course items with accompaniments, and two desserts including fresh fruit salad. There are always bhel puri and masala dosa.

Soups plus 20 hot and cold starters are all £4.95. Main course curries and specials £6.95-£7.95 include some unusual ones such as Lilotri Sak slow cooked Kenyan style aubergines, broad beans, green beans, peas and potatoes with spices; or Undia aubergine, peas, guvar, valour, tindora, pigeon peas and potato slow cooked with fried fenugreek balls. Rani dosa £4.95-

£8.95. Thali £12 with your choice of curry from the menu, chola, pilau rice, chapattis or pooris, dal, pickle and chutney.

Set meals £35 for two sharing gets you papadums, any two starters, dal, any two curries, bread and/or rice, soup, mango chutney and raita.

Excellent stuffed breads such as paratha stuffed with potato mix, or mithi roti, a sweetened lentil mix with cardamon and saffron, parcelled in unleavened dough, roasted in vegetable ghee, sprinkled with poppy seeds.

Fruit salad £4.95 is the only vegan dessert..

House wine £2.95 small glass, 175ml £3.95 medium, £14.95 bottle. Small Cobra Indian beer £3, large £4.95. Fresh juices £4.50 glass, £15 jug; soft drinks £2.20. Tea or coffee £2.

10% service charge. Reservations advised after 7.30pm and for large groups. Children welcome, best to come early evening and let them know to expect you. 10% off above £12 for take-away collections. Free delivery within 7 miles, minimum order applies. Parties and weddings up to 120 people. Outdoor catering for up to 200.

Vitality Bay
Vegan restaurant

- 818 High Road, North Finchley N12 9QY
- 020 3026 1776
- M-Sa 10.00-22.00, Su closed
- Finchley Central
- vitalitybay.co.uk
  Facebook Vitality Bay
  instagram.com/vitality_bay

They describe it as plant-based natural healing food and drink therapy.

Food includes all day breakfast, beanburger, lentil biryani, mogo chips, pani puri, banana cake.

Juices and smoothies.

Falafel Bar, Finchley Central
Vegetarian falafel take-away

- 3 Long Lane, Finchley N3 2PR (next to Rani)
- 020 8248 0932
- M-F 11.00-21.00, Sa-Su 11.30-21.00
- Finchley Central
- falafelbar.co.uk
  facebook.com/falafelbarlondon

Rani in 2015 added a falafel and salad bar take-away next door.

Green, spicy or plain falafel in pita with salad and sauce £3.20. In a box small £3.20, large £3.90. Meal with side and drink £5 sandwich, £6 box. Potato or sweet potato wedges in small or large size £1.50-£3.50. Salads £2.50-£4. Baba ghanoush aubergine dip or plain, red pepper or chilli hummus £2.50. Canned drinks 80p.

Also in Harrow.

Rani

Rani

NORTH

FINCHLEY

Vitality Bay

Falafel Feast
Vegetarian cafe & take-away

- 377 Regents park Road N3 1DE (opposite Station Road)
- (020 8346 3361
- M-F 07.00-19.30, Sa-Su closed
- Finchley Central
- falafelfeast.co.uk
  facebook.com/falafelfeastcatering
  instagram.com/falafelfeast

Delicious falafel in pitta to take-away, plus imited seating inside. All the food is vegetarian but only the falafel in pitta seems to be suitable for vegans, £5.50 with salads and hummus, £6 on a plate. However they have introduced vegan shawarma kebab in pitta £6 with hummus, chili, salad and tahini!

Hot or cold dishes to order include warm lentil salad, tabouleh, couscous salad, green beans with flaked toasted almonds, sweet potatoes roasted with onion and walnuts, spiced roasted carrots, butternut squash wedges roasted with olive oil and thyme, chard and red onions with green lentils, Israeli couscous pasta with onions and mushrooms and nuts and sultanas and herbs, broccoli and cauliflower roasted, beetroot salad, hummus, salads.

Cold and hot drinks £1.50-£2 include Cafe Botz Israeli black coffee, can be with cardamon.

A few seats inside. Party and event catering, menu on website.

Meera's Xpress
Vegetarian Indian cafe & take-away

- 43-145 Ballards Lane, Finchley N3 1LJ
- (020 8371 8677
- Su-Th 11.00-21.30, F-Sa 11.00-22.00
- West Finchley, Finchley Central
- meerasxpress.com

Around 100 menu items, all between £1.50 and £4.99. Chaat, bhajias, mogo chips, north Indian curries, south Indian dosas and uttapam, Indo-Chinese dishes like chilli tofu.

Man Chui III
Chinese omnivorous restaurant

- 84 Ballards Lane, Finchley Central N3 2DL
- (020 8349 2400
- M-Su 12.00-14.30, 18.00-23.30
- Finchley Central

Chinese restaurant near the tube station with extensive and tasty vegan section on the menu. Apart from the tofu and veggie dishes, there are many fake meat items. Two set vegetarian menus £15.80 or £17.80 per person for two or more people for around 10 dishes. Children welcome, high chairs.

B Green Health Food Plus
Health food shop & take away food

- 104-106 Ballards Lane N3 2DN
- (020 8343 1002
- M-Sa 9.00-18.00, Sun 11.00-16.00
- Finchley Central
- bgreenhealthfoods.co.uk

Wholefood shop with many gluten-free and special diet products. Lots of yogurt and cheese including Sheese, Violife, Tofutti, Follow your Heart. Organic dressings, veganaise. Free and Easy organic soups. Taifun, Cheatin, VegiDeli, many kinds of tofu and tempeh. In the freezer you can find Amy's vegan rice'n mac or lasagna, Clive's pies, Fry's sausages and burgers, Booja-Booja ice cream. Bars from Creative Nature, Pulsin, Organix Punk'd for children, Ombar, Vego, Conscious and other chocolates.

Cruelty-free toiletries include Weleda, Green People, Sukin, Akin, Lavera, Jason, Dr Hauschka, Faith In Nature (without sodium lauryl sulphate). Inika makeup. Whole Ecover range. Nelsons, New Era and Weleda homeopathy. There is always someone to help with nutritional advice.

Natural Health
Wholefood store

- 339 Ballards Lane N12 8LJ
- 020 8445 4397
- M-Sa 9.00-18.00, Su 11.00-16.00
- Woodside Park
- facebook.com/NatHealth

Vegan ice creams and cheeses such as Follow your Heart, Vegusto, Tofutti, Violife and ranges from Cheatin, Tofurky, VBites. Vitaquell organic spreads, Follow your Heart vegenaise, vegan honey mustard, spreads and sauces. Vegan eggs. Meat substitutes like The Vegetarian Butcher with many vegan options, Clive's Pies and Amy's lasagne. Swedish Glace, Coyo and Booja-Booja ice cream. Sojade and Provamel yogurt. Booja Booja truffles and chocolate. Gluten-free and special diet ranges. Big selection of chocolate and teas including Triple Leaf tea, Natur Boutique, Rio Amazon, Birt & Tang.

Bodycare by Green People, Avalon, Weleda, Jason, Faith in Nature and Dr Bronner. Kids' section with Green People, Bioskin, Jason, Weleda, Lavera, Organic Babies and Earth Friendly Baby. Cleaning products including Ecover and BioD.

Vitamins by Viridian, Solgar, Wild Nutrition, Pukka, Biocare, superfood by Synergy Natural and protein powders. Homeopathic and herbal remedies, aromatherapy oils.

Mahavir Sweet Mart
Vegetarian Indian sweet and savoury

- 136, Ballard Lane N3 2PA
- 020 8346 9884
- Tu-Sa 10.30-18.45, Su 9.00-17.00, M closed
- Finchley Central
- mahavirsweetmart.com

Take away only. Thali special £4.99: 2 curries, 3 puris and a choice of samosa or dhokra. Many snacks and sweets, make sure you ask for the vegan options because nothing is labelled. Credit card minimum order £10.

Holland & Barrett, N Finchley
Health food shop

- 748 High Road, North Finchley N12 9QG
- 020 8446 9346
- M-Sa 9.00-18.30, Su 10.00-16.30
- Woodside Park

Fridge and freezer.

FINSBURY PARK

& Stroud Green

Jai Krishna
Vegetarian South Indian restaurant

- 161 Stroud Green Road N4 3PZ
- 020 7272 1680
- M-Sa 12.00-14.00, 17.30-23.00, Su closed
- Finsbury Park
- no website

Vegetarian South Indian and Gujarati restaurant at the end of the foodie haven that Stroud Green Road has become. Very good value and can get busy, so worth booking for big groups especially Fri- Sat evening.

There is a wide range of starters £2.25-£5.25 such as pakoras, kachories (lentils in puff pastry) and peas or masala dosas a panacake made from rice and gram flour filled with potato, fried onion served with coconut chutney and sambar £4.95-£5.25. Uttapam £5.50 lentil and rice pancake topped with fresh tomato, ginger, green pepper and served with coconut chutney and sambar.

Mains such as dosas, 35 kinds of curry, £3.55-3.95. Thalis £7.95 for 1 person and the special Thali for 2 people £19.95. Try the coconut and lemon rice, and they have brown rice. There are lots of special dishes such as pumpkin curry £3.25.

Fresh mango £3.50.

Corkage £1.25 bottle of wine, 40p a bottle or can of beer, and there's an off-license opposite. Take advantage of the extremely knowledgeable staff at Jack's across the street to get an unusual variety of wines and beers from around the world. Coffee or tea £1.25, no soya milk. Soft drinks £1.50.

Children welcome, no high chairs. No credit cards, only cash or cheque with card.

St Gabriel Cafe, Finsbury Park
Omnivorous Ethiopean omnivorous cafe

- 12 Blackstock Road N4 2DW
- 020 7226 1714
- M-Su 09.00-20.00 or later
- Finsbury Park
- stgabrielcafe.co.uk

This tiny cafe has lovely vegan salads and roast vegetables, which you wrap in Ethiopian injera flatbread and eat with your hands. Selection of vegan dishes with injera for £8, which is probably enough to share. It's smaller than the Kennington branch (south London). Dishes include cabbage and carrot, chickpea, or lentil, spinach or beetroot watch out for the spicy one.

They also have individual plate for £7 such as spice red lentil, yellow spit pea, or spiced chickpea stew. Spiced chickpea stew with salad £8.50. Green pepper, lentils, garlic, onion, lemon juice with Ethiopian mustard

£7.50, salad £2.50.

Hot drinks £1-£1.50. Canned soft drinks £1 and bottled soft drinks £1.50.

During Lent for 40 days they go vegan.

Deliveroo. Another branch near Elephant & Castle, South London.

Yard Sale Pizza
Omnivorous pizzeria

- 54 Blackstock Road N4 2DN
- 020 7226 2651
- M 17.00-22.00, Tu-Th 17.00-23.00, F 16.00-23.00, Sa 12.00-23.00, Su 12.00-18.00
- Finsbury Park
- yardsalepizza.com

All pizza can be made vegan and gluten-free with or without vegan cheese. From the classic pizza such as margherita with tomato and cheese to a unique one like kool Keith with cayenne kale, kalamata olives and artichoke. 12 inch pizza £7.50-£11 and 18 inch £14.25-£21 fpr a giant Texas VBQ Gluten-free base add £2.50, 12" only. Vegan cheese add £2, £3.80.

Side salads £4, garlic bread with rosemary and sea salt £4, olives £3.50, dips £1-£2.

Soft drinks and juices £2-£3. Bottled beers £4-£5.50. Wine £4.50 small glass, £12 carafe, £16.50 bottle.

From dough to door, minimum delivery order £15 and £2.75 delivery charge to N4, N5, N7 and N16.

Arsenal Food and Wine, N4
Eclectic off-licence and grocer

- 68B Blackstock Road N4 2DW (corner Ambler Rd)
- 07703 730050
- M-Su 09.00-23.00
- Finsbury Park

Small off-licence with an amazing variety of vegan, organic and gluten-free goods. Stocks soya, oat and coconut milks, loose pulses, musli, rice sold by weight. Nuts, seeds, dried fruit and superfood. Macrobiotic section. Pukka, Yogi, Clipper. The bread section includes Biona rye and gluten-free rice breads, gluten-free pasta. Geo Organic Mayo plain or with chilli and Plamil Mayo.

Take away fridge from £1.49-1.99 a big selection of salads including red kidney beans; chickpea; couscous with chargrilled vegetables; 3 beans; tabule; falafel; lentil; and guacamole; aubergine; avocado and hummus dip £1.49.

In the fridge tofu, VBites, Taifun sausage and cutlet, Sheese, Violife, and at least one vegan margarine, Provamel single cream, San Amrosia hummus, different mediterranean paste, Booja Booja chocolates and truffle, Sojade, Coyo and Alpro yogurt. Coyo and Booja Booja ice-cream in the freezer.

Household cleaning includes an Ecover bulk refill area as well as other biodegradable household items such as Ecoleaf, BioD and Nature Care nappies.

The beer selection includes the vegan Brooklyn Lager and Goose Island beers.

STROUD GREEN

Cats Cafe des Artistes
Omnivorous Thai restaurant

- 79 Stroud Green Road N4 3EG
- 020 7281 5557
- M-Su 12.00-24.00
- Finsbury Park
- cats-cafe-des-artistes.co.uk
  Facebook Cats Cafe Des Artistes

Very eccentric and quirky interior mostly imported from Thailand.

Starters £4.30-£5.30 include chilli sweet corn cakes, spring rolls, golden basket vegetables, gyoza, deep fried tofu with chilli and ground peanut, mushroom spicy soup with lemongrass and chilli, coconut soup with galanga, lemongrass and lime juice. Mixed vegetable starter for 2 people £8.50.

Mains £5.70-£7.60 such as 4 kinds of tofu stir-fried, tir-fried spring greens fried tofu in red curry paste, rice noodle with vegetable or tofu, various veg or tofu curry. Coconut, jasmine or lemongrass rice £1.80-£3.50. Any vegetable dishes with oyster sause can be made vegan by replacing it with soya sauce.

Lemon, mango and strawberry sorbet £1.50, coconut in the shell £4.20.

Wines are all under £20 and a bottle of prosecco £15.45.

Highchairs. Wifi. Take away.

Q&T
Omnivorous Vietnamese restaurant

- 57 Stroud Green N4 3EG
- 020 7561 0474
- Tu-We 17.30-22.30, Th-Sa 12.00-15.00, 17.30-22.30 Su 12.30-22.00, M closed
- Finsbury Park
- qandtvietnamesekitchen.co.uk

Cosy little gem run by husband and wife.

Starters £5.50-£5.90 including grilled aubergine, green papaya salad with tofu and tofu with garlic and chilli. Mains £7.20-£7.90: aubergine and tofu with black bean sauce; pak choi with garlic, broccoli with tofu and fresh tomato; mixed vegetable and tofu; morning glory with garlic; oyster mushroom with pak choi; tofu with lemongrass and chilli, wok fried flat rice noodles with tofu.

Rice vermicelli salad with tofu, lemongrass and chilli served with salad, roasted peanuts and dipping sauce £7.50. Coconut rice, mixed vegetable fried rice £2.90-£6.90.

Glass of wine £3.50, bottle £14. Beer from £3.30. Homemade lemonade £3.50, soft drinks £1.80-£3.50. Tea and Vietnamese coffee £1.50-£2.70, iced coffee £3.50.

BYOB is also available.

Highchairs, wifi and take away. 10% service charge is added to the bill.

Urban Native
Wholefood shop

☛ 188 Stroud Green Road N4 3RN

☎ 07769 721366

🕐 M-Sa 8.00-21.00, Su 08.30-20.30

⊖ Finsbury Park

↖ facebook.com/urbannativeorg

Mordern and bright store with a coffee shop at the back with tables outside.

Manna vegan cakes and snacks including lemon, blueberry, raspberry double chocolate, chocolate brownies and cupcakes. Coffees £1.60-£2.80, teas £1.85-2.20, fresh juices and smoothies £3.50.

In the fridge is great food: aromatic Moroccan kofta and falafel, spinach and pine nuts bites, sweet potato pakora. Taifun, Biona nuggets, burgers, lucky stars, falafel balls, India moons and quinoa mini burger. Seitan burger, tempeh and soya. Laura's Idea meals. Coyo, Nash, Coconut Collaborative, Soyade yogurt. Booja Booja, Coyo and Jollyum ice cream.

Fruit and veg. Loose Mejool dates £1.30 per 100gr; fresh olives £1.20 per 100gr.

Fresh bread, gluten-free pasta, organic raw pesto and pasta sauces. Asparagus, artichoke, olive and zucchini spreads Meridian and macrobiotic section. Lentil chips, veggie and kale chips, hummus chips and quinoa puffs.

Supplements by Pukka, Higher Nature, Viridian and Biocare. Bodycare by Weleda, Sukin, Organic Surge, Urtekram, Avalon, Lavera, Faith In Nature and Dr Brenner's. Clearning by Ecover, BioD, Ecozone, and Attitude. Minimum card payment £5 or 20p extra.

GOLDERS GREEN

North London

Golders Green is renowned as a Jewish area, where the grocery stores have lots of vegan chocolate, cakes and ice-cream. It's not just falafels and hummus, though they are the best in London, you can also find Oriental, East European and Middle Eastern restaurants, shops and delis.

Taboon
Vegetarian kosher café & take away

- 🖝 17 Russell Parade, Golders Green Road NW11 9NN (corner Alba Gardens)
- ☎ 020 8455 7451
- ◑ Su-Th 09.00-23.00, F 9.00-between 14.00 and 17.00 depending on time of year, Sa closed
- ⊖ Brent Cross, Golders Green

The speciality at this late-night cafe is falafel in pitta with a self-service salad bar and hot sauces, all vegan apart from mayonnaise. Small seating area. Fantastic value for London.

Falafel £3.50 in pita, £4.50 in lafa flatbread. Drinks £1-£2.50 include fresh orange juice small or large, cola, water, lemonade, sometimes Israeli drinks, tea, coffee, Turkish coffee, hot chocolate.

Hummus Bar
Omnivorous Kosher Mediterranean restaurant

- 🖝 82 Golders Green NW11 8LN
- ☎ 020 3872 3777
- ◑ Su-Th 12.00-23.00, F-Sa closed, open Sa evening in wineter
- ⊖ Golders Green
- hummus-bar.co.uk
- ↖ facebook.com/hummusbaruk

This Middle Eastern and burger restaurant clearly labels vegan dishes and does massive portions. Trendy, buzzy and vibrant place. Vegan dishes are £7.50-£9.50 such as homemade hummus with two pittas plus mushrooms or falafel balls; falafel mezze with hummus, braised cauliflower and salad; Israeli salad; ciabatta wrap with braised cauliflower.

Sides £3.50 such as salad, rice or mash; sweet potato fries £4.50.

Soft drinks and juices £2.95. Draft beers £3.45 half pint, £4.95 pint. Turkish coffee £2.50. Tables outside.

Balady
Vegetarian Israeli café

- 750 Fincley Road, Temple Fortune NW11 7TH
- 020 8458 2064
- M-Th 11.00-21.00, F 10.00-16.30, Sa closed, Su 11.00-21.00
- Golders Green
- Facebook Balady
  instagram.com/baladylondon

Kosher falafel cafe, full of Israelis. Falafel in pita £5.50, with lafa flatbread £7, on a plate £7.50. Cauliflower shawarma £7, £8.50, £10.50. Other dishes £3-£7.50 such as chips, chilli chips, rice and beans £4.50, soup, tahini aubergine, full mademes broad beans, salad.

Hummus or baba ganoush (aubergine purée) plates £7-£11.50 in regular or large, come with your choice of mushrooms, chickpeas, ful, falafel balls.

Kid's falafel and chips £5, chips and corn schnitzel £6.

Soft drinks £1.50-£2.50 such as sodas, malt beer, Moroccan tea or coffee.

Pita
Omnivorous cafe & take-away

- 🚩 102 Golders Green Rd, NW11 8HB
  (corner of Hoop Lane by railway
  bridge over the main road)
- 📞 020 8381 4080
- 🕐 Su-W 11.00-24.00, Th 11.00-01.00,
  F 11.00 one hour before sunset, Sa
  one hour after sunset - 04.00
- ⊖ Golders Green
- 🏹 pita.london
  facebook.com/pitagoldersgreen
  instagram.com/pita_london

Not veggie, but it is great value. Falafel with
hummus £5 with pitta, £6 with laffa
flatbread, £9 as a meal. Other nice take-
aways such as salads £2 small, £3.50
medium, £6 large. Extra portions £3-£3.50
such as chips, rice, aubergine, Israeli salad,
falafel, mini hummus, soup. Hummus with
pitas £5.50 and you can add tahini, broad
beans, chickpeas or falafel balls. Lunch deal
falafel in pita with chips and soft drink £8,
with laffa bread £9.

Soft drinks and juices £1.50-£2, Turkish or
cardamon coffee or mint tea £2. Israeli
Goldstar beer from £3. Parties and events.

Sushi Haven
Omnivorous sushi restaurant

- 🚩 98a Golders Green Road NW11 8HB
- 📞 020 8123 0555
- 🕐 Su-W 11.00-23.00, Th 11.00-13.00,
  F 11.00-14.30, Sa 18.30-01.00
  (winter), 22.00-02.00 (summer)
- ⊖ Golders Green
- 🏹 sushihaven.co.uk

Most Japanese style restaurants have a
handful of vegan options if you're lucky, this
one has dozens. Sushi rolls with many kinds
of vegetable inside or tropical fruits, 8
pieces £3.20-£4.75. Also platters to serve
up to 18 people. Hot food £3.50-£8.15
includes miso soup and udon noodles with
tofu, vegetables, wakame and scallions;
seaweed salad, sesame noodle salad and
avocado salad; grilled veg skewers with
brown rice; tempura veg. Edamame, teamed
white or brown, sweet potato tempura fries,
crispy avocado fries £2.75-£5.50.

Lunch deals, not for take-out, regular £7.10
with 2 regular rolls, snack box and any
choice of can or water; Healthy lunch £9.99
2 regular rolls, edamame, seaweed salad,
cucumber salad and miso soup.

High chairs. Wifi. Delivery and collection.
Deliveroo.

Soyo

Omnivorous Kosher Mediterranean restaurant

- 94 Golders Green Road NW11 8HB
- (020 8458 8788
- Su-Th 08.30-24.00, F 08.30-14.00, Sa 19.00-03.00,
- Golders Green
- soyo.co.uk
  facebook.com/soyolondon
  instagram.com/soyoldn

Hip and trendy fusion restaurant where you can just meet for coffee or have a 3-course meal or a full cooked vegan breakfast. Yummy mummies love the kids' play zone with games and toys. Open kitchen.

Vegetan breakfasts served till 4pm £7-£11 include full cooked featuring chickpea omelette, homemade spreads, bread, side salad and orange juice or hot drink; Soyo muesli served with berry, confiture and chia seeds; organic açaí with banana, pineapple and coconut; porridge with walnuts, coconut, banana, cinnamon and chia seeds.

Savoury dishes £4.50-£12 include mushroom or tomato and rice soup; vegan sandwich with fried tofu, mushrooms, salad and Asian dressing; spaghetti with asparagus, broccoli, peas and courgettes; rice noodle stir-fry veg with spring rolls; salads; tabouleh salad with lentils. There is a vast range of ingredients from which to create your own salad.

Cold driks £2.50-£5 include freshly squeezed juices and super smoothies. Teas and coffees £2-£3. They have soya milk. Beer £3.95. Wine £4.50 glass, £18.50 bottle.

High chairs. Wifi. Catering for private functions up to 60 people.

Du Eat

Omnivorous Chinese buffet restaurant

- 22 Golders Green Rd NW11 8LL
- (They don't give out their number
- M-Su 12.00-22.00
- Golders Green

Previously the vegan restaurant CTV, then Tao which went omnivorous. Eat as much as you like for £8.50, with a £5 charge if you waste food, take away £5. Fill up on noodles, curry, special fried rice, sweet and sour balls, black beans soya chicken, sea-spiced aubergines, spring rolls, vegetable tempura, Singapore noodles, lemon grass pot, crispy seaweed, steamed veggies, salad, fruit and more.

Tea £1.50 including Tai ginseng, sweet ginger, red date logan lotus, jasmine and green tea. Soft drinks and juice £1.80, fresh juice £2.50.

High chairs.

Buy 2 Save
Intenational supermarket

- 24-26 Golders Green Rd NW11 8LL
- (020 8455 8839
- M-Su 24 hours
- ⊖ Golders Green
- ⟋ no website

Fruit and vegetables heaven. You can find 20 different types of dates, also loose dried figs, apricots and mango strips. Fresh olives, jars of pickled vegetables, garlic, onions, jalapeño, gherkins, beetroot, red cabbage, cucumber with chilli and more, also jars of peppers and aubergine. Tins and jars of beans. There is a long shelf packed with dried beans, lentils, grains, flours, seeds, nuts and dried fruits. Bodrum spices, Afghan and Persian bread, date syrup and Pukka teas.

Well Natural
Health food shop

- 17 Temple Fortune Parade, set back from Finchley Road NW11 0QS (opposite Hampstead Way)
- (020 8458 6087
- M-F 9.00-18.00, Sa 9.00-17.30, Su 11.00-16.00
- ⊖ Golders Green
- ⟋ wellnatural.co.uk
  Facebook Well Natural Temple Fortune

Previously called Temple Health Foods.

Holland & Barrett, NW11
Health food shop

- 81 **Golders Green Rd** NW11 8EN
- (020 8455 5811
- M-Sa 9.00-20.00, Su 11.00-18.00
- ⊖ Golders Green

Freezer.

- 20 **Temple Fortune**, Finchley Road NW11 0QS
- (020 8455 5091
- M-Sa 9.00-18.00, Su 10.00-18.00
- ⊖ Golders Green

Fridge and freezer.

- Unit Y10, **Brent Cross** Shopping Centre, Prince Charles Drive NW4 3FE
- (020 3302 8623
- M-Sa 9.00-20.00, Su 12.00-18.00
- ⊖ Golders Green

Fridge and freezer.

Jewish Vegetarian Society

- 855 Finchley Road NW11 8LX
  (south of the tube station)
- 020 8455 0692
-
- Golders Green
- jvs.org.uk
  Facebook The Jewish Vegetarian
  Society
  twitter.com/JewishVegSoc
  tinyurl.com/jvscentre

Headquarters welcome all to cookery
demonstrations, film screenings, communal
meals and talks. JVS also holds events in
the local area, including low-cost mystery
cooking classes and a pop-up café with
guest chefs. Vegan food available at every
event.

HAMPSTEAD

The Village and Hampstead Heath

Hampstead is a suburb that feels like a village. The adjoining Hampstead Heath is a park so huge and wild, it feels like you're in the countryside. There are three different ponds where you can swim on hot days in the summer, mixed, men's, and women's. You'd have to be pretty rich to buy a house here, but it's a fun place to spend a Sunday afternoon or a summer evening. There are plenty of places to eat and drink, or you can get picnic food and chill on the grass.

You can get to Hampstead on the regular 24 bus from Pimlico, via Trafalgar Square, The West End and Euston. Alternatively get the tube (Northern Line) or an Overground train to Hampstead Heath.

They call it the Beverly Hills of London. Hampstead is renowned for the famous people living here, especially in the past, with writers like Keats, George Orwell, Leigh Hunt, D.H. Laurence, Karl Marx, dancers like Anna Pavlova, painters like John Constable, and today many tv stars, musicians and footballers reside here such as Ridley Scott, Ricky Gervais, Boy George, Liam Gallagher, Annie Lennox etc.

Still today In Hampstead the air is thick with culture. There is the Pentameters theatre, Hampstead theatre (Swiss Cottage), Everyman independent cinema. And many museums such as the stunning Kenwood House packed with art including a Rembrandt self-portrait, Keats' house, Freud museum, Burgh House and Fenton House.

There are a lot of independent shops especially in the little alleys off the main street.

Top places to eat are Woodlands vegetarian Indian restaurant and London's oldest falafel stall, Friendly Falafels, on Thur-Sun evenings plus Sunday afternoons.

Woodlands, Hampstead
Indian vegetarian restaurant

- 102 Heath Street NW3 1DR
- (020 7794 3080
- M closed; Tu-Th 18.00-10.45; F-Su 12.00-15.00, 18.00-11.00
- ⊖ Hampstead
- woodlandsrestaurant.co.uk

One of three branches of this excellent chain with chefs from India. Separate vegan menu. Seating for 55, warm red and brick walls. They have also gluten-free and Jain (no garlic and onion) food.

Small plates £4.60-£5 such as tomato sonsommé, chaat, poori, bhel, idli, medu vada, samosa, onion bhajia.

Dosas an uthappam £9.50. Curries around £8 include okra, mushroom, chickpea, aubergine, veg jalfrezi, spinach and potato, tarka dal, jackfruit rogan josh. Steamed, brown, pulao or lemon rice £3.50-£4.90. Tandoori roti £2.90. Thali £19.

House wine £21 bottle, glass £6, organic and vegan ones are marked. Beers from £3.90. Plum and ginger cider £5.50 made from Surrey apples. Soft drinks and freshly squeezed juices £3.20-£4.30.

They do a special Woodlands lunch box for £5.95

Discretionary 12.5% service charge. Minimum £25 for groups of 12 or more when ordering a la carte.

Events and party bookings. Children welcome, high chairs. Wifi. Also in Soho and Marylebone.

NORTH

HAMPSTEAD

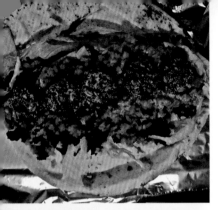

Friendly Falafels
Falafel stall

- 15-17 South End Rd NW3 2PT (In front of House of Mistry shop)
- Th-Sa, M 20.00-24.00, Su 13.00-21.00, Tu-W closed. Closed approx end Dec-end Mar or early April, depending on weather, check Facebook for when they reopen in Spring. Also closed in atrocious weather.
- Hampstead Heath BR, Belsize Park
- Facebook Friendly Falafels

Since 1989, London's pioneering, first falafel stall is next to Hampstead Heath, almost opposite Hampstead Heath overground, in front of House of Mistry health food shop. You can grab a meal for around £4-£6.

Falafel £6, add hummus 50p, aubergine with lentils £1. You can also get something lighter such as salad in pitta, or a box of 6 falafel balls.

Sometimes they have soft drinks and water, otherwise there is a grocery store adjacet. The Garden Gate pub opposite has vegan beers.

Event catering for parties, weddings etc. Call or text Joe on 07713 186030 or Anat on 07720 326279.

Wagamama, Hampstead
Omnivorous Japanese restaurant

- 58-62 Heath Street NW3 1EN
- 020 7433 0366
- Su-Th 11.30-22.00, F-Sa 11.30-23.00
- Hampstead
- wagamama.com

Les Filles Cafe-Deli
Omnivorous Australian cafe

- 95-97 Heath Street NW3 6SS (opposite Woodlands)
- 020 7794 8600
- M-F 07.00-17.00, Sa-Su 08.00-17.30
- Hampstead
- facebook.com/LLSCafe
  lesfilles.co.uk/hampstead-store
  www.instagram.com/lesFillesldn

A cosy cafe with a mix and match of shabby chic and Provençal furnitures in the heart of Hampstead. Their display of cakes in the window is very inviting. Les Filles are sisters Sonia and Hayet, who developed this clean eating idea to help their mum deal with diabetes, with an all-day menu full of "free from" dishes.

For breakfast £3.50-£7.95 you can have toasted sourdough bread served with berries, plums and chia jams; choco chia pudding topped with cacao and coconut whipped cream; quinoa granola porridge with coconut cream and baked plums; pancake with red fruits, chia jam and date syrup.

Soup of the day £5.90. Their original layered jar salads £9.95 are for take-away too, 75p jar deposit. Walnut pesto salad sandwich £6.50.

Most cakes are raw and organic from £5, such as spirulina slice, aphrodisiac, tiramisu, cake, purple carrot. Matcha or turmeric energy balls £1.60-£1.70. Brownies £2.90.

Juices and smoothies £3.50-£4. Teas, coffees and fancy lattes £1.70-£3.30. Almond, oat and soya milk.

Previously called LLS Cafe-Deli. Also in Lancaster Gate W2.

Waterstones Cafe
Omnivorous cafe in bookshop

- 68-69 Hampstead High St NW3 1QP
- 020 7794 1098
- M-Sa 9.00-18.00, Su 11.30-17.00
- Hampstead
- waterstones.com

This cosy cafe is situated on the first floor inside Waterstones book store. Coffees £1.90-£2.90, with almond and soya milk. Pot of tea £1.90. Soft drinks £1.95-£2.50.

One or two vegan cakes served daily. Quite big seating area surrounded by books. Wifi.

House of Mistry
Health food shop and pharmacy

- 15-17 South End Road NW3 2PT
- 020 7794 0848
- M-F 9.00-18.30, Sa 9.00-18.00, Su closed. Shop M-Sa till 20.00, Su 11.30-17.30.
- Hampstead
- houseofmistry.com
  facebook.com/houseofmistryUK

Opened as a pharmacy in 1975 on the right, then adding an interconnected health food shop next door on the left in 1978. Owner Dr Mistry is a renowned vegetarian health food nutritionist, chemist and pharmacist who produces organic products such as insect repellent for plants and humans. He won the Rashtriya Rattan Award (Gem of India, equivalent of an M.B.E.) for his outstanding achievements with neem, an Indian tree from which many products are made. There is a catalogue of products which are available by mail order worldwide.

All the usual wholefoods. Lots of gluten-free

and diabetic products. Fridge with take-away pasties including gluten-free , Delphi pots, tofu, tempeh, falafels, burgers, cold drinks. Bread by Celtic Bakers. Everfresh sprouted wheat bread. Pulsin and other snack bars. Chocolate includes Booja Booja truffles and Vego hazelnut bars.

Cosmetics and bodycare include Mistry's and Weleda. Supplements by BioCare, Bio-Health, Lamberts, Mistry's, Nature's Own, Nature's Plus, Solgar, Vogel. Bach flower remedies.

They can advise on products suitable for diabetics, blood pressure, IBS, psoriasis and eczema, and we saw the pharmacist expertly advising customers on all sorts of conditions and recommending products.

Revital Health Shop
Health food shop

☛ 197 Haverstock Hill, Belsize Park NW3 4QG (between Belsize Ave and Glenloch Rd)

☏ 020 7443 5725

🕐 M-F 9.30-19.00, Sa 9.30-18.00, Su 11.00-16.00

⊖ Belsize Park

↸ revital.co.uk

At the back of the shop in the fridge you can find falafel, tempeh, Sheese, Vegenaise, Tofutti sour cream and yogurt. Booja Booja and Coyo ice cream.

Many chocolate bars such as Ombar, Seeds & Beans, Conscious, Organic Raw, Doysy & Dam, Plamil and Raw Chocolate Co. Big selection of "superfood" powders including camu camu, lucuma, buckthorn, maca, ashwaganda, plus apricot kernel.

Bodycare and natural beauty products including Dr Hauschka, Green People, Sukin. Big range of bodycare for kids.

Lots of supplements including Revital (most vegan), Lamberts, Viridian, Terranova, Nature's Plus. Sports nutrition. Herbal and homeopathic remedies. Aromatherapy. Books. Staff are trained in nutrition and products.

HENDON

and Brent Cross and Colindale

Tapuach
Kosher supermarket

- 108-110 Brent Street NW4 2HH (corner Bell Lane)
- 020 8202 5700
- M-W 07.00-23.00, Th 07.00-23.45, F 07.00-17.30, Sa closed, Su 08.00-22.00
- Hendon Central
- tapuach.co.uk
  facebook.com/tapuach.hendon

Big kosher supermarket with lots of vegan products.

Huge fruit and vegetable section by the door. Fridge with mixed antipasti, aubergine, tomato and mixed olives, marinated olives such as garlic and chilli; lemon and coriander and Nocellara Sicilian; pickled vegetables, fresh pesto, vegetable soup, tabouleh salad, roasted potato with paprika, roasted potato and green beans in sesame oil. Fresh sushi prepared in store daily such as avocado, cucumber, mixed vegetables and sweet potato.

The freezer is packed with vegan delights: Booja Booja ice-cream; Alpine big box of sorbets in lemon, passion fruit, strawberry; also from Alpine vanilla, double chocolate, fudge, caramel swirl and cappuccino ice-cream; Tofutti cuties pack of 8 with biscuits at the top and at the bottom vanilla, mint chocolate chip, biscuits and cream, and just chocolate; also from Tofutti chocolate fudge treats. Also Fry's veggie mince. schnitzel and traditional burgers.

Non-dairy topping cream and coffee creamer. Doves Farm organic gluten-free and soya- free stem ginger, lemon zest and chocolate cookies. Gluten free flapjacks. Home Free gluten-free mini cookies.

Spreads and sauces, dairy free pesto, sweet tangy onion relish, black olive, sweet or hot harissa and filfel chuma hot sauce. Sauerkraut, vine leaves, tins and jars of olves.

Spelt pizza bases, matzos, organic rye bread and 3-grains bread, rice cakes, maize or durum wheat pasta, lasagne and noodles. Clearspring macrobiotic range. Plant milks.

Big baby section with Organix snacks, muesli, baby rice and purée, Ella's Kitchen, Beech-Nut oatmeal fruit drinks with no sugar.

Lots of dry roasted and raw nuts and with dried fruits. Elite and Carmit Candy chocolate and Naked bars. Eat Real hummus and lentil chips.

White House Express
Omnivorous restaurant & take-away

- 63 Brent Street NW4 2EA
- (020 8203 2427
- M-F 12.00-90 mins before sunset, Sa closed, Su 10-00-23.00
- Hendon Central
- whitehouseexpress.com

Opposite Tapuach is this licensed kosher restaurant, very spacious with lots of seats.

Starters £4.50-£8 include hummus, tahini and falafel, hummus and mushrooms, onion rings.

Mediterranean salad platter for 2 people £10, 4 people £18.

Falafel in pita £4, in laffa £6, with hummus, tahini, chilli, salad, pickles, aubergine, red cabbage, fresh and fried onions and matbucha (tomato, pepper and chilli salsa).

Bread 50p-£3.50 including pitta, Iraqui, za'atar (mixed herbs such as oregano, thyme, and basil) Iraqi, garlic Iraqi and sesame Iraqi.

Dessert only tropical fruit salad £4.

Tea and coffee £3, they have soya milk. Soft drinks £1.75-£2, imported beers £3, malt beer £3, spirits £4-£6, wine glass £4, bottle £20.

Optional 10% service charge. Wifi. High chairs.

The Kanteen
Omnivorous Israeli & American kosher restaurant & coffee shop

- Lower Mall, Brent Cross Shopping Centre, Prince Charles Drive NW4 3FD
- (020 8203 7377
- M-W 9.00-20.00, Th 9.00-21.00, F 9.00-15.00, Sa closed, Su 12.00-19.00
- Brent Cross
- thekanteen.com
  brentcross.co.uk/eating/restaurants-bars/the-kanteen

On the ground floor, this kosher restaurant makes everything fresh so you can get a lot of vegan options. Falafels, salads, pasta.

Breakfast £3.95-£65 can be toast and jam or organic porridge with almond milk, walnuts, almonds and coconut. Alas the "light & healthy" fruit oat bowls all come with honey.

Starters £5-£8 such as edamame, hummus falafel, bruschetta, soup, roasted cauli or aubergine with tahini, tomatoes and parsley. Mains £11-£15 include salads, crispy green Thai stir-fry, spaghetti arrabiata.

Fresh juices £3.50-£4.50. Fruit smoothies £5. Soft drinks £3-£4. Wine £12 half bottle. Beer £4. Coffee £2.50-£3.75, pot of tea £2.75, herbal tea £3.50.

High chair. Wifi.

Chick
Omnivorous falafel bar

- 📍 Lower floor, Brent Cross
- ☎ 020 8202 8095
- 🕐 M-Sa 11.00-20.00, Su 12.00-18.00
- ⊖ Brent Cross
- ⚲ facebook.com/chickfalafelbrentcross
  brentcross.co.uk/shops/
  cafes-takeaways/chick

On the lower floor of Brent Cross shopping centre, next to each other, are falafels, cupcakes, and coffee stalls.

Falafel in white or wholemeal pitta with salad and sauce £5.60. Hummus with salad, salsa and pitta £5.15. Falafel with salad, sauce and pitta £3.80. Extra guacamole dip and aubergine 60p.

Also worth mentioning: Lush, The Body Shop, Waitrose and M&S are on level two (Upper Mall). Leon, Wagamama, Pizza Express, and Pret a Manger are on level three (top floor).

Lola's Cupcakes
Cake and coffee shop

- 📍 Lower Mall, Brent Cross Shopping
  Centre NW4 3FQ
- ☎ 020 8203 1339
- 🕐 M-Sa 9.00-20.00, Su 11.00-18.30
- ⚲ lolascupcakes.co.uk

Big stall with seats. Five types of vegan cupcakes: chocolate and pistachio, lemon and raspberry, chocolate, coconut and passionfruit, coconut and strawberry, also a chocolate brownie, all £3. Coffee £1.70-£3. They have soya and almond milk. Vegan hot chocolate £3.75.

All day cupcake and hot drink deal £3.95.

Holland & Barrett, Brent Cross
Health food shop

- 📍 Unit Y10, Brent Cross Shopping
  Centre, Prince Charles Drive NW4
  3FE
- ☎ 020 8202 8623
- 🕐 M-F 10.00-20.00, Sa 9.00-20.00,
  Su 12.00-18.00

Fridge with VBites, Tofurky, Cheatin, Veggie Deli, Drangonfly tofu, Sheese, Violife and Provamel. Frozen Fry's, VegiDeli, Okobay coconut ice-cream.

Veggie Wok
Vegetarian Indo-Chinese restaurant

- Bang Bang Oriental Foodhall, 399 Edgware Road NW9 0FH
- 020 3417 5460
- M-Th 12.00-21.30, F-Sa 11.30-22.00, Su 11.30-21.30
- Colindale
- veggiewok.co.uk
  Facebook Instagram veggiewokuk
  bangbangoriental.com

Assemble your meal here at the only vegetarian stall at this food court with shared tables. Food here is steamed or tossed in a wok.

All dishes include cabbage, barrot, bean sprouts, peppers, starting at £4.95, then add your choice to make Exotic Veg or Protein Boost £7.75 or Signature Creation £8.95, selecting from a dozen Chinese and British veg, mock duck, tofu, jasmine or brown rice, four types of noodles, and Oriental sauces. Specials £8.95 with rice and veggies such as tofu chilli.

Side dishes £4.25-£5.95 include Chinese samosa, spring rolls, masala or chilli garlic chips.

Drinks £1.20-£3.50 are still water, ice tea, Limca Indian lemonade or fresh coconut.

HIGHGATE

North London

Queens Wood Cafe
Omnivorous cafe

- In Queens Qood, 42 Muswell Hill Road, Highgate Woods N10 3JP
- 020 8444 2604
- May-Oct M-F 10.00-17.00, Sa--Su 9.00-18.00; Nov-Apr M-F 10.00-16.00, Sa-Su 9.00-17.00
- Highgate. Bus 43, 134.
- queenswoodcafe.co.uk
  Facebook Queen's Wood Cafe

Community cafe and gardens, with some nice vegan dishes. It is in the middle of a tranquil wood with a lovely relaxing vibe to the place, a cute sofa at one end, verandah tables with a sense of woodland energy.

Cooked breakfast £8.70 can be vegan. Main courses £6-£10.80 such as organic soup of the day with toast, falafel salad with hummus, Jamaican chickpea and sweet potato curry with herb rice and naan bread. Cakes are not vegan.

Teas, coffee, cappuccino, latte, Whole Earth and Fentimans drinks, around £2. Soya milk available. Beer £3.50. Bottle of wine, litre of Pimms or sangria, £19. glass of wine £4.50 small, £5.50 large.

Kids' meals and parties. Well-behaved dogs welcome under tables on the veranda, water bowls provided. Events and venue hire.

HOLLOWAY ROAD

From Highbury & Islington to Archway

Jake's Vegan Steaks
Vegan take-away and pub-restaurant

- 102 Holloway Road N7 1XH
- 07428 723 390
- Su-Tu 12.00-21.00, W-Sa 12.00-22.00
- Holloway Road, Drayton Park BR
- jakesvegansteaks.com
  facebook.com/jakesvegansteaks
  instagram.com/jakesvegansteaks/
  thehoratia.co.uk

Brick Lane and vegan markets heroes Jake's Vegan Steaks opened their first permanent take-away shop here in summer 2019, and are also supplying the food for the Horatia pub next door. The food being Philadelphia style cheezesteaks, made of shredded seitan steak with melted cheeze in a baguette, with various toppings and loaded fries. Your non-vegan pals will love it too, seitan is really "meaty".

Reckon on £8-£10.45 for a seitan steak main, £3.50-£8.25 for fries depending on just how much loading you're up for.

Specials £5-£10.45 include chick'n nuggets with BBQ and sweet chilli sauces,; BBQ chick'n cheeze fries; pepperoni pizza steak with tomato pizza sauce, shredded BBQ seitan, melted mozarellla and crispy pepperoni.

Soft drinks £1.65. Combo box £11.55 with cheezesteak, loaded fries, sweet mustard, slaw, drink.

Also at Vegan Nights in Brick Lane, in East London.

Loving Hut, Archway
Vegan Chinese restaurant

- 669 Holloway Road N19 5SE
- 020 7281 8989
- Tu-F 12.00-15.00, 18. 00-23.00; Sa-Su 18.00-23.00; M closed
- Archway
- archway.lovinghut.co.uk

The queen of London's Chinese vegan restaurants, vegans and vegetarians converge here from all over for birthdays and parties, it's a fantastic venue for around 20 friends right in the middle of north London near Archway tube. Previously called Peking Palace, now part of the Loving Hut group but still retaining its own distinct identity. The inside has been redesigned and the gigantic à la carte menu simplified from 100 to a still astounding 70 dishes including new Vietnamese specials and burgers.

Mon-Fri lunch buffet with 18-20 dishes £6.80 eat in, take-away box £4.20 small, £5.30 large. Dishes include sweet and sour soya chicken, dumplings, spring rolls, crispy seaweed, salty and spicy veg, tempura, curry, soya beef in black bean sauce, gluten stew.

Lots of a la carte starters £3-£5.90 and main £5.50-£7 including soups and vegan versions of just about any Chinese dish you've ever had including sizzling Szechuan veggie chicken, veggie duck with fruity sauce, yellow curry, braised aubergine, chow mein. Make the choice simple by going for one of their multi-course set meals £16.50-£21 each for 2+ people.

A la carte specials are all under £7.20 such as Vietnamese rice pancake with veggie meat, lettuce and peanut hoi sin sauce; rice noodle salads; Tom Yam fried rice with spicy veggie chicken; Singapore rice noodles with veggie chicken and prawns; ho fun noodles with vegetables, chicken, beef, lamb, bean sprouts; roast veggie duck; veggie chicken with asparagus in oyster sauce; Pad Thai chicken, prawns and tofu with vegetables, tamarind sauce and peanuts; hot pot with chicken, lamb, tofu, shiitake mushrooms, yam and vegetables.

Vegans missing fast food can have their signature fish and chips £9.50 with salad, coleslaw, ketchup and mayo. Burgers £5.10 are veggie chicken, fish or spicy bean with all the trimmings. Add vegan cheese 65p, chips £2, wedges or salad £2.50.

Desserts £4.30-£5.60 include lemon cheesecake, chocolate cake with buttercream and chocolate sauce, carrot cake, pineapple and banana fritters, toffee apple or banana with ice cream, and selection of ice-cream.

No MSG. Alcohol-free restaurant. Non alcoholic beers £2.20, healthy freshly pressed juices £3.50, smoothies and milkshakes £3.90, hot drinks £1.60-£2.90.

Children welcome, high chairs. Credit card payments accepted over phone above £6.

*TIP: Great place for large dinnr parties

Cookies and Scream
Vegan gluten-free cake bakery & cookie bar

- 🐀 130 Holloway Road N7 8JE (corner Drayton Park)
- ☏ 07778 691 519
- 🕐 M-Su 10.00-20.00, F-Sa 21.00
- ⊖ Holloway Road, Drayton Park BR
- ⬉ cookiesandscream.com
  Facebook Cookies and Scream

Opened here October 2016. Yummy fresh baked cookies, cakes, brownies, donuts and cupcakes, plus hot drinks. If a healthy vegan diet is 80% wholefoods and 20% fun food, then here comes the fun. Every last squidgy, chocolaty treat is dairy, egg and gluten free, but you wouldn't know it from the taste. It's less hectic than the original counter in Camden Market (now sadly closed after a huge fire gutted their building), with a variety of spaces - at the bar, window, a snug, by the back window, and a garden.

Banoffee pie, cookie sandwich filled with vanilla cream, brownie, square donuts, chico pie, peanut butter and jam chiquita, £2-£4.

Teas, coffee, cappuccino, latte, macchiato, mocha, chai latte, hot choc £1.80-£2.50.

Milkshakes £3.50-£4.50, soya based including vanilla old school, salted caramel, bourbon (whiskey and toffee), cookie dough, affogato (espresso), brownie, peanut butter, zombie, or mix any two.

Gift boxes to order, minimum 4 items such as cookies, brownies, pies.

Note their disclaimer: "Cookies and Scream bakes are so yummy, many of our customers have become hooked. These long-term users, or 'scream-addicts', are found begging for more outside of our kitchen. You have been warned!"

The Owl And The Hitchhiker
Omnivorous food pub

- 471 Holloway Road N7 6LE
- 020 8161 0150
- Pub: M-W 17.00-23.00, Th-F 12.00-23.00, Sa 12.00-02.00, Su 12.00-22.30.
  Kitchen M-W 17.00-22.00, Th-Sa 12.00-22.00, Su 12.00-21.00.
- Archway, Holloway Road (midway)
- owlandhitchhiker.pub
  facebook.com/OwlHitchhiker

Voted best pub in north London for their craft beers, ales, wines, bottomless brunches and a food menu that is 75% vegan. Not to mention themed pub quiz such as Star Wars or Friends, drag bingo, Drag Race pub quiz, Taylor or Britney Brunch, this place is FUN.

Burgers with fries £11-£13 come in crispy seitan, chickenish with smokey facon, or soy beefless with facon and cheese sauce. Tacos filled with seaweed wrapped tofu pr cjoclemosj seotam strips £6.50-£7.50. Salads £7.50.

Small sharers £3.50 are crispy seitan chickenish strips, white truffle oil mac n chese with smoky facon, or salt n pepper crispy cauliflower with pickled chillies and onions.

Sunday sturlers £6-ish are mushroom paté with onion jam and toast, or creamed leeks with pine nuts and sambal. Main course mushroom paté Wellington £14 with gravy, roast potatoes and veg, seitan burger with loaded fries and slaw £13. Dessert £5.50 chocolate truffle torte or carrot and nut cake. 2 courses £19, 3 £23.50.

Half price on all food Mondays.

Keren View
Vegan Eritrean restaurant

- 🕿 201 Holloway Road N7 8DG (corner Liverpool Rd)
- ☎ 020 3802 3600
- 🕐 M-Sa 12.00-22.00, Su 13.00-22.00
- ⊖ Holloway Road, BR Drayton Park
- ▸ keren-view.business.site

Great value vegan restaurant and take-away opposite London Metropolitan University. Various dishes are served on injera flatbread, which is more like a thin pancake, and you eat by hand with pieces of injera.

Soups £4.50 such as lentil or mixed beans with veg, served with brown bread. Salads £4.50.

Main dishes served with basmati rice, £5 for one, £6 for two, £7 for three, include spinach with garlic in olive oil, green beans and carrot, split yellow peas with onion and garlic and turmeric, brown lentils with molokhia leaves, red lentil stew, potato and green pepper stew, sweet potato with spinach stew, potato in tomato sauce with onion mixed pepper, molokhia slowly stewed with garlic and onion and tomato, slow cooked okra with onion and cumin.

Other dishes £7-£8.50 include penne arrabiata pasta, blackeye and aduki beans with rice and two sides. A good idea is to get a selection of dishes, such as Beba'Aynetu, five dishes for £8.50, or Me'Adi six dishes for three people to share for £26. Extra injera or rice £1. Steamed brown basmati rice or barley or sorghum or mixed beans £3.

Desserts £3. Teas £1.50, masala tea £3, various teas made with fresh spices. Coffee £2. Cold drinks £1.50-£3. 20% student discount.

EZ & Moss
Vegetarian cafe

- 183 Holloway Road N7 8LX (near Mackenzie Road)
- 020 7619 9523
- M-F 08.00-17.00, Sa-Su 9.00-17.00
- Hollway Road, Highbury & Islington
- facebook.com/ezandmoss
  instagram.com/ezandmoss

This industrial/vintage looking cafe has been open since 2013. Most of the furniture is from recycled material. It's very popular for the weekend all-day breakfast.

Quinoa porridge £5 with goji berries, pumpkin seeds, coconut, almond flakes, prunes and apple compote, add 30p for soya milk, 50p almond milk. Homemade granola £5.50, but if you want soya yogurt it's 50p extra. Chia pudding £5 with coconut milk, nuts, fresh fruits, organge juice, maple syrup and berry coulis. A unique twist on avocado toast £6 with chilli-coriander relish, watercress and dukkah. Vegan mushroom-onion omelette £7.50 with avocado and salad. French toast with fruits £8.20.

Grilled sandwich with Mediterranean roasted veg and peanut butter £6.80. Lentil and quinoa burger £8.50 with sweet potato wedges and green salad, optional vegan cheese £1.20. Soups are almost all vegan, and salads £8 can be. Veganwarma £8.50 with flatbread, coleslaw, potato salad, tahini and pickles. Daily specials such as beetroot falafel platter.

4 or 5 cakes such as matcha muffin, nut seed roll, plum cake, pecan date slice with rose water. Gluten-free vegan apple tart £3.20.

A vast range of coffees, which can be enjoyed with homemade almond, oat or soy milk. Freshly squeezed juices or smoothies.

There are around 25 seats. Prices do not include service.

Thai Corner Cafe
Omnivorous Thai restaurant

- 236 St Paul's Road N1 2LJ
- 020 7704 8227
- M-Tu 17.30-22.30, W-Sa 12.00-15.00, 17.00-23.00, Su 17.30-22.30
- Higbbury & Islington (then walk 5 mins towards Dalston)
- thaicornercafelondon.com

Excellent value, authentic Thai cuisine with a Thai chef and manager. Separate vegetarian menu.The dishes are clearly labelled for all kind of allergies.

Starters £4.25 include deep fried tofu with peanut sauce, fried sweet corn cakes, spring rolls with sweet chilli sauce. Main courses £6.95 include red or green curry with tofu, pa naeng curry with tofu, jungle curry with tofu and pad gra prao aubergine. Sides includes stir-fried broccoli, stir-fried mixed vegetables, coconut rice and rice noodles. Set menu starter and main course £7.45.

Small selection of white, red and rose wines. Liqueurs are available. Juices £2 including orange, apple and cranberry. Non-alcoholic cocktails £4 including virgin mojito, cocolada, passion tropic, sand island and some alcoholic cocktails £6.50 like mojito, pina colada, sex on the beach and zombie. Coffees £1.75 to £2.35. Peppermint, green, jasmine and fresh ginger tea for £2.

You can order online from Just Eat, Deliveroo and Hungry House. Outdoor patio in summer.

La Taberna
Omnivorous Italian restaurant & bar

- 🕿 1A Roman Way, Barnsbury N7 8XG (corner Offord Road)
- ☎ 020 7607 3519
- 🕔 M-Sa 10.30-22.30, Su closed
- ⊖ Caledonian Rd & Barnsbury overground, Caledonian Rd, Highbury & Islington
- ↖ latabernarestaurant.co.uk facebook.com/ latabernaristoranteitaliano

Family owned Italian fine dining, opened April 2016. They have always had vegetarian options and now vegan ones too, including vegan cheese and cream sauces, though these are not always marked on the menu. Some outside tables.

Dear Pizza
Omnivorous Italian organic restaurant

- 🕿 36 Highbury Park N5 2AA
- ☎ 020 7354 9309
- 🕔 M-Sa 12.00-23.30, Su 12.00-23.00
- ⊖ Highbury & Islington
- ↖ dearpizza.uk

Big separate vegan menu with dishes £7.50-£10 such as super food salad, vegan smoked Gouda cheese salad, roast aubergine salad with hummus, pasta and pizza dishes with vegan Gouda or mozzarella, vegan ham, vegan mince, calzone. And vegan tiramisu! 3 course deal with soup, main and tiramisu £13.50.

Children welcome.

Mother Earth, Highbury
Organic wholefood store

- 🕿 282 St Pauls Road N1 2LH
- ☎ 020 7354 9897 shop
  020 7704 6900 centre
- 🕔 M-F 08.00-20.30, Sa 09.00-19.00, Su 10.00-18.00
- ⊖ Highbury & Islington
- ↖ facebook.com/MotherEarthLondon thehealthylivingcentre.co.uk

Large range of organic food such as artisan breads, fruit, veg and sprouts, healthy takeaways, baby foods and natural bodycare products.

The fridge has some take-away food including Taste Matters, Hoxton Beach also Biona spring rolls, Taifun and locally produced Clean Bean tofu, San Amvrosia hummus, Soyade yogurt, Sheese, Violife and sauerkraut. Dairy-free ice-cream from Booja Booja. Apricot slices, and sugar-free muffins. Bottled and sparkling juices.

They sell loose herbs, spices and superfood like lucuma and maca. Also loose nuts, seeds and dried fruits sold by weight.

Eco-household products including Bio-D which are available for refill too.

Bodycare includes Barefoot Botanicals, Dr Hauschka, Weleda, Green People and Sukin.

Supplements include Nature's Own, Viridian, Higher Nature, Terranova, Pukka. Omega oils. Homeopathy, aromatherapy.

Juicers and sprouters. They sell organic bamboo Ecowear underwear for mens and women and their baby range.

The Healthy Living Centre upstairs offers

beauty treatments, acupuncture, Alexander technique, aromatherapy, Ayurvedic and herbal medicine, NLP, counselling, psychotherapy, chiropractic and osteopathy, homeopathy, hypnotherapy, kinesiology, craniosacral (for children, mother and baby and M.E.), various massages, shiatsu, rolfing, lymphatic drainage, meditation, naturopathy (with food, vitamin and blood testing), nutrition, pilates, reflexology yoga and meditation.

Also in Stoke Newington.

Fiveboys
Health food shop

- 17 Highbury Park N5 1QJ
- 020 7359 3623
- M-Sa 10.00-20.00, Su closed
- Highbury & Islington

Small but well-stocked health food shop. Large chilled section with many vegan products such as Redwood and Scheese, tofu, tempeh, Swedish Glace, milk alternatives. Vegan Parmazano. Speciality breads such as hard rye and other grains.

Cosmetics, hair colour. Cleaning stuff. Organic baby food, nappies and wipes. Lots of herbs. Homeopathy. Health related books. Hardware.

Holland & Barrett, N7
Health food shop

- 452 Holloway Road N7 6QA
- 020 7607 3933
- M-Sa 9.00-19.00, Su 10.30-16.30
- Archway

Fridge and freezer.

HOLLOWAY ROAD
CS Cookies & Scream
JV Jake's Steaks
KV Keren View

EZ EZ & Moss

dp Dear Pizza
ta La Taberna
tc Thai Corner Cafe

5 Five Boys
me Mother Earth

vegan
vegetarian
omnivorous
shop

ISLINGTON
AT Al Turath falafel
Co Copperhouse Choc
ON Om Nom (2020)
WF Wild Food Cafe
am Amorino
Ga The Gate
In Indian Veg
ap Appestat
ch Chilango
gb Gallipoli Bistro
ga Gallipoli Again
gl Ginger & Lime
ka Katsute 100
su Sutton & Sons
ts Thai Square
cw The Coffee Work Project
wa Wagamama

cm Chapel Market
er Erbolario
H1 Holland & Barrett
H2 Holland & Barrett
po Planet Organic

HOLLOWAY ROAD

ST PAUL'S RD.

NEWINGTON GREEN

CANONBURY

STREET

HIGHBURY & ISLINGTON

UPPER

ESSEX RD.

NEW NORTH RD.

ESSEX ROAD

LIVERPOOL ROAD

STREET

Waterstones
Tesco Metro

UPPER STREET

ANGEL

Sainsbury's
Waitrose

PENTON ST

WHITE LION ST.

CITY RD.

JOHN STREET

THE CITY

ROSEBERY AVE.

AMWELL ST.

RD.

404

ISLINGTON

North London

Islington is a shopping and cafe area that's great for designer gifts and antiques. The major vegan opening here in 2019 was the second, much larger branch of Covent Garden's **Wild Food Cafe**.

Other excellent restaurants in the area are gourmet vegetarian **The Gate**, and at the other end of the price scale and down the end of Chapel Market, friends converge from all over to chat over a £7.95 all-you-can-eat buffet with vegan lassi at **Indian Veg**. Opposite, **Copperhouse Chocolate** is a vegan chocolate cafe! Also in Chapel Market is **Al Turath** vegan falafel stand.

Gallipolli are a pair of Turkish restaurants, just north of Islington Green, in the long street of restaurants running all the way to Highbury & Islington tube. Although they are omnivorous, they offer lots of middle eastern vegan options, each in its own characterful setting with unique decor and a vibrant atmosphere in the evenings.

There's a cluster of cafes with vegan options in the antiques and bric-a-brac High Street, set back from Upper Street just above the tube station.

As well as two branches of **Holland & Barret**, on the fringes of Islington are two gorgeous wholefood stores: **Planet Organic** in Essex Road, and **Mother Earth** at Highbury Corner (see Holloway Road chapter). Keep walking north from Planet to **Sutton & Sons** for vegan "fish" & chips.

Opening in 2020 will be **Om Nom** vegan restaurant at Islington Square.

WILD FOOD CAFÉ

Wild Food Cafe, Islington
Vegan restaurant

☛ 269-270 Upper Street N1 2UQ

☎ 020 8036 3990

◑ M-F 11.30-22.00, Sa 10.00-22.00,
Su 10.00-20.00

⊖ Highbury & Islington

⇡ wildfoodcafe.com
facebook.com/WildFoodCafe
instagram.com/wildfoodcafe_islington

Joel and Aiste Gazdar's restaurant in Neal's Yard, Covent Garden, specialising in raw food, is always packed, so in December 2018 they opened this much bigger one, with some new dishes.

Starters £7-£9 include steamed aubergine with pickled mooli, wakame and cucumber; BBQ jackfruit with saffron pine nut mayo and squash curry cream; white polenta with chanterelle, squash foam and truffle; oyster mushroom scallops with seaweed tartare.

Main courses £12-£14.50 suich as Wild Green Burger made from raw pink olive and shiitake mushroom with sundried tomato and pepper ketchup, served with kale chips; Wabi Sabi Kale Salad with pickled mooli, kimchi, activated teriyaki almonds, chestnuts, oyster mushrooms, nori, avocado, butternut squash, broccoli, sunflower seed sour cream dressing; Queen of the Forest coconut-seared plantain with wild rice, amaranth, cacao nibs, Brazil nuts, camu-camu and romanesco; Dillicious Carbonara courgette noodles with cashew cream sauce, garlic, mushrooms, kale, parsley, chives and white wine. 12-inch pizzas with toppings that can include pine nut parmesan, wild leaf pesto, cashew mozzarella, smoked chilli cashew cheese, macadamia ricotta, olives, artichoke, marinated and dehydrated mushrooms, truffle oil, olive pepperoni. Pizza bases are made of in-house protein rich gluten-free flour which contains amaranth, sprouted chickpeas, teff, quinoa and vegetables, cooked in a wood fire, while toppings are raw for maximum freshness and flavour.

Sides and nibbles include pickles, olives, teriyaki almonds, flatbread with wild leaf pesto, raw crackers, cheese and onion kale chips, green leaves.

Desserts £5-£9.50 feature baked doughbuts with seasonal toppings, double choc and coffee cake with raw cacao ganache and vanilla ice-cream, raw chocolate tart with date caramel, matcha moss cheesecake with wild nettle and kombucha, nut cheeses board with fruit and crackers.

Weekend brunch menu till 3pm £7-£9 includes granola; banana bread toast with walnuts, dates and coconut yogurt; sild avocado on buckwheat toast. The main menu adds quinoa dosa pancakes £9 with either tikka mushroom, kale tabouleh and salsa verde, or slow cooked aubergine, hummus and mango-fennel chutney.

Green and other vegetable and fruit juices £6.50, carafe £12. Superfood smoothies £7. Soft drinks £3-£6 such as cola, ginger beer, passionfruit or ginger kombucha, coconut.

Organic wines from small growers from £4.25 medium glass, £15.50 carafe, £22 bottle. Beer and cider from £5.50, spirits £3, cocktails £8.

Luxurious hot drinks £4-£6.50 include chai spice; white hot chocolate; mystic mushrooms; matcha with hemp seeds, Irish moss, caco butter and cinnamon.

Copperhouse Chocolate
Vegan chocolate-themed cafe

- 1 Chapel Market N1 9EZ
- 020 7278 7777
- Tu-Su 10.00-16.30, M closed
- Angel
- copperhousechocolate.co.uk
  facebook.com/copperhousechocolate
  instagram.com/copperhousechocolate

New chocolate themed cafe opposite Indian Veg. As well as chocolate drinks and cakes, there are healthy breakfast, savoury lunch items, and waffles and smoothies for a weekend brunch.

Smoothie bowls or granola yogurt pot £4.50. Dark rye sourdough toast and preserves £2.50. Exotic toast £4.50, topped with nut butter, banana, berries and cocoa shavings. Toasted bana bread with vegan butter or preserves or nut butter £2.50-£3.50.

Weekend brunch specials £7-£9 till 3pm: French toast in coconut, almond and banana batter served with fruit and compote; orange zest pancakes; fruit, oat and almond crumble served with coconut yogurt or ice cream; cooked breakfast hash of spicy potatoes with blackbean sausage, pepper and kale, smoky aubergine rashers and avocado.

Savoury cornbread waffles £7, topped with black bean chilli, avocado and roast tomatoes, or with beer-marinated mushrooms and spinach. Black bean chilli £6 in savoury chocolate, pepper and tomato sauce served with bread.

Two sweet waffles £4.50 with dark chocolate sauce, add toppings for 50p-£2 each, choose from whipped coconut cream, cinnamon cocoa dust, nuts, marshmallows, granola, caramel sauce, choc chips, cocoa nibs, banana, fresh berries, orange slices, ice cream, fruit compote. Other desserts £2-£4.50 include ice cream, ice cream cookie sandwich , warm brownie and ice cream with chocolate sauce, banoffee pie glass with a biscuit base.

Chocolate fondue £12 for two to share, £5 extra each for more people, with fruit, brownie chunks, pretzels and marshmallows for dipping.

The counter is covered in cakes £1.50-£3.80 eat in, £2.10-£3.20 take-away, tend to be chocolatey and most are vegan such as chocolate orange, chocolate coconut tart with almond-date crust, banana bread, flapjack. Cookies, and fudge bites in coconut or pecan £1.50.

Hot chocolate drinks £3 from African and South American countries, with extras £3.50 such as orange, cardamon and cloves, or cinamon, nutmeg, allspice and ginger. Kids portions can be smaller and sweeter. Monmouth coffees £2-£2.70. Tea £1.50. They have almond, oat, soy and coconut milk and whipped coconut cream. Coffee and chocolate can be iced. Also soft drinks £2 and milkshakes £4.50 made with coconut ice cream.

Chocolates in bars and packets to take away, including Booja Booja truffles, Origin hot chocolate.

Friday happy hour 3-4pm, slice of cake for £1 or a free cookie with every coffee or hot chocolate.

Dogs welcome. Free wifi. Portable ramp for disabled access, toilet downstairs. Booking recommended for groups of 5+. Formerly called Jaz & Jul's Chocolate House.

The Gate, Islington
Vegetarian international restaurant

- 370 St John Street EC1V 4NN
  Opposite Saddlers Wells theatre. Turn left out of Angel tube, walk south across the big junction towards Rosebery Ave.
- 020 7278 5483
- M-Su 12.00-23.00; lunch 12.00-14.30 last orders. Dinner 18.00-22.30 last orders. Weekend brunch 10.00-15.00
- Angel
- thegaterestaurants.com
  facebook.com/TheGateVeg

This big, elegant, second branch of Michael Daniels' (pictured) top class international vegetarian restaurant opened here in June 2012, a stone's throw from Sadler's Wells theatre. It's popular with famous veggies. Vegan and gluten-free options are clearly marked on the menu, which changes frequently with the seasons.

Starters £5-£6.25 such as soup of the day; wasabi potato cake stuffed with roasted shitake mushrooms and spices and served with pickled vegetables and seaweed salsa; plantain fritters; slow baked artichoke salad with French beans, oven-dried tomatoes and roasted walnuts.

Mains £12.50-15.50 such as root veg and chickpea tagine; red Thai curry; aubergine teriyaki on stir-fried noodles with pickled ginger and mango salsa; tortillas; salads.

Mezze (not available during weekend brunch) choose 1 for £4, 3 for £10, 5 for £15 such as falafel, grilled aubergine, roasted sweet ptotato, noodle salad, artichoke salad.

Sumptuous desserts £5-6 such as apple and Calvados crumble with vegan ice-cream, or poached pear stuffed with fig compote.

Two course set menu for lunch and until 7pm £12.50 such as mushroom consommé followed by potato gnocchi.

Extensive wine menu, most vegan, some organic. House wine £16.25 bottle, £4.15 glass. Cocktails £7.50. Dessert wine £2.50-£4.50. Beers include Freedom lager £3.60. Freshly squeezed juices from £3.25.

Children welcome, high chairs.

Also in Marylebone (Centre), Hammersmith (West London), and St John's Wood (North).

thegate

vegetarian restaurant

Pure Vegetarian and Wholefood Restaurant

INDIAN VEG · BHELPOORI HOUSE · Fully Licensed · Tel: 0207 833 116

0207 837 4607 · BHELPOORI HOUSE · Fully Licensed

EAT AS MUCH AS YOU LIKE
from a selection of 20 Dishes, Chutneys & Samosas

We are an Oasis in the desert... an invitation
to indulge in all you can eat for just £5.95

It's Healthy
It's Economical
It's Compassionate
It's Noble
It's Peace

Press Reviews on Indi

GOING VEGGIE · VEGETARIAN FOOD

412

Indian Veg Bhelpoori House
Vegetarian Indian restaurant

- 92-93 Chapel Market N1 9EX
- 020 7837 4607
- M-Su 12.00-23.30
- Angel
- theindianveg.wordpress.com
  vimeo.com/25119227 (video)

All-you-can-eat-buffet that runs all day long. Fantastic value for money here on the edge of trendy Islington, where you could easily stretch your wallet beyond the total bill here by going to nearby Upper Street for just starters or a couple of drinks. The food is basic, but filling.

Indian Veg promotes the benefits of a vegetarian diet and were serving organic brown rice long before it ever got fashionable in this part of town. Come to think of it, how many Indian restaurants can you think of that even serve it or have non-dairy lassi?

Eat as much as you like for £7.95 from the buffet which has brown, white and pilau rice, chickpea dal, spicy mashed potato, bread salad, mixed dal, aloo potato peas, mixed veg curry, onion pakora, onion bhaji, poori and some raw veg salads. You can go back as many times as you like. The food is basic but filling.

One of the few Indian restaurants that will make fresh vegan lassi for you with soya or rice milk in different flavours such as sweet lassi or mango lassi £2.95. There's a fridge full of canned and bottled soft drinks. Tea £1.25.

They use vegetable oil not butter ghee. Bring your own alcohol (but not other drinks), no corkage.

Om Nom
Vegan restaurant, goa and wellness space

- Islington Square, 116 Upper Street N1 1QP
-
- M-Sa 9.00-19.00, Su 9.00-15.00 (provisional)
- Highbury & Islington, Angel
- omnom.com
  facebook.com/omnomlondon
  instagram.com/omnom
  islingtonsquare.com/shop/omnom/

Healthy vegan restaurant opening 2020 in the Islington Square complex, a new place to eat, drink and shop, situated in North London's old postal sorting office. The day we went to press with this book, Om Nom posted a video on their instagram of builders plastering and putting in the fittings for this exciting, colourful new VEGAN healthy restaurant.

Breakfast, lunch, dinner, coffee and drinks. Children welcome. Good for groups or parties.

Dishes will include jackfruit tacos, sweet potato and bean burger in avocado bun, smoothie bowls. As pictured to the left.

Amorino
Gelateria (Italian ice-cream parlour)

- 110 Upper Street N1 1QN
- 020 7226 8717
- Su-Th 12.00-22.00,F-Sa 11.00-23.00
- Angel
- amorino.com

Italian authentic ice-cream parlour some original flavours of sorbet including pistachio Mawardi sublime, lime & basil, mango Alphonso from India, limone femminello di Sorrento, raspberry heritage, passion fruit, strawberry camarosa, organic chocolate sorbet, organic sicilian citrus, and banana nanica from Brazil, make this ice-cream parlour quite unique.

Chilango, Islington
Omnivorous Mexican café

- 27 Upper Street N1 0PN
- 020 7704 2123
- Su-Tu 11.30-22.00, W-Sa 11.30-23.00
- Angel
- chilango.co.uk

Mexican fast food with vegan options that include salads, burritos, tacos and totopos with fillings such as guacamole, black or pinto beans, peppers and chili. Vegan pot £3.95 with beans, rice, peppers and guacamole.

Gallipoli Bistro
Omnivorous Turkish restaurant

- 102 Upper Street N1 1QN
- 020 7359 0630
- M-Th 12.00-23.00, F 12.00-24.00, Sa 10.00-24.00, Su 10.00-23.00
- Angel, Highbury & Islington
- gallipolicafe.co.uk

Busy bistro full of interesting artwork and artifacts covering walls and ceiling. During daytime, offers veg breakfast £6.95, falafel salad wrap £6.95, and extras such as chips and mushrooms at 95p each.

Evening menu includes veggie mezze items £4.50-£5.50 or a nine-item platter for £9.95 and at lunch time an eight-item platter for £6.95 which can be vegan. Mains include imam bayildi aubergine stuffed with chickpea, mushroom, peas and onions, served with rice and salad; falafel meal, both £10.95. Wine from £4.10 glass, £15.95 bottle.

Gallipoli Again
Omnivorous Turkish restaurant

- 120 Upper Street N1 1QP
- 020 7359 1578
- M-Th 11.00-23.00, F 11.00-24.00, Sa 09.30-24.00, Su 09.30-23.00
- Angel, Highbury & Islington
- gallipolicafe.co.uk
  facebook.com/cafegallipoli

Another venue full of quirky character and chandeliers, with a garden out back for alfresco dining. Menu same as Bistro.

Ginger & Lime
Juice bar

- 191 Upper Street N1 1RQ
- 07469 232625
- M-F 7.00-18.00, Sa 8.00-18.00, Su 9.00-18.00
- Angel, Highbury & Islington
- gingerandlime.co

Small shop on busy Upper Street with 86 different types of juices, probably the biggest selection of juices in the country says the owner.

Juices, smoothies, breakfast smoothies, pure greens med, protein shakes, with stacks of superfoods and shots, in small, medium or large, £3-£5.50.

Thai Square
Thai omnivorous restaurant & bar

- 347-349 Upper Street N1 0PD
- 020 7704 2000
- M-F 12.00-15.00, 18.00-23.00 (Fri -23.30), Sa-Su 12.00-23.30
  M-Th 12.00-15.00 18.00-24.00, F -23.30, Sa 12.00-24.00 Su 12.00-23.00
- Angel
- thaisq.com

Big classy Thai restaurant with a whole page of veggie dishes. 6 starters £6.25-8.75 such as tempura, fried bean curd, crispy seaweed, spring rolls, corn cake with sweet chilli sauce, or have a mixed selection £13 for two people. 2 soups £5.95.

8 main courses £8.25-8.95 such as green or extra hot jungle curry, spicy basil fried bean curd with long beans & mixed vegetables; sweet & sour mixed vegetables bean curd; stir-fried tofu bean curd with cashew; and tofu bean curd with ginger; spicy aubergine in yellow bean sauce and pad Thai. Rice sticky, steamed or with coconut, brown rice £2.75-3.50. You can ask for extra veg.

House wine £19.95 bottle, £5.50 glass. Beer £4.00, spirits, ports, liqueur, aperitifs, whiskey £3.50, classic cocktails £10.50, martini cocktails £8.95, long drink cocktails £16.50 pitcher and £8.95 glass, champagne £7.50 glass, bottle £32-185. Soft drinks from £2.75.

Branches in Covent Garden, Fulham, Hanover square, Putney bridge, Richmond, Mansion House, South Kensington, St Albans, the Strand, Trafalgar square,

Children welcome, no high chairs.

Katsute100
Omnivorous Japanese tea room

- 100 Islington High St N1 8EG (Camden Passage)
- 020 7345 8395
- M-Su 12.00-19.00
- Angel
- katsute100.com

Opened at the end of 2016, this is basically a Japanese tea house for teas and light snacks with around 20 seats.

Traditional Japanese green tea leaf infusions are served in a teapot £3.60-£5 including asamushi sencha, genmaicha with roasted brown rice, hojicha low-caffeine, fukamushi sencha, gyokuro and kabusecha. Also flavoured infusions with flowers and fruits £4-£4.50 a pot such as citrusy yuzucha, kyoho sencha, lichee black tea with lychee, and caramel hojicha.

Sakuracha cherry blossom non-leaf tea £5.20 by the cup, served with a sakura mochi dessert that complements the flavour; the tea is made with salted, pickled sakura, naturally caffeine-free.

Japanease teas by the cup £2.80-£3.60 include green gyokuro, kuromame cha (black bean tea), ume kombu (plum and sea kelp tea), ume shiso bancha (plum and shish herb tea), organic molokheiya (Egyptian spinach), gobo cha (burdock), biwa cha (Japanese loquat tea), Japanese vegetable tea (kabocha, onion peel, black bean, sweet potato, burdock, corn and carrot), sencha (green tea) and hojicha (low caffeine roasted tea). These tea infusions are also available for take away but allow some extra time for preparation.

Apart from tea you can get different drinks like matcha latte and hojicha latte for £3.80.

Snacks and treats are onigiri £2.50, hiziki edamame salad £3.50, wakame sesame seaweed £3.50, sakura mochi £1.40, chocolate mochi £2.40.

The Coffee Works Project
Omnivorous coffee shop

- 96-98 High Street N1 8EG (Camden Passage)
- (020 7424 5020
- M -F 07.30-18.00, Sa 9.00-18.00, Su 10.00- 18.00
- ⊖ Angel
- offeeworksproject.com
  Facebook The Coffee Works Project
  instagram.com/thecoffeeworksproject

Busy, Independent, family run coffee house with salads, two vegan cakes, and soya and almond milk for drinks.

Appestat
Omnivorous cafe, deli and pantry

- 102 Islington High Street N1 8EG (Camden Passage)
- (020 7226 5457
- M-F 7.30-19.30, Sa 9.00-18.00, Su 10.00-18.00
- ⊖ Angel
- appestat.co.uk

This vibrant deli has a range of coffee by Climpson & Sons £2-£2.80 for espresso, cortado, macchiato, flat white, americano, latte, cappuccino, mocha, mint mocha, chai latte, iced latte, iced mocha, iced chai latte, served with almond, oat and soya milk (Bonsoy). Fine Tea Co. teas £2.20-£3.50; pot of fresh mint tea £3.50.

Freshly squeezed juices with fruits and vegetables £3.50. They have energy balls for £2.50 and vegan chocolate cake and almond pecan cake. Wifi. Check their website for special events. They have a pop up gallery too.

Wagamama Islington
Omnivorous Japanese restaurant

- First floor, The N1 Centre, Parkfield St, Islington N1
- (020 7226 2661
- M-Sa 12.00-23.00, Su 12.00-22.00
- ⊖ Angel
- wagamama.com

Inside the N1 shopping centre at the junction of Upper Street and Liverpool Road, on the first floor. See Chains section. Disabled access.

Sutton & Sons, Islington
Omnivorous fish n chip shop

- 356 Essex Road N1 3PD (top end between Englefield & Ockendon Rd)
- 020 7359 1210
- Su-Th 12.00-22.00, F-Sa 12.00-22.30
- Essex Road BR, Canonbury
- instagram.com/suttonandsonsvegan
  suttonandsons.co.uk

After the success of the vegan menu at their Stoke Newington branch, owner Danny Sutton expanded it to the Hackney Central and Islington branches. The fish fillet is made from tofu or banana blossom, a flour popular in Asia cooking, marinated overnight in seaweed and samphire, then spiced with cumin and garlic powder, and fried in egg-free batter. Vish and chips £8.50. Fish burger and chips £8.95. Fish cake £4.95.

Scampi and chips £8.50. Young Vegans pie and mash £8.50. Battered sausage and chips £6.95. Battered calamari strips £5.95. Classic prawn cocktail £.95.

Sides 65p-£3.95 include onion gravy, curry sauce; pickled onion, gherkin, mushy or garden peas, seasonal salad, pickles.

Cheesecakes £4.50. Black Milq ice cream £2.95, two scoops £5.50.

Soft drinks include Coke, Fentimans and Dalston's (lemonade, fizzy apple, ginger beer, dandelion & burdock). Bottled beers around £4, pint of Guiness £4.95. 187ml bottle of wine £5, Prosecco £6.

Planet Organic, Islington
Natural & organic supermarket & cafe

- 64 Essex Road N1 8ER (near junction Packington St)
- 020 7288 9460
- M-Sa 08.00-21.00, Su 10.00-20.00
- Angel
- planetorganic.com

A short walk up Essex Road from Islington Green, this is Islington's ethical supermarket alternative, with a wide selection of vegan foods, supplements and natural bodycare, and a mini café. Fresh fruit, veg and bakery items, kitchen essentials, sweet and savoury raw snacks, vegan chocolate, veggie wines and plant milks.

The fridges have quick meals such as Laura's Idea pancakes and Hoxton Beach falafel and salad boxes, as well as chilled vegan staples such as hummus, tofu, dairy-free spreads, burgers and sausages, yogurts and desserts, raw vegan cakes.

The cafe section has a coffee and juice bar, and hot and cold food counter. Two tables inside, and several more outside. Mix-and-match food box £5.50, £7.50 or £8.50. Soup and seeded bread £3.50, £4.99. Vegan gluten-free banana and walnut muffins and protein balls.

Teas and herbal teas £1.95 and a range of coffees £1.60-£2.95 in regular or large. Speciality lattes £3.15-£4 such as cacao, chai, hot choc, charcoal, turmeric, mango matcha, or dragon fruit. Almond, coconut, hazelnut, oat and soya milk at no extra cost. Organic classic and 'super' juices and smoothies £4.50-£5.95 and wheatgrass shots £3.60 single, £3.95 double. Brown rice miso £1.95.

Bodycare shelf labels indicate if vegan,

including Organic Bloom, Jason, Green People, Dr Hauschka, Sukin, Pai, Urtekram, Weleda, John Master Organics, Inika make-up. Small range of holistic books. Supplements including Terranova, Viridian, Biocare, Pukka herbal remedies. Friendly and knowledgeable staff.

L'Erbolario
Bodycare shop

- 📍 106 Upper Street N1 1QN
- 📞 020 3601 8130
- 🕐 M-Sa 10.00-18.30 Su 12.00-18.00
- ⊖ Angel, Highbury & Islington
- ↖ erbolario.com

If you are looking for a gift for him, her, the little ones and your companion animal, this is the place. Erbolario (herbalist in Italian) has been around since 1978 and has always been cruelty-free and eco-friendly. They have a vast range of body, face, hair products, make-up and sun lotion. They do mini sizes good for travelling. For your home you can find candles, fragrances for scented wood, home fragrance diffusers, incense and scented sachets. One or two products contain bee pollen or royal jelly, ask at the counter.

Chapel Market
Yer actual London street market

- 📍 Chapel Market (a street), N1
- 🕐 Tu-W, F-Sa 9.00-18.00; Th, Su 9.00-16.00
- ⊖ Angel

Full on London street market with all sorts of bargains for the home, fruit and veg, clothing, and great cheap veggie eateries nearby. Look out for Al Turath vegan falafel.

Holland & Barrett, Angel
Health food shop

- 📍 31 Upper St, Islington N1 0PN
- 📞 020 7359 9117
- 🕐 M-F 08.30-20.00, Sa 9.00-19.00, Su 10.00-19.00
- ⊖ Angel

Fridge with grab and go light lunch things and freezer.

Holland & Barrett, Islington
Health food shop

- 📍 212 Upper Street N1 1RL
- 📞 020 7226 3422
- 🕐 M-F 9.00-19.00, Su 11.00-17.00
- ⊖ Highbury & Islington

Fridge and freezer.

Butternut squash, onions, peppers and olives
served w/ salad £5.00

Coconut & Raspberry Bakewell
Wheat free
Refined sugar free 2.20

PEAR, CHOCOLATE & CARDAMOM 2.90

The GODFATHER... Returns...
smoked courgette, sweet potato, red onion chutney, rocket, pesto, grilled mushrooms, nigella seeds
4.90

Everyone round here gets their coffee here

The Fields Beneath
by Gillian Tindall

COFFFFFEE ALL DOUBL
ESPRESSO   2
MACCHIATO
FLAT WHITE   2.60
CAPPUCCIO   2.60
LATTE   2.70
MOKHA
DECAFFF 3.0
               ORANGE 3.0

LOOSE LEAF TEAS   1.80
HOME MADE CHAI   2.80

HOT CHOC   2.80
HOT MILK   1.80
HOT GINGER   1.80

COLD DRINKS
JUICE, FIZZ, WATER
COFFEE BEANS SOLD

BREAKFAST POTS
Bircher Muesli   £2.20
Chia Seed Pudding
Granola + Greek Yog

KENTISH TOWN

and Tufnell Park

Just a walk or rapid bus ride north of Camden Town but much quieter, with three excellent sit-down vegan eateries, some fabulous Ethiopian restaurants, and superb vegan food shopping.

The Fields Beneath, Kentish Tn
Vegan cafe

- 52a Prince of Wales Road NW5 3LN
- 020 7424 8838
- M-F 07.00-16.00, Sa 08.00-16.00, Su 9.00-16.00
- Kentish Town West
- thefieldsbeneath.com
  facebook.com/fieldsbeneath
  nstagram.com/fieldsbeneath

This cafe originally opened 2012 at the entrance to Kentish Town West overground station, and was made completely vegan in March 2017 by owner Gavin Fernback. The name references a history book about Kentish Town. The rustic interior has a wooden floor, big Moroccan style tiled counter and an open prep kitchen.

The light bites menu £4.90-£5.50 changes often and might include raw Pad Thai with courgette ribbons, red cabbage, red pepper, spring onions, edamame with homemade dressing with kohlrabi, toasted peanuts and lime; cauliflower buffalo wings wrap with pickled onions, iceberg, celery, ranch dressing, red cabbage and onion slaw; the Godfather sandwich with smoky tomato sauce, grilled mushrooms, courgettes, watercress and pickled onions; farina butternut squash, onions, peppers and olives served with salad. Check the board for daily special such as Bombay Pot with rice £5.50.

Cakes and snacks £1.50- £2.80 including plain and chocolate croissants; pear, chocolate and cardamom flapjack; coconut and raspberry Bakewell; choccy chip cookie; Bill Gates millionaire flapjack (ginger, date, salted caramel, dark chocolate ganache); majestic balls (dates, coconut, hemp, seeds, maple syrup, cacao, no nuts); toasted banana loaf.

Hot drinks £2-£3.20 include loose leaf tea, coffees, turmeric golden milk, hot chocolate, hot milk and hot ginger, with almond, Bonsoy, coconut, hazelnut or oat milk. They sell coffee beans too which they roast in collaboration with Coffee by Tate.

Wifi. Seats inside and outside. Take-away. Another branch opened 2019 in Camden.

Engocha
Vegan Ethiopian restaurant

- 📞 143 Fortess Road NW5 2HR
- ☎ 020 7485 3838
- 🕐 M-Sa 10.00-20.00, Su 10.00-19.00
- ⊖ Tufnell Park
- ↖ Facebook Engocha Grocery

Choose injera Ethiopian flatbread or basmati rice plus 3 items £4, 4 £6.99 or 5 £8.99. Select from gomen spinach, misir kik spiced lentil stew, tikil gomen curry potatoes with cabbage and carrot, ater kik split peas simmered with spices and herbs sauce, shiro chick peas, azifa whole lentils, fesollia mixed veg stew.

Hot drinks include hot chocolate with soya milk.

Arancini Factory Cafe
Vegan Italian restaurant

- 📞 115A Kentish Town Road NW1 8PB
- ☎ 020 3583 2242
- 🕐 M-F 08.00-21.30, Sa-Su 09.30-21.30
- ⊖ Camden Road, Kentish Town West, Kentish Town, Camden Town
- ↖ arancinibrothers.com

This Italian take-away and eat in restaurant turned vegan in 2018 and serves unusual vegan dishes. If you fancy a change from falafels then do go try their arancini, deep-fried rice balls which they serve with or in everything.

Vegan recovery breakfast wrap £5.50-£6.80 baby spinach, roast tomato, mushrooms, eggplant and tomato sauce, maple syrup.

Veganist wrap £5.70-£7.20 served with risotto balls and salad with tomato and eggplant sauce. One tasty vegan risotto burger £7.50-£8 comes with mushroom and zucchini risotto patty organic bap with tomato eggplant sauce, onion jam, crispy onions and fresh tomato; Vegan box £5.50-£6.90 includes 4 risotto balls, salad, eggplant tomato sauce and onion jam. Mushroom zucchini risotto balls served with chutney 5 balls £4-£5, 7 £5-£6.20, 12 £7-£8.40. Extras 50p-£3 are small and large fries, side salads, chutney, eggplant tomato sauce.

Hot drinks £1.70-£2.50, almond milk extra 50p. Cold drinks £1.70-£2.50. Juices £2.50-£3.80.

Summer garden. Wifi. Catering. Also in Dalston (East London), Old Street (The City) and Maltby Street (London Bridge). At the time of printing this branch was closed for renovations.

Lalibela

Omnivorous Ethiopian restaurant

- 137 Fortess Road NW5 2HR
- 020 7284 0600
- Tu-Sa 18.00-23.00, Su-M 18.00-22.00
- Tufnell Park
- lalibelarestaurant.co.uk
  facebook.com/lalibelalondon
  instagram.com/lalibela_london

If you want Ethiopian after 8pm, when Engocha closes, this is the place to go. Vegan dishes are marked on the menu. As well as injera, you can eat with turmeric and herb rice, spinach rice or flavoured couscous.

Salads £4-£5. Start with injera with dips or soaked in spicy tomato and onion sauce, or lentil samosas, under £5.

Main dishes ££7.95-£9.95 such as lentils, spinach and mushrooms, spinach and potato stew, chickpea stew, grilled aubergine and chickpeas in spicy tomato stew, mushroom and okra, slow cooked pumpkin chunks in spicy tomato based stew.

Side dishes £3.95 include spiced potatoes with carrots and green beans, fried spinach with herbs and garlic, gomen greens, okra with tomato, azifa whole green lentils.

Soft drinks from £2. Bottled beers and strawberry cider around £4. Wine from £5.50 large glass, £14.95 bottle. Traditional Ethiopian coffee ceremony, mint or spiced tea.

423

Earth Natural Foods
Wholefoods shop and take-away

☞ 200 Kentish Town Road NW5 2AE (corner Gaisford St, opposite Rio's health spa)

☎ 020 7482 2211

◷ M-Sa 08.30-19.00, Su 11.00-17.00

⊖ Kentish Town, Kentish Town West BR

🖊 earthnaturalfoods.co.uk

Fabulous and huge wholefood store, more like a mini-supermarket, set up by people who used to work at Bumblebee. Packed with organic vegetarian wholefoods, bodycare, cleaning products and a big range of organic vegan wine.

Lots of organic fruit and vegetables, herbs and spices, also loose, fresh wheat, rye and gluten free bread. Pasta made from kamut, spelt, rice and corn, rice quinoa. Self-serve nuts and seeds, pulses, grains, tea and coffee beans which you can have fun grinding in their electric grinder. Soya, rice, oat, hazelnut and even quinoa milk. Stacks of vegan margarines, cooking creams, dips, nut butters. Japanese foods.

Chocolate such as Rapunzel, Demeter, Plamil, Viviani, Doisy and Dam, New Tree, Green & Blacks. Vegan ice-cream includes Booja Booja, B'Nice, Swedish Glace. Some vegan cake slices and croissants.

Deli counter at back with salad bar and hot food £3.60 small, £5.90 medium, £8.30 large carton, point to what you want. Soup £1.50 small, £2.75 large. Antipasti £1.50 per 100gr including olives, sun dried tomatoes and roasted artichokes.

In a hurry? There are grab-and-go fridges in the middle of the shop with vegan stuff such as Laura's Idea tofu spinach pancakes, croquettes, sushi, Soupology, Cheatin, VegiDeli, Taifun, Coyo, The coconut Collaborative, Sojade and Provamel. Sheese and Tofutti. Booja Booja truffles. Ploughshares slices.

Big organic wine section, mostly vegan and labelled, beers and ciders, juices.

Supplements include Biocare, Viridian, Terranova, Nature's Plus. Magazines. Baby section.

Bodycare includes Desert Essence, Jäson, Faith In Nature, Weleda, Urtekram, House of Mistry, Green People, Alba Botanica, Lavera, Avalon, Avena. Organic cottonwool and buds. Insect repellant.

Cleaning products by BioD, Earth Friendly, Ecolino, Ecover refills.

Phoenicia
Mediterranean cafe and food hall

- 186-192 Kentish Town Rd NW5 2AE (corner Patshull Rd, opposite Somerfield)
- 020 7267 1267
- M-Sa 9.00-20.00, Su/BH 10.00-18.00
- Kentish Town
- phoeniciafoodhall.co.uk/

Great Lebanese cafe and grocery with deli counter. Starters include rice, lentils, tabouleh salad, green beans, mushrooms, hummus, aubergine dips and spicy couscous. Main dishes: roast veggie mix, aubergine, okra stew and chilli, potato and peppers. You can get falafel with sides, veggies mezze plate, Lebanese or Moroccan wrap. Juices, smoothies, soft drinks, hot drinks, all at lower prices than down in Camden.

Meat is out of sight in a separate section. Chilled section has various antipasti and homemade dips, also tofu and plant milks. The big groceries area includes 25 kinds of self-serve (stuffed) olives by weight, sundried tomatoes, chilli and garlic. Fruit and veg, fresh herbs, Mediterranean breads. Wholefoods and organic section on the far left. 30 kinds of halva. Lots of olives, coconut, avocado, organic sesame oils.

Outside catering. Seats, children welcome, no high chairs. Delivery service.

Natural Coffee Lounge
Organic Mediterranean ood store and omnivorous cafe

- 136-138 Kentish Town Road NW1 9QB
- 020 7813 1179
- M-F 07.00-19.00, Sa-Su 8.00-19.00
- Kentish Town
- naturalcoffeelounge.co.uk facebook.com/Naturalcoffeelounge

Two floors of cafe with a wholefood shop on the right hand side.

Salads £4.90 to £5.90, soup £3.90-£4.90, vegan cheese avocado panini £3.90-£4.90. Tea and coffee £1-"2.80. Smoothies £3.90.

Desserts £1.40-£3 include carrot, orange and coconut loaf, double chocolate loaf, lemon poppy seed, chocolate fudge brownie and peanut butter brownie.

At the back in the fridge are Great Food Uk gluten-free range, Moroccan koftas, spinach and pinenuts bites and Tuscan bites; Tideford organic soups; lots of tempeh and tofu. Couldron, Taifun, Tofurky, Cheezly, Violife, Sheese, Vegusto, Provamel, Sojade and Koko yogurts. Sprouts too.

In the freezer is great selection of ice cream by Swedish Glace, Okobay, Food Heaven lemon sorbet, Jollyum and Sweet Rebellion. Clive's pies.

Organic fruit and veg. Big range of organic wholefoods. Really Healthy pasta, soya noodles, vegan pesto, Plamil Mayo, Cookies, chocolate bars, flapjacks, biscuits, protein bars and Booja Booja truffles. Go Vegan chocolate and nut spreads.

Organic vegan wines, beers and ciders.

Baby food and bodycare by Biocare,

Biohealth and Salus.

Cleaning products by Ecover, Ecozone, BioD and Faith in Nature. Yarrah vegan snacks and food for dogs.

On the top floor and outside are tablest. Wifi. High chairs. Community board. There is always someone to provide advice.

Franco Manca
Omnivorous pizzeria

- 337 Kentish Town Road NW5 2TJ
- 020 3026 5717
- M-Th 11.30-22.30, F-Sa 12.00-23.00, Su 12.00-22.30
- Kentish Town
- francomanca.co.uk

Sourdough pizza bases, vegan cheese, and all their wines are vegan.

The Queen of Sheba
Omnivorous Ethiopian restaurant

- 12 Fortess Road NW5 2EU
- 020 7284 3947
- M-Sa 18.00-23.30, Su 12.00-22.30
- Kentish Town
- thequeenofshebarestaurant.co.uk
  instagram.com/
  thequeenofsheba_restaurant

Family business, great atmosphere with a unique setting with typical Ethiopian furniture and art.

Starters £4.50-£6 such as mixed salad, Azifa lentil salad, kategna cripy injera with chilli; Misir injera lentil wrap served cold; ingudai ti's sauté mushrooms with spices; sambossa stuffed with your choice of vegetables marinated with herbs and spices.

Main courses £7-£9.50 include vegetable stew served in a clay pot; hot red lentil stew; whole green lentil stew with turmeric and black pepper; mushroom stew marinated with onion, garlic, ginger, with red pepper and wine sauce; split yellow pea with ginger and green chilli; spinach with onion, garlic, ginger and jalapeño; cabbage with potatoes and carrot; whole beans with carrot and spices.

Sides £3.50-£5.50 such as spicy potato wedges; sauté mushrooms with spices; stutted green chilli.

Fruit salad £3.90. Tea, coffee and Ethiopian coffee £1.90-£3.50. Wine £4.25 glass, £13 bottle. Beers £3.95 including Ethiopian Bati, St George and Castel. Champagne £8.50 glass, £39 bottle. Soft drinks £2.

KINGS CROSS

North London

Kings Cross has many veg*ns living in the neighbourhood, the very authentic Japanese vegan restaurant **Itadaki Zen**, **Temple of Camden** vegan fried chick'n restaurant by the canal, and vegan street food stalls. Look out for **Arabica Food & Spice** in front of Kings Cross station selling Mediterranean salads, dips and mezze March-November, W-F 12.00-19.00.

It's an eclectic neighbourhood and the first part of London many people see when arriving by train from Europe, or from the north. It's very multicultural and has lots of small shops. As well as kebab shops there are Japanese, Ethiopian and Indian restaurants.

The area has recently been modernised and redeveloped. The new West concourse at Kings Cross station replaced the ugly old one with a tree-lined public square, new shops, offices and flats.

Behind St Pancras station and the Eurostar terminal, much is brand new. But it doesn't have just a modern feel, they kept the old buildings too, giving a quite industrial look with Regent's Canal going across. The Granary Building from 1851, where wheat was stored, is part of the Goods Yard complex with the Train Assembly Shed and the Eastern transit shed, now being used by Central Saint Martins University, while the Western transit shed is occupied by shops and restaurants. **Granary Square** is in the middle with its jumping fountains and usually has one or two vegan street food stalls such as **Little Leaf Pizza**. This part of London has a brand new postcode N1C.

St Pancras station has been completely renewed with Eurostar trains going to Paris, Brussels and Amsterdam. St Pancras Hotel, established in 1873 with the most beautiful renaissance facade, has been refurbished.

On the west side of St Pancras, the modern British Library serves as a work base for writers and researchers. Meanwhile the old La Scala cinema on Pentonville Road is now an events and gigs venue. Google, The Guardian and Observer newspapers, and Universal Music have all moved here.

On a sunny day you can sit by the canal and either bring your own food or get a take-away from the many places this area has to offer. There is also a Waitrose supermarket with its own tables outside. Afterwards you can stroll along the canal to Camden.

Other new openings are the third branch of **Mildreds** vegetarian restaurant, and **Thenga** Indian vegetarian cafe.

Harry Potter fans can find Platform 9 3/4 at Kings Cross. Look out for the luggage trolley embedded in the wall between platforms 9 and 10. You can also browse the Harry Potter shop. In St Pancras concourse you can play the piano.

▸ kingscross.co.uk

EUSTON

ST. PANCRAS RD.

CALEDONIAN ROAD

LIVERPOOL ROAD

PENTON ST.

WHITE LION ST.

AMWELL ST.

ROSEBE

KING'S CROSS

ST. PANCRAS

PENTONVILLE RD.

GRAYS INN RD. A201

KINGS CROSS RD. A201

BLOOMSBURY

Sainsbury's
Waitrose

NORTH

KINGS CROSS

KINGS CROSS
IZ Itadaki Zen
Te Temple of Camden

Mi Mildreds Kings Cross
Th Thenga Cafe
ad Addis
di Dishoom
va La Valle
Q   Le Pain Quotidien
le Leon
me Mediterraneo
rt Royal Thai

ms Marks & Spencer
ne Neal's Yard
so Sourced Market
wa Waitrose

li Life After Hummus

ISLINGTON
AT Al Turath
Co Copperhouse Choc
In Indian Veg
cm Chapel Market

⬤ vegan
⬤ vegetarian
⬤ omnivorous
⬤ shop
⬤ cookery class

429

Itadaki Zen
Vegan organic Japanese restaurant

- 139 Kings Cross Road WC1X 9BJ
- 020 7278 3573
- Tu-F 12.00-14.15, M-Sa 18.00–22.00 (last orders 15 minutes before closing); Su, bank holidays closed
- Kings Cross
- itadakizen-uk.com
  Facebook Itadakizen London

With its 'food as medicine' and slow-food philosophy, this organic vegan restaurant offers nurturing and beautifully presented dishes to eat in or take away. Delicately-prepared rice, root vegetables, seaweeds, soya beans and seasonal vegetables form the basis for a dazzling choice on the full evening menu, including all kinds of sushi, noodle dishes, and tempura. The interior is elegantly decorated in Japanese style with natural wood walls and tables throughout and there is a downstairs private dining room for groups.

If you don't want to narrow down to one or two a la carte items, treat yourself to their recently increased range of multi-dish set dinners such as the Tanno set £17 which comprises a mixed rice dish, cabbage-leaf spring roll, seasonal vegetables with marinated peanut dressing, tofu with Yangyeom sauce, three vegetable dishes and miso soup. Other set dinners £13 to £28 include sushi set, tempura with sushi and dessert, or vegetable dishes with noodles and sushi.

Amazing sugar-free desserts £4-£5 include Japanese pumpkin muffin with jujube and chestnuts, topped with tofu and vanilla cream; and their new matcha cake. £20 for a whole Zen cake for parties – must be ordered in advance.

Fast lunch menu £6-£7 such as udon noodles with fried tofu or tempura, or Korean style sushi. Bento box of tempura £10. Side dishes £1-£3 include marinated seaweed, spring roll, miso soup, kimchi, tofu steak.

10% service charge from 7pm. Wine from £5 glass, £23 bottle.

Children welcome, one high chair. 10% discount for students.

Temple of Camden
Vegan fried chick'n restaurant

- 103A Camley Street N1C 4PF (Behind St Pancras, next to the canal)
- no phone
- M-Sa 12.00-21.00, Su 11.00-18.00
- Kings Cross, Camden Road, Camden Town, Mornington Crescent
- templeofseitan.co.uk
  facebook.com/templeofseitan
  instagram.com/templeofseitan

Opened 31st January 2017 with the same menu as the original Temple of Hackney, plus some new items. The original shop in Hackney only had seating outside, this branch is much bigger with plenty of seating inside. Vegan Londoners flock here for a fun fast food fix of fake fried fowl, mac n cheez, or vegan egg and bacon bagel.

Main dishes £6-£7.50 include various flavours of fried chick'n burger with extras that include bacon, cheese, chipotle mayo, coleslaw, jalapenos, sriracha, pickles; a quarterpounder cheeseburger with bacon; or hot dipped, buffalo or BBQ wings; Add fries or coleslaw and a drink for £2.50, large portion £3.50. Mac 'n cheese £4, large £6. Top up with an extra burger, popcorn bites, coleslaw, gravy, extra bacon or cheese, pot of mayo (chipotle, ranch, classic, or lemon pepper).

Lots of desserts £3 on display in a glass cabinet such as choc brownies, peanut butter cookie sandwich, marshmallow chocolate cookie, carrot cake, cinnabuns, summer berry slice, croissant, pain au chocolat, pain au raisin.

Dark Arts coffee, latte, cappuccino, flat white, cortado £2-£2.60. Teapigs tea £1.50. 30p discount if you bring your own cup. With Oatly or Bonsoy. Cans £1.50.

To get there from Kings Cross station: Walk up Pancras Road, between Kings Cross and St Pancras, which becomes Camley Street and branches left under railway lines then over the canal. Uber Eats.

TEMPLE
OF
CAMDEN
→
NOW SERVING BREAKFAST
MON-FRI 9:00-11:45
AND SPECIALTY COFFEE
FRIED CHICKEN FROM
12:00 ON MON-FRI
11:00 ON SAT-SUN
100% VEGAN

TEMPLE
OF
SEITAN

ANY ALLERGIES?
PLEASE ASK ABOUT ALLERGENS

CINNABUNS £3
(WHEAT, GLUTEN, SOYA NUTS, TREE NUTS)

GLUTEN FR
SUMME
(SOYA, NUTS)

£2.5

BROWNIES £3
(WHEAT, GLUTEN, TREE NUTS, NUTS)
SESAME SEEDS

CHOC MARSHMALLOW
COOKIES £2.5
(WHEAT, GLUTEN, NUTS, TREE NUTS)

PEANUT
BUTTER
COOKIE
SANDWICH
(PEANUTS, NUTS
WHEAT, GLUTEN
SESAME SEED)

PAIN AU £2.5

PAIN AU £2.5
CHOCOLATE
(GLUTEN, SOYA, WHEAT, TREE, NUTS)

433

Mildreds Kings Cross
Vegetarian restaurant

- 200 Pentonville Road N1 9JP
- 020 7278 9422
  kingscross@mildreds.co.uk
- M-F 11.00-23.00, Sa 10.00-23.00, Su 10.00-22.00
- Kings Cross,
- mildreds.co.uk
  facebook.com/mildredskingscross

The third branch of Mildreds opened in 2016. We love that their menu, which changes throughout the year, marks the items which are *not* vegan.

Industrial interior with an open kitchen. 90% of their food and drinks are vegan, they use organic ingredients when possible.

Weekend brunch runs till 15.00, £6-£10. The big brunch £13 has scrambled tofu, sausage, oak smoked house beans, roasted tomato and mushroom, toasted sourdough. slow roasted tomato. Waflles E8 with strawberries, chocolate sauce and ice cream. BLT with aubergine bacon £8.50.

Olives and bread £5. Starters £5-£9 such as soup with bread; gyoza dumplings; celeriac skordalia with leeks and pumpkin; porcini arancini; hummus with rose harissa and pinenuts; chargrilled Roman style artichoke; porcini arancini.

Burgers £8-£9 feature teriyaki chick'n, Polish beetroot white bean with pickled red cabbage and gherkins. Add cheese, avocado, fries or sweet potato fries for £1.50-£4.50.

Main courses £12-£13 such as Soul Bowl with veggies, quinoa, kale, avocado cashew cheese, toasted seeds; Levant chick'n kebabs with butterbeans and spinach; Sri Lankan sweet potato coconut curry with roasted cashews and pea basmati rice; parsnip apple sausages with borlotti beans, mustard mash; gochujang tofu with oriental veg and furikake Shanghai noodles or black venus rice.

Desserts £6-£7 such as cheesecake with blackberry sauce, clementine and pistachio cake with blood orange sorbet, chocolate cherry cake with coconut chantilly, coffee infused creme caramel. Spiced rum truffles £3.

Wines are vegan organic, from £6.50 glass, carafe £18, bottle £23. Pale ale and lager £4.95. Cocktails from £7.50. Organic juices £4 or £4.50. Soft drinks £2.50-£3.50 include kombucha, Pimento ginger beer, cola. Organic coffee.

There are two big long tables in the middle and a few tables outside. High chairs. They only take bookings for parties of 10 to 12, so enjoy a drink at the bar if there is a queue. Take-away and delivery direct or through Deliveroo.

Also in Camden, Soho (Central London) and Dalston (East London).

Thenga Cafe
Vegetarian Indian cafe

- 120 Cromer Street WC1H 8BS
- (020 3817 9919
- Tu-F 10.00-18.00, Sa 10.00-16.00, Su-M closed
- ⊖ Kings Cross
- ⦚ thengacafe.com
  facebook.com/thengacafe

Great value new cafe in the back streets towards Kings Cross. Thali £4.95. Menu changes every day, most dishes are vegan including cakes £1.80, biscuits. Tea £1.50, organic coffee £2, large £2.40, they have almond milk.

To get there, walk south down Judd Street (opposite St Pancras) and Cromer Street is third on the left.

Leon, Kings Cross Station
Omnivorous World food takeaway

- Western Concourse King's Cross Station, Euston Road N1C 4AH
- (07973 259 924
- M-W 06.00-23.00, Th-F 06.00-24.00, Sa 07.00-24.00, Su 07.30-22.00
- ⊖ Kings Cross
- ⦚ leon.co

Now with heaps of vegan options such as jack wings, burger, lentil masala, Brazilian black beans, hummus, baked fries, crushed pea salad, slaw.

Another branch behind this station at 6 Pancras Square N1C 4AG. Open M-F 07.30-21.00, Sa-Su 10.00-17.00.

Le Pain Quotidien, St Pancras
Omnivorous Belgian cafe and bakery

- Unit 4, St Pancras International Station, Euston Road NW1 2OL
- (020 7486 6154
- M-Sa 05.30-22.00, Sa 02.00-24.00, Su/BH 06.30-22.00
- ⊖ Kings Cross
- ⦚ lepainquotidien.com/store/st-pancras

Get in the mood for a trip on Eurostar to Paris, Brussels or Amsterdam with a meal at this vegan-friendly Belgian cafe chain. Highlights are porridge, mushroom or avocado toast, soups, chilli sin carne, vegetable curry, veggie bowl, blueberry muffins. They have almond and oat milk.

La Valle

Omnivorous restaurant

- 260 Pentonville Road N19JY
- 020 7278 7887
- M-F 08.00-22.00, Sa-Su 9.00-20.00
- Kings Cross
- foodilickingscross.co.uk
  facebook.com/foodilic

Previously part of the Foodilic chain, now independent but still specialising in raw food and a big salad bar. Tremendous value.

All you can eat buffet breakfast £6.50, lunch and dinner £7.50, take-away box £4.50. See the list of dishes below, plus vegan moussaka. Raw vegan desserts £3.50 are carrot cake or papaya cake, though they'd sold out by the time we got there in the evening.

Kombucha and soft drinks. Organic Fairtrade hot drinks £1.60-£2.30 include all kinds of coffees, hot choc, mocha, tea, Earl Grey, camomile, peppermint. Almond, oat or soy milk.

Mediterraneo

Omnivorous Italian restaurant

- 112 Kings Cross Road WC1X 9DS
- 020 7837 5108
- Su-Th 17.00-23.00, F Sa 17.00-23.30
- Kings Cross
- themediterraneo-kingscross.com

Bruschetta £6. Spaghetti with vegan meat balls in tomato sauce, or penne alla primavera with grilled mediterranean vegetables in a tomato garlic sauce, both £8.95. Gnocchi Napoletano £8.50. Fully licensed. Minimum card payment £10.

Dishoom

Omnivorous Indian street food restaurant in Bombay style

- Granary Square, 5 Stable Street N1C 4AB
- 020 7420 9321
- M-W 08.00-23.00, Th-F 08.00-24.00, Sa 09.00-24.00, Su 09.00-23.00. Open BH except Christmas.
- Kings Cross
- dishoom.com/vegan-main

Set in a huge restored Victorian building on 3 floors, the biggest of the chain and is also the biggest restaurant in Kings Cross. This branch is called Dishoom Godown which in India means a warehouse, and is another building inside the Western Transit Shed. The decor and the atmosphere take you back to the colonial era in old Bombay, every detail is so perfect, even the music, that you cam forget you are in modern London. The substantial separate vegan menu ranges from street food snacks to a banquet.

Cooked breakfast £13.90 with Beyond Meat sausages, vegan black pudding, tofu akuri scramble, grilled field mushrooms and tomato, masala beans and vegan buns; or just akuri and buns £7.20. Other options £5.50-£7.20 are naan sausage roll with cheese and chilli tomato jam, coconut granola, banana and date porridge, fresh fruit and coconut yogurt,

Samosas, okra fries, bhel, grilled corn on the cob, bowl of greens, vada pav like a chip butty £2.90-£4.70. Fried lentil puris with a hearty bowl of potato and chickpea curry £10.50. Pomelo salad ££7.90 with kale, pistachios, date and tamarind chutney. Gunpowder potatoes £6.90. Chickpea and couscous salad £8.90.

For dessert, kala khatta gola fluffy ice flakes £3.50 steeped in kokum fruit syrup, with blueberries, chilli, lime, white and black salt. Basmati rice pudding £5.90 with coconut milk, cardamon and cashews and blueberry compote.

Wine from £6 medium glass, £16.70 carafe, £23.50 bottle. Beers and cider from £4.50. Cocktails. Soft drinks £2.90-3.50. Freshly squeezed orange juice £3.90. Teas and coffees £2.50-£2.90.

It's a busy place, especially at the end of the week, so a good idea to book. Though if you are stuck in a queue don't worry as complimentary drinks are offered. Tables outside. Take-away.

Addis
Omnivorous Ethiopian restaurant

- 40-42 Caledonian Road N1 9DT
- 020 7278 0679
- M-F 17.00-23.00, Sa-Su 12.00-23.00
- Kings Cross
- addisrestaurant.co.uk

Ethiopian restaurant with several vegan dishes. Starters and sides £2.99-£3.99 include salads, herby spicy potatoes, humus, lentils, beans, cabbage with potato and carrot. Mains cost £6.50-£8.95 are various combinations of vegetables, spices and chickpeas, also falafel. Beware that one dish (yetesom beyaynetu special) listed as vegetarian contains fish; read the menu carefully.

Bar with wine, beer, juices, Ethiopian coffee.

Licenced bar. Take-away. Catering. Children welcome. Wifi.

Royal Thai
Omnivorous Thai restaurant

- 50 Caledonian Road N1 9DP
- 020 7837 7755
- M-Su 12.00-15.00, 17.00-23.00, last order 22.00
- Kings Cross
- royalthai-res.co.uk

Starters, soup and salads £4.95-£6.95 include corn cake with chilli sauce; papaya salad with crushed peanuts; tofu glass noodle salad; glass noodle soup, mushroom and tofu soup cooked in coconut milk. Mixed starters £10.95 for two people.

Red or green tofu curry £6.95. There are also noodle dishes, both glass and Pad Thai with tofu, tofu fried rice, and brown, coconut, sticky and steamed jasmine rice.

Wine from £4.70 medium glass, £6.50 large, £19.30 bottle.

When you reserve a table for more than 4 people you get 10% off your bill on Monday and Tuesday evenings.

Life After Hummus
Healthy vegan international cookery classes

- Somers Town Community Centre, 150 Ossulston Street NW1 1EE
- 020 7833 3524
- Evenings from 18.30
- Kings Cross, Euston, Mornington Crescent
- lifeafterhummus.com
  facebook.com/lifeafterhummus

Free and very low cost ultra-healthy vegan cooking classes. Calendar on Facebook.

Sourced Market
Omnivorous deli/grocer

- ☛ St Pancras International station (under Eurostar departures board) NW1 2QP
- ☎ 020 7833 9352
- 🕐 M-F 07.00-21.00, Sa 08.00-20.00, Su 9.00-20.00
- ⊖ Kings Cross

A large outlet, that brings Borough Market style artisan foods to the station, quite a change from the average corner shop. On one side it is very meaty and cheesey but on the other side is much better for us.

In the food to go fridge are salads, pots and falafel wraps by Laura's Idea, Hoxton Beach, and Pollen & Grace, and Pudology desserts. At the counter you can have a soup for £4, avocado pistachio and chocolate cake slice £3.

On the shelves are organic raw chocolate brownies, and chcolate bars by Montezuma, Organic Raw and Ombar. Squirrel Sisters snack bars.

Coffees and teas £1.50-£2.80. Juices and smoothies counter, made to order for around £4-£5.

Waitrose
Omnivorous supermarket

- ☛ Granary Square, 1 Wharf Road N1C 4BZ
- ☎ 020 7372 5330
- 🕐 M-Sa 8.00-22.00, Su 12.00-18.00
- ⊖ Kings Cross
- ↖ waitrose.com

This Waitrose is quite unique, being in the restored listed Midland Goods Shed. It's spacious and very bright with brick walls and high ceilings, a coffee shop, juice bar, bakery and wine bar. Tables inside and out.

You can find salads, sushi, sandwiches, falafels and anything you need to make your own sandwich like spreads, antipasti, greens, salads etc.

If you have a Waitrose card you can have a free coffee or organic herbal tea. Also juice blends and smoothies £3.95.

There are many vegan wines on the shelves, pay an extra £7.50 if you want to drink it at the wine bar, or take it with you by the canal or outside on the grass. There is a wine specialist and a catalogue to tell you which ones are vegan.

Neal's Yard, St Pancras
Organic health & beauty shop

- ☛ Unit 17c, St Pancras International Station, Euston Road NW1 2QP
- ☎ 020 7833 3524
- 🕐 M-Sa 07.00-21.00, Su 9.00-19.00
- ⊖ Kings Cross
- ↖ nealsyardremedies.com

Also inside St Pancras station are Marks & Spencer, Pret a Manger, Starbucks, Hamleys toy shop, Hatchards bookshop and WH Smith newsagent.

MILL HILL

The Broadway

Brewed Eatery
Omnivorous cafe

- 103 The Broadway NW7 3TG
- 020 3909 9270
- M-F 08.00-18.00, Sa 9.00-18.00, Su 9.00-17.00
- Mill Hill Broadway BR
- brewedandeatery.co.uk (menu) facebook.com/brewedeateryuk instagram.com/brewedeatery

New cafe in Mill Hill Broadway. Mostly vegetarian with plenty of vegan food. Some outside seating.

Morning dishes include matcha chia pudding with coconut milk; oats and quinoa porridge with banana and almond flakes. All day dishes such as soup of the day; yellow coconut curry; brown and wild rice with veggies and tofu; falafel wrap; avocado toast with truffle oil, pea shoots, tomato and omega seeds; salads with ingredients that include kale, black beans, olives, sweet corn, red and white quinoa, sweet potato, broccoli, green beans, edamame; Mezze Bowl with baked sweet potato falafel, onion humus; raw zucchini linguini salad.

Raw vegan cakes include tiramisu, peanut butter, strawberry and many more. Colourful vegan protein shakes.

Children's gluten-free penne with tomato sauce, or plain pasta with olive oil. Deliveroo, Uber Eats.

Pizza Express, Mill Hill
Omnivorous Italian restaurant

- 92 The Broadway, Mill Hill NW7 3TB
- 020 8959 3898
- Su-Th 11.30-22.30, F-Sa 11.30-23.00
- Mill Hill Broadway BR
- pizzaexpress.com

Vegan cheese. Disabled access. Baby facilities.

Love a drink? Pop into **Mill Hill Wines** at 85 Mill Hill Broadway where they have vegan labelling on many items as well as knowledgeable and friendly staff. Huge selection of beers, wines and some very interesting spirits. Lychee liqueur anyone?

MUSWELL HILL

Hopper & Bean
Omnivorous independent cafe

- 152 Fortis Green Rd N10 3DU)
- 020
- M-Sa 08.00-17.00, Su 9.00-16.00
- Finsbury Park, then W7 bus
- hopperandbean.com
  facebook.com/hopperandbean

Vegan breakfast £9.80 with mushrooms, falafel, avocado, spinach, grilled cherry tomatoes, homemade beans and organic sourdough toast. Toast with spreads £3.

Falafel and hummus wrap £7. Falafel and mixed bean Mediterranean salad £9.

Smoothies £4.80. Tea, coffees £1.80-£3. Plant milks.

Cilicia
Omnivorous Turkish cafe-restaurant

- 400 Muswell Hill Broadway N10 1BS
- 020 8444 7172
- 365 days M-F 10.00-23.00, Sa 09.00-23.00, Su 09.00-22.00
- Highgate then 43 bus
- thecilicia.com
  facebook.com/thecilicia
  instagram.com/ciliciacafe

Vegan meze around £5 nclude hummus, aubergine caviar, broad beans, mango salad, tabouleh, sautéed mushrooms, falafel. Mains £9.50-£10.50 like broadbean and chickpea falafel tabouleh and salad; stuffed peppers; rice and aubergine boat. No vegan desserts. Children welcome.

Pizza Express, Muswell Hill
Omnivorous Italian restaurant

- 290 Muswell Hill Broadway N10 2QR
- 020 8883 5845
- M-W 11.30-23.00, Th-Sa 11.30-23.30, Su 11.30-22.30
- Finsbury Park, then W7 bus
- pizzaexpress.com

Vegan cheese.

Planet Organic, Muswell Hill
Health food shop & omnivorous cafe

- 111/117 Muswell Hill Road N10 3HS
- 020 8442 2910
- M-Sa 07.30-21.30, Su 11.00-17.00
- Highgate then 43 bus
- planetorganic.com

Just past the main part of Muswell Hill lives this ethical supermarket alternative. This shop has a wide selection of vegan foods, supplements and natural bodycare, and a mini café with both indoor and outdoor seating. Fresh fruit, veg and bakery items, kitchen essentials, sweet and savoury raw snacks, vegan chocolate, wines and plant milks.

The refrigerated section includes quick meals such as Laura's Idea and Hoxton Beach falafels, pots and salad boxes, as well as chilled vegan staples such as hummus, tofu, dairy-free spreads, burgers and sausages, yogurts and desserts.

The cafe section has a coffee and juice bar, and small hot and cold food counter. Two tables inside, and seven more outside.

Herbal teas, coffees such as mocha. Soya and rice milk at no extra cost. Organic classic and 'super' juices and smoothies and wheatgrass shots.

Mix-and-match food box £5.50, £7.50 or £8.50. Soup and seeded bread. Vegan gluten-free banana and walnut muffins.

Bodycare includes Organic Bloom, Jason, Green People. Small range of holistic books. Supplements, herbal remedies. Friendly and knowledgeable staff.

Holland & Barrett, Muswell Hill
Health food shop

- 155 Muswell Hill Broadway N10 3RS
- 020 8444 7488
- M-Sa 9.00-18.00, Su 10.00-18.00
- Finsbury Park, then W7 bus

Fridge and freezer.

TIP: There's no train or tube in Muswell Hill, so take 43 or 134 from Highgate tube, W7 from Finsbury Park or 144 from Tuffnel Park.

ST JOHN'S WOOD

& Swiss Cottage

This is an upmarket residential area, on the northwest side of Regent's Park, which now has its first vegan market stall and is about to get its first vegetarian restaurant.

The standout local attractions are Lord's Cricket Ground and the legendary Abbey Road Studios, where Beatles fans recreate the 1969 album cover on the zebra crossing at Grove End Road.

Work up an appetite with a stroll in Regent's Park or up Primrose Hill.

The Gate opened here spring 2019, the fourth branch of the London chain of top class, elegant, big, international vegetarian restaurants. Vegan and gluten-free options are clearly marked on the menu, which changes frequently with the seasons, and these days it seems like almost everything is vegan. All their wines are vegan.

The Gate, St John's Wood
Vegetarian international restaurant

- 📞 87 Allitsen Road NW8 7AS
- 📞 020 7833 0401
- 🕐 M-F 08.30-22.15, Sa 10.00-22.15, Su/BH 10.00-21.15
- ⊖ St John's Wood (Jubilee Line)
- ➤ thegaterestaurants.com

Weekday breakfast and weekend brunch, such as American style banana and berry pancakes £8.50, sourdough toast with toppings £8, full English £12, granola and seasonal fruits with coconut yogurt £6.50.

Eight a la carte starters £7.50-£9.50 are all vegan such as avocado and beetroot tartare, crispy marinated tofu with salsa, three-onion tart, artichoke terrine infused with truffle and hazelnut, wild mushroom and truffle arancini, miso glazed aubergine.

Mains £13.50-£16.50 such as Green Dragon tofu salad, black bean tortillas, wild mushroom risotto cake with creamy cep sauce, red Thai curry, beetroot cheese burger with raw vegn salad.

Outstanding desserts £6-£8 such as sticky toffee pudding, tiramisu with salted caramel ice cream, mango cheesecake, plum and pecan crumble with brandy crème anglaise, peanut buttter brownie with ice cream and chocolate sauce. Trio of desserts £15.

Vegan wines from £6.50 medium glass, £17 carafe, £21 bottle. 12.5% discretionary service charge which is divided across the entire restaurant team. Book online for up to 10 people. For parties of 11+, email them. A deposit of £10 per person is required for bookings of 7 and above and on special occasions.Also in Islington (North), Hammersmith (West) and Marylebone (Centre).

Holland & Barrett, St Johns Wood
Health food shop

- 📞 55 High Street NW8 7NL
- 📞 020 7586 5494
- 🕐 M-Sa 9.00-18.00, Su 1.00-17.00
- ⊖ St John's Wood

No fridge or freezer in this branch.

Holland & Barrett, Swiss Cottage
Health food shop

- 📞 11 Harben Parade NW3 6JP
- 📞 020 7586 3756
- 🕐 M-F 9.00-19.00, Sa 9.00-19.00, Su 11.00-18.00
- ⊖ Swiss Cottage

Fridge and freezer.

Valerie Veg
Vegan bakery

- 📞 Goldhurst Terrace NW6 3HS
- 📞 07532 743 272
  hello@valerieveg.com
- 🕐 M-F 9.00-17.00
- ⊖ South Hampstead BR, Swiss Cottage
- ➤ valerieveg.com
  facebook.com/valerievegbakery
  instagram.com/valerie.veg.bakery

Vegan raw artisan bakery specialising in gluten-free, soy-free, organic desserts. Cupcakes, mini loaves, muffins, whole cakes, cheesecakes, bespoke such as two tier chocolate ganache cake with chocolate roses with personalised iced message. Delivers in and out of London.

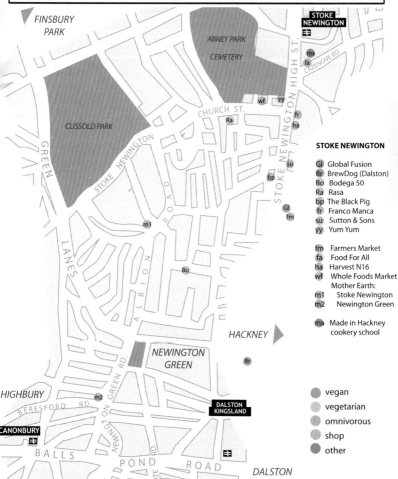

STOKE NEWINGTON

& Newington Green

FINSBURY PARK

ABNEY PARK CEMETERY

STOKE NEWINGTON

CLISSOLD PARK

CHURCH ST.

GREEN

STOKE NEWINGTON ROAD

ALBION ROAD

LANES

HACKNEY

NEWINGTON GREEN

HIGHBURY

BERESFORD RD.

NEWINGTON GREEN RD.

DALSTON KINGSLAND

CANONBURY

BALLS POND ROAD

DALSTON

ISLINGTON

SOUTHGATE RD.

ESSEX RD.

NORTH

STOKE NEWINGTON

- Gl Global Fusion
- Br BrewDog (Dalston)
- Bo Bodega 50
- Ra Rasa
- bp The Black Pig
- fr Franco Manca
- su Sutton & Sons
- yy Yum Yum

- fm Farmers Market
- fa Food For All
- ha Harvest N16
- wf Whole Foods Market
  Mother Earth:
- m1 Stoke Newington
- m2 Newington Green

- ma Made in Hackney
  cookery school

- vegan
- vegetarian
- omnivorous
- shop
- other

445

Rasa

Bodega 50

Bodega 50
Vegetarian cafe

- 50 Allen Road N16 8SA
- (020-7683 3869
- M-Su 08.00-16.00
- Bus 73
- Facebook Bodega 50
  instagram.com/bodega50

Stokey's best kept secret is this charming coffee shop featuring locally roasted coffees and a variety of vegan cakes, sandwiches and snacks, all made on site. Everything is vegan except milk.

Breakfast granola or muesli £3.50-£4. Salads £7 to which you add two ingredients such as roasted vegetables, artichokes, dolmas, turmeric sauerkraut. Sandwiches £3.80-£4.50 such as hummus and carrot, or toasted tofu, mustard, tomato and rocket;. Soups and dal £4-£4.20.

Cakes include banana, pecan, date spelt loaf and fruit loaf, both sugar free, orange and carrot loaf, and a gluten-free orange and polenta cake, 5 types of muffins.

Smoothies around £4, fresh juices around £3, kombucha £3. Coffee £2.-2.90 and tea £2.20. Soya, almond, or oat milk.

Lots of games to keep children entertained, and a separate children's menu.

Small retail section that sells gluten-free goods, coffee that can be ground to suit your machine, and a variety of organic and vegan goodies. The cafe also has a rather charming dog, Bruce, who on our visit insisted on showing me to my seat.

High chairs. Tables inside and out.

Rasa N16
Vegetarian South Indian restaurant

- 55 Church Street N16 0AR
- (020-7249 0344
- M-Th 18.00-22.45; F 18.00-23.30 (last orders); Sa 12.00-15.00,18.00-23.30; Su 12.00-14.45, 18.00-22.45
- Stoke Newington BR, Bus 73 from Angel
- rasarestaurants.com
  facebook.com/rasaveg

One of London's top licensed vegetarian restaurants and great for parties. Rasa means taste, and not only of the food. Here you experience a taste of Kerala's villages and dishes from other south Indian states. The atmosphere is relaxed with classic Indian music in the background, with pink walls and tablecloths. Dishes that don't seem vegan can be veganized.

Starters £4.50 such as banana boli with plaintain slices in a batter of rice and chickpea flour, seasoned with black sesame seeds and served with peanut and ginger sauce; medhu vadai spongy urad bean and chilli dumpling. Two soups such as peppery lentil broth with garlic, tomatoes, spices and tamarind or a combo of three different lentils with tomato, garlic, coriander and black pepper.

Main courses feature dosa (stuffed pancake) selection and some unusual curries £5.95-£7.95.

Salad and side dishes £4.50-£4.95 such as amazing Kerala salad of guava, avocado, stir-fried Indian shallots, fresh coconut, lemon juice and chilli powder; Vendakka Masala of okra fried with shallots; blackeye beans curry. 6 kinds of rice from £3 include boiled, Kerala brown, tamarind, lemon, coconut, tomato with cashew.

Vegan desserts £3.50-£4.25 include ice cream, mango sorbet. and mango halva flavoured with cashew nuts and raisins.

Kerala vegan feast £22.50 per head with pre-meal snacks, starters, curry selection, side dishes, breads and a traditional Keralan sweet.

Optional service charge 12.5%. Children welcome, no high chairs.

Yum Yum
Omnivorous Thai restaurant

- 📍 183-187 Stoke Newington High Street N16 0LH
- 📞 020 7254 6751 restaurant
- 🕐 M-Th 12.00-15.00, 18.00-23.00, F 12.00-15.00, 18-24.00, Sa 12.00-24.00, Su 12.00-23.00
- 🚇 Stoke Newington BR
- ➤ yumyumthain16.co.uk instagram.com/YUMYUMN16/

In a stunning Grade II listed Georgian building with seating for over 200, with entry through a Thai garden where you can drink cocktails on a summer evening at their hand carved cocktail bar. They make their own coconut milk and curry pastes in-house and have introduced seasonal specials menus. Vegetarian dishes marked on menu.

Starters £5.50-£7.75 such as spring rolls, tempura, sweet corn cakes, crispy tofu with peanut sauce, mashed vegetable on toast, tofu apple salad with palm sugar, Thai herbs and peanuts, or have a platter for two £16.75. Thai soups around £7. Curries £8.50 such as pumpkin curry with tofu, green or red or jungle curry. Nine vegetable dishes around £7.

Banan fitter with coconut ice cream £5. Exotic sorbets £4.75.

Thai express menu. starter amd main course 12.00-15.00 daily from £7.55, such as srping rolls then monk's vegetables on toast, or Pad Thai or tofu mushroom potato mussomon curry with mixed veg..

Set vegetarian menu for two, £25 per person, with assorted starters, srping rolls, sweet corn cakes, deep fried tofu, tempura veg on toast, main course red curry with veg. For four or more people add main course stir-fried mushrooms with tofu, stir-fry long beans, Pad Thai noodles with veg, jasmine rice.

Wine from £4.75 medium glass, £6.25 large, £17 bottle. Beers from £3.75. Cocktails £8-£12.

Children welcome, high chairs. Evening deliveries. Outside catering. Downstairs lounge bar with large screen TV for private events. Deliveroo.

Franco Manca
Omnivorous pizzeria

- 📍 176 Stoke Newington High Street N16 7JL
- 📞 020 7241 4057
- 🕐 M-Sa 12.00-23.00, Su 12.00-22.30
- 🚇 Stoke Newington BR
- ➤ francomanca.co.uk

Sourdough pizza bases, vegan cheese, and all their wines are vegan. Some outside seating. Disabled access. Baby changing

The Black Pig With White Pearls

Omnivorous Spanish tapas restaurant & bar

- 61 Stoke Newington High Street N16 7JL
- 020 7249 1772
- M-Sa 18.00-23.00, Su closed
- Stoke Newington BR
- blackpigwithwhitepearls.co.uk
  Facebook BlackPigwithWhitePearls
  Instagram blackpigwithwhitepearls

Separate vegan menu with a dozen types of tapas in this candlelit Spanish restaurant on two floors with a bar area, complete with subtle background flamenco music.

£3.50-£5 for Spanish omelette made with chickpea flower; patatas panaderas or bravas; slider burger made wtih seitan, oats, quinoa, beetroot; sourdough toast with olive oil, garlic, fresh tomato and parsley.

£6.50-£7 for cauliflower tempura; black truffle and wild mushroom croquettes made with almond milk and olive oil; roasted red peppers and aubergine; empanadillas ratatouille; quinoa lollipops; tomato tartare with avocado; padron peppers; marinated beetroot and walnuts salad.

Sutton & Sons, Stoke Newington

Omnivorous fish & chip shop

- 218 Grahjam Road E8 1BP (at Tyssen Road)
- 020 7249 6444
- Su-Th 12.00-22.00, F-Sa 12.00-22.30
- Rectory Road BR, Stoke Newington BR
- instagram.com/suttonandsonsvegan
  suttonandsons.co.uk

After the success of the vegan menu at their Stoke Newington branch, owner Danny Sutton expanded it to the Hackney Central and Islington branches. The fish fillet is made from tofu or banana blossom, a flour popular in Asia cooking, marinated overnight in seaweed and samphire, then spiced with cumin and garlic powder, and fried in egg-free batter. Vish and chips £8.50. Fish burger and chips £8.95. Fish cake £4.95.

Scampi and chips £8.50. Young Vegans pie and mash £8.50. Battered sausage and chips £6.95. Battered calamari strips £5.95. Classic prawn cocktail £.95.

Sides 65p-£3.95 include onion gravy, curry sauce; pickled onion, gherkin, mushy or garden peas, seasonal salad, pickles.

Cheesecakes £4.50. Black Milq Ice cream £2.95, two scoops £5.50.

Soft drinks include Coke, Fentimans and Dalston's (lemonade, fizzy apple, ginger beer, dandelion & burdock). Bottled beers around £4, pint of Guiness £4.95. 187ml bottle of wine £5, Prosecco £6.

Harvest N16
Vegetarian cafe and omni wholefood shop

📍 172-174 Stoke Newington High Street N16 7JL

📞 020 7249 7268

🕐 M-Sa 07.00-22.00, Su 09.00-21.00

🚇 Stoke Newington BR

🔖 harvestn16.com
facebook.com/harvestn16
instagram.com/harvestldn

Big, bright and and airy space with a coffee shop at the front in the picture windows with rustic wooden tables, light snacks, and a stunning array of vegan cakes. It's a lot less hectic than the nearby Whole Foods Market, but also has a huge range of products.

Salads £4.50, sandwiches £4 such as cherry tomato, pesto cheese and mixed leaves; mushroom and leek sausage roll £2.95.

Many vegan cakes and sweets £1.80-£3.95 beautifully displayed and you'll find it difficult to leave without having one, such as raspberry or bluebrery cheesecake, coffee and walnut cake, carrot, coconut and orange cake, pear and pecan loaf, chocolate loaf, lemon and poppy loaf, chocolate and almond brownie, apricot and pumpkin or cranberry and coconut flapjack, apple, walnut and cinnamon muffin, almond raspberry or double chocolate or coffee and walnut muffin.

Coffees £1.80-£3. Superfood lattes include spirulina, açai berry, cinnamon chai, turmeric and ginger, green tea matcha, red velvet beetroot. Fresh juices and super smoothies 2.90-£4.

In the big shop behind the cafe are fruit and veg and lots of fridges with Laura's Idea, Hoxton Beach falafels, VegiDeli, Sojade, Provamel, Coyo, Coconut Collaborative, Nush, Chia Pods, Violife, Follow Your Heart, Sheese, Taifun, Tofurky, Dragonfly, Soupology.

Frozen Amy's, Fry's, Forest Food, Clive's Pies, Booja Booja, Swedish Glace.

Huge section with chocolates, bars and truffles. Many teas and plant milks.

At the back in the health and bodycare section are brands like Jason, Sukin, Green People, Lavera, Antipodes, Ren, Faith in Nature, Avalon, Dr Bronner and Weleda. Supplements by Pukka, Terranova, Viridian, Wild Nutrition, Biocare and Solgar. Protein powders.

Big kids' section next to cleaning products by Faith in Nature, Ecozone, BioD, Ecover, Sodasan.

Tables outside and inside. Wifi. High chairs. Another branch in Dalston.

Food For All
Vegetarian wholefood store

- 📞 3 Cazenove Road N16 6PA
- ☎ 020 8806 4138
- 🕐 M-F 9.00-18.00, Sa 10.00-18.00, Su 11.00-16.30
- ⊖ Stoke Newington BR
- ↖ foodforall.co.uk

Popular and friendly veggie wholefood shop with alternative medicine, herbs and spices. Grains sold by weight, measure out what you want such as rice, quinoa, porridge,, lentils, millet, buckwheat, sesame, sunflower seeds, pumpkin seeds. They specialise in superfoods. Great chilled section with vegan cheeses including Vegamigo, Violife, Sheese and Tofutti. Taifun, VegiDeli, Biona, tempeh and spreads. Koko, Sojade and Provamel yogurt. In the freezer Booja Booja and Fry's.

Around 250 kinds of herbal remedies, and dried herbs sold by weight.

Some supplements and herbal remedies by Viridian, Terranova, Pukka, Vogels. Pulsin protein powder.

Bodycare by Weleda, Avalon, Mistry's, Dr Bronner and Green People.

Cleaning products including Ecover and BioD refills, Ecozone, Faith in Nature, Green Scent.

There is a free noticeboard in the shop and a yoga centre upstairs run by Ananda Marga, also meditation and tantra classes.

Made In Hackney Local Food Kitchen vegan cookery classes in the basement.

Also check out Volt, the vegan run BMX bicycle shop opposite. voltbmx.com

Whole Foods Market N16
Wholefood supermarket, cafe and juice bar

- 32-40 Church Street N16 0LU
- (020 7254 2332
- M-Sa 07.30-21.30, Su 08.00-21.30
- Stoke Newington BR, Bus 73, 476 from Angel, 106 from Finsbury Park
- wholefoodsmarket.co.uk

Big food shop and café concentrating on organic produce. No artificial colourings, sweeteners, preservatives or hydrogenated fat. Large range of vegan food, natural remedies department, an area devoted to natural skincare and supplements. Trained advisers are on hand to answer all queries.

Deli section with freshly prepared organic hot food, macrobiotic and raw selections, and a cake section where you can buy juices, coffee, capuccino and tea. Cake ingredients are clearly labelled. Outside cafe seating for around 25 people.

Highlights include a dozen kinds of tofu, vegan ready meals, wheat-free pasta, breakfast cereals, organic juices, non-dairy cheeses and yogurts, hemp and soya ice cream. Big selection of organic fruit and veg as well as organic herb plants, organic wine, beers and ciders with clear vegan labelling.

Another area is given over to all kinds of toiletries, aromatherapy oils, supplements and herbal remedies, most of which are vegan, including Dr Hauschka and Ren. There is always a staff member who can advise you, and a file of local complementary health practitioners.

Well stocked range of books on many subjects adjacent to the toiletries counter. There is a small bulletin board at the front of the shop for local events.

If you like this then don't miss their other stores in Soho, Clapham, Camden, Fulham, Richmond, and the Whole Foods superstore in Kensington.

Farmers' Market, N16
Omnivorous organic food market

- outside St Paul's Church, 182 Stoke Newington Road N16 7UYt
- (020 7502 7588
- Saturday 10.00-14.30
- Stoke Newington or Rectory Rd BR
- growingcommunities.org/market

100% organic and biodynamic fruit & veg stalls, grown close to London, including Britain's only biodynamic mushroom farm, fermented veg, plus hemp products, bread.

Global Fusion
Vegan creole bakery market stall

- at Stoke Newington Farmers Market, St Paul's Church N16 7UY
- (020-8252 4066
- Saturday 10.00-14.30
- Stoke Newington or Rectory Rd BR
- Facebook: Global Fusion Vegan Creole Bakery

Organic vegan baked goods made in Stokey. 15 fruit and seed loafs including gluten-free, soda bread. Sweet and savoury Cajun style tarts. Vegetable gumbo made with local farm veg, okra, sweet potatoes. Rich bean salad. Hot veg, banana or apple fritters. Cakes. Chilli sauce.

Hornbeam Bakers Collective

Growing Communities
FARMERS' MARKET
HERE EVERY SATURDAY
10 am til 2·30pm

· www.growingcommunities.org ·

Global Fusion

Freshly baked fruit or
vegetable bread, low
cholesterol, but with that
delicious Creole taste

Whole loaf £4
Half Loaf £3
Quarter Loaf £2

MADE IN HACKNEY

Christian Sinibaldi

———————— LOCAL FOOD KITCHEN

PROVIDING ACCESS TO HEALTHY, AFFORDABLE FOOD THAT'S GOOD FOR PEOPLE AND PLANET

- Cooking and food growing courses
- Pay-by-donation community classes
- Programme of masterclasses
- Meaningful volunteer opportunities
- Training for ethical food start-ups

This course has changed my eating habits for life
— Seema

INFO@MADEINHACKNEY.ORG   020 8442 4266
WWW.MADEINHACKNEY.ORG

Peticia Niven patricianiven.com

@Made_In_Hackney   f MadeInHackneyLocalFoodKitchen

Made In Hackney is a project of charity AMURT UK 327216

MADE IN
HACKNEY

LOCAL FOOD KITCHEN

Made In Hackney
Plant based community cookery classes

- Food For All basement, 3 Cazenove Road N16 6PA
- 020 8442 4266
- Stoke Newington BR
- madeinhackney.org
  facebook.com/
  MadeInHackneyLocalFoodKitchen

Educational community kitchen and cookery school where you can learn about use of local food, composting, growing your own, foraging, cooking (mainly vegan).

Run by vegan journalist Sarah Bentley who is also part of Growing Communities vegbox scheme. Since launching in 2012 they have helped 11,000 Londoners eat well, cheaper, and improve their health at the same time.

Classes are free or pay by donation, with a theme such as Feed 4 for £3, 15-minute Meals, Healthy Baking, Indian, Gluten-Free Baking, Bread Making, Fermentation, Nut Cheeses, Preserving, International Cuisine.

Catering service. Kitchen can be hired for small-scale food producers, for workshops and photoshoots.

photo Tanya Harris

Mother Earth, Stoke Newington / Albion Parade
Organic wholefood shop & take-away

- 5 Albion Parade, Albion Rd N16 9LD
- 020 7275 9099
- M-Sa 9.00-20.00,
  Su 10.00-19.00
- Bus 73
- facebook.com/MotherEarthLondon

Colourful wholefood shop with organic fruit and veg, macrobiotic and organic products. Bread and assorted vegan snacks. Bulk produce to weigh and pay, discount on cases. Baby and kids' foods.

The freezer section has vegan ice cream such as Fry's, Bio-ice, Booja Booja, Coyo , and fruit ice-lollies in various flavours. Amy's and Fry's savoury food.

The fridge has Sojade, Coyo, Violife, Sheese, Tofutti, Clive's Pies, hummus, tofu and tempeh. Take-away prepared food such as superfood salad or Spanish chickpea and spinach stew. Cakes and sweets.

Booja Booja truffles and a big section of chocolates and bars.

Cruelty-free toiletries such as shampoos, lip balms, soaps and vegan toothpaste from Weleda, Sukin, Mistry's and Faith in Nature.

Natural remedies and friendly advice. Homeopathy, herbal. Supplements such as Viridian, Vogel. Superfoods including goji berries, maca, spirulina.

Cleaning by Ecover, Faith in Nature, and BioD refills.

Also in Newington Green (next page) and at Highbury Corner (see Holloway Road).

Mother Earth, Newington Gr
Vegetarian café and wholefood shop

- 101 Newington Green Road N1 4QY
- 020 7369 7353
- M-Sa 10.00-19.30, Sa-Su 10.00-19.00
- Cannonbury BR. Bus 73,476,293.21/
- Facebook Mother Earth Newington Green

Veggie café and food shop. Eat in or take away. Outside and inside seating.

Around 4 salads, various pies and pastries, soup all made on the premises with vegan and gluten-free options. The deli has a gourmet selection of olives. Cakes. Herb teas and coffees.

Chilled section wtih Provamel, Sojade and Coyo yogurt; Violife and Sheese; Taifun, VBites, tempeh, Biona and Pure spreads. In the freezer The Vegetarian Butcher, Amy's, VegiDeli and Fry's. Organic baby food.

The shop next door is for zero packaging food sold by weight such as spices, dried fruit, nuts, pulses, grains, and a huge selection of herbs.

Packaged and loose superfoods. Also protein powders.

Some supplements by Higher Nature, Viridian and Terranova.

Bodycare by Lavera, Green People, Sukin, Weleda, Dr Bronner, Jason and Faith in Nature.

Clearning by Ecover, Ecoleaf, and BioD refills.

Incense, oil diffusers, rock lamps and jute bags.

WEST HAMPSTEAD

Brew & Wild
Vegetarian coffee shop & take-away

- 🖙 134 West End Lane, West Hampstead NW6 1SA
- ✆ hannah@brewandwild.com
- 🕐 M-F 07.00-15.00, Sa 9.00-15.00, Su 9.30-15.00. Times may vary.
- ⊖ West Hampstead
- 🏹 facebook Brew and Wild instagram.com/brewandwild

Cute grab and go place opened summer 2017, offering a huge selection of drinks and treats. The food is homemade or locally sourced, and all packaging is made of recycled material. Everything is vegan apart from some cakes, honey in porridge and cow's milk.

Overnight oats or granola pots with any milk, seasonal fruit, chia seeds, raisins and nuts £3.50.

Homemade soup with olive roll or gluten-free brioche £5. Rainbow hummus with sweet pop crackers made from dried juice pulp £3.50. Savoury items such as vegan pizza, Mexican bean roll, gluten-free cornbread.

All sweets and cakes £1.50-£2.50 are gluten- and sugar-free including peanut butter cups, gingerbread man, hardhoo raw brownie, tahini and banana cookie, matcha cookie, oat and raisin cookie, cinnamon bun, energy ball, muffins such as bran and flaxseed breakfast, fruit loaf, cacao loaf, truffle, bounty bar in matcha or blueberry.

Juices £4.50 such as Unbeatable Beets with beetroot, carrot, apple and lemon; Immunity Magic with carrot, lemon, ginger, turmeric; Daily Greens with kale, spinach, cucumber, celery, apple and lemon; Morning Metabolism with pink grapefruit, mint and lime.

Hot drinks £2.20-£3.50 include chai latte, gingerbread hot chocolate, spirulina mango tea, matcha almond latte, tumeric/beetroot latte. Campbell & Syme coffee £2-£2.50, decaf add 20p. Plant milks 30p extra: soya, oat, almond, rice, hemp, coconut, cashew, hazelnut. Teas £2. Bring your own cup for 20p discount. Sweeten with date, maple or agave syrup 10p.

Breakfast table with three stools, one table outside. Wifi.

Curled Leaf
Vegetarian tea house, cafe and yoga studio

☛ 98 Mill Lane NW6 1NF

☎ 020 7794 6296

🕐 M-Sa 9.00-17.00

⊖ West Hampstead

↖ curledleaf.co.uk
facebook.com/curledleaf
instagram.com/curledleaf

This tranquil tea heaven has a cosy and calm atmosphere with a fireplace and low lights. They serve 52 types of teas: herbal, mixed spiced, black, organic, oolong, green, white and chai. Each has a detailed description on their website, but the knowledgeable staff can advise you on which is more suitable for you according to your taste and mood. They also serve all different types of coffee from independent, ethical and sustainable company Climpson & Sons. A selection of fresh smoothies £3.50 to £4, and again they can help you to make a selection.

The beautifully presented food (just take a look at their instagram!) is Mediterranean style healthy, with lots of veggies and salads, plus cakes and treats, as organic as possible with plenty of vegan options. They don't really do menus, so point to whatever you fancy, around £3 per portion. For example peppers mixed with five beans, aubergine, roasted baby tomatoes topped with onions; roasted butternut squash, mixed baby leaves with chickpeas, tahini and black sesame seeds. For a meal it could be mixed roasted vegetable soup with sourdough bread £6; roasted mixed vegetable stew served with their homemade spelt bread, organic hummus, mixed salad and pomegranate £7.50.

Variety of treats £2 made with chocolate,

dates, cashew, peanut butter, almond, almond butter, ginger and coconut.

Owner Alketa Mripa is a yoga teacher and artist, while husband Luli is an acupuncturist and Chinese herbalist who originally trained as a doctor. You'll get a lot more individual attention here than in big centres with huge classes, especially if you have a baby or young children. Rooms for acupuncture for adults and kids; yoga one to one or small groups of up to 5, with classes for kids, and mums with babies. You can hire the space for 12, 30 or even 60 people with the garden. They cater for outside private events. Wifi and newspapers.

Banana Tree, West Hampstead
Omnivorous South-east Asian restaurant

- 237-239 West End Lane NW6 1XN
- 020 7431 7808
- M-Sa 12.00-23.00 (22.45 last orders), Su/BH 12.00-22.30
- West Hampstead
- Bananatree.co.uk
  facebook.com/bananatreerestaurants

Food from the lemongrass growing countries of south-east Asia: Vietnam, Cambodia, Laos, Thailand, Malaysia. Vegan dishes are clearly marked and mains are all under £10. Their Vegan Bites are high protein soya nuggets. Tofu Is lightly fried to intensify its flavour and texture then it absorbs its sauces. Vegan Satay is marinated skewers of soya protein nuggets. The only downer is that the only vegan dessert is sorbet.

Small plates include edamame with garlic spiced salt, sweet fritter balls with chilli dipping sauce, spring rolls, gyoza dumplings with sweet chilli dip, grilled aubergine half, Singapore Laksa coconut soup

Noodle dishes include Pad Thai and Laksa. Thai green curry, Malaysian red coconut kari with aubergine and tofu, bun bo noodle salad, sweet and sour stir-fry, tamarind spicy aubergine, stir-fry veg with cashew nuts.

Add steamed, sticky or spiced rice, sweetcorn fritter balls, stirfry broccoli.

Express lunch menu Mon-Thu till 6pm gets you a meal for around £6.

Raw juices £3.85. Wine from £3.50 small glass, £4.50 medium, £15.95 bottle. Cocktails £7.50.

Kids welcome, baby seats.Outside tables, dogs welcome there.

Peppercorn's
Health food shop & take-away

- 260 West End Lane NW6 1LG
- 020 7317 7000
- M-F 10.00-20.00, Sa 10.00-19.00, Su 11.00-18.00
- West Hampstead
- Peppercornshealthstore.com

Organic wholefood store, now in much bigger new premises with a larger product range, by the green in the centre of West Hampstead, selling everything for vegans including tofu and tempeh, every kind of pasta and health food. They have added some organic fruit and veg.

Wide selection of take-away and macrobiotic specialities from around the world, some organic, including sushi, tofu parcels, aduki pies, spring rolls, rice rolls, Laura's Idea, organic hummus, cottage pies, sausages, rice and curry, cakes and flapjacks. Most dishes, snacks and cakes have ingredients displayed and if they're gluten-, sugar-free or vegan.

Supplements include Solgar, Viridian, Terranova, Nature's Own, Lamberts, Biocare, Pukka Ayurvedic.

Bodycare including Jason and Weleda, Faith in Nature, Barefoot Botanicals, Organic Essence, Nova Scotia, Weleda Baby and Green People Baby.

Ecover and BioD cleaning products and baby-suitable ones by Bentley Organics.

Staff are well trained and have in depth knowledge of what's what. 10% discount for Vegetarian and Vegan Society members, and senior citizens on Wed.

HARA Health Store & Natural Therapy Centre
Health, nutrition and therapy centre

- 231 Finchley Rd, NW3 6LS (between O2 centre and tube)
- 020 7794 5486
- M-F 9.30-18.30, Sa 9.30-17.30, Su closed
- Finchley Road
- harahealthstore.business.site

If you want expert advice on choosing products, the owner here is a former pharmacist, and the staff include a medical herbalist and a nutritional therapist.

Small selection of health foods. No take-away. Organic snacks such as sugar- or wheat-free. Raw living. Speciality teas.

Organic natural beauty and bodycare, hair dyes, Ayurvedic products. Supplements, sports nutrition, herbs and homeopathy. Magazines What Doctors Don't Tell You, and Natural Lifestyle magazine (free).

Downstairs therapy rooms for a soothing session with a physiotherapist or massage therapist, reflexologist, cranio-sacral, nutritional therapist, medical herbalist, biofeedback.

Lemon & Limes
Fruit, veg and wholefood store

☛ 243 West End Lane NW6 1NX
☎ 020 7443 9799
🕐 M-Su 08.00-21.00
⊖ West Hampstead
🖉 lemonandlimes.co.uk

A cut above the average grocer. Also in Turnham Green (see Chiswick, West London).

WOOD GREEN

and Hornsey, Turnpike Lane & Alexandra Park

Pomodoro e Basilico
Vegan Italian street slow food stall

- ☛ **Alexandra Palace Farmers' Market**, at either Alexandra Palace Park, near Muswell Hill entrance N10 3TG
  or occasionally at Campsbourne School if an event at Ally Pally
- ☎ 07866 194 403
- 🕐 Sunday only 10.00-15.00
- ⊖ Bus W3, short walk from Alexandra Palace BR, 30 minute walk from Turnpike Lane or Bounds Green
- ↖ facebook.com/PomoBasilico
  instagram.com/pomodoro_e_basilico
  weareccfm.com (market organisers)

In the market in the park surrounding Alexandra Palace.

Italian chef Sara worked for several vegan restaurants and bakeries before starting her own vegan food business out of a passion for made-from-scratch slow vegan food with seasonal ingredients.

Sara brings burgers, pizzas and vegan cakes to the market with bags of enthusiasm.

Also at South Kensington Farmers Market Tuesday (West London), Bloomsbury Farmers Market Thursday (Centre), and usually at Portobello Vegan Night Market in Notting Hill (West).

Vegan Life Live
Vegan huge annual exhibition

- ☛ **Alexandra Palace**
- 🕐 Sa-Su 14-15 March 2020, 10.00
- ⊖ Alexandra Palace BR, Wood Green then free shuttle bus
- ↖ veganlifelive.com
  alexandrapalace.com

Huge annual weekend event organised by *Vegan Life* magazine early in the year at Alexandra Palace. In 2020 it's on Sat 14th 10.00-18.00, Sun 15th 10.00-17.00.

Caterers serving pizza, kebabs, pasta, curry, soul food, ice creams, cakes. Three areas with cookery demos and talks. Over 200 vegan exhibitors offering food, cheese, chocolate, footwear, cosmetics and more.

One-day £12 and two-day £19 tickets from the website. Concessions for students, senior citizens, disabled, benefits, proof may be required at the door. Under-16 free with an adult. Carers free with the person they are caring for.

Free shuttle buses during the show from Wood Green tube station and Alexandra Palace train station from 30 minutes before the show until 30 minutes after.

Karamel

Vegan restaurant, bar, live music venue and night club

- 🖝 4 Coburg Road, Wood Green N22 6UJ
- ☎ 020 3146 8775
- ⏱ W 10.00-22.00, Th 10.00-24.00, F-Sa 10.00-01.00, Su 12.00-20.00, M-Tu closed
- ⊖ Wood Green (Piccadilly), Alexandra Palace BR
- ↖ karamel.london
  facebook.com/KaramelLondon.N22
  instagram.com/karameln22

"Some of the best vegan food London has to offer" The Guardian (24.9.16) This Time Out award-winning vegan venue is a fabulous big place, with a 100% vegan bar including organic craft beer, well worth a trip. Karamel is unique, and every night is different, from live music, comedy, art and theatre shows, to club nights, private parties, socials, meet-ups and weddings.

Moving Mountains burger £8 comes with fried onions, salad and mayo in a brioche bun, served in three versions: with cheeze; with gherkins, beetroot relish and pickled red cabbage; with jalapenos and siracha.

Handmade stone baked pizzas £9-£13.50 have toppings that include mushrooms, courgette, pepper, aubergine, olives, chillies, jalpenos, red onion, tomatoes, soya chicken, salami, sweetcorn.

Starters and sides are all £3.50 or 3 for £10, choose from 4 samosas, 8 mini spring rolls, chips, triple fried per peri potatoes, marinated olives, side salad, chilli minted peas, smokey beans.

Proper British vegan Sunday Roast £13 with all the trimmings features almond Wellington or sausage roast, served with roast potato medley, braised root veg, red and green cabbage, peas, stuffing and luscious gravy.

Other dishes and specials £8-£10 have included curry bowl with rice with cashews and salad, tofish and chips with minty mushy peas and tartar sauce, spaghetti puttanesca, soya chiken and veg stir-fry, Indian thali.

Apple and vanilla crumble with custard £5.50.

The Pitfield beer range includes Eco Warrior, N1 Wheat Beer and London Porter on draught, plus Indian Pale Ale and Chocolate Stout in bottles. The house cocktail is a vegan White Russian for £5.

Weekly programme of live music, top quality jazz, art exhibitions, vegan comedy nights.

Families weocme, kids' menu, regular kids' activities and children's theatre.

Social highlights include London Vegan Drinks – Europe's biggest vegan social – on the first Saturday of every month from 7pm-midnight, with free entry, food, drinks, DJs and dancing. Second Sunday lunch 2pm-5pm. Second Saturday Wood Green Geekstravaganza for boardgaming and meeting vegans from 1pm. Check the Karamel website events calendar to see what's on before visiting, or the events at

- ↖ meetup.com/londonvegan

Sunday Vegan Roast.

Charlie's Cafe
Omnivorous cafe

- 169 High Rd, Wood Green Shopping Mall N22 6BA
- 020 8881 9766
- M-F 08.00-18.30, Sa 08.30-18.30, Su 9.00-18.00
- Turnpike Lane (20 mins walk) or Hornsey rail station. Bus 144,W3,41.
- charliescafebakery.co.uk
  Facebook.com/charliescafebakery
  instagram.com/charliescafebakery

Cafe and bakery with a separate, substantial vegan menu.

Religiously Vegan cooked breakfast £8.50 of spinach, hand-picked mushrooms, roasted peppers, avocado mash, falafel mix, zucchini, hummus, beans with their special arctic flatbread and vegan cheese. Porridge and cereals with toppings, açai granola bowl with fruits

Vegan shaksuka with cannellini beans, Salads under £7, falafel wrap.

Filled filo pastries, vegan croissants heck yeah can come with cheese and tomato.

Six vegan cakes such as coffee and walnut, chocolate fudge, lemon poppy seed, carrot coconut and orange, blackcurrant crumble, organic almond brownie.

Fresh juices and smoothies around £4 or less. Teas. regular and large coffees, mocha, hot choc, fancy lattes like beetroot, iced coffees £1.80-£3.50. Almond, coconut, oat and soy milk.

Deliveroo.

Harmless Store
Vegan zero-waste shop

- 📍 79 Tottenham Rd, Hornsey N8 9BE
- ☎ 07377 322 426
- 🕐 Tu-Th 11.00-19.00, F 11.00-18.00, Sa 11.00-17.00, Su-M closed. Will be open 7 days and evenings.
- ⊖ Hornsey BR
- ➤ harmlessstore.co.uk
  facebook.com/harmlessstore
  instagram.com/harmless_store

Opened April 2018 in Wood Green at Blue House Yard, River Park Road N22 7TB. While we were printing this book, Tami was moving to and fitting out her new much bigger shop. We've given the opening times for the old address, though Tami is aiming to bring in more like-minded people and open 7 days a week and into the evenings. The new shop is actually closer to Crouch End than Wood Green.

Plastic-free, low impact, vegan convenience store. Bring your own containers and fill up on household basics including vegan food, cleaning and personal care. Grains, pulses, cereals, nuts, seeds, herbs, spices, plant oils, beans, peas, lentils and soy dried food stuffs. Loose tea and coffee and brewing equipment. Shampoos, conditioners, cleaning products.

The new shop will have fridges and be able to sell artisan cheeses, plant--based salmon, kimchi, tofu and sweet treats.

Plastic and toxic free: feminine products, toothbrushes, straws, coffee cups, water bottles, food wrap, cutlery, pet feed products.

And with all the extra space, the new shop will be able to host workshops. Check the internet for latest details of this exciting, trailblazing project.

Ambala, Turnpike Lane
Vegetarian sweet shop

- 📍 61 Turnpike Lane N8 0EE
- ☎ 020 8292 1253
- 🕐 M-Su 10.00-20.00
- ⊖ Turnpike Lane
- ➤ ambalafoods.com

This modern and bright take away shop is handy for picking up Indian savouries by the kilo such as samosas and pakoras.

Holland & Barrett, Wood Green
Health food shop

- 📍 66-68 High Road, Wood Green N22 6YA
- ☎ 020 8889 2131
- 🕐 M-Sa 9.00-19.00, Su 10.00-18.00
- ⊖ Wood Green

Three fridges, two freezers.

- 📍 129-131 High Street, Wood Green N22 6BB
- ☎ 020 8881 5508
- 🕐 M-Sa 9.00-19.00, Su 10.00-17.00
- ⊖ Wood Green

Fridge and freezer.

Islands
Omnivorous coffee shop and deli

- 104 Hornsey High Street N8 7NT
- 07931 038 003
- M-Sa 08.00-17.00, Su 10.00-16.00
- Turnpike Lane (20 mins walk) or Hornsey rail station. Bus 144,W3,41.
- Facebook.com/IslandsinHornsey instagram.com/islands_in_hornsey

A little gem with a lot of vegan and gluten-free food run by two young friendly guys, Panos and Theo.

All the salads come with bread, they can all be made vegan, cheese can be replaced with hummus, beetroot and avocado £5-£6.

With the sandwiches you can choose your bread for £1.25 and then ingredients for 50p to 75p including hummus, onion mango chutney, olive paste, mixed peppers, sweetcorn, rocket, spinach, beetroot and avocado for £1.50.

They normally have one vegan cake such as chocolate, or red velvet cupcake £2.

Juices £2.50 and smoothies all with plant milk £4. Teas, coffees, Greek coffee £1-£3.

They sell fresh bread such as cranberry, Mediterranean, basil, rye etc, some gluten-free. Also chocolate, Rhythm 108 biscuits, hummus chips, Greek olive oil and traditional giant beans, Sativa olive paste, barley rusk, pesto, chargrilled artichoke, herbal Greek loose teas with unique flavours such as Cretan mountain, sage, lemon verbena and nettle.

Seating inside and out. Wifi. Dogs welcome. High chairs. On a sunny day you can take your food next to church and enjoy your meal in the garden.

HERTFORDSHIRE

and rest of North London

BARNET

Pizza Express, Barnet
Omnivorous Italian restaurant

- ☛ 242-248 High St, Barnet EN5 5TZ
- ☎ 020 8449 3706
- 🕐 Su-Th 11.30-22.30,
  F-Sa 11.30-23.30
- ⊖ High Barnet
- ↖ pizzaexpress.com

Right at the top of the high street, on the edge of Hadley Common. Vegan cheese. Baby facilities. Disabled access.

Health Matters London
Health food shop with juice bar & clinic

- ☛ 121 High St, High Barnet EN5 5UZ
- ☎ 020 8441 8335
- 🕐 M-Sa 9.00-18.00, Su 12.00-16.00
- ⊖ High Barnet
- ↖ healthmatterslondon.co.uk
  facebook.com/healthmatterslondon

Great health food store run by practitioners. Organic fruit and veg, which they use for juices and smoothies made to order; the bestseller is Green Panda with spinach, broccoli, carrot, banana, watercress and apple, which you can enjoy on the sofa. Lots of bodycare such as Faith in Nature. Herbal pharmacy. Treatments including massages, herbal medicine, homeopathy.

Daniel Field
Vegan hairdresser

- ☛ 5 Greenhill Parade, Station Road,
  New Barnet EN5 7ES
- ☎ 020 8441 2224
- 🕐 M, Th 09.00-21.00; Tu 9.00-17.00;
  W 9.00-20.00; F-Sa 9.00-18.00;
  Su 10.00-16.00
- ⊖ High Barnet
- ↖ danielfield.net (salon)
  danielfieldmailorder.co.uk

Celebrity hairdresser who is also a chemist and has developed his own range of hair care products now certified by the Vegan Society, with a 1984 testing cut-off date, no animal ingredients, hypo-allergenic, toxin-free, Fairtrade and with minimal packaging. 10 freelance stylists, or be styled by the man himself if you book well ahead. There is also a private studio if you need privacy. Free parking.

Holland & Barrett, Barnet
Health food shop

- ☛ 15 High Street, Barnet EN5 5UZ
- ☎ 020 8449 5654
- 🕐 M-Sa 9.00-18.00, Su 10.00-17.00
- ⊖ High Barnet

Fridge and freezer.

Simple & Good
Vegan cafe & take-away

- 4 St. Onge Parade, Genotin Road (north end), Enfield EN1 1YU
- 020 8364 5955
  simpleandgoodsocial@gmail.com
- M-Sa 08.00-20.00, Su 10.00-18.00. Times may vary.
- Enfield Town BR (opposite)
- facebook.com/simpleandgoodenfield
  instagram.com/
  simpleandgood_enfield

Enfield's first vegan eatery opened January 2019, and has an awesome menu.

Food includes full English breakfast wrap, smoothie bowl, choc peanut butter porridge, Moving Mountains burger or hot dog, sausage rolls, cauliflower chickpea and spinach curry, Mexican rice bowl, toasted wraps, smashed avo and coconut bacon toastie, cassava fries

Lots of cakes including gluten-free, cookies, artisan ice creams and sorbets in cone or cup, waffles, milkshakes and smoothies, or try a peanut butter, banana and Vego spread toastie.

Artisan coffees, fancy lattes like beetroot or chai. Soft drinks, juices and kombucha.

Children welcome. Deliveroo.

Capel Manor Gardens
Garden centre café

- Bullsmoor Lane, Enfield EN1 4RQ
  (next door to Middleton House)
- 08456 122 122
- Centre Mar-Oct M-F 10.00-17.30,
  last ticket 16.00; Oct-Feb M-F only
  10.00-17.00, last ticket 15.30..
  Closed Xmas-New Year. Restaurant
  open M-F till 16.00, hot meals
  11.45-14.00, Sa-Su till 17.00, meals
  12.00-15.00
- Turkey Street BR (0.8km)
- capelmanorgardens.co.uk
  facebook.com/capelmanorcollege

Gardeners will be in heaven. Horticultural college with 30 acres of beautiful themed gardens open to the public, including Australian, Japanese, historical, jungle and even an Italianate maze. £6 entry, concessions £5, children £3, under-5 free.

Bring a picnic or enjoy the café serving vegan soup, vegan pasta, jacket potato and salad, vegan bakes. The restaurant seats 200 and there is also outdoor seating with picnic benches and tables. It gets busier during term time.

Pizza Express, Enfield
Omnivorous Italian restaurant

- 2 Silver Street, Enfield EN1 3ED
- 020 8367 3311
- Su-Th 11.30-22.30,
  F-Sa 11.30-23.30
- Enfield Town BR
- pizzaexpress.com

Vegan cheese. Baby facilities. Disabled toilet. Wifi.

Village Wholefood Store
Vegetarian wholefood shop

- 23 Forty Hill, Enfield EN2 9HT
- M-Sa 9.00-17.30, Su closed
- 020 8366 5108
- Gordon Hill BR. Bus 191, W10
- villagewholefood.co.uk
  facebook.com/
  thevillagewholefoodstore

Excellent shop with organic fruit and veg delivered arrives mornings and non-organic twice a week. Veg boxes for collection. Specialists in vegan foods including cakes and pastries. Chilled and frozen. Raw foods. Supplements. Bodycare. Cleaning products. Home brewing.

Holland & Barrett, Enfield
Health food shop

- Unit 34 Palace Gardens, Enfield
  EN2 6SN
- 020 8363 4253
- M-Sa 9.00-18.00, Su 10.30-16.30
- Enfield Town

Fridge and freezer.

Holland & Barrett, Edmonton
Health food shop

- Unit 2C South Mall, Edmonton
  Green shopping centre N9 0AL
- 020 8803 4538
- M-Sa 9.00-18.00, Su 10.30-17.00
- Edmonton Green

Fridge and freezer.

SOUTHGATE & PALMERS GREEN

Pure Health Store
Wholefood shop

- 56 Chase Side, Osidge N14 5PA
- 020 8447 8071
- M-Sa 9.00-18.00, Su closed
- Southgate
- villagewholefood.co.uk
- facebook.com/Purehealthsouthgate

Wholefoods, cosmetics, bodycare and vitamins. Some take-away food. Herbal and homeopathy, ayurvedic, sports nutrition. Cleaning products. Clinic with massage, osteopathy, chiropody.

Holland & Barrett. Palmers Green
Health food shop

- 250 Green Lane, Palmers Green N13 5TU
- 020 8886 1669
- M-Sa 9.00-17.30, Su 11.00-17.00
- Palmers Green BR

Fridge and freezer.

Holland & Barrett, Southgate
Health food shop

- 88 Chase Side, Southgate N14 5PH
- 020 3784 8029
- M-Sa 9.00-17.30, Su 11.00-17.00
- Southgate

Fridge and freezer.

The Orange Tree Totteridge
Omnivorous pub

- ☛ 7 Totteridge Village N20 8NX
  N20 8NX
- ☏ 020 8343 7031
- ◔ Pub: M-Th 12.00-22.00, F 12.00-23.30, Sa 09.00-23.30, Su 10.00-21.00
  Food: M-Th 12.00-22.00, F 12.00-22.30, Sa 09.00-22.30, Su 10.00-21.00.
- ✪ Totteridge & Whetstone
- ⇗ theorangetreetotteridge.co.uk
  facebook.com/
  TheOrangeTreeTotteridge

Country dining pub in the heart of Totteridge Village with a separate vegan menu, including an impressive choice of desserts.

Nibbles and starters £6.25 include warm artisan breads with olive oil and balsamic vinegar; nocellara olives; miso aubergine bao buns; hummus and toasted ciabatta with pine nuts and pomegranate; homemade soup of the day with ciabatta.

Main courses £8.95-£13.95 feature Nourish Bowl of Warm lentil falafel, roasted butternut squash, avocado, crispy chickpeas, pickled rainbow vegetables, baby spinach, slow-roasted tomato dip and soft tortilla; Poke Bowl of Pickled rainbow vegetables, sesame roasted aubergine, avocado, edamame beans, jasmine rice, soy & mirin dressing; Moroccan Bowl of giant couscous, baby spinach, roasted chickpeas, pomegranate & coconut tzatziki, topped with an aubergine, lentil and chickpea stew, optional tofu; burger with coconut tzatziki and slow-roasted tomato tapenade and side salad; slow roasted tomato, basil and almond bake; mezze. Extra veg £3.50.

Desserts £4.95-£6.75 are served with coconut vanilla ice cream: apple, plum and damson crumble; blackcurrent mousse with biscuit base and strawberries; salted caramel billionaires bar with a chocolate chip cookie base, salted caramel and dark chocolate ganache; treacle and pecan tart.

Children welcome. Outside seating.

VEGAN NORTH LONDON © Copyright

1st edition by Alex Bourke
EAN 978-1-902259-16-1
Published January 2020
by Vegetarian Guides Ltd
www.veganlondon.guide

2 Hilborough Court, Livermere Road, London E8 4LG, UK
Tel: 020-3239 8433 (24 hrs)
International: +44-20-3239 8433

Distributed in UK by Bertrams, Gardners, Marigold
In USA/Canada by Book Publishing Company, TN. www.bookpubco.com
Updates to this guide at: vegetarianguides.co.uk/updates
Link and earn 10% commisssion: vegetarianguides.co.uk/affiliate

In the same series:
VEGAN CENTRAL LONDON
VEGAN EAST LONDON
VEGAN SOUTH LONDON
VEGAN WEST LONDON
VEGAN LONDON comprehensive edition

Printed by Buxton Press, England

VEGAN SOUTH LONDON

1st edition

The complete insider guide to the best vegan food in London

Alex Bourke
Vegetarian Guides

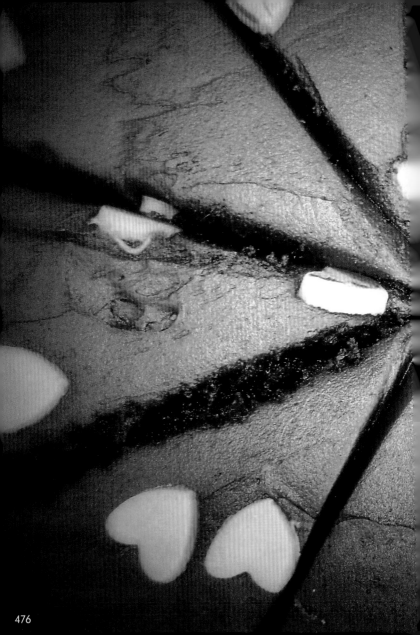

SOUTH LONDON

* OUR TOP 5 - BEST OF SOUTH LONDON *

Brixton Saturday
Eat of Eden
Habesha Village
KataKata
Ms Cupcake
Picky Wops at the Queens Head

Dining Out
Amrutha Lounge, Tooting
By Chloe, Bermondsey/Greenwich
Bonnington Cafe, Vauxhall
Cafe Van Gogh, Oval
Vegan Express, Tooting

Cafes
Blue Brick, Dulwich
Deserted Cactus, Peckham
Retreat Cafe, Richmond
The Waiting Room, Deptford
Wholemeal Cafe, Streatham

Fast Food
Borough Market, South Bank
The Full Nelson, Deptford
Halo Burger, Brixton
The Waiting Room, Deptford
What the Pitta, Croydon

Indian
Hullaballo, Deptford
Saravanaa Bhavan, Croydon
Saravanaa Bhavan, Tooting
Santok Maa's, Thornton Heath
SWAD, Thornton Heath

Lunch
Amrutha Lounge, Tooting
The Retreat, Richmond
Tide Tables, Richmond
Wholemeal Cafe, Streatham
Zionly Manna, Peckham

Markets
Borough Market
Brixton Vegan Market
Greenwich Market
Peckham Rye Market
Tooting Indoor Market

Pubs
The Amersham Arms, Deptford
Brewdog, Brixton
The Bird's Nest, Deptford
The Full Nelson, Deptford
The Queen's Head, Brixton

Vegan Cake/Dessert
Blank Brixton
Ms Cupcake, Brixton
The Retreat Kitchen, Richmond
Riverside Vegetaria, Kingston
Ruby Tuesday, Greenwich

Wholefood Shopping
Brixton Wholefoods
Greenlands, Greenwich
Hetu, Battersea
Planet Organic, Wandsworth
Whole Foods Market, Richmond

HABESHA VILLAGE
ETHIOPIAN AND ERITREAN FOOD
vegetarian . vegan . gluten free
55
EÑO

Brixton Market

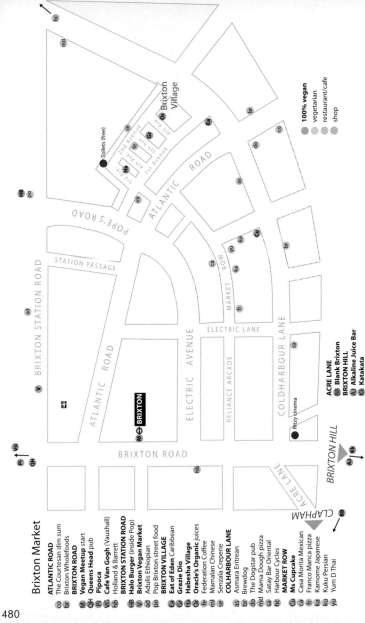

ATLANTIC ROAD
co The Courtesan dim sum
br Brixton Wholefoods
BRIXTON ROAD
M   Vegan Meetup start
QH Queens Head pub
Pi Pipoca
VG Cafe Van Gogh (Vauxhall)
hb Holland & Barrett
BRIXTON STATION ROAD
HB Halo Burger (inside Pop)
Brixton Vegan Market
V   Adulis Ethiopian
ad Pop Brixton street food
po **BRIXTON VILLAGE**
Ea Eat of Eden Caribbean
Gr Grazie Dio
HB Habesha Village
Or Oracle's Organic juices
fe Federation Coffee
ml Mamalan Chinese
se Senzala Creperie
COLHARBOUR LANE
as Asmara Eritrean
br Brewdog
do The Dogstar pub
md Mama Dough pizza
sa Satay Bar Oriental
hc Harbour Cycles
MARKET ROW
Cu Ms Cupcake
ca Casa Morita Mexican
fr Franco Manca pizza
ka Kamome Japanese
ku Kuku Persian
yu Yum D Thai

ACRE LANE
BB Blank Brixton
BRIXTON HILL
AJ Alkaline Juice Bar
Kk Katakata

100% vegan
vegetarian
restaurant/cafe
shop

480

BRIXTON

Vegan Hotspot by Catherine Laurence

Brixton is abuzz with character day and night, with its markets, gig venues, independent cinemas and pedestrianised areas bustling with locals and visitors alike.

As well as concerts at the famous Brixton Academy and the Ritzy cinema with its lively upstairs performance space, Brixton is home to other great live music venues like Plan B and Electric Brixton, and the fantastic Whirled Cinema under the railway arches down at Loughborough Junction.

Nearby Brockwell Park is a huge green space, boasting an Olympic size lido that's open April to September, locally known as "Brixton's beach". Brixton is also a thriving Transition Town, complete with its own local currency, the Brixton Pound - one of many initiatives for transitioning towards local resilience as we kick the fossil fuel habit.

Brixton Market is huge and falls into three main areas: shops, street markets, and covered arcades containing restaurants and cafes from around the world, many offering some vegan dishes.

Vegan in the market: On Coldharbour Lane is the devilishly good **Ms Cupcake** cakes shop with tables outside in the arcade; at the back of the market in *Brixton Village* are four vegan restaurants and cafes: **Oracle's Organic** rasta juice and food bar; Caribbean **Eat of Eden**; Ethiopian **Habesha Village**; and Italian **Grazie Dio**. Just outside is **Halo Burger**.

To the south, half way along Brixton Hill is

KataKata arts cafe, and just before it **Alkaline Juice Factory**.

Head north up Brixton Road for dinner at **The Queen's Head** 100% vegan pub which has pizzas and Italian food by Picky Wops, **Pipoca** vegan pancake restaurant and zero waste wholefood shop, and further still (see Vauxhall & Oval chapter) **Cafe Van Gogh** vegan restaurant. West towards Clapham along Acre Lane is **Blank Brixton** vegan cafe and bakery.

London Vegan Meetup do a monthly Saturday afternoon market walkabout. There are usually at least 20 people and it's a great way to make new friends. Jess who hosts these free tours also hosts **Brixton Vegan Market** on Brixton Station Road on summer weekends and less often in winter, and occasional indoor vegan fayres at the Dogstar pub.

Ital is vital

One of the reasons Brixton qualifies as a vegan hotspot is the 'ital' food. Ital is pronounced to rhyme with 'vital', which is actually the root of the word, denoting the living plant-based diet followed by many in the Rastafarian movement. Always virtuous but never boring, look out for Oracle's raw berry cake and tasty salads and sandwiches, often with a spicy kick, or try Eat of Eden.

We have created separate entries for the top places, and also included a summary by the staff at Ms Cupcake of what to eat at the best of the rest.

481

Picky Wops Vegan Pizzeria at the Queen's Head Vegan Pub
Vegan Italian restaurant in 100% vegan pub

- 144 Stockwell Road SW9 9TQ
- 074 2707 6525 (Andrea)
  075 5208 5472 (Cristiano)
  pub 020 7737 3519
- Wops M closed, Tu-F 17.00-22.30,
  Sa-Su 13.00-22.30
  Pub M closed, Tu-Th 16.00-23.00, F
  16.00-01.00, Sa 13.00-01.00, Su
  13.00-23.00
- Brixton, Stockwell
  facebook.com/pickywops
  instagram.com/pickywops
  queensheadbrixton.co.uk
  facebook.com/brixtonqueenshead
  instagram.com/thequeensheadbrixton

Pub landlord Eoin McCullagh made all his drinks vegan in 2019 and brought in Italian vegan pizza legends Picky Wops, previously in Fulham and Peckham until they hit landlord issues, to run this pub kitchen. It's a beautiful traditional English pub with a fireplace and out back there's lots more seating in the covered garden.

Cristiano and Andrea opened up a restaurant in Fulham in 2016 with only one vegan pizza, but early the following year both lads went vegan and in April 2017 their industrial look eat-in and take-away vegan pizzeria followed. These two picky Italian wops (not our words, it's how they define themselves), both pizzaioli (pizzaiolo - man who makes pizza), seemed to be doing everything else too as they were there every day of the week from morning till night. In December 2018 they opened another branch in Peckham. Following landlord "issues" at both locations, they then moved into here in early 2019.

The unique point about the pizzas here is that the bases are very varied. You can choose from type 2 or 00 white flour, or for £3 extra choose burned wheat, multigrain or turmeric, for £3.50 spirulina and hemp, or £4.50 kamut and plantain.

Pizzas or calzone £6-£12 are topped with coconut modern moxxarella cheese, select from **Rossa** with tomato and oregano (no cheese); **Maggie** with tomato; **Greenman** with courgettes, olives, onion, modern parmezan; **Victory** with courgette, mushroom, olives and peppers; **Protein Punch** with tempeh and pesto; **Parmigiana** with aubergines, onion, modern parmezan, pesto.

Tagliatelle alla Bolognese £8, courgetti spaghetti with pesto (cold) £7, pasta with pesto £8.

Top up with garlic bread multigrain £4, add hemp or seaweed £6. Fries £4. Green salad £5.

For dessert there is tiramisù £6.

Vegan wines from £5 medium glass, £19 bottle. Draft beers include Camden Hells, Chieftain, Gamma Ray, Brixton Low Voltage IPA, Rekorderlig, Rebel Red, La Trappe, Aspall cider

481

Pipoca
Vegan gluten-free crperie/restaurant and zero waste shop

- 224 Brixton Road SW9 6AH
- 020 7501 8539
- M-Tu closed, W-F 11.00-22.00, Sa 10.00-22.00, Su 10.00-19.00
- Brixton
- pipocavegan.com
  facebook.com/pipocavegan
  instagram.com/pipocavegan

Vegan creperie restaurant on the right, dry and organic foods shop on the left.

All day brunch/breakfast £7-£10.50: **Brixton Brunch** is spiced Caribbean black beans, roasted cajun spiced sweet potatoes, gluten-free fritters, fried plantain, turmeric and cumin seeded breadfruit, cassava, steamed spinach, garlic mayo, banana ketchup and tomato. **Pipoca Brunch** is homemade pinto baked beans, cajun spiced sweet potatoes, aubergine, courgette, mixed peppers, cherry tomatoes, guacamole, seeded sourdough toast. **Mezze bowl** with chickpea and potato croquette, roasted Meditteranean veggies, seeded sourdough toast. **Tex Mex sweet potato pancake**, shredded jackfruit, chillies, sour cream, mango vinaigrette. Avocado toast.

Small dishes £3.20-£5 include croquette, turmeric cassava chips, chilli olives.

Savoury galettes £7-£10.50 £7-£10.50 filled with various veggies, vegan cheese, chilli olives, almonds, black beans, guacamole, scrambled tofu, jackfruit, plantain and banana ketchup.

14 kinds of sweet galettes £4-£8 with one or a combination of chocolate, maple, peanut butter, almond butter, vegan Nutella, caramel.

Smoothies ££3.50-£4.50. Fizzy drinks and kombucha £3. Teas £2. Coffees, iced latte, hot choc, mocha, matcha or chai latte £2-£3.50. Almond, oat and coconut milk.

The zero-waste **shop** has a wall of self-serve grains, pulses, nuts, seeds, dried fruit. Nut butters. Flours including coconut, quinoa, spelt. Plant milks. Organic apple or red grape juice. Sauces. Balsamic vinegar.

Faith In Nature refills for body wash, shampoos and conditioners.

Refills for laudry liquid, fabric conditioner, washing up liquid, multi surface spray, glass cleaner, liquid hand soap, dishwasher powder, toilet cleaner, white vinegar.

Soap, hairbrushes, bamboo toothbrushes, razors.

Ms. Cupcake
Vegan cake shop and café

- 📢 408 Coldharbour Lane SW9 8LF
- ☎ 020 3086 8933
- 🕐 M-Th 11.00-20.00, F-Su 10.00-20.00
- ⊖ Brixton
- ↖ mscupcake.co.uk
  facebook.com/Ms.CupcakeUK

Ms. Cupcake burst onto the Brixton scene in 2011 with London's first vegan cake shop, rising rapidly to fame and winning the Baking Industry Rising Star Award within six months of opening. A team of sixteen serve up their amazing freshly-baked vegan cakes, savouries and other sweet treats seven days a week to their dedicated fans from far and wide, as well as all manner of local residents, workers and passers-by, achieving awesome feats of vegan-advocacy-through-cake on a daily basis. The delightful 1950s-style bakery and shop is open plan so everything is baked and decorated fresh on site in front of customers.

At least eight cupcake flavours of the day, from a repertoire of over 150, are displayed at the front counter. £3.30-£3.90 per cupcake. Try the decadently moist and crunchy peanut and chocolate or wildly popular "Ferrero Rocher", a.k.a. the Ambassador. Other flavours range from sophisticated sticky toffee ginger or raspberry cheesecake, through classics such as red velvet or carrot cake, to nostalgic confectionary-themed Oreo, Bounty or Rocky Road.

As well as her famous cupcakes, Ms Cupcakes menu features cookies, squares, tray-bakes, layer cakes, muffins, and even marshmallows, £2-£4 per portion. For an insane sugar rush, go for a chocolate chip cookies "sandwich" with chocolate or vanilla cream £3.60. Other cookie sandwich flavours also available.

Rendezvous with a mischievous friend and linger at the shared tables in the covered Market Row while you blow your sugar ration. You can also take away, or pre-order for pick-up, or choose delivery around the UK. Cupcakes keep three days and freeze for three months.

No refined sugar, soya and gluten-free options available, and they do bespoke orders too, so if you have a unique idea just ask, and they can conjure it into cake form. Whole cakes £45-£80 depending on size.

If you fancy something savoury, they sell a range of tasty vegan snacks and sandwiches.

The shop also sells various brands of vegan chocolates, sweets and snacks. Also ice cream by Swedish Glace, Naturli', Northern Bloc, Booja Booja, and vegan Magnums. Cold drinks.

Hugely popular masterclasses are held in London a few times per year.

Also on UberEats and Deliveroo.

*TIP: Before opening in Brixton, Ms Cupcake had devotees at markets around London. You can also pick up her cupcakes in Whole Foods Market branches across London.

RASPBE
CHAMPAGN

offer
classes!
Sign up HERE!

We have
Gift Vouchers!

SALE!

THE NAUGHTIEST VEGAN CAKES IN T♥WN...

If you're looking for places to get delicious vegan food there are loads of vegan friendly options in Brixton, take a look at some of our top picks below! Please note the majority of these places are <u>NOT fully vegan</u>, *so please do ask for the vegan options when you get there*, as recipes may have changed since this list was written.

Market Row (the market Ms Cupcake is in)

- **Kuku – 14-E Market Row, Brixton, SW9 8LD**
  Persian inspired kitchen, serving home cooked food, salads and desserts. *Top Tip: try their homemade sausage rolls, made fresh each day!*

- **Yum D – 14-D Market Row, Atlantic Road, Brixton, SW9 8LD**
  Thai deli and café with lots of vegan options on the menu! Everything is made from scratch including gyoza dumplings, tempura vegetables and Thai curries.

- **Kamome – 14-C Market Row, Brixton, SW9 8LD**
  Casual restaurant serving home style, Japanese food at low prices. The vegan options are clearly labelled on the menu, including seaweed salad and tofu teriyaki!

- **Casa Morita – 9 Market Row, Brixton, SW9 8LB**
  Classic Mexican dishes which can be made vegan on request. They also serve a range of cocktails and have a happy hour from 5pm-7pm!

- **Franco Manca – 4 Market Row, Brixton, SW9 8LD**
  Neopolitan style pizzeria famous for their sourdough pizzas. Pizza Number 1 is vegan, or ask for any of the their vegetarian ones to be made without cheese to make it vegan.

Brixton Village

- **Senzala Creperie – 42 Coldharbour Lane, Brixton, SW9 8PS**
  French crepes with Brazilian flair! There's savoury and sweet options, and all of the vegan dishes are clearly marked on the menu. *Top Tip: make sure you try the Acai bowl for dessert – it's been tested and approved by one of our Brazilian team members!*

- **Federation Coffee - Unit 77-78 Coldharbour Lane, Brixton, SW9 8PS**
  Local café serving speciality coffee plus freshly made snacks, cakes and savoury dishes! They use Bonsoy milk as an alternative when making your coffee. *Top Tip: try their hot chocolate, its delicious!*

- **The Oracle's Organic Juice Bar - 60 Brixton Village Market, Brixton, SW9 8PS**
  Fully vegan café and juice bar serving mostly raw and organic food. They have a variety of freshly made juices, smoothies and salads!

- **Mama Lan - 18 Brixton Village Market, Coldharbour Lane, Brixton, SW9 8PR**
  Small Chinese street food restaurant serving handmade dumplings, noodle soups and salads. The vegan options are clearly marked on the menu.

- **Eat of Eden - Unit 4, 63 Brixton Village Market, Coldharbour Lane, Brixton, SW9 8PS**
  Fully vegan café offering patties, burgers and wraps.

Surrounding Area

- **Satay Bar - 447 Coldharbour Lane, Brixton, SW9 8LP**
  Pan-Asian restaurant serving Thai, Malay and Chinese food. Lots of vegan options on the menu and great cocktails to choose from!

- **The Courtesan - 69-73 Atlantic Road, Brixton, SW9 8PU**
  Dim Sum restaurant with modern and classic dishes. There are plenty of vegan options as well as cocktails and teas.

- **Mama Dough - 354 Coldharbour Lane, Brixton, SW9 8QH**
  Great tasting sourdough pizzas and a selection of homemade desserts.

- **Pop Brixton - 49 Brixton Station Road, Brixton, SW9 8PQ**
  A selection of street food restaurants with lots of different cuisines available. Most of the stalls have vegan options and it's a great place to hang out just for drinks as well.

- **Brixton Wholefoods - 59 Atlantic Road, Brixton, SW9 8PU**
  Health food store selling organic fruit and vegetables plus herbs, spices and supplements.

- **Café Van Gogh - 88 Brixton Road, SW9 6BE** (seeVauxhall & Oval chapter)
  Fully vegan café with a brand-new menu serving up breakfast, lunch and dinner. Try the Huevos Rancheros or the signature sticky seitan ribs.

Habesha Village
Vegan Ethiopian & Eritrean restaurant

☛ 55 Granville Arcade, Coldharbour Lane SW9 8PS

☎ 020 7738 4513

🕐 M closed, Tu-F 12.00-22.00, Sa 09.00-22.00, Su 12.00-22.00

⊖ Brixton

↖ habesha-village.business.site
facebook.com/habesha.village
instagram.com/habesha.village

Opened 2018 in Brixton Village at the abck of the market. One of the great cuisines of the world for vegans, Ethiopian food is based on stews, lentil dishes and salads, served with injera, a fermented pancake-like flatbread made from teff flour that you use to eat the food with your right hand.

You can start with samosa £2.50 or mixed salad £4.50.

Individual dishes £7, £8 or £11, such as spinach, split peas, collard greens, split lentils, whole lentils, or cabbage with carrot and potatoes, all slowly cooked with onion, garlic and spices. Shiro Wat £12 is a stew made with powdered chickpeas.

Best value is a combination of four dishes for £15 for one person, or six dishes for £28 for two people.

They have some handsome cakes.

Cold drinks £2-£3.25. Tea, Ethiopian spiced tea, herbal teas, Ethiopian jebena coffee, regular coffee, latte cappuccino £2-£3.20. Beers £3.50-£4.45. Wine £5.90 glass, £20 bottle. Spirits.

Sometimes live Ethiopian music.

Eat of Eden
Vegan cafe

- Unit 4, Brixton Village Market, Coldharbour Lane SW9 8PS
- 020 7737 7566
- M 11.00-18.00, Tu-Su 11.00-22.00
- Brixton
- eatofeden.co.uk
  Facebook Eat of Eden
  instagram.com/eatofeden

Opened 2017 where Atlantic Road meets Coldharbour Lane. The inside is tiny but there's lots of outside seating. Healthy Ital food and plenty to choose from.

The platter for £12.95 gets you 8 items including salad, for two people £22.50. Choose from chickpea curry, pumpkin curry, lentil stew, ackee, callaloo, quinoa, rice, bulgur, wheat, plantain, macaroni pie, wheat meat, fried dumplings, seaweed fritters, salad. Take-away version large (6 items) £9.95, small (4 items) £7.50.

Curry, stew or ackee portion £5, with a grain, side and salad £8.95. Burger £4.95, with sweet potato fries and salad £7.75. Wraps £4.80, with fries and salad £7.50. Callaloo, dal or veg patties £2.20.

Sides £1.50-£4.50 include plantain, fritters, dumplings, callaloo, macaroni pie, quinoa, bulgur, African rice, red rice, salads.

Cakes £4-£4.95 such as almond, banana walnut, cocoa orange, raw chocolate or lemon torte, coconut ginger cookie, apple crumble, . Ice-cream £1.75, 2 scoops £3.

Home-made juice drinks, fresh juices, smoothies, punches £3.50-£4.95. Teas £1.95 include regular, green, moringa, sorrel, matcha, sour sop, echinacea, liquorice. Coffee, latte, hot choc £2-£2.95.

SOUTH

BRIXTON VILLAGE

491

Grazie Dio
Vegan Modern Italian restaurant

☛ Brixton Village unit 81, 5th Avenue, SW8 8PS

☏ 07703 365 146

🕐 M-Tu closed, W-Th 11.00-22.00, F 11.00-23.00, Sa 09.00-23.00, Su 09.00-21.00

⊖ Brixton

↖ facebook.com/graziedioitsvegan

In the heart of Brixton Village Market, this Italian restaurant went fully vegan summer 2019, with food by Picky Wops and The Fish Out. Here are some sample dishes.

Breakfast items £4-£7.50 include chia pot; black quinoa porridge poke with berries; sourdough toast with mushrooms and cheddah cheese, or crushed avocado, hummus, chilli and pumpkin seeds; sausage sarnie in a croissant with onion chutney and sauerkraut; salm'n bagel; scrambled tofu bac'n bap with ackee; Full English poke with sourdough, mushrooms, tomatoes, sausage and bac'n, baked beans, scrambled tofu.

Boozy brunch £29.95 one course, £34.95 two, with unlimited prosecco for 90 minutes.

Mains £9 such as white Sardinian lasagna with Carasau bread, crushed potatoes, smoked gouda and blue cheese sauce. Gluten-free plantain tacos with salsa, caper berries, onions, black olives, tomato. Calzoncini with alternative flours such as hemp. Pasta with a beer £10.

Cashew and pineapple tiramisu or mango chia seeds pot £4.

Just Eat deliveries.

Halo Burger
Vegan fast food cafe & take-away

- Inside Pop, 49 Brixton Station Road SW9 8P (corner Pope's Road)
- 020
- Su-Th 12.00-22.00, F-Sa 12.00-23.00
- Brixton
- facebook.com/haloburgeruk
  instagram.com/haloburgeruk
  haloburger.co.uk
  popbrixton.org

Inside the Pop Brixto building that houses creative spaces and little bars with shared seating. Look at the back for the unobtrusive red shopfront.

They sell vegan burgers £5.50-£9.50 such as hamburger, cheeseburger, quarter pounder with cheese, or the "bleeding" Beyond Meat Halo burger. Pink salty fries £2.50, Don't Have a Cow fries £4. Sauces £1.

Vegan Magnum ice cream £2.50. Beer £4.50. Karma Kola or lemonade £2.50. Water £1.50.

Deliveroo.

Oracle's Organic Juice & Foods
Vegan café

📞 Shop 90, 6th Avenue, Brixton Village
SW9 8PS

📞 07584 240 909

🕐 M-W 10.00-18.00, Th-Sa 10.00-
23.00, Su 10.00-17.00

⊖ Brixton

Gorgeous rasta vegan café and juice bar, mostly raw and organic, the perfect place for a bite to eat before going on to a gig at Brixton Academy, a local pub or bar, or perhaps some live music at the nearby Agile Rabbit, also in Brixton Village market (see below).

You can sit inside the small shop at benches along the walls, or at the tables outside. Everything is also available to take away, so you can always buy a stash of their tasty offerings and perch elsewhere. On sunny days, the large seating area at the Coldharbour Lane entrance to Brixton Village Market is a great spot.

Very reasonably priced - substantial sandwiches such as avocado healthy bite, carrot delish and soya-free vegan cheese £2.50, or salad meals such as crunchy walnut and avocado mountain £3.50, are all served with big smiles by the owner Ifa-tunde who swiftly befriends new customers. Warm raw soups £3 such as spinach, carrot and avocado, or carrot soup with herbs.

Healthy herbal teas and chicory coffee with plant milks to sip with a generous slice of decadent but virtuous raw cake £3, such as chocolate with hemp, carrot and ginger, or mango, strawberry and coconut. Raw chocolate mousse £2.50, kids love this. Individual handmade raw chocolates.

"Liquid meals" smoothies and power juices £3-£5 with ingredients such as spirulina, avocado, banana, cashew nut milk, dates and sea moss.

They also sell a small selection of vegan wholefoods, books and supplements.

If you like this you'll probably like Negril rasta-rant on Brixton Hill.

Brixton Vegan Walkabout
Vegan Saturday foodie walkabout

- Meet at underground station entrance
- For stalls email via the Facebook page
- Usually second Saturday of the month 12.30.
- Brixton. Bus 45,59,109,118, 133,159,250,333
- meetup.com/londonvegan

Come rain, shine or snow, discover the many vegan delights south of the river with around 20 or 30 other vegans. Gather 12.30-12.45 outside Brixton tube station, then walk to Brixton Station Road from where we explore the market and surrounding areas. Highlights include Saba's Ethiopian food stall, Bean & Bun vegan burger stall with sweet potato or curly fries, Dosa stall, and the vegan cafes.

2pm head to Ms Cupcake. 3pm head to one of these pubs on Coldharbour Lane: The Dogstar, The Prince Albert, or The Market House, or Effra Social & Hootenanny on Effra Road, or The Windmill off Brixton Hill which serves Pitfield vegan beer, or The White Orse which has Moretti Italian beer, La Gunias and, in bottles, Becks and cider. Alternatively in nice weather there is Brockwell Park with a walled garden.

You could also head off north up Brixton Road to vegan Cafe Van Gogh (see Vauxhall and Oval) or south down Brixton Hill to KataKata vegetarian restaurant and music venue.

Started in 2012 and organised by Jessica Stella Fox. Check the Meetup web page for the next evemt.

Adulis, Brixton
Omnivorous Eritrean restaurant

- 21 Brixton Station Road SW9 8PB
- 020 3417 2810
- M-F 17.00-23.00, Sa-Su 12.00-23.00
- Brixton
- adulis.co.uk, facebook.com/ AdulisEritreanRestaurant

See Clapham branch for menu. Also in Oval (see Vauxhall section).

Holland & Barrett, Brixton
Health food shop

- 490 Brixton Road SW9 8EQ
- 020 7326 4577
- M-F 07.30-20.00, Sa 08.30-19.00, Su 10.00-18.00
- Brixton

Small shop with no fridge or freezer but if Brixton Wholefoods is closed you might want to nip in here on a Sunday to pick up basics like supplements, shampoo, dried fruit, nuts and chocolate.

Brixton Markets
Indoor and street markets

☛ Behind Brixton underground station

🕐 Shops M-Su 08.00-19.00 or later.
Electric Ave & Pope's Rd 08.00-18.00, W till 15.00, Su closed.
Brixton Village & Market Row arcades 08.00-23.30, M till 18.00, Su open.
Brixton Station Road outdoor markets:
Street food all week lunch times;
Friday market 10.00-17.00;
Themed Sat markets 10.00-17.00;
Sunday Farmers' Market and Vegan Market 9.30-14.30;

⊖ Brixton

↖ brixtonmarket.net

This market is much bigger than it at first seems and falls into various areas both indoors and out. Loads of fruit and veg on Electric Avenue and Pope's Road, especially Caribbean stuff like yam and plantain. There are arcades and a covered market full of shops.

Indoors: The market arcades, comprising Reliance Arcade, Market Row and Brixton Village Market as you head east from Brixton Road, are open daily, and are home to numerous quirky little places where you can find food, drink and entertainment. Top of the list are of course the pure vegan Ms Cupcake (on the Coldharbour Lane corner of Market Row) Oracle's Organic and Habesha Village in Brixton Village Market, and Eat of Eden on the outside of that part.

There are also cheap and tasty vegan eats of all kinds at various omnivorous places dotted throughout the arcades. For example, in Brixton Village Market you can have Mexican at Casa Morita. In Market Row there's also great Thai food at Yum-D where virtually everything can be veganized with tofu versions and minus the fish sauce.

Outdoors: The Brixton Station Road Saturday outdoor markets are always worth a potter, especially as there is a regular falafel stall. There's a different theme each week. First Saturdays are the Bakers & Flea Market with bread, cakes, antiques and secondhard art, jewellery, books, ceramics, collectables. Second Saturdays are the Makers' Market with crafts, contemporary art and independent fashion. Third Saturdays are Retro & Vintage clothes plus jewellery and furniture. Fourth Saturdays are Brix Mix with stalls from all three markets plus hot food from around the world. Every so often there are specialist markets too.

Every Sunday in Brixton Station Road is the Farmers' Market 9.30-14.00, not very vegan apart from fruit and veg and Zinglefoods falafel wraps. Except that on some Sundays there is Brixton Vegan Market, see next entry.

There is also a Friday Market with street food stalls, crafts, retro and vintage clothes.

Brixton Vegan Market
Outdoor vegan street markets

- 🕿 Brixton Station Road SW9 8QQ
- ☏ For stalls email via the Facebook page
- 🕐 Sunday 11.00-16.00 approximately every two weeks Apr-May, every week June-mid Oct, less often in winter. From summer 2019 they are also trying Saturdays.
- ⊖ Brixton
- ↖ facebook.com/BrixtonVeganMarket
  instagram.com/BrixtonVeganMarket
  twitter.com/BrixtonVeganMkt

Started in 2017 by Jessica Stella Fox, who

also organises on Facebook the monthly London Vegan Meetup Brixton walkabouts and vegan fayres at the Dogstar pub. A typical lineup of at least a dozen traders could include Twinz Kitchen curry and mac n cheese, Vogococo raw chocolate energy balls, Bear's Doughnuts, Sara Sechi art, Las Vegans meatballs and salads, Lele's vegan patisserie, Vegan Sweet Tooth cakes and savoury food, and more. See the Facebook event page for who's at the next one.

Brixton Wholefoods
Wholefood shop

- 🕿 59 Atlantic Road SW9 8PU
- ☏ 020 7737 2210
- 🕐 M-Sa 9.30-17.30, M -19.00, F -18.00, Su closed
- ⊖ Brixton
- ↖ brixtonwholefoods.com

Great wholefood store behind Brixton market with fresh take-away. Organic fruit and veg. Large range of vegan foods including non-dairy cheese, tofu, tempeh and ice-cream. Food to go such as vegan sausage rolls and spicy veg pasties £1.60, Paul's vegetable and tofu samosa £1.05, and a delectable selection of Manna vegan cakes such as orange and almond polenta cake, £2.58 for a generous slice. Lots of raw superfoods and chocolate.

Huge range of 'serve yourself' herbs and spices which you weigh so you can have as little or as much as you want.

Bodycare including Faith in Nature, Urtekram, Jason, Weleda. Homeopathic remedies. BioD and Earth Friendly cleaning products. MC, Visa, Brixton Pound.

COLDHARBOUR LANE

Harbour Cycles
Vegan popup dinners in bicycle shop

- 📍 200 Coldharbour Lane,
  Loughborough Junction SE5 9QH
- ☎ 020 7274 5008
- 🕐 M, Sa 9.30-18.30, Tu-F 08.30-
  18.30, Su 12.00-18.30
- ⊖ Loughborough Junction BR (adjacent),
  Brixton, Denmark Hill
- ➤ harbourcycles.co.uk
  facebook.com/pg/theharbour.cycles/
  events

Cycle shop and workshop opened summer 2015 by top bike mechanic Mark and mechanical engineer Brenton who is also a youth/community worker. They also host occasional vegan popup dinner evenings. At the last two the chefs were raw food master Denisa Ratulea and south London vegan restaurant Cafe Amrutha (see Tooting).

Fresh coffee available till midday with almond milk while they look over your bike.

You can hire the space for your own birthday party, community group celebration or friends' get-together, for 20 people (or 26 at a squeeze) over 4 tables. Vegan and vegetarian chefs and a local florist available.

The shop sells fully refurbished secondhand bikes from £75 to £800, new and used parts, accessories, and offers a comprehensive repair service. Bike maintenance evening classes.

To get there, head east from Ms Cupcake towards Camberwell.

Asmara
Omnivorous Eritrean restaurant

- 📍 386 Coldharbour Lane SW9 8LF
- ☎ 020 7737 4144
- 🕐 M-Su 17.30-24.00
- ⊖ Brixton
- ➤ zomato.com/london/asmara-brixton

Handy for concerts at Brixton Academy and with a good reputation for catering for vegetarians and vegans. It's the usual no cutlery salads and lentil dishes eaten by hand with enjera bread that is actually more like a pancake. Set vegan meal £30 for two people. Licensed.

The Dogstar
Pub

- 📍 389 Coldharbour Lane SW9 8LQ
  (corner Atlantic Rd, near Ms Cupcake)
- ☎ 020 7733 7515
- 🕐 M closed, Tu-W 16.00-23.00, Th
  16.00-02.00, F 16.00-04.00, Sa
  12.00-04.00, Su 12.00-22.30
- ⊖ Brixton
- ➤ dogstarbrixton.com
  facebook.com/DogBRX

The London Vegan Meetup monthly Brixton walkabout on a Saturday usually ends up here, though if it's sunny they might go to Brockwell Park. There are vegan pizzas, and vegan drinks include Apples and Pears cider, Stowford Press, Heineken, Blue Moon, Becks, Peroni.

Occasional weekend vegan fayres are held here in the function rooms on the first and second floors.

Brewdog, Brixton
Pub with mainly vegan craft beers

- 419 Coldharbour Lane SW9 8LH
- 020 3026 2500
- M-W 16.00-24.00, Th 12.00-01.00, F 12.00-02.00, Sa 11.00-02.00, Su 11.00-24.00. Kitchen till 22.00.
- Brixton
- brewdog.com
  facebook.com/BrewDogBrixton

Most beers here are labelled vegan. The food menu £9.50-£11 includes BBQ Hail Seitan steak, Clucky This Time southern fried seitan, Buffalo cauliflower burger, and the Beyond Meat burger, which comes with chipotle slaw, vegan Gouda cheese, roasted red peppers, baby gem and pickles in a beetroot brioche bun. Add fries £2.50 or sweet potato fries £3. Superfood salad £8.

On Vegan Mondays they do 2-fo-1 on vegan mains. Also a tofu dog £9.50 with avocado hummus, broccoli, scallions and carrot in a brioche bun.

Brunch menu served weekends and bank holidays until 4pm, offerss Veggie Haystack £9 with bbq seitan steak, smashed avocado, chargrilled padron peppers, hash brown, Boston beans, forest mushroom, vine tomato and sourdough toast.

As well as beers galore, they also do cafetiere coffee and teus. Children welcome until 8pm. Dogs welcome all day. Food and beer on Deliveroo and Uber Eats.

BRIXTON HILL

Heading south towards Streatham are these places.

KataKata
Vegetarian art cafe

- ☛ 132A Brixton Hill (middle of) SW2 1RS
- ☎ 020 3490 1160
- ◑ M-Su 10.00-22.00, last order 20.30
- ⊖ Brixton (15mins walk). Bus 45,59,109
- ↖ katakatabrixton.com
  facebook.com/KatakataBrixtonHill

Colourful community space half way along Brixton Hill, with African art, walls inside and out brightly decorated by local artist Nebula, and sofas to relax on. There is a huge garden at the back with permaculture vegetable beds. It is an oasis of calm after the bustle of central Brixton, the perfect place to relax outside in summer or inside anytime. Sometimes there is live music. Owner Franklin also owns vegetarian cafe Maloko in Camberwell which also specialises in pancakes.

French galettes £4-£6.90, a traditional buckwheat savoury pancake, with a vegan base made from chickpeas, tahini and herbs from their garden, served with mushrooms, sweet potato, asparagus, peppers; or aubergine, tomato, spinach, mushrooms; or Caribbean style jerk tofu, sweet potato, mushrooms, aubergine. They also serve crepes, but those are not vegan.

Daily freshly pressed juices £2.95 such as apple, carrot, beetroot and ginger. Add a shot of spirit £1.50. Teas and coffees £1.80-£2.95. Local beers £3.75. Wine £4.50 large glass, £12 bottle.

Alkaline Juice Factory
Vegan organic shop, smoothie & juice bar

- ☛ 100b Brixton Hill SW2 1AH (at Glanville Rd)
- ☎ 020 8678 6900
- ◑ M-Sa 07.00-19.00, Su 10.00-18.00
- ⊖ Brixton
- ↖ facebook.com/alkalinejuicefactory
  instagram.com/alkalinecleanse

Slow pressed juice bar and healthy foods such as quinoa and sea moss porridge, pancakes, salads, cooked meals such as spicy kamut grain and butternut squash risotto with portobello mushroom and chickpea sauce, avocado, rocket and cherry tomato salad; or coconut curry.

Nut-free raw vegan cakes £4 such as chilli and cacao with banana, or acai and coconut.

A couple of seats at the bar.

Negril

Omnivorous Caribbean restaurant

- 132 Brixton Hill SW2 1RS
- 020 8674 8798
- M-F 17.00-22.30, Sa-Su 12.00-22.30
- Brixton
- negrilonline.co.uk

There's a great selection of vegan food at this Caribbean restaurant with a big front garden set back from Brixton Hill and background reggae music. The dedicated Ital vegan section has a range of mains £7.95 based on fresh veggies and spices, such as tofu curry; Ital Stew with beans, sweet potato, carrots, pumpkin and coconut milk. Ital salad £11.95 with smoked tofu, carrots, avocado, tomato and mixed leaves. Homemade bean burger with chickpeas and blackeye peas £8.95.

Or you might be tempted by dishes elsewhere on the menu, such as roti wrap £7.95 stuffed with mixed bean curry and spinach - vegan if you ask for it without mayo. Plenty of salads, starters and sides for us too, such as plantain wedges £3.25 and sweet cornmeal dumplings £2.95.

Smoothies such as Caribbean Queen £3.25 with papaya, pineapple, mango and coconut milk. Various juices including fresh coconut £1.95-2.95. Soft drinks £2.95. Coffees and hot chocolate around £2.40, soya milk available. Beers £3.95-£5.95. Wine from £4.95 glass, £19.95 bottle. Rums from £5.50. Cocktails £7.50.

Home delivery from 6pm week days, noon weekends, free for orders over £15.

S.G. Manning
Health food shop and pharmacy

- 294 Brixton HiW2 1HT
- (020 8674 4391
- M-F 9.00-19.00, Sa 9.00-14.00, Su closed
- Brixton or Streatham Hill BR
- sgmanningpharmacy.com

Small health food store in a pharmacy towards the south end of Brixton Hill with vegetarian owner. An astonishing range of wholefoods, non-dairy cheese, organic bread, frozen foods including vegan ice-cream, nut and chocolate spreads. Bodycare including Faith in Nature, Urtekram, Natracare. Cleaning products such as Veggi Wash. Great for vegans.

Blank Brixton
Vegan Antipodean cafe

- 144 Acre Lane SW2 5UT (after Lidl on the opposite side)
- (07788 602 119
- M-F 06.00-17.00, Sa 07.00-17.00, Su 9.00-17.00
- Brixton
- facebook.com/Blankbrixton instagram.com/blankbrixton

Sam and Kiwi husband Warner's lovely cafe, on the road that links Brixton to Clapham, serves plant based food for everyone - 80% of customers are omnivores. They use lots of Brixton produce. Everything is made in house including pastries and cakes.

Main means £9-£12.50 include The Works, their version of an all day full English, with avocado on toast, mushrooms, tomatoes and sausages. All Worked Up is the bigger breakfast, replacing sausages by beans and hash browns. Sweetcorn fritters come with avo, tomatoes and mango chilli sauce. Sweet potato and kale fritters are served with red pepper sauce, hummus and salad. Pancakes include seasonal fruit, coconut yogurt and maple syrup.

For something lighter around £6 have toast topped with avo, mushrooms, smashed banana and syrup, scrambled tofu or baked beans. Or porridge with either mixed berry and chocolate, peanut butter, or banana and syrup.

Grab and grow sandwiches £4-£5 such as Marmite and cheese toastie, BBQ jackfruit with mushroom and cheese, or pesto with tomato and cheese toastie.

Cakes and cookies £2-£3.20 incldue oat chip cookie, banana bread, choc chip banana bread.

Cold drinks £3-£4 include pressed juices, kombucha and cans.

They roast their own coffee £2-£3.80 served with Minor Figures oat milk from Hackney, or you can have almond or coconut milk. Choose from espresso, cortado, flat white, cappuccino, latte, mocca, hot choc, chai or dirty chai or turmeric latte. And tea of course, this is Britain. Add CBD oil £1.20.

Event space downstairs. Kids' section with toys and books. Dogs welcome. Deliveroo, Just Eats.

SUNDAY
@blankbrixton

BRIXTON

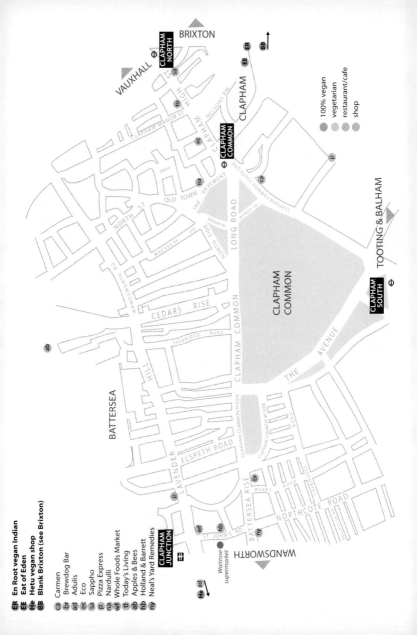

ER En Root vegan Indian
EE Eat of Eden
He Hetu vegan shop
BB Blank Brixton (see Brixton)

ca Carmen
br Brewdog Bar
ad Adulis
ec Eco
sa Sappho
p Pizza Express
na Nardulli
wf Whole Foods Market
tl Today's Living
ab Apples & Bees
hb Holland & Barrett
ny Neal's Yard Remedies

100% vegan
vegetarian
restaurant/cafe
shop

BRIXTON

VAUXHALL

CLAPHAM NORTH

CLAPHAM COMMON

CLAPHAM

CLAPHAM SOUTH

CLAPHAM COMMON

TOOTING & BALHAM

BATTERSEA

CLAPHAM JUNCTION

WANDSWORTH

Waitrose supermarket

CLAPHAM MANOR ST

NELSONS RW

CLAPHAM COMMON SOUTH SIDE

OLD TOWN

THE PAVEMENT

NORTH ST

MACAULAY RD

NORTH SIDE

WANDSWORTH RD

LONG ROAD

CLAPHAM COMMON N SIDE

CLAPHAM COMMON W SIDE

CEDARS RISE

TAYBRIDGE ROAD

CLAPHAM COMMON

THE AVENUE

HILL

LAVENDER

ELSPETH ROAD

BATTERSEA RISE

WEBBS ROAD

NORTHCOTE ROAD

ST JOHN'S RD

CLAPHAM

& Battersea

Battersea (around Clapham Junction station) and Clapham (towards Clapham Common station) are well endowed with green open spaces, the Omnibus and Bread & Roses theatres, and the Clapham Picturehouse independent art house cinema showing foreign, cult and classic movies with a funky bar.

There are various vegan-friendly eateries and stacks of wholefood stores, including a completely vegan one.

New in 2019 are a pair of adjacent vegan cafes on the right side of the map. **En Root** vegan Indian is brilliant for take-aways and delivery. Next door is **Eat of Eden**, the new branch of the Caribbean cafe at the back of Brixton Market. A bit further along Acre Lane towards Brixton is **Blank Brixton** vegan cafe, see the Brixton chapter.

Hetu was London's very first zero-single-use-packaging vegan shop where you fill up bags and jars with produce. If you don't have any containers with you, they have some in the store. We especially like the Mylkman plant milks in glass bottles - no more Tetrapaks!

Today's Living is the long established and well-stocked independent wholefood store by Clapham Common. **Apples & Bees** is an independent health food shop towards the river.

For wholefood supermarkets, there is a **Whole Foods Market** with a café and juice bar. In adjoining areas you can find **Planet Organic** in Wandsworth (see Putney & Wandsworth chapter), and down in Balham (see Tooting) is a branch of **As Nature Intended**.

Eco is a regular pizza restaurant that really likes vegans and can serve a vegan calzone on request. **Carmen** is a fun tapas bar with plenty of vegan options. We really like **Sappho Meze Bar** for home cooked Greek dishes and a relaxing atmosphere. **Adulis** Ethiopian is great for eating with your fingers. Hipster craft beer monsters should head for **Brewdog**, which also does some vegan fun food.

Not far from Clapham is Brixton (previous chapter), with its indoor markets that have many vegan cafes, and other bigger vegan places nearby including a 100% vegan food pub. Or catch a bus down to new veggie hotspot Tooting for its many vegetarian Indian shops and restaurants and some new vegan eateries, or head to **Wicked Vegan** in Balham.

Eat of Eden
Vegan cafe

☛ 6 Ascot Parade, Clapham Park Road,
SW4 7EY (corner Bedford Road)

☏ 020 7737 7566 (Brixton)

🕐 M 11.00-18.00, Tu-Su 11.00-22.00

⊖ Clapham North, Clapham Common

↖ eatofeden.co.uk
instagram.com/eatofeden

Their first branch is at the back of Brixton
Market, this new one opened in 2019.
Healthy Ital food and plenty to choose from.

The platter for £12.95 gets you 8 items
including salad, for two people £22.50.
Choose from chickpea curry, pumpkin curry,
lentil stew, ackee, callaloo, quinoa, rice,
bulgur, wheat, plantain, macaroni pie,
wheat meat, fried dumplings, seaweed
fritters, salad. Take-away version large (6
items) £9.95, small (4 items) £7.50.

Curry, stew or ackee portion £5, with a
grain, side and salad £8.95. Burger £4.95,
with sweet potato fries and salad £7.75.
Wraps £4.80, with fries and salad £7.50.
Callaloo, dal or veg patties £2.20.

Sides £1.50-£4.50 include plantain, fritters,
dumplings, callaloo, macaroni pie, quinoa,
bulgur, African rice, red rice, salads.

Cakes £4-£4.95 such as almond, banana
walnut, cocoa orange, raw chocolate or
lemon torte, coconut ginger cookie, apple
crumble. Ice cream £1.75, 2 scoops £3.

Home-made juice drinks, fresh juices,
smoothies, punches £3.50-£4.95. Teas
£1.95 include regular, green, moringa,
sorrel, matcha, sour sop, echinacea,
liquorice. Coffee, latte, hot choc £2-£2.95.
This branch also has wine, beer and
cocktails.

EAT of EDEN
-VEGAN CUISINE-

En Root

Vegan Indian fusion restaurant & take-awayt

- 📍 5 Ascot Parade, Clapham Park Road, SW4 7EY (corner Bedford Road)
- 📞 020 8001 6603
- 🕐 Th-Tu 12.00-22.00, W closed
- 🚇 Clapham Common, Clapham North
- 🔗 enrootldn.co.uk/ourroots (menu)
  facebook.com/enrootldn
  instagram.com/enrootldn

Indian food with no dairy anywhere, including the naan, lassi and chai! They started with a popup in Herne Hill in 2016, then a vegan food van in 2017 which is still touring festivals, and added this restaurant and take-away May 2019.

Small bites £3-£4 include 4 pani puri filled with sweet potato, red onion chickpeas and date tamarind chutney (8 for £5); dal and avocado crumpet; power porridge with banana, cacao, chia and coconut.

Mains £6-£10 feature **Raja Wrap** with rainbow salad, refried Daily Dal, bhajia falafel and avocado; **En Root Select** mix and match goodness plate with golden basmati rice, Curry inna Hurry and Daily Dal served with rainbow salad, avocado and bhajia falafel; **Don Dada Platter** (bestseller) is the En Root Select upgraded with two pani puri, a paratha and root veg; **Hearty Root Salad** with a dollop of Daily Dal, bhaji falafel, avocado and sunflower seeds; **Naanza** naan bread topped with veg and roast roots.

Extras £2 include paratha, naan, avocado, poppadum with chutneys.

Cake of the day £3 such as banana and carrot or chai lemon drizzle; Mango lassi cheesecake £4 has a raw oat and coconut based. Energy balls £1.50, 4 for £5.

Drinks £1.50-£4 include Rubicon street drinks, ginger beer, green smoothie, coconut water, coconut creamed mango lassi with cardamon, chai with oats and banana, cacao chai; moringa, rooibus, Yorkshire or peppermint tea.

Call directly for collection or local delivery.

Hetu
Vegan zero waste store

- 201 St Johns Hill SW11 1TH
- 07391 700816
- M closed, Tu-Th 11.00-19.00, F-Su 11.00-17.00, Sa-Su 11.00-17.00
- Clapham Junction
- hetu.co.uk
  facebook.com/hetu.vegan.zero.
  waste

London's beautiful and bright, pioneering, vegan, zero waste store is on a mission to change the world with one of the most powerful tools at our disposal, our buying power. They offer sustainable household items and wholefoods without unnecessary single-use packaging. Even their furniture, equipment, decorations and plants (repotted in recycled food jars and cans) are secondhand, and wall paint is non-toxic. Cardboard boxes that food arrives in bulk in are picked up by a company that returns them to the suppliers.

Most of the food is kept in glass jars or tin containers, and you scoop the quantity you need and weight it.

Wholefoods include arborio, brown, wild and jasmine rice; British quinoa, red quinoa, wholemeal penne, fusilli with turmeric, hemp fusilli, wholemeal and white couscous; black turtle beans, red kidney beans, butter beans, cannellini, soya, chickpeas, green and red split peas, brown lentils; pumpkin, hemp, sunflower and mixed seeds; hazelnuts, pecans, walnuts, pine kernels, peanuts, chocolate covered almonds and mulberries, goji berries; popcorn; dried fruits such as banana or mango chips, figs, dates, chopped apricot, fruity jerky, juice pulp crackers, raw cacao nibs; arrowroot, soya chunks, bicarbonate and baking

Carmen

powder, maca.

Herbs and spices include mixed spice, onion or garlic powder, ginger, chilli, sage, nutmeg, cinnamon, fennel seeds, thyme, cumin, parsley, oregano, basil, turmeric.

Organic almond, hazelnut or cashew butter. Tamari. Apple cyder vinegar. Kitty's kombucha brewed in oak barrels. Mylkman plant milks in returnable glass bottles feature almond, oat, cashew, choc oat. Vegan cheese. Dairy-free yogurt. Loose tea and coffee are coming soon.

Fruit and veg. Energy bliss balls.

Organic shampoo, soap bars, liquid soap, toothpaste. Golden turmeric skin cream from Suneeta London. Earthconsciousuk lavender and citrus deodorant. A bigger section of "refill" beauty is coming soon.

Greenscent refill such as multi surface spray, washing up liquid, laundry liquid and conditioner.

They encourage you to bring your own containers which can be sterilised free of charge, but if you forget you can buy empty bottles for refilling and small and medium glass jars. No bags are provided.

Eco items on sale include reusable produce bags, cloths, toothbrushes, bottles, KeepCup coffee cups amd Who Gives A Crap toilet paper.

Carmen
Omnivorous Spanish tapas restaurant

- 6 Clapham Common South SW4 7AA
- 020 7622 6848
- M-Th 18.00-24.00, F-Sa 12.00-24.00, Su 12.00-23.30
- Clapham Common
- carmenbardetapas.com

Andalusian-style tapas restaurant with Spanish staff. If you've ever been to Spain you will think you are there again. Almost half the menu is vegetarian and half of that is vegan or vegan-option. Ask for the separate version of the menu showing what is vegan and vegan option, wheat-free, or has nuts. There are warm yellow walls, covered with Spanish pictures, posters and a few farm tools. Wooden tables, discrete lighting, long bar. Don't wait for a table, you can eat at the bar like in Spain.

Vegan tapas and salads £5.50-£6.50 include patatas bravas, lentil or chickpea casserole, garlic mushrooms and asparagus. Pimientos de padrón (on main menu only) are mixed mild and hot peppers, so you can have fun with your friends trying to guess which ones are hot.

One vegan dessert £6, pears cooked in red wine and cinnamon without the cream.

Wine from £6 medium glass, carafe £12.50, bottle £16.50. Beers £3.20-£3.80. Sangria glass £5, jug £17.50. Soft drinks £2.20. Tea/coffee £1.90-£4. No soya milk. They have a restaurant licence therefore alcohol cannot be served without food.

They love children, one high chair. 10% service charge for parties of 6+. No drinking without food.

SOUTH

CLAPHAM

509

Eco
Omnivorous pizza restaurant

- 162 Clapham High Stree SW4 7UG
- 020 7978 1108
- M-Th 12.00-23.00, F 12.00-23.30, Sa-Su 09.00-23.30
- Clapham Common
- ecorestaurants.com
  facebook.com/EcoRestaurant

The best pizzas are vegetarian according to the manager, and the pizza base is dairy free. This is a pizza place with panache, smartly decorated in light wood and sculptured steel. Allow £4.75-£9.95 for a pizza. The calzone (vegan on request) is great with pepper and aubergine. The garlic bread is done in olive oil not butter. Salads £2.30-£3.95, main course £8.75-£14.95.

They also serve breakfast on weekends and bank holidays from 9.00 to 12.00. Totally vegan breakfast £7.95 with smashed avocado, courgette frittes, vine tomatoes, field mushrooms, smokey house beans and grilled sourdough.

£13.95-£21.95 for a bottle of wine or £3.95 a glass. Gets pretty crowded so reservations advisable and you are encouraged to leave after an hour and a half, but great fun if you've got the energy. Wifi and highchairs.

Brewdog Clapham Junction
Bar with vegan beers

- 11- 13 Battersea Rise, Battersea SW11 1HG
- 020 72 236 346
- M-Th 16.00-24.00, F-Sa 12.00-24.00, Su 12.00-23.30
- Clapham Junction BR
- brewdog.com/bars/uk /clapham-junction
  facebook.com/brewdogclapham

The first south London branch of the national chain with lots of vegan craft beers. They also do sourdough pizzas, and the Hero £9.50 is vegan with wild mushrooms, courgette ribbons, pine nuts, smashed Nupoli tomatoes and fresh rosemary. Children welcome till 8pm. Board games.

Nardulli
Italian ice-cream parlour

- 29 The Pavement SW4 0JE
- 020 7720 5331
- Winter mid Oct to mid Mar M-F 14.00-21.00, Sa-Su 11.00-22.00. Summer M -Th12.00- 22.00, F 12.00-23.00, Sa 11.00-23.00, Su 11.00-22.00.
- Clapham Common
- nardulli.co.uk

Italian gelateria by the east side of the Common, with many vegan sorbets like apricot, banana, blackcurrant, blueberry, lemon, mango, mandarin, passion fruit, peach, raspberry, strawberry and chocolate flavours.

Sappho Meze Bar
Omnivorous Greek restaurant

- 9 Clapham High Street SW4 7TS
- 020 7498 9009
- M-Sa 17.30-23.30, Su closed
- Clapham North
- facebook.com/smbclapham

This restaurant is owned by a Greek chap called Louis who, apart from being very wise and knowledgeable, is the chef, waiter and entertainer and has been running the place for over 20 years. He shops for ingredients in the morning, prepares in the afternoon and serves in the evening. I'ts a big place with 40 seats and an open kitchen. There is no menu, you just say you are vegan and he keeps on bringing food.

At least 8 mezze starters £5.50 including olives, koulouri sesame bread, hummus, fava beans, fassoles beans, mushrooms, spinach and chickpeas. Soup £7. At least 4 meze main courses £8.50 from salads, vegan moussaka, vegetable stew, rice dishes and potatoes dishes. Both courses £12.50.

Glass of wine £3.50, bottle £13.50. Beer £3, 1 litre £5. Greek brandy, ouzo and liqueur £4.50. Soft drinks £1.50 and water £2.50. Tea and coffee £1.50.

High chairs, wifi. He keeps the prices low so please pay cash.

Apples & Bees
Health food shop

- 258 Battersea Park Rd SW11 3BP
- 020 7223 3330
- M-F 9.00-18.00, Sa 9.30-17.00, Su closed
- Clapham Junction
- applesandbees.com
  Facebook Apples & Bees

Independent family run shop with lots of organic, vegan, gluten-free and raw products.

Fridges full of vegan cheeses, yogurt, sausages, burgers, seitan, tempeh, yogurts. Also ice cream.

Bodycare by REN, Dr Hauschka, Green People, Weleda. Cleaning products.

Supplements by Biocare, Higher Nature, Nature's Plus, Quest, Solgar, Terranova, Viridian. Sports nutrition.

Dogs welcome. Mail order from website.

Today's Living
Health food shop

- 92 Clapham High Street SW4 7UL
- (020 7622 1772
- M-Sa 9.00-18.30, Su/BH closed
- Clapham Common
- www.todaysliving.co.uk

Well stocked health food store that won the Annual Industry Awards for best new health food shop in 2004. Plenty of vegan, organic and gluten-free food. Chilled food includes Taifun, Tofurky, tempeh, vegan bacon, Violife, Sheese, Tofutti, oat, soya and almond cooking cream, Isola Bio rice or millet cream, Vegenaise. In the freezer are meat substitutes and vegan ice-cream by Booja-Booja and Coyo.

Lots of organic wholefoods. Meridian spreads. Treats from Raw Chocolate Pie company, Seed & Bean, Ombar, Doisy & Dam, and Pulsin protein bars.

Skincare by Green People, Sukin, Weleda, Dr Haushka.

Supplements including Biocare and Viridian, lots of Bioforce, body building products. Natural and homeopathic remedies, Bach flower, aromatherapy oils.

Ecover cleaning and washing products.

Neal's Yard Remedies, Clapham
Herbs and bodycare

- 6 Northcote Road, SW11 1NT
- (020 7223 7141
- M-F 10.00-20.00, Sa 9.00-18.00, Su 11.00-17.00
- Clapham Junction BR
- nealsyardremedies.com

Mostly organic, lots of Fairtrade. Herbs and spices by weight, organic teas, organic toiletries, natural remedies. Also therapy rooms offering healing treatments. Supplements by Viridian.

Holland & Barrett, Clapham
Health food shop

- 51-53 St Johns Road SW11 1QW
- (020 7924 1028
- M-F 08.30-19.00, Sa 08.30-18.30, Su 11.00-17.00
- Clapham Junction BR

Fridge with VBites, Cheatin, Tofurky, Vegout, Vegi Deli, Dragonfly tofu, VBites, Cheezly, Sheese, Violife. Freezer with Fry's, Vegideli, VBites pizza, Booja Booja.

Whole Foods Market, Clapham Junction
Natural & organic wholefood supermarket, deli & omnivorous cafe

---

🚩 305-311 Lavender Hill, Battersea SW11 1LN

📞 020 7585 1488

🕐 M-Sa 07.30-21.30, Su 11.00-17.00

⊖ Clapham Junction BR, Clapham Common then bus

↖ wholefoodsmarket.co.uk

Big wholefood supermarket with a cafe and a huge range of organic produce, fruit and veg. Take-away food such as Hoxton Beach burrits and falafels, Laura's Idea pots, salads, mezze, babaganoush, olives, tapenade, salsa, guacamole. Lots of gourmet, artisan and specialist foods including fresh bread, gluten/wheat free foods. Organic and vegan wines.

Café, juice bar and deli with seats and tables. Heaps of hot and cold food, some made daily by the in-store chefs. Hot food £1.91/ 100g, salad bar £1.59/100g. Cold or hot lunch deal, one main and two sides such as brown rice, onion bhajia, Asian cucumber salad, eat in or take away £6, the cold one is cheaper as a take-away £5.49. Soup large £3.99 or small £2.99, with a roll 50p. Tostada, burrito and nachos with salad £4.00-£5.95.

Sandwiches made daily £2.99-£5.99.

Coffee £2.00-3.50, Pukka tea £1.50-£3, matcha and iced matcha latte £2.50, iced matcha tea and matcha cucumber water £2. Juices and smoothies £1.99.

The natural remedies and bodycare section has some qualified naturopaths. Health, body and skincare includes Avalon, Lavere, Dr Bronner, Sukin, Nourish, Akin, Pai, Dr Hauschka, Ren, Weleda, Faith in Nature, Jason, Urtekram, Green People. Also aromatherapy, herbs, probiotics, flax oil and supplements such as Viridian, Pukka, High Nature, Nature's Plus, Terranova and Lambeth. And a section for babies with Lavera, Green People, Organic Babies, Weleda and Earth Friendly Baby. There is always a staff member who can advise you. On Saturdays there are often visiting masseuses who offer massage in store.

You can order anything that is not in store but is in the main branch in High Street Kensington. Customer toilet.

CROYDON

and Thornton Heath and Sutton

Croydon is easily the best outer London borough for variety and quality of vegan eating out, at any time of day.

The **Boxpark** mall is outstanding for meeting up with friends. You and your mates can get food and drink from a big range of places at great prices, then all sit together at the shared tables. Top of the list has to be the very filling doners at 100% vegan kebab shop **What the Pitta**.

In town head straight for **Follow Burger** fast food cafe just off Surrey Street. For a sit-down meal, the top places are **Coffee Shotter** vegetarian cafe and **Saravanaa Bhavan** vegetarian Indian restaurant.

We also love **Smoothbean!** cafe which has a mighty five vegan cakes.

Pick of the pubs is **The Oval Tavern**, a real ale pub with a landlady who goes out of her way to provide vegan grub. There is a beer garden, and kids' activities on Saturdays.

Chain restaurants **Pizza Express** and **Zizzi** now offer vegan cheese.

Coughlans bakeries all over the borough specalise in vegan cakes and are constantly expanding their range. For a romantic gift, head to **Cozy Glow** vegan candles and gifts shop in Coulsdon.

Thanks to local vegans Tracey Hague, Scarlet Hughes, Shivani Parikh, Hannah Thrush and Maeve Tomlinson for recommending places here.

What The Pitta
Vegan kebab take-away

- ☛ Boxpark unit 8, 99 George Street, Croydon CR0 1LD
- ☎ 07912 860293
- 🕑 Su-W 11.30-21.00, Th-Sa 11.30-23.00
- ⊖ East Croydon
- ➤ whatthepitta.com facebook.com/whatthepitta

London's first vegan doner kebab take-away started in Shoreditch then opened their second branch here, with the third opening in 2018 in Camden. Fantastic. Yet another opens in Brighton in November 2018.

Huge doner £7.95 contains an impressive 37g of protein, mainly in the form of spiced soya chunks, and comes either in a wrap, or as a salad box on couscous, with hummus, tzatziki, salads and chilli. Or have it as doner and chips with mixed salad.

Lamacun Turkish pizza also £7.95, a round, thin piece of dough topped with minced soya, minced veg, herbs and spices.

For dessert £2.50 you can have vegan baklava, or artisan ice cream £3.50 in salted caramel, mint choc chip or chocolate.

£10 meal deal gets you any doner main or pizza plus a baklava and a cold drink. £12 deal adds chips.

If you're not into doner, the mixed meze £10.95 with hummus, tzatziki, mixed olives, two freshly made breads.

Organic cold drinks include elderflower, ginger, cola, lemonade, still or sparkling water.

Ubereats, Deliveroo.

Also in Boxpark:

Chilango does Mexican burritos, tacos, salads.

Greek on the Street does lunchtime specials till 3pm for £5.50, falafel with three sides from gigantes beans with tomato sauce, rice, new potatoes, chips, couscous salad, mixed leaf salad.

Indigo does Indian street food including samosas, chaat, dosas, biryani, dal, aubergine curry. Mains £9.

Oatopia does coconut porridge, oat and bean burger, energy balls, flapjacks and smoothies.

YO! Sushi has tofu katsu curry.

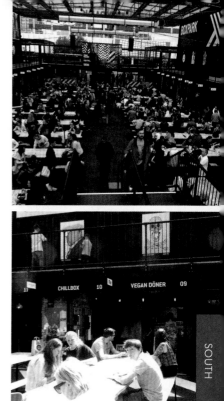

SOUTH

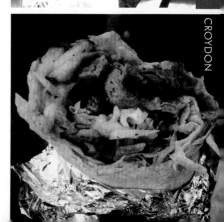

CROYDON

RAVeOLI
LUNCH BOX

5 × RAVeOLI of the day
+
Garlic & Evo Oil Bread
+
1 Side

£ 5

"Doble it Up" +£3

516

Raveoli

Vegan Italian take-away & restaurant

- Boxpark unit 39, 99 George Street, Croydon CR0 1LD
- 020 3873 2761
- M-Th 12.00-22.00, F-Sa 12.00-23.00, Su 12.00-21.30
- East Croydon
- raveoli.co.uk
  facebook.com/raveoliuk
  instagram.com/raveoliuk

Opened late 2018 in Croydon Boxpark. Watch ravioli (squares of filled pasta) made in front of you in eight flavours to eat at the shared tables, have it delivered by Deliveroo, or buy raw to cook at home.

Step 1: choose from seven kinds of ravioli, some of them gluten-free, £10.95-£15.95: Mamma Patata with potato, rosemary, onion, EVO oil, seasonings; Mushroom and Cheese; Zucotti Pumpkin with almonds, mustard, nutmeg, breadcrumbs; Spinach and smoked tofu with nutritional yeast, potato flakes; Mafia e Mandolino with capers, olives, cherry tomato, almonds, sundried tomato, basil, sugar; Bolognesi with seitan, soya meat, nutritional yeast, lentils, garlic, nutmeg; Porcini Mushrooms & Truffle with mixed mushrooms, potato flakes, truffle sauce. Also two gluten-free £10.45, either Rustic ravioli with creamy sauce and mushrooms, or potato gnocchi in tomato and basil sauce.

Step 2: choose a sauce from green pesto, tomato & basil, sage & E.V.olive oil, white cream and pepper.

Step 3: add toppings 50p each from chilli paste, vegan cheese shavings, smoked tofu shavings, truffle oil.

Step 4: choose sides £4-£4.50 such as rosemary and garlic roasted potatoes, sautéed mushrooms, chickpeas in tomato sauce, Italian mixed salad.

There are Deliveroo starters £3-£4.50 such as marinated olives, bruschetta, garlic bread with tomato and mushrooms or aubergines

Cakes £4.50 include chocolate, forest fruit, Sicilian lemon, and tiramisù.

There are deals in Boxpark such as lunchbox ravioli of the day with garlic bread and side £7, £5 deal five ravioli of the day plus garlic bread, or double up the box for £3 extra.

Also artisan Italian coffee and fine Italian wines.

Follow Burger
Vegan fast food cafe

- 1 Matthews Yard, Croydon CR0 1FF (just off Surrey Street)
-
- W-Th 12.00-21.00, F-Sa 12.00-22.00, Su 12.00-18.00, M-Tu closed
- West Croydon, East Croydon
- instagram.com.followburgergrill

The Green Grill started a burger stall in Surrey Street Market, then set up in Mathews Yard cultural and community hub, and in 2019 handed the business on to the Follow Burger girls.

Moving Mountains burgers, cheeseburger, double burger, Mexican style with guac, salsa and jalapeños; Bacon Supreme with bacon, hash brown, onion ring and crispy onions; The Big Boy triple cheeseburger, an outrageous 13cm thick.

Milkshakes such as chocolate or strawberry shortcake.

Coffee Shotter
Vegetarian cafe & coffee shop

- 71 High Street (south end), Croydon CR0 1QE
- M-F 08.00-17.00, Sa 10.00-15.00, Su closed
- West Croydon, East Croydon
- coffeeshotter.co.uk
  instagram.com/coffeeshotter

An independent coffee shop opened March 2018, providing stacks of vegan food from Laura's Idea such as breakfast pots, light spicy soba noodles, wild rice salads, gluten-free and vegan sandwiches, to indulgent tofu cheesecake and doughnuts (be sure to get the syringe filling!).

Ethically sourced coffee from Horsham Coffee Roasters, accompanied by Bonsoy and Oatly, the kings of plant milks. Suki Tea teas and herbal teas. Free wifi.

Saravanaa Bhavan, Croydon
Vegetarian South Indian restaurant

- 18 George Street, Croydon CR0 1PA
- 020 8286 9940
- M-Su 11.00-22.00
- George Street tram
- saravanabhavanlondon.co.uk

Opened in 2017 with about 100 seats and huge menu. See Tooting for menu. No vegan desserts and only managerial staff appear to be sure about what is and is not vegan.

Smoothbean!
Omnivorous coffee shop and juice bar

- 2-3 Dingwall Road, Croydon CR0 2NA
- 020 3754 2412
- M-F 07.30-15.30, Sa-Su/BH closed
- East Croydon
- smoothbean.co.uk
  facebook.com/Smoothbean23

An omnivorous restaurant near the Boxpark that makes a real effort and clearly marks vegan food on the menu. They usually have a vegan sandwich, a salad, a Buddha bowl £7.50 such as Thai coconut, two vegan mains such as beetroot and spinach lasagne £7.50 and Goan veg curry with wholegrain basmati rice £6.90. The soup is also vegan 3 out of 4 weeks, such as sweet pepper soup £5.30 with toasted artisan sourdough or multigrain bread. Greek chopped salad with chickpeas and olives £6.70 full plate, small plate £4.79, portion with sandwich £3.

An impressive five vegan cakes and five types of plant milk, so you could pop in here for weekday afternoon dessert after doing lunch in the Boxpark. Cakes include apple and maple, coffee and walnut, Glynde fruit, vegan bites.

Juices and smoothies are freshly made to order. Organic coffee beans from Peru roasted locally by Volcano Coffee Works. Eleakat loose leaf teas.

Wine and craft beers from 12.00. Tables inside and out. Free wifi.

The Oval Tavern
Omnivorous food and real ale pub

- 131 Oval Road, Croydon CR0 6BR
- 020 8686 6023
- M-Th 12.00-23.00, F-Sa 12.00-24.00, Su 12.00-22.30
- East Croydon
- theovaltavern.co.uk
  facebook.com/theovalcroydon

Superb real ale pub with a walled beer garden and a landlady, Esther Sutton, who has introduced vegan dishes like all day cooked breakfast £9.95, avo toast £4.75, chocolate chili and nachos £8.25, falafel salad £7.75, ratatouille £6.95, African sweet potato stew £8.25, loaded chips £3 with chilli £2, Sunday nut roast £13 with all the trimmings. Food served 12.00-21.00, from 13.00 on Sunday.

Events most days such as evening live music from jazz to ska to rock, DJs, Wednesday quiz. Well-behaved children welcome till 9pm. Saturdays 1-3pm stories and crafts for children aged 3-8, entry by donation, see Facebook for this week's theme. Dogs on a lead welcome. "Cats can come and go as they please." Books, newspapers, board games.

Wagamama, Croydon
Omnivorous Japanese chain restaurant

- 4 Park Lane, Croydon CR0 1JA
- 020 8760 9260
- M-Th 11.00-22.00, F-Sa 11.00-23.00, Su 12.00-22.00
- East Croydon
- wagamama.com

Baby changing, disabled toilet, braille men.

Pizza Express, Croydon
Omnivorous pizza chain restaurant

- 48 George Street, Croydon CR0 1PD
- 020 8681 2550
- 11.30-22.30, Tu-Sa 11.30-23.00, Su 11.30-22.00
- East Croydon, West Croydon

- Unit 2, Valley Leisure Park CR0 4YA
- 020 8686 2888
- M-Sa 11.30-23.00, Su 12.00-22.00
- Ampere Way tram stop
- pizzaexpress.co.uk

Both branches offer garden dining, baby facilities, disabled toilet. Vegan cheese.

Zizzi, Croydon
Omnivorous pizza chain restaurant

- 57 South End CR0 1BF
- 020 8649 8403
- M-Sa 11.30-23.00, Su 11.30-20.30
- South Croydon
- zizzi.co.uk

Also in Croydon:

Byte Cafe at 75-77 High Street CR0 1QW does sandwiches, salad, stew, cake and energy balls. Open M-F 07.30-16.30.

Parklife Cafe in Lloyd Park does a "veganista" breakfast, smoothies, and a vegan cake such as carrot or chocolate. M-Su 08.30-17.30.

Coughlans Bakery
Omnivorous bakery & take-away chain

🏠 220 High Street, Croydon CR0 1NE
📞 020 8688 6020
🕐 M-Sa 07.30-16.30, Su closed

🏠 502 London Road, Croydon CR7 7HQ
📞 020 8684 6433
🕐 M-Sa 07.30-17.30, Su 10.00-15.00

🏠 259 Brighton Road, South Croydon, CR2 6EL
📞 020 3302 0102
🕐 M-Sa 07.00-17.00. Su 9.30-15.00
🔗 coughlansbakery.co.uk
facebook.com/coughlansbakery

This family owned bakery chain of 24 shops in the Croydon area, founded 1937, are really keen to attract vegans. Throughout 2019 they kept adding and adding vegan goodies to the vegan list on their website, which now scrolls across two computer screens or severl on your phone. They post photos of new vegan treats on our Facebook page *Vegetarian London* that supplements this book, "search this group" on Coughlans.

Loaves include wholemeal, farmhouse, bloomers, sandwich, baguettes, wholemeal, multi-seed, rolls, sourdough.

Approaching 30 cakes, slices, biscuits, buns, donuts, flapjacks, muffins, Danishes. And they make celebration cakes to order.

Lunches include several kinds of sausage rolls, sandwiches, sourdough toasties, pasties, soup, Wellington for 4.

Coffees with Oatly Barista or Alpro soya milk. Hot chocolate. Frozen gelato.

Party platters can be ordered for next day collection, with mini sausage rolls, savoury turnovers, sandwiches.

At Christmas they do gingerbread, mince pies, truffles, fruit cake, stollen.

Also in Addiscombe, Banstead, Beckenham, Caterham (two branches), Chessington, Chipstead, Coulsdon, Epsom, Forestdale, Godstone, Lingfield, Oxted, Purley, Reigate, Stoneleigh, Sutton, Wallington (two branches), Warlingham, West Wickham.

Holland & Barrett, Croydon
Health food shop

🏠 1098-99 The Mall, Whitgift Centre CR0 1UU
📞 020 8681 5174
🕐 M-W 9.00-18.30, Th 9.00-20.00, F-Sa 9.00-19.00, Su 10.30-17.00

Fridge and freezer.

🏠 53-54 North End CR0 1TG
📞 020 3417 2182
🕐 M-Sa 08.30-19.00, Su 10.00-18.00

Fridge and freezer.

Lush, Croydon
Cruelty-free cosmetics

- 58 North End, Croydon CR0 1UG
- 020-8681 7332
- M-W, F-Sa 10.00-18.00, Th 10.00-18.30, Su 11.00-17.00
- West Croydon
- lush.co.uk

Hand-made cosmetics, most of them vegan.

Cozy Glow
Vegan candle shop

- 160 Brighton Rd, Coulsdon CR5 2NE (near Aldi)
- 020 3697 0273
- M-Sa 10.00-17.00, Su closed
- ,Coulsdon Town BR
- cozyglowcandles.com
  facebook.com/CozyGlow

Pals Ashley Cooke and Kristian Matthews were disappointed with the standard of candles in shops, so started designing, making and selling vegan organic scented candles from soy wax, burning for up to 50% longer at a lower temperature than paraffin and hence without giving off nasty soot and carcinogenic chemicals. There are over 50 scents in 6.5oz and 13oz sizes in jars, including aromatherapy favourites, foods, and seasonal ones. Sea Breeze is the most popular in the shop, and Coconut online.

Also reed diffusers, room sprays, 16 types of bath bombs, face masks, body washes, jute gift bags, home décor and gifts.

Check out the range in their online shop and at amazon.co.uk/cozyglow

Croydon Vegans & Vegetarians
Local social group

- facebook.com/groups/
  CroydonVegetariansVegans

One of the oldest vegetarian groups in the UK, established in 1886. Follow the Facebook page for latest news about eating out vegan.

Croydon Vegan Outreach
Local outreach group

- Thursday 13.00-17.00
- croydonveganoutreach.com
  Facebook Croydon Vegan Outreach

Website to help anyone transitioning to a vegan lifestyle. The Croydon Vegan Outreach Team are on the High Street every Thursday afternoon around Holland & Barrett, with posters and leaflets and laptops, speaking with the public. Check the Facebook page for a link to this week's outreach event page.

Scarlet's Nutrition
Vegan nutritionist

- scarletthughes.net
  scarletsnutrition@gmail.com

Local vegan nutritionist Scarlet Hughes holds a BSc in Nutrition Sciences. Services include nutrition consultations, interviews, presentations, nutrional analyses and labelling.

THORNTON HEATH

Santok Maa's
Indian vegetarian restaurant

- 848 London Road, Thornton Heath CR7 7PA
- 020 8665 0626
- Th-Tu 12.00-19.30 last entry, W closed
- Thornton Heath BR, Norbury BR

North and South Indian dining and take-away, with some spicy Chinese dishes like stir-fries. Nearly 100 dishes of which nearly 90% are vegan.

Starters average £3.50, main courses £4.50, rice £2.50.Desserts include vegan jelabi, ladoo, and sometimes ice-cream £3.

Bring your own wine, £1.50 per person corkage. Children welcome, high chairs. Outside catering.

Swad
Indian vegetarian take-away

- 850 London Road, Thornton Heath CR7 7PA
- 020 8683 3344
- Tu-Sa 10.30-19.00, Su 10.30-17.00, M closed
- Thornton Heath BR, Norbury BR
- swadsweets.com
  facebook.com/swadsweets

On the main London to Brighton Road, previously a restaurant, now take-away tiffin service. Take-away tiffin £4 for four items: rice, dal, curry and three rotis. They can make vegan options on request, although quite a few dishes are vegan already.

They provide food for other restaurants in the area and also do wedding and outdoor catering.

SOUTH

London Borough of SUTTON

Pizza Express has branches in Sutton, Wallington, and Worcester Park.

Some options at The Hope in **Carshalton** on West Street. Sutton's first community run pub. Has won Sutton & Croydon CAMRA awards, real ale. Alternatively, **The Sun** at 4 North Street has a vegan menu.

In Sutton, Zizzi Italian restaurant at 13 High Street, Sutton SM1 1DF has vegan cheese. **Heen's** Chinese restaurant, opposite Sutton station on Mulgrave Road, has many vegan dishes £6-£9.50

In **Cheam** try Chinese and Thai restaurants for vegan options.

Sutton Community Farm
Veg box scheme

- 40a Telegraph Track, Wallington SM6 0SH
- 07722 156097
- suttoncommunityfarm.org.uk

Worcester Park Vegans
Local social group

- Thursday 13.00-17.00
- Facebook Worcester Park Vegans

Monthly meetings.

CRYSTAL PALACE

AOK
Vegetarian juice and salad bar

- 18 Church Road, Crystal Palace SE19 2ET
- 07397 115 211
- Tu-Sa 11.30-18.00, Su-M closed
- Crystal Palace
- ageoldknowledge.co.uk
  facebook.com/AgeOldKnowledge

Age Old Knowledge opened October 2018, a mostly vegan restaurant based on whole foods, yoga and Ayurveda.

Meals £3-£12 range from a pie or falafel through jackfruit in pitta to main course salads or pie and salad.

Snacks such as sweet potato crackers, pitted dates. Juices and activated nut milk smoothies £5. Deliveroo.

Return to Shashamane
Vegan world food stall

- 🪧 Crystal Palace Food Market, Haynes Lane SE19 3AP
- 📞 07714 512 208
- 🕐 Fortnightly Saturday 10.00-15.00
- ⊖ Crystal Palace
- ⚲ Facebook Return to Shashamane crystalpalacefoodmarket.co.uk

Vegan organic box £6, wrap £5, deli pot £4. Choose from kidney beans with cardamon seeds and parsley; chickpeas with wakame seaweed and mustard seeds; butter beans with basil, parsley and spring onions; quinoa with linseed, coconut and sunflower seeds; tabouleh or quinoa with sprouts, mint, basil and pomegranate; hummus; red cabbage with vegan mayo.

Also at this market **Afrikoko** vegan food from Benin.

Made From Plants
Vegan take-away, bakery and shop

- 🪧 120A Anerley Road, Crystal Palace SE19 2AN (corner Hamlet Rd)
- 📞 07850 356 434
- 🕐 Th-F 9.00-18.00, Sa-Su 11.00-17.00, M-W closed
- ⊖ Crystal Palace, Anerley
- ⚲ madefromplants.co.uk facebook.com/madefromplants instagram.com/madefromplantsldn

Vegan bakery and shop opened 2017, selling sweet and savoury baked goods, cakes, juices, shakes, hot drinks, and groceries. Load up here with treats to enjoy in Crystal Palace Park and at home, or salivate first over the photos on their social media.

Savouries feature sausage rolls, pesto stuffed crust pizza, No Chick in Pie.

Highlights of the sweet delights are orange and chocolate brioche, cinnamon buns, cookies, chocolate orange cupcakes, lemon drizzle cake, gluten-free Bakewell tarts, gluten-free salted caramel peanut butter truffles, sticky toffee bundt cake, cheesecake.

Tea, coffee £2, hot choc, chai £1.50-£2.50, with soya, almond or oat milk. Banana, peanut butter, chocolate mylkshake £3.

Groceries include fake meats, vegan cheeses such as Tyne Chease, and tofu.

10% off if you bring your own containers. Private catering orders and birthday cakes.

Planta Health, Crystal Palace
Health food shop

- 32 Westow Hill SE19 1RX
- 020-8761 3114
- M-F 9.30-19.00, Sa 9.30-18.00, Su 11.00-17.00
- Crystal Palace
- planta.co.uk

A nice and fairly well stocked store with wholefoods such as wholegrain bread and pasta, beans, sauces and seaweed. Soya alternatives, readymade meals, cereals, juices, ice-cream and chocolate. Organic products, skincare and washing products.

The wbsite is an online shop and lists bodycare by Barefoot Botanicals, Green People and Weleda. Supplements by Solgar, Lamberts and Viridian.

A therapy clinic is attached to the shop offering massage, osteopathy, Alexander technique acupuncture, hypnotherapy.

Deptford

& New Cross, Lewisham, Catford & Brockley

Deptford and adjacent areas to the west (New Cross) and south (Lewisham, Brockley, Catford) is an up and coming area. Like Dalston in north London, it's no longer dominated by betting shops, pound shops and greasy spoon caffs. There are new wholefood stores, lots of indie and veggie cafes, music pubs and even a vegetarian fast food pub. There is a strong anti-gentrification movement, and in keeping with its fiercely independent spirit and strong community ethos that demands to be respected, they even pushed out Subway - this is simply not the place to open a chain.

With 9,000 hungry students at Goldsmiths in New Cross, there's plenty of great value vegan food in the area. **The Full Nelson** vegetarian food pub on the main road serves up burgers, mac 'n' cheese and fiery seitan ribs with ale.

There's also great vegan pub food at **The Amersham Arms**.

Round the corner from The Full Nelson on Deptford High Street proper, head to the new **Hullabaloo** south Indian street food restaurant where you can stuff yourself silly for less than half the price of a central London restaurant. On the same street, **The Waiting Room** veggie cafe does tasty vegan treats like sausage rolls and cakes, and is also a right bargain.

Deptford Does Art is the only completely vegan place, a beautiful arty cafe with a bar that stays open till 10pm on exhibition nights, usually Friday or Saturday.

If you've just staggered out of an all night party on a Saturday morning, head for smoothies at **The Greenhouse**.

Another omni place we love is **The Bird's Nest** music pub, which oozes that Deptford community feel with its friendly party vibe at night, and does Sunday lunch vegan roasts.

The Full Nelson
Vegetarian food pub

- 47 Deptford Broadway SE8 4PH
- no phone
- Tu-Sa 16.00-23.00 (food till 21.45), Su 11.00-16.00, M closed
- Deptford Bridge DLR, New Cross
- facebook.com/thefullnelsondeptford
  instagram.com/thefullnelsondeptford

This pub is now owned by the same people as The Waiting Room. The bar and kitchen serve craft beer, cocktails and vegetarian junk food, all of which can be made vegan. Previously a hairdresser, the building is long and narrow, more like a European bar, with the bar along the right side, tables along the left wall, and the kitchen at the back.

Burgers £6 can come with BBQ sauce, spicy cheese, jalapenos and onion served on toasted brioche. Seitan "ribs", £6 or £8, are really meaty and come with fries and coleslaw. The macaroni cheese £4 is fairly bland, just like you remember from before you were a vegan, but when you add some pieces of ribs it's divine. Beer battered cauliflower £4 comes in sweet chilli BBQ glaze with lime and sesame seeds. Chicken flipper fries £4.50 are pieces of crispy fried "chicken" on more fries. Burger, beer and fries £10.

For dessert try Oreo speed wagon £2, double stuffed oreo deep fried in a cornmeal sweet batter and served with ice-cream.

Punk IPA draft ale £4.50 pint. Pitcher of beer £15. Cider £3. Cocktails £7, or two for £10 on Wednesday.

Look out for burger, beer and fries for £10.

The Amersham Arms
Pub with vegan kitchen

- 388 New Cross Road SE14 6TY
- 020 8469 1499
- Su-W 12.00-24.00,
  Th-Sa 12.00-03.00
- New Cross (opposite)
- theamershamarms.net/kitchen
  facebook.com/amersham.arms

6 vegan Sunday roasts in a traditional souf-east London pub! Yeah.

City of Seitan, who already supplied meat replacers to places in Deptford and New Cross such as The Full Nelson, The Waiting Room and the Bird's Nest pub, took over the kitchen at the Amersham Arms and turned it vegan, starting on Sundays with vegan roasts, then followed by a bigger choice all week.

British mains £11: seitan stake and Guinness pie, or chikken and leek pie, or Buff Wellington (mushroom, nuts, soy and cranberry); all served with roast potatoes veg, yorky pudding, cauliflower cheeze and red wine gravy. Also £11 jerk jackfruit cornbread pie, or BBQ seitain and jackfruit ribz, served with coconut mash, roast peppers, plantain, garlicky kale, and gravy.

Dessert of the week £4. Brewdog Punk IPA on tap.

10% student discount. Order at the bar. They host events including fortnightly comedy (with comedians you've seen on tv like vegan Sara Pascoe), live music, theatre and DJs. The events space at the back can hold an audience of 300. Art gallery space upstairs. Outdoor seating.

On call Ambulance Staff always go to the front of the queue!

The Waiting Room
Vegetarian cafe

- 134 Deptford High Street SE8 3PQ
- 020 3601 0100
  M-F 08.00-16.00, Sa 9.00-17.00, Su/BH 10.00-16.00
- Deptford BR (opposite), Deptford Bridge DLR (5 mins), New Cross (10 mins), Bus 53, 453, 47, 199, 188
- Facebook The Waiting Room instagram.com/waitingroomse8

A few minutes walk in between studenty New Cross and touristy Greenwich, Deptford High Street is proper south London.

If they ever make a veggie version of the Hairy Bikers, this is it, a great little cafe run by tattooed and bearded Alec and Kevin with down to earth food at very low prices and loads for vegans. You can have a meal for under a fiver.

For breakfast two toasts and toppings; muffin or bagel with sausage, optional bacon, fish finger roll on ciabatta with tartare sauce and cheese; granola bowl. Vegan croissants, pain au choc, pain au raisin and ham 'n' cheese.

The vegan leek, thyme and mushroom sos rolls are a big hit. Specials £5 or less such as hummus falafel in tortilla; spicy bbq tofu; barmy bahn mi sweet bbq seitan ribs with peanut sauce; VLT bacon, lettuce with mayo on an oaty grain sub. Luscious hot dawgs. Bagels and sandwiches such as BLT. Winter soup and summer salads.

Vegan cakes, cupcakes, brownies, cookies, flapjacks and loaf.

Milkshakes and smoothies such as coconut, banana and chocolate. Organic Fairtrade teas, coffee, hot choc with chilli, mint or amaretto and cinnamon. Iced tea or coffee. They have soya, almond and oat milk and no vegan tax. Save 10p when you bring your own cup.

Children welcome. Seats in the garden. Book exchange. Wifi. Dogs weclome. Cash only, or credit card over £6 and there is a charge of 50p.

Hullabaloo
Vegetarian South Indian restaurant

- ☛ 111b Deptford High Street SE8 4NS (near Douglas Way)
- ☏ 020 7018 4747
- ◐ Su-Th 12.00-22.30, F-Sa 12.00-23.45
- ⊖ Deptford BR
- ↖ facebook.com/hullabaloodeptford

Fantastic value Indian street food restaurant opened February 2017, after doing a street stall, with 35 vegan dishes. Everything "non vegan" is clearly labelled, we like! And they do take-away. Chef Baloo previously worked in Michelin star restaurant Tamarind in Mayfair and is from the Punjab region. The interior is very characteristic with Bollywood posters and Bangra music to welcome you.

Starters £2-£3, side dishes £4.49, including Bombay potato, saag aloo, chana masala, coconut beans, tarka dahl mixed lentils with cumin seeds and ginger and garlic, mixed vegetables etc.

Mains £5.99, some classic dishes such as korma, tikka masala, bhuna, Madras, jalfrezi, rogan josh, have them with vegetalbles or tofu. Biryani £6.49. Mushroom, coconut and pilau rice £2.99. Garlic, onion or plain naan, tandoori roti £1.99-£2.99.

At lunchtimes you can get a nan poulty (nan, rice, vegetables and curry) for £5, or vegan curry tower.

Soft drinks and vegan masala chai with coconut milk for £1.

Sister Midnight
Vinyl record shop, live music venue, bar, cafe and gallery

- 📨 4 Tanners Hill, Deptford SE8 4PJ
- 📞 07930 421 113
- 🕐 M closed, Tu-W 12.00-18.00, Th-Su 12.00-22.00, M closed
- 🚇 Deptford Bridge DLR, New Cross, Deptford BR
- 🔗 sistermidnightrecords.co.uk
  facebook.com/sistermidnightrecords
  instagram.com/sistermidnightrecords
  twitter.com/vinylDeptford/media

New and secondhand vinyl records and cassettes shop for all tastes, with art on the walls for sale, and performances at night.

Vegan sandwiches, bar snacks and cakes, all made in store.

Who could resist hot chocolate with vegan whipped cream £2.75? The bar is stocked with beers from £2.50 Pilsners to the latest South London craft brews.

Seats inside and out. Events calendar on Facebook. Previously called Vinyl, now under new ownership since summer 2018 but very much as before.

Deptford Does Art
Vegan cafe, bar and art gallery

- 28 Deptford High Street SE8 4AF
-
- W-Su 10.00-18.00, -23.00 on event night such as F or Sa, M-Tu closed
- Deptford Bridge DLR, Deptford, New Cross
- instagram.com/deptforddoesart

Beautifully decorated arty cafe, with local artists on the walls to buy

Sandwiches, light brunch/lunch, cakes, ice cream, coffees and colourful superfood lattes. Loose leaf teas. Cocktails.

The Bird's Nest
Omnivorous food & music pub

- 32 Deptford Church St,reet SE8 4RZ
- 020 8692 1928
- Su-Th 12.00-23.00, F-Sa 12.00-01.00
- Deptford Bridge DLR, Deptford BR
- thebirdsnestpub.co.uk
  facebook.com/thebirdsnestpub

One street east of Deptford High Street, an old skool pub, with a stage for live music every evening, an art gallery and a male only hostel.

On Sunday there is vegan roast £10, seitan stuffed with leek and mushrooms, served with veggies and roast potatoes.

Burgers £3.50-£6 can be made vegan with mock beef or chicken. Double burger add £2.50. Wrap £6 such as mushroom, veg and pesto. Bowl of roast potato, triple cooked crunchy chips or skinny fries £3.

Bar menu £3-£4 features batons and dips, mixed salad, and multi-veg healthy fries.

Wifi. Tables outside. Kids welcome 12.00-17.00. Happy Hour M-F 5-7pm all pints, bottles and glasses of wine £3.

Japanese style capsule pods hostel upstairs, £75/week, plus two weeks deposit, "ideal for builders and backpackers." facebook.com/thebirdsnestguesthouse Your pod is a lockable private bunk bed with personal reading light and electric sockets inside. TV lounge, self-catering kitchen, free wifi.

The Greenhouse
Omnivorous cafe

- 481 New Cross Road SE14 6TA (corner Watson Street)
- info@greenhousedeptford.co.uk
- M-F 08.00-17.00, Sa 9.00-17.00, Su 9.00-16.00
- New Cross, Deptford Bridge
- greenhousedeptford.co.uk facebook.com/greenhousedeptford

Independent coffee shop midway between New Cross station and the start of Deptford High Street. serving speciality coffee and healthy food.

Breakfast £7.50 includes half a sliced avocado, roasted vegetables, mushrooms, homemade hummus, yiachini potatoes. sourdough toast with olive oil, salad and tomato salsa.

Homemade soup with sourdough £4.75. Mediterranean sandwich £4.75 with avocado, hummus, courgette and sundried tomato, can be gluten-free. Roast veg salad £6.50 with toasted seeds, add nutritional yeast 50p.

Smoothies £4 are a meal in themselves. Sugar and gluten-free bar £2.50. Alchemy coffee £1-£3, with almond and soya milk.

High chairs. Wifi. Outside tables.They support local, eco-friendly and independent suppliers. Packaging is compostable, they don't use plastic, and use Ecotricity green electricity.

Deli X
Wholefood shop and omnivorous cafe

- 156 Deptford High Street SE8 3PQ
- 020 8691 3377
- M-F 9.00-18.30, Sa 9.00-18.00, Su closed
- Deptford
- facebook.com/DeliXltd

Shop at the front, cafe at the back. They sell fruit and veg and the full range of wholefoods from Infinity distributors, and can order in for you, with discounts on bulk. In the fridge Violife, tofu, coconut oil, various milks and drinks including Biona pomegranate or tart cherry juice.

Italian cold pressed extra virgin olive oil refills £14.50 for a litre, £9.50 for half. Organic agave syrup 1 litre £9.

The cafe does breakfasts £1.99-£7.99 such as muesli, granola, porridge with toasted seeds and agave syrup, (gluten-free) toast with spreads, scrambled tofu on toast with avocado.

Sandwiches £3.95-£4.50. Soup and bread £4.95. Baked butternut squash stuffed with mushroom, baby spinach and vegan pesto, plus side salad £6.45. Mixed olives £2.95. Focaccia, sourdough bread or pitta served with hummus £3.50, add olives and sun blushed tomato £5.99. Salads £6.95 such as wholemeal couscous with squash; or quinoa and Camargue red rice salad with apricot, beetroot, mango, tomato salsa dressing.

Cakes £2.50-£3, chocolate and banana, chocolate and raspberry, tropical fruit, mixed berries and carrot cake. They also sell fresh bread.

Hot drinks £1.75-£3.10, cold coffee or

tea £2.50-£3, fresh juices £2.95 and smoothies £2.20.

Dogs welcome. High chair. Wifi. Outside garden.

Buster Mantis
Omnivorous Jamaican bar and restaurant

☛ 3-4 Resolution Way, Deptford SE8 6NT

☎ 020 8691 5191

🕐 Tu-Th 17.00-23.30, F-Sa 17.00-01.30, Su 14.00-23.30, M closed

⊖ Deptford BR

🏹 bustermantis.com

Named after the first prime minister of Jamaica. Rum cocktails, Red Stripe, local keg and bottle beers from small independent brewers. Food includes chickpea and butternut squash curry £8.50, pulled jackfruit wrap with chips £8, fried planatin or rice and peas£3.

Also on Deptford High Street:

London Velo bike shop cafe-bar at 18, SE8 4AF has vegan options and a courtyard. Falafel lunch £6.50.

Green Onions
Health food and records shop

- 6 Clifton Rise SE14 6JP
- 07474 537570
- M-F 10.00-19.30, Sa 10.00-18.00, Su 11.00-17.00
- New Cross, New Cross Gate
- facebook.com/ greenonions.newcross

Cute little shop with rock 'n' roll, soul, funk, hip pop, blues, reggae and jazz records for sale at the back. They have a record player in the shop with great music playing all the time.

Fruit and veg, fresh bread, and the usual wholefoods. Lots of chocolate and Goody Good Stuff sweets. Unusual butters such as apricot or olive and avocado. Extra virgin olive oil refills £6.90 for half litre.

Fridge with Tofutti, Violife, Mozzarisella, Taifun, tofu, sprouts and Booja Booja truffles.

Brownies £1.50.

Some bodycare such as Faith in Nature, Lavera and Weleda.

Bio-D refills, Earth Friendly.

They sell beautiful plants, textile bags, cards, incense sticks and holders and organic tea lights. Small book section.

Everest Curry King
Omnivorous South Indian / Sri Lankan restaurant

- 24 Loampit Hill SE13 7SW
- 020 8691 2233
- M-Su 10.00-23.00
- Lewisham BR, St Johns BR

Lots of vegan dishes at this authentic, great value place. Curries £2.25 small, £3.50 medium, £5.50 large. Set meal £5.95 has four curries, rice and popadoms.Unlike other south Asian restaurants they use seasonal veg so the dishes change.

Sheel Pharmacy
Health food shop & pharmacy

- 312-314 Lewisham Road, Lewisham SE13 7PA
- 020 8297 1551
- M-F 9.00-19.00, Sa 9.00-18.00, Su closed
- Lewisham BR & DLR
- sheelpharmacy.com

Not just a pharmacy, they have savoury take-aways and cakes, including vegan and a wide range of vegan foods and cosmetics. Homeopathy. Ecover, BioD and Earth Friendly cleaning products.

Chiropodist and osteopath by appointment, tattoo removal. They have another branch nearby, but this is the one to come to for wholefoods.

Mission Green
Vegan zero waste wholefood shop

- ☛ 182 Hither Green Lane SE13 6QB
- ☎ 07453 680879
- ◐ M-Tu, Th -F 10.00-19.00, W 13.00-18.00, Sa 10.00-18.00, Su 11.00-16.00
- ⊖ Hither Green BR
- ↖ facebook.com/missiongreen182

Bring your own containers from home to fill up with dry food, nuts, dry fruits, baking ingredients, toiletries, cleaning products. Full list of products at the top of their Facebook page.

Holland & Barrett, Lewisham
Health food shop

- ☛ 67 Riverdale Court, Lewisham SE13 7ER
- ☎ 020 8297 9559
- ◐ M-Sa 9.00-18.30, Su 11.00-17.00
- ⊖ Lewisham BR & DLR

Fridge and freezer.

Lewisham Vegans
Local group.

- ↖ facebook.com/LewishamVegans

Social and campaigning meetups and news about what's new for vegans in the area. Over 500 members.

Joy's Health Sanctuary
Vegan health food shop, smoothie and juice bar

🖝 29 Winslade Way, Catford SE6 4JU

📞 020 3719 9223

🕐 M-F 08.30-17.30, Sa 9.00-17.00, Su 10.00-16.00

⊖ Catford Bridge BR, Catford BR

▸ facebook.com/joyshealthsanctuary
  instagram.com/joyshealthsanctuary

Opened February 2018.

Food such as vegetable or callaloo patties, organic brown basmati rice with butterbean, sweet potato and spinach curry.

Vegan, sugar-free and gluten-free cakes such as pumpkin and walnut, chocolate orange, fruit cake, or sugarless banana cake made with organic spelt flour and coconut oil.

Juices and smoothies made in front of you. Try Joy's Green Special with kale, cucumber, barley grass, wheatgrass, spirulina and chlorella.

The shop sells organic health foods, and herbal remedies. Previously in Rushey Green.

Daun's Deli
Vegan cafe & delicatessenr

- in Catford Mews cinema, 32 Winslade Way SE6 4JU
- (70481 535 768
- M-Su 12.00-20.00
- Catford, Catford Bridge
- daunsdeli.com
  facebook.com/daunsdeli
  instagram.com/daunsdelir

Opened by Rickard Daun from Linköping in Sweden, Catford's plant-based deli offers daily seasonal hot dishes with Scandinavian, Mediterranean and Middle Eastern twist, salads, open sandwiches, nibbles and comfort foods. All day weekend brunch.

Daily dish £6-£7 such as creamy linguine with kale, chard and setan; burger and mash with peas and gravy. Soup £4 such as spiced pumpin with roasted fennel and sunflower seeds and bread.

Located in Catford Mews, the new 3-screen cinema and bar, cafe in the centre of Catford.

In the same place is Bears Dough selling all-vegan doughnuts, which are also without soy or nuts. Tu-Sa 10.00-18.00.

- .daunsdeli.com

Holland & Barrett, Catford
Health food shop

- 33 Winslade Way, Catford SE6 4JU
- (020 8690 3903
- M-Sa 9.00-17.30, Su 10.00-16.00
- Lewisham BR & DLR

Fridge and freezer.

BROCKLEY

The Broca
Vegetarian cafe and wholefood shop

- 4 Coulgate Street, Brockley SE4 2RW
- (020 7277 7888
- M-Tu 07.00-19.00, W-F 07.00-22.00, Sa 08.00-18.00, Su 08.30-18.00
- Brockley (just outside)
- facebook.com/thebroca

Shabby chic veggie cafe and coffee shop with a wholefoods mini-shop, opposite the station. Lots of vegan and gluten-free options.

Brunch £5-£7.50 such as full Broca breakfast £7.50 with smokey molasses beans, wedges, red onion sausages, marinated tofu and tomato; avocado on sourdough toast; sweet potato quesadilla with avocado, pineapple salsa and cashew sour cream, add grilled tofu £1. Lunch special such as pulled pork jackfruit burger on ciabatta; spinach quiche or tofu scramble with lentils.

Evening popups include Olfactory Brockley on Thursdays, dishing up starters £3-£6 such as Caribbean sweet fried dumpling, seitan smoked jerk wings, mac 'n' cheese, jalapeno sweet corn fritters. Mains £7.50-£8 could be chickpea potato curry, seitan butterbean stew, jerk bbq jackfruit bowl with sweet fried plantain.

Vegan cakes £4 such as rum and ginger, chocolate coconut, gluten-free doughnuts

For Veganuary they made vegan lattes cheaper than the non-vegan ones. We like.

Lager £2.50. Margarita £6.

DULWICH

South London

Blue Brick Cafe
Vegetarian cafe

- 14 Fellbrigg Road, off Northcross Road, off Lordship Lane SE22 9HH
- 020 8299 8670
- M, W-Su 9.00-17.30, Tue closed
- East Dulwich BR
- instagram.com/bluebrickcafe

Great café with restaurant quality food and a chef who used to be at Carnevale. They use lots of fresh herbs, seeds, and often cook to order.

All day breakfasts £3.50-£9 are massively popular at weekends, from muesli or lightly spiced dried fruit with (soya) yogurt through to full cooked with homemade beans, vegan sausage, sauté mushrooms, roasted tomatoes, spinach, bubble and squeek, and sourdough toast.

Starters around £5 like salads or soup with sourdough bread.

Mains £8-£8.50 such as roasted garlic, squash and saffron risotto; spicy chickpea stew with sausage, rice and salad; tomato and ginger curry with brown rice; main course salads.

Proper desserts £4 include apple crumble, chocolate pot with poached rhubarb. Cakes £1.50-£3.50 such as vegan chocolate mint cake and eccles cake.

Smoothies £3 such as mango lassi or berry and pineapple. Juices, Whole Earth lemonade and cola, spiced hot apple and elderflower £1.80. Climpson & Sons coffee (roasted in east London), cappuccino, latte, mocha £1.90-£2.50. Hot choc £2.50. Pot of tea for one £1.90, two £2.90. They have soya milk. They have just started serving their own kombucha.

Bring your own alcohol, £2.50 per bottle corkage.

Children's portions, two beautiful vintage high chairs. Dogs welcome. Outside tables in summer. Cash only, cash machine nearby.

The Guava Kitchen

Vegetarian Caribbean healthy cafe, deli and take-away

- 16 London Road SE23 3HF
- 07483 387 059
- M-F 08.00-18.00, Sa 9.00-17.00, Su 10.00-17.00. May vary.
- Forest Hill BR
- theguavakitchen.com
  facebook.com/theguavakitchen
  instagram.com/theguavakitchen

Opened Septemberr 2019 where there used to be a Santander bank. Jenny Campbell's healthy plant based deli and catering service with a Caribbean tropical twist.

Breakfast served till 10.00 weekdays, 12.00 weekends, such as Full English Caribbean with sausages, plantain, basil tomatoes, herb mushrooms, callalloo and butterbean baked herbs; smashed avo on toasted charcoal bread, add mushroom or sausage 60p; ackee scramble on toasted sourdough; sourdough bread with Scotch bonnet and coriander vegan butter; açai bowl with yogurt, granola, apricot, sultanas, pumpkin and chia seeds, coconut.

Lunch 12.00-16.00 includes plantain balls with sweet and sour sauce; curried chickpea wrap; BBQ pulled jackfruit in organic brioche bun; pea soup stew with dumplings, sweet potato and yam; blackeye fritters with vegan cheese fondue; pea fritters with avo dressing; salads such as three bean and lentil with callalo; coconut spicy curry with sweet potato and yam served with black bean rice; plantain lasagne with green salad; Calypso Macro Bowl with plantain balls, quinoa and passionfruit sweet and sour sauce; wild mushroom and thyme parcels with mango chutney and herb leaf salad. Top up with sweet potato chips, fried plantain.

For dessert there are cakes, caramelised pears, and black rice pudding with coconut milk. Juices, coffee.

High chairs. Private hire for parties and events. Deliveroo.

Also recommended in Dulwich:

Romeo Jones deli at 80 Dulwich Village SE21 7AJ has vegan cake and will do vegan sandwiches etc.

Dulwich Clock Cafe in the park has some dishes marked vegan on the menu, pizza with vegan bases, and a separate fryer for chips including sweet potato. There is plenty of indoor and outdoor seating and water bowls for dogs. Worth a half day outing to the park.

Healthmatters
Health food shop & therapy rooms

- 47 Lordship Lane, Dulwich SE22 8EV
- (020 8299 6040,
  020 8299 4232 therapies
- Shop M-Sa 9.00-18.30, Su 10.00-18.00. Therapies M-F 9.00-20.00, Sa closed, Su 12.00-15.00
- East Dulwich BR
- dulwichhealthmatters.com
  dulwichtherapyrooms.co.uk

Wholefoods including wheat-free, organic, Fairtrade. Vegan chocolate and carob. Fridge with drinks. (For vegan chilled and frozen foods go to SMBS.)

This is the best place in Dulwich for cosmetics, eco-cleaning, supplements and homeopathy. Bodycare includes Jäson, Dr Hauschka, Organic Pharmacy, Weleda, Lavera, Natracare and baby products.

Supplements include Solgar, Biocare, Nature's Plus, Viridian, Nature's Aid. Herbal remedies, homeopathy.

BioD and Ecos clearning products and refills, also Earth Friendly. Yoga mats and blocks.

Dulwich Therapy Rooms are in the same building and treatments include acupuncture, chiropractic, Alexander Technique, aromatherapy, counselling, craniosacral, facials, herbal medicine, homeopathy, hynotherapy, massage, nutritional therapy, osteopathy, reflexology, shiatsu. Classes include Feldenkrais, meditation, pilates, pre and post-natal.

SMBS Foods
Vegetarian grocery and wholefood shop?

- 75 Lordship Lane SE22 8EP
- (020 8693 7792
- M-F 9.00-18.30, Sa 9.00-18.00, Su 9.00-17.00
- East Dulwich BR

Lots of Indian, health, organic, Fairtrade, vegan chilled and frozen, organic fruit and veg and a great selection of exotic fruits. Incredibly busy at weekends and evenings.

Fridge and freezer with great variety of vegan delights such as cheese, yogurt, meat substitutes, tofu, tempeh, ice-cream by Swedish Glace, Tofutti, Booja Booja, cream, custard. Lots of chocolate by Plamil, Divine, Organica, Montezuma, Booja Booja etc.

Some bodycare, supplements, cleaning.

Fashion Conscience
Women's shoe shop & ethical fashion

- 28 Grove Vale, East Dulwich SE22 8EF (corner Melbourne Grove)
- (0871 384 1180
- M, F 10.00-18.00; Tu-Th, Sa 10.00-19.00, Su 11.00-17.00
- East Dulwich
- fashion-conscience.com
  Facebook Fashion-conscience.com
  instagram.com/fconscience

Founded by a former fashion and celebrity journalist for UK high-end women's glossy magazines. Shoes from UK, North America, Brazil and Europe. 200 kinds of vegan shoes, boots, heels, sandals and trainers in all styles £15-£90, either in store or on their website. Also bags and Fairtrade clothing. Check their instagram to see what's hot right now.

ELEPHANT & CASTLE

& Kennington

This is a young area, with the London College of Communication, South Bank University, and famous clubs Ministry of Sound and Corsica Studios. The historic Elephant & Castle pub was the birthplace of UK Garage. There is also a strong South American community.

In October 2019 Ethiopian restaurant **Beza** became the area's first vegan restaurant, while **Electric Elephant Cafe**.**Electric** dropped meat (though not fish).

The area's best kept secret is the vegetarian **Courtyard Garden Cafe** in the Jamyang Buddhist Centre. If you've been there in the past and been as disappointed at the lack of vegan cakes as we were (the owner was an ex dairy farmer), now they have them!

Mercato Metropolitano is an indoor Italian food court with bars, cafes and a big grocer, located in an old paper factory located in the new Sobo area or South of Borough.

For omnivorous dining with great vegan options, head to **St Gabriel** Ethiopian cafe or **Electric Elephant Cafe**.

 getlivinglondon.com
  /elephant-and-castle
  elephantandcastle.org.uk

Courthouse Garden Cafe
Vegetarian cafe & accommodation

 Jamyang Buddhist Centre, The Old Courthouse, 43 Renfrew Road SE11 4NA (off Kennington Lane

 020 7820 8787

 M-F 10.00-16.00, later when courses on, Sa-Su closed

 Kennington, Elephant & Castle

 jamyang.co.uk

Enjoy the tranquility of a Buddhist Centre in an old courthouse and courtyard with a cafe open to the public, tables inside and in the garden. They make everything, even pasta, and with old varieties of wheat and rye. Biodynamic veg. Most food is organic.

The main menu changes daily with seasonal ingredients and they rarely cook the same main dish £7.80 twice. British, Indian and Italian style food such as stuffed mushrooms with leek, hazelnut and apple sauce; spicy dishes such as curries; walnut dumplings with paprika sauce; chickpea croquettes with tahini pomegranate sauce. Mains come with salads, which in summer use ingredients from the garden.

There is not always a vegan main but usually W-F, ring to be sure. Always vegan soup such as pea and mint £4.25 with organic sourdough bread. Salad platter £1.70 scoop, £4.60 small, £5.70 regular.

Some cakes £3.15 are vegan such as pear and ginger. Chocolate blackcurrant truffles £1.60.

Monmouth coffee, latte etc £2-£3. Bottomless cup of tea for the day £3.95. They have soya and oat milk. James White organic juices £2. Aspalls apple juice, Luscombe lemonade £1.60-2.90.

No alcohol. Children welcome, no high chairs. Classes in meditation, tai chi, yoga, Buddhism. Beautiful meditation hall. Rooms for hire. Courses such as bread-making. Outside catering and weddings. MC, Visa £5+.

Also accommodation for quiet adults in four single cells of the old courthouse £35, shared bathroom, one single room with desk, maximum stay one week. Kitchen where you can cook.

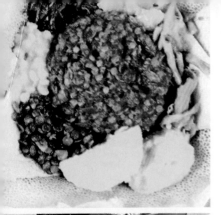

Beza
Vegan Ethiopian restaurant

- 8A Sayer Street, Elephant Park SE17 1FH
- 020 7483 2489, 07833 463095
- M-F 11.00-22.00, Sa-Su 10.00-18.00
- Elephant & Castle
- bezaveganfood.com
  facebook.com/Bezarestaurant
  instagram.com/bezaethio

Opened October 2019 in their own vegan restaurant, following a two year popup in the now closed Artworks.

Vegan plate of food (see photo), eat in £7.50 regular, £8.50 large, take-away £6, £7. Dishes, cooked with garlic, turmeric and red onions, include yellow split peas, brown lentils, string beans, white cabbage, potato, spinach, all served with rice or of course injera flatbread made from wheat or gluten-free teff.

Vegan beer. Wine.

You can book on the website.

Electric Elephant Cafe
Vegetarian and fish cafe

- 186a Crampton Street SE17 3AE (corner Iliffe Yard)
- 020 7277 4433
- M-F 07.30-17.00, Sa 900-17.00, Su 10.00-16.00
- Elephant & Castle
- electricelephantcafe.co.ukt
  Facebook Electric Elephant Cafe

In October 2019 this formerly omnivorous cafe got rid of meat apart from fish. A lot of dishes still contain cheese or eggs and vegan items are not yet marked on the online menu so you might want to phone ahead, but hey it's early days and they are definitely making a big move in the right direction which we applaud.

Full English cooked vegan breakfast £12.40 (photo left) with sausage, avocado, spinach, baked beans, grilled tomatoes, garlic mushrooms, hash brown, bubble & squeak, toast. Extra portions £1-£2.

Soup with organic bread £5. Salads £7.50 eat in, £6.25 take-away, include falafel and hummus with veggies, cooked beetroot and olives. Daily specials. (Toasted) sandwiches and panini £3-£5.40.

Freshly squeezed juices £3.79, homemade Sicilian lemonade £2.80.

Teas, coffees £1.70-£3.70. Pot of tea for two £3.60, free refill.

Dogs welcome.

St Gabriel Cafe, SE11
Ethiopian omnivorous cafe-deli

- 154 Newington Butts, Kennington, London SE11 4RN (in an alley along the back of the triangular junction of Newington Butts, Kennington Lane and Kennington Park Road, next door to Sisay Hairdresser)
- 020 7587 0199
- M-Su 10.00-20.00
- Elephant & Castle, Kennington
- just-eat.co.uk/restaurants-st-gabriel-cafe-lambeth (menu)

Lovely vegan salads, lentil dishes and roast vegetables, some with quite a lot of oil, which you wrap in Ethiopian enjera flatbread and eat with your hands. Have a veggie selection plate for £8, which is probably enough to share with a friend. Juices, Ethiopian coffee £2, tea £1. Also some groceries. They have a smaller branch in Finsbury Park, north London.

Mercato Metropolitano
Omnivorous indoor Italian food market

- 44 Newington Causeway SE1 6DR
-
- Tu-Sa 11.00-23.00, Su 11.00-22.00, M closedf
- Elephant & Castle, Borough
- mercatometropolitano.co.uk

New Italian indoor market with shared tables, food stalls, bars, craft beers, coffee bars, an Italian food shop Prezzemolo & Vitale, and a cinema. The best bet for vegan dining is Leggero, who specialise in gluten-free, or try the Lebanese falafels and mezze stall. Dogs welcome on a lead.

Enoteca organic wine shop has a couple of vegan ones for £22 drink in, 15% discount to take home..

Leggero, Mercato Metropolitano
Omnivorous gluten-free Italian restaurant

- 42 Newington Causeway SE1 5DR
- 020 7403 0930
- Tu-Sa 11.00-23.00, Su 11.00-22.00, M closed
- Elephant & Castle
- leggero-london.com

Counter service, then take your food to eat at the shared tables in the market. Like their original branch in Old Compton Street, Soho, they have gluten-free vegan pasta, bread and dessert.

Courgette burger with homemade bread and vegan cheese £6. Focaccia with vegetables and vegan cheese, or olives and rosemary, £3.50. Sorghum basil tagliatelle £9 with almond flakes, pesto and tomatoes. Chickpea coquettes £1.50.

Raspberry mousse £4.50 served with choco chips and crunchy sponge.

Soft drinks £2.75. Water £1.50. Gluten-free beer £4.90. All wines are vegan, small glass £5.50, medium £7, bottle £24.

For a bigger range of gluten-free vegan food check out their main restaurant in Soho.

Prezzemolo & Vitale
Omnivorous Italian supermarket

- 44 Newington Causeway SE1 6DR (in Mercato Metropolitano)
- 07778 067221
- Tu-Sa 11.00-23.00, Su 11.00-22.00, M closed
- prezzemolovitale.com
  facebook.com/Prezzemoloevitaleuk

Family owned grocery chain from Palermo with a lot of niche products that you won't find elsewhere in London. Beautiful rustic interior.

Boxes of vegan croissants. Unique organic jams with no sugar by Rigoni di Asiago like dog rose, raspberry, sour cherry, pomegranate, lemon, apricot and peach. The hazelnut spread is fantastic too.

Organic coffees and herbal teas. Bottled organic juices like pomegranate and apple, apple and mango, plum, blueberry. Cold teas like lemon, peach, and green. Alice Nero organic vegan drinks like oat and soybean.

Organic cooking cream from Probio like vegan bechamel and Sarchio rice cream.

From the counter you could have some olives, sundried tomatoes, mix of mushrooms, 98p-£1.80 per 100gr . If you'd rather avoid the meaty cheesy counter you can find a lot of antipasti and patés on the shelves, most organic. Their own label Giugiu has amazing spreads like wild fennel, capers and tomatoes, artichoke, green with black olives.Their chutneys from Ladle & Larder are also very different: rhubarb and ginger, apple and ginger, and chilli and pineapple. Original pesto like zucchini; raisins and pinenuts; aubergine and almond. Vast range of gluten-free and organic pasta, such as rice pasta, and organic tomato sauce.

Old grains flour like buckwheat, spelt and kamut. mostly organic and other flours like chickpea for gluten-free pizza and bread. The flour with porcini mushroom is good for making a quick polenta. Also seeds, dried fruit, pulses, soup mixes. Lots of fresh vegetables, fruits, fresh herbs, and truffle products.

Be sure to read the ingredients because they are not labelled as vegan.

Baldwin's Health Food
Health food shop

171/173 Walworth Road SE17 1RW

020 7703 5550 enquiries, mail order
020 7701 4892 office

FB says M-Sa 09.00-18.00, Th 19.00, Su closed

Elephant & Castle

baldwins.co.uk online shop
facebook.com/BaldwinsUK

Well stocked and great value wholefood shop since the eighties, good for Japanese Clearspring, gluten-free, lots of vegan stuff and organic. It's actually two shops, the second one being G Baldwin herbalist (trading since 1844) which has dried herbs, essential oils, candles, incense, bodycare, soap-making products. The only thing they don't sell is organic fruit & veg, which you can get from FareShares.

Hot and cold take-away selection of sweet and savoury goodies including sandwiches, pasties, ready meals. Organic bread. Vegan cheeses (Sheese, Violife), Tofurky, yogurts, ice-cream, meat substitutes.

Vegan chocolate by Organica, Ombar, Seeds & Bean, Happy Kitchen, Plamil, John Adams, Booja Booja at Xmas and Easter, Montezuma.

Bodycare includes Weleda, Wild Rose, Jason, Aubrey, Barefoot, Laughing Bird, Dead , Sea Magic, Faith in Nature, Theraneem, Alva, Green People, Natracare, Sukin, Weleda baby, Green People Baby, Bambo.

Supplements include their own label, Quest, Bioforce, Viridian, Nature's Plus, Solaray, FSC, Nature's Aid, Solo, Terranova, Pukka and lots of others.

Kids supplements available too. Homeopathic remedies by Weleda, Nelsons, Helios, and Bush Flowers and Bach Flower remedies.

BioD, Ecover and Earth Friendly cleaning products. Herbatint and natural Henna. Health, diet and herbal books. Bulletin board.

FareShares Food Co-op
Vegan organic wholefood cooperative

- 🢒 56 Crampton Street SE17 3AE
- ☏ none
- 🕐 Th 14.00-20.00, F 16.00-19.00, Sa 15.00-17.00, Su-W closed
- ⊖ Elephant & Castle, Kennington
- ⭢ fareshares.org.uk
  56a.org.uk, fareshares@activix.org

Established by local people back in 1988, FareShares is a self organised, non-profit community-run food co-op which aims to make healthy food affordable. They buy in bulk and resell at minimal mark-up to cover some expenses. Bring your own bags, weigh and price up what you want. Donations help to cover bills too.

They stock a range of dry goods such as grains, beans and pulses sold in bulk and wholefood from Suma, Infinity, Meridian, Biona, some chilled vegan food, fresh organic fruit, veg, bread, culinary and medicinal herbs, and various household products. All stock is sourced as locally and ethically as possible, much of it is organic and all produce is animal-, sugar- and GMO-free.

SOUTH

FareShares relies on individuals' time and energy and everyone is a volunteer. They always welcome new people to get involved and as well as doing shifts, there are plenty of other ways to help out. They operate as a collective, with meetings every month. They are always on the lookout for volunteers.

Also here is the 56A Infoshop, a DIY social centre with a massive radical politics archive, and selling radical books and zines.

And 56a Bikespace, a DIY repair bicycle workshop with cheap new and secondhand parts.

ELEPHANT & CASTLE

GREENWICH

& North Greenwich / Peninsula & The O2

Greenwich makes a great day out. Top attractions are the **Cutty Sark** sailing ship museum, **Greenwich Observatory** at the top of the park, **National Maritime Mueum.**

The covered **market** has several vegan food stalls ranging from burgers or pizzas to plates of Ethiopian food to cakes. At the back is the excellent wholefood shop **Greenlands** on two floors.

The only vegan cafe is **Yummzy**, up by the park, a vegan dessert cafe! For a vegan restaurant you'll need to head up to North Greenwich to the new branch of **By Chloe** that opened in summer 2019.

Away from the market, there are no strictly vegetarian or vegan places, but there are the usual chains like Pizza Express where you can get a vegan bite. Our top tips for restaurants are Mevali and Tai Tip Mein. But if you like fast food, you should head straight to **The Lost Hour** pub up by the park which has stacks of vegan options like burgers, kebabs, loaded fries, even dessert.

The most fun way to get to Greenwich is on the river boat from the Tower of London, Charing Cross or Westminster. Cutty Sark is the most central tube station, on the Docklands Light Railway.

Greenwich Market
Indoor market

- Greenwich Church Street SE8 3BU
- Market stalls M-Su and bank holidays 10.00-17.30. Most shops, pubs and restaurants open every day.
- Cutty Sark DLR
- greenwichmarket.london

The covered market has various vegan food stalls, each trading on different days, surrounded by shops including the excellent Greenlands wholefood store. The market is full of art, handcrafted toys, fashion, jewellery, fruit and veg. Wed, Sat, Sun are art and craft days; Tue, Thu, Fri antiques and vintage.

As well as the stalls listed overleaf, look out for Vivienne's Fruit & Veg on Wednesday and Thursday, all locally grown in Kent and Sussex; Brazilian churros Th-Su, which are labelled vegan but the caramel sauce is not vegan so go for chocolate sauce and cinnamon and sugar coating; Blowing Dandelion at weekends have some vegan chocolates and cakes.

Yummzy
Vegan healthy cake cafe and shop

- 9 Nevada Street, Greenwich SE10 9JL
- 020 8858 6028
- M-F 08.00-20.00, Sa 9.00-19.00, Su 10.00-19.00
- Cutty Sark DLR, Greenwich
- yummzy.co.uk
  facebook.com/Yummzy.Desserts
  instagram.com/yummzy_desserts

Opened November 2018, serving up cakes, donuts, cupcakes, cookies and other desserts, savoury treats and healthy drinks. But these are super-healthy treats, with less than 5 grams of carb per serving, no added sugar, gluten-free and high in protein.

10% discount Mondays with a pram, Tuesdays for seniors and their friends, Wednesday with a gym pass, every day with student ID.

Ethiopian Vegetarian Food
Vegan Ethiopian food stall

- 🛵 Greenwich Market SE10 9HZ
- 📞 07957 926123
- 🕐 W-Su 11.00-16.00
- 🔗 greenwichmarket.london/guide/detail/ ethiopian-vegetarian-food

If you like the Ethiopean stalls in Brick Lane, you'll love this. Plate of curries, veg and salads £5 served with rice or injera pancakey flatbread to mop it all up with.

Little Leaf
Vegan pizza stall

- 🛵 Greenwich Market SE10 9HZ
- 🕐 Tu-Sa. 10.00-17.00, sometimes at other markets such as as Soho, check first
- 🔗 facebook.com/littleleaffood

Whole pizzas £7 topped with rosemary or basil or pesto with courgettes. Also cookies.

Ruby's of London
Vegan cake stall

- 🛵 Greenwich Market SE10 9HZ
- 📞 020 8858 6618 (orders), 07947 271487
- 🕐 Sa-Su 10.00-17.30
- 🔗 rubysoflondon.com
  Facebook Rubys of London

Artisan vegan bakery also specialising in products additionally free from wheat, gluten, sugar, nuts and soya. Ruby uses organic wheat flour and Fairtrade products. Banana bread, fudge brownies, almond and cherry loaves, biscuits, small birthday cakes, cupcakes, donuts and seasonal products.

You can also order on the website for delivery across London or collect from the stall.

Vegan Garden
Vegan savouries, cakes and muffins

- 🍴 Greenwich Market SE10 9HZ
- 🕐 Sa-Su 11.00-17.30
- 📍 Facebook Vegan Garden London

Kaya serves up cakes, biscuits, tarts, savoury tartlets, soups, salads, quiche, alternative vegan savouries, raw and cooked

Selection of salads £4.50 small, large £6.60. Polenta bake including spinach and mushroom £3.50, and £6.50 with 2 salads; quiche such as courgette, spinach and tomato or sweet potato, spinach and pea, or rainbow roast £4.50, and £6.50 with 2 salads; lasagna £6, and £8 with 2 salads. Look out for the special of the day. Soups in winter £3.50.

Cakes £2.50-£3.50 such as plantain and carrot, plum and almond, raspberry and coconut, lemon and blueberry.

Veganauti
Vegan cake stall

- 🍴 Greenwich Market SE10 9HZ
- 🕐 Days vary, check Twitter or Instagram
- 📍 facebook.com/veganauti
  Instagram or Twitter veganauti

The newest vegan stall in Greenwich Market. Check their instagram or Twitter for which days they are serving this week. Fabulous burgers with lots of colourful veg in them too, masala crisps, shakes. Try a pakora burger or smokey beet and bean burger topped with shrooms, caramelized red onions and their own BBQ sauce.

Panzerotto Blues
Omnivourus Italian pizza pockets

- 🍴 5b Greenwich Market SE10 9HZ
- 📞 07440 279823
- 🕐 M-F 10.30-17.00 plus 2 weekends a month
- 🚇 Cutty Sark DLR
- 📍 facebook.com/panzerottoblues

First Italian panzerotto in London, an Italian artisan street food savoury turnover from Puglia, made from pizza dough, like a small calzone in the shape of a pastie, fried in seed oil. They have a vegan one £6 with tomato, mixed peppers, courgette, mushroom, black olives and capers.

Royal Teas
Almost vegetarian cafe/coffee shop

☛ 76 Royal Hill, Greenwich SE10 8RT

☎ 020 8691 7240

◑ M-Sa 9.30-17.30, Su 10.00-17.30

⊖ Greenwich DLR

↖ royalteascafe.co.uk

Vegetarian cafe and tea house, apart from salmon in the cream tea and one sandwich.

Breakfasts on toast with one item £3.25, additional items £1-1.25, such as avocado, mushrooms, tomatoes, baked beans. Porridge oats with apricots or banana £3.75. Huevos bravos £5.75 can be made vegan.

Jacket potato with one filling £4.25, extra filling £1, such as baked beans, red onions, roasted vegetable, hummus and chipotle bean mix. Salad £4.75 served with baguette or pitta, hummus and crudités, and you can add falafel. They can make up something special for vegans from whatever is in the kitchen.

Sandwiches and cakes are made with dairy or eggs, few things can be made vegan. However if you just want to relax with a cuppa after doing the Observatory, then this place is the business, with lots of teas and coffees to choose from. Tea by the cup £1.70. Pot for one £2.20, two £4.40, three £5.40. Coffee by the cup £1.80-£2, pot of coffee for 1 £2.20, for 2 £4.50, for 3 £5.40. Hot chocolate with vegan cocoa powder £2.20. They have soya milk.

They also sell their loose teas and coffees which are ground there.

Fresh juices £1.50-£2.75.

High chairs. Dogs welcome.

The Lost Hour
Omnivourous pub

☛ 217-219 Greenwich High Rd SE10 8NB

☎ 020 8269 1411

◑ Su-Th 11.00-24.00, F-Sa 11.00-01.00

⊖ Greenwich BR, Cutty Sark DLR

↖ social-squirrel.com/
   thelosthourgreenwich
   facebook.com/TheLostHour/

It's a regular pub grub menu, with awesome vegan options £4.95-£9.45 and terrific value, like the burgers come WITH fries.

All day breakfast £4.95 with two vegan Quorn sausages, Kansas bean burger, tater tots, baked beans, grilled mushroom and tomato, toast. Breakfast pot £3.25 with sausage, hash brown, button mushrooms, grilled tomato, baked beans and spinach.

Mains £7.45 or £9.45 are BBQ pulled jackfruit kebab, tikka masala with rice, BBQ jackfruit wrap, grilled cheese sandwich and skinny fries, roasted red pepper and onion macaroni. Moving Mountain B12 burger comes with skinny fries, trade up to sweet potato fries for £1, smoky soya fries £1.50.

BBQ loaded pulled jackfruit fries for sharing £6.75, topped with Violife grated mature cheese and spring onion. Loaded smoky soya sloppy Joe fries £6.25. Hash brown bars topped with Violife, red chilli and jackfruit or sloppy Joes £7.95.

For dessert salted caramel torte with chocolate flavoured sauce £3.45. Fruit and veg smoothies £3.25. Wine from £3.65 medium glass, £4.60 large, £12.50 bottle. Real ale. Cocktails. Children welcome till 8pm. Baby changing. Disabled toilet. Sky TV and Sports. Pool table. Outside area. Function area.

Mevali
Omnivourous Lebanese cafe

- 🐾 17 Church Street SE10 9BJ
- ☎ 020 3490 4342
- 🕐 M-Su 11.00-23.00
- ⊖ Cutty Sark DLR
- ⬥ facebook.com/Mevali.Greenwich

Very nice sit-down restaurant for when you want to take your time instead of scurrying around the market. Middle Eastern interior and decoration, with a back garden and courtyard with tables. Bring your own alcohol.

Meze dishes £4.50, cold ones include hummus, roasted aubergine, tomato, moutabel mashed grilled aubergine, tabouleh; fattoush salad. Hot mezze such as patata harra diced potato with garlic, coriander and chilli; chickpea and broad bean falafel; vine leaves; ful medames broad beans. Falafel wrap £3.95.

Soft drinks £1.50-£1.80. Coffee £1.90-£2.10, cup of tea £1.50, pot £2.50. Matcha £2.50.

Pizza Express, Greenwich
Omnivorous Italian restaurant

- 🐾 4 Greenwich Church Street SE10 9BG
- ☎ 020 8853 2770
- 🕐 M-Th 11.00-23.00, F-Sa 11.30-23.30, Su 11.00-22.00
- ⊖ Cutty Sark DLR
- ⬥ pizzaexpress.com

Vegan cheese. Baby facilities. Disabled access.

SOUTH

GREENWICH

Tai Tip Mein
Omnivorous Oriental restaurant & take-away

- 39 Greenwich Church Street SE10 9BL
- 020 8858 1668 / 2688
- M-Su 11.30-23.00
- Cutty Sark DLR

Cheap, cheery and delicious noodle house, a little gem of Greenwich with plenty for vegans even though it's not explicit on the menu, and they are happy for you to mix and match. The most expensive thing is £6.95. Servings are huge and they have some of the best East/South-East Asian food in London. They don't do tofu, nor do they have anything explicitly vegan on the menu, but a local vegan recommends fried ho fun (flat rice noodles) with vegetables and black bean sauce with no egg.

Fruit juices £3 are freshly squeezed and they also do a range of Asian beers £2.40-£4.80 and Chinese tea for just £1.20. House wine £3.80 glass, £13.80 bottle. No service charge. Cash only.

Greenlands Health
Wholefood shop

☛ 14 Greenwich Market SE10 9HZ
📞 020 8293 9176
🕐 M-Su 9.00-18.30
⊖ Greenwich

Fantastic wholefood store on two floors on the edge of the market, jam packed to the ceiling with delights.

Fridge and freezer with soups, Laura's Idea take-aways, Sheese and Vegusto, Tofutti, Follow your Heart, Provamel, Sojade yogurts Rhythm vegan kefir, meat substitutes by Cheatin, Taifun, VegiDeli, Fry's, Clive's Pies, sprouts, Laurie's beet kraut and sauerkraut, Booja Booja truffles. Ice-cream from Booja Booja and Coyo.

Vegan chocolate by Plamil, Divine, Organica, Montezuma, Booja Booja.

Head downstairs for bodycare by Weleda, Alba Botanica, Avalon, Tisserand, Mistry's, Nourish, Dr Bronner's, Dr Hauschka, Green People, Faith in Nature, Jason, Lavera. Make up including Lavera and BWC.

Protein section. Supplements such as Biocare, Optibac, Solgar, Lambets, Nature's Plus, Viridian.

Homeopathy by New Era, Bach, Weleda, Nelsons. Bush flower remedies Essential oils and incense.

Cleaning by Ecover and refills, Method, Earth Friendly, BioD, Greenscent and Ecozone.

Baby food, bamboo nappies.

On Monday there is a nutritionist in store.

Peninsula & The O2

To the north-east along the river Thames is Greenwich Peninsula, containing the new urban Greenwich Millennium Village and the O2 arena (not to be confused with the O2 centre in Finchley), formerly called The Dome, which hosts big shows and concerts, a cinema and exhibitions.

North Greenwich underground station is on the Jubilee line, or arrive in style with great views on the Emirates Air Line cable cars from the Royal Docks on the other side of the river. The adult cash fare is £4.50 adult, £3.50 with an Oyster or Travelcard, and £17 for a "frequent flyer" pass for 10 trips.

Restaurants inside the O2 include Ask Italian, Busaba Eathai, Las Iguanas, Pizza Express, Wasabi, Zizzi. Outside in Peninsula Square is the new vegan restaurant **By Chloe** and a branch of Wagamamma.

- greenwichpeninsula.co.uk
  theo2.co.uk
  emiratesairline.co.uk

By Cloe, ICON at the O2
Vegan restaurant

- ICON at the O2, Ground Floor, Peninsula Square SE10 0DX
- 020
- M-W 10.00-20.00, Th-Sa 10.00-22.00, Su 12.00-18.00
- North Greenwich
- eatbychloe.com

The fourth branch opened summer 2019. **For menu see Covent Garden branch.** Also at Oxford Circus (Fitzrovia, opens 7am weekdays), Tower Bridge (South Bank). Deliveroo, To-go by Chloe.

Cafe Pura
Vegetarian cafe

- 48 Newton Lodge, Oval Square (Greenwich Millennium Village), West Parkside SE10 0BA
- 020 8312 8383
- M-F 07.00-19.00, Sa 08.00-18.00, Su/BH 10.00-17.00
- North Greenwich (Jubilee), bus 108, 129
- AyurvedaPura.com

Cafe in the same building as the Ayurveda Pura health spa and beauty centre, which has three therapies rooms and a yoga room.

Light meals and snacks £2.85-£4.75 such as samosas, chana dal (lentils and spices), soup, salads, sandwiches to order.

You can create your own salad by choosing the base from mixed salad leaves or baby spinach or couscous, then toppings such as vegetables or avocado or garnish, and finally a dressing.

Hot drinks £1.80-£2.80 include tea, organic Ayurvedic herbal teas, coffee, latte, cappuccino. Juices, freshly made smoothies, soft drinks. Soya milk.

High chairs. Wifi. Seats inside and outside.

Pizza Express, O2
Omnivorous Italian chain restaurant

- Unit 8, Entertainment Avenue, The O2, North Greenwich SE10 0DY
- 020 8293 5071
- M-Sa 11.30-23.00, Su 11.30-22.00
- North Greenwich
- pizzaexpress.com/greenwich-the-o2

Glass frontage looking into the O2. It gets busy when there is a concert so allow plenty of time to eat. Baby facilities. Disabled access.

KINGSTON

-upon-Thames

Riverside Vegetaria
International vegetarian restaurant

☛ 64 High Street, Kingston-upon-Thames KT1 1HN

☎ 020 8546 7992

◑ Kingston BR

⊖ M-Su 12.00-23.00

↖ riversidevegetaria.co.uk
facebook.com/RiversideVegetaria

Superb riverside vegetarian restaurant with large windows that open out over the Thames. Idyllic in summer but well worth the trip at any time of year. Head there after a walk along the river or before seeing a play at the nearby Rose Theatre. In warm weather you can eat under the sky in the outdoor area on the towpath, watching the swans gliding around as the sun sets. 90% vegan and 80% gluten-free, with many local, organic and Fairtrade ingredients. Irresistible for lovers of vegan cakes and desserts.

Choose from the extensive a la carte menu, or daily specials listed on the colourful chalk board. For starters you could have nutty parsnip soup, spicy veg balls with coriander sauce, garlic mushrooms, falafel with hummus, or vegetable fritters with mango chutney among others (£5.95-7.50).

Main dishes (£8.95-£10.75) could be masala dosa; string hopper biriyani with fine noodles; tofu marinated in teriyaki sauce; African-style sweet potato and aubergine in peanut sauce; four bean & potato pancake, and lots more, all served with veg, salad and/or rice. A truly great vegetarian restaurant, memorable for its fabulous home-made desserts, many of which are vegan and organic. These include classic fruit crumble, baked figs with orange and brandy, and awesome cakes - try chocolate fudge, apricot and almond, or apple and cinnamon (£5.95 each). These can be accompanied with vegan ice cream or even soya custard.

Organic and vegan wines from £5.15 medium glass, £20.95 bottle. Lots of soft drinks, including freshly squeezed orange and grapefruit juice. Liqueurs, organic and gluten-free beer and cider. Teas, coffees and hot chocolate.

Take-away including frozen soup by the litre, and new range of home-made ready meals for sale at the restaurant itself and at the nearby Food for Thought wholefood shop (next page).

Ever popular since its launch in 1989, Riverside scooped London's Best Veggie Restaurant Award 2012 (Jellied Eel Magazine & Ethical Eats) and was a finalist in the Vegetarian Society's award for Britain's Best Vegetarian Restaurant 2010, among a series of other well-deserved accolades over the years.

Kids welcome, 5 high chairs. Gluten and wheat-free no problem. Book ahead for weekends and outside. Outside catering.

The Cheeky Pea
Omnivorous hummus bar

- Ground Floor, Eden Walk Shopping Centre, Eden Street, Kingston-upon-Thames KT1 1BL (near Union Street entrance)
- 07501 974411
- M-W 10.00-18.00, Th 10.00-20.00, F-Sa 10.00-19.00, Su 11.00-17.00
- Kingston BR
- thecheekypea.wix.com /the-cheeky-pea
  facebook.com/TheCheekyPea
  edenwalkshopping.co.uk /outlets/22/ cheeky-pea

New hummus bar with falafel, fava beans etc and salads in warm pitta or wrap. Most items are vegetarian or vegan. The local vegan group sometimes meet up here for lunch.

Small and large wraps from £2.80 to £6 can include your choice from falafel, hummus, tahini, fava beans, salsa, hot mushrooms, guacamole, salad, pine nuts.

Side dishes £2.40-4.00 such as tabouleh, fries or chips, roasted red peppers, lentil salad, fried cauliflower, smoked aubergine..

Desserts £1-2.30 are chocolate balls, knafeh or baklava - are any vegan?

Hot drinks £1.50-£2.20 include Turkish coffee, fresh mint tea, green or Moroccan tea. Juices, smoothies and cold drinks 90p-£1.80..

Children welcome. Free wifi.

Wagamama Kingston
Omnivorous Japanese chain restaurant

- 16-18 High St, Kingston-upon-Thames KT1 1EY
- 020 8546 1117
- M-F 12.00-23.00, Sa 11.30-23.00, Su 11.30-22.00
- Kingston BR
- wagamama.com

Omnivorous fast food Japanese noodle bar with veggie dishes.

Food For Thought, Kingston
Wholefood shop

- 38 Market Place, Kingston-upon-Thames KT1 1JQ
- 20 8546 7806
- M-Sa 9.00-18.00, Su 11.00-17.00
- Kingston BR
- foodforthoughtuk.com

Lots of organic, Fairtrade and gluten-free. Fridge with hummus, beansprouts, pies, tofu, lots of raw foods and superfoods including their own brand, Bonpom.

Bodycare ranges from Sukin, Jason, Faith in Nature, Lavera, Green People and more.

Supplements, homeopathy, aromatherapy. Qualified holistic health practitioners in-store (homeopath, nutritional therapist).

Cleaning products include Earth Friendly and Faith in Nature. Different promotions every month.

Panacea Health, Kingston
Health food store

- ☛ Unit G29 The Bentall Centre, Wood Street, Kingston KT1 1RF
- ☎ 020 8549 8341
- ◖ M-W, F 9.30-18.00, Th 9.30-21.00, Sa 9.00-19.00, Su 11.00-17.00
- ⊖ Kingston BR
- ↖ panaceaonline.co.uk
  twitter.com/PanaceaK
  thebentallcentre-shopping.com

Fridge with tofu, hummus, Taifun and Redwood meat replaceers and vegan cheeses, Sojade yogurts. No freezer. Wide range of dry foodstuffs including wheat-free and diabetic sugar-free sections.

Some unique pioneering products from overseas such as candida, IBS, weight loss and skincare products, including Evolve, and Lavera vegan make-up. Hemp and pea sports nutrition.

Herbal remedies. No cleaning products. Qualified herbalist in store. Visa, MC.

Previously called Millenium, now part of Panacea with branches in Muswell Hill, Edgware and Watford.

Holland & Barrett, Kingston
Health food shop

- ☛ 12-13 Apple Market, Kingston-upon-Thames KT1 1JF
- ☎ 020 8541 1378
- ◖ M-Sa 9.00-17.30, Su 9.00-18.00
- ⊖ Kingston BR

Fridge and freezer.

Peckham

Made famous by BBC sitcom Only Fools & Horses, Peckham is on the way up, evidenced by the opening of some vegetarian and vegan cafes.

Most of the interest is around the overground train station and Peckhamplex cinema, where you can see the latest blockbusters for only a fiver. Close by is Peckham Levels, opened December 2017, a 7-storey concrete car park converted into a cultural hub and community space with art, photography and yoga studios, and the top two floors open to the public for eating and drinking.

ɭ peckhamlevels.org

The Odds
Vegan cafe & cheesemonger

- 🖎 28 Choumert Road SE15 4RE
- 📞 07428 745 674
- 🕐 Su-W 9.00-17.00, Th-Sa 9.00-21.30
- ⌖ Peckham Rye BR
- ɭ instagram.com/theodds.peckham

Opened July 2019 by Alina and Sean Fenne; open evenings too from Nov 2019.

Weekend brunch from £6 up to £11 for the full English with sausage, scrambled tofu, red haricot baked beans, Portobello mushroom, tomato, leek, avocado and bread; moong dal with beetroot raita and

flatbread; scrambled tofu and f-ish smoked salmon on toast; roasted chestnut mushrooms, cashew cream, crispy onions and fresh herbs on toast; avocado, kimchi, black tahini on toast; jackfruit, avo and cheese toastie; coconut spelt pancakes with blueberries and toasted hazelnuts; açai bowl.

During the week you can also get salads, sandwiches, toasties, panzanella, croissants, pain au chocolat, cake, muffins, donuts, miso brownie and ice cream.

Opening sample evening menu snacks £3-£3.50 include olives,or sourdough with olive oil and apple cider balsamic. Dishes £7.50-£14 are roasted cauliflower steak with sumac, tahini and chilli sauce; beetroot carpaccio; radicchio, pear and walnut salad with veganzola; battered banana blossom fish with mushy peas; pumpkin, potato, spelt and chestnut flour gnocchi with yellow chanterelles, garlic cashew cream sauce. Affogato dessert £4.50, add kahlua £3. Three cheeses with oat cakes, flaxseed crackers and chutney £11.

Fresh cold pressed juices £4. Coconut water or kombucha £3.50. Teas, coffees £1.50-£2.90. Cocktails.

Dogs welcome. Discretionary 12.5% service charge at weekends. They sell artisan cheeses and vegan butters.

567

Zionly Manna
Vegan Afro-Caribbean rastarant

- ☛ Unit 41, 48 Rye Lane Indoor Market, Peckham SE15 5BY (between Highshore Rd and Elm Grove)
- ☎ 07831 136 705
- 🕐 M-Sa 10.00-18.00, Su closed
- ⊖ Peckham Rye
- ➹ Facebook Zionly Manna Vegan Rastarant

Vegan cafe at the back of the market, run by charismatic vegan rastaman Jahson Peat, owner of various African inspired art and antiques businesses and now this. Unique blend of spices and herbs mixed with a creative adventure of foods from Africa and the Caribbean. Selection of raw food and salads, hot vegan meals and soups.

Big portions. £5 for a plate of three items such as chickpea dumplings, pilau rice, vermicelli, spicy callallo, fried plantain, ital stews such as smutton with crunchy veg and soya meat, salad.

Wraps, roti, panini and pittas. Soups.

Double chocolate cake £2; cupcakes £2.50 include lemon and rum, gluten-free chocolate cupcake. Soya or not soya based ice-cream.

Unusual juices and smoothies such as ginger and clove. Roots tea and tonic. Rasta root beer. Fresh coconut water.

Deserted Cactus
Vegan Caribbean cafe

- ☛ Holdrons Arcade units 23 & 25, 135a Rye Lane SE15 4ST
- ☎
- 🕐 Tu-Th 13.00-16.30, F 13.00-16.00, Sa 13.00-18.00, Su-M closed. Check instagram to confirm this week's times.
- ⊖ Peckham Rye
- ➤ londonafrovegan.com
  instagram.com/deserted_cactus
  copelandpark.com/holdronsarcade

Tiny cafe with a couple of tables and an astonishingly awesome savoury soul food menu packed with spices and flavours that changes every day.

Feast your eyes on the daily instagram posts such as shepherds pie with puy and green lentils and three types of mushrooms in a rich sauce; spiced green lentil, butterbean, spinach and mushroom stew with rice and kidney beans, plantain balls and salad; fried dumpling jerk tofu burger with smoked baked plantain, slaw, salads and smoky tamarind sauce; spinach noodle bowl with spring rolls and fried crispy seaweed; or southern fried jackfruit with sides that will satisfy non-vegan KFC fans.

Level Six Cafe
Vegetarian cafe and yoga centre

- ☛ Floor 6, Peckham Levels, 95a Rye Lane SE15 4ST (turn right in front of PeckhamPlex cinema and walk down the green alley to black door on left)
- ☎ 020 3941 1950
- 🕐 Cafe M-Su 9.00-16.00, also M-W 18.00-21.00. Studio, see class schedule
- ⊖ Peckham Rye
- ➤ levelsixstudios.co.uk/food
  peckhamlevels.org

Yoga centre offering many styles, workshops, pilates classes, treatments, and a healthy vegetarian, gluten-free cafe open to all, with lots of comfortable cushions if you feel like settling in for the afternoon to use the wifi. They make almost all their own food including almond milk and raw vegan flapjacks and use only seasonal fruits and veg.

Cold pressed juices and smoothies.

Breakfasts include porridge with almond milk, chia seeds, fruit compote, toasted nuts and seeds and banana chips; avocado seed toast, rainbow chard, wild mushrooms and pine nuts.

For lunch The House with satay, brown rice, plantain, sprouting broccoli; Rice Bowl with black rice, roasted sweet potato, kale, hummus, cherry tomato; soup of the day such as spiced pumpkin with seed toast; marinated aubergine steak with new potatoes, sunflower mayo and autumn slaw.

Fairtrade teas by the Rare Tea Company.

2 Girls' Cafe
Vegetarian cafe

- 24a Peckham Rye SE15 4JR
- 07753 432163
- M-F 08.00-17.00, Sa-Sun 9.00-17.00
- Peckham Rye
- facebook.com/2girlscafe
  instagram.com/2girls_cafe

Cafe and art gallery showcasing the work of local artists.

All day breakfast such as spirulina smoothie bowl. Vegan quiche, burrito, sandwiches, Buddha bowl, beetroot and quinoa burger. Buckwheat crete with fruits. Gluten-free banana and chia seed pancakes.

Pecan cheesecake, chocolate and raspberry cake £3.25.

Smoothies £3.50 such as green, purple with berries, beetroot power. Coffees, cappuccino, latte, chai latte, mocha, hot choc, ice-hot choc and berries, regular or large, £1.50-£3.40. Lattes can come with matcha, lavender, turmeric, beetroot, rose, charcoal, even maca mushroom. Loose leaf teas £2.30, tea bag £1.60.

Free wifi. Dogs welcome. Available for hire for yoga classes, birthday parties. They can do a buffet evening menu for a party of up to 50 people.

Persepolis
Vegetarian cafe & Persian grocer

- 28-30 Peckham High Street SE15 5DT
- 020 7639 8007
- M-Su 10.35-21.00
- Peckham Rye BR (from Victoria), Queen's Rd Peckham (for Lon Bridge)
- foratasteofpersia.co.uk
  Facebook Persepolis in Peckham

If you haven't yet been to the veggie cafe in Peckham's Persian landmark Persepolis, you're in for a treat. The cafe is run by Sally Butcher ("Mrs S.") and the shop by her Persian husband Jamshid ("Mr Shopkeeper"). Vegan mezze, hot chocolate, knickerbocker glory, Persian dishes with tofu and all in a beautiful and delicious-smelling shop. Sample dishes and then buy the ingredients to make them at home, or snack while you shop. In the evening they light candles and you can bring your own alcohol.

Meze platter £4, for two £4, with basket of warm bread. Wraps £4.75. Hotpot of the day wtih rice and salad £7.50. Soup with warm bread £4.50. Vegan knickerbocker glory or sundaes £3.50.

Juices and smoothies £1.50-£2.75. Teas £1.50-£2 include fragrant Persian with cardamon, Afghan green (which they say separates the men from the boys), and ginger with orange, lemon and mint. Coffee, Turkish/Greek coffee, date and cardamon latte, hot choc with carob and spices £1.50-£2.75.

Not sure what to order? Go for meze dishes and share them. The tasting menu is £20 a head with starters and a soft drink and the equivalent of a main course and dessert and coffee, plus no need to choose from the menu or split the bill.

Reservations recommended evening and weekend, deposit required if you are more than 6 people. Service note included, optional 10% service charge for parties of 5+.

The shop has lots of vegan food and they have their own huge Middle Eastern cookbook called Veggiestan. Head for the fridge for dips such as besara smoky broad bean mash, olives, stuffed peppers, baby aubergines stuffed with dates and garlic and walnuts, felafel, salad. Great for posh presents like argan oil, truffles, saffron, backgammon.

One Organic Peckham
Health food shop

- ☛ Holdrons Arcade unit 24, 135a Rye Lane SE15 4ST (opposite Deserted Cactus)
- ☏ 07539 086 783
- ◑ Tu-Sa 10.00-18.00, Su-M closed
- ⊖ Peckham Rye
- ↖ twitter.com/one_organic

Wholefoods. Yogi and Pukka teas. Some bodycare and Ecover products. Fresh juices £2.50 such as "green lean", "liver flush" or "blood clean". The owner Hellinda sources ingredients for supplements mainly from Latin America and has her own label organic superfoods like acai berry, chlorella, moringa powder, mauby (suppress sugar craving), mulberry. She also prepares her own tinctures and homeopathic and herbal remedies. A small selection of books. Cash only.

Naïfs
Vegetarian restaurant

- 56 Goldsmiths Road SE15 5TN
- 020 3490 2422 (16.00-18.00_
- W-Su 18.00-23.00, last orders 21.30. M-Tu closed.
- Peckham Rye BR (from Victoria), Queen's Rd Peckham (for Lon Bridge)
- naifs.co.uk
  facebook.com/naifsfood
  instagram.com/naifsrestaurant

Vegetarian evening bistro-style restaurant opened October 2019 by owners Tom and Anne and his brothers Max and Finn.

The initial menu, £39 per person, includes dishes such as fava hummus with flatbread, house pickles, olives with green orange and fennel, kohlrabi and pear caesar with olive crumb, fried celeriac with smoked apple and mustard and koji (a bit like miso), mushroom broth with semolina dumplings. For dessert almond and barley ice cream sandwich with fennel caramel, or chocolate mousse with smoked hazelnuts. You can also order dishes individually for £3-£12.

Wines from £4-£7 small glass, £22-£50 botle. Brick Brewery beers £5 can. Cocktail £7-£8.50. Unusual pirits £3.50-£8.

Soft drinks £2.50-£4. Teas, coffee £2.50-£4. Reservations recommended. Maximum table 8 people.

Holland & Barrett, Peckham
Health food shop

- Unit 9, The Aylesham Centre, Rye Lane, Peckham SE15 5EW
- 020 7639 3354
- M-Sa 9.00-18.00, Su 10.00-16.00
- Peckham Rye BR

Fridge and freezer.

Peckham Vegans
Social group

- Facebook Peckham Vegans

For vegans living or working in Peckham and nearby. Socials at local cafes and restaurants, campaigns and more.

Putney
& Wandsworth

Foodilic
Omnivorous cafe

- 85 Putney High Street SW15 1SR
- 020 8704 1503
- M-Sa 08.00-22.00, Su 08.00-22.00
- Putney BR, Putney Bridge
- foodilicputney.co.uk
  facebook.com/foodilicputney

The newest in a chain of four great value vegan-friendly places, also in Brighton and Kings Cross (now called La Valle) , founded by chef Peter Ilic. Lots of salads and raw vegan desserts.

Brunch menu served all day. Organic porridge £4.85 with fresh fruit and soya, oat or almond milk. Baked butterbeans or crushed avocado on sourdough toast £4.85. Spinach, walnut pesto and pignolio (pine nut) cheese stuffed chestnut mushroom, which is raw vegan, £6.50. Vegan full English breakfast £7.50 with sausage, pignolio stuffed chestnut mushroom, button mushrooms, spinach, baked tomato, butterbeans and toast.

Salads are mostly raw vegan, two for £3.80, four for £7.20. Raw vegan sushi, spicy raw falafel, beetroot falafel, each £4.20.

Raw vegan cakes £4.85 feature carrot, chocolate, several cheesecakes and chocolate brownie.

Fresh juices £3.50. Fairtrade organic coffees £1.50-£2.10. Teas £1.50.

Blåbär
Omnivorous Swedish restaurant & home shop

- 3a Lacy Road, Putney SW15 1NH
- 020 8780 2723
- M-Sa 08.00-18.00, Su 9.00-17.00
- East Putney
- blabar.london

Cosy Nordic coffee and shop hidden at the back of the High Street, on two floors where you can enjoy a bite and buy whatever you see around. They sell soft furnishings, decorative items and artefacts, all made by small independent companies or artists from back home. It's quintessential *hygge* (cosy).

If you fancy some *fika* this is the place. *Fika* is a social institution in Sweden, it means taking a proper relaxing break with coffee or tea and maybe some cake. Central to Nordic life it is a cherished time to spend with friends, family or just on your own.

Smashed avocado on Danish rye bread £4.50. Coconut milk porridge with chia seeds £3.50. Gluten-free soup of the day with bread £6.

Gluten-free sweet potato brownie or banana and walnut muffins £1.80-£2.80.

At weekends 9am to 3pm they do brunch £8 with banana and cinnamon buckwheat pancakes, served with blueberry compote, coconut yogurt and maple syrup.

Organic Fairtrade coffee £2.20-£2.80.

Almond, coconut and oat milk 50p extra, soya milk 30p. Hot chocolate and chai £2.85 can be made vegan. Pot of tea £2.50.

Cold drinks £1.80-£2.20 include homemade ginger lemonade, kombucha with lemon, pineapple, strawberry and ice.

On the counter are Pana chocolate, salty liquorice and typical sourdough crispbread.

Seating outside, wifi.

Thai Square, Putney Bridge
Omnivorous Thai restaurant

- 2-4 Lower Richmond Road SW15 1JN
- 020 8780 1811
- M-F 11.00-15.00, 18.00-23.00, Sa 12.00-23.00, Su 12.00-22.30
- Putney Bridge (across river), Putney BR
- thaisq.com

Beautiful location overlooking the river, it feels like you are on a boat. They have a separate vegetarian menu which is mostly vegan.

Starters £7.25-£9.95 including raw papaya with ground cashew nuts, peanuts, tomato, long beans, carrot and lime juice; corn cakes; mixed grilled vegetables and bean curd with peanut sauce; spicy mushroom soup; coconut mushroom soup. Platter of mixed starters £15.

Mains £11.95-£12.50 feature green curry, jungle curry, sweet and sour vegetables with tofu, bean curd with cashew nuts. aubergine with basil leaves, and pad kra pow crispy tofu with long beans, oyster mushrooms, peppers, garlic and chillies.

Wine medium glass £6.25, large £7.95,

bottle £21.95.

Wifi. High chair.

Wagamama Putney
Omnivorous Japanese restaurant

- 50-54 High Street, Putney SW15 1SQ
- 020 8785 3636
- Su-Tu 11.00-22.00, W-Su 11.00-23.00
- Putney Bridge
- wagamama.com

Revital, Putney
Wholefood shop

- 75 Putney High Street SW15 1SR
- 020 8780 0809
- M-F 9.00-19.00, Sa 9.00-18.00, Su 11.00-16.00
- Putney BR
- revital.co.uk

Lots of organic food, a wide range of toiletries and cruelty-free cosmetics.

In the fridge Nush, Coyo and Sojade yogurts, Chia Pod, Booja Booja truffles, Soupology, Biona, Great Food, tempeh and tofu, Tofutti, Follow Your Heart, Violife.

In the freezer Coyo, Booja Booja and Swedish Glace ice-cream, Fry's and Clive's pies.

Bodycare including Dr Hauschka, Weleda, Noah, Dr Bronner's, Khadi Natural, Lavera, Green People and Sukin. Vitamins and minerals such as Viridian, Terranova, Pukka, Wild Nutrition, Biocare and lots of sports nutrition. Herbal and homeopathy including Bach flower remedies and Ainsworth.

Aromatherapy. Cleaning products by Ecover, Ecos, Ecozone, Sodasan and Greenscent. There is always a qualified member of staff who can help you. Kids' section.

Holland & Barrett, Putney
Health food shop

- 99-101 High Street, Putney SW15 1SS
- (020 8785 7401
- M-F 08.30-20.00, Sa 08.30-19.00, Su 10.00-18.00
- Putney BR, East Putney

Fridge and freezer.

WANDSWORTH

Southside Wandsworth shopping centre has a Waitrose supermarket, Cineworld, Virgin Active health club and restaurants including Wagamama and Rosso Pomodoro, which does a couple of vegan pizzas for £12.95. For the two new vegan restaurants Amrutha Lounge and Vegan Express, head down Garratt Lane towards Earlsfield and Tooting. (see Tooting chapter)

Planet Organic, Wandsworth
Wholefood supermarket & omnivorous cafe

- Southside Shopping Centre, 52 Garratt Lane SW18 4TF
- (020 8877 8330
- M-Sa 07.30-21.00, Su 09.00-21.00
- Wandworth Town BR, East Putney
- planetorganic.com

Very bright shop in the newly renovated shopping centre. Check out the store's promotional offers on the tables in the entrance.

Cafe and take-away food. Small bowl or box of hot and cold food £5.50, medium £7.50, large £8.50. Menus change every 2 to 3 months using seasonal veg. Choose for example from cauliflower curry, veg korma, turmeric dal, sprouted brown rice, sweet potato wedges, roast potatoes, winter roast veg, tofu stir-fry, falafel and hummus, and salads like beetroot & cranberry with raspberry vinaigrette, buckwheat & roasted veg, Mexican quinoa, plus dressings like cashew caesar, kimchi, omega 3 seeds mix.

Mexican chilli pie and open sandwich with teriyaki aubergine, hummus, sundried tomato and sprouts on rye bread. Vegan soup. They have a vegan pastry range.

Large selection of juices and smoothies, with three types of plant based protein versions such as The Bench Press, Green and Lean and PB Powerhouse, as well as vegan specialty hot drinks. 7 types of plant milks which are not charged as extra, unlike the "vegan tax" in certain coffee bars.

In the take-away fridge are savoury and sweet snacks such as Laura's Idea, Hoxton, Yummy Tummy, Planet Organic mezze bowls, açai and chia pots, sweet potato flapjack, cakes and bars.

There is a small fruit and vegetables section, next to the huge range of chilled food which includes Taifun, Clearspring, Biona, Florentin, White Rabbit pizza, Real Olive Co., Modir Jord (jars of turnip salad, kimchi, sauerkraut, cabbage and kale, kohlrabi). Follow Your Heart and Violife. Yogurts by Abbot Kenney, Coyo, Nush, Coconut Collective and Sojade.

Frozen food by Goodlife, Amy's vegan lasagne; Pack'd smoothies; Lily's Hanna's raw , Booja Booja and Coconut Collective ice cream.

Lots of macrobiotics, coconut oils, unusual pastas such as red lentil or sprouted spelt, various kinds of vegan pesto.

Chocolate such as Pacari Raw, Goodio Chocolate, Loving Earth, Coco Chocolatier and many more.

Health and bodycare at the back by Sukin, Green People, Weleda, Barefoot Sos, Jason, Faith In Nature, Evolve, John Masters, Urtekram, Ren, Dr Hauschka, Neal's Yard, Nourish, Lavera and Pai. Inika makeup.

Big baby and kids section with food by Ella's Kitchen, Organix, Biona, Holle, and bodycare including Weleda, Jason, Organic Children, Earth Friendly Baby, Bioskin, and

Jack & Jill bio-degradable nappies.

Supplements by Pukka, Living Nutrition, Biocare, Viridian, Terranova, Solgar and Pukka. Protein powder by Sunwarrior, Vega, Aduna, Naturya, Green Origins and Pulsin.

Cleaning and washing products from Greenscent, Attitude, Ecos and Ecover. Yarrah cats and dogs food. Sage and Vitamix blenders.

High chairs. Wifi but you need to register online. On the first floor there is a fitness studio separate from Planet Organic.

Wagamama, Wandsworth
Omnivorous Japanese chain restaurant

- ☛ Southside shopping centre, 90-92 Garratt Lane SW18 4DJ
- ☏ 020 8 875 0653
- ◑ Su-W 11.00-22.00 Th-Sa 11.00-23.00
- ⊖ Wandsworth Town BR
- ↖ wagamamma.com

Holland & Barrett, Wandsworth
Health food shop

- ☛ SU93, Southside Shopping Centre, Wandsworth SW18 4DG
- ☏ 020-8871 1021
- ◑ M-Sa 9.00-19.00, Su 11.00-17.00
- ⊖ Wandsworth Town BR

Fridge and freezer.

RICHMOND

upon Thames

You can enjoy a nice walk by the river, stopping off at an outside table at the long established vegetarian cafes **Tide Tables** of **Hollyhock**, or the new vegan **Retreat Kitchen** or **Bhuti**, and perhaps finishing at a pub.

Richmond Park is a nature reserve and the largest of London's royal parks, where at least 600 wild deer live. Plenty of space for picnics.

Kew Gardens are a royal botanical garden of 300 acres and 30,000 species of plants. Keep an eye out for events and exhibitions/ A day ticket is £15. Apart from some salads and coffee at the White Peaks cafe and some bits and bobs from Orangery restaurant, there is not much for vegans, so stock up before you go in at Olivers Wholefood.

There are many shops nearby, most of them independent ones.

Other attractions are Richmond Theatre and some art galleries.

The Retreat Kitchen
99% vegan cafe

- 🖅 16 Hill Rise, Richmond TW10 6UA
- ☏ claire@theretreatkitchen.co.uk
- 🕐 Tu-F 08.30-17.00, Sa-Su 9.00-17.00, M closed
- ⊖ Richmond
- ⭢ theretreatkitchen.co.uk
  facebook.com/TheRetreatKitchen

New vegan cafe (apart from the option of dairy in hot drinks) in the centre of town, near the river, park and shops, opened February 2017. Founders Claire and Maggie met the year before in Thailand on the BBC2 whole person makeover show *The Retreat* presented by Nick Knowles (currently on Netflix). In the programme everyone followed a plant-based diet and did yoga, fasting, exercise and counselling for 28 days.They were ready for a change of careers and returned home with a new zest for life, bringing *The Retreat* with them, and swapping ready meals for raw vegan in their new kitchen.

Weekday breakfasts till 10.30 £6-£8.50 can be berry and oat smoothie bowl topped with fresh fruit, chickpea omelette, ciabatta sausage sandwich, scrambled tofu and spinach wrap with sautéed potato, smashed avocado on rye toast. Weekend brunch till 3pm adds to this a pancake stack, and a full English cooked breakfast £9 with scrambled tofu, sausage, smokey beans,

garlic mushrooms, hash brown, tomato, sourdough toast or gluten-free bread.

Weekday lunch till 3.30pm £6-£9 features soup of the day with sourdough, falafel, savoury open sandwiches, salad plate, quiche and salad, hot dish of the day.

Lots of amazing cakes and treats.

Juices £4, smoothies £4.50. Pot of organic loose leaf tea £3. Coffees £2-£3.20 with almond, soy, coconut or oat milk. Soft drinks £1.50-£2.

Vegan organic wine, beer and Prosecco by vegan supplier Vintage Roots.

Sometimes open evenings, such as mezze wine evening, £22.50 for a mezze board and a bottle of organic vegan wine for two to share. To book for more than 4 people email Maggie@ or Claire@ theretreatkitchen.co.uk.

Events and private hire.

Tide Tables
Vegetarian café

☛ 2 The Archways, Richmond Bridge, Richmond, Surrey TW9 1TH

☏ 020 8948 8285

🕐 Mo-Su daylight hours

⊖ Richmond

↑ tidetablescafe.com

Vegetarian café under the arch of Richmond Bridge near the town centre, with beautiful views of the Thames, a riverside terrace and outside seating in summer, though people sit ouside year round for the view. Child and dog friendly, a nice place to meet friends for lunch or stop off after a bike ride in Richmond Park, or a boat trip on the river.

The menu marks what is gluten-free, organic and vegan.

For a sustaining breakfast you could have a fruit smoothie £4.50 and a round of toast and jam £2.50.

For lunchtime and evening meals £2.90-£7.90 there are samosa, vegan soup or gazpacho, bean and veg chilli on brown rice, Moroccan harissa flatbread, falafel plate, filled baked potato. Everything is served with salad.

Vegan cakes £3.50 such as lemon and poppyseed or gluten-free brownie with orange. Tubs of lemon sorbet £2.30.

Fairtrade teas, coffees, hot chocolate, e.g. £2.90 for a latte or cappuccino, add 30p for soya milk. Juices, freshly squeezed orange juice £3.50 for half pint, smoothies £4.50. Organic wine £5.50 medium glass. Organic cider £4.95 pint. Beers include Becks, London Pride, Peroni £3.95 and organic German lager £4.95

A great 'coffice' for students and footloose workers, who are welcome to plug in to the free wifi and hang out all day. Child friendly, high chairs. Party hire.

Hollyhock Café
Vegetarian café

☛ Petersham Road, Richmond TW10 6UX

☎ 020 8948 6555

🕐 M-Su daylight hours

⊖ Richmond

Another vegetarian café, linked to Tide Tables, in the middle of the Terrace Gardens park overlooking the Thames, with really lovely views. Good vegan labelling, and many items Fairtrade and organic.

Very child friendly, parents sit on the veranda while kids play on the grass. Dogs welcome outside, water dishes are kept replenished. In winter they provide blankets and hot water bottles so you can sit outside, or you can stay inside at one of the indoor tables or on the sofa as the wood-burning stove works up a cosy fug. Free wifi and relaxed atmosphere make this a great place to bring a laptop and work.

Main meals include baked potato with various fillings, with or without salad, £5.50-£8.50: substantial falafel plate with 3 falafels, salad, hummus and bread roll; vegetable samosa with salad; chickpeas in Tandoori sauce with naan bread. Mixed salad plate £4.70 with choices such as spinach, rocket and sunflower seed, mixed beans. Plenty of sundries such as samosa £2.90, hummus with toast £2.95. Miso soup £2.50 and hearty soup with organic bread roll £5.50, all year round.

Cakes such as lemon poppy seed and gluten-free brownie with orange £3.50.

Coffee, hot chocolate and herbal teas all Fairtrade, from £2 for an espresso to £2.95 for a mocha, add 30p for soya. Filter coffee £2.40, free refills weekdays. Fresh smoothies £3.50-£4.50, squeezed orange juice and carrot, apple and ginger £3.50. Other soft drinks in fridge. No alcohol.

Menu has vegan and gluten-free sections, as well as kids' favourites. High chairs. Party hire. Wifi.

Bhuti
Vegan tea room and eco wellbeing centre

- 50 Hill Rise, Richmond TW10 6UB
- 0330 400 3108
- M-Su 08.00-18.00
- Richmond
- bhuti.co
  facebook.com/bhutilondon

New vegan cafe with an open kitchen. 100% organic, gluten-free and refined sugar-free.

Brunch £6.50 to £8 served all day features porridge bowl, buckwheat paleo toast with avocado and lemon and chilli or nut banner and banana, granola bowl, buckwheat and banana pancakes, soup of the day.

Main menu £8-£12: soup of the day with buckwheat bites; hot dish and raw dish of the day; Smorgasbord, a selection of all of the dishes of the day. Bhuti bowls can contain quinoa or rice, seasonal leaves, roasted Mediterranean veg, raw slaw, curried cauliflower, sweet potato wedges, herby falafel, spicy beanburger, miso-glazed mushroom. Topped with toasted cashews, avocado, coconut bacon, house hummus, toasted pumpkin seeds, pomegranate, satay sauce, cheesy turmeric, maple mustard.

Snacks £2-£5: homemade raw vegan cakes and cheesecake, banana bread, macaroons, cookies, raw chocolate doughnut energy balls, trail mix.

Classy smoothies and juices £5, large £7, with ingredients such as hemp, quinoa milk, nut butter, maca and. Top up with superfood shots £1-£3.

Hot drinks £3 to £3.50 can be made with quinoa, hemp, almond, soya, coconut and rice milk such as matcha or chicory or golden elixir latte and hot chocolate. Infusions £3.50 include ginger, lemon, turmeric, mint, lemongrass and ginger.

Members have their own room where they can eat and/or work on their laptop. Once a month they organise a supper club event with 3 course menu, which you can book online.

The manager is a nutritional therapist.

As well as the food side there is a day spa with many holistic treatments such as facials, massage (aromatherapy, deep tissue, Indian head, reflexology, shiatsu, Swedish, Thai yoga, orthopaedic and sport), body scrubs, waxing, pedicure and manicure. Ayurveda, acupuncture, homeopathy and naturopathy consultations. They even have a package for brides and grooms. For yoga and pilates lovers there are studios with skylight windows.

The shop at the front has some vegan and organic products such as makeup from Inika and Ila face and bodycare. Yoga and pilates clothes.

Wagamama, Richmond
Omnivorous Japanese restaurant

- 3 Hill Street, Richmond TW9 1SX
- 020 8948 3990
- M-Sa 11.00-23.00, Su 11.00-22.00
- Richmond
- wagamama.com

See Chains for details.

Olivers Wholefood
Wholefood shop

- 5 Station Approach, Kew Gardens, Richmond TW9 3QB (next to tube)
- 020 8948 3990
- M-Sa 9.00-20.30, Su 10.00-20.30
- Kew Gardens
- oliverswholefoods.co.uk

Open since 1989 this wholefood shop has a wide selection of produce, not all veggie. Pick up munchies for a trip to Kew Gardens such as sandwiches, wraps, pastries, salads by Laura's Idea, and sweet treats such as raw vegan chocolate cake slices, tubs of mousse, Booja Booja truffles and chia pots.

Organic fruit and veg. Bakery section. Fridge has tempeh, tofu and fake meats such as Vegideli, Oasis, Taifun, Tofurky. Biona mini burger, unusual falafel mixes like beetroot and walnut. Freezer has veggie burgers, sausages, Amy's Kitchen ready meals, and ice-cream by Booja Booja, Coyo and Swedish Glace. Vegan wines.

Large bodycare range includes Jason, Lavera, Sukin, Ren, Nourish, Tisserand and Faith in Nature. Lip balms from the Visionary Soap Company and Green People.

Cleaning products include Ecomil and Greenscent.

Supplements such as Terranova, Viridian, Pukka and Floradix. Herbal and homeopathic remedies. Books on healthy and green living. Trained nutritionist and beauty therapist for advice.

Regular lectures in-store on topics like living food and digestive health.

Revital Health, Richmond
Health food shop & juice bar

- 2 The Quadrant House, The Quadrant, Richmond TW9 1BP
- 020 8334 1049
- M-Sa 9.30-18.30, Su 11.00-16.00
- Richmond
- revital.co.uk

Near the HQ of the Institute for Optimum Nutrition, handy for their students and clients.

Range includes wholefoods, raw, and a well-stocked fridge with tofu, tempeh, meat-free slices, vegan cheese, spreads, yogurt and raw Booja Booja truffles.

Bodycare and natural beauty including Faith in Nature, A'kin.

Supplements by Viridian, Higher Nature, Pukka, Biocare, Revital own brand. Homeopathy. Essential oils. Health books.

Cleaning by Ecover, Sodasan, Ecos, Earth Friendly.

Whole Foods Market, Richmond
Omnivorous wholefood supermarket

- 1-3 George St TW9 1AB
- 020 8334 4130
- M-Sa 08.00-21.00, Su 11.00-17.00
- Richmond
- wholefoodsmarket.com/stores/richmond

Seating inside and outside. Salad bar. All kinds of wholefoods. Bodycare and health.

Two hours free parking at the Paradise Car Park on Paradise Road TW9 1SQ when you purchase over £25 in store.

Home delivery service.

Holland & Barrett, Richmond
Health food shop

- 51/52 George St, Richmond TW9 1HJ
- 020 8940 1007
- M-Sa 08.30-19.00, Su 10.00-18.00
- Richmond

Big chilled section with Soupology, Vegi Deli, Cheatin, Sheeze, Violife, Cheezly and Provamel. Frozen food by Tofurky, Okobay and Booja Booja ice-cream.

Neal's Yard Remedies, Richmond
Herbs and cruelty-free bodycare

- ☛ 15 King Street, Richmond-upon-Thames TW9 1ND
- ☏ 020 8948 9248
- ◖ M, W-Sa 10.00-18.00, Tu 10.00-20.00, Su 12.00-17.00
- ⊖ Richmond
- ↖ nealsyardremedies.com

Herbs and spices by weight. Organic toiletries. Natural remedies. Supplements by Viridian. Also therapy rooms offering over 20 kinds of treatments from acupuncture to Swedish massage.

For smoothies and juices try **Joe & The Juice** on George Street. Open daily 07.00-19.00, Su from 08.00. There is also a **Leon** at 35 Lower George Street.

STREATHAM

Wholemeal Café
Wholefood vegetarian restaurant

- 📞 1 Shrubbery Road SW16 2AS
- 📞 020 8769 2423
- 🕐 M-Su 12.00-22.00 (last order), closed bank holidays
- ⊖ Streatham BR, Streatham Hill BR
- ↖ wholemealcafe.com (menus)

Wholefood veggie restaurant opened 1978, with Thai, Indian, Mediterranean and world cuisine. Large vegan selection.

7 starters and snacks include garlic mushrooms with pitta £5.25, or soup of the day £3.25, usually vegan. 13 main dishes £7.95-£9.50 include French ratatouille or aubergine and veg Burgundy casserole, Hungarian goulash stew, Thai sweet and sour veg, Thai coconut curry, Cajun veg casserole, nut burgers with salad and salsa and roasted potatoes, homity pie, Moroccan chicpea stew, large mixed salad, Mediterranean savoury nut crumble.

Meal deals £6.50 Mon-Fri 12.00-16.00 such as bake or casserole of the day with brown rice or salad.

Desserts £3.95-£4.25 such as sponge cake with soya custard, or wholemeal bramley apple fruit crumble.Freshly squeezed juices £3.50. Pot of green or jasmine tea £2.20, coffees £2.20. They have soya milk. Organic vegan alcoholic drinks such as wine from £4.95 glass, £20 bottle, Samuel Smith beer and pale ale £4.95.

Child portions, high chair.

Maitri Health
Vegetarian health food shop

- 📞 252 Streatham High Road SW16 1HS (near Wholemeal Cafe)
- 📞 020 8769 0065
- 🕐 M-Sa 9.30-18.30, Su 11.00-16.00
- ⊖ Streatham, Streatham Hill BR
- ↖ holistic-well-being.co.uk
  facebook.com/MaitriHealth

Two floors with a very large range of foodstuffs on the lower floor, while on the upper floor are supplements, remedies, aromatherapy oils, green products, stationery and cruelty-free cosmetics.

Ecover and Ecofriendly cleaning products. People come from a long way to shop here.

There's plenty for vegans including the whole Plamil range.

Herbal dispensary with western and ayurvedic herbs, and an in-store herbalist.

Holland & Barrett, Streatham
Health food shop

- 📞 210 Streatham High Rd SW16 1BW
- 📞 020 8769 1418
- 🕐 M-Sa 9.00-18.00, Su 10.00-17.00
- ⊖ Streatham Hill BR

Fridge and freezer.

Tribe V
Vegan cafe

- 22 Streatham High Road, Streatham Hill SW16 1DB
- 07341 937 812
- M-F 10.00-20.00, Sa closed, Su 10.00-20.00
- Streatham BR, Streatham Hill BR
- tribev.co
  facebook.com/tribe.streatham.1
  instagram.com/tribe_streatham

New vegan cafe, juice bar and co-working space. There's lots of wood and plants and the tables have power points, bring your laptop or a book to work or chill.

Light breakfasts till midday £3.90-£6.80 include jerk beans on toasted sourdough; quinoa porridge; tofu and almond French toast topped with berries; quinoa porridge; fried plantain sandwich with sweet chilli hummus.

All day breakfast £10 with sausages, jerk beans, mushrooms, sweet onion and avocado.

Appetisers £2.50-£4 such as Lincolnshire sausage roll, cauliflower bites, mac n cheese, sweet potato fries.

Mains £7.50 such as seasoned rice with mixed veg and plantain stew; jollof and plantain stew with bulgar wheat, extra large portion £10.50. Fried tofu salad £5.90.

Donuts, brownies, raw cake, nut ball £2-£4.20. Ice cream £1 per scoop.

Drinks £2-£3 include ginger beer, J20, kombucha. Coffee and herbal teas from £1.90.

TOOTING

Balham and Earlsfield,

Tooting Market is a mishmash of world cultures where you can find fascinating and unique places selling music, ladies' and men's fashion, arts and crafts, furniture, hair and nails. There is a lot of food from fruit & veg stalls to the vegan cafes **Get Juiced** and **V-Belly**, pizza at Frano Manca, coffee shops, a falafel stall (Meza) and zero-packaging food store **BYO**. Also this is the place for getting anything repaired. Market open Su-Th 08.00-22.00, F-Sa 08.00-23.00.

▶ tootingmarket.com

The Broadway and Upper Tooting Road have lots of bargain shops, various restaurants, Indian take-aways and Asian sweet shops. **Saravanaa Bhavan** is a big, authentic Indian vegetarian restaurant.

Towards Earlsfield are what this area has always needed, a couple of excellent new vegan restaurants **Vegan Express** and **Amrutha Lounge**.

Up in Balham, **Wicked Vegan** is a new fast food vegan cafe.

Get Juiced
Vegan smoothie & juice bar, restaurant

- 🢒 Tooting Market, Unit 15a, 21-23 Tooting High Street SW17 0SN
- ☎ 07857 803781
- 🕐 Tu-W 9.00-17.00, Th 9.00-17.30, F-Sa 9.00-18.00, Su 10.00-17.00
- ⊖ Tooting Broadway
- ↖ facebook.com/getjuicedbar
  instagram.com/getjuicedbar
  tootingmarket.com

Great value, colourful place in the L-bend of the market with wooden tables shared with the bar next door.

For breakfast, smoothie bowls £6 or £8, porridge £4.50 or £6.50. Gluten-free wraps and toasties £6.50 filled with lots of veggies plus coconut cream cheese and chickpea chuna or jerk jackfruit or sprouted hummus.

Sweet and savoury pancakes £5.95-£8.45, each with several fillings such as jerk jackfruit and avocado with veggies and sundried tomato, or assorted fruits, or cinnamon apple sauce topped with crumble. You can add ice cream.

Soup £4.50, large £6.50. Hearty pumpkin, chickpea and coconut stew or Jollof quinoa salad £7.95.

Banana bread £3, raw Snickers £3.50.

Mixed veg and fruit juices, smoothies and sugar cane juice made to order in four sizes £2.50-£7.50. Coconut water £3. Herbal teas £1.50. Lattes £2.50-£4.50 can come with chai, turmeric, matcha, moringa or hemp.

V Belly
Vegan British cafe

- 🢒 Tooting Yard Market Unit T13, 20 Totterdown Street SW17 8TA
- ☎ 07966 057566
- 🕐 Tu-Sa 12.00-22.00, Su 12.00-19.00, M closed
- ⊖ Tooting Broadway
- ↖ Just Eat / Deliveroo VBELLY,

Tooting's hidden gem of a little vegan restaurant is right at the back of the Yard Market, with shared tables and an entrance with service counter inside, and their own outside tables and another entrance on the street.

Nibbles £4.50-£6.50 like wild mushroom croquettes with garlic cashew dip, nachos with melty vegan cheddar and black beans, and beer-battered celeriac with curry sauce.

Belly Thumpers £7-£9 such as burger with crispy onions and cheese in a beetroot bun, Moving Mountains burger with all the trimmings, spiced seitan kebab, tomato and aubergine stew with kale and butter beans and garlic cream, nuts bean squash with creamy satay sauce and cauliflower rice.

Sides £1-£3.20 include sauces, slaw, fries.

Soft drinks £2.20. Beers £3.50. Bottle of wine £14.

Vegan Express
Vegan restaurant

- 913 Garratt Lane SW17 0LT
- 020 8127 6560
- M-F 17.00-23.00, Sa-Su 12.00-23.00
- Tooting Broadway
- veganexpress.co.uk
  Facebook Vegan Express
  instagram.com/vegan.express

Family run business opened by husband and wife Charles and Ulrika Diallo in 2016. Charles has 20 years experience as a chef in kitchens in the UK and abroad. Their motto is making vegan mainstream. Everything is homemade and they also cater events. The restaurant is very spacious and bright and has a vast selection of dishes. The menu is divided into pizzas, lunch, evening and children's.

Pizzas, £10.50 to £13, feature Margherita, artichoke and spinach, Garden, seitan salami, rosso with tofu cottage cheese, cashew ricotta, pine nut white sauce, mushroom white sauce, butternut rosso.

Lunches include soup of the day £4.50-£6.50; salad bar £7.50; gluten-free red lentil or seitan or spinach-potato-cashew cheese and veg patties with triple cooked chips or season roasted vegetables £9.50-£10.50; gluten-free burger £11.50 with skinny potato wedges; black bean broccoli mushroom burger or red lentil cauliflower burger. Vegan fish & chips £12.50 is made from tofu marinated with seaweed, served with triple cooked chips and mushy peas.

Evening starters £5.50-£6.50 include grilled pepper with papaya and mango salad and basil dressing; kelp noodle avocado sea salad with miso dressing; fruit ceviche soup with Thai basil oil.

Evening mains £11.50-£13.50 feature wild mushroom & potato pavé with golden polenta cubes with tomato coulis, red wine and herb oil; grilled marinated tofu with puy lentil salsa, spinach and red pepper; roasted beef tomato stuffed with quinoa, chanterelle, pine nuts and crushed sweet pea sauce; butternut squash, lentil and cauliflower moussaka with garlic bread & salad; seitan Portobello stroganoff with rice.

Dessert £5.50-£5.80 such as raw tiramisu, rich chocolate tart with ice-cream, chocolate mousse, raw zucchini cheese cake, raw pomegranate coconut mousse, chocolate and raspberry gateau, Victoria sponge.

The children's menu comes with side salad. For main course £5.50-£7.50 the kids could have spaghetti and vegan meatballs in tomato sauce, mini margherita, vegan fish fingers or mini falafel burger with chips. For pudding £4.50-£6.50 there are waffle with ice-cream and fresh fruit, ice cream cup, chocolate mousse or fruit salad. Freshly squeezed fruit juices (8oz) £1.50.

12oz smoothies and juices £4.50. Homemade chocolate, strawberry or vanilla milk £2.50 made with almond, coconut, oat or soya. Coconut water £1.80. Teas and coffee £1.90-£2.50.

Wine from £4.25 glass, £16.50-£34 bottle. Organic beers £6 such as Eco Warrior or London Porter.

High chairs. Wifi.

VEGAN EXPRESS
www.veganexpress.co.uk   020 8127 6560

Amrutha Lounge
Vegan soul food restaurant & take-away

- 326 Garratt Lane, Earlsfield SW18 4EJ (near Earlsfield Road)
- 020 8001 4628
- Tu 18.00-22.00; W-F 12.00-15.00, 18.00-22.00, Sa 13.00-22.00, Su 13.00-21.00, M closed
- Earlsfield BR, Southfields
- amrutha.co.uk
  facebook.com/AmruthaUK

Opened February 2018, specialising in Indian and Thai food, and already getting rave reviews everywhere for quality and fantastic value for money. Take-away box £5, large £7, eat in £12. Selection buffet £15 per person, minimum two people, great for your first visit, grand selection £20.

Mains include Buddha Box with chickpea, lentil and coconut curry, brown rice, sesame slaw, crispy pakoras, satay and sweet chilli dips; Rasta Box with sweet potato and bean stew, plantain, dumkkplings, collard greens and brown rice; noodle stir-fry with roast mushrooms, broccoli and crunchy peanut sauce; Thai green curry with nori fritters and satay dip; big salad with marinated mushrooms, cashew cheese sauce, chilli jam and raw onion bread. Side of crispy pakoras, tofish tempura, polenta or sweet potato fries £4.

Desserts £5 include chocolate and raspberry brownie with ice-cream, and raw cheesecakes such as coffee and cinnamon, blueberry and lemon, chocolate and orange, and lemon and lime.

Soft drinks £3.50. Juices and smoothies such as Choco Heaven with brazil nut milk, date, lucuma, maca and cacao. Teas and coffees. Bring your own alcohol.

Saravanaa Bhavan, Tooting
Vegetarian South Indian restaurant

- 254 Upper Tooting Road SW17 0DN
- 020 8355 3555
- M-Su 10.00-22.30
- Tooting Broadway
- saravanabhavan.com

Part of a worldwide chain, headquartered in Chennai, India with UK branches in Croydon, East Ham, Ilford, Soho, Southall and Wembley. This Tooting branch opened in 2011 and is a large, bright, informal cafe-style restaurant, popular among the local Indian community.

Starters £1.50-£3.95|. Lots of south Indian specialities such as adai avial £3.25, a pancake made of pulses and lentils, served with Kerala style sauce of fresh vegetables, coconut paste and spices. Chinese options such as mushroom Manchurian.

Impressive range of dosas £2.75-£4.75 such as kara dosa, a rice crepe with spicy onion and potato filling. Uttapam lentil pizzas £2.95-3.75. South Indian meal £6.95 with curries, rice, salad, side dish, chappathi or poori and sweet. North Indian thali £7.95 with soup, salad, pilao, 3 side dishes, dal, kattol, fried papad, 3 chappatis and sweet. Business meal £4.25.

The manager told us that all desserts contain dairy (though one staff member had told us some were vegan).

Juices £2.75. Fizzy drinks 95p. Tea or coffee £1. Dairy milk only. No alcohol.

Children welcome, high chairs.

Pooja
Vegetarian take-away

- 168-170 Upper Tooting Road SW17 7ER (corner Hebdon Rd)
- 020 8672 4523
- M-Su 09.00-21.00, 365 days a year
- Tooting Bec, Tooting Broadway
- poojasweets.com

Family owned Indian bakery with a wide selection of Asian savouries and sweets, most of them are gluten-free and some sugar-free also. Lebanese and Turkish sweets. Dry pulses and nuts sold by weight.

Breakfast, lunchtime meals, take-away only. Lunch thali from £3.50. They do next day delivery when ordered before 12.00 (excluding weekends).

They cater events and at festivals.

Holland & Barrett, Tooting
Health food shop

- 3 Mitcham Road SW17 9PA
- 020 8767 8552
- M-F 08.30-20.00, Sa 08.30-19.00, Su 10.00-18.00
- Tooting Broadway

Fridge and freezers.

Wicked Vegan
Vegan fast food take-away

- ☛ 14 Hildreth Street, Balham SW12 9RQ
- ☏ 020 8673 4163
- ◷ Tu-Sa 11.00-21.00, Su 11.00-18.00, M closed
- ⊖ Balham
- ↟ wickedvegan.uk
  instagram.com/wickedveganuk

Opened May 2018, giving fried chicken and burgers a vegan makeover.

Burgers £8.50-£9.50 include deep fried jackfruit; black bean patty with baba ganoush, spinach, scallion, gherkins, cashew nuts; chicpea and barley with red onion tartar and shichimi mayo; cargrilled carrot and lentil with guacamole, roasted kale.

Baps and wraps £7-£7.50 such as grilled avocado, marinated beans, cream cheese, black beans; beer marinated aubergine with miso heritage carrots, deep fried sage, spinach and tomato; Fresh italian tomatoes with homemade basil pesto and Japanese pepper; blueberry BBQ marinated jackfruit.

Sprcials £5-£7.50 feature deep fried jackfruit wings with sauce; Machos with gaucamole, black beans, cheese, jalapeño; loaded chips with pulled jackfruit, chipotle mayo, chilli; mac & cheese.

Skin on or sweet potato fries, coleslaw, rice crackers £3-£4. Sauces £1.

Raspberry and chocolate cake £3.50, flajpack £2.90.

Shakes and smoothies £5.50. Teas £2.50.

As Nature Intended, Balham
Organic and health food shop

☛ 186 Balham High Rd SW12 9BP)
☎ 020 8675 2923
◕ M-Sa 9.00-21.00, Su 10.00-20.00
⊖ Balham
🔦 asnatureintended.uk.com

Organic store that aims to combine the variety of a supermarket (over 5,000 products) with the product range found in traditional health food shops. Not completely vegetarian but many vegan items, including Japanese and tofu-based foods and tempeh. Vegan wines are clearly labelled.

Many items are suitable for those with food allergies such as sugar-, gluten-, salt- or yeast-free. Bread and gluten-free muffins. Raw foods and superfoods. Sandwiches and pies in fridge to take away. Raw vegan brownies, and plenty of chocolate. Freezer has veggie burgers and several vegan ice cream brands.

Following a renovation in 2018, they added bulk (zero packaging) foods like grains, cereals, nuts, coffee and dried fruits. Also bulk cleaning products, laundry detergent and softener, shampoo, conditioner, shower gel and bath salts.

Beauty and skincare products including Tisserand, Jason, A'kin, Faith in Nature, Earth Friendly Baby. Inika and Lavera makeup.

Supplements. Herbal and homeopathic, aromatherapy oils. There is a qualified nutritionist in the remedies section, and an experienced advisor with in-house training. Lots of information on recommended treatments for various conditions on their website.

The Health Store
Health food store

☛ 246 Upper Tooting Road SW17 7EX
☎ 020 8672 5417
◕ M-Sa 9.30-18.30, Su closed
⊖ Tooting Broadway
🔦 nutritionandbeauty.org.uk

Large range of wholefoods, gluten-free,and vegan. Chilled and frozen include tofu, Meridian spreads, cheeses like Violife, Sheese and Tofutti. Lots of herbal teas.

Many supplements such as Viridian, Biocare, Pukka, Solgar. Protein powders including hemp, pea, rice and soya. Lots of other sports nutrition and supplements.

Lots of organic bodycare by Green People, Weleda, Thursday Plantation, Faith in Nature. Hair dyes and henna.

Cleaning products include Ecover and Method.

Natural and herbal remedies, ayurvedic products, homeopathy, aromatherapy and essential oils. Diffusers and candles, some books. Two qualified staff for all aspects of natural health and nutrition.

Holland & Barrett, Balham
Health food shop

☛ 190 Balham High Rd SW12 9BP
☎ 020 8675 1894
◕ M-F 9.00-20.00, Sa 9.00-18.00, Su 11.00-17.00
⊖ Balham

Fridge and freezer.

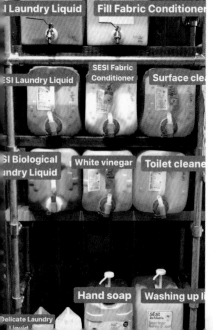

BYO
Vegan zero waste food shop

- Tooting Market 21-23 Tooting High Street SW17 0SN
- tanya@byo.london
- M closed; Tu, F 10.00-17.00; W-Th 11.00-19.00; Sa 11.00-17.00, Su 11.00-16.00
- Tooting Broadway
- byo.london
  facebook.com/london.byo
  instagram.com/byo_london/

Bring your own containers and bags, weight, fill, pay, easy. Or buy a sustainable container from them.

Full product list on the website by categories: containers, cereals, chocolate, cleaning, dried fruit, grains, oil & vin, pasta, pulses, seeds, spicers, sweeteners, toiletries, other edible stuff like pesto, seitan, tempeh and tofu.

VAUXHALL

Oval and Camberwell

Opposite Parliament across the river, but a completely different vibe with lots of community cafes. Highlights of the area are the iconic **M.I.6 building** as seen in James Bond films, the Oval cricket ground, and New Covent Garden wholesale fruit and veg market.

Stroll along the river for fabulous views and photos of Parliament, or across the river to visit Tate Britain.

Friends converge for a fabulous value night out at **Bonnington Cafe**. It's even bring your own booze. Booking is essential in the evening, it's always full for both sittings.

Also good for a bargain lunch is **The Ragged Cangeen.**

Other new arrivals offering incredible value for money are **Lovage Project** and **Ila**.

Cafe Van Gogh is a wonderful vegan restaurant in an old church down past The Oval.

Bonnington Café
Vegetarian international wholefood restaurant

☛ 11 Vauxhall Grove SW8 1TA

📞 020 7820 7466 (10.00-21.00)

🕐 M-Su 12.00-14.00, 18.30-22.30

⊖ Vauxhall

➤ bonningtoncafe.co.uk
Facebook Bonnington Cafe

Vegetarian wholefood restaurant and garden in a quiet square. Run by a cooperative of member cooks from all over the world, with a different cook and their recipes each night, such as Japanese, French, Italian or new American. The atmosphere is very laid back and it's incredible value for a three course dinner. Regulars love the candlelight, burning fire in winter, and community feel.

Visit their website for a map of the exact location behind Vauxhall underground/rail station, and for tonight's chef's email and phone number for enquiries such as the availability of vegan food and reservations. Bookings are essential, and are not confirmed until you receive a reply from the cook.

Vegan nights are Tuesday, Thursday, Saturday and Sunday.

There are normally two options for each course. Starters £3.50, main courses £9, desserts £3.50-£4. On the day mains were roast pepper, red onion and rocket pizza with salad; and spinach and blackeye bean tart with roast potatoes and salad.

Bring your own alcohol, corkage is free and you can buy booze at the off-licence opposite, but they ask for a donation of 50p per person for glass hire as someone is washing these up don't you know. Thursday and Saturday no corkage charge.

Cash only. There is somethimes piano or other music. Individual cooks may set a minimum charge or service charge on large bookings.

Ila Vegan & Veg
Vegetarian restaurant & take-away

- 📍 Unit.2, 125-131 Westminster Bridge Road SE1 7HJ (behind Waterloo station)
- 📞 020 3129 9348
- 🕐 M-Th 09.00-22.00 (food served till 21.00), F-Sa 09.00-24.00 (22.00), Su 11.00-22.00 (21.00)
- ⊖ North Lambeth
- 🔗 ilavegan.co.uk
  Facebook Ila Vegan & Veg

Insanely cheap for central London, this new place does breakfast vegan porridge for £2.20, and main course meals for just £4.99 such as Brazilian tomato and black bean with cashew and quinoa; butternut lentil and spinach stew; West African peanut and chickpea with red rice; mushroom stroganoff stew; Thai green jackfruit stew; north Indian red lentil veg and dal; pulled jackfruit BBQ burger.

Also smoothies for £3.50. Vegan cakes and pastries. Two tables. Vegware compostable plates and cutlery.

Lovage Project
Vegan cafe

- 📍 Vauxhall Gardens Community Centre, 5 Glasshouse Walk SE11 5ES
- 📞 020 793 1110 (centre)
- 🕐 M-F 9.00-15.00, Sa-Su closed
- ⊖ Vauxhall
- 🔗 instagram.com/lovage_project
  vgcc.org.uk

Just across the river from Parliament, this fantastic value, zero waste social enterprise opened in September 2019.

Soup of the day £3. Stew of the day £4. Salad bar £3, big £4.50. Pasta with pesto or tomato £5.50. Daily mains are all £6.50 such as, all available on one day, mac no cheese with greens and cauliflower sticky wings; burger of the week; special of the day such as sweet potato and courgette croquettes with spiced rice and sweetcorn guacamole.

Cakes £3 such as chocolate, rocky road, carrot. Croissant £1.50.

Van Gogh Cafe
Vegan cafe-restaurant

- at Christchurch, 88 Brixton Road SW9 6BE (corner Mowll Street)
- 07546 966554
- Tu-Sa 10.00-21.00, Su 12.00-17.00, M closed
- Oval
- cafevangogh.co.uk
  facebook.com/cafevangoghbrixton
  instagram.com/cafevangogh01

This no-profit cafe and coffee shop with a hidden courtyard is part of a beautiful church. The Dutch post-impressionist artist Vincent Van Gogh used to lodge just around the corner in the 1870s. There is a dining area downstairs and upstairs with a dark blue painted ceiling with gold stars. Also a huge outdoor space at the front and back in the garden. It's popular with big groups of vegans having a night out.

Well-travelled chefs from around the world blend a unique and original mix of ingredients on their ever-changing summer and winter menus. Owner Steve Clarke, who turned the restaurant 100% vegan in 2017, is always available for a chat.

Brunch weekdays till 12.00, Saturday till 3pm, £8.95 for a full English cooked breakfast, or vegan shakshuka, or tofu rancheros with tofu scramble, smokey beans, homefries and toast. Beans or tofu scramble or mushrooms on two toast £5.50. Extra portions £2.

Lunch served 12.00-16-00 £6.95, features a special of the day, or any pasta with salads. Soup plus special £9.

Small plates £3.50-£5.50 include dal and flat bread, mac 'n' cheese, soup of the day, baked paprika homefries.

Large plates £5.95-£10.99 feature seitan sticky ribs with braised red cabbage, roasted squash and IPA gravy (perfect for a Sunday roast); bangers and mash; buger of the day with homefries and salad; lentil bolognese; jerk plantain with smoky beans, seasoned rice, pineapple salsa.

Sunday lunch specials include their mushroom bouguigon Wellington £10.95 with roast potatoes, roast veg and gravy. Three courses for £18.99.

Desserts £4.95 such as sticky toffee pudding with hot toffee sauce and cream, or pannacotta. Cakes and muffins £2.50-£3.95.

Tea £2 and herbal £3, coffee £2.20 to £2.75, iced turmeric latte £2.75. Apple juice, elderflower, rhubarb ginger beer and apple and ginger £2.20-£2.40. Oat and soya milk.

Bring your own wine, corkage £2 per person, but soon they will have their licence. Wifi. Dogs welcome. 10% discount for students and NHS staff. Vegan catering, private parties. There is a great secondhand shop next door.

The Ragged Canteen
Vegetarian cafe in arts centre

- ☛ Beaconsfield Gallery, 22 Newport Street SE11 6AY (off Black Prince Rd)
- ☏ 020 7582 6465
- ◑ M-F 10Sa-Su 11.00-17.00. Closed most of Aug, and Xmas to mid Jan.
- ⊖ Vauxhall, Lambeth North, Waterloo
- ↖ beaconsfield.ltd.uk/cafe
  facebook.com/RaggedCanteen
  instagram.com/raggedcanteen

Loved by arties and young mums with children, always art exhibitions on here and it's very contemporary. Weekday lunches served 12.00-14.00. Also open Sat-Sun for all day brunch, coffee and cake during exhibition periods only. The menu is changed daily, with ethically sourced and seasonal food. Beautiful seating area outside.

Weekday hotpots, served with rice or homemade bread, such as South African sweet potato stew £6.80, spinach daal and salad £5.50, Mexican 'Mole' chili £6.80. Soups with bread £4.50 such as Thai squash and coconut. Mixed plates £7.20: baba ganoush, hummus, harissa, salad and sourdough bread (from a local bakery). Lentil, chestnut and spelt pasty £5.80.

Weekend all day brunch such as Mexican brunch plate £7 with homemade refried beans, red peppers, fritata, nachos; add guacamole £1. Soups of the day £2.50 or £4.50 such as red lentil veg dal, add £1 for bread. Winter porridge £5 (bayleaf infused rice pudding with spicy plum compote & winter dried fruits & nuts). Mexican salad plate £3.50-£7. Open sandwich £4.50 (beetroot hummus, grilled mushroom and micro sorrel). Bread & olives £3.

Cakes £2-£3.50 have a gluten-free and

vegan option.

Chegworth Valley juices £1.70. Monmouth organic coffee £2, latte or cappuccino or hot chocolate £2.50, soya milk available. Fairtrade teas £1.20-£1.50 Juices £1.70-£1.80. Craft beer £3.20. Glass of wine £4.10 (150ml), bottle £19, Prosecco £4.90, £26.

Children welcome, high chair, baby changing. Books and puzzles. Plenty of space for buggies. Disabled toilets. Outside seating, dogs welcome there. Wifi, newspapers, art magazines.

Locals can get on the email list to receive daily menus and order ahead for collection. Rooms for hire.

Maloko
Vegetarian creperie

- 60 Camberwell Church Street SE5 8QZ
- (020 3305 8913
- ● M-Su 08.00-22.00
- ✆ Denmark Hill
- ✈ facebook.com/mymaloko

Vegetarian, shabby chic, creperie near the big junction of Camberwell Green, with the same owner as Katakata in Brixton. The house speciality is buckwheat galettes, a big, free from everyting, savoury pancake vegan wrap with all sorts of fillings. The Vegan Route £6.25 is filled with chestnut mushrooms, baby spinach, sweet potato and quinoa. Other fillings include asparagus and pineapple.

Sweet £4.70, though none are vegan, but they will make you a sweet vegan galette with fillings like jam, lemon and sugar, or jam, banana and coconut.

Bring your own alcohol. Freshly squeezed juice £2.95. Tea, coffee, latte, cappuccino, mocha, hot chocolate £1.80-£2.50. They have soya milk.

Wifi. Deliveroo.

Adulis, Oval
Omnivorous Eritrean restaurant

- 44-46 Brixton Road SW9 6BT
- (020 7587 0055
- ● M-F 17.00-24.00, Sa-Su 12.00-24.00
- ✆ Oval
- ✈ adulis.co.uk, facebook.com/ AdulisEritreanRestaurant

See Clapham branch for menu. Also in Brixton.

Holland & Barrett, Camberwell
Health food shop

- Unit 12, Butterfly Walk Shopping Centre, Camberwell Green SE5 8RW
- (020 7252 6707
- ● M-F 9.00-19.00, Sa 9.00-18.00, Su 10.00-16.00
- ✆ Tooting Broadway

Fridge and freezer.

On the edge of the area is iklectic vegetarian cafe, see the South Bank chapter of Central London.

WIMBLEDON

South London

Lu-Ma Cafe
Omnivorous dairy-free cafe

- ☛ Justin James Hotel, 43 Worple Road SW19 4JZ
- ☎ 020 8296 6714
- ◐ M-F 07.00-16.30, Sa-Su 08.00-16.30
- ⊖ Wimbledon
- ↖ lu-ma.co.uk
  facebook.com/lumacafe

Lucy (Lu) and Maria (Ma) are a mother and daughter team who decided to open a healthy cafe incorporating macrobiotic principles. Food is made fresh for you and they don't use dairy or a microwave.

Breakfast and brunch till midday weekdays and all day at weekends. Granola with soya yogurt, bery coulis and fruit; acai smoothie bowl £6.15-£9.45 with granola, blueberries, apple and coconut flakes; vegan protein brekkie £9.45 with quinoa, veggies, avocado and spirulina dressing.

Soup of the day £5.75, add sourdough 90p. Spiralized veg with avo in rice paper rolls with goji berry sauce £5.75. Main dishes £8.25-£10.50 such as white bean burger in gluten-free bun with sweet potato fries £10.50; miso noodle bowl; sharing platter with vegan cheddar, salad, olives, hummus and gluten-free crispy bread; vegan meatballs with gluten-free spaghetti in tomato sauce; sweet jacket potato with homemade baked beans, sweetcorn or red lentil curry; chickpea and veg mild mini curry with brown rice; open sourdough sandwich with falafel or humus and salad; Caesar salad with tempeh bacon and vegan piquant cheese £8.75.

Vegan desserts incude nut balls, brownies and cheesecake. Booja Booja ice-cream £3.50.

Smoothies £4.95 include almond milk chocoholic with maca and cashew, or mixed berries. Teas, Barleycup and latte £1.60-£3.50.

Organic wines £4.75 medium glass, £18.50 bottle.

Every first and third Friday of the month they open late until 21.30, call to book.

Sticks n Sushi
Omnivorous Japanese restaurant

- 58 Wimbledon Hill Road SW19 7PA
- 020 3141 8800
- Su-Tu 12.00-22.00, W-Sa 12.00-23.00
- Wimbledon
- sticksnsushi.com

Although the menu is predominantly non-veggie, their veggie offerings are excellent. Classy Japanese decor with Scandinavian twist: lanterns, high ceilings, exposed brick wall, shared tables and central bar.

Sides £2-£6 include seaweed salad, fried cauliflower, Jerusalem artichoke, grilled corn, edamame beans and rice. Yakitori skewers £2.20-£2.80 include king oyster mushroom, or grilled sweet potato with teriyaki. Maki (sushi) are £6.50 for 8 pieces filled with avocado and cucumber, rolled in chives and soy sesame. Veggie salad qirh tofu £9.50.

The Green Keeper meal £22 consists of salad, nigiri, maki, hosomaki inside-out with greens, king oyster mushroom and sweet potato skewers, spicy edamame beans, grilled corn and seaweed salad. Also good is the Greengate salad £15, with grilled king oyster mushrooms, sweet potato and tender stem broccoli, on a salad of gem leaves, veggies, quinoa and pine nuts.

For dessert try a yuzu sorbet £3.40.

Wine from £3.10/£4.10 glass, £16.50 bottle. Soya milk available for hot drinks.

Children welcome, they can have hosomaki sushi with cucumber and avocado. High chairs. Wifi.

Le Pain Quotidien
Omnivorous Belgian restaurant

- 4-5 High Steet, Wimbledon Village SW19 5DX
- 020 3657 6926
- M-Sa 07.00-19.00, Su/BH 08.00-19.00
- Wimbledon
- lepainquotidien.co.uk

Kids' corner. Outside seating. Wifi. Catering.

Wagamama, Wimbledon
Omnivorous Japanese restaurant

- 46-48 Wimbledon Hill Road SW19 7PA
- 020 8879 7280
- M-Sa 11.00-23.00, Su 11.00-22.00
- Wimbledon
- wagamama.com

Omnivorous fast food Japanese noodle restaurant with a separate vegan menu and huge portions.

Health Zone Ltd
Health food shop & complementary health clinic

- 🖝 30 Wimbledon Hill Road SW19 7PA (corner of Worple Rd, opposite library)
- ☎ 020 8944 1133
- 🕐 M-F 9.00-19.00, Sa 9.30-18.00, Su 11.00-17.00
- ⊖ Wimbledon
- ⭡ healthzoneuk.com
  healthzoneclinic.co.uk

More than your average health food shop, with complementary therapy clinic attached. They stock a wide range of vegan foods, many organic, including raw foods and superfoods.

Fridge has Soupology, Tofurky, Taifun, VBites, Great Food, Florentin, Biona, Follow your Heart, Violife, Tofutti, Sheese spreads, vegenaise. tofu, tempeh, sprouts. Sojade, Provamel, and Coyo yogurt and Chia Pods .

Frozen food by Forest Food nut roast, Secret Sausage and Clive's Pies. Booja Booja, Coyo and Naturally Coconuts ice-cream.

Spreads from Meridian, Biona, Carley's organic raw, Profusion pasta, vegan pesto and sauces. Macrobiotic section.

Huge selection of chocolate such as Belvas Belgian thins, Natural carob, Mini Moos, Go Do and Yogi Q. Bars by Love Raw, Squirrel Sisters, Creative Nature, Trek, Rude Health, Aduna, Rawcha, Square Organics. Raw Health balls. Vegan marshmallow.

Kids and baby section with lots of food.

Bodycare by Sukin, Antipodes, Weleda, Green People, Lavera, Natura Siberica, Avalon and Faith In Nature.

Method and Ecozone cleaning products.

Supplements by Viridian, Terranova, Pukka, OptiBac and Vogel. Homeopathic remedies from Weleda, Dr Bronner, New Era, Nelsons and Bach flower.

Clinic treatments include acupuncture, massage, sports massage, Indian head massage, hot stone massage, aromatherapy, osteopathy, reflexology, Reiki, acupuncture, cupping, homeopathy, nutritional therapy, NLP, hypnotherapy. The clinic is open the same times as the shop.

Holland & Barrett, Wimbledon
Health food shop

- 🖝 Unit 106a, Centre Court Shopping Centre, Queens Road SW19 8YE
- ☎ 020 8947 0001
- 🕐 M-F 9.00-19.00 (Th 20.00), Sa 9.00-18.00, Su 11.00-17.00
- ⊖ Wimbledon

Fridge and freezer.

Neal's Yard, Wimbledon Village
Vegan bodycare, remedies and treatments

- 95 High Street, Wimbledon Village SW19 5EG
- M-F and Sa 10.00-18.00, Sa 9.30-18.00, Su 10.30-17.30
- 020 8947 3155
- Wimbledon
- nealsyardremedies.com

Remedies, bodycare and therapy rooms.

Lush, Wimbledon
Cruelty-free cosmetics

- 5 Wimbledon Bridge SW19 7NH
- 020 8944 1299
- M-F 10.00-17.00, Th 20.00, Sa 9.30-18.00, Su 11.00-17.00
- Wimbledon
- lush.co.uk

Hand-made cosmetics, most vegan.

Boho Beach Fest
Women's fashion shop

- 15 High Street, Wimbledon Village SW19 5DX
- 020 8944 7375
- M-Sa 9.30-18.00, Su 11.00-17.00
- Wimbledon
- bohobeachfest.com

Independent boutique with a lot of Bohemian style clothes from kaftans to maxi dresses, beach bags and throws, flip-flops and beautiful vegan shoes from Holster Australia.

Vital NRG
Vegan coffee shop

🚩 Bellingham Station, Randlesdown Road SE6 3BT

📞 07496 913 286

🕐 M-F 06.00-18.00, Sa 10.00-18.00, Su closed

⊖ Bellingham Thameslink

↟ vital-nrg.com
facebook.com/vitalnaturalrawgoodness
instagram.com/vital_nrg

After working in hospitality for six years, Rania Bakr opened Vital Natural Raw Goodness next to Bellingham station in May 2019, serving coffee, superfood smoothies and healthy meals and snacks.

Sandwiches £4.50 or £5 such as TLT wtih grilled smoked tofu, lettuce, tomato, avocado; spiced chickpea tuna and veggies; grilled garlicky aubergine, spicy hummus and salad. Toasted sandwiches £5 with melted vegan cheese, spinach, herbss, and sundried tomato or garlicky mushrooms.

Soups and salads £3-£6 with ingredients like marinated tofu feta, Egyptian fava beans cooked with olive oil. Callaloo or dal patties £1.80.

Cakes and treats £2-£3.50 include cupcakes, chocolate cake, chia seed pudding, protein balls.

Superfood smoothies £4 and £6. Teas such as moringa or cinnamon leaf 85p. Coffees £1.50-£2.30, hot choc £3. Coconut, hemp, oat or tiger nut milk.

The counter and shelves are made with reclaimed wood. Cups, lids, bags and straws are compostable.

By Chloe, Tower Bridge
Vegan American fast food restaurant

- One Tower Bridge, 6 Duchess Walk SE1 2SD
- 020 3883 3273
- Su-W 08.00-22.00, Th-Sa 10.00-23.00
- London Bridge, Tower Hill, Bermondsey
- eatbychloe.com
  facebook.com/eatbychloeuk

This American chain landed early 2018 in Covent Garden, then in June opened this branch on the south side of the river right next to Tower Bridge, opposite the Tower of London. Big salad bowls, soups, burgers, pasta, sandwiches and lots of cakes.

Most main dishes are just under £10. Salads such as Kale Caesar, spicy Thai, quinoa taco with spicy seitan chorizo and black beans, Greek. Burgers come in tempeh-lentil-chia-walnut, black bean-quinoa-sweet potato, pesto meatball. Tofish n' chips with mushy peas and tartar sauce. Roast celery root with veggies, thyme potatoes, Yorkshire pudding and rosemary gravy. Ground seitan shepherd's pie with mash and veggies.

Mac n' cheese or avocado-cashew pesto pasta £4.80. Air baked original or sweet potato fries £4. Pea and vegan ham soup.

BLT or chickpea tuna sandwich takeout around £5.

Brunch Sa-Su till 4pm, dishes £4.80-£9 include morning oats with quinoa and flaxseed and fresh berries; granola and berries smoothie bowl; raw almond butter and banana toast; various forms of Full English such as with scrambled tofu, spinach, maple sausage, walnuts, greens, 7-grain toast; quinoa hash browns with tofu sour cream; daily pancake with coconut whipped cream.

Desserts include sticky toffee pudding with coconut whipped cream, banana walnut bread, muffins, cookies, cupcakes.

Organic oat pupcakes and peanut butter bones for your dog.

Lots of cakes such as banana walnut, cupcakes, chocolate chip pecan cookies £2-£3.90.

Smoothies, juices, lemonade, kombucha, coffees and iced coffees, teas.

Deliveroo deliveries. Also in North Greenwich, Covent Garden and Fitzrovia.

Love Gift Vegan
Vegan Caribbean restaurant

- 🖝 386 Lee High Road SE12 8RW (A20, at Langmead Road)
- ☏ 07958 308 397
- 🕑 W-Th 12.00-20.00, F-Sa 12.00-21.00, Su 12.00-19.00, M-Tu closed. Times may vary.
- ⊖ Train: Lee, Blackheath, Hither Green
- ➤ lovegiftvegan.co.uk
  instagram.com/lovegiftvegan
  facebook.com/lovegiftvegan

Previously in Brockley, so don't be fooled by the wrong address in most references to this place on the net. Before that, Maya Matanah from the island of Grenada ran Spirited Palace vegan restaurant in Crystal Palace. The food here is similar, super-healthy and terrific value.

Rainbow platter of vegetable stew or curry with quinoa, or mac & cheese with rice, served with steamed greens. You can add fried plantain, spelt dumplings, seaweed fritters, potato wedges, wheatmeat.

Also soups such as lentil and sweet potato, wraps filled with spicy beans and/or mixed veggies, pubrgers in Portobello or bean or BBQ tofu or Tower, veg topped pizzas with vegan cheese and a pitta or ciabatta base, spelt or wholewheat bread sandwiches.

Desserts include banana cake sweetend with dates and topped with chocolate and vanilla,, pineapple crumble, spelt coconut rock cakes, chocolate chip cookies, banana chia seed cake, mango and strawberry cheesecake, pear and walnut cake. They can be served with ice cream or custard.

Ginger beer, pink lemonade, fresh juices. Tea, herb teas, chai with coconut milk.

Vegan food workshops.

Mantanah Thai, South Norwood
Omnivorous Thai restaurant

- 2 Orton Buildings, Portland Rd, South Norwood SE25 4UD
- 020 8771 1148
- Tu-Sa 18.00-23.00, Su 12.00-15.00, 17.30-22.30, M closed
- Norwood Junction BR
- mantanahthai.com
  facebook.com/MantanahThai

Like many Thai restaurants, this one has as many vegan dishes as some vegetarian restaurants.

Starters £4.50-£4.95 such as spring rolls, mixed veg tempura, sago dumpling, tom khar spicy mushroom soup, or mixed starters for two people £11.95.

Main dishes £6.50-£6.95 include the Thai classics of red or green curry, jungle curry with mock chicken and jackfruit, stir-fried aubergine with mock chicken in soya and black bean sauce, deep fried bean curd with tamarind sauce, papaya salad with crushed peanut.

Wine by the glass or bottle. Beers include Thai Singha.

In **West Norwood** on Knights Hill you can always find something vegan at The Cul de Sac at number 2, Otter bistro at 17, or Pintadera Cafe at 50.

Well Being Foods, Sydenham
Wholefoods and organic shop

- 19 Sydenham Road SE26 5EX
- 020 8659 2003
- M-Sa 9.00-18.00, Su closed
- Sydenham BR
- Facebook Well Being Health Foods

Complete selection of whole foods and organic fruit and veg. Take-away samosas, rotis and pasties. Fresh bread from Blackbird bakery daily, and some cakes including vegan slices. Good freezer selection.

Bodycare and household products. Natural remedies, homeopathy, vitamins, and Melvyn the in house Herbinator to assist you.

Shop Without Packaging
Vegetarian organic zero-waste food shop

- 7 Burnt Ash Road, Lee Green SE12 8RG
- 020 3689 5233
- M-F 08.30-18.00, Sa 10.00-18.00, Su 10.00-16.00
- Lee BR, Blackheath BR
- swop.market/stock (products list)
  facebook.com/SWOPZeroWaste
  instagram.com/swopzerowaste

Mums Claire and Jess were so fed up with plastic and packaging littering our world that they set up this shop. It's also organic, Fairtrade, and where possible local. Dried loose grains, seeds, beans, pulse and nuts in hygienic gravity dispensers. Coffee beans, loose leaf tea, fruit and veg, unwrapped bread and patisserie. Shampoo and beauty products. Detergent and cleaning refills.

Village Pizza, Ewell
Omnivorous pizza restaurant & take-away

- ☛ 5 Castle Parade Ewell, KT17 2PR (junction of A24 London Rd and Ewell By-Pass)
- ☎ 020 8393 9123
- ◑ M-Su 11.00-23.00
- ⊖ Ewell West, Stoneleigh, Ewell East BR
- ↖ villagepizzauk.com (menu)

Separate vegan menu on the website or Just-Eat of pizzas made with vegan style chicken, tika or Mexican chicken, pepperoni, garlic sausage, spicy kidney beans.

Also in Surbiton at 7 Claremont Road, Tel 020 8399 2293.

Holland & Barrett, Blackheath
Health food shop

- ☛ 31 Tranquil Vale, Blackheath SE3 0BU
- ☎ 020 8318 0448
- ◑ M-Sa 9.00-17.30, Su 10.00-16.00
- ⊖ Blackheath BR

Fridge and freezer

Well Bean, Blackheath
Organic health food store

- ☛ 9 Old Dover Road, Blackheath SE3 7BT
- ☎ 020 3538 3617
- ◑ M-Sa 9.00-18.00, Su closed
- ⊖ Westcombe Park, Maze Hill, Blackheath
- ↖ facebook.com/wellbeanhealth

The original vegan manager's son-in-law and daughter have taken over the store since our last edition. Plenty of vegan grub including icre-cream cheeses, yogurts; meat substitutes such as Redwood, Frys, Biona, Taifun; Clearspot and Cauldron tofu; sprouts. Gluten-free range. No take-away.

Bodycare ranges include Green People, Faith in Nature, Pitrok, Weleda, Savakan, Zambesia, Botanica. Supplements include A Vogel, Nature's Plus, Viridian, Nature's Own, Nature's Aid, Weleda, Solaray, Lifeplan and others.

Ecover, BioD and Ecolino cleaning products and Veggiewash.

South East London Vegans
Facebook groups

- ↖ facebook.com/groups/ SELondonVegans

Tips on where to eat and shop in south-east London.

VEGAN SOUTH LONDON © Copyright

1st edition by Alex Bourke
EAN 978-1-902259-17-8
Published January 2020
by Vegetarian Guides Ltd
www.veganlondon.guide

2 Hilborough Court, Livermere Road, London E8 4LG, UK
Tel: 020-3239 8433 (24 hrs)
International: +44-20-3239 8433

Distributed in UK by Bertrams, Gardners, Marigold
In USA/Canada by Book Publishing Company, TN. www.bookpubco.com
Updates to this guide at: vegetarianguides.co.uk/updates
Link and earn 10% commisssion: vegetarianguides.co.uk/affiliate

In the same series:
VEGAN CENTRAL LONDON
VEGAN EAST LONDON
VEGAN NORTH LONDON
VEGAN WEST LONDON
VEGAN LONDON: THE KNOWLEDGE
VEGAN LONDON comprehensive edition

Printed by Buxton Press, England

VEGAN WEST
LONDON

1st edition

The complete insider guide to the best vegan food in London

Alex Bourke
Vegetarian Guides

WEST LONDON

* OUR TOP 5 - BEST OF WEST LONDON *

All-you-can-eat Buffet
222 lunch, West Kensington
Bombay Spice, Kingsbury
Pradip, Kenton
Sakonis, Harrow/Wembley
Tai Buffet, Shepherd's Bush

Cafes
Ahimsa, Pinner
Cafe Forty One, Bayswater
Green Bottle, Twickenham
Planet Organic, Bayswater
West Six, Hammersmith

Dining Out 100% Vegan
222, West Kensington
Farmacy, Bayswater (photo)
Kiss My Grass, West Kensington
Tell Your Friends, Fulham
Wulf & Lamb, Chelsea

Fast Food
Earth Brgr, West Kensington
Portobello Vegan Market
Super Singh's Feltham/Hounslow
Super Singh's, Southall

Indian Veg Restaurants
Harrow
Hounslow
Kenton/Kingsbury/Queensbury
Southall
Ealing Road, Wembley

Raw Food
Paradise Plantbased, Queens Park
Rainforest Creations, Chelsea (Sa)
Rainforest, Hammersmith (Th)
Redemption, Notting Hill
Tanya's, Chelsea

Independent Shops
Eden Perfumes, Notting Hill
GreenBay, West Kensington
Organic for the People, Ealing
Windfall Natural, Chiswick

Days Out
Animal Aid Xmas Fayre (Dec)
Cloud Twelve spa, Notting Hill
Natural History Museum (then
Tanya's or Wulf & Lamb, Sloane)
Portobello (Vegan) Markets
Vegfest London (autumn)

619

MY CHELSEA

SLOANE ZONE

West London

The area between Hyde Park and the river Thames, from Victoria and Knightsbridge in the east to Kensington and Fulham in the west, is posh London. There are stacks of fashion stores that are magnets for Sloane Ranger "It girls", embassies, multi-million pound apartments, the Royal Albert Hall, Science Museum, Victoria & Albert Museum, Natural History Museum (dinosaurs!). But in our last edition of *Vegetarian London* not a single meat-free restaurant.

How things change! In the last few years lots of vegan eateries have appeared, especially raw food cafes such as **Tanya's**, which is located on the ground floor of the boutique *My Chelsea hotel*, and places like CPress and JuiceBaby.

And now at last the area has some proper sit-down big vegan restaurants that you can take non-vegans to. **Wulf & Lamb** opened October 2017 near Sloane Square, followed by **Tell Your Friends** down in Parsons Green. Then in the

summer of 2019, East London vegan legend King Cook opened a new branch of **Cook Daily** right in front of Victoria Station.

If you're in Chelsea on a Saturday, don't miss **Rainforest Creations'** point-to-what-you-want huge raw food salad boxes and cakes.

Top of the shops has to be the gigantic **Whole Foods Market** over three floors on Kensington High Street. It's ten times the size of the next biggest wholefood store. There is also a "smaller" branch in Fulham, which is still several times the size of most other wholefood stores.

There are also stacks of upmarket ethnic restaurants in the area with vegan dishes, especially Lebanese, and chains such as Wagamama which has a separate vegan menu. Le Pain Quotidien is always a good bet for a chain cafe, with vegan soups, salads and muffins, and lovely wooden tables.

Cookdaily, Victoria
Vegan restaurant

- Market Hall Victoria, 191 Victoria Street SW1E 5NE
- 07498 563 168
- Cookdaily M-Su 12.00-22.00. Building M-F 07.00-23.00, Sa 09.00-23.00, Su 09.00-22.00
- Victoria.
- cookdaily.co.uk
  instagram.com/cookdailyvictoria
  instagram.com/kingcookdaily
  markethalls.co.uk/market/victoria
  instagram.com/markethallvictoria

London's trailblazing East London vegan restaurant opened a new location in summer 2019 in this new three-storey food hall right in front of Victoria Station, behind the bus terminus. Enter from Victoria Street or Terminus Place. Cook Daily is upstairs.

Cook Daily's range of dishes is impressive, building on founder King Cook's Laotian heritage plus influences from around southeast Asia. With all dishes priced at £9 to £10.50, it's terrific value for central London.

Choose from:

Yoga Fire mild oil-free curry with sweet potato, turmeric and chickpea dal simmered in golden coconut milk, served with Japanese brown rice.

Yaki Bowl fried vegan chickn bites coated in chef's famous teriyaki glaze, served with a crunchy sesame slaw and Japanese brown rice smothered in gravy.

The Infamous King's mum's green curry recipe with brown rice and a choice of just veggies, tofu and veg, chickn and veg, or chickpeas and veg.

C.D.P. Cookdaily Vegan Pho. Flat rice noodle soup broth infused with their aromatic tea bag and fresh herbs topped with crispy shallots. Choose from veg, tofu or vegan chickn.

House Pad Thai flat rice noodles stir-fried with cabbage, carrot and beansprout, flavoured with sweet tamarind "egg" tofu and vegan fish sauce served with crushed peanuts. Choose from veg, tofu or vegan chickn.

Extras: teriyaki vegan fried chickn coated in chef's house teriyaki glaze and sesame seeds.

Meal deal 1 add butterfly pea flower iced tea £2.

Meal deal 2 add teriyaki bites £4.

Meal deal 3 add butterfly pea flower iced tea and teriyaki bites £6.

No reservations, but there is ample seating both inside and outside on the terrace.

Other traders in the building include Press coffee shop, The Bar which is full of independent British beers, and Rooftop Bar (weather permitting).

Cook Daily's dedicated restaurant, with a more extensive menu, is at London Fields, East London. In November 2019 they opened a third branch near Oxford Circus in the new Market Hall West End at 9 Holles Street, Marylebone W1G 0DB, open Su-M/BH 11.00-22.00, Tu-Sa 11.00-24.00, kitchen closes one hour before.

Wulf and Lamb
Vegan restaurant

- 243 Pavilion Road, Chelsea SW1X 0BP
- 020 3948 5999
- M-Sa 08.00-22.00, Su 09.00-21.00
- Sloane Square
- wulfandlamb.com
  facebook.com/wulfandlamb
  twitter.com/wulfandlamb
  Instagram @wulfandlamb

Big, bright, beautiful new contemporary vegan restaurant on two floors with 70 seats inside and out, opened autumn 2017 near Sloane Square. Open long hours for breakfast, lunch, dinner, drinks and coffee. Fast casual, no reservations. Head chef Franco Casolin was formerly at Vanilla Black.

The original and fabulous breakfast menu starts with full English cooked £12.95 with potato layer cake, borlotti ragoût, scrambled ackee, lemon spinach sautéed peppers, mushrooms and toasted sourdough. Or try scrambled ackee £10.95 with herb-roasted datterini tomatoes, mushrooms, spinach, peppers and toasted sourdough. Smashed avo on toasted sourdough with lemon and beetroot hummus £12.95. Fluffy American pancake stack £9.95 with maple syrup, mixed berries and vanilla cashew cream. Sourdough cheese toastie £6.95. House granola with spicy pineapple and coconut yogurt £4.50.

On the counter are hot and cold sandwiches. Seasonal soup £6.95 with toasted sourdough.

Lunch and dinner mains £11.95-£14.95: Wulf Burger made from seitan, served with cashew aioli, sauerkraut and wedges; spicy veg burger; jackfruit and lentil stew pie with mash and baby carrots; chilli non carne; creamy linguine with white wine and parmesan sauce and sliced seasonal veg; green coconut curry with sweet potato mash and vegetables, aromatic Thai roots, spices and coconut cream with jasmine rice; open burrito with sautéed ackee, black beans, red rice, cherry tomatoes, peppers and cashew sour cream; Tex Mex salad; seasonal roots and leaves with pear, toasted hazelnuts, walnuts and pumpkin seed; roasted winter veg in a creamy cheese sauce. Sides £4.95-£6.95 include mac 'n' cheese, roasted herby wedges.

Desserts £7.95 such as mango and passionfruit cheesecake on a base of macadamia, pistachio and sesame topped with rasperry crumble; raw almond cream tiramisù on a chocolate and nut base with coffee meringue and a decadent brandy and vanilla cashew cream.

Cakes by Ruby's such as triple chocolate cupcake or rose pistachio donut. Also brownies, doughnuts, croissants and muffins..

Wines from £6.50 glass, £24 bottle. Beers from £5 include Brixton Reliance pale ale, Camden Hells lager, Green's gluten-free Dry Hopped lager or Glorious pilsner. Aspall draught cider. Budvar and Lucky Saint non-alcoholic beers. Cocktails.

Coffees adn teas with homemude almond milk.

You can hire the restaurant in whole or part.

Dogs welcome.

Tell Your Friends
Vegan restarant and bar

- 📞 175 New King's Rd, Fulham SW6 4SW
- 📞 020 7731 6404, 07453 566215
- 🕐 M-F 10.00-22.00, Sa 10.00-16.00, 17.00-22.00, Su 10.00-19.00
- ⊖ Parsons Green
- 🗲 tellyourfriendsldn.com
  facebook.com/tyfldn
  instagram.com/tyfldn

Opened by vegan sisters Lucy and Tiffany Watson, stars of *Made In Chelsea*, and their dad Clive, who has run chains of pubs. Even the beer is vegan.

Breakfast served till midday and brunch at weekends till 4pm. Full English £13 with sausages, aubergine bacon, sautéed mushrooms, grilled tomato, house baked beans, ackee scrambled egg, hash brown, sourdough and coconut butter. Other options £7-£9 include superfood chia pudding, smashed avo on sourdough with toasted seeds, ackee scramble, fluffy Scoch pancakes with chocolate spread or berries.

Small plates £6 such as hemp and sunflower crumbled jackfruit "chicken" bites with BBQ sauce, mac 'n' cheese (or large £10.70), or mushroom and bambook shoot gyoza. nMains £12-£14 such as Buddha bowl, pan-fried gnocchi with sundried tomato and artichoke heart, or the Moving Mountains B12 burger with cheddar cashew cheese, sundried tomato ketchup and chips.

On Sundays there is a choice of three all-day roasts £13-£15 made from seitan, or green lentil and oat baked loaf, or Portobello mushroom stuffed with buckwheat, pine nuts, garlic and parsley; all served with steamed kale, braised red cabbage, cauliflower cheese, roasted carrots and maple parsnips, roasties, Yorkshire pudding and gravy.

Desserts £6.5-£8.50 such as warm peanut butter blondie with nice cream, vanilla cheesecake with berry coulis, chocolate and avocado mousse. Also cakes and donuts from the counter.

Kids' menu £7.50-£8.50: mac 'n' cheese, or jackfruit chicken nuggest with chips and BBQ sauce, or beanburger with chips and ketchup.

Cold pressed fruit and veg juices £4, power shots £2. Smoothies £4.90-£6. Bottled soft drinks £2.60-£4 including various kombucha, Belvoir. Coffees and teas £2-£3.20 with almond, coconut, oat or soya milk. Coloured lattes £4.

Wine from £5 medium glass, £7.20 large, £21-£34 bottle. Beers, ciders and non-alocholic beers £4-£6. Cocktails £8-£9, mocktails £4.

Deliveroo. Gift vouchers. Downstairs room for parities, breakfast meetings, yoga classes, events.

175

tell
your
friends

RESTA

Tanya's
Vegetarian raw restaurant and bar

- Ground floor at My Chelsea hotel, 35 Ixworth Place, Chelsea SW3 3QX
- 020 7225 7500
- M-Su 07.00-23.00 every day of the year as it's in a hotel
- South Kensington (7 mins walk), Sloane Square (12 mins), Victoria (taxi 10 mins). Metered parking.
- tanyasliving.com
  facebook.com/TanyasLiving
  myhotels.com/chelsea

Wellness coach and healthy plant-based pioneer Tanya Maher's raw food grab 'n' go restaurant is just inside the entrance of a beautiful boutique hotel. It's almost all vegan, apart from cow milk in hot drinks. Everything is free from gluten, wheat or refined sugar. Grab your food from the fridges on the right then settle into the big seating/bar area with a glass roof.

Living mains £11.55-£13.45 include lasagna made with organic courgette pasta, herbed cashew almond ricotta, sundried tomato marinara, and marinated walnut "meat" and basil pesto; temaki nori sushi roll filled with rice, buckwheat, sauerkraut, pickled carrots, veg and herbed almond cashew paste; activated sunflower seed and cashew burger with baked sweet potato wedges, pink beet ranch sauce and herbed cabbage and kale salad; jackfruit caesar salad with coconut bacon, spiced chickpeas adn creamy raw cashew dressing; Adventure Salad Bowl with herbed cashew almond cheeze. Sides around £4 include herbted cabbage and kale, probiotic sauerkraut, Korean shredded carrot marinated in garlic pepper dressing, guacamole dipping pot.

Peek into a fridge full of desserts £2.50-

£5.90 that might include raw chocolates, peanut butter cups, matcha squares, coconut slice, chocolate brownie, salted caramel slice, and cheezecakes such as strawberry, blueberry pie, keylime pie.

Raw dessert heaven. Cheesecake slices £6.20 made with creamy cashew include strawberry and date or blueberry and lemon on a coconut and walnut base, tiramisu with a hazelnut and cacao base, choc and peanut butter, cookies and cream. Raw bar slices £4.95 such as coconut and raspberry topped with a layer of chocolate, salted caramel on millionaire shortbread, fudgey brownie with walnuts, pecans and almond butter. Mr Prempy's CBD oil truffles. Choc bars such as Ombar, Pana Chocolate. Booja Booja truffles.

Whole cakes small £53 (serves 8-10), large £72 (serves 12-16).

Snacks, around £3-£4, include coconut jerky or chips, BBQ spiced mixed activated nuts, pili nuts, Clearspring seaveg crispies/

Organic cold pressed juices, Jarr Kombucha, Rebel Kitchen raw organic coconut water, all £6.95.

Hot drinks £3-£4. like teas or coffees with almond, oat or soya milk; latte with chai, turmeric or matcha or Reishi, Chaga and Cordyceps mushrooms; hot chocolate.

These prices include 20% VAT for dining in (it's the law), take-away prices in fridges are lower. 12.5% discretionary service charge when eating in. Deliveroo. Uncookery workshops and you can buy Tanya's The Uncook Book.

Rainforest Creations

Pomodoro e Basilico

JuiceBaby

Rainforest Creations Chelsea
Vegan raw food stall in market

- Chelsea Market, Duke of York Square, Kings Road SW3 4LY
- 07985 235 219 (M-F 9.00-17.00)
- **Saturday only** 10.00-16.00
- Sloane Square
- rainforestcreations.co.uk

Range of raw, vegan food dishes such as sprouted chickpea hummus, sprouted mungbean salad and tropical coleslaw. Sweet treats include carob ginger sweets and raw chocolate cake. Big box of salad and savouries for £6, salad roti £5, cakes £3, sweets £1. See Spitalfields (East London) for more info, or their website.

In the market there is also a Caribbean lady selling vegan cakes, breads and chocolate.

Pomodoro e Basilico
Vegan Italian street slow food stall

☛ **South Kensington Farmers Market**, by Queens Lawn and Queens Tower, Imperial College Road, Imperial College university campus. (Behind the Natural History Museum, also behind the Royal Albert Hall). Sometimes at Princes Gardens, off Exhibition Road (behind the Victoria and Albert Musuem).

☎ 07866 194 403

🕐 **Tuesday only** 9.00-14.00

⊖ South Kensington

🔖 facebook.com/PomoBasilico
instagram.com/pomodoro_e_basilico
lfm.org.uk

Italian chef Sara worked for several vegan restaurants and bakeries before starting her own vegan food business out of a passion for made-from-scratch slow vegan food with seasonal ingredients.

Sara brings burgers the size of a Shaggy Sandwich, pizzas and vegan cakes to the market with bags of enthusiasm.

Also at:

Thursday Bloomsbury London Farmers Market (Central London)

Sunday Alexandra Park London Farmers Market (Wood Green, North London)

and usually at Portobello Vegan Night Market in Notting Hill.)

JuiceBaby
Vegan raw cafe & juice bar

☛ 398 Kings Road SW10 0LJ (near Milman's Street)

☎ 020 7351 2230

🕐 M-Sa 08.00-19.00, Su 9.00-19.00

⊖ Fulham Broadway

🔖 juicebaby.co.uk
facebook.com/juicebabyuk

Juice bar and cafe towards the Fulham end of Kings Road, near Triyoga and next door to Chelsea Health Store. It's great for healthy breakfasts, raw lunches and desserts. All vegan and mostly gluten-free.

Cold-pressed juices and nut milks £4.25 qtr litre, £6.95 half-litre. Smoothies £6.25 half-litre.

Breakfasts £5.50 like millet porridge, avo chilli toast, nut butter and chia jam sandwich. Açai bowls around £8.

Lunch choices £5.95-£9.75 include tomato or green gazpacho, soup of the day with multi-seed spelt bread, kale salad, taco bowl, dragon veg bowl with steamed quinoa, glow bowl with sweet potato and herby quinoa, winter tahini bowl, super greens salad, sandwiches such as red pepper hummus or spicy sunflower spread with salad.

Lots of raw snacks and desserts £3.75-£5.75 include lemon blueberry cheesecake, pumpkin pie, Brazil nut brownies, chocolate krispies, goji 5-seed bars, sticky toffee balls, almond and coconut cookies, cacao macaroons, superfood truffles.

Teas, organic coffees, latte, iced latte, matcha latte, hot choc £1.75-£3.60.

Also in Notting Hill.

CPress, Fulham Road
99% vegan juice and salad cafe

- ☛ 285 Fulham Rd SW10 9PZ (between Beaufort St & Elm Park Gardens)
- ☎ 020 7352 7568
- ☽ M-Sa 07.00-22.00, Su/BH 08.00-20.00
- ⊖ South Kensington, Goucester Road
- ↖ cpressjuice.com

Of the new raw juice and salad dens around Chelsea, this is the only one certified organic by the Soil Association. Raw, cold-pressed, mixed vegetable and fruit juices with big clear labels listing ingredients, 300ml £4.95, 490ml £6.50-£8.50.

Salads £6.50 take-away, £7.80 eat in, are all raw except for things like quinoa. Try Five Seasons with sweet potato and quinoa falafel, marinated avocado, veggies, quinoa, pumpkin and chia seeds, lime juice, marinated celeriac with cashew. Chia pots £3.75 (£4.50).

Desserts such as banoffee pie, or key lime pie £4.50 (£5.40) with a buckwheat, walnut sunflower and dates base and a filling made from almond milk, coconut oil, cashews, avocado, lime, agave and vanilla. Energy balls £1.95. Kale chips, activated nuts.

Teas, coffees, drip coffee, ice coffee, latte with almond milk £2.30-£3.90.

Also in Fitzrovia (Central) and Canary Wharf (East London).

Raw Press Chelsea
Cold-pressed juice cafe

- ☛ 3 Ellis Street SW1X 9AL (off Sloane St)
- ☎ 020 7730 4347
- ☽ M-F 08.00-17.00, Sa 9.00-18.00, Su 9.00-17.00
- ⊖ Sloane Square
- ↖ rawpress.co
  facebook.com/rawpressco

New juice, healthy breakfasts and salad cafe just north of Sloane Square.

Breakfast bowls till 11am £4.50-£9 include almond milk porridge with blueberries, frozen coconut yogurt with toppings, Bircher muesli, chia pot, granola, açai bowl, fruit salad, or fill your own from the bar with grains, yogurts, fruit, nut butters and "superfoods". Also toast with avocado, jams, hummus and nut butters, and waffles.

Lunches £6.60-£12.60 feature soup of the day, nacho platter, small and regular salads served with or without daily hot options.

Desserts and treats £2-£4 such as energy balls, and raw brownies maded with walnuts, dates, coconut oil, cacao, rice malt syrup, almond butter, maca and lucuma.

Cold pressed raw organic juices and nut milks £5.50 250ml, £7.50 half litre.

Coffee, iced coffe, iced matcha latte £3-£4.

Also in Dover Street, Mayfair (Central).

CPress

SLOANE VEGAN

WEST

RAW PRESS

Big Sister Cafe
Vegetarian cafe

- ☛ The Auction Rooms, 71 Lots Road, Chelsea SW10 0RN
- ☏ Cafe 07961 016090
  Auction room 020 7376 5800
- 🕐 Sunday only 11.00-16.00
- ⊖ Fulham Broadway
- ⭠ lotsroad.com
  facebook.com/lotsroad.auctions

Vegetarian cafe at the back of an antiques auction room, offering a very different Sunday out. The cafe cannot be seen from the street. International and Sri Lankan dishes are prepared by the proprietor Roma who is a life vegetarian and uses lots of beans and root veg.

Normally one of the main dishes £7 is vegan such as Mexican bean stew with corn cakes, or South Indian curries. Occasionally vegan cake £3. Organic teas, coffee and alternatives £2.50, plant milks available. Children welcome.

See website for a calendar of what's coming up at the auction house and a catalogue. Viewing Sa 10.00-17.00, Su from 09.00, W 18.00-20.00, Th 9.00-18.00, F 9.00-17.00. If you buy anything huge you have until Tuesday to collect it or they can recommend carriers.

Falafel Zaki Zaki
Vegetarian falafel stall

- Strutton Ground Market
- 07867 426997
- M-F 11.30-15.00, Sa-Su closed
- Victoria

Falafel wrap with 3 falafels, salad and hummus £5, large with 4 falafels and aubergine too £5.50, whole shebang with 6 falafels in wrap or box £6.50. Drinks £1.

Jakob's

Comptoir Libanais
Omnivorous Lebanese cafe-deli

- 1-5 Exhibition Road, **South Kensington** SW7 2HE
- 020 7225 5006
- M-Sa 08.00-24.00, Su 08.30-18.00
- South Kensington
- 77A **Gloucester Road** SW7 4SS
- 020 3355 0856
- M-Sa 08.00-23.30, Su 09.00-22.30
- Gloucester Road
- 53-54 **Duke of York Square, Chelsea** SW3 4LY
- 020 7657 1961
- M-Sa 08.00-22.00, Su 08.00-20.00
- Sloane Square
- lecomptoir.co.uk
  facebook.com/lecomptoirlibanais

All day cafe and deli serving Beirut street food close to tube stations. Vegetarian dishes are labelled and many are vegan.

Cold and hot mezze starters £4.95-£5.75 eat in including dips (hummus, labneh), salads, falafel. Dips or mezze platter £8.95. Main course falafel wrap £8.50, salads £9.45, aubergine tagine £10.45.

Vegan orange and almond cake £5.50.

Fruity home-made lemonades £2.95-£3.75. Wine from £4.50 medium glass, £6.50 large, £18.95 bottle. Teas, coffees £1.95-£2.65, almond and soya milk.

Children's menu. Take-away slightly cheaper. Outside seating.

Hare & Tortoise, Kensington
Omnivorous Japanese restaurant

- 373 High St, Kensington W14 8QZ
  (between Warwick Gardens &
  Warwick Rd, near Olympia)
- 020 760 8887
- Su-Th 12.00-23.00, F-Sa 12.00-
  23.30 (last order 30 mins before)
- Olympia
- hareandtortoise.co.uk

Huge portions and low prices. Mostly sushi,
maki, noodle and ramen dishes with several
vegan options, plus tempura and salads.
No dishes are labelled as vegan, but many
of the vegetarian ones are vegan or can be
made so by changing the type of noodles.

Starters from £3.40 include edamame,
pumpkin croquette, spring rolls, tofu duck
rolls. Mains from £8.40 such as deep-fried
tofu and vegetable Lo Mein, or tofu and veg
ramen. Maki £3.80-£5.70 for six such as
avocado and asparagus.

Freshly pressed juice £3.20. Oriental beer
from £3.40. Hot sake, japanese fruit
liqueur (ume shu), plum wine spritzer. Wine
from £4.60 medium glass, £6.10 large,
£15.20 bottle.

Take-away menu available. 30p charge for
cards under £10. Optional 10% service
charge for groups of 5+.

Also in Blackfriars, Bloomsbury, Chiswick,
Ealing, Putney.

Jakob's
Omnivorous Mediterranean restaurant

- 20 Gloucester Rd SW7 4RB (north
  end towards Hyde Park)
- 020 7581 9292
- M-Su 08.00-23.00
- Gloucester Road
- facebook.com/JakobsOfficial

A selection of mostly vegan Persian,
Armenian and Mediterranean dishes,
around 65-70% organic. Choose your food
at the counter from 25 salads, 3 choices on
a small plate £8 lunch, £6 dinne (from 7pm)
r, take-away £4-£4.50; 6 choices £11.50,
£12.50, £7.50-£8.50.

Dairy-free cakes, some without eggs.
Organic wine and beer. Children welcome,
high chair. Pay and display parking, free
after 18.30. Outside catering.

Mango Tree
Omnivorous Thai restaurant

- 46 Grosvenor Place, Belgravia SW1X 7EQ (behing Buckingham Palace)
- 020 7823 1888
- M-W 12.00-15.00, 18.00-23.00, Th-Sa 12.00-15.00, 18.00-23.30, Su 12.00-22.30
- Victoria, Hyde Park Corner
- mangotree.org.uk/menu facebook.com/MangoTreeLondon

Separate vegetarian menu where all the starters and stir-fries are vegan. Dishes include vegetarian appetisers platter £11.95 each, minimum two people, with papaya salad, mushroom satay skewers, deep-fried tofu and veg tempura; Thai green curry £13.95 with tofu and aubergine, stir-fried rice noodles, papaya salad and deep fried tofu with spicy vegetables.

They have some vegan desserts £5.50-£10 including honey mango (a type of mango, not honey!) with coconut milk and sticky rice, fresh Thai mango, sorbets (including lavender rose, chilli lemongrass and mango, and seasonal exotic fruit platter with mango sauce).

There is a separate bar and comfy seating area where you could have a drink before or after a meal.

Wine from £23.50 bottle, fine wines from £7.85 medium glass, £11.25 large, £32 bottle. Cocktails from £10.50.

High chairs. Cloakroom. 12.5% discretionary service charge. Some long tables suitable for large groups.

Maroush Bakehouse
Omnivorous Lebanese restaurant

- 131 Earls Court Road SW5 9RQ
- 020 7370 4324
- M-W 08.00-24.00, Th-Sa 08.00-01.00, Su 08.00-23.30
- Earls Court
- maroushbakehouse.com

Lebanese and Mediterranean food to eat in or take away. Same owners as Randa in Kensington and similar dishes.Lots of vegetarian options labeled on the menu and many are vegan.

10 of the mezza starters £4.50-£7.50 are vegan such as hummus, falafel, tabbouleh, baba ghanoush. Lentil soup and two salads, £5-£6, are also vegan. The only vegan main is aubergine stew with rice £15..

Coffee and tea £1.75-£2.40. Soft drinks, fresh juice £2.50. No alcohol. Children's menu, high chairs. Breads (vegan) and pastries (not) to take away. Gluten-free options. No service charge.

Maroush Beauchamp Place
Omnivorous Lebanese restaurant

- 38 Beauchamp Place, Knightsbridge SW3 1NQ (near Harrods)
- 020 7581 5434
- Su-W 12.00-03.00, Th-Sa 12.00-04.30
- Knightsbridge
- maroush.com

Very similar to Randa. Maroush II really gets going after 10pm, especially at weekends with post-clubbers. Vegetarian items are marked and are usually vegan. Soup, salads and mezze £5-£7.50. Aubergine, okra or green beans stew with vermicelli rice £15.

Sharing vegan set menu for two £70 with humus, moutabal, Maroush salad, falafel, batata hara, followed by moussaka with rice.

Juices £3.50. Wine £4.75 glass, £19 bottle.

Mango Tree

Randa by Maroush
Omnivorous Lebanese restaurant

- ☞ 23 Kensington Church Street Kensington W8 4LF
- ☎ 020 7937 5363
- ◐ M-Su 11.30-24.00 (last orders 23.30)
- ⊖ High Street Kensington
- ↘ maroush.com

Many vegan labelled hot and cold mezze starter dishes £4.50-£7.75 such as such as hummus, baba ganoush, tabouleh and moussaka, plus soups, savoury pastries and salads. Main courses £14.50-£16 include aubergine, okra or green beans stew with rice.; pumpkin kibbeh.

Lots of wines, champagne, liqueurs and spirits. Wine from £5 glass, £20 bottle.

Maroush Bakehouse

Randa

Maroush Bakehouse

Le Pain Quotidien
Omnivorous Belgian cafe and bakery

- 9 Young St, **Kensington** W8 5EH (next to Whole Foods Market)
- (020 3657 6942
- M-Sa 07.30-18.30, Su/BH 09.00-18.00
- ⊖ High Street Kensington

- 201-203 Kings Rd, **Chelsea** SW3 5ED (corner Oakley St, opposite fire station)
- (020 3657 6941
- M-F 07.00-20.00, Sa 08.00-20.00, Su/BH 08.00-20.00
- ⊖ South Kensington, Sloane Square

- 15-17 **Exhibition Road**, South Kensington SW7 2HE
- (020 3657 6940
- M-Su 08.00-20.00
- ⊖ South Kensington, Gloucester Road

- 128 Wilton Rd, **Victoria** SW1V 1JZ
- (020 3657 6945
- M-Su 08.00-21.00
- ⊖ Victoria

- 212 **Fulham** Road SW10 9PJ
- (020 3823 4510
- M-F 07.30-18.00, Sa-Su 08.00-18.00
- ⊖ Fulham Broadway

- 70 **Parsons Green Lane** SW6 4HU
- (020 3657 6937
- M-F 07.00-20.00, Sa 08.00-20.00, Su 08.00-18.00
- ⊖ Parsons Green
- ↖ lepainquotidien.com

Menus vary slightly from one restaurant to another, but there are lots of clearly labelled vegan options (except at breakfast, only a fruit salad or avocado toast) and staff are happy to adapt veggie dishes to make them vegan. You can see detailed menus for each branch on the website with a carrot marking vegan dishes.

Breads are all organic and vegan. Vegan dishes include avocado toast £8.45, organic soup with breads £5.95, and mains £10.95-£11.95 that include lentil, avo and chickpea salad; Lebanese mezze; chilli sin carne; cauliflower and butternut coconut curry. (However don't bother with breakfast, there's only a fruit salad.)

Best of all are the vegan blueberry muffins £2.95, chocolate cake £4.45.

Organic wine from £4.80 medium glass, £6.45 large, £19 bottle. Free wifi in all branches.

Wagamama

Omnivorous Japanese restaurant

🖝 **Victoria branch**: Roof Garden
Level, Cardinal Place (off Victoria
Street) SW1E 5JE

📞 020 7828 0561

🕐 M-Sa 11.00-22.00, Su 11.00-21.00

⊖ Victoria

🖝 Upper Level, **Fulham Broadway**
Shopping Centre SW6 1BW

📞 020 7386 8017

🕐 Su-Tu 11.00-22.00, W-Sa 11.00-
23.00

⊖ Fulham Broadway

🖝 26 **High Street Kensington** W8
4PF

📞 020 7376 1717

🕐 Su-W 11.00-22.00, W-Sa 11.00-
23.00

⊖ High Street Kensington

🏃 wagamama.com/vegan

Separate vegan menu includes edamame
green soya beans with chilli or salt, miso
soup with pickles, yasai steamed gyoza, raw
salad, udon noodles with curried veg, tofu
glass noodle salad, vegatsu curry with sticky
rice, pad Thai, yaki soba udon or rice
noodles, yasai samla tofu curry.

Unfortunately they forgot to veganize the
desserts apart from sorbet, but the mains
are so huge you won't have space anyway.
Wine from £4.50 medium glass, £5.75
large, £14.95 bottle.

Wagamama
vegan take-out

Made In House

Thai Green Grilled Tofu Curry

Tofu, Coconut Milk, Green Curry Paste (garlic, Onion, Lemongrass, Cilantro, Ginger, Chili Flakes, Jalapeno Pepper, Salt, Pepper), Date Syrup, Tamari (soya Beans), Lime Leaf

allergens: soya

Whole Foods Market Kensington
Omnivorous wholefood supermarket & cafes

- ☛ 63-97 High Street Kensington W8 5SE
- ☎ 020 7368 4500
- ◐ M-Sa 08.00-22.00 (restaurants close 30 mins before), Su cafe and shop open for browsing 11.00, sales 12.00-18.00
- ⊖ Kensington High Street
- ⚲ wholefoodsmarket.co.uk

This flagship UK branch of the US chain is ten times the size of any other UK wholefood store at 75,000 sqare feet. There is a staggering range of healthy foods on the ground floor and basement, and a vast cafe area upstairs (though with a lot of animal products), including a salad bar.

The **ground floor Provision Hall** has a bakery, olives, take-away, flowers and 28 checkouts. The bakery makes artisan breads and has biscuits, tarts, muffins, cookies, pies, cakes and pastries. Look out for vegan sushi £3.75 in the chiller by the take-away section, and Cat and the Cream vegan cupcakes and vegan chocolate cake.

The **basement Market Hall** has a huge array of great value basic wholefoods that you weigh and pack yourself, and a vast range of organic fruit, veg and herbs, much of it delivered from small local producers or sourced in London markets. The long line of fridges and freezers are packed with a zillion kinds of tofu, meat substitutes, soya yogurts and vegan ice cream.

The chocolate counter is dazzling.

Bodycare by Faith in Nature, Dr Hauschka, Weleda, makeup by Lavera and UNE.

Huge range of supplements. Cleaning products. Eco-clothing. Vegan cookbooks, health and lifestyle.

Upstairs are several cafes around the sides, but compared to when they first opened, it's gotten incredibly meaty, for example the sushi restaurant has only one vegan option. Wok Street does a veg tofu bowl with rice or noodles £6.50. However there is something excellent in the middle, an impressive self-serve salad bar, £1.59 per 100g take-away; £1.91 eat in. Dishes are clearly labelled with all ingredients, and might include all of these: squash with cranberries, Szechuan lentil salad, green beans with peas, quinoa and corn, rosemary potatoes, mixed fruit, roasted spicy cauliflower, Lebanese freekeh salad, beetroot vinaigrette, ratatouille, Mediterranean veg salad, quinoa with kidney beans, quinoa with chickpeas and sundried tomato, lemon and mustard quinoa with azuki beans and peas. Most have a dressing such as olive oil, lemon juice, salt and black pepper, and maybe herbs.

Also treatment and community rooms.

Whole Foods Market, Fulham
Omnivorous wholefood supermarket, cafe and juice bar

- 2-6 Fulham Broadway SW5 1AA
- 020-7386 4350
- M-F 07.30-22.00, Sa 08.00-22.00, Su 11.00-17.00 (coffee bar opens at 10.00)
- Fulham Broadway
- wholefoodsmarket.co.uk

On two floors with the bodycare department and a seating area upstairs.

Counter selection of cold and hot food £1.49-£1.91 per 100 grams, including beans, veg, quinoa salad, noodle salad, tofu, superfood salad, spinach and kale falafel, seaweed and original hummus, stuffed vine leaves, olives, Brussels sprouts with hazelnut, green beans with crispy shallots, veg stir-fry, broccoli sesame and chilli, roasted aubergine, butternut squash with cranberry.

Another counter with burritos and tostadas £5.95-£6.95 including different kinds of rice, soya mince, pinto and black beans, pepper and onion, guacamole, salsa, jalapeño, coriander, lettuce and lime juice.

Teas and coffee £1.60-£3.10.

Fridges with vegan cheeses and dairy by Sheese, Follow Your Heart, Violife, Nush, Coyo, The Coconut Collaborative, Isola Bio, Soyatoo (whipped cream), Sojade, Provamel, Alpro, Rude Health, Rhythm coconut mango kefir. Biona, Tofurky, pizzas. Olives and antipasti £1.99 per 100 grams.

Take-away by Laura's Idea, Pollen and Grace, such as kelp noodles and miso, beetroot quinoa and tahini, Tideford and own brand soups, San Amvrosia, seaweed salad.

Ice cream by Booja-Booja, Frill, Lilly & Hannah, The Coconut Collaborative chocolate dip snowconut sticks, Coyo, Dream, Nobo.

Great selection of vegan Italian, French and world wines. Vegan almond Baileys.

Loose grains, cereals, pulses, nuts, seeds, berriest.

Sections for superfoods, macrobiotics, herbs and spices, baby and kids. Huge selection of chocolate.

Supplements including Viridian, Terranova, Biocare, Pukka, Solgar, Vogel. Protein powders.

Bodycare by Antipodes, Neal's Yard, Trilogy, Pai, Mio, Dr Hauschka, Ren, Green People,Avalon, Faith in Nature, Jason, Dr Bronner, Sukin. Dr Hauschka, Benecos and Lavera make up and Pacifica nail varnish. They have a big sink where you can try some of their products.

Bach flower remedies. Absolute Aroma essential oils and incense sticks. Yoga accessories.

Cleaning by Method, Ecover, Attitude, Ecozone.

On the top floor "the living room" is a community space to learn, think and do, which you can book, projector and catering can be arranged. Free wifi. Amazon pick up point. High chairs. Community board.

Nearby up North End Road are 222 and Kiss My Grass vegan restaurants and Rabbit Hole vegan hairdressert. See Hammersmith - West Kensington.

Chelsea Health Store
Health food shop

- 400 Kings Road SW10 0LJ (near Triyoga)
- 020 7352 4663
- M-F 9.00-19.00, Sa 9.00-18.00, Su 11.00-18.00
- Fulham Broadway
- chelseahealthstore.com
  Facebook Chelsea Health Store

Independent health food shop with a huge range, next door to JuiceBaby. Fry's and VBites meat replacers. Amy's ready meals. Vegan cheeses such as Violife, yogurts and ice-creams including Booja Booja. Stacks of vegan chocolate.

Lots of supplements including BioCare, Lamberts, Viridian. Bodycare by Faith in Nature, Dr Hauschka, Jason, Lavera, Weleda, Earth Friendly Baby. Cleaning by Ecover. Treatment room for reflexology and massage.

Health Craze
Health food shop & take-away

- 24 Old Brompton Road, South Kensington SW7 3DL (opposite tube)
- 020 7589-5870
- M-F 9.30-22.00, Sa 10.00-20.00, Su 12.00-20.00
- South Kensington

Lots of organic wholefoods including nuts and snack bars like Trek and Nakd. Fridge with Taifun tofu and vegan burgers; coconut and soya yogurt; Tofutti, Sheese and Cheezly vegan cheese. Non-dairy milks. Biona vacuum packed rye bread.

Some bodycare such as Faith in Nature, Weleda, Sukin. Ecover clearning. Huge range of supplements, homeopathic and herbal remedies.

The owner is a pharmacist so can offer advice about health problems and using natural remedies.

Health Foods
Health food shop & take away

- 767 Fulham Road, London SW6 5HA
- 020 7736 8848
- M-Sa 9.00-18.00, Su closed
- Parsons Greenark
- aetherius.org/locations/london/
  health-foods-shop

Health foods since 1966 with take-away snacks, some vegan. Vegetarian (but not vegan) sandwiches and meals such as couscous with lentils.

Gluten-free and yeast-free and organic breads from different bakers. Freezer section with vegan ice-cream.

Cruelty free toiletries like Dead Sea Magik. Big mother and baby section. Ecover and Biogreen clearning products. A few books.

Lots of vitamins including A Vogel, Lambert's, Solaray, Nature's Own, Biocare, Nature's Gold. Homeopathy, Tisserand aromatherapy.

They have always been big on helping people to help themselves with natural healing and lifestyle. Top homeopathic practitioner available by appointment, also reflexologist, colour healing, kinesiologist/nutritionist. Centre for self-development, with courses for the giving and teaching of spiritual healing and counselling.

10% discount to senior citizens Thursday and Friday, and for everyone every day 9-10a.m.

Queens Health Shop
Health food shop

- 64 Gloucester Road SW7 4QT
- 020 7584-4815
- M-Sa 9.00-19.00, Su 11.00-16.30
- Gloucester Roade
- facebook.com/QueensHealthShop

Organic ranges and pre-packed vegan food to take away such as muesli, flapjacks and chocolate, but no fresh food available.

Large selection of vitamins, skin and body care. Ecover cleaning products.

Revital, Chelsea
Wholefood shop

- 83 King's Road, Chelsea SW3 4NX (opposite Markham Street)
- 020 7351 6593
- M-F 9.30-19.00, Sa 9.30-18.00, Su 11.00-16.00
- Sloane Square
- revital.co.uk

Lots of organic food, a wide range of toiletries and cruelty-free cosmetics. They have a take-away section with pies, sos rolls, cutlets, salads and burgers, some of which are vegan.

Bodycare including Dr Hauschka, cleaning products, vitamins and minerals, lots of sports nutrition, herbal and homeopathy, aromatherapy. Healthnotes touch-screen information kiosk which you can browswe and ask them to print out any pages.

Revital Health Place, Victoria
Health food shop

- 3a The Colonnades, 123/151 Buckingham Palace Rd, Victoria SW1W 9SH

  (entrance on Belgrave Rd, behind Victoria train station at entrance to Megabus & Green Line)
- 020 7976-6615
- M-F 9.00-19.00, Sa 9.00-18.00, Su 11.00-16.00
- Victoriae
- revital.co.uk

A great place to stock up before a coach or train journey. Fresh food counter, some vegan and gluten-free, such as pasties, date slice. Fridge with sprouts, hummus, lots of tofu, vegan cheeses, soya yogurts, coconut water and cold drinks. Freezer with vegan Booja Booja, Amy's, Swedish Glace, Fry's, Linda McCartney, Clive's pies, vegan gluten-free pizzas.

Gluten and dairy-free ranges including bread, organic and vegan foods, organic chocolates, carob bars, sugar-free sweets, raw snacks. Macrobiotic foods, lots of sea vegetables. Huge range of teas.

Organic bodycare including Dr Hauschka, Pukka, Aubrey, Natracare, Weleda Baby. Aromatherapy.

Food and herbal supplements. Sports nutrition. Trained staff can advise on products and you can book a free consultation with their qualified nutritionist. Lots of books. Healthnotes touch-screen information kiosk. Ecover and other cleaning products.

St James Health & Beauty
Beauty and vitamin shop

- 11-13 Strutton Ground, off Victoria Street, Victoria SW1P 2HY
- (020 7222 8442 / 5902
- M-W 10.00-19.00, Th-F 10.00-20.00, Sa 10.00-17.00, Su closed
- ⊖ St James's Park
- ↘ stjamesbeauty.co.uk

Formerly Greens health food shop, now transformed into a salon that also sells vegetarian and vegan supplements, homeopathic, naturopathic remedies, bodycare such as Dr Hauschka, Jason and Weleda. Onsite doctor of naturopathy for free onsite advice. Treatments include massage, beauty, aromatherapy, all male and female waxing, facials."

Lush
Cruelty-free cosmetics

- Victoria Rail Station,, by base of escalators and platforms 15-19, Unit 42B, Lower Concourse, 115 Buckingham Palace Road SW1V 9SJ
- (020 7630 9927
- M-Th 8.00-20.00, F 08.00-21.00, Sa 10.00-20.00, Su 11.00-20.00
- ⊖ Victoria
- ↘ lush.co.uk

Hand-made cosmetics, most of them vegan.

Holland & Barrett, Victoria
Health food shop

- Unit 2/3, **Victoria Shopping Centre**, Buckingham Palace Rd SW1W 9SA (just before the back entrance/exit)
- (020 7828 7663
- M-F 07.30-20.00, Sa 9.00-20.00, Su 10.00-19.00
- ⊖ Victoria

At the back right of Victoria rail station upstairs in the shopping centre where you can stock up on the way to the National Express and Eurolines coach station. Fridge and freezer. Sainsbury's supermarket opposite and Leon cafe next door.

- 73 **Kings Road**, Chelsea SW3 4NX
- (020 7352 4130
- M-Sa 9.00-19.30, Su 11.00-18.30
- ⊖ Sloane Square

No take-away, fridge or freezer. Monthly allergy testing, call ahead.

- 192 **Earls Court** Rd, SW5 9QF020
- (020 7370 6868
- M-Sa 9.00-19.00, Su 11.00-17.00
- ⊖ Earls Court

Fridge and freezer, vegan snacks, sos rolls.

- 220 **Fulham Road**, SW10 9NB
- (020 7352 9939
- M-F 9.30-18.30, Sa 9.30-18.00, Su 11.00-17.00

No take-away, fridge or freezer.

- 2-10 Jerdan Place, **Fulham** SW6 1BW
- (020 7386 5568
- M-Sa 9.00-19.00, Su 11.00-17.00
- ⊖ Fulham Broadway

Fridge and freezer but no take-away.

- 📪 167 **Kensington High St** W8 6NA
- 📞 020 7603 2751
- 🕐 M-F 9.00-19.00, Sat 10.00-19.00, Sun 11.00-18.00
- ⊖ High Street Kensington

Handy for the park, small store with fridge and freezer, drinks, pasties, yogurt, tofu.

- 📪 94a Brompton Road, **Knightsbridge** SW3 1ER
- 📞 020 7581 3324
- 🕐 M-F 9.00-20.00, Sa 10.00-20.00, Su 12.00-18.00
- ⊖ Knightsbridge

Freezer.

- 📪 10 Warwick Way, **Pimlico** SW1V 1QT
- 📞 020 7834 4796
- 🕐 M-Sa 9.00-18.30, Su 10.00-17.00
- ⊖ Victoria, Pimlico

Fridge and freezer, sos rolls and pasties.

- 📪 161 **Victoria Street** SW1E 6SH
- 📞 020 7233 6105
- 🕐 M-Sa 08.00-19.00, Su 11.00-18.00
- ⊖ Victoria, St James's Park

Fridge.

- 📪 86 **Victoria Street** SW1E 5JL
- 📞 020 7828 6147
- 🕐 M-F 07.30-20.00, Sa 10.00-18.30, Su 10.00 18.30
- ⊖ St James's Park, Victoria

Fridge and freezer.

Animal Aid Christmas Fayre
Annual one day vegan festival

- 📪 Kensington Town Hall, Hornton Street W8 7NX
- 🕐 First or second Sunday in December 10.00-16.30
- ⊖ High Street Kensington
- 🖱 animalaid.org.uk/events/animal-aids-christmas-fayre-2 (2018 website) Also on Facebook

Annual vegan event that is perfect for doing your Christmas shopping. Around 100 stalls, a big hall for talks by celebs and activists, several vegan caterers.

You can meet the people behind favourite vegan products, try samples of new ones before you buy, stock up on chocolate, cosmetics, shoes, and discuss where to eat out and shop at the Vegan London (the people behind this book) stall and London Vegan Meetup social group.

Admission £3. The 2019 event is on 9th December. Stallholders include Vegetarian Guides, publishers of this book, so come and say hello and find out what's new.

BAYSWATER

Notting Hill, Portobello Road & Ladbroke Grove

If you visit **Portobello Market** on a Sunday for antiques and clothes, make it the 2nd or 4th one of the month and take in the new **Portobello Vegan Farmers Market**. On the 2nd and 4th Wednesday evenings is **Portobello Vegan Night Market**. At other times you can feast on falafels and at **The Grain Shop** and pick up supplies at **Portobello Wholefoods**.

Around Westbourne grove are some high end vegan restaurants that specialise in raw. **Farmacy** is an absolutely beautiful, elegant restaurant with a bar. Nearby **Redemption** is a high raw, no alcohol restaurant and mocktail bar. Also in the area is **Café Forty One** vegan restaurant in La Suite West boutique hotel, specialising in French patisserie and afternoon teas. For a healthy vegan cafe, head to **JuiceBaby**.

Cloud Twelve spa off Portobello Road has a vegan brasserie, open to all even if you're not having your body thoroughly pampered.

You can load up on picnic supplies and snacks at **Planet Organic** store, which has a veggie cafe, or stroll across Hyde Park to Whole Foods Market in Kensington.

Paddington, between Bayswater and Edgware Road, has lots of hotels. Around the station of the same name, trains go west to Reading, Bath, Bristol and beyond, and you can catch the 15-minute Heathrow Express (though the Piccadilly line is a lot cheaper if you're not in a hurry).

Café Forty One
Vegan hotel & French, British & international restaurant, afternoon tea & pâtisserie

- 🛏 In La Suite West boutique hotel, 41-51 Inverness Terrace, Bayswater W2 3NJ
- 📞 020 7313 8484 contactus@lasuite-hotel.com
- 🕐 M-Su breakfast 07.00-11.00, lunch 12.00-15.00, afternoon tea 12.00-17.00, all-day desserts 08.00-17.00. Last orders 30 minutes before.
- ⊖ Bayswater, Queensway
- 🦅 lasuitewest.com/hotel-dining-london

The restaurant, previously called RAW then Nosh, in La Suite West boutique hotel on the north side of Hyde Park, got a boost with the arrival of French chef and pâtissière Clarisse Flon, who was trained in French pâtisserie then veganized it. Her specialities include meringues made from aqua faba chickpea water, and smoked salmon and cream cheese made with seaweed, miso and liquid smoke infused carrot.

Sample vegan breakfast: Continental buffet £9.95 with pastries, banana muffin, foccacia, hummus, fruit salad, soya yogurt. Full English breakfast £12.95 with sausages, roasted portobello mushrooms, baked beans, 'bacon', sliced avocado, sourdough toast, roasted tomatoes, filter coffee or pot of tea. Avocado on sourdough toast £9 with sundried tomatoes, caramelised onion chutney, sliced almonds, fried shallots and roasted cherry vine tomatoes. Savoury mushroom & black bean porridge £6 with button mushrooms, black beans, carrots and onions topped with bacon. Coconut Bircher muesli with caramelised bananas £5. Brioche french toast with roasted plums £7.50 plus yogurt, sliced almonds, vegan honey. Add vegan salmon £3.50.

Main courses £9.50-£13.50 include vegan salmon salad with quinoa; potato and cheese ravioli; sweet potato dauphinois with crispy pulled aubergine; truffle polenta and wild mushrooms with roasted winter veg; mushroom Bourguignon pie with mash and gravy; onion tart and Mediterranean salad.

Afternoon tea, £35 midday till 5pm, comes with four kinds of sandwiches such as cream cheese and smoked carrot salmon, patisserie of the week, non-alcoholic bubbly, coffee or loose-leaf tea, and raisin and plain scones served with homemade berry compote, vegan honey and clotted cream. Mocktails £5.

All day desserts 8am till 5pm, £8-£9.25, such as chocolate and praliné millefeuille, roasted figs and almonds honey rice pudding, poire belle-Hélène, coconut and grapefruit bergamot, quince and apple tatin tart served with chestnut cream and apple crisps and redcurrant curd.

The hotel was designed by famous British designer Anouska Hempel on the north side of Hyde Park. The garden with trees, hedges and plants is perfect for mocktails or afternoon tea. Rooms and suites with 4-poster bed, marble bathroom and breakfast from £175.

Children welcome; high chairs. Outside seating in summer; dogs welcome there. Free wifi. Some outside tables. Meeting room.

Redemption, Notting Hill
Vegan restaurant and alcohol-free bar

- 6 Chepstow Rd W2 5BH
- 020 7313 9041
- M-F 12.00-22.30, Sa 10.00-22.30, Su 10.00-21.30, last orders in the kitchen approx 1 hour before close
- Notting Hill, Bayswater, Royal Oak
- redemptionbar.co.uk

All vegan and gluten-free, some raw, they claim to be London's healthiest restaurant, so you can spoil yourself without spoiling yourself in a space away from temptation that still feels like a treat. Menus change during the year, here are sample dishes.

Weekday small dishes £7.50-£8.95 served on toasted sunflower and flaxseed break, choose from chunky guacamole with tomato and micro greens, or black bean chichurri, or marinated medicinal mushrooms (shitake, chestnut, nameko and golden needle).

Weekday mains £8.95-£9.75 feature buckwheat or sweetcorn and red pepper pancakes, brown rice penne pasta bolognese, or Carlifornication roasted sweet potato and red onion hash with mushrooms, kale, spinach.

Burgers £12.95 come in an oat bun with turmeric superslaw and chunky sweet potato fries, choose from pulled barbecued jackfruit or shitake with black bean and ruby beet.

Main course salads £10.75-£14.50 include Kale Caesar, raw courgette spaghetti with pumpkin seed pesto, or Tokyo with brown rice.

The evening menu adds soup, grilled aubergine and tahini, Vietnamese summer rolls, asparagus and pea black rice risotto.

On weekends before midday you can have the weekday small dishes and mains plus smoothie bowls £6.95, then it's the full regular menu from 12.00.

Extras £2.75-£4.50 such as small salads, turmeric hummus, slaw, sweet potato chunky fries, chunky guacamole, coconut yogurt, extra berries.

Luscious desserts £5.75-£7.50 include key lime cheesecake made with cashew cream and a coconut and almond crust; banoffee pie made from medjool date salted caramel, banana and coconut yogurt cream and an oaty biscuit base; seasonal berries selection with crème Chantilly; ruby forest gateau with a nutty chocolate base, raspberries and Chantilly; bliss balls made with raw dark chocolate and date truffles rolled in coconut.

Non-alcoholic drinks £4-£5.95 include Fitbeer beer, mocktails such as apple mockjito, juices and smoothies and shakes, such as the protein-rich superhero with almond milk, banana, blueberries, chia and hemp seeds, cacao powder and date syrup. Bees Knees alcohol-free sparkling wine £4 glass, £18.50 bottle.

Pots of tea are great value at £2.95, the same price for any type of coffee. Skinny cacao £3.75. Turmeric, matcha or guarana coconut latte £4.95.

Discretionary service charge 12.5%. Call for bookings of more than 6. Children welcome. Well-behaved dogs welcome outside, inside under the table at their discretion. Free wifi.

Another branch in Old Street, Shoreditch East London, and a third opemed at the end of 2018 in Covent Garden.

Made in Notting Hill

Farmacy

Vegan organic restaurant

📍 74-76 Westbourne Grove W2 5SH

📞 020 7221 0705

🕐 M-F 09.00-17.00, 18.00-22.00;
Sa 10.00-16.00, 18.00-22.00;
Su 09.00-16.00, 18.00-21.30

🚇 Bayswater, Queensway, Royal Oak

🔗 farmacylondon.com
facebook.com/Farmacyuk

Opened April 2016 by Camilla Fayed, daughter of Harrods' boss Mohammed Al Fayed and previously owner of high end fashion brand Issa, who is moving on from fashion into the vegan restaurant business. Her aim is to bring to London the type of ultra-healthy vegan food more commonly found in vegan restaurants in New York and Los Angeles, which she says has improved her health. They make their own almond milk, and cashew cheese for pizza.

Breakfasts £9-£14 range from avocado sourdough toast with dukkah and herbs; sprouted beans on sourdough toast; rawnola; berry bowl with lucuma, spirulina and maca; probiotic cashew yogurt jars; buckwheat pancakes with fresh fruit, coconut yogurt, caramelised pecans and maple syrup; chocolate chip waffles; chickpea omelette; full cooked English. The weekend brunch menu adds some of the main menu dishes such as falafels, salads, bowls, burgers and pizza.

The weekend brunch menu has the usual breakfasts plus starters, sharing plates and mains £7.50-£15.50 that include rice pasta mac 'n' truffled cheese, artichoke pizzetta with macadamia cheese, nachos, sweet potato falafels, salads, Mexican bowl, kimchi bowl with soba noodles, winter veg bowl with sprouted spiced buckwheat,

Farmacy burger (millet, black bean and mushroom) with potato chips or sweet potato fries. The weekday menu adds soup, seasonal curry, mushroom and Jerusalem artichoke pie with sweet potato mash, loaded mushroom tacos, kamut spaghetti bolognaise.

Desserts £7-£11 include banana bread and peanut butter pudding; pumpkin tart; nice cream brownie sundae; chocolate cup; warm chocolate chip cookie with a glass of almond milk; cardamon and orange spiced rice pudding; probiotic jars. Add chocolate or vanilla cashew nice cream £2.

Luxurious high tea £42 per person.

Superfood smoothies and cold pressed juices £7. Unusual hot and cold drinks £4-£7 such as coconut matcha, maca or chai latte; coconut hot chocolate with vanilla, cinnamon and nutmeg; turmeric coconut milk with black pepper and cardamon; coconut lemonade; iced green tea with orange and lemon juice and berries; berries punch; syringe shots £5. Herbal teas and coffees £4 with oat or coconut milk.

Wines £5-£12.50 medium glass, £20-£70 bottle, they know which are vegan though it's not marked on the menu. Freedom vegan beers £5. Cocktails £10.

12.5% discretionary service charge is shared amongst all staff. When we visited mid morning, the power points around the walls were popular with laptop users coffeeing. Private dining room for up to 20 people, breakfast or brunch £25, lunch or dinner £35 or £45 set menus.

FIL THY VEGAN JUNK FO

AKE CARDS - ASK FOR ALLERGENS

NGIN' WINGZ

A SUGARCANE SPEAR, CHOOSE
BON INFUSED BBQ SAUCE

MON SWEET CHILL, MISO MAYO
STED NUTS

TWO PIECE 5
THREE PIECE 6.5

ACKED FILLET
BURGERS

ATHER JACK
BACON JAM / FRIED ONION RINGS   7.5
ESE / BOURBON BBQ SAUCE / ICEBERG

MUEL HELL JACKSON
BO CHIPOTLE SLAW / BURGER CHEESE   7.5
PEÑOS / MAPLE CHIPOTLE SAUCE

CAJUN FRIES AND PICKLES
IN DUSTED FRIES PORTION   2
        COLD DRINK   1.5

FFS JACK SHACK

WE'RE
CARD ONLY

FIL THY VEGAN
BURGERS

VEGAN

BURGERS

TIPPLE ON TAP

Portobello Vegan Night Market (Wednesdays)
Vegan street food market

- ☞ 281 Portobello Road W10 5TZ (north end by the Westway
- 🕐 2nd & 4th Wednesday 18.00-22.00
- ⊖ Ladbroke Grove, Westbourne Park

Portobello Vegan Farmers Market (Sundays)
Vegan food market

- ☞ All Saints Catholic College, 75 Saint Charles Square W10 6EL (5 blocks north of the Vegan Night Market)
- 🕐 2nd and 4th Sundays 10.30-14.30
- ⊖ Ladbroke Grove
- ➴ portobellovegan.com
  facebook.com/plantbasedevents

Run by entrepreneur JP McCormack, aka Portobello Vegan. The night market features 20+ traders showcasing vegan street food plus an artisan corner for fresh produce, juices and smoothies, cakes, treats, cheese, superfoods, sauces, ice-cream, clothing, beauty and home products. Vegan DJ playing reggae, ska, roots, soul and funk. A typical lineup could include En Root, Yim Food, Comptoir V, Little Leaf, Rebel Tapas, Oh My Gulay, Elusive Juices, Rainforest Creations, Pomodoro e Basilico, Portobello Mushroom Man, Rainforest Creations, Valerie Veg Bakery, Dark Arts Vegan, Hemp Botanics, Tipple on Tap, Self Care Co, Eat Moringa, Vraps.

On Sundays the UK's first and only vegan farmers' market is free of stinky meat and dairy stalls, but full of organic fruit and veg, vegan cheese, condiments, suuperfoods, clothing, beauty and bodycare, and some vegan street food traders.

Cloud Twelve

Luxury spa and salon with organic vegan brasserie

📍 2-5 Colville Mews W11 2DA

📞 020 3301 1012

🕐 M-W, F-Sa 9.00-19.00, Th 9.00-20.00, Su 9.00-18.00

⊖ Ladbroke Grove, Notting Hill Gate

🔖 cloudtwelve.co.uk
facebook.com/CloudTwelveClub

Wellness and lifestyle club on three floors, to the east of the middle of Portobello Road along Lonsdale Road. There is an indulgent spa, hair and nails salon using vegan Evo and Nailberry products, holistic wellness clinic, and a brasserie which is open to non-members. There are fantastic facilities for you to bring your children along too, where they can play and learn with you, or with Ofsted registered assistants while you watch and unwind in the lounge.

The brasserie, open to non-members, centres on mezze and Spanish tapas using recipes by Stu Henshall of The Alternative Kitchen plant-based consultancy.

All day breakfasts £6-£8 include overnight Bircher muesl, açai bowl, avo sourdough toast, trio of smoked carrot gravadlax with tempeh chorizo and scrambled tofu, and you can add soy-braised chestnut and shiitake mushrooms. Pastries and cakes.

From midday: soup of the day with sourdough £9; hot and cold small plates £6, 2 for £11, 3 for £15, such as roasted veggies with tofu feta, broad bean and peas orzo pasta, salad special, shepherdess pie, puy lentil stew with roasted squash in coconut and tahini broth, ratatouille, weekly warmer special.

Superfood smoothies £6. Kombucha £4. Pot of leaf tea £4 with plant milks. Coffees £2.50-£4 include turmeric, matcha or chai latte.

Organic wines £6-£14 small glass, £8-£24 medium, £31-£9 bottle. Pale ale, apple or pear cider.

Afternoon tea for two £70, or £90 with a glass of champagne. Feast elegantly on devilled scrambled tofu tart, truffled sausage rolls, sandwiches that include chickpea tuna, smoked carrot gravadlax and BLT, black bean brownie bites, fruit scones with in-house fig and blueberry jam and cream, rose macaron with buttercream filling, passionfruit Victoria sponge, citrus and leaf mousse. Plus a choice of medicinal, green and breakfast teas.

Family Space with crèche/play zone for children 0 to 11. Educational toys and books, play area, apparatus and ball pit, supervised by qualified, professional play buddies, wih a focus on drama, singing, stories and rhymes, games and activities.

Children's healthy vegan cafe and lounge focusing on dark green veg, wholegrains, pulses, dark chocolate, dried fruit, tofu and other soy products, nuts and seeds. Breakfasts £2-£4, smoothies £3, lunch £3.50-£5, download menu on the website.. Dishes include crunchy baked tofu faux fish fingers, mac and cheese, baby broth.

The spa, open to non-members, offers sauna, steam and salt rooms, massages, facials, pre- and postnatal rituals, men's treatments, and a couples' suite equipped with Dolomites quartz beds. Over-16 only, children over 6 welcome till 1pm. Gift vouchers. Wellness clinic with acupuncture, reflexology, herbal and Chinese medicine, nutrition, osteopathy, craniosacral etc.

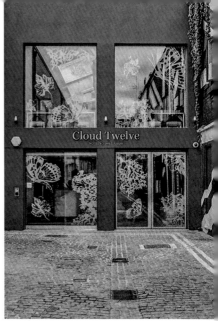

JuiceBaby, Notting Hill
Vegan juice bar and salads cafe

- 181 Westbourne Grove W2 2SB
- 020 7221 2144
- M-F 07.30-19.00, Sa 08.00-19.00, Su 08.00-18.00
- Notting Hill
- juicebaby.co.uk

Great pitstop for for healthy breakfasts, raw lunches and desserts. All vegan and mostly gluten-free.

Cold-pressed juices and nut milks £4.25 qtr litre, £6.95 half-litre. Smoothies £6.25 half-litre.

Breakfasts £5.50 like millet porridge, avo chilli toast, nut butter and chia jam sandwich. Açaí bowls around £8.

Lunch choices £5.95-£9.75 include tomato or green gazpacho, soup of the day with multi-seed spelt bread, kale salad, taco bowl, dragon veg bowl with steamed quinoa, glow bowl with sweet potato and herby quinoa, winter tahini bowl, super greens salad, sandwiches such as red pepper hummus or spicy sunflower spread with salad.

Lots of raw snacks and desserts £3.75-£5.75 include lemon blueberry cheesecake, pumpkin pie, Brazil nut brownies, chocolate krispies, goji 5-seed bars, sticky toffee balls, almond and coconut cookies, cacao macaroons, superfood truffles.

Teas, organic coffees, latte, iced latte, matcha latte, hot choc £1.75-£3.60.

Also in Fulham Broadway, Sloane Zone.

The Grain Shop
Vegetarian cafe, bakery & take-away

- 269a Portobello Road W11 1LR (in Portobello market, opposite Tavistock Rd)
- 020 7229 5571
- M-Sa 10.00-18.00, Su 10.00-17.00
- Ladbroke Grove

Vegetarian take-away and bakery with bar seats along the wall. They use organic flour. 16 hot dishes, 13 of which are suitable for vegans, such as tofu stir-fry, veg curry, as well as salads all made on the premises. Medium mixed box £4.99 (eat in £5.39), large £6.50 (£6.90).

Specialist breads and cakes for allergy free diets, also sugar-free items.

Organic sourdough bread £1.50, £2.75.

Lots of vegan and sugar-free cakes £1.80, brownies £1.90.

Lots of cold drinks. MC, Visa 80p charge.

Happy Vegetarian
Vegetarian falafel stall

- In front of Tesco Metro, 224 Portobello Road W11 1LJ (opposite Hayden's Place), pitch 104 in Portobello Market, just south of Westway flyover
- 07984 721 115
- M-W, F 11.00-17.00; Sa 10.15-18.00; Th, Su closed
- Ladbroke Grove
- Facebook Happy Vegetarian

Falafels £3-£5. Extra salad or sauce 50p. Water or soft drink £1.

Falafel Stall
Vegetarian falafel stall

- 94 Golborne Road W10 5PS, north of the flyover
- 07956 813119
- M-W, F 11.00-16.00; Th, Sa-Su closed
- Ladbroke Grove

Falafels, hummus, lentil soup, salad box. On Thursdays they are at Hammersmith Market.

Holland & Barrett
Health food shop

- 32 Queensway W2 4QW
- 020 7727 6449
- M-F 9.00-20.00, Sa 10.00-20.00, Su 11.30-20.00
- Queensway

Fridge and freezer.

- 130 Notting Hill Gate W11 3QG
- 020 7243 2470
- M-Sa 9.00-19.00, Su 11.00-18.00
- Notting Hill Gate

Fridge and freezer.

- 162 Portobello Road W11 2EB
- 020 3441 6725
- M-F 9.00-18.00, Sa 08.30-18.00, Su 10.00-17.00
- Ladbroke Grove

Fridge and freezer.

Planet Organic, W2
Natural/organic supermarket & veggie cafe

- 42 Westbourne Grove W2 5SH (Queensway end)
- 020 7727 2227
- M-Sa 07.30-21.30, Su 12.00-18.00
- Bayswater, Queensway, Royal Oak
- planetorganic.com

Organic wholefood supermarket with a juice bar and café. Most dishes, snacks and cakes have ingredients displayed and if they are gluten-, sugar-free or vegan.

Picnic heaven. Load up here with every kind of veggie food and heaps you never even knew existed, alcoholic and non-alcoholic drinks. A long row of fridges at the front is packed with take-away food and drink including salads, falafel, sushi, wraps, curry, soups, hummus, vegan Violife cheese, chia pots, Bircher muesli, soy and coconut yogurts, juices, smoothies, almond shakes, green tea.

Juice and coffee bar. Hot food bar and salads, point to what you want, small bowl or take-away box £5.50, medium £7.50, large £8.50. Hot soups. Lots of cakes and desserts, many vegan and raw. Breakfast porridge until 11am.

Juices and smoothies £4.50-£5.95. Hot drinks in regular or large £1.65-£2.95, speciality lattes £3.15-£4, choice of several plant milks. Filtered water free.

Huge section devoted to health and body care, including vitamins, herbs, tinctures, floral essences, aromatherapy oils, suncream, makeup, shampoos and conditioners, including Barefoot Botanicals, Dr Hauschka, John Masters, Lavera, Living Nature, Green People, Jäson, Neal's Yard Remedies, Urtekram, Weleda.

Staff are very friendly and well-trained to deal with customer queries, many being practitioners or in training.

Household goods including Ecover, Attitude, Greensense. Organic baby section. A great place for presents like pretty candles and incense, chocolate and other treats. Books section includes cookery, dietary, mother and baby and Veggie Guides.

Children welcome.

Portobello Wholefoods
Vegetarian wholefood shop

- 266 Portobello Road, Ladbroke Grove W10 5TY (Junction with Cambrige Gardens just under the Westway; north end of market)
- 020 8968 9133
- M-Sa 9.30-18.00, Su 11:00-17.00
- Ladbroke Grove
- facebook.com/portobellowholefoods

Excellent large wholefood shop in Portobello market area. They pack all their own dry products like nuts, dried fruit, grains and beans, make their own muesli, and have extended the range of organic fruit and veg. Non-dairy cheeses and ice-cream.

Big fridge with tortillas, pies, sushi wraps, salads, Laura's Idea vegan healthy breakfast granola pots.

Vitamins and supplements. Large range of toiletries including soaps and moisturisers. Biodegradable cleaning products, Ecover refills.

Clothes market opposite on Sundays on Portobello Green. (see Portobello Market)

Eden Perfumes|
Vegan perfume shop

- 📍 203 Portobello Road W11 1LU (north end before Westway)
- 📞 01273 696 866
- 🕐 Tu-Sa 11.00-18.00, Su 11.00-17.00, M 11.00-18.00
- 🚇 Ladbroke Grove
- 🔗 edenperfumes.co.uk
  facebook.com/edenveganperfumes

Their first shops were in the Brighton area, and now they have a devoted following in London. Vegan, paraben free, not tested on animals, refillable, affordable, handmade, SLS free. 200 lovely vegan perfumes for men and women such as rose-vanilla, their best seller.

Neal's Yard Remedies, Notting Hill
Herbs and complementary health

- 📍 9 Elgin Crescent W11 2JA (off Portobello Rd, 2/3 of the way up)
- 📞 020 7727 3998
- 🕐 M-Tu, F 10.00-19.00, W-Th 10.00-19.30, Sa 9.00-19.00, Su 11.00-18.00. Closed M bank holiday.
- 🚇 Ladbroke Grove, Notting Hill Gate
- 🔗 nealsyardremedies.com

Herbs and spices by weight, organic toiletries, natural remedies, books on homeopathy and remedies. All products tested on human volunteers, not animals. Mostly organic, lots of Fairtrade. They also have therapy rooms offering many kinds of massage and other treatments.

Portobello Market
Huge street market

☞ Portobello Road, W11

🕐 Summer most stalls set up 8-9am, finish 5-6pm. Winter and bad weather from 9-10am till 4-5pm. Closed bank holidays except Good Fri. Closed Th afternoon. M-Th fruit & veg, F-Sa antiques, Su fashion.

⊖ Ladbroke Grove, Notting Hill Gate

↖ portobelloroad.co.uk
portobellomarket.org
shopportobello.co.uk (handy map)

Gigantic market, competing with Walthamstow for the title of longest in Britain. The market is packed with stalls from Westbourne Grove all the way up to and along Golborne Road, and across under the Westway out to Ladbroke Grove. Come early to discover the best finds and avoid the crowds!

M-W plus Th morning, Portobello Rd from Elgin Crescent to Westway: fruit & veg, household goods. Golborne Rd: fruit & veg.

Friday is the second busiest day with antiques in south Portobello Road; food, new fashion and household in the middle; and vintage clothing and bric-a-brac at Portobello Green and North Portobello.

Saturday is the big one, as Friday plus more antiques in Westbourne Grove to Kensington Park Road, the Antiques Arcade off Portobello Road is open between Chepstow Villas and Westbourne Grove, and more new fashion and less vintage at Portobello Green.

On Sundays on Portobello Green (opposite Portobello Wholefoods), there is another market with vintage and new clothes, secondhand jewellery, crystals and cards.

Fresco
Omni Lebanese restaurant

- 25 Westbourne Grove, W2 4UA
- (020 7221 2355
- M-Su 09.00-22.00
- Queensway, Bayswater, Royal Oak
- eat-fresco.co.uk

A cross between a fresh juice bar and a small Lebanese restaurant, Fresco serves a variety of juices and smoothies, alongside wraps like falafel and hummus with tabouleh, salad boxes, vegetable tagine, lentil soup, and a mixed mezze platter.

Around Paddington station these Indian restaurants are open every day for lunch and dinner: Connoisseurs at 8 Norfolk Place W1 1QL is great value, and the more upmarket Bombay Palace at 50 Connaught St W2 2AA.

Leafwild Cafe
Vegetarian cafe

- 156 Ladbroke Grove W10 5NA (just north of the Westway)
- (020 3417 6616
- M-F 07.30-18.00, Sa 08.00-18.00, Su 9.00-18.00
- Ladbroke Grove
- leafwild.co.uk

Opened May 2018 in a beautifully designed space created by the architect and interior designer owners. Almost all vegan apart from eggs, and gluten-free.

Breakfast and brunch includes oat or quinoa porridge with seeds, nuts, fruit, granola; tofu scramble or avocado and cashew pesto on sourdough £8; acai bowl £8; Asian toast £9.50 with carrot roasted salmon, mashed edamame, roasted seaweed, vegan caviar and toasted sesame on charcoal sourdough; full English £13 with scramble, organic baked beans, roasted tomatoes, mushrooms, avocado, toast. Buddha bowl £10 with sweet potato and black beans. Buckwheat pancakes £10 with coconut cream, fresh berries and activated pecans.

Children's breakfast £4-£5.50.

Lunch soup £4.50, stew of the day £5.50

Raw desserts such as hazelnut bar, flapjack, orange polenta cake, protein tofu cake (nuts, tofu, raw cacao),

Smoothies £7.20. Coffees £2.30-£3.70. Super lattes £3.95 with turmeric or cacao or matcha or beetroot or maca mushroom, plus other goodies, can be made with coconut, almond or hazelnut milk. Teas £3.

Dogs welcome. All packaging is recyclable or compostable.

Firezza, Notting Hill
Omnivorous pizzeria

- 12 All Saints Road W11 1HH
- 020 7221 0020
- M-Th 17.00-23.00, F-Sa 12.00-24.00, Su 12.00-23.00
- Ladbroke Grove
- firezza.com

They have vegan cheese! Carne Vegana pizza comes with vegan chorizo, pepperoni and stacks of veggies for around £10 or £14. Mango sorbet £1.99.

CHISWICK

Angies Little Food Shop
Omnivorous cafe-restaurant

- 📍 114 Chiswick High Road W4 1PU
- 📞 020 8994 3931
- 🕐 M-F 07.30-19.00, Sa 08.30-19.00, Su/BH 10.00-18.00
- ⊖ Turnham Green
- ✦ angieslittlefoodshop.com

Angie Steele, the owner and chef, previously worked as a private chef to celebrities and with Gordon Ramsay for 8 years, and while the main menu is distinctly unvegan, she is also big on healthy salads and cold-pressed juice.

Salads, small up to 3 portions £8.80, large up to 5 £10.70, choose from eight salads, each with at least five ingredients. The base could be red rice, black quinoa, soba noodles, and then several more ingredients such as roasted butternut, red pepper, aubergine, red onion, courgette and mizuna leaves. And there are some pure veg salads too like artichoke, asparagus, samphire, runner beans with chilli tarragon dressing.

Soup of the day £7. Avocado on toast £5.75.

Wine medium glass £7 glass, £28 bottle. Cocktails around £5. Beer £4.75.

Fresh juices £3.10, cold pressed juices £4.40. Soft drinks, coffee. They have almond, rice and soya milk.

Beautiful handmade ceramics on display, imported from Angie's native South Africa. The walls are adorned with pictures from London artist Millie McCullum and everything is for sale.

Big table at the back is ideal for meetings or working. Seats outside. High chairs. Wifi. Very dog friendly. No reservations.

Franco Manca, Chiswick
Omnivorous chain Italian restaurant

- 📍 144 Chiswick High Road W4 1PU
- 📞 020 8747 4822
- 🕐 M-F 12.00-23.00, Sa-Su 11.30-23.00
- ⊖ Turnham Green, Stamford Brook
- ✦ francomanca.co.uk

Vegan pizza sourdough bases. They let the dough rest for 20 hours, good for people who have trouble digesting fast-rising pizza and end up having to spend all night drinking water. Vegan cheese and all wines.

Hare & Tortoise, Chiswick
Omnivorous chain noodle & sushi restaurant

- ☛ 156 Chiswick High Rd W4 1PR
- ☎ 020 8747 5966
- ◑ M-F 12.00-23.00, Sa 11.30-23.00, Su 11.30-22.30, last order 30m before
- ⊖ Turnham Green
- ➤ hareandtortoise.co.uk

Vegan dishes include fake duck with hoisin sauce, spring rolls, edamame, maki, sauté bean curd with mixed veg lo mein.

Pizza Express, Chiswick
Omnivorous chain Italian restaurant

- ☛ 252 Chiswick High Road W4 1PD
- ☎ 020 8747 0193
- ◑ Su-Th 11.30-23.00, F-Sa 11.30-24.00
- ⊖ Turnham Green, Chiswick Park
- ➤ pizzaexpress.com

Small patio at the front for outside dining. Vegan cheese. Baby facilities. Disabled toilet. Wifi.

Zizzi, Chiswick
Omnivorous chain Italian restaurant

- ☛ 235 Chiswick High Road W4 4PU
- ☎ 020 3302 2126
- ◑ M-Sa 11.30-23.00, Su 11.30-22.30
- ⊖ Turnham Green, Chiswick Park
- ➤ zizzi.co.uk

Vegan mozzarella in original, smoked, cheddar and blue. Pizza and calzone. Lush vegan desserts. Outdoor area. Free wifi.

Windfall Natural Goods
Wholefood shop

- ☛ 1-3 Turnham Green Terrace W41RG
- ☎ 020 8742 1640
- ◑ M-Sa 9.00-19.00, Su 11.00-17.00
- ⊖ Turnham Green
- ➤ facebook.com/WindfallNatural
  instagram.com/windfallnaturalgoods

Friendly, independent wholefood shop near Turnham Green underground, previously at number 41 where it was called Health My God Given Wealth and was just one fifth the new floor area. The store is packed to the ceiling with a big range of hand-picked organic and natural products, avoiding synthetic preservatives, and which the staff use themselves.

Wide range of wholefoods, organic breads. Lots of Fairtrade including Palestinian olive oil.

In the fridges: Vegan cheeses include New Roots Free-the-Goat, Happy Cheese, Violife. Taifun sausages and tofu. BOL salads. Press soups. Fresh organic tempeh. Natural Jackfruit. Slo Good Living oganic nut milks in pecan, pistachio, cashew, almond blends. Rhythm coconut kefir, Biomel coconut milk drinks, Coyo coconut yogurts. Karine & Jeff fine French cuisine, Tideford Organics.

Ice cream by Booja Booja; White Rabbit vegan pizza.

Bodycare by Pai, Weleda, Jäson, Barefoot Botanicals, Green People, Green Baby, Neal's Yard, Dr Hauschka, Faith in Nature, Dr Bronners, Ameliorate, John Masters Organics, Fushi, Absolute Aromas. Grace and Green organic biodegradable cotton pads and tampons; Organic Cup menstrual cup.

Supplements by Solgar, Biocare, Viridian, Pure Encapsulations, Terra Nova, Wild Nutrition, Pukka, Minami.

Natural remedies including Nature's Plus, Bioforce tinctures.

I Love Skin beautiful facial and scar oils that are formulated by a local naturopath.

Wide range of CBD products, oils, sprays, balms, teas, including London Botanists and KIKI CBD oils, Mr Moxye's CBD mints, OTO luxurious 20% CBD roll on blends with essential oils - they are the very first store to stock these.

Cleaning products by Bio D, Method, Ecover, Green Frog organic soap nuts.

Ecoffee cups from bamboo fibre, Chilly's water bottles. Holistic London vegan candles poured locally in Chiswick. Liforme yoga mats.

Three in house nutritionists providing free consultations every day.

As Nature Intended
Organic & health food shop

- 201 Chiswick High Road W4 2DR
- 020 8742-8838
- M-Sa 9.00-20.00, Su/BH 10.00-19.00
- Turnham Green
- asnatureintended.uk.com

Newly refurbished 95% organic store that aims to combine the variety of a supermarket (over 5,000 products) with the product range found in traditional health food shops. Many items are suitable for those with food allergies such as sugar-, gluten-, salt- or yeast-free. Not completely vegetarian.

Wide range of sandwiches and pies to take away: Laura's idea, Yummy Tammy, Bol. Many Japanese and tofu-based foods and tempeh. Taifun, Tofurky and Clearspring. Cheese from Violife, Sheeze and Cheezly. Fresh olives, artichokes, sun dried tomatoes, garlic in oil £1.69 per 100gr. Bread and gluten-free muffins.

Refill nuts, grains and beans. Separate section for baby/kid's food..

Vegan and wines are clearly labelled and there is a leaflet in case you're unsure what constitutes a vegan wine.

Herbal and homeopathic remedies, aromatherapy oils, beauty and skincare such as Pai, Green People, Weleda, Avalon, Faith in Nature, Akin also Green People, Weleda, Pai for kids. Vitamins and minerals including Veridian, Terranova, Pukka, Biocare, solgar. Lots of books. Ecover (refill), Ecosystem, Earth Friendly.

Everyone in the remedies section is a practitioner or has had training. Certain days therapists offer treatments. Lots of information on recommended treatments for various conditions on their website. Pay and display car park at front.

Lemon & Limes
Fruit, veg and wholefood store

- 88 Turnham Green Terrace W4 1QN
- 020 8995 9077
- M-Su 08.00-21.00
- Turnham Green
- lemonandlimes.co.uk

Apart from the wide selection of fruit and veg both organic and not, there are lots of wholefoods from Infinity, Biona, Suma and Clearspring. Loose nuts, dried fruit including pineapple, sharon fruit, melon, cantaloupe, mango etc. Organic herbs. Pea protein. Vegan mayo.

Fresh green and fruit smoothies £3.95 such as kale with cavolo nero, spinach, parsley, apple and pear. Unusual fruit such as Chinese pear, kiwano melon, prickly pear, dragon fruit, guava and a lot more. Stop there in the summer for the watermelon.

Also in West Hampstead (North London).

Holland & Barrett, Chiswick
Health food shop

- 350 High Road, Chiswick W4 5TA
- 020 3638 3718
- M-Sa 08.30-19.00, Su 11.00-18.00
- Chiswick Park, Turnham Green

Fridge and freezer.

Carley's Organic
Raw Hemp Seed
Butter
£3.20
250g

Carley's Organic
Sunflower Seed
Butter
£2.60
250g

Carley's Organic
Mixed Nut Butter
£3.85
250g

Carley's Organic
Sesame Seed Butter
£2.90
250g

Carley's Organic
Cashew Butter
£3.85
250g

y Store & Deli • Fairtrade • Vegan • Gluten Free • Affordable Organics

Organic for the people

THE UK'S ONLY 100% ORGANIC HIGH STREET STORE

Organic for the People
Vegan organic wholefood shop and deli

- 🖝 29-30 High Street W5 5DB
- ☎ 020 3581 1080
- 🕐 M-Sa 08.00-20.00, Su 09.00-18.00
- ⊖ Ealing Broadway
- ⬥ Facebook Organic For The People

New shop that is adored by local vegans and people who travel into London to visit. As well as the usual wholefoods, they sell organic fruit amd veg and hard to find items like Vego nutty chocolate bars. They say it is the first shop in the UK to be 100% organic and vegan, and they will keep the prices low so they can encourage more people to be vegan and eat organic.

There is a big section of chocolate by the till so you can't escape from temptation. Many old and new brands such as Rawr, Iswari, Chocolate & Love, Mulu, Love Raw and Wild Things. Booja Booja truffles.

Another packed section with plant milks and cooking cream. Everything you need for breakfast.

Many types of flour and pasta from La Bio Idea, Castagno Bio etc. Terra Vegane mac 'n' cheese. Lots of noodles. Quinola organic Fairtrade quinoa.

Soups from Geo, Essential Organic, Amy's and Free & Easy.

Spice things up with Geo paste, Kitchen Garden basil paste, chilli paste and mint sauce; Real Organic mushroom and red wine, Thai green and Thai red curry.

Bread, crackers and grissini (Italian breadsticks), most gluten-free.

The Kombu Seaweeed Company sea salad, kombu of course, sea spaghetti, sea green and dulse. Macrobiotic section.

Fruit, veg and Hatton Hill herbs.

Impressive organic baby and kids section with Organix, Holle, Quinola range, Pip, Little Pasta and sauces, Pumpkin Tree sauces.

Behind the till are bodycare and supplements such as Earth Friendly Baby, Green People for kids and adults, Urtekram, Dr Bronner, Organii, Emma Noel soaps, Pukka. Aromatherapy.

(Just as we loaded the book up to our printer, we discovered that the shop VeganHQ in Ealing had closed. So here is a space. Really sorry about that. But remember that for every vegan place that closes in London, at least three more open.)

Falafel Box
Vegan falafel trailer

- ☛ Ealing Broadway, Oak Road W5 5AW
  (opposite HSBC and Lloyds Bank)
- ☏ 07782 502660
- 🕐 M-Sa 11.00-19.00, Su closed
- ⊖ Ealing Broadway
- ➤ facebook.com/ealingw5

Falafel wrap £3.80. Falafel box £5 with potato, cauliflower, aubergine and vine stuffed leaves, sauces. Also seitan kebabs.

Soft drinks £1.

The Humble Veg
Vegan take-away

☛ 135 Northfields Avenue W13 9QT
   (corner Leyborne Avenue)

📞 020

🕐 Tu-Sa 12.00-18.00, Su-M closed

⊖ Northfields

↖ facebook.com/thehumblevegealing
   instagram.com/thehumblevegealing

Eco-friendly, 100% vegan, grassroots take-away opened 2019, with vegan Vegware and Fiesta Green packaging made from plants. Bring your own Tupperware or travel cup and get 20p off your meal/tea.

Hot rice boxes £5 come with coconut and cumin lentils, or chunky veg stew, or corn on the cob, sweet pepper and kidney beans in spiced tomato sauce. Special £5-£6 such as spicy Gochujang stir-fry with rice and salad; or mushroom, walnut, veg in a creamy sauce, topped with mash potatoes, served with greens.

Jac's Wrap £4.50 with jackfruit, garlic mayo, lettuce, gherkin, onion. Cheeky Chicks wrap £4 with with crispy chickpeas, hummus, olive and sundried tomato tapanade, salad.

Salads £5 such as Rainbow Cous Cous with chickpeas, or Eat Yo' Greens with spinach, broccoli, peas, green lentils, potatoes, sweetcorn, spring onion, seeds.

Snack box £3 of crackers, crudités, hummus, olives. Nachos £3. Sandwiches £3 such as cheese and pickle.

Sweet treats such as cashew and sultana chocolate tart £1.20, nutty tart pudding pot £2, fresh fruit pot £3, salted caramel coconut ice cream. Drinks £1.Pukka teas £1.20.

Triyoga Ealing Cafe
Vegan cafe in yoga & pilates centre

- ☛ Unit 30, Dickens Yard, Longfield Avenue, Ealing W5 2UQ
- ☏ 020 3362 0688
- ◷ M-F 06.00-21.00, Sa 07.00-20.00, Su 09.30-20.00
- ⊖ Ealing Broadway (closest), West Ealing, South Ealing
- ⇣ triyoga.co.uk/locations/triyoga-ealing

Dogs welcome. Body and energy treatments. Yoga shop. Far-infrared sauna.

Previously run by CPress, the cafe is now grab and go with vegan gluten-free food by Pollen & Grace and Mira's Kitchen such as chia pots, dal pot, salads, cold brew coffee, Super Square biscuity snacks, Livia's Kitchen biccy bombs, bottled orange juice and activated charcoal lemonade.Water and complimentary herbal tea from an urn.

Butler's Thai Café
Omnivorous Thai restaurant

- ☛ 14 St Mary Rd, Ealing Green W5 5ES
- ☏ 020 8579 8803,
- ◷ W-Sa 12.00-15.00, 18.00-22.00, Su 18.00-21.00, M-Tu closed
- ⊖ South Ealing
- ⇣ butlersthai.co.uk

Vegan starters £4.95-£5.50 include spring rolls, steamed edamame beans, hot and sour mushroom soup with lemongrass, or coconut soup with Thai herbs. Lots of vegan mains dishes £5.95-£7.25 such as Som Tum spicy salad, fried bean curd salad, 5 types of curry: red, green, jungle, dry jungle, Masaman. Stir-fries with tofu and ingredients such as cashew nuts, mushrooms, pineapple sweet and sour. Sweet and sour veg or with chili and basil £4.95-£5.95. Express lunch eat in or take away £5.95.

Singha, Chang Thai or Kopparberg fruit beers £3. Wine medium glass £3.80, large £5.25, bottle £14.50.Water and juices £1.50-£2.75.

Free delivery within 3 miles for orders over £15.

Beehive

Omnivorous Middle Eastern cafe and shop

- 📍 26 The Green W5 5DA
- 📞 020 7998 0962
- 🕐 M-Sa 8.00-19.00, Su 9.00-17.30
- ⊖ Ealing Broadway
- ↖ beehiveonthegreen.co.uk
  facebook.com/Beehiveealing

Don't be fooled by the name, vegans can find a lot here. One box with up to 5 choices £5.50 take out, eat in £7.95.

Salads include lentil, onion and parsley; okra, tomato, onion and cucumber; brown rice with turmeric; roasted roots and veg; spinach, tomato and chickpeas; baba ganoush; broccoli; beetroot; pasta etc.

Vegan wraps or sandwiches £3.25-£5.75 include vine leaves, hummus and salad; falafel plus hummus and salad or grilled veg or potato with chilli chutney and cabbage.

Cakes £2.50-3.25 such as pumpkin and coconut or vegan brownie.

Milkshakes can be made with soya and almond milk for an extra £1. Fruit and veg juices £3.50-£4. Hot drinks £2.25-£2.50.

They sell fruit and veg, Meridian spreads, coconut oils, organic seeds, nuts, spices, lentils, gluten-free pasta, Infinity foods, Eat Real quinoa and lentil crisps, rye bread, plant milks, Clipper and Pukka organic teas, organic jams and Whole Earth drinks.

Seats inside and out. Disabled toilet. Baby changing. Wifi. Student discount 10%, falafel wrap and drink plus crisps £4.95.

Firezza, Ealing

Omnivorous pizzeria

- 📍 15a Bond Street W5 5AP
- 📞 020 8840 3030
- 🕐 M-Th 17.00-23.00, F-Sa 12.00-24.00, Su 12.00-23.00
- ⊖ Ealing Broadway
- ↖ firezza.com

Theyy have vegan cheese! Carne Vegana pizza comes with vegan chorizo, pepperoni and stacks of veggies for around £10 or £14, or create your own with three toppings. Spinach and olives salad £4.95. Tomato focaccia £3.95. Mango sorbet £1.99.

Hare & Tortoise, Ealing

Omnivorous Japanese restaurant

- 📍 38 Haven Green, Ealing W5 2NX
- 📞 020 8810 7066
- 🕐 Su-Th 12.00-23.00, Fr-Sa 12.00-23.30, last order 30 minutes before
- ⊖ Ealing Broadway
- ↖ hareandtortoise.co.uk

Huge portions and good prices. Starters £3.40-£6.10 include green salad, Gomadare tofu salad, tofu "duck" pancakes, spring rolls, Chinese greens, edamame steamed soy beans, seaweed salad. Miso soup £3.20. Vegan mains £8.40-£8.90 include deep-fried tofu and vegetable ramen in soup (like the massive bowls at Wagamama only cheaper); lo mein with tofu and Chinese veg; satay mixed veg and tofu with noodles and sesame.

Freshly pressed juices £3.20-£3.40. Wine from £15 bottle, £4.60-£6.10 medium glass. Sake or plum wine £5.50. Orientall beers £3.40. Tea £1.20-£1.40.

Monty's Tandoori
Omnivorous Nepalese & Indian restaurant

- 18 The Mall, Ealing Broadway, W5 2PJ (in the Royal Institution of Chartered Surveyors building)
- 020 8567 8122, 020 8567 5802
- M-Sa 12.00-14.45, 18.00-24.00, Su 12.00-15.00, 18.00-23.00
- Ealing Broadway
- montysoflondon.co.uk
  facebook.com/MontysRestaurant

The menu sections are divided into vegetarian and non-veg, staff can advise if there are egg or dairy. Bhajia, spring roll or samosa £3.60. Veg or mushroom biryani £9.20. All kinds of vegetables bhajees and curries £5.55-£6.30.

Ealing Animal Charities Fair
Omnivorous pizzeria

- Hanwell Methodist Church, Church Road W7 1DJ
- Around the first Saturday in March
- Hanwell BR
- ealinganimalsfair.london

Annual event that has been running for over 40 years. The 2019 one is on Saturday 2nd March, 10.00-16.00. It used to be called the Ecology and Animal Welfare Bazaar until 2010.

Stalls, speakers, music, vegan catering (apart from cow's milk). Free admission.

As Nature Intended, Ealing
Organic & health food shop

- 17-21 High Street, Ealing W5 5DB
- 020 8840 1404
- M-F 08.00-20.00, Sa 09.00-20.00, Su/BH 10.30-18.00
- Ealing Broadway
- asnatureintended.uk.com

Sister to the Chiswick store with the same gigantic range.

Holland & Barrett, Ealing
Health food shop

- 61/62 Ealing Broadway W5 5JY
- 020 8566 1338
- M-Sa 08.00-19.00, Su 11.00-18.00
- Ealing Broadway

Freezer.

- 61 The Broadway, West Ealing W13 9BP (corner Melbourne Avenue)
- 020 8840 7558
- M-Sa 9.00-18.00, Su 11.00-17.00
- West Ealing

Fridge and freezer.

Queen of the Suburbs
Ealing what's on website

- queenofthesuburbs.org

This online guide to Ealing is like a mini *Time Out* magazine compiled by local people. Includes markets, shops, pubs, upcoming music and art events, galleries, cinema, theatre, kids activities, family days out, pilates and yoga, sport, and a list of veggie and vegan-friendly places.

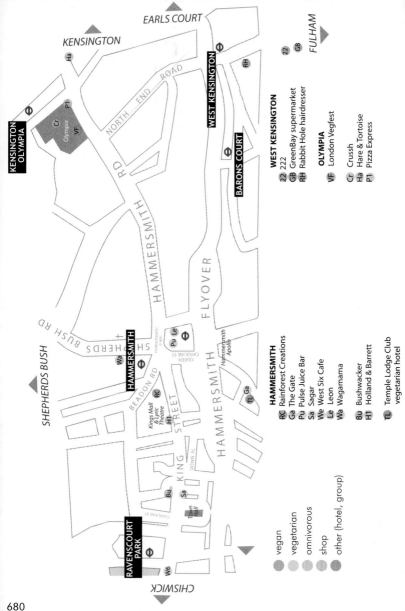

WEST KENSINGTON

22 222
GB GreenBay supermarket
RH Rabbit Hole hairdresser

OLYMPIA
VF London Vegfest

Cr Crussh
Ha Hare & Tortoise
Pl Pizza Express

HAMMERSMITH

RC Rainforest Creations
Ga The Gate
Pu Pulse Juice Bar
Sa Sagar
We West Six Cafe
Le Leon
Wa Wagamama

Bu Bushwacker
H1 Holland & Barrett

TL Temple Lodge Club
   vegetarian hotel

- vegan
- vegetarian
- omnivorous
- shop
- other (hotel, group)

HAMMERSMITH

inc. Olympia & West Kensington

HAMMERSMITH, between Shepherds Bush, Kensington and Chiswick, is the western gateway to the capital. Beneath the giant flyover that leads to the M4 motorway, it's a hotspot for entertainment and eating out.

See top bands at the **Apollo**, also home to tv's flagship standup comedy show *Live At The Apollo*. Or try the **Lyric Theatre** or new **Riverside Studios**, reoping in 2019 after a 5-year renovation. It's a short bus ride or walk to **Olympia** exhibition centre, home of London's biggest vegan festival **Vegfest** every autumn.

There are fabulous walks by the peaceful Thames, and some great British waterside pubs.

Terrific vegan dining possibilities abound. **The Gate** is one of London's longest established vegetarian restaurants, quite up-market and popular with celebs, and with now with a far higher proportion of vegan food in than In Its early days, indeed they went 100% vegan for Veganuary 2019. In the same building is the vegetarian hotel **Temple Lodge**.

Raw food fans can get their fix from the **Rainforest Creations** stall on Thursdsay lunchtimes. Look out for amazing salads and cakes.

Sagar is a great value south Indian vegetarian restaurant.

Green fingered vegans will love the area's best kept secret, the **West Six** vegetarian cafe in a garden centre.

For grab 'n' go food by the tube, try **Pulse Juice Bar**. Also **Leon** is perfect for an early breakfast, or neutralising a late night munchies attack on the way home.

WEST KENSINGTON, midway between Olympia and Fulham, is home to a cluster of three of London's groundbreaking vegan icons. **222** was one of the capital's first truly awesome vegan restaurants, years before we became cool, and offers a fabulous lunchtime buffet, 7 days a week. At night you'd best reserve for a la carte. A few doors along is **GreenBay**, our first vegan supermarket, opened summer 2016. In 2018 they were joined by **The Rabbit Hole** vegan hair salon which relocated from Shepherds Bush. Lady vegans flock here for stunning styling and colouring using only vegan products.

OLYMPIA exhibition centre hosts trade and consumer shows of all kinds. You can eat inside at **Crussh**, or outside at **Pizza Express** or **Hare & Tortoise**. Though if there's time we would always walk down to **222**, just be sure to call ahead in the evenings.

The Gate

Vegetarian international restaurant

📍 51 Queen Caroline Street W6 9QL

📞 020 7833 0401
reservations@thegaterestaurants.com

🕐 M-F 12.00-14.00, 18.00-22.00 (last orders), Sa 12.00-22.00, Su 12.00-21.15

🚇 Hammersmith

🔗 thegaterestaurants.com
facebook.com/TheGateVeg

Everyone should treat yourselves to dinner at the celebs' favourite elegant, award-winning vegetarian restaurant The Gate. Especially at the outside courtyard tables in summer. It is a unique setting in an artist's studio with modernist leanings. Many vegan and gluten-free options, clearly marked on the menu, which changes frequently with the seasons. For Veganuary 2019 they made the entire menu vegan.

This is the original of four branches, and there is the vegetarian hotel Temple Lodge Club in the same building, handy for London Vegfest in the autumn.

Fixed price weekday lunch two courses £15, three £18, with three choices for each course. Extra side veggies £4.

Sunday roast menu £19.50 2 courses, £22.50 three, again with a choice of threee dishes for each course, inclduing root vegetable, chestnut and sage Wellington with roasted potatoes, season veg and Madeir sauce.

A la carte starters £6-£8 could include plantain fritters with creamy sweet chilli sauce; miso glazed aubergine with toasted cashew nuts and ponzu sauce; soup of the day; or a sharing starters platter for two £22.

Mains £11-£16 such as aubergine and cashew cheese schnitzel with roasted veg; Green Dragon glazed tofu and oriental veg; tortillas filled with black bean, sweet potato, sweetcorn, soft onion, coriander, with a tomato sauce with guacamole and sweet pepper salsa; Thai red curry; wild mushrooms risotto cake; sweet potato and pomegranate salad; pad Thai.

Sides £4 include chunky herb polenta chips with garlic aioli; or cauliflower with smoked paprika tahini, pomegranate and pine nuts.

Sumptuous desserts £6-£8 such as tiramisu flavoured with coffee liqueur and mocha cream, prune and apple crumble with Armagnac crème anglaise, cranberry and vanilla cheesecake, peanut butter brownie with vanilla ice cream and chocolate sauce. Trio of desserts £15.

All drinks are vegan. Wine £6.50-£9 medium glass, £21-£44 bottle.Beers £5, ciders £6. Mocktails £3-£5. Freshly squeezed juices £4. Cola £2.50.

Kids two-course menu £6.50 starts with a choice of seitan nuggets with mushy peas and chips, or bulgur and beetroot burger with chips, or pasta of the day; followed by ice cream sundae; and a glass of cordial.

High chairs. Wifi. Discretionary service charge 12.5% is divided across the restaurant team. Book at least 2 days ahead at the weekend: Deliveroo.

Also in Marylebone (Central London), Islington (North London) and St John's Wood (North London).

West Six Cafe

Vegetarian cafe in garden centre

- 17 Ravenscourt Avenue W6 0SL
- 020 8563 7112
- M-F 08.30-17.00, Sa-Su 9.30-18.00
- Ravenscourt Park
- w6gardencentre.co.uk
  facebook.com/W6gardencentre
  instagram.com/westsixcafe

A peaceful escape from the intensity of central London, opened 2011 under the railway arches of Ravenscourt Park tube station. This cosy cafe is in a garden centre, which has to be the most plant based location for miles. The cafe was originally omnivorous, then vegetarian, and with them backing Vegan Month (November) and Veganuary, plenty is now vegan, especially the cakes.

Breakfast £4 served until 11am such as organic porridge with berry compote, or peanut butter and banana on sourdough toast.

All day brunch £5-£6.50 such as crushed avo and cucumber on sourdough; homemade hummus and olives on sourdough; tamari mushrooms and cashew cream. Baguette £5 filled with mushroom, pickled beetroot, hummus, onion relish and walnuts.

Top up or snack on Bites £1.50-£4 such as sourdough, avocado, garlic and parsley potatoes, tamari mushrooms, hummus, side salad.

Mains £6.50-£12 such as wild mushroom soup; carrot and cashew tart; chorizo-style burger; smoked almond risotto with squash terrine and foraged mushrooms; smoked pear and celeriac carpaccio salad with hazelnut cream, dukah and crispy kale.

They have been making vegan sausage rolls for much longer than Greggs and without receiving any complaints from Piers Morgan.

Children welcome, kids snacky menu £3-£4.50 such as garlic and parsley potatoes; hummus and veg bowl; hummus and avocado pitta pocket with cerry tomatoes.

Organic desserts £2.50-£3.50 are almost all vegan (and half of those gluten-free) including double chocolate muffin, apple and cinnamon muffin, raspberry jam muffin, sugar-free banana and walnut loaf, lemon and poppy seed loaf, almond and orange polenta cake, coffee and walnut cake, carrot and coconut cake, berry flapjack.

Smoothies £4-£4.50. Classy cold drinks £1.50-£3 include raw coconut water, cactus water, cold pressed orange or green juice, Belvoir lemonades, Fentimans, Karma cola, James White apple or pear or carrot apple juice,

Teas and coffees, mocha, superfood or iced latte £2-£3.20. Kids hot drink or smoothie £1-£2.

Dogs welcome. Private functions. Their horticulturalists and designers can sort you out some plants for roof terraces, balconies, window boxes, retail spaces, restaurants, offices and co-working spaces, entrances and doorways. In 2017 the centre was awarded best boutique garden centre at the industry's Garden Retail Awards.

"Vegan sausage roll, Piers?"

Rainforest Creations
Raw vegan food stall

- 📍 Farmers' Market, Lyric Square, King Street W6 0ED
- 🕐 Every Thursday 10.00-15.00
- ⊖ Hammersmith
- ↖ rainforestcreations.co.uk
  instagram.com/rainforestvegan

Vegan raw food heaven with a big box of salads and savouries for £6. The various box options include spinach flan, lentilburger, lentil sprouts, tropical coleslaw, angel kale, coleslaw, hot dressing; chickpeas, tropical slaw, dressing. Salad pot £4.

Rotis £5 are made with cornmeal, lentils and wholewheat flour and filled with the same items as boxes.

Raw cakes £4 such as mango and banana or chocolate and berry. Energy balls £1 such as pumpkin & coconut; carob & ginger; beetroot & fennel; omega hemp.

Drinks £3-£4 are jelly coconut, ginger, Caribbean sorrel.

Also at:

Oval Market Sa 10.00-15.00

Chelsea Market Sa 10.00-16.00

Herne Hill Market Su 10.00-16.00

Alexandra Palace farmers market Su 10.00-15.00.

Pulse Juice Bar
Vegetarian take-awayh

- 📍 Broadway Shopping Centre, Hammersmith Station, Hammersmith Broadway W6 9YE
- 📞 07468 604 366
- 🕐 M-F 07.30-19.00, Sa 11.00-19.00, Su 11.30-18.00
- ⊖ Hammersmith (District/Piccadilly)
- ↖ pulsejuicebar.co.uk
  instagram.com/pulsejuicebar

Fabulous take-away with stacks of grab 'n' go vegan food, inside the shopping centre that houses the District and Piccadilly tube lines. (The Hammersmith & City line ends in the other Hammersmith tube station, north of this one.)

Juices, fruit crushes, low fat smoothies, protein shakes.

Vegan toasties include "egg" tofu salad; BLT with tempeh bacon.

Grilled wraps such as falafel; chickpea and salad; detox rainbow.

Salads boxes include roasted veggie and superfoods with turmeric quinoa; Kew Garden veggies.

Sagar, Hammersmith
Vegetarian Indian restaurant

🐀 157 King St, Hammersmith W6 9JT

📞 020 8741 8563

🕐 M-F 12.00-15.00, 17.30-23.00, Sa 12.00-23.00, Su 12.00-22.00

⊖ Hammersmith, Ravenscourt Park

↖ sagarveg.co.uk

Good value South Indian vegetarian restaurant near the Town Hall.

Starters from £4.95 such as idli (dumpling) and you can have them steamed, fried or with green chilli, pepper and cashew nuts; medu vada fried lentil doughnuts; samosa; potato bonda; kebab bhajia fried onions with coriander seeds, pappadam and dal soup.

Main courses £5.25-8.95 include 7 types of dosas (rice and lentil pancake) and 7 of uthappam (lentil pizza). Curry dishes include channa masala, aloo gobi, bhindi bhajee, brinjal bhajee, fried dal, sambar and onion sambar, suki bhajia, zeera aloo and potato palya. Thali set meal £16.95 with starters, curries, rice and dessert.

Vegan mango sorbet dessert.

Wine £3.95 glass, £15.95 bottle. Spirits and liqueurs £2.95-£3.45. Juices £2.25 and freshly squeezed orange juice £3.25. Tea and coffee £1.95-£2.45.

Also in Covent Garden, Fitzrovia and Harrow.

Children welcome, 1 baby chair

HAMMERSMITH

WEST

Leon, Hammersmith
Omnivorous cafe

- ☛ Unit 27 The Broadway Shopping Centre, Hammersmith W6 9YD
- ☎ 020 8222 8732
- 🕐 M-Th 06.30-23.30, F 06.30-24.00, Sa 07.30-24.00, Su 08.00-22.00
- ⊖ Hammersmith (Piccadilly/District)
- ⚲ leon.co

Open from dawn till midnight for porridge, toast, falafels, Lebanese mezze salad, burgers, vegan meatballs, lentil masala, Brazilian black beans, sweet potato falafel hot box, bummus, crushed pea salad, slaw, baked fries, flatbread. All kinds of coffee, ginger kombucha, juicy water; carrot, apple and ginger juice. Kids can have toast and banana, or falafel rice box.

Wagamama, Hammersmith
Omnivorous Japanese restaurant

- ☛ The Old Firestation, 244 Shepherds Bush Road W6 7NN
- ☎ 020 8741 9814
- 🕐 Su-W 11.00-22.00, Th-Sa 11.00-23.00
- ⊖ Hammersmith (Hammersmith & City)
- ⚲ wagamama.com

Separate vegan menu. Free wifi, bar, outside dining, baby facilities, braille menus. Fully accessible, disabled toilet.

Bushwacker Wholefoods
Vegetarian wholefood shop

- 132 King Street W6 OQU
- 020 8748 2061
- M-Sa 9.30-18.00, Su/BH closed
- Hammersmith, Ravenscourt Park

Completely GM free, with plenty for vegans. Speciality ranges include macrobiotic, gluten-free and Fairtrade. Organic fruit and veg.

Good range of take-away ready-to-eat meals and salads, Laura's idea sandwiches and salads, Paul's Bakery organic tofu and arame pasti and tofu cutlet, samosas. Wheaty chorizo salami.

Non-dairy cheese including Vegusto and Violife. Vegenaise. Organic chocolate cake and Booja Booja truffles.

In the frozen section you can find Sojade, Swedish Glace and Coyo ice-cream and Fry's range such as schnitzel, sausage and strips. Great selection from Infinity Foods and Meridian.

If you are a tea lover this is the right place for you with stacks of brands including Pukka, Clipper, Dalgety (moringa teas), Floradix, Yogi, Organic India, Slimatee, Heath & Heather, Clearspring, Dragonfly, Qi, Dr Stuart and Celestial Seasonings. Coffee by Grumpy Mule, Equal Exchange and Union.

Chocolate brands include Pana, Ombar, Vivani, Seed & Bean, Montezuma. Aso bars such as Nakd, Organica, Siesta carob, Aduna, Raw Bites, Meridian and Pulsing.

Skin and bodycare by Weleda, Faith in Nature, Avalon and Urtekram. Books, natural remedies and aromatherapy oils.

Vitamins include Solgar, Biocare, Vogel (Bioforce.

Household cleaning products include Ecover, Ecolino, Earth Friendly, Ecos and Citrus Magic.

Holland & Barrett
Health food store

- Unit 33-34, Kings Mall shopping centre, King Street W6 9HW
- 020 8748 9783
- M-Sa 08.30-18.30, Su 11.00-17.00
- Hammersmith

Fridge and freezer.

Temple Lodge Club
Vegetarian hotel

- 51 Queen Caroline Street W6 9QL
- 020 8748 8388
- Hammersmith
- templelodgeclub.com

Situated in a very quiet location and very close to the underground, this Georgian listed building has a peaceful garden. Most of the bedrooms, the library and dining room overlook the garden, and with no television, how rare and cool is that nowadays? There are 11 rooms, single and double and twin, with and without bathroom, from £68 to £121. Vegetarian breakfast buffet with dairy alternatives is included.

No children below 12 years old because the rooms in this historic building are sensitive to the noise.

WEST KENSINGTON

and Olympia

GreenBay vegan supermarket
Vegan supermarket

- 228 North End Road W14 9NU
  (close to 222 vegan restaurant)
- 020 7385 8913
- M-Sa 10.00-20.00, Su 10.00-18.00
- West Kensington, West Brompton
- greenbaysupermarket.co.uk
  facebook.com/GreenBayLDN

Opened August 2016, this is more than a grocery store, with many hard to find products and unusual vegan brands. Well worth a special journey with a big bag or ruksac. Here are some of the highlights.

Fridges packed with tofu, Tofurky, vegan Quorn, tempeh, seitan, and VBites in far more flavours than you'll find in other shops and at good prices. Veggyness doner kebab and Topas bio salami.

Over 100 vegan cheeses include Sheese, Violife, Follow Your Heart and Vegusto. Tofutti cream cheese and Mouse's Favourite Cream.

Sojade yogurts. Desserts such as Rebel Kitchen.

Frozen ready meals such as Clive's Pies, Amy's Mexican burrito, Fry's curry pie, chicken style strips and crispy style prawns, Wicken Fen sausages.

Ice-cream by Coyo, Swedish Glace and Booja Booja.

Fruit and veg such as Cauli Rice. Pasta and sauces such as Zest, Geo and Mr Organic. Spreads. Tinned pulses. Yeast flakes Vegenaise and Plamil mayo. Follow Your Heart salad dressings and Vegan Egg.

Muesli, granola. Wholewheat croissants. Everything for baking. Jam.

Go Vegan chocolate and hazelnut biscuits. Chocolate by Moo Free, Seed & Bean, Vivani, Loving Earth, iChoc and Clif protein bars. Kale chips in jalapeño cheddar and white cheddar.

Coffee by Grumpy Mule, Percol and Whole Earth. Herbal teas. All kinds of plant milks.

Pitfield beers. Aspall premium organic ciders. Lots of wines, most organic. Utkins organic vodka. Soft drinks.

Nature's Own supplements.

Bodycare by Lavera, Avalon, Urtekram, Faith in Nature and Pravera. Hair colours by Tint of Nature.

Cleaning products by Earthly Friendly, Green Scents, Faith Laundry, Pravera, Sodasan and Ecozone.

Dog food by Yarrah and Benevo, also with grain-free vegetable. Candles.

222

International gourmet vegan restaurant

- 222 North End Road, West Kensington W14 9NU
- 020 7381 2322
- M-Su 12.00-15.30 buffet only, 17.30-22.30 a la carte
- West Brompton, West Kensington, Fulham Broadway
- 222veggievegan.com facebook.com/222veggievegan

One of London's first vegan restaurants, opened in 2004. Ghanaian chef Ben Asamani was previously at Country Life, and is legendary amongst London vegans and beyond for pioneering healthy, fabulous, global vegan food at his vegan restaurant between Olympia and Fulham. There is a superb lunchtime all-you-can-eat buffet every day; or go a la carte in the evenings but be sure to book as it's always full.

The lunch buffet has a selection of hot dishes and salad, but if going to a nearby exhibition you really should treat yourself to dinner afterwards. The desserts are out of this world. Raw and gluten-free folk will love it too.

Lunch buffet £11.50 eat in, £9.50 take-away, with a selection of hot dishes and salad. For a lighter lunch have soup £4.50 eat in, £3.50 take-away.

Starters £5.50-£6.50 include soup of the day with house-baked gluten-free bread; sautéed artichoke hearts with roast pepper sauce; bean and tofu pancake; cauliflower and polenta bake with a pistachio and olive tapenade; almond cheese with raw crackers and julienned vegetables; raw, chilled avocado and watercress soup; mezze selection. Salads £5.

Main courses £12 such as vegan roast with all the trimmings; seitan stroganoff; Ben's special veg with seitan or marinated tofu and brown rice or noodles; pumpkin and pine nut risotto; oyster mushroom and spinach raclette with tofu cottage cheese; asparagus and petits pois burger with oven-baked chips; chef's salad; seitan medallions with potato and parsnip mash, steamed veg and onion gravy; African Egusi made from ground melon seed, served with baked yam; pumpkin and courgette noodles with fresh coconut, veg, Brazil nuts, lime and ginger dressing. Gluten-free spaghetti with quinoa and spinach "meat balls" and roasted tomato sauce £10.50.

Side dishes £3-£4 include garlic bread, baked plantain or sweet potato, okra, oven-baked chips.

London's finest vegan dessert menu £6.50 includes tofu and almond blueberry and vanilla cheesecake with chestnut purée; apple crumble; ice-cream pancake with warm vanilla-chocolate custard; chocolate gateau served warm with ice cream or coconut whipped cream; raw cashew and almond spice island pie on a crunchy nut and coconut base; banana cake; chocolate ganache torteon almond and date base. Maple roast pineapple with ice cream or coconut whipped cream £5. Ice cream £4.

Organic house wine £5.50 glass, £18.50 bottle. Freedom and Sam Smiths lager £4.50-£6.50. Freshly made juices, smoothies, soft drinks, kombucha style kefir £3-£6. Hot drinks £2.50-£3.50 include teas, coffees, matcha green tea, with almond, rice, coconut or soya milk.

Children welcome, high chairs. Vegan Society 10% off mains. Wedding and party buffet catering.

Kiss My Grass
Vegan restaurant and cafe

- ☛ 123 Lillie Road SW6 7SX (A3218, just west of North End Road)
- ☎ 020 7386 9444
- 🕐 W-F 12.00-22.00, Sa 09.00-22.00, Su 10.00-18.00, M-Tu closed
- ⊖ West Brompton, West Kensington, Fulham Broadway
- ➤ kissmygrass.co
  facebook.com/KissMyGrassUK
  instagram.com/kissmygrass_uk

Opened April 2019 by English couple Stephanie and Ben, just round the corner from 222 and GreenBay. Completely original healthy vegan dishes with no meat substitutes, choice of wines, and weekend brunches, what's not to like?

They're not really into starters and sides, so dive straight in with a choice of six main courses £10-£14 that include **crispy corn gnocchi** with pan fried exotic mushrooms and cherry tomatoes in herbed green sauce; **oven-roasted baby aubergine** with garlic and ginger, served with bulgur, pumpkin seeds and pan fried veg, topped with croutons and creamy avocado sauce; **Scotch Bonnet and lemongrass cassava dal** with paratha, soya yogurt and green herb dressing; **sweet corn and potato fritters** with pan fried baby gem lettuce, soy sauce and seet masala soya yogurt dressing; **Anaheim pepper packed with oven roasted cauliflower**, green lentils and tomatoes, on a bed of cauliflower purée with pomegranate seeds, Chinese cabbage and a sunflower seed slaw; seasoned **heirloom tomatoes** in balsamic dressing, served on toasted porridge bread with courgette and rocket salad.

Desserts £2-£3 include doughnut in cinnamon sugar, chocolate doughnut with strawberry glaze and edible flowers, peanut butter brownie with dark chocolate, fig and date brownie with fennel and turmeric, banana bread.

Lunches specials may be on the way.

Brunch weekends till 2pm: cinnamon, cardamon and fennel **granola** £5.50 with figs, dates, cranberries, turmeric and date yogurt with homemade coulis; **toasted banana bread** £6.50 with poached saffron plums, cinnamon apple and pears, cinnamon butter, oat cream and cinnamon sugar; pan fried **spinach and mixed mushrooms** £8 toasted Middle Eastern tomato and garlic bread with relish; **tomato and garlic bread sandwich** £10.50. with cheeze, mushrooms, special sauce, koftes, pickled cucumber, cherry tomatoes. Add bottomless prosecco £20, valid for 1.5 hours.

Wines £4.50-£6 small glass, £20-£29 bottle. A wall fridge full of dinks including ciders, beers, G&T £5-£5.50, Longflint ginger and rum fuego or rhubard and vodka £6, soft drinks £2 such as Karma Cola, Nix and Kix cucumber mint or mango ginger, Chari teas £2.50.

Coffees and teas £1.25-£2.25 drink in or with your own cup, add £1.25 take-away for one of their reusable cups. Almond, oat or soya milk.

20 seats. Counter service. Children welcome, high chairs. Dogs welcome. Card payments only. They can host parties and private events.

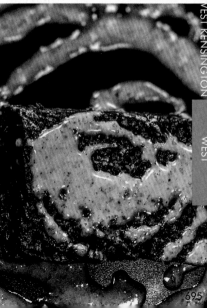

The Rabbit Hole
Vegan organic hairdresser

- 6A Charleville Road W14 9JL
- 07450 225230
- By appointment M closed, Tu-F 11.00-19.00, Sa 11.00-18.00, Su 12.00-17.00
- West Kensington
- therabbitholelondon.com
  facebook.com/veganhairsalon
  instagram.com/veganhairsalon

At West London's vegan hairdresser, near 222 vegan restaurant and Greenbay vegan supermarket, they believe no one should suffer for gorgeous hair, so use organic and vegan hair colours, hair care and finishing products. You can even enjoy complimentary tea or coffee with plant based milk and vegan biscuits. Haircuts start from £60.

They sell products by Spa Ritual and Organic Colour System.

By appointment only, message on Facebook or by email.

Dogs welcome. Where else can you have your pup on your lap during colouring? Like London based vegan travel writer Caitlin Galer-Unti here with her adorable poodle sidekick Benito. They compiled the dog-friendly chapter in *Vegan London*.

Earth Brgr
Vegan food stall

- North End Road Market, SW6 1NN
- 07867 697 203
- W-Sa 11.00-18.00, Su-Tu closed
- West Kensington
- instagram.com/earth_brgr

Possibly the best fast food stall ever. Check out their instagram for mouthwatering food porn photos of their quarter pounder cheeseburger, jerk chickn burger, BBQ or crispy fried or red hot wingz, mac n cheese with chick'n poppers, fried chickn and chips, falafel in a salad box with sweet potato fries, grilled or battered plantain, lentil Sloppy Joe salad, even chickpea scrambled egg with cheese and sausage in a muffin.

Also juices such as rhubarb with raspberry and apple, and blue lemonade, which you can add CBD oil to.

All packaging, from straws to burger boxes, is biodegradable and recyclable.

OLYMPIA

London Vegfest
Britain's biggest vegan festival

- 🐀 Olympia Exhibition Centre,
  Hammersmith Road W14 8UX
- 🕐 Autummn weekend, Sa 10.00-18.00,
  Su 10.00-17.00
- ⊖ Kensington Olympia
- ↖ london.vegfest.co.uk
  vegfest.co.uk/event/
     plant-powered-expo-2020
  facebook.com/vegfestuk

The best vegan day or weekend out in Europe. The 2019 event was 26-27th October. Around 300 stalls, 14 rooms of free talks, health, vegan sports and fitness stars, comedy, music, cookery demos, kids' entertainment. Book online from August for two for one and buy one get one half price deals and no queuing. In 2020 they are adding a second event called **Plant Powered Expo, 1-2 February.**

Crussh, Olympia
Omnivorous juice bar and cafe

- 🐀 Olympia Exhibition Centre,
  Hammersmith Road W14 8UX
- 📞 020 7602 8994
- 🕐 during exhibitions
- ⊖ Kensington Olympia
- ↖ crussh.com

Conference centres and exhibitions are generally rubbish for veggies and even worse for vegans. You might find a hummus sandwich if you're lucky and they haven't sold out. But at Crussh they make juices in front of you, have vegan soup, salads and sandwiches to eat in or take away.

Hare & Tortoise, Kensington
Omnivorous Japanese restaurant

- 🐀 373 High Street Kensington W14 8Q
- 📞 020 7603 8887
- 🕐 Su-Th 12.00-23.00, F-Sa 12.00-
  23.30, last order 30 mins before
- ⊖ Kensington Olympia
- ↖ hareandtortoise.co.uk

Plenty vegan at this chain restaurant such as noodle dishes.

Pizza Express Olympia
Omnivorous Italian restaurant

- 🐀 The Addison Rooms, Olympia
  Exhibition Centre W14 8UX
- 📞 020 7602 6677
- 🕐 M-Su 11.30-22.00
- ⊖ Kensington Olympia
- ↖ pizzaexpress.com

On the south-east corner of Olympia, near the tube. Pizzas with vegan cheese. Baby facilities. Disabled toilet.

There are Middle Eastern shops opposite Olympia where you can pick up nuts, pitta or flat bread and hummus, and fruit. For a fabulous buffet lunch walk down North End Road to 222 vegan restaurant. Or walk or bus west to Hammersmith. At night you could take the bus (but not in rush hour) or tube to Soho for a big choice of veggie and vegan places, pubs, cafes and cinemas. Our favourite there is the buffet at Vantra, just off Leicester Square.

HARROW

North Harrow, South Harrow, West Harrow, Kenton

Aumkar
Vegetarian Gujarati fast food cafe

- 319 Station Road, **Harrow** HA1 2AA
- (020 8427 3864
- M-Sa 10.00-20.00, Su 11.00-19.00
- Harrow-on-the-Hill

Amazing value in the centre of town. It does get a big packed at lunchtime. Thali £3.50, biryani £2-£3, rice and curry £2.50. Curries £1.50-£2.75. Rice £1.50-2. Street snacks £1.50-£2.50 such as dabeli, vada pav, puris, various chaat. Tea £1.

Dabeli Hut
Vegetarian Indian café

- **St George's Shopping Centre**, St Ann's Road, **Harrow** HA1 1HS
- (020 8419 8161
- M-W 12.00-19.00, Th-Sa 11.00-19.00, Su 12.00-17.00
- Harrow-on-the-Hill
- dabeli-hut.com, Facebook Dabeli Hut

Originally in Wembley, then moved to Harrow. Dabeli, a popular street food in the Kutch region of Gugarat, is a burger bun filled with potatoes, masala, chutney, bright pomegranate and crunchy bits like peanuts and chaat. It's soft, it's crunchy, it's juicy, it's sweet and it's spicy all in one. And it's a bargain lunch.

Dabeli start at £2 and nothing is over £4, including samosas, wada pav potato patty, pani puri, bhel puri, chaat, and they can do Jain versions too.

Ketraj
Vegetarian Indian take-away

- 146 Station Road, **Harrow** HA1 2RH
- (020 8427 7787
- Tu-Sa 10.00-20.00, Su 09.30-18.00, M closed
- Harrow & Wealdstone, Harrow- on-the-Hill
- facebook.com/ketrajH

Starters such as Punjabi samosa, onion or chilli bhajia, dal vada, dhokla, batada vada, medu vada, pakora, spring roll, dal or pea kachori, 30p-40p each.

5 curries daily such as dal, cauliflower with mixed veg, dry potato with cashew nuts, spinach and chickpea. One curry and rice £2.50. Thali £3.75 with 2 curries, dal, rice, 2 chapattis. Falafel with bhajia and chapatis £3.50.

Dried fruit sweets, more during Diwali from October to November. Soft drinks 75p. Outside catering.

Miriam's Munchies
Vegetarian bakery and coffee shop

- 405-7 Station Road, **Harrow** HA1 2AT
- 020 3730 4605
- M-F 08.00-17.00, Sa 10.00-16.00, Sun/BH closed
- Harrow & Wealdstone
- miriamsmunchies.co.uk
  facebook.com/MiriamsMunchies

Very cosy, bright and modern, and no curry, just vegan cakes galore.

Soup with sourdough bread £4, sandwiches on sourdough or focaccia £4.20 with hummus, beetroot, and spinach.

Cakes and snacks pecan and banana or chocolate cake £2.60-£3, peanut or coco-choco bars £2.20.

Teas, Fairtrade artisan Monmouth coffee, hot chocolate, £1.85-£3.40. Juices abd lemonade £1.95-£2.25. Soya and coconut milk 40p.

They sell focaccia, sourdough and seeded bread, and local products such as chutneys, jam and sauces. Crisps. Birchall herbal teas.

Wifi. Tables outside and 12 seats inside. Take away. Books and magazines. Deliveroo, JustEat. They trade at farmers' markets and supply vegan to cafes and individual orders.

Mumbai Local, Harrow
Vegetarian Indian restaurant

- 207 Station Road Central Parade HA1 2TP (at Hindes Road)
- 020 8427 7960
- M-F 12.00-15.30, 17.30-22.00; Sa-Su 12.00-22.00
- Harrow-on-the-Hill, Harrow & Wealdstone
- mumbailocal.co.uk

Like the Wembley and Rayners Lane branches, but this one also has some Kathiyawadi dishes.

Thali lunch M-F £9.95, evening £12.95, with two curries, dal, rice, chapatis, a fried favourite such as pakora, pickles, salad, popadums.

Chaat and starters £1.50-£5.95 such as dabeli, masala pav, bhajia or samosa in pav, Chinese bhel crispy noodles, bhajias, samosas, spring rolls. Sandwiches and toasties £3.50-£4.95 such as peanut butter, masala potato dabeli with peanuts and pomegranate.

South indian dishes £3.95-£4.75 such as dosa, uttapam, medu vada and idli. Curries £5.95-£7.95. Rice £3.50-£5.95.

Indo-Chinese dishes £5.95-£7.95 such as chilli or stir fry tofu with veg, noodles with veg.

Finger sliced potato deep fried chips £2.75-£4.95 such as with chilli sauce, or garlic and pepper.

Soft drinks £1.50. Jug of passion fruit juice £13.95.

Bottled beers from £2.95. Wine £4.95 for 187ml..

Delivery to HA0, HA9, UB6 12.00-20.30. Deliveroo. Also in Wembley and Rayners Lane.

Radhika Sweet Mart
Vegetarian Indian cafe & sweet shop

- 63 Station Road, **Harrow** HA1 2TY
- 020 8424 2752
- M-Tu, Th-Su 10.30-20.30, W closed
- Harrow & Wealdstone
- radhikasweetmart.com
  Facebook Radhika's

Stacks of Indian snacks, plus dosas and curries, most under £5. Lunch thali £4.50.

Outside catering.

Saburi
Vegetarian Indian café & take-away

- 359 Station Road, **Harrow** HA1 2AW
- 07946 6791197
- M-Sa 10.00-20.00, Su 11.00-19.00
- Harrow-on-the-Hill
- facebook.com/saburiltd

Great value, specialists in chaat like pani puri, set puri vada-pav, bhel puri, pav bhajia, samosa chaat and aloo tikki chaat £1.50-£2.50. Snacks 40p-£1.50 such as kachori, chilli bhajia, cutlets, aloo tikki, methi gota, pakora. Thali £3.50. Curries £2.75 -£4.50. Bread £1-£1.50. Indo-Chinese dishes £3.50 small, £4.50 large.

Coffee £1.25-2. Cold drinks 75p-£1. Cash only. 10% off when you spend £20 or over. 16 seats. Catering.

Sakonis, Harrow
Vegetarian Indo-Chinese restaurant

📍 5-8 Dominion Parade, Station Road, **Harrow** HA1 2TR

📞 020 8863 3399

🕐 M-Su 12.00-22.00

🚇 Harrow & Wealdstone, Harrow-on-the-Hill

🔗 sakonis.co.uk
facebook.com/sakonisharrow

Same menu as Wembley branch with Indian and Chinese dishes. Buffet 12-3pm £10.90, child 4-10 £6, under-3 free; 6.30-9.30pm £13.50, child £6.50; plus 10 service charge for eat in. The buffet is a combination of the whole menu with 40+ items including chaat, pooris, pizza, curries such as chickpea, spinach, rice, chips, sticky veg noodles, salad, chutneys, sauces and fruit. Everything on the buffet with dairy products is clearly labelled.

A la carte South Indian dishes £3.99-£6.95 such as idli, bhajias, biryani, uttapam, dosas, curries. Plain rice £3.75. Snacks and starters £2.95-5.75 such as mogo crisps, samosas, kachori, potato wedges.

Curries £4.25-6.95; rice £3.95-6.95; wrap with chilli, tofu and falafel £5.50 and pizza with green peppers, olives, onion and jalapeño or create your own £7.99.

Chinese dishes £3.49-£7.95 include several soups, fried vegetables and rice or noodles, and Indo-Chinese style chilli mushroom, stir-fry aubergine or triple hakka with noodles, fried ice and stir fried vegetables.

Juices £3.50. Fresh coconut £3.95. Soft drinks £1.50 All hot drinks £1.50. All drinks except coconut water and sugar cane are half prices.

Most items can be prepared hot, medium, mild or without onion or garlic. Children welcome, 7 high chairs. No alcohol. Cards below £10 minimum charge of 50p. 10% eat in charge. Also in Wembley.

Free delivery on minimum order of £25 within 3 mile radius from 15.00-21.00.

SKVP, Harrow
Vegetarian Mumbai street food restaurant

📍 55 Station Road, **Harrow** HA1 2TY

📞 020 8538 0474 / 5

🕐 M-Su 11.00-21.00

🚇 Harrow & Wealdstone

🔗 skvp.co.uk
facebook.com
/shreekrishnavadapavharrow

Mumbai street food £1-£3.50 such as vada pav, which is like a potato burger, vada plate, potato bhajia pav, samosa pav. Dabeli spiced boiled potato served with peanuts and pomegranate. Idli chutney.

Chowpatty chat £2.50-£4 includes bhel puri and set puri, samosa chat, ragda pattice, and khasta kachori. Bhajiva wrap (without cheese), Bombay wrap and samosa wrap £3.75

Deliveroo. Just Eat. Also in West Harrow, Hounslow and Slough.

Pizza Express, Harrow
Omnivorous Italian restaurant

- 📍 St George's Shopping Centre, **Harrow** HA1 1HS
- ☎ 020 8427 0982
- 🕐 M-Tu 11.30-22.00, W-Sa 11.30-23.00, Su 11.30-21.00
- ⊖ Harrow-on-the-Hill
- ⬀ pizzaexpress.com

Vegan cheese available. Baby facilities. Disabled toilet. Wifi.

Holland & Barrett, Harrow
Health food shop

- 📍 Units 3-4 St Anns Shopping Centre, St Anns Road, **Harrow** HA1 1AS
- ☎ 020 8863 4250
- 🕐 M-Sa 9.00-18.00 (Th 19.00), Su 11.00-17.00
- ⊖ Harrow-on-the-Hill

Fridge with VegiDeli, Cheatin, Tofurky, Veg Out, Sheese, Cheezly, Violife, Pudology, Chia Pods and Provamel. Freezer with Fry's, Tofurky, VBites, Clive's Pies, Amy's and Booja Booja.

There is also a Pizza Express in this shopping centre.

HARROW

WEST

Jai Durga Mahal
Vegetarian Indian restaurant & take-away

📞 64 Station Road, **North Harrow** HA2 7SJ

📞 020 8863 3593

🕐 M-Th 12.00-14.30, 17.00-22.00, F-Sa 12.00-22.30, Su 12.00-22.30

⊖ North Harrow

📞 18 Watford Road, **Sudbury Town** HA0 3EP (by Butler's Green)

📞 020 8904 7848

🕐 M-F 12.00-15.00, 17.00-22.30, Sa-Su 12.00-22.30

⊖ Sudbury & Harrow Road BR, Sudbury Town

↖ jaidurgamahal.co.uk

85% is vegan on the gigantic menu and marked V next to it. Almost everything comes in three sizes, small, medium and large. Lots of Chinese dishes too and create your own pizza.

Indian snack starters £2-£7.95 include samosas, kachori, wada, spring rolls. Bhel, sev and pani puri. Plus Chinese soups, Shanghai tofu, garlic mogo, even Chinese falafel.

Dosas and uttapam lentil pizzas £3.75-£5, and you can crfeate your own uttapam by choosing five from 11 toppings. Other Indian main meals £3-£6 such as idli, pav bhaji (toasted buns with minced mix veg curry), puri masala, chola bhatura (big fluffy fried bread with chickpea curry).

Around 14 Indian and 9 Chinese curries £4.50-£5. All Indian and most Chinese rice

dishes £2.75-£5 are vegan. Noodle dishes £3.25 up to £8 for a Triple Haka with fried rice, veg and black beans. Roti and chappathi £1.50-£1.75. Naan not vegan.

Thali £6 with rice, 2 vegetable curries, dal, papadom and a roti or chapati.

Fresh fruit juice £2.75-£3, soft drinks £1.25-£1.50. Beers £3-£3.25, wine bottle £13.50, spirits £2.75-£3.50.

High chairs. Minimum charge £10. Free parking at the rear at Harrow. Party and outdoor catering.

Sagar, North Harrow
Vegetarian Indian restaurant

- 57 Station Rd, **North Harrow** HA2 7SR
- 020 8861 5757
- Su-Th 12.00-22.00, F-Sa 12.00 -22.30
- North Harrow
- sagarveg.co.uk
  facebook.com/sagarharrow

South Indian vegetarian food in this bright and modern branch, beautiful decor. They have a separate vegan menu.

Starters £3.25-£4.95 include idli steamed rice dumplings; Kancheepuram idli rice and lentil dumplings with green chilli, pepper and cashew nuts; medu or rasa vada lentil doughnuts; samosas; potato bonda; vegetable kebab; onion bhajia. rasam soup; dal; bhel puri; pani puri; mogo chips.

Mains £5.25-£7.75 feature dosas, uthappam rice and lentil pizzas, curries. Rice £2.95-£4.45.

Thali £13.95. Veg biryani £6.25.

Tea, coffee, hot choc £1.95-2.45. Soft drinks and juices £2.25-£2.45. Beers from £3.45. Vegetarian wine £3.55 glass, £13.95 bottle. Spirits around £3.

Wifi. High chairs. Also in Hammersmith, Covent Garden and Fitzrovia.

SOUTH HARROW

Natraj
Vegetarian Indian café & take-away

- 341 Northolt Road, **South Harrow** HA2 8JB
- 020 8426 8903
- M-Tu, Th-Sa 10.00-19.45, Su 9.30-17.30, W closed
- South Harrow

Great value Indian vegetarian take-away with plenty for vegans. Starters/snacks such as bhajias, sweets, samosas etc.

6 curries each day are vegan such as spinach and chickpea, okra and potato, cabbage and potato, soya bean, kidney bean and butterbean mix. A regular take-away box of curry and rice is £2.75, large £3.75. Thali £3.50 with rice, 2 vegetable curries, dal, 2 chapati or puri. Box of rice £2 and £3. Dal £3 and £4. Snacks and savouries £7.50 per kilo including kachori, samosa, falafel, vada pav, spring rolls, mix veg bhajia etc. Soft drinks 60p.

Children welcome, high chairs. Cards minimum £5. Parties and events. Also at Rayners Lane.

WEST HARROW

Falafel Bar, Harrow
Vegetarian cafe & take-away

- 273 Pinner Rd, **West Harrow** HA1 4HF (opposite Cornwall Road)
- (020 8930 2748
- M-Sa 12.00-21.00, Su 12.00-17.00
- ⊖ West Harrow
- falafelbar.co.uk/menu/harrow
  facebook.com/pg/falafelbarlondon

Started in Finchley two years ago, this second branch opened here March 2018, and has just won Harrow Times' Restaurant of the Year award. Falafel in wrap, pitta or box, salad boxes, £4.50-£7. Chips, spicy chips, sweet potato chips, £2.50-£3.50. Hummus.

Vegan raw cakes £3.50.

Soft drinks and juices £2-£3.50. Teas and coffees around £2.50.

SKVP, Pinner Road
Vegetarian Mumbai street food restaurant

- 152 Pinner Road, **West Harrow** HA1 4JJ
- (020 8538 0476 / 7
- Tu-Su 10.00-21.00, M closed
- ⊖ West Harrow
- skvp.co.uk
  facebook.com/SKVPExpress

Mumbai street food £1-£3.50 such as vada pav, which is like a potato burger, vada plate, potato bhajia pav, samosa pav. Dabeli spiced boiled potato served with peanuts and pomegranate. Idli chutney.

Chowpatty chat £2.50-£4 includes bhel puri and set puri, samosa chat, ragda pattice, and khasta kachori. Bhajiva wrap (without cheese), Bombay wrap and samosa wrap £3.75

Deliveroo. Just Eat. Also in Harrow, Hounslow and Slough.

RaRa Cakes & Catering
Vegan catering business

- facebook.com/RaRaCakesCatering
  facebook.com/rena.shah2

Vegan cakes, bakes, desserts and catering business based in Harrow.

Harrow Vegans
Social group

- facebook.com/groups/harrowvegans

Social group for vegans living in and around Harrow. Meet up and share local finds. Over 400 members

HEATHROW

Airport

Landside: the area that is open to the public.

Airside: the area beyond security checks and passport and customs control.

Some outlets offer a "15-minute menu" served within 15 minutes, including Comptoir Libanais, Giraffe, Pret, Wagamama. Pret, all over the airport, is great for grab-and-go items.

🔖 heathrow.com

TERMINAL 2 AIRSIDE

Leon
Omnivorous global cafe & take-away

🛫 Terminal 2 airside TW6 1EW
📞 020 8976 7528
🕐 M-Su 05.00 till last departing flight
🔖 leon.co

Vegan menu include beetroot and quinoa burger, jackfruit curry, gyozas, chocolate and coconut torte with ice-cream. Children welcome, kids' menu Leon

EAT and Pret also have vegan options.

TERMINAL 3 LANDSIDE

Best bet here is Pret a Manger, and possibly Giraffe Stop.

TERMINAL 3 AIRSIDE

Try EAT or Pret.

TERMINAL 4 AIRSIDE

Leon
Omnivorous global cafe & take-away

- Terminal 4 airside TW6 2GW
- 020 8745 0877
- M-Su 05.30-21.00
- comptoirlibanais.com

Soups, baguettes, salads, coconut poridge, Chakalaka bean and veggies wrap, chia pot, acai bowl, falafel.

TERMINAL 5 LANDSIDE

Giraffe
Omnivorous global restaurant

- Terminal 5 landside TW6 3XZ
- 020 3117 5532
- M-Su 05.00-21.00
- giraffe.net/news/vegan-menu

Beetroot and quinoa burger, jackfruit curry, gyozas, chocolate and coconut torte with ice-cream. Kids' menu.

TERMINAL 5 AIRSIDE

Giraffe
Omnivorous global restaurant

- Terminal 5 airside TW6 3XZ
- 020 3117 5500
- M-Su 05.15-21.30
- giraffe.net/news/vegan-menu

Veganuary menu included beetroot and quinoa burger, jackfruit curry, gyozas, chocolate and coconut torte with ice-cream. We hope they keep these dishes going!

Wagamama, Heathrow 5
Omnivorous Japanese restaurant

- Terminal 5 departures TW6 2GA
- 020 8283 6186
- M-Su 05.30-21.30
- wagamama.com

Very filling seperate vegan menu. Eat in or take-out to the plane. In 2019 they introduced a full English cooked breakfast.

Super Singh's vegetarian pizzeria and fast food is right next to Heathrow Airport on the east side, near Hatton Cross tube station. See Hounslow section.

HOUNSLOW

& Feltham and Hatton

Chini Chor, Hounslow
Vegetarian Indian restaurant, take-away & sweet shop

- 348 Bath Rd, Hounslow TW4 7HW
- 020 8570 3500
- M-Su 10.00-22.00
- Hounslow West
- chinichor.com

Great value south Indian food. All the usual starters, chaats, samosas, pakoras, bhajias, soups £1-£3.50. Curries £3.50-£6. Chinese dishes such as chilli tofu £3-£6. South Indian dosas and uttapam £2.75-£4.50. They can make food without onion or garlic.

Mini meals £5-£7 such as curry with puri or Indian bread.

They preferred not to tell us if any desserts were vegan, so we'll take that as a no then.

Soft drinks and teas £1, coffee £1.25-£2.25. Freshly made juices £3.50.

Take-away is slightly cheaper. Also in Southall.

Mr Singh's
Vegetarian fast food restaurant

- 431 Great West Road TW5 0BY (by Lampton Rd)
- 020 3475 0217
- M-Su 11.00-23.00
- Osterley, Hounslow East, Houslow Central
- mrsinghspizza.co.uk
  facebook.com/Mrsinghs

Opened 2018, their fifth branch following others around Brimingham and in Slough. They love vegans and have vegan cheese, vegan options marked on the menu, and during Veganuary 2019 they even gave 10% discount on vegan items.

Pizzas in 7, 10, 12 or 14 inches from £3.99 to £14.99 with toppings that include cheese, various veggies, chillies, pepperoni, sausage, tandoori fake chicken, olives, pineappe. Also calzone £4.99-£8.99.

Burgers £3.25 in chicken style, chilli chicken, spicy soya, add fries £1, curly fries or wedges £1.25. Double burger or quarter pounder £3.75, half pounder double cheese double burger £4.75, mega burger £4.75 with veg bacon rashers, triple cheese and bbq sauce.

Sizzler mixed grill of soya chunks and veggies £3.99.

Tortilla wraps £4.75 filled with salad and either chicken style nuggets with Thai sweet chilli sauce or spicy soya chunks with cheese and bbq sauce. Or create your own filling.

Sides £1.75-£4.95 include crispy coated garlic mushrooms; wedges, fries or curly fries in small or large, 75p to load them with pizza toppings like cheese, beans, chicken, sausage etc; onion rings; hotdog; nuggets; curried beans; garlic bread, can be with cheese; salad, loaded salad, garlic cheese tortilla.

No-garlic/onion options. Deliveries from 6pm.

Sangeetha, Hounslow
Vegetarian South Indian restaurant

- 320 Bath Rd, Hounslow TW4 7HW
- 020 8570 1888
- M-Su 10.30-22.30
- Hounslow West
- sangeetharestaurants.com

The majority of the dishes on the menu can be made vegan. Soups and starters £2.99-£4.99. Curries £4.50-£5.49. Plain rice £1.99, special rice or Chinese or biryani or noodles £4.50-£5.50. Dosas £3.99-£6.99. Utthapam £4.49-£5.99. Rice and noodles £4.99-£5.25. Thali £7.49. Indian bread and naan can't be made vegan.

Cobra beer £4.50, spirits £2.99-£3.95. Freshly squeezed juices £3.49 such as orange, pomegranate or pineapple. Hot drinks £1.75-£2.50.

Wifi. High chair. Minimum card payment £20 and there is a 5% service charge for eat in. Free delivery minimum order £20. Catering.

Vegology
Vegetarian fast food restaurant

- 30 Bath Road (eastern end), Hounslow TW3 3EB
- 020 8569 5402
- M-Su 10.00-22.30
- Hounslow Central
- vegologyldn.com (links to) facebook.com/vegologyldn instagram.com/vegologyldn

Fancy a change from Indian? Awesome fast food restaurant opened October 2018 by the owners of Thakers, and already getting rave reviews from the locals. All day full English and Indian breakfasts, stonebaked pizzas, no-fish and chips, jackets, wraps, stacked burgers. Vegan items are marked on the menu and most things can be veganized..

Cooked breakfast £5.95 includes sausages, hash browns, mushrooms, grilled tomato, sourdough toast and baked beans. The Indian version is spicy. Extra items £1-£1.75.

Lunch offer M-F 10.00-17.00: chik'n salad or oven roasted jacket potato or any wrap with chips, £4.95. Stone baked pizza with two toppings, or any burger and chips, £6.50.

Burgers £6.50, either Classic or Hot Hawaiian. Add fries, peri peri fries or sweet potato fries £2-£3. Fried, Buffalo or BBQ Tings (like wings) £4.50-£4.95.

No-fish and chips £9.95 with crushed peas, tartar sauce and lemon. Bangers and creamy mash £7.50 with green peas and gravy. Flame grilled peri peri or sheesh skewers £9.95 with charred marinated veg, rice, salad and chilli garlic sauce.

Stone-baked pizzas £6.95-£9.95. Toppings include all kinds of veggies, vegan ham, pepperoni, sausage, grilled chicken, peri peri chik'n, jalapeno. Sides £2.50-£3 include olives, onion rings. Chik'n salad £5.50.

Gourmet jacket potatoes £6.50-£6.95 with either Tex-Mex 5-bean chilli, chopped salsa, jalapeno, and avocado drizzle; or roast chik'n, chopped leek, broccoli and gravy.

Falafel, sheesh, or peri peri chik'n wraps £3.95-£4.95.

No vegan desserts.

Soft drinks £1.95. Bottled beer £3.50. Wine £3.95. Hot drinks £1.75-£2.35.

Children welcome. Minimum card payment £15. Uber Eats.

Thakers Vegetarian Soul Food

Vegetarian Indian restaurant

- ☛ 162A High Street, Hounslow TW3 1BQ
- ☏ 020 8577 6130
- 🕐 Su-Th 10.00-21.00, F-Sa 10.00-22.00
- ⊖ Hounslow Central
- ↖ thakersfood.com
  facebook.com/thakersfood

Gujarati and Mumbai (Bombay) food with East African influences, very clean and modern. You will be drawn in by the Bhangra music playing inside and the great food smell. Indian/British staff who are pretty cool. Vegan dishes marked on the menu.

Saver menu items £1.50-£2.50 include vada pav burger, samosa pav, Tikki pav, aloo potato mash stuffed paratha.

Appetisers £2-£5.75 such as Kenyan style chips with chilli, salt and lemon rub; masala chips; crispy fried mogo; samosas; pitta pizza; chilli cauliflower gobi in Indo-Chinese sauce; potato and onion bhajia with tomato chutney; crispy battered mushrooms; fried coated okra. Also pani puri or sev puri and other chaats.

Pizza veg sandwich £3.95.

Signature dishes £5.95 such as their best seller Chole Bhature chickpea curry with 2 bhature; masala puris with breakfast potato bhaji; Kala Chana plan puris with traditional black chickpea curry.

Thali tiffin changes every day with two curries, two rotis, rice and salad £6.95; half thali with one curry, one roti, rice and salad £5.95. Curry and rice £4.95.

No vegan desserts.

Passion fruit juice £2.50. Nimbi Pani ice cold fresh lime with sugar, black pepper and black salt £1.95. Coffees £1.50.

3 long tables and benches plus a small table inside, and outside can accommodate 14 people. High chairs. Wifi. Air conditioning. Minimum card payment £5. They also own Vegology.

HOUNSLOW

WEST

717

Super Singh's
Vegetarian pizza take-away

☛ Monrepos, Faggs Road, Feltham
   TW14 0NB

☏ 020 8384 3132

🕐 M-Su 12.00-22.00

⊖ Hatton Cross

↖ supersinghs.co.uk
   Facebook Super Singh's

Opened 2012, close to Hatton Cross tube. Punjabi interiors. Pizzas and burgers. Handy for picking up something on the way to the airport.

Pizzas 7, 9, 10, 14, 18 inches. For example 18 inch is £7.99, two 14 inch pizzas for £15 iincluding chips and 2 litre bottle of drink.

Vegan pizzas include Hawaiian, Shanghai, Chili Wala, BBQ, and Mexican which comes with vegan chicken, kidney beans, mixed peppers, red onion, sweetcorn, jalapenos and fresh tomato. Extra toppings 50p-90p.

Lunchtime special M-F 12.00-16.00, 7inch pizza and a can of drink £2.99, 9 inch pizza and a can of drink £4.99.

Also veggie burgers, grilled vegetable wrap £2.49-£4.99.

Side dishes £1.49-£3.99 include mini spring rolls, garlic bread, chicken nuggets, chicken satay skewer breaded drumstick, nachos, masala fish. Warrior fries with masala chips, mixed veg, veggie chicken, melted cheese, tomato and chilli.

Children welcome. Also in Southall.

Shree Krishna Vada Pav
Vegetarian Mumbai street food restaurant

- 121 Hounslow High Street TW3 1QL
- 020 8538 0470 / 71
- Su-Th 10.00-20.00, F-Sa 10.00-22.00
- Hounslow East, Hounslow Central
- skvp.co.uk
  facebook.com/ShreeKrishnaVadaPavUK

Started here in 2010, now another in Slough and two in Harrow. The place for genuine Mumbai street food such as vada pav for just £1 (pictured), dabeli, bhel and pav bhajia.

£1-£3.50 such as vada pav, which is like a potato burger, vada plate, potato bhajia pav, samosa pav., idli Dabeli spiced boiled potato served with peanuts and pomegranate. Idli chutney.

Chowpatty chat £2.50-£4 includes bhel puri and set puri, samosa chat, ragda pattice, and khasta kachori. Bhajiva wrap (without cheese), Bombay wrap and samosa wrap £3.75

Deliveroo, Just Eat. Catering.

Ambala, Hounslow
Vegetarian Indian sweet shop

- 123 Kingsley Road, Hounslow TW3 4AJ (junction Taunton Ave)
- 020 8569 6578
- M-Su 10.00-20.00
- Hounslow East
- ambalafoods.com

Indian sweets and savouries.

Jay Sweets Mart
Vegetarian Gujarati sweet shop

- 276 Staines Road TW3 3LX (junction A3063 Wellington Road)
- 020 8570 0982
- M 9.00-17.00, Tu-F 10-19.00, Sa 9.30-19.00, Su 9.00-18.00
- Hounslow West
- jaysweetsmart.co.uk

No vegan sweets but some savoury food such as 4 different types of bhajia £5.20 half kilo; spring onions, okra and dhokry £9 for 1 kg, samosa spicy or mild £1.20 for four, spring roll 50p, kachori £1.20 per 3.

Lots of snacks/savoury £3.60-£4 400 gr.

Holland & Barrett, Hounslow
Health food shop

- 233-235 High Street, **Hounslow** TW3 1EA
- 020 8570 4101
- M-Sa 08.30-19.00, Su 10.00-17.00
- Hounslow Central

Fridge and freezer.

- Unit 9a The Longford Centre, High Street, **Feltham** TW13 4BH
- 020 8751 4474
- M-Sa 9.00-18.00, Su 11.00-17.00
- Feltham BR

Fridge and freezer.

KENTON

Chennai Srilalitha
Vegetarian South Indian restaurant

- 196 Kenton Road, **Kenton** HA3 8BX (next to Pick & Save supermarket)
- 020 8907 7737 / 9299
- M-F 11.00-15.30, 17.30-22.30; Sa-Su 11.00-22.30
- Kenton
- chennaisrilalitha.co.uk
  facebook.com/ChennaiSriLalitha

All day South Indian buffet M-F £8.99, Sa-Su £10.99, plus 10% eat in charge. Choose from idli, sada dosa, masala dosa, uthappam, onion chili uthappam, medhu vada, sambar vada, rasa vada, kichadi, upma, jeera or plain rice, salad.

A la carte all the usual Indian starters £2.99-£5.25 plus gobi Manchurian cauliflower, baby corn. Huge range of dosas, uthappam, curries, biryani, coconut rice, most dishes around £4-£6. Madras thali £8.49 only Sat-Sun.

Soft drinks, juices £1-£3.49, jug of juice £12.99. Tea and coffee £1.99.

Just Eat, Uber Eats. Outdoor catering, weddings and parties. Previously called Sangeetha.

Pradip
Indian vegetarian restaurant & sweet shop

- 152-156 Kenton Road, **Kenton** HA3 8AZ
- Restaurant 020 8909 2232
  Shop 020 8907 8399
- Restaurant Tu-F 12.00-15.00, 18.00-22.00, Sa-Su 12.00-16.00, 18.00-22.00
  Shop Tu-Sa 10.00-19.00, Su 9.00-18.00, M closed.
- Kenton
- pradipsweet.co.uk menus
  Facebook Pradips

Indian vegetarian restaurant with sweet shop next door. They specialise in Gujarati food from the west of India. You can eat well here for under £10. They use vegetable ghee in cooking but butter ghee in sweet. However next door in the shop all the savouries are good for vegans because they use vegetable ghee.

All day buffet Fri-Sun £9 includes starter, main course and dessert, children up to 10 £8, no sharing, only available for a grou pof 4 or more. Eat as much as you like from two starters, select two curries of the day, rice and dal, green salad, poppadom and pickle, bhatura and naan, a dessert.

A la carte starters £1.90-£3.30, mains £3.50-4.50. Thalis £5.60, or £6.60 with a starter, £7.50 with dessert too.

Soft drinks, juices and hot drinks £1.40-£3,

jug of juice £6-£8.

No alcohol. Children welcome, 2 high chairs. Outside catering. The restaurant takes party bookings of up to 110 people outside normal opening times.

Ram's
Vegetarian Indian Surti Gujarati restaurant

- ☛ 203 Kenton Road, **Kenton** HA3 0HR
- ☎ 020 8907 2022
- 🕐 M-Su 12.00-23.00
- ⊖ Kenton 5 mins
- ⮞ ramsrestaurant.co.uk
  facebook.com/RamsRestaurant

Gujarati, South Indian and Surti vegetarian cuisine from the city of Surat. They use butter ghee, but vegetable ghee is available.

Lunch thali M-F 12.00-17.00 £6.90 with 2 veg, 3 puri, dal, rice, papadom, pickle; dinner £9.90 M-F up to 21.00 starter, 2 veg, 3 puris, chapatti, dal, rice, kichdi, papad, pickle.

Starters £2.99-£5.49, mains £4.99-£5.99, dal and rice £4.90-£5.90, breads £1.70-£3.10.

Desserts include vegan carrot halva.

Juices £2.90, jug £11, soft drinks £1.70-£2.90, hot drinks £1.50

Wine, Indian beer, spirits.

Wheelchair access and toilet. Cards minimum £10. 10% service charge. Very child friendly, high chairs. Catering. Home delivery within 2 miles. They also have a party hall.

KENTON

WEST

721

KILBURN

& Cricklewood, Harlesden, Willesden

Olive Tree
Vegetarian cafe and wholefood shop

🖛 152 Willesden Lane NW6 7TH
(opposite Kimberly Road)

📞 020 7328 9078

🕐 M-Tu, Th-F 10.00-18.00, W 12.30-
18.30, Sa 10.00-17.30, Su closed

⊖ Brondesbury Park, Brondesbury,
Kilburn

🖊 theolivetreehealth.co.uk
facebook.com/TheOliveTreeHealth

A wholefood store since 1993, they have
added a lunchtime vegetarian cafe and
take-away at the front with four tables. All
organic ingredients.

Small meal £5.30, large £6.30, come with
brown rice and salad. Choose from sweet
potato stew, Hungarian goulash, Indian
spicy veg, chickpea potato stew, black bean
stew with tofu sausages, savoury lentil donut
with mild chilli jam sauce, homemade
falafel, sweet potato with seaweed and
sesame patty.

Vegan gluten-free apple tart £3.20, flapjack
£2.40, raw cheesecake.

Juices and smoothies £4.10-£4.65 made
with fruit,berries, greens and veg.. Teas,
coffees, latte, cappuccino, mocha. £1.50-
£2.60.

The shop sells the full range of Laura's Idea.

Bodycare by Weleda, Urtekram, Jason,
Avalon, Lavera make-up.

Supplements by Solgar Nature's Own,
Ainsworth. Flower remedies.

Ecover and some refills.

All displayed in a charming old worldly style
wooden interior.

Bhavna's
Indian vegetarian take-away

- 237 High Road, Willesden NW10
- 020 8459 2516
- M-Su 10.00-20.00
- Willesden Green, Dollis Hill

Indian vegetarian and vegan take-away with 7 seats. Large portions of curry with rice £2.30, with naan £3.20. Parathas, bhajias and sweets.

Everything is made with sunflower oil except the sweets which use butter ghee.

Don't get there too late in the day in case all the best stuff's been scoffed, or pre-order your food by phone. They are even open on Christmas Day and New Year's Day if you feel like something different!

Firezza, Willesden Green
Omnivorous pizzeria

- 76 Walm Lane NW2 4RA
- 020 8459 3311
- M-Th 17.00-23.00, F-Sa 12.00-24.00, Su 12.00-23.00
- Willesden Green
- firezza.com

They have vegan cheese! Carne Vegana pizza comes with vegan chorizo, pepperoni and stacks of veggies for around £10 or £14, or create your own with three toppings. Spinach and olives salad £4.95. Tomato focaccia £3.95. Mango sorbet £1.99.

Abyssinia
Omnivorous Ethiopian restaurant

- 9 Cricklewood Broadway NW2 3JX (just north of Walm Lane)
- 20 8208 0110
- M-Th 12.00-23.45, F-Sa 12.00-03.00, Su 12.00-02.00
- Kilburn, Cricklewood BR
- abyssiniarestaurant.co.uk
  facebook.com/abyssinialondon

One of the oldest Ethiopian restaurants in London. Vegan options include salads £4, soup £4, and main dishes £7.50 -£8.90 including Gomen greens in mild onion and garlic sauce; Mesir Wot lentils in berbere sauce; Shero Wot ground split peas; Ater Kilk split peas; Aleecha Dinech cabbage, carrot and potato with onion; Ingudai Tibs mushrooms; Yetsom Beyaynetu mixed veggies.

Vegan grand combo for 3 people £26.50. Lunch offer main plus drink £16, two mains and two drinks £16. Kids vegetable rice £7.

Soft drinks £1. Mango juice £3. Hot drinks £1.50-£2.75 include tea, coffees, Abyssinian black tea, and unusual teas such as Kemem Shay mixed spices, Ginger Shay, hibiscus, and green Arengude Shay.

Bottled beer £3, house wine £12.90 bottle. Weekdays happy hours 25% off drinks 16.30 till 18.30.

Lounge for live bands and dancing. Private functions and parties. Outdoor seating in summer. Take-away and delivery. Children welcome.

Rubio
Omnivourus coffee, eats and beats restaurant

- 📍 43 Park Parade, Harlesden NW10 4JD
- 📞 020 8961 9630
- 🕐 M closed, Tu-F 08.00-22.30 Sa-Su 09.00-22.30
- ⊖ Willesden Junction, Harlesden
- ➤ rubio.co.uk
  facebook.com/RubioLondon
  facebook.com/theshapeshifters

As well as great food, there is definitily some groove going on in the atmosphere of this indie place, opened in 2016 by Max Reich of the Shapeshifters, who topped the UK charts with house hit Lola's Theme. There is a wall full of vinyls and plenty of great music. They are very vegan friendly and the chef is vegan.

Brunch until 3pm such as full English cooked breakfast, £8.90, spicy mixed beans on toast £4.90, or the healthyVegan Breakfast £7.90 with truffle oil mushrooms, kale, avocado, spinach, red pepper, baby plum tomatoes and sourdough toast.

Soup of the day £4.20. Smashed avo on toast with chili, basil and lemon £4.90. Sweet potoato wedges £2.90.

From 5pm till 10pm sourdough pizzas £8.50.-£12 can be made with vegan cheese and gluten-free.

Always a vegan dessert.

House wine £4.60 medium glass, £12 half litre carafe. Bottled beers from £4.

Freshly squeezed juices £2.90-£3.60. Soft drinks £2.50. All coffees, chai, green organic matcha and loose leaf teas, with soya or almond milk.

Tale-away. Deliveroo. Live music events. DJ nights.

Newcare Pharmacy & Health Food
Health food shop and pharmacy

- 📍 16-18 Station Parade, Willesden Green NW2 4NH
- 📞 020 8450 7002
- 🕐 M-Sa 9.00-19.00, Su/BH closed
- ⊖ Willesden Green
- ➤

Not much has changed from the previous shop called Mistry. It's all in one now, with the health food shop on one side, and on the other the pharmacy, plus a homeopath and sometimes acupuncture.

Take-away food includes vegan sandwiches. Vegan cheese by Violife and Sheese; Taifun and Cauldron range. Big range of wholefoods, herbal teas and chocolate. Anila's concentrated curry sauces.

Supplements and remedies by Vogel, Viridian, Solgar. Bodycare by Weleda, Avalon, Green People and of course Mistry. Also ayurvedic products.

Revital, Willesden
Health food shop

- 📍 35-37 High Road, Willesden NW10 2TE (near Walm Lane)
- 📞 020 8459 3382
  Mail order 0800 252 875
- 🕐 M-Sa 9.30-19.00, Su 11.00-16.00
- ⊖ Willesden Green
- ➤ revital.co.uk

Lots of organic and special diet foods.

In the fridge are Violife, Vegusto, Sheese, Sojade, Coyo, raw sauerkraut, organic tofu ravioli, Tofurky and Taifun range.

In the freezer pies and pasties, ice cream from Booja Booja and Coyo.

Chocolate by Green & Black, Ombar, Seed & Bean, Raw Chocolate Company, Conscious. Energy bars.

Really Healthy organic and gluten-free pasta such as penne or fusilli made with red lentils, mung beans, buckwheat, chickpeas or black beans.

Bodycare for adults and kids including Weleda, Sukin, Green People. Cleaning products by Ecover, Enviroclean, Earth Friendly.

Supplements include Pukka, Terranova, Viridian, Higher Nature, Biocare. Their nutritionist gives free advice on supplements. Sports nutrition.

Aromatherapy oils and homeopathic remedies such as Ainsworth, Weleda and Nelsons. Bach and Bush flower and herbal remedies like Bioforce.

Meera's Health Food Centre
Health food shop

- 2 High Street, Harlesden NW10 4LX
- 020 8965 7610
- M-Sa 10.30-18.00, Su closed
- Willesden Junction, Harlesden BR

No fresh take-away but they have dried fruits, nuts and seeds, flapjacks. All sort of dry soya and a big selection of herbal teas. Freezer with soya ice-cream and in the fridge are some soya drinks.

Behind the counter is a wide range of dried loose herbs, some ayurvedic remedies too. Free advice on products.

Supplements include Solgar, Now, Health Aid, Salus and Nature's Aid.

Bodycare. Ecover. Spiritual bath crystals £4.50 a jar, and incense powder £3.50.

Holland & Barrett
Health food shop

- 106A Kilburn High Road NW6 4HY
- 020 7624 4567
- M-Sa 9.30-18.00, Su 11.00-17.00
- Kilburn High Road BR

Freezer.

- 96-98 Kilburn High Road NW6 4HS
- 020 7624 2648
- M-Sa 9.00-20.00, Su 11.00-10.00
- Kilburn High Road BR

Fridge and freezer.

- 69 High St, Harlesden NW10 4NS
- 020 3784 9525
- M-Sa 9.00-18.00, Su 11.00-10.00
- Willesden Junction BR, Harlesden BR

Fridge and freezer.

KINGSBURY

Rose Vegetarian
Vegetarian Indian restaurant

- 532-534 Kingsbury Road NW9 9HH
  (corner Brampton Road, near HSBC)
- 0208 905 0025, 0800 583 8905
- M-Su 12.00-21.30 (last orders)
- Kingsbury (opposite)
- rosevegetarian.co.uk

North and South Indian and Chinese vegetarian restaurant and take-away. Gigantic menu, over 100 dishes. Excellent value.

Dishes containing dairy are marked, which is quite a lot of them including many that would be vegan in other restaurants, and some paneeer dishes are not marked D, so best to check everything. There are no vegan desserts. Jain options.

Starters £2.99-£6.99 such as kachumber salad with mango; crispy potato, bhindi or onion bhajia; four samosas or two large spicier Punjabi samosas; spring rolls; mogo chips; potato wada.

Vegetable, spicy, or tofu burger with chips £3.50-£3.99.

Bombay chaat £4.99-£5.99 such as bhel sev, or pain puri, samosas or cutlets topped with hot chickpea sauce, black chana.

South Indian mains £4.99-£6.99 such as idli, medu wada lentil doughnuts, dosas and a Chinese one stuffed with Hakka noodles.

Note that some of the dosas and all the uttapams contain dairy.

North Indian specialities £4.99-£6.49 feature spicy veg kofta, karahi soya mince, various potato or vegetable curries in the style of mutter, methi or masala, dals, Punjabi kidney beans curry, veg jalfrezi, tofu masala, Kenyan mogo curry, spinach with chickpeas paalak chole.

Plain rice £2.50. Again all the other rices appear to contain dairy, as too do most of the Indian breads.

Chinese starters £2.99-£6.99 such as soups, chilli mogo, mushrooms, crispy battered corn and spinach. (Beware tofu dishes contain dairy!)

7 different types of noodles, 8 fried rice dishes, and three Chinese curries (but again the tofu one is not vegan), all £6.75-£6.99.

Eat as much as you like buffet lunch Mon-Fri 12.00-15.00, £7.99, varies every day, includes Chinese soup of the day, Chinese dish, two North Indian curries, daal or Punjabi kadhi, nan or roti, plain or pulau rice, green salad, roasted papad.. Children under-6 £3.50. Take-away box £6.99 with three curries, rice dish, large naan or roti.

Juices £2.99-£4.99. Cans 99p. Tea and coffee £1.50-£1.99. No alcohol.

10% charge for eat-in customers. Children welcome, high chairs. Catering.

Gayatri Sweet Mart
Vegetarian Indian take away

- ☛ 467 Kingsbury Road, Kingsbury NW9 9DY
- ☏ 020 8206 1677
- 🕐 M-Sa 10.00-18.00, Su 9.00-16.00
- ⊖ Kingsbury
- ↟ gayatri.co.uk, gayatrisweet.com

46 dishes, snacks and mixes £7.50-£14 per kilo. Savouries such as samosa 50p, bhajias, dhokra, kachori. Vegan sweets include kaju katti and anjeerlak £12.50-13.50/kg. Credit cards over £10.

Supreme Sweets
Vegetarian Indian take-away / cafe

- ☛ 706 Kenton Road Kenton HA3 9QX
- ☏ 020 8206 2212
- 🕐 M-Tu, Th-F 10.00-19.00, W closed, Sa 09.30-19.00, Su 08.30-17.30
- ⊖ Kingsbury
- ↟

Sweets and savouries such as bhajias £7 per kilo, samosas and pakoras from 50p.

Also frozen products like samosas, kachoris and spring rolls, £7.99-£8.99 for 25 pieces. 75% of items are vegan, vegetable oil in savouries, but butter ghee in sweets. Soft drinks. They have a few seats.

Catering for weddings and parties, you collect or they deliver for over 100 people.

Bombay Spice
Vegetarian Indian street food restaurant

- 560 Kingsbury Road NW9 9HJ)
- 020 8204 7009
- M-Tu, Th-Sa 10.30-19.30, Su 10.30-18.45, W closed
- Kingsbury

Bombay street food such as pani puri, sev puri, plain and masala chips, bateta poha, samosas, potato vada, methi bhajiya, dahi puri and chole puri 50p-£3.50.

Eat in buffet, eat as much as you like for £5 Mon-Sat 12.30-16.00. Every day different food for example on Monday they have roti, dal, vegetable curry and rice.

For card payment there is a charge of 50p. Tiffin £3.50.

Kingsbury Fruit & Veg Ltd
Greengrocer

- 477-481 Kingsbury Road NW9 9EA
- 020 8905 0295
- M-Sa 08.00-19.00, Su 08.00-17.00
- Kingsbury

Huge food store with tons of fruit and vegetables from all over the world. Also spices, pulses, chutneys, pickles, olives, oils, dates, flour, seeds.

Health First
Health food shop

- 664 Kingsbury High Road NW9 9HA
- 020 8238 9336
- M-Sa 9.30-19.00, Su closed
- Kingbury (opposite

Chilled food includes Cheezly, Sheese and Tofutti cheese; Taifun and Clearspring tofu. No take-away. Frozen by Fry's, Food Heaven ice cream and Booja Booja.

Wholefoods by Infinity. Some macrobiotic foods. Superfood such as apricot kernels, raw cacao, raw goji berries, maca powder or root.

Bodycare by Faith In Nature, Weleda, Avalon, Green People, Alba Botanica, Dr Bronner's, Avalon, Mistry and Jason.

Supplements and herbs such as Lambert's, Solgar, Biocare, Nature's Plus, Nature's Answer and Vogel.

Homeopathy New Era and Weleda. Nature by Nature essential oils. Bodybuilding. Ecover

PINNER

Organically Foodspot, Pinner
Vegetarian organic cafe

- 🠶 40-42 High Street, **Pinner** HA5 5PW
- ℂ 020 8966 9424
- ◐ M-Sa 9.00-17.00, Su 10.00-16.00
- ⊖ Pinner
- ⟍ organically.uk.com
  facebook.com/OrganicallyFoodSpot
  instagram.com/organicallyfoodspot

Coffee specialists with almond, coconut, oat or soya milk. Breakfasts such as granola bowl and lunches. Panini, toasties, sandwiches, wraps such as falafel and hummus in flatbread, salads. Vegan cakes such as chocolate or apricot and almond. Smoothies. Also in Teddington (Twickenham section, with food photos).

Bodywise Health Foods, Pinner
Health food shop

- 🠶 65 Bridge Street, **Pinner** HA5 3HZ
- ℂ 020 8429 1336
- ◐ M-Sa 9.00-18.00, Su closed
- ⊖ Pinner
- ⟍ bodywiseuk.com

Chilled foods by Cheezly, Tofutti, Violife, Taifun, Cheatin, Dragonfly, Sojade. Frozen by Coyo, Booja Booja, Swedish Glace, Coppa della Maga ice cream, Amy's, Thank Goodness, Fry's, and Clive's Pie.

Wholefoods. Meridian sauces, Zest, Plamil mayo. Soup by Amy's and Free & Easy. Whole Earth and Meridian spreads. Chocolate bars and protein bars.

Bodycare by Faith in Nature, Weleda, Mistry's, Jason, Green People, Dr Hauschka, Urtekram, Weleda Kids, Green People, Earth Friendly Baby and Bioskin. Ecover cleaning.

Supplements by Terranova, HealthAid, Viridiun, Solgar, Lamberts, Higher Nature, Biocare and Vogel. Homeopathy by Nelson's, New Era, Shuessler Tissue Salt.

Complementary therapies clinic. Books and magazines.

There is a **Pizza Express** at 33-35 High Street, Pinner HA5 5PJ. Conference rooms.

PINNER

WEST

729

Ahimsa
Vegan cafe

☛ 7 Red Lion Parade, **Pinner** HA5 3JD
(Bridge Street, near Love Lane)

☎ 020 7018 2133

🕘 M 9.00-16.00, Tu-Th 9.00-20.00,
F-Sa 09.00-21.30, Su 9.00-20.00

⊖ Pinner

⚲ ahimsathevegancafe.com
facebook.com/AhimsaTheVeganPinner

Vegan cafe opened December 2016 by four friends with different background (banker, scientist, nurse and communications). They met through Mohanji, a spiritual master who has been supporting them throughout their new venture. Ahimsa means non-violence and is the purpose of this place, respect for all living things and loving each other. It definitely has that feel, with a great vibe and luminous clean space. They aim to offer a healthier alternative to fast food.

Breakfast £3.90-£7.90, served till midday and possibly a bit later, includes full English, porridge with chia seeds and coconut milk, scrambled tofu and sausage wrap, blueberry pancake stack, or toast topped with beans and vegan cheeze or avocado smash or peanut butter and banana or scrambled tofu with roasted peppers.

Wraps from 11.30a.m., medium £5.70 or large £6.70, are served warm, such as Mediterranean superfood; Lebanese falafel; chilli tofu; Mexican black bean and coriander rice; Caribbean jerk Quorn; Bombay potato.

Construct yourself a Health or Hot bowl, medium £6.70, large £7.90. Choose from brown rice or quinoa, add one of the wrap fillings or vegetable curry, then some salads and dressing.

Filled jacket or sweet potato around £6 with beans or chilli and cheeze. Side dishes £2.50-£4.90 such as chunky chips, sweet potato fries, falafel with hummus, nachos.

Dinner menu from 5pm. Prices are considerably lower than in central London. Burgers £6.50. Quesadillas £5.50 come in Mexican, Indian with Bombay potatoes, or Mediterranean with smashed avo, salsa, cheeze and sweetcorn.. Mac & cheeze £6.50. Pizzas £8.50-£10.50 include the Meat-Free Paradise starring Caribbean spiced Quorn, with veggies, jalapenos and mozzarella.

For vegan cakes galore, some organic, this is the best place in Harrow. £3.20 gets you chocolate fudge, raspberry, coffee and walnut, apple cinnamon and walnut, orange polenta, carrot orange, or coconut loaf. Also brownies in chocolate almond or date and polenta. Ice-creams, sorbets and cones £1.95-£2.95.

Juices and smoothies £3.20-£3.70. All kinds of coffees £1.70-£2.95. Pot of tea £3.70.

Freshly squeezed juices £2.50, large £3.50, such as apple, beetroot, carrot and ginger; hydration special with cucumber, lime, green apple, celery, and basil leaf.. Smoothies £ 2.90, large £3.90, such as pineapple, spinach, banana and almond; or soya milk, almond butter with banana, avocado, spinach and ice cubes. Coffees £1.50-£ 2.70, with almond or soya milk. Herbal teas £1.60, large £1.90.

Disabled toilet. Around 26 seats and more outside in summer. Reservations only after 5pm.

Ahimsa theVegancafe

OPEN

LOVE LANE
HA5

QUEENSBURY

Two Peas
Vegan American fast food restaurant

- 242 Streatfield Rd, HA3 9BX (Honeypot Lane end)
- 020 8204 4660
- M-Su 12.00-23.00 (last orders 22.30)
- Queensbury
- two-peas.co.uk
  facebook.com/twopeasdiner
  instagram.com/twopeasdiner

The area's first vegan restaurant opened March 2019, next door to Only Parathas. No curries here, though there are plenty of spicy BBQ options. It's vegan comfort foods all the way like pizza, Beyond Burgers, fries, cauli nuggets. Gluten-free options.

Vegans rejoice. Unlike most of north-west London's vegetarian Indian restaurants, here they won't offer you ten dairy desserts and, possibly, a watery sorbet or frustrating fruit salad. Oh no, Two Peas serve up luscious *proper* vegan desserts and ice creams. And they have vegan alcohol.

Beyond Meat burgers £7-£8 in Classic with cheese, red onion, pickles and house sauce; Big BBQ with cheese, pickles, bbq sauce, crispy onions, onion rings and mayo; or Mexican with chilli cheese, onion slices, jalapeños, chipotle mayo and nachos.

Pizzas £9-£11 include classic Margherita; mushroom & kale; American BBQ with soy chilli mince, peppers, charred sweetcorn; Sicilian Aubergine with olives, capers, pine nuts; Hot Pepper Love with red onions. Also calzone.

Also weekly and monthly specials

Sides £6 include finger licking battered buffalo cauliflower florets with garlic aioli dip; load crispy fries topped with pimento cheese, soy chilli, jalapenos, chopped tomatoes, red onions; loaded nachos; okra fries in chick pea batter. Skin on or sweet potato fries with choice of dip, or garlic bread, all £4.

Desserts £6 such as salted caramel brownie with ice-cream, apple tart, cheesecake, 3 scoops of assorted ice creams.

NoMilk shakes £6 are made with coconut ice cream and oat milk, in vanilla, chocolate, salted caramel or strawberry.

Soft drinks £3 such as Karma Cola, Lemony lemonade, Gingerella ginger beer, OrangeAde Summer.

Vegan wine coming soon.

Beers £5 such as Brewdog American Red, Camden Hells, Hop House, Guiness, Meantime London lager. Spirits. Cocktails and hard shakes £8.

Children welcome. Deliveroo. Uber Eats.

Meera's Village Restaurant
Vegetarian Gujarati Indian restaurant

- 📍 36 Queensbury Station Parade, Queensbury HA8 5NN
- ☎ 020 8952 5556
- 🕐 M 18.00-22.00, Tu closed, W-Th 12.00-15.00, 18.00-22.00, F-Sa 12.00-22.30, Su 12.00-22.00
- ⊖ Queensbury
- ➤ meerasvillage.com

Fully licenced Indian restaurant with wide variety of choices and a fabulous buffet. Beautiful and rustic interior to bring you back to a typical Indian village, all the staff wear traditional clothing.

Starters £3.99 include soups, pani puri, bhel puri, dhokra, samosa chaat, sev roll, corn palak roll, dhaal bhajia. Sides £2.50-£5.50 such as 4 samosas, 3 spring rolls, kachori, pav bhajia, methi gota, plain and masala mogo. Dosas, uttapam and mains £3.99-£5.99.

Huge thali plate that you assemble yourself from the all you can eat buffet, evening £13.99, lunch W-F £6.99. Thalis cannot be shared unless under 5 years old. Between 5-10 years half price.

Dishes are marked on the menu for milk, gluten, nuts, sesame, soya, mustard.

Kids' meals £2.50 include noodles, chips or mogo.

Fresh juices £3-£3.50, jugs £8.99-£10.99. Soft drinks £2.50. Tea and coffee £2.50.

Cocktails £6.25, mocktails £3.50-£3.99. Beer £1.60-£3.99. Champagne £20-£65 Spirits £2.50-£3.50.

12.5% service charge.

Meera's Xpress, Kenton
Vegetarian Indian take-away

- 📍 205 Streatfield Road, Kenton HA3 9DA (Honeypot Lane end)
- ☎ 020 8206 0022
- 🕐 Su-Th 11.00-21.30, F-Sa 11.00-22.00
- ⊖ Queensbury
- ➤ meerasxpress.com

They say Kenton, but it's actually much closer to the Queensbury tube so we've listed it in this section. Around 100 items on the menu, all priced between £3 and £5. Chaat, bhajias, mogo chips, north Indian curries, south Indian dosas and uttapam, Indo-Chinese dishes like chilli tofu.

Lunch thali M-W, F £4.50. Kathiyawadi thali Thursday £4.99.

Soft drinks £1. Also in Finchley.

Only Parathas
Vegetarian Indian & Chinese restaurant

- 238-240 Streatfield Rd HA3 9BX
  (opposite Portland Crescent)
- 020 8732 2621
- Tu-F 12.00-15.00, 18.00-22.30,
  Sa-Su 12.00-23.00, M closed
- Queensbury
- onlyparathas.co.uk
  facebook.com/Onlyparathas

Fancy a change? This big restaurant, seating over 120, specialises in made to order parathas, Szechuan dishes and Mumbai street food.

Starters £3.50-£5.50 include soups, bhajias, mogo, kachori, samosas, chaats. Mains £4.50-£6.50 feature parathas made with just about anything, including green peas, mushroom, or babycorn with onion, plus the usual South Indian curries, uttapam, dosas, Chinese dosa, noodle dishes, garlic bread, pizzas. They also have hummus or spicy hummus with pita, and falafels.

Fresh juices £3.75. Soft drinks £1.50.

QUEENSBURY

WEST

Shay Naiy Sweet Mart
Vegetarian Indian take-away

- 11 North Parade, Mollison Way HA8 5QH
- 020 8905 6677
- Tu-F 10.00-19.00, Sa 10.00-18.00, Su 9.00-16.00, M closed
- Queensbury
- shaynaiysweetmart.co.uk
  facebook.com/ShayNaiySweetMart

Set meal deal (thali) £4.25 with choice of veg curry of the day, daal and rice with 2 chapatis or thepla flatbreads.

Savouries are all vegan 40p-£1.75 including bhajias, rotis, kachori, khichi, mogo, samosas, spring rolls. None of the Indian sweets are vegan.

Drinks 50p-£2.50. Outside catering.

Sri Rathiga, Queensbury
Vegetarian South Indian restaurant

- 21 North Parade, Mollison Way HA8 5QH
- 020 8952 4411 / 4440
- M closed, Tu--Su 12.00-23.00
- Queensbury, Burnt Oak
- srirathiga.com

Opened late 2012. Specialising in dishes from the southern states of Tamil Nadu, Kerala, Karnataka and Andhra Pradesh, with some dishes you won't find elsewhere.

Starters £2/50-£5.50 such as medu vada fried lentil doughbuts, bhajias, samosas, mogo chips, bhel puri, sev puri, pani puri, Manchurian mushrooms, deep fried plantain, Manchurian veg, deep fried chilli idli. Snacks platter £9.99. Platter of assorted mini dosas and uthappam £13.99.

Main course curries £4.50-£6 such as coconut milk veg kurma, Madras potatoes, Chettinad fiery veg curry, peas and mushroom, dal and spinach, sambar lentils and veg in tamarind sauce, black lentil and tomato dal makhani. Dosas, uthappam, biryani and noodle dishes £3.50-£6.99. Plain rice £2.50, or try lemon, coconut, pilau, jeera, mushroom fried, Szezwan, even tamarind rice £2.50-£4.99.

South Indian thali £8.50, take-away £5.99. Mini tiffin £7.99 with drink, mini masala dosa and uthappam, idli, vada, upma and chutneys.

Soft drinks, juices, tea and coffee £1.50-£3.25. Beers £2.49. Wine from £9.99 bottle, £3.50 medium glass. Spirits from around £2.50.

Tamu Tamu
Vegetarian Indian Kenyan take-away

- 🌮 40 South Parade, Mollison Way HA8 5QL
- ☎ 020 8951 4322
- 🕐 M-Th 10.00-18.00, F-Sa 10.00-19.00, Su 08.30-16.00, BH 9.00-14.00
- ⊖ Queensbury
- 🏃 tamutamu.co.uk
  facebook.com/tamutamuuk

Chaluka Kenyan style food. Indian sweets, savouries, curries, snacks and take-aways, nothing over £5, including maize flour cakes with greens, beans and maize, some unusual bhajias, (such as banana, green chilli and spinach), toasted masala veg

sandwich with chips, puris, samosas, spring rolls, masala mogo (cassava), falafel with chutney, idlis.

They sell Pukka and Numi tea.

You can call in advance to place your order and collect within 25 minutes. Diwali and Christmas hampers. Catering for 10 to 1,000.

The Regency Club
Indian/Kenyan omnivorous restaurant & bar

- 🌮 18-21 Queensbury Station Parade HA8 5NR
- ☎ 020 8952 6300
- 🕐 M18.00-22.30, Tu-Th 12.00-14.30, 18.00-22.30, F-Sa 12.00-14.00, 18.00-23.00, Su 12.00-22.00.
- ⊖ Queensbury
- 🏃 regencyclub.co.uk

You will be amazed by this place, when you walk in you think you are in an old, well kept traditional English pub. Although the main

menu is pretty meaty, we love that they have a separate vegan menu. Family run business since 1991.

Starters £2.55-£5.95 include mogo cassava chips tossed in a special chilli and garlic sauce; button mushrooms sautéed in Indo-Chinese sauce; crispy okra or potato bhajia; samosas; kachori filled with spiced peas; deep fried mushy peas; spring rolls; deep fried lentil dumplings.

Main curry dishes £6.45 feature some unusual ones such as soya mince curry, kidney bean masala, black lentil curry, as well as potato with fenugreek, Karahi or Dhansak mix veg, sweetcorn, chickpea and potato, okra in caramelised onion gravy.

Bread and rice £2.30-£3.10.

Three vegan beers £3.30-£5.50, Guinness, and three vegan wines £4.20 medium glass, bottle £17. Any wine can be served by the glass and they seal the bottle afterwards. Aperitifs, spirits, cocktails and mocktails.

Sky Sports HD with two boxes on different screens around the venue for football, cricket (of course!) or rugby, surround sound. Use their app or book online. Over 18 years old ecxept afternoons, and all day Sunday and bank holidays. Private room. 35 members of staff. Wifi.

Triple A
Vegetarian Indian supermarket

- 217-219 Streatfield Road, Kenton HA3 9DA
- (020 8204 6812
- M-Sa 9.00-18.30, Su 10.00-18.00
- Queensbury

Vegetarian Indian grocery

Shambhu's Vegan Caterers
Vegan caterer & cookery classes

- Based in Queensbury
- (020 8931 0030
  contact@shambhus.co.uk
- shambhus.co.uk
  facebook.com/
  ShambhusVeganCaterers

Chef Nishma Shah and husband Mahersh provide the food at London Vegans monthly meetings, and you'll find them at big events such as Vegfest. They can also cater your events, including AGMs, meetings, seminars, yoga classes, conferences, parties, weddings.

Dishes include sandwiches, bagels, burritos, pizzas, samosas, pakoras, spinach cannelloni, lasagna, penna all'arrabiata, biryani, spinach and cashew nut rice, vegan raita, Iranian adas polow (rice, dates, currants, green lentils), tangy tofu, tofu tikka masala, Thai green curry, chickpea curry, creamy tofu veg curry, vegan spinach paneer, vegetable jalfrezi, blackeye bean curry, mung bean curry, daal, salad, Greek salad, green lentil salad, coleslaw, chutney. And then there are the desserts! Cheesecakes come in chocolate and coconut, lemon and coconut, chocolate orange, mint choc chip , or mixed berries. Also chocolate fudge slice, flapjacks.

Juices and hot drinks.

Gujarati cooking classes and summer holiday classes for children.

QUEEN'S PARK

& Kensal Rise

Comptoir V
Vegan international & Moroccan restaurant

- 1 Keslake Mansions, 12 Station Terrace NW10 5RU
- 020 3092 0047
- M-Su 12.00-23.00
- Kensal Rise
- comptoirv.co.uk
  facebook.com/ComptoirVLondon
  instagram.com/comptoir_v

New international vegan restaurant that is already many people's favourite. Many Moroccan dishes. You can share some small plates tapas style, or go for big ones.

Small plates mostly £4.75 include spicy beetroot hummus, chickpea and broad bean falafel, sautéed Moroccan spinach, aubergine zaalock arrot smash, curried chickpeas, shakshooka roasted peppers. Tempura battered "dynamite" shrimp in sriracha aioli £6.75. Sharing platter £19.95.

Mains £7.50-£11.95 feature salad, Moroccan Buddha bowl, mushroom burger, three bean jerk patty burger, khadija daily special, sweet potato and lentil island curry, Aunty Esi Caribbean curried chickpeas with Moroccan ghife bread, mac 'n' cheese with steamed garlic kale and southern style battered bbq mushroom ribs.

Side dishes £1.95-£4.75 include ghife bread, skin on or sweet potato fries, festive rice, wholewheat couscous, seasoned avocado, fried plantain, salad, mac 'n' cheese.

Diners adore their desserts, £5.95-£6.50. Banana and date crumble with pecan nuts and banana caramel custard. Moroccan pancakes filled with caramelised biscuit spread, maple syrup, ice cream with chopped nuts. Cheesecake. Add ice cream £1.95.

Cold pressed juices £3.95-£4.50. Soft drinks £2.95 include Karma cola, Lemony lemonade, gingerella. Fresh Moroccan mint teas £2.75-£7.95, breakfast or herbal tea £2.20-£2.30. All kinds of coffees £2.50-£2.75.

Biodynamic vegan wines, lots of beers around £4, cocktails £7.

They also have a larger omnivorous restaurant Comptoir Mezze at number 20.

CV — COMPTOIR V —

LL DAY DINING   020 3092

Paradise Plantbased
Vegan and raw cafe

- 59 Chamberlayne Road, Kensal Rise NW10 3ND
- 020 8968 8321
- M, W-Sa 9.00-17.00, Tu closed
- Kensal Rise
- paradiseplantbased.com
  facebook.com/paradiseplantbased

Opened August 2016 as Paradise Unbakery, and specialising in raw vegan cakes and cheesecake. Everything is free from eggs, dairy, grain, gluten, soya, agave and refined sugar, it's basically guilt-free and cruelty-free. With a background in art and design, everything looks beautiful.

They have a selection of salads, which can be warmed up. The small salad bowl is £6 up to 3 choices and £8.50 for 6 choices. Salads and main is £8.50. Also for take away the mix & match salad is priced by weight, 100gr £1.70.

Raw and cooked savoury food like pizza, lasagna, moussaka, tartlets, quiche, soup, breads and vegan cheeses.

Break your fast: berry smoothie bowl; and cacao smoothie bowl £6.90; apple pancake £7; waffle £7; porridge £5.50; cinnamon bagel £4; avo on toast £4.50; bagel & beans £7; chickpea omelette £7.

Many cakes £3.30 to £3.80 such as raw raspberry, chocolate cashew ; raw lemon poppy seed cashew ; chocolate banofee; rich chocolate, vanilla & banana cake and many more.

Slow cold press juices for £3 and smoothies £4.50: cat cow aka cacao (nut milk, banana, raw cacao, chia & coconut sugar); raspberry dreams (nut milk, raspberry, banana, lacuma, chia & coconut sugar); witness the fitness (nut milk, blubbery, peanut butter gluten-free oats, chia, banana & coconut sugar). Homemade kombucha by the glass £3.

Hot drinks from £1.60 to £3.50, lots of alternative coffee like barley, chicory and dandelion; matcha latte and turmeric latte; pink mangosteen latte. Milk includes oat, soya, almond and coconut.

On the counter you could find chocolate bars by Love Earth, Coco Caravan, Ombar, the Chocolate Vanoffe, also their own brand of coconut bacon and probiotic crackers.

There are around 30 seats inside and 8 outside.

Take-away, deliveries and event catering Celebration cakes for any occasion. Workshop & events like cooking and crafting. Wifi and baby changing facilities.

Mount Olive Supermarket
Omnivorous take-away and food shop

- 69 Salusbury road NW6 6NJ
- 020 7328 7191
- M-Su 09.00-22.00
- Queen's Park

Possibly the best falafels in London, served from 11.30a.m. every day except Sunday. You can have your falafel in a wrap, a salad box, or just have the salad. Portions are generous, including whatever you like from their vast selection of at least 20 salads made fresh on site every morning. A big box of mixed salads is £5 and the huge wrap is £4.50. Their own homemade babaganosh and hummus.

It works on a first come first served basis, and they tend to run out pretty quickly because at lunch time it gets really busy, sometime the queue extends outside the shop, but don't worry the wait is not too bad because the staff are very efficient and fast. If there are any salads left later, you'll find them in a take-away box in the fridge.

Also a counter with just fruit and vegetables for juices, for £3-£3.50 you can have a mixture of both, tutti-frutti, energy or green.

The shop sells fruit and veg, organic and wholefoods, even kale chips and mulberries. Lots of dried herbs, fresh olives by weight. Alcohol.

Salusbury Foodstore
Omnivorous Italian cafe & deli

- 56 Salusbury Road NW6 6NN
- 020 7328 3287
- M-Th 08.00-22.30, F-Sa 08.00-23.00, Su 08.30-22.30
- Queen's Park, Brondesbury Park
- thesalusburyfoodstore.co.uk
  facebook.com/SalusburyFoodstore

There are up to four vegan salads every day and one of the soups is normally vegan. Eat in small salad £4.95, medium £7.50, large £10.95. Take-away salad box £7.45 can include falafel, tabouleh and lentils.

Huge range of mixed green and veg juices 400ml £4.95, litre £10 such as Brocosaurus (kale, cucumber, celery, apple, fennel, ginger, spinach, lime), Rooster (wheatgrass, spirulina, turmeric, macha, Udo's oil, chia and hemp protein) and many more. Smoothies 600ml £4.95 such as Breakfast (banana, dates, spinach, oats, frozen berries) or Tropi-kale (kale, mango, pineapple, ginger, lime, almond milk). Lascombe organic drinks.

Teas and coffees £2 -£3.20 with almond or soya milk.

In the evening from 17.00 they serve sourdough pizza from £9.50 which can be made gluten-free and dairy-free.

Some snacks from the shelves like quinoa, lentil and hummus chips; tamari roasted Sicilian almonds; pumpkin seeds; or seeds and soya. Ollybars energy bars.

Wine from £4 medium glass, £6.10 large, £12 carafe, £18 bottle. Beer from £4. There are many seats inside and a few outside. Wifi. Baby changing, high chair. Deliveroo pizzas, 10% discount for collection.

Pomodoro e Basilico
Vegan Italian dining popup & caterer

- ☏ 07866 194403
- ⊖ Queen's Park
- ↖ facebook.com/PomoBasilico

You've probably seen Italian chef Sara's vegan food stalls at markets and vegan events all over London. She also runs cookery and pasta making classes, popup and private dinner parties at her home in Queens Park. Check out her Facebook page for what's coming up.

Also at these weekly markets: Tuesday South Kensington (Sloane Zone), Wednesday Swiss Cottage (North), Thursday Bloomsbury (Centre), Saturday Ladbroke Grove (see Notting Hill).

Jivita Ayurveda
Organic spa, apothecary and wholefoods

- ☛ 89 Chamberlayne Rd NW10 3DN
- ☏ 020 8964 4993
- ◕ M-F 10.00-19.00, Sa 10.00-18.00, Su closed
- ⊖ Kensal Rise
- ↖ jivitaayurveda.com
  nstagram.com/jivitaayurveda

Vast list of relaxing treatments, including massage, facial and beauty, detox, diet and lifestyle consultations.

They stock organic wholefoods, loose dry herbs, Meridian spreads, miso, Biona bread, gluten-free flour, pasta, plant milks, Pukka coconut oil, hemp seed oil, herbal teas. Small fridge with plant milk and some soya products. Chocolate by Doisy & Dam, Booja Booja and Raw. Bodycare from Pai and supplements from Pukka. Some Ecover.

Books. They also run Ayurveda training courses.

Bombshell Nails
Vegan owned nails and beauty salon

- ☛ 93 Salusbury Rd, NW6 6NH
- ☏ 020 7625 7546
- ◕ M-W & F 9.00-20.00, Th 9.00-21.00, Sa 9.00-19.00, Su 9.00-18.00
- ⊖ Queen's Park
- ↖ bombshellnails.co.uk
  facebook.com/bombshellnailsltd
  sparitual.com

This vegan owned nail bar & beauty parlour offers many treatments for men and women. SpaRitual products and polish are 100% vegan and eco-friendly. Any treatment with these products can be arranged on request. They sell some bags which are vegan too

Planet Organic, Queen's Park
Wholefoods supermarket

- ☛ 117-121 Salusbury Road NW6 6RG
- ☏ 020 3985 5410
- ◕ M-Sa 07.30-21.30, Su 09.00-21.00
- ⊖ Brondesbury Park overground, Queen's Park (midway between them)
- ↖ planetorganic.com/
  planet-organic-queens-park

The eighth branch of Planet Organic opened here in August 2019, with a cafe area for fresh juices, coffee, hot food and salads. Lots of food to go in the fridges. Organic fruit and veg. "Unpackaged" section for weighing out things like grains and pulses into your own containers. Body care section with trained adviers. See Bayswater branch for more details.

RAYNERS LANE

Mumbai Local, Rayners Lane
Vegetarian Indian restaurant

- 453 Alexandra Ave HA2 9SE (corner High Worple, opp Zoroastrian Centre)
- 020 8357 2902
- M-F 12.00-15.30, 17.00-22.30; Sa-Su 12.00-22.30
- Rayners Lane
- mumbailocal.co.uk

Like the Wembley and Harrow branches, but this one has some

Thali £9.95 M-F, weekend and bank holiday £12.95, with two curries, dal, rice, chapatis, a fried favourite such as pakora, pickles, salad, popadums.

Chaat and starters £1.50-£5.95 such as dabeli, masala pav, bhajia or samosa in pav, Chinese bhel crispy noodles, bhajias, samosas, spring rolls. Sandwiches and toasties £3.50-£4.95 such as peanut butter, masala potato dabeli with peanuts and pomegranate.

South indian dishes £3.95-£5.95 such as dosa, uttapam, medu vada and idli. Curries £5.95-£7.95. Rice £3.50-£5.95.

Indo-Chinese dishes £5.95-£7.95 such as Szechuan mushrooms.

Finger sliced potato deep fried chips £2.75-£4.95 such as with chilli sauce, or garlic and pepper.

Soft drinks £1.50-£2.95. Jug of passion fruit juice £13.95. Bottled beers from £2.95. Wine £4.95 for 187ml.

Delivery to HA0, HA9, UB6 12.00-20.30. Deliveroo. Also in Wembley and Harrow.

Natraj
Vegetarian Indian café & take-away

- 467 Alexandra Avenue, **Rayners Lane** HA2 9RY (by the tube)
- 020 8617 3858
- M-Sa 10.00-20.00, Su 9.30-18.00
- Rayners Lane

Great value Indian vegetarian take-away with plenty for vegans. Starters/snacks such as bhajias, sweets, samosas etc.

6 curries each day are vegan such as spinach and chickpea, okra and potato, cabbage and potato, soya bean, kidney bean and butterbean mix. A regular take-away box of curry and rice is £2.75, large £3.75. Thali £3.50 with rice, 2 vegetable curries, dal, 2 chapati or puri. Box of rice £2 and £3. Dal £3 and £4. Snacks and savouries £7.50 per kilo including kachori, samosa, falafel, vada pav, spring rolls, mix veg bhajia etc. Soft drinks 60p.

Children welcome, high chairs. Cards minimum £5. Parties and events. Also at South Harrow.

Saravana Bhavan, Harrow
Vegetarian South Indian restaurant

- ☛ 403, Alexandra Avenue, **Rayners Lane** HA2 9SG
- ☎ 020 8869 9966
- ◐ M-Su 11.00-23.00
- ⊖ Rayners Lane
- ✦ saravanabhavanlondon.co.uk

Same menu as other branches such as Wembley. Check for ghee in some dishes.

Mystic Masala
Vegetarian Indian restaurant

- ☛ 242 Imperial Drive, Rayners Lane HA2 7HJ
- ☎ 020 8062 2104
- ◐ M closed, Tu-Su 12.00-22.30
- ⊖ Rayners Lane
- ✦ mysticmasalaharrow.co.uk
  facebook.com/mysticmasalarestaurant

Contemporary licensed Indian restaurant opened October 2018. Huge menu includes Mexican and Chinese dishes. Vegan and Jain options are marked.

Starters and chaat £1.95-£4.75 include masala chips, mogo cassava chips, bhajias, chilli mushroom, Manchurian veg balls, spring tolls, samosa, corn on the cob, crispy fried okra, blvel puri, sev puri, pani puri, Chinese soups.

Mini meal Chole Bhatura chickpea curry with Indian bread £4.95.

Main dishes £4.75-£7.95 include malai kofta veg dumplings, veg Jaipuri, curries, yellow tadka dal, veg biryani with gravy, Fada Ni Khichdi wheat and yellow dal with veg, chilli tofu or Quorn with peppers, Palak or Kadai tofu with creamy spinach sauce, Quorn korma, Chinese garlic or Hakka noodles and veg, garlic fried rice, Burmese Khow Suey curried soup with noodles, Mexican nachos with refried beans, enchilladas. Rice £2.25-£2.75.

No vegan desserts. Soft drinks £1.95-£2.75 include fizzy, lime soda, juices. Coffee, green tea £1.50-£1.65.

Sugar & Spice
Vegetarian Indian take-away

- ☛ 399 Rayners Lane, HA5 5ER
- ☎ 020 8866 3909
- ◐ M-Sa 10.00-19.30, Su 09.00-19.00
- ⊖ Rayners Lane (very close)
- ✦ facebook.com/
  SugarAndSpiceTakeaway

The usual samosas, spring rolls, kachori.

The Village Inn
Omnivorous pub- restaurant

- ☛ 402 Rayners Lane HA5 5DY
- ☎ 020 8868 8551
- ◐ Su-W 08.00-23.00, Th 08.00-24.00, F-Sa 08.00-00.30
- ⊖ Rayners Lane
- ✦ jdwetherspoon.com

Wetherspoons pub with some vegan food such as five-bean chilli with rice and tortilla chips, even fulll cooked breakfast. Children welcome. Wifi. Outdoor area. Step free access. TV screens.

SHEPHERD'S BUSH

and Westfield Shopping Centre

Tai Buffet
Vegan Chinese buffet restaurant

- 86 Uxbridge Road, W12 8LR (middle of north side of Shepherd's Bush Green)
- (07850 663328
- M-Su 12.00-22.00
- Shepherd's Bush

All you can eat Chinese and Thai vegan buffet £6.50 Mon-Sat till 5pm, £6.60 evenings, Sundays and bank holidays, including 10% service charge. Take-away boxes £3.50, £4.50 large. Hot and cold buffet counters with around 30 dishes including veg chow mein, green curry, sweet and sour soya chicken, yelllow curry soya lamb, black bean soya chicken, crispy soya duck, Singapore nooldes, spring rolls, dim sum, lots of vegetables, soup, salads, tapioca pudding with coconut milk, fruit salad. Also sauces.

Chinese hot teas £1.50 including tai ginseng, sweet ginger, lemon plum, and mountain dandelion. Soft drinks £1.50 like mango juice, red guava juice, iced lemon tea. Fresh juices £ 2.50 such as apple, carrot, mixed. Chinese Tsingtao beer £2.50. Wine £3.50 glass, bottle £14. You can also bring your own drinks and pay corkage. Cash only.

Mr Falafel
Vegetarian falafel cafe

- Units T4-T5, New Shepherd's Bush Market, 13 Uxbridge Road W12 8LH
- (07440 557681
- M-Sa 11.00-18.00; Su, BH closed
- Shepherd's Bush Market (opposite)
- mrfalafel.co.uk
  facebook.com/mrfalafellondon

Big cafe in the New Market, which is parallel to the Old Market. Cheap, big portions, wholemeal wraps available, and the only non-vegan item is cheese. Classic falafel wrap with salad £4.75, £5.75 extra large. Then there are lots of variations for £1 more that you won't find in other falafel places, such as with fried cauliflower and fried potatoes with aubergine, spicy hot potato cubes with coriander and onion, ful medames mashed broad beans, olives, avocado, or a mixture of several of these. If you don't fancy falafel, you can have a vegetable cocktail wrap £4.25 or £5 XL with fried cauliflower florets, potato, aubergine, garlic sauce, lemon, pickle and sauces.

Fries £2, come with tahini sauce and pomegranate syrup or chilli sauce. Falafel platter £8. Cold drinks 75p-£1.30. Deliveroo.

Ankh Wellbeing Centre
Vegan shop and cafe

- ☛ 10 Adelaide Grove W12 0JJ (off Uxbridge Road, towards Acton)
- (020 8743 1985
- ◕ M-Th 10.00-18.00, F-Sa 10.00-20.00, Su closed
- ⊖ Shepherd's Bush Market
- ↑ Facebook ANKH Wellbeing Centre

ANKH stands for Afrikan Natural Konnection to Health, primarily a shop. They source from the African and Caribbean communities so you will find lots of products that you don't see elsewhere. Whole foods. Lots of loose herbs. Akamuti organic skincare. Hidden Garden supplements. Gifts such as jewellery, bags, crystals. Books, cards and crafts.

The cafe helps to introduce people to the products. section has a couple of tables and does herbal teas £1 cup, pot £2.50, organic Marley coffee £2. Juices and smoothies. Snacks are vegan. Bulghur wheat pattie with veg, or spelt and kamut patty filled with pumpkin and spinach, or kale, or lentils, samphire £2.50. Cakes £2 include sweet potato, chocolate, pineapple, or fruit.

Lectures on food such as vegan cookery or raw food or a particular product promotion, workshops such as yoni eggs, film screenings, business networking evenings. Children's activities. Vitamin and mineral testing. Occasional pamper days when therapists come in.

SHEPHERD'S USH

WEST

Carol's Organic Kitchen
Vegan healthy cookery classes and nutritionist

- Loftus Road W12 7EN (book ahead to receive the door number)
- (07757 662 448
- Shepherd's Bush Market
- Facebook Carol's Organic Kitchen
  carolsorganickitchen.com
  instagram.com/carolsorganickitchen

Carol Organic demonstrates how to cook healthy vegan, wholefood, organic recipes at her home in Shepherd's Bush, followed by sitting down to dinner with like-minded people. She can help you to create a wholefood plant-based lifestyle.

Also nutrition assessment, personal and family nutrition planning and counselling, weight management, anti-inflammatory detox.

Visit the website and social media for further details of the workshops and to book your place.

These workshops are for you if you are seeking to transition, learn more about nutrition and foods that heal or need more innovative ideas in maintaining a healthy diet.

Brewdog, Shepherd's Bush
Omnivorous bar

- 15-19 Goldhawk Road W12 8QQ (near the Shepherd's Bush Empire)
- (020 8749 8094
- M-Sa 12.00-24.00, Sa 11.00-24.00, Su 11.00-22.30
- Goldhawk Road, Shepherd's Bush Market, Shepherd's Bush
- brewdog.com/bars/uk/shepherds-bush
  facebook.com/brewdogshepbush

Most Brewdog craft beers are Vegan Society certified, and they do some vegan pub food.

Seitan or southern fried seitan burger or tofu hotdog £9, add fries £2, sweet potato fries £2.50. Buffalo cauli wings, small £6, regular £8, share £12. Superfood salad £8.

Weekend brunch Bircher muesli with passion fruit and pistachio £4.50; full English cooked breakfast £9 with bbq seitan steak, crispy kale, smashed avocado, chargrilled padron peppers, bbq pit beans, forest mushroom, tomato and sourdough toast.

Nutcase
Vegetarian shop

- 352 Uxbridge Rd W12 7LL (nr ANKH)
- (020 8743 0336
- M-Sa 10.00-20.30, Su 10.00-17.00
- Shepherd's Bush Market

Around 30 types of loose raw and roasted nuts, roasted pulses to snack on, and raw pulses to cook at home, dried fruits, many types of dates. 40 kinds of spices. Date juice. Liquorice roots.Superfoods such as chia, goji, mulberry, lucuma, maca. Gifts such as chess, coffee makers, music.

Holland & Barrett, Shepherd's Bush
Health food store

- In W12 Shopping Centre, 112 Shepherds Bush Green W12 5PP (opposite Central Line tube)
- (020 8743 1045
- M-F 9.00-19.00, Sa 9.00-18.00, Su 11.00-17.00
- Shepherd's Bush

Fridge and freezer.

Holland & Barrett, White City
Health food store

- Unit 1096 Westfield Shopping Centre, Ariel Way, White City W12 7GB
- (020 8740 5959
- M-Sa 10.00-22.00, Su 12.00-18.00
- Shepherds Bush

Fridge and freezer.

Market Place
Vegetarian health food shop

- 8A Market Place, Acton W3 6QS
- (020 8993 3848
- M-Sa 9.00-17.45, Su closed
- Acton Town

Fridge and freezer with veggie-burgers, sausages, vegan ice-cream. No take-away. Lots of sports nutrition stuff. Big range of vitamins, especially Solgar and children's. Cosmetics, especially Avalon. Aromatherapy supplies.

Holland & Barrett, Acton
Health food store

- 122 High Street, Action W3 6QX
- (020 8752 0333
- M-Sa 9.00-18.30, Su 11.00-18.00
- Acton Central

Westfield

Upstairs in the huge Westfield Shopping Centre (behind Shepherd's Bush tube station, not to be confused with Westfield Stratford in east London) is The Balcony where there are lots of food places with shared seating in the middle, high chairs and wifi, including Pret a Manger. There are more restaurants outside opposite Waitrose.

ᛏ uk.westfield.com

Comptoir Libanais, Westfield
Omnivorous Lebanese chain restaurant

☞ The Balcony, Westfield W12 7GE
☎ 020 8811 2222
◔ M-Sa 11.00-22.00, Su 11.00-17.00 (closed for refurbishment until Spring 2019)
ᛏ comptoirlibanais.com

Have a selection of mezze dishes £4.95-£5.95 each, or a mixed platter for £9.95, one person, £18.95 for two. Falafel wrap with salad and pickles £5.95.

Vegan orange and almond cake £4.95.

Homemade lemonades £2.90, large £3.55, are unusual, made with pomegranate and orange blossom, or apple, mint and ginger, or lemon and lime with rose syrup. Juices made to order £3.45, £3.95. Non-alcoholic Laziza fruit beers £2.95. Hot drinks £1.95-£2.65.

Wine £4.50 medium glass, £6.50 large, £18.95 bottle. Almaza Lebanese or Casablanca Moroccan beer £3.95, £4.50.

Mandaloun
Omnivorous Lebanese restaurant

☞ Southern Terrance, outside Westfield (opposite Waitrose)
☎ 020 8749 8845
◔ M-Sa 11.00-24.00, Su 12.00-24.00
ᛏ mandaloun.com

Upmarket restaurant with beautifl interior, some vegan dishes, seats inside and out (where they'll give you a blanket if it's cold). The usual Lebanese hot and cold mezze dishes, salads and soups, £4.75-£5.75, platter of eight £21.50.

Soft drinks and juices £2.75-£4.75, coffees £2.50-£3, organic artisan tea and mint tea £3.50. Laziza non-alcoholic fruit beers £3.50.

Shawa
Omnivorous Lebanese cafe

☞ The Balcony, Westfield
☎ 020 87491832
◔ M-Sa 11.00-22.00, Su 12.00-19.00
⊖ Shepherd's Bush
ᛏ shawa.co.uk

Falafel £4.95 with pickled turnip, tomato, red onion, lettuce. Mezze £2.45-£4.25 such as hummus and pitta, falafel bites with tahini, vine leaves, Shawa salad, seven-spiced Lebanese rice with golden sultanas, Lebanese fries with paprika and cumin, pickles and olives; free sauces. Mezze platter £11.95.

Soft drinks £1.50-£3.25. Almaza Lebanese beer £3.85. Mint tea £1.95.

Tossed
Omnivorous salad bar chain

- The Balcony, Westfield W12 7GF
- 020 8740 3058
- M-Sa 11.00-22.00, Su 12.00-19.00
- tossed.uk.com

Lots of juices. Vegan wraps £5.99 such as Piri Protein with avocado salsa, piri piri sauce, pickled kale, red cabbage and rainbow slaw; Muscle Mezze with falafel, hummus, mint, pickled red onion, pomegranate, pickled kale, red cabbage and rainbow slaw. Vegan Greek salad £6.99.

Create your own salad and wrap £8.49 from around 20 ingredients.

Juices and smoothies £3.99-£5.29.

Wagamama, Westfield
Omnivorous Japanese restaurant

- Southern Terrace, Westfield W12 7SL
- 020 8749 9073
- M-Sa 11.00-23.00, Su 11.00-22.00
- Shepherd's Bush
- wamama.com

Separate vegan menu. Baby facilities. Disabled toilet. Free wifi.

Lola's Cupcakes
Vegetarian cake cart

- First floor, Westfield W12 7GD
- M-Sa 10.00-22.00, Su 12.00-19.00
- lolascupcakes.co.uk

Five kinds of vegan cupcake £3 such as pistachio and chocolate, chocolate, strawberry and coconut, passionfruit and coconut, chocolate and raspberry; brownie £2.75.

Super Singh's, Southall
Vegetarian restaurant & take-away

- ☛ 5 Western Road UB2 5HA (King St end)
- ☎ 020 8574 4471
- 🕐 M-Su 12.00-23.00
- ⊖ Southall BR
- ↖ supersinghs.co.uk
  facebook.com/SuperSinghsSouthall

Following the huge success of the original branch in Feltham by Heathrow airport (see Hounslow), this second branch opened April 2016.

Pizzas 7, 9, 10, 14, 18 inches. For example 18 inch is £7.99, two 14 inch pizzas for £15 iincluding chips and 2 litre bottle of drink.

Vegan pizzas include Hawaiian, Shanghai, Chili Wala, BBQ, and Mexican which comes with vegan chicken, kidney beans, mixed peppers, red onion, sweetcorn, jalapenos and fresh tomato. Extra toppings 50p-90p.

Lunchtime special M-F 12.00-16.00, 7inch pizza and a can of drink £2.99, 9 inch pizza and a can of drink £4.99.

Also veggie burgers, grilled vegetable wrap £2.49-£4.99.

Side dishes £1.49-£3.99 include mini spring rolls, garlic bread, chicken nuggets, chicken satay skewer breaded drumstick, nachos, masala fish. Warrior fries with masala chips, mixed veg, veggie chicken, melted cheese, tomato and chilli.

Children welcome. Cash only. Just Eat, Uber Eats, Deliveroo. Look out for offers on their Facebook page.

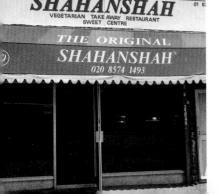

Chini Chor, Southall
Vegetarian Indian restaurant & sweet shop

- 86 South Road, Southall UB1 1RD
- 020 8574 1807
- M-Su 08.30-22.00
- Southall BR
- chinichor.com

Great value south Indian food. All the usual starters, chaats, samosas, pakoras, bhajias, soups £1-£3.50. Mixed pakora platter £7. Curries £3.50-£6. Chinese dishes such as chilli tofu £3-£6. South Indian dosas and uttapam £2.75-£4.50. Bread 75p-£2.50, rice £1.50-£2.25. The masala dosa is great value at £3.75.

Take away prices are slightly cheaper.

Soft drinks, tea, coffee £1-£2.25. Freshly made juices £3.50.

Take-away is slightly cheaper. Also in Hounslow.

Delhi Wala
Vegetarian Indian restaurant and snack shop

- 11 King Street, Southall UB2 4DG
- 020 8574 0873
- M-Su 08.00-22.00
- Southall BR

South of the station away from the Broadway.

Punjabi and South Indian dishes from £1 starters such as samosa, dal, onion baji, chaat, mogo chips and pakora.

Around 23 main dishes are vegan £5.50-£10 and include soya mince. Dosas £4-£5 and uthappam £5-£5.50. Rice £2-£2.50, biryani £6.50. The special menu includes pilau or boiled rice, 3 vegetable curries, bhatura or naan and salad £5.

Chinese mains £4.25-£6.50 such as mushroom chow mein with fried rice, vegetable Manchurian.

Very unusual for an Indian places to have some of the sweets dairy-free including kaju burfi, besan burfi, besan ladoo, patisa, pista roll etc.

Soft drinks £1, passion fruit or orange juice £2.50-£3.50. Coffee £1.25-£2.

Children welcome, two high chairs. Air conditioning. No alcohol. Card minimum £5. Catering for all occasions.

Shahanshah
Vegetarian North Indian restaurant, take-away and sweet shop

- 60 North Road, Southall UB1 2JL
- 020 8574 1493
- M-Su 10.00-20.00
- Southall BR

Starters £1-£2 such as two samosas (take-away 45p each) or pakora (take-away £7.50/kg). Main meal £3.50 such as curry and rice. Dosa £2.25-£2.95 Some food is vegan as they use butter ghee, groundnut and sunflower oil.

Cold drinks 80p, coffee and tea £1.

Around 30 seats inside. Children welcome. No alcohol. No cards. They cater for parties and weddings.

Saravanaa Bhavan
Vegetarian Indian restaurant

- Glassy Junction, 97 South Rd UB1 1SQ
- 020 8843 0088
- M-Th 10.30-23.00
- Southall BR
- saravanabhavanlondon.co.uk

Opened June 2012, this is a very good vegetarian restaurant, part of a UK and international chain with branches in East Ham, Harrow, Ilford, Tooting and Wembley. 200 seats, open kitchen, specialising in parties and weddings. Huge menu. There is a party hall for groups of 30 to 100, and party menus from £13 to £20 for 3 courses, no hire fee.

Starters £2.95-£4.95 including Chinese items such as chili mushrooms and vegetable Manchurian.

Main courses include of course dosas £3.45 to £4.45 for a tailor made one with your choice of three fillings. Uthappam £3.45-£4.25.

South Indian meal £7.25 with 2 curries, rice, salad, side dish, sambar, rasam soup, chappathi, appalam (Tamil for papadom) and pickle. North Indian thali £7.95 with soup, 2 chappathis, salad, dal, biryani, 3 side dishes, spring rolls, fried papad and pickles. Business meal £5.45.

Chinese main courses £4.95 including mushroom fried rice and noodles, steamed noodles sautéed with shredded vegetables and topped with shredded apples, cauliflower with Manchurian sauce.

Rice £1.75-£3.40, bread £1.25-£1.95.

No vegan desserts.

Wine £5 glass, £13.50 bottle. Beer £1.95-£3.75, champagne and sparkling £18.50-£35.

Juices £2.75. Fizzy drinks 95p. Tea or coffee £1, no soya milk.

Children welcome, high chairs. No take-away.

Barfi
Vegetarian Indian sweet shop

- ☛ 96 South Road UB1 1RB
- ☎ 0208 574 8594
- ⏱ Tu-Su 9.30-19.00, M closed
- ⊖ Southall BR
- ➤ facebook.com/barfico

Good range of Indian sweets and savouries, some vegan.

Mor Foods
South Asian supermarket

- ☛ 100 South Road UB1 1RB
- ☎ 020 8571 3661
- ⏱ M-Sa 07.30-20.00, Su 12.00-18.00
- ⊖ Southall BR
- ➤ morfoods.co.uk

Established since 1989 this supermarket is full of local and exotic fruits and veggies. They do fruit baskets and gift wrapping too.

Lots of South Asian groceries including lentils, beans, grains, dried fruit, nuts, flours, spices, and the colours are just fantastic.

Also at 266 Yeading Lane, Hayes UB4 9AX.

Quality Foods
Grocery superstore

- ☛ 47-61 South Road UB1 1SQ
- ☎ 020 8917 9177
- ⏱ M-Sa 08.00-19.30, Su 12.00-18.00
- ⊖ Southall BR
- ➤ quality-foods.co.uk

A local vegan tells us they sell a great range of vegan groceries, including many Indian snacks, some ready made curries labelled vegan, Nature's Choice cereals, tofu, plant milks, some frozen savouries and Sri Lankan frozen deserts. Not to mention all the nuts, seeds, rice, flours, lentils, Asian vegetables, fruit, jackfruit both fresh and tinned, soya chunks and mince.

Definitely worth a visit! They are expanding their organic range too.

Holland & Barrett, Southall
Health food shop

- ☛ 34 The Broadway UB1 1PT
- ☎ 020 8571 1225
- ⏱ M-Sa 09.00-20.00, Su 11.00-20.00
- ⊖ Southall BR

Fridge with Violife, Cheezly, Tofurky, VegiDeli, Provamel, Pudology and Chia Pods. Freezer with Fry's, Clive's pies, VegiDeli and Booja Booja.

The Green Bottle Cafe
Vegetarian cafe

- 37 Crown Road, St Margarets TW1 3EJ
- 020 3632 0248
- M-F 07.00-17.00, Sa-Su 08.00-17.00, hours may vary
- St Margarets BR
- greenbottlecafe.com
  facebook.com/greenbottlecafe

Finally Twickenham has a vegetarian venue, opened April 2019 by Mehr Kosravi, with the green ribbon cut by local MP and Lib Dem leader Sir Vince Cable!

Breakfast include organic gluten-free porridge £4.50 with berries, banana and toasted almonds; full cooked £8.25 with vegan scrambled eggs, two sausages, sautéed wild mushrooms, grilled cherry tomatoes; guacamole / sliced avocado on sourdough rye bread £4.50.

Hot dishes £9.95 include spinach lasagna, or stuffed peppers with wild rice and veg. Dishes come with two sides.

Mix of 4 salads £5.95, 5 £6.96, 6 £7.95.

Falafel and hummus wrap. Salads include mixed bean and paprika; chickpeas with artichoke and mixed peppers; beetroot and pickled onion; baby potato and cauliflower; Heritage tomato; and several more.

Vegan sausage roll £2.

If you're wondering if it's worth visiting from other areas, then consider the awesome cakes! Vegan cakes and muffins £2.25-£3 nclude carrot, banana vanilla loaf, orange carob loaf, raw blueberry and lemon, raw nutty choc bar with coconut, raw tiramisu, raw choc raspberry.

Juices and smoothies £2.99-£5.50, such as Mr Peanut with peanut butter, banana, cacao nibs, dates, almond milk.

Teas, coffees, mocha, hot choc, special lattes with matcha, turmeric, charcoal, chai, cacao, £2-£3.90. They have MCT and CBD oil.

Children welcome, high chairs, baby changing. Dogs welcome. Outdoor seating.

Vegan banana vanilla loaf

Vegan carrot cake

Vegan sausage roll

BREAKFAST

Organically Foodspot, Teddington
Vegetarian organic cafe

- 97 High Street **Teddington** HA5 5PW
- (020 8977 0421
- M-Sa 9.00-18.00, Su 10.00-17.00
- Teddington
- organically.uk.com
  facebook.com/OrganicallyFoodSpot
  instagram.com/organicallyfoodspot/

Coffee specialists with almond, coconut, oat or soya milk.

Breakfasts such as granola bowl and lunches.

Panini, toasties, sandwiches, wraps such as falafel and hummus in flatbread, salads.

Vegan cakes such as chocolate or apricot and almond. Smoothies.

Also in Pinner.

Village Pizza
Omnivorous Italian restaurant

- 49 London Rd, Twickenham TW1 3SZ
- 020 8891 2345
- Su-Tu 11.00-01.30, W 11.00-02.00, Th-F 11.00-03.00, Sa 11.00-03.30
- Twickenham
- villagepizzauk.com

Separate vegan menu on the website or Just-Eat of pizzas made with vegan style chicken, tika or Mexican chicken, pepperoni, garlic sausage, spicy kidney beans.

Also wedges, Kentucky or Cajun or Tikka nuggets, olives, salads, filled baked potato scoops, dips.

Vegan chocolate and coconut tart, blackcurrant slice. Ben & Jerry's vegan ice cream.

Also in the area: Pizza Express at 21 York Street, Twickenham TW1 3JZ and 11 Waldegrave Road, Teddington TW11 8LA; **Zizzi** at 36 York Street, Twickenham TW1 3LJ. Or head east across the river to Richmond (South London) for more vegan and vegetarian cafes and Wagamama, or north-west to Hounslow for Indian food.

Gaia Wholefoods
Wholefood shop

- 123 St Margarets Rd, Twickenham TW1 2LH
- 020 9892 2262
- M-F 9.30-19.00, Sa 9.30-17.00, Su closed
- St Margarets BR (next door)
- gaiawholefoods.co.uk

Wholefood shop opened 1983 by the current owners Dave Kennington and Doe Murray, influenced by macrobiotics and raw guru Ann Wigmore. 60% organic.

Organic fruit and vegetables, Japanese macrobiotics, organic bread, gluten-free products. Some vegan take-aways such as pastries. Dried herbs.

Also bodycare. Eco cleaning products. Vitamins. Herbal tinctures, flower remedies, homeopathy, aromatherapy.

Holland & Barrett, Twickenham
Health food shop

- 13 King St, Twickenham TW1 3SD
- 020-8891 6696
- M-Sa 09.00-17.30, Su 10.30-16.30
- Twickenham BR

Fridge and freezer.

- 63 Broad St, Teddington TW11 8QZ
- 020 8977 7470
- M-Sa 09.00-17.30, Su 10.00-16.00
- Teddington BR

Fridge and freezer.

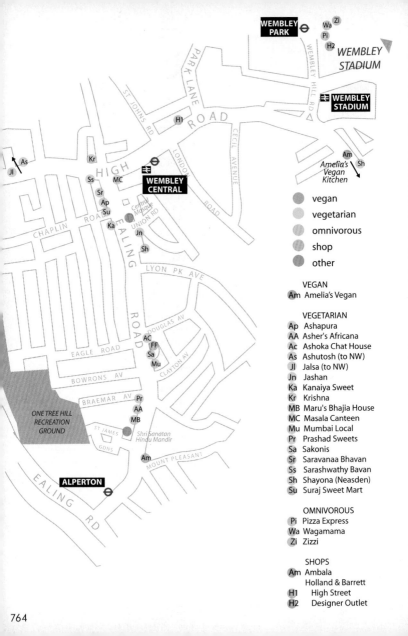

WEMBLEY PARK

Wa Zi
Pi
H2

WEMBLEY STADIUM

WEMBLEY STADIUM

Amelia's Vegan Kitchen

Am
Sh

WEMBLEY CENTRAL

Kr
Ss
MC
Sr
Ap
Su
Ka
Jn
Sh

ONE TREE HILL RECREATION GROUND

AC
FF
Sa
Mu

Pr
AA
MB

Shri Sanatan Hindu Mandir

Am

ALPERTON

Central Masjid

- vegan
- vegetarian
- omnivorous
- shop
- other

VEGAN
Am Amelia's Vegan

VEGETARIAN
Ap Ashapura
AA Asher's Africana
Ac Ashoka Chat House
As Ashutosh (to NW)
Jl Jalsa (to NW)
Jn Jashan
Ka Kanaiya Sweet
Kr Krishna
MB Maru's Bhajia House
MC Masala Canteen
Mu Mumbai Local
Pr Prashad Sweets
Sa Sakonis
Sr Saravanaa Bhavan
Ss Sarashwathy Bavan
Sh Shayona (Neasden)
Su Suraj Sweet Mart

OMNIVOROUS
Pi Pizza Express
Wa Wagamama
Zi Zizzi

SHOPS
Am Ambala
     Holland & Barrett
H1 High Street
H2 Designer Outlet

764

Wembley is home to a large Indian community and you won't be disappointed by the huge selection of authentic food available here, whether you come for the Sunday market, a concert, conference, or to support your team in the final at Wembley Stadium.

Near the stadium and market, there are vegan options at Pizza Express, Wagamama and Zizzi. But for a street full of completely vegetarian restaurants head down Wembley High Road to **Ealing Road**, which has veggie zones at the north and south ends. There are stacks of Gujarati and other Indian vegetarian restaurants, many with Chinese and East African dishes too. Huge competition ensures that menus are packed with gastronomic sensations and prices are great value.

Long established favourites are **Sakonis, Saravanaa Bhavan, Sarashwathy Bavans, Jashan, Asher's Africana** and **Maru's**.

Newer places include **Krishna, Masala Canteen** and **Mumbai Local**.

All Indian restaurants welcome children

For cheap food to eat at home or work, head for the Indian take-aways and sweet shops. You can pick up a fast lunch on the run or crunchy snacks at **Ashapura, Ashoka Chat House, Kanaiya Sweet, Prashad Sweets** or **Suraj Sweet Mart**.

If you're all curried out, head east (off the map) to Tokyngton to take-away **Amelia's Vegan Kitchen** for vegan fast food and wholefood dishes. Or have them delivered. Further on in Neasden is **Shayona** vegetarian restaurant at the Swaminarayan Mandir.

Also off the map to the north-west, in North Wembley and Sudbury, are **Ashutosh** restaurant and **Jalsa** take-away.

On the High Road **Holland & Barrett** health food shop has a few take-away items in the fridge.

Amelia's VK burger

Ashoka

Amelia's Vegan Kitchen
Vegan take-away

🖝 in Monks Park Health Centre, 2
Monks Park, Tokyngton HA9 6JE
(opposite Grittleton Avenue)

(020 3002 0577
0790 388 9411 VK

🕑 M-Su 11.00-23.00

⊖ Stonebridge Park

🏹 ameliasvegan-kitchen.co.uk
facebook.com/ameliasvegankitchen
facebook.com/vkburgers

Vegan caterer. Smoothies £4 and £6.
Starters £3.50 such as fried pak choi,
calallo and lentils in coconut dumplings,
sweet potato salad, avocado mash with bell
peppers and olives, chickpeas or mushroom
wrap, avo salad, falafel balls.

Breakfast £3.50 small, £4.50 large, such
as regular, cornmeal or peanut butter
porridge made with oat or coconut milk.

Mains £5.50 small, £7 large, include
butterbean and quinoa soup; lentils quinoa
with chickpeas and spinach; butterbean and
kale gluten-free pasta with vegan;
mushroom stir-fry; vegetable soup with
coconut milk and blackeye peas; specials
such as okra or chickpeas and kale stew;
callaloo and green banana with pumpkin;
falafel pie and sweet mash with peas;
chickpea coconut curry with rice or quinoal;
basghetti - mushroom and beansprout or
butterbean and pak choi spaghetti ball. Side
dishes £3.

Desserts £2.99.

They also run VK Vegan King burgers on
Deliveroo and Just Eat. Massive range of
burgers, dogs and falafels £5.50-£8. Sweet
fries £1.99-£2.99. Salads. Kids' meals.
Drinks.

Ashapura
Vegetarian Indian take-away

- ☛ 42 Ealing Road HA0 4TL
- ☎ 020 8902 9900
- 🕐 M-Su 9.00-20.00
- ⊖ Wembley Central

New sweets and savouries shop opened October 2012. They have a bar table along one wall where you can eat standing.

Samosas and spring rolls 3 for £1.10. Chilli bhajia 2 for £1. Chapatis, methi goda, medu vada, kachori 3 for £1.

Daily thali £3 with 2 curries, dahl, rice and 3 chapati. Vegetable curry box small £1, medium £1.70, large £2.20.

Hot drinks 70p. All the sweets have ghee.

Asher's Africana
Gujarati and South Indian restaurant

- ☛ 224 Ealing Road HA0 4QL
- ☎ 020 8795 2455
- 🕐 M-Su 12.00-22.00
- ⊖ Wembley Central

You know it's good when it's full of Indian people! A relaxed place decorated with pictures of Hindi gods.

20 starters £2-£2.50. Thalis £5.50-£7.50. Curries £3.50 with rice, roti or paratha. masala dosa £4. Chips £2. Poppadoms 30p.

Desserts £2-3. Carrot juice £2, orange juice £1. No alcohol.

Also take-away frozen samosas, spring rolls etc. in packs of 5 or 10.

Ashoka Chat House
Vegetarian Indian take-away

- ☛ 105A Ealing Road HA0 4BP (at front of Muzik Zone Asian music store)
- ☎ 020 8795 1266 (boss's number)
- 🕐 M-Su 10.00-21.00

Amazing value. Dosas £2. Uttapam £2.50. Lots of chaat £3. Pani puri big box £3 and 7 pieces £7. Also some Chinese dishes £3-£5. Outside covered seating.

Jashan
Vegetarian Gujarati Indian restaurant

- ☛ 1-2 Coronet Parade, Ealing Road HA0 4AY (corner of Union Road)
- ☎ 020 8900 9800
- 🕐 Su-Th 12.00-22.30, F-Sa 12.00-23.00
- ⊖ Wembley Central
- ➤ jashanvegetarian.co.uk

Huge menu of North and South Indian and Chinese dishes for around £3-£7.99.

South Indian dishes include idli and medu wada £4.25, uttapam £3.99. They have a dosas "corner" all served with sambhar, (lentil and tamarind thin soup) and coconut chutney, £3.50-7.50. A long list of curry dishes £5.50-£6.99.

Around 19 Indo-Chinese dishes £3.50-8.50 such as Szechuan hakka noodles, Nanking fried rice, veg balls in hot garlic sauce.

Many cold drinks such as fresh lime juice with soda water £1-£2.50. Tea and coffee £2, hot chocolate £2.25. No alcohol.

Children welcome, high chairs. Minimum card payment £10.

Kanaiya Sweet
Gujarati Indian vegetarian sweets & savoury take-away

- 📍 50b Ealing Road HA0 4TQ
- ☎ 020 8902 8008
- 🕐 M-Su 09.00-20.30
- ⊖ Wembley Central, Alperton
- ⬈ Facebook Kanaiya Sweets

Gujarati vegetarian sweets and savoury take-away with bar table with stools. Everything made on the premises.

Lunch box with curry, dahl and rice for £1 small, £1.50 medium and £2 large. Tiffin £3.50 with 2 curries, rice, dahl and 4 roti. Aloo chana chat rice, potato, chickpea, onion and chilli and bhel puri (roti, chickpea, fresh chilli and coriander) £2.50.

Savoury: 4 onion bahji £1, 2 spring rolls £2, 4 soya samosa £4, 3 methi thepla (wheat, fenugreek, sesame and basil) £1, 5 roti £1, bajra rotla (pearl millet flour bread) £1.

Snacks mostly vegan £2 per pack. They have a couple of vegan sweets.

Soft drinks 50-60p, tea and coffee 50p.

Children welcome. Minimum card £10. Outside catering.

Krishna
Vegetarian Indian café

- 📍 590 High Road HA0 2AF
- ☎ 020 8903 9672
- 🕐 M-F 11.00-15.00, 18.00-23.00; Sa-Su 11.00-23.00
- ⊖ Wembley Central

New restaurant almost opposite the top of Ealing Road. Punjabi, South Indian, Gujarati/Kathiyawadi and Indo-Chinese dishes. Gujarati thalis £10-£11.50. Lunch thali Mon-Fri £8. Vegetable biryani £6.99. Deliveroo.

Maru's Bhajia House
Vegetarian Indian café

- 📍 230 Ealing Road HA0 4QL
- ☎ 020 8903 6771, 8902 5570
- 🕐 M-Th 12.30-20.30, F-Su 12.30-21.30
- ⊖ Alperton, Wembley Central
- ⬈ marubhajia.com

Ealing Road has a number of inexpensive Gujarati and south Indian restaurants. Maru's Kenyan Asian cuisine has been a firm favourite since 1976 with bhajias of course, samosas, maize and assorted snacks. Before that the family had a restaurant in East Africa from 1949 to 1972.

The Maru bhajia, single portion £5 and double portion £9.60, has always been the main item on the menu, made from potato slices mixed with gram (chickpea) flour fried with spices, with their special tamarind sauce.

Asian film stars fill up here on pani puri, kachori and vada, £4.10 for a portion.

Juices £2.20-£3.90 include fruit juice cocktail, passion fruit , mango or pineapple. Soft drinks £1.20. Tea and coffee £1.50. No alcohol.

This is a café with seating for 30 people and gets very busy. Children welcome, high chair. £10 minimum card payment.

Masala Canteen
Vegetarian North & South Indian restaurant

- 529 High Road HA0 2DN (corner Ealing Rd)
- 020 8702 2222
- M-Su 11.00-23.00
- Wembley Centrall
- masalacanteen.co.uk

Opened March 2018, by the people who previously owned Kailash Parbat around the corner. It's quite upmarket looking inside. Dishes containing dairy are marked, which appears to include all the curries, naan, and Indian rice other than steamed basmati, plus all the desserts.

Street food £3.95-£5.45 such as bambaiya pani puri fried puff pastry balls filled with spiced mashed potato, served with spiced mint water and tamarind juice. Also sev batata puri, Bombay bhel puri.

Mumbai street classics £4.95-£7.45 such as chole bhaturas fried Indian bread with chole masala chickpeas curry and onions. Bombay vada pav burger in a bun.

South Indian specials £3.45-£5.95 include idli rice and lentil cakes, medu vada fried lentil doughnuts, dosas, uthappam lentil and rice thick pancake.

Masala Canteen

Sweet corn or Manchow soup £4.45. Indo-Chinese mains £5.45-£7.95 include Veg Manchurian deep fried balls in soy, tomato and chilli sauce; fried rice; Hakka noodles stir-fried with veggies.

Weekday lunch thali £7.99.

Passion fruit juice, Indian lemonades £3.45. Cans £1.25. South Indian filter coffee £2.45.

Catering. Delivery. Children welcome.

Sakonis

Mumbai Local, Wembley
Vegetarian Indian restaurant

- 141 Ealing Road HA0 4BP
- 020 8903 5577
- M-Su 11.30-21.00 (last order)
- Wembley Central, Alperton
- mumbailocal.co.uk

Fresh look and decor at this authentic place which has a big open kitchen.

Thali changes daily, £9.95 M-F, weekend and bank holiday £12.95, with two curries, dal, rice, chapatis, a fried favourite such as pakora, pickles, salad, popadums.

Chaat and starters £1.50-£5.95 such as dabeli, masala pav, bhajia or samosa in pav, Chinese bhel crispy noodles, bhajias, samosas, spring rolls. Sandwiches and toasties £3.50-£4.95 such as peanut butter, masala potato dabeli with peanuts and pomegranate.

South indian dishes £3.75-£4.75 such as dosa, uttapam, medu vada and idli. Curries £5.95-£7.95. Rice £3.50-£5.95.

Indo-Chinese dishes £5.95-£7.95 such as chilli or stir-fry tofu with veg, noodles with veg.

Finger sliced potato deep fried chips £2.75-£4.95 such as with chilli sauce, or garlic and pepper.

Passion fruit juice £3.75, jug £14.95. Freshly juiced orange, pineapple, watermelon, carrot £3.75. Coffee £1.75.

High chairs. Wifi. 10% service charge. No minimum spend. Deliveries 12.00-20.30 to HA0, HA9, UB6. Deliveroo. Also in Harrow and Rayners Lane

Prashad Sweets
Vegetarian sweet and savoury take away

- 222 Ealing Road HA0 4QL
- 020 8795 1734, 8902 1704
- M-F 10.00-21.00, Sa-Su 09.00-21.00
- Wembley Central, Alperton

Very busy place. Their hot counter has 15 different dishes: curries, rice, dahl, vegetable biriyani and so on, £1 for a small box and £1.50 for a large one. Bhajia and chips £2.25-£2.75; rice £2-£2.50; Chinese dishes £2.50-£2.75. £1.50 for puri, samosa, kachori and pav; 4 roti or chapati for £1.20 or 35p each Their snacks are £1.75-£2.50. Cash only. Also private events.

Sakonis
Vegetarian Indian restaurant & take-away

- 127-129 Ealing Road HA0 4BP
- 020 8903-9601 / 1058
- Breakfast Sa-Su 09.00-11.00, M-Th 12.00-22.00, F-Su 12.30-22.00
- Wembley Central, Alperton
- sakonis.co.uk
  facebook.com/SakonisUK

Vegetarian Indian snack bar, take-away and big restaurant, with an extensive menu of over 100 Gujarati, North Indian and Chinese dishes. Outdoor tables. Everything on the buffet and on the menu with dairy is clearly labelled.

Sat-Sun and bank holidays 9.00-11.00a.m. buffet south Indian breakfast £6, includes idli, masala dosa, puri, potato curry etc.

Every day buffet eat as much as you like, lunch £11.99 from 12.00 to 16.00, evenings £14.99 from 18.30 (weekends 17.00) to 21.00, children 3-10 half price, under-3 free. Choose from over 30 items from starters to desserts.

A la carte starters and bites £3.25-£6.30 such as sev puri, pani puri, bhel puri, Punjabi samosa, kachori, potato vada, methi gota (chickpea flour and fenugreek, garnished with sesame seeds, coriander, and green chilli served with coriander chutney), khandvi, khichi (rice flour steamed with spices), ferrai cutlet.

Main dishes £5.75-£7.50 such as plain or masala or chutney or Mysore or pav baji dosa, uttapam, puri bhaji, idli, curry, dal of the day. Chinese dishes, £4.99-£7.50 prepared Indian style include chilli tofu in tangy Chinese sauce, hakka noodles tossed with vegetables, mixed Szechuan vegetables noodles in sweet and sour sauce, chow mein noodles, vegetable balls.

All chips and mogo £2-£6.25 in different styles such as garlic chilli, spicy Szechuan, chilli and lemon etc. Extras £1.95-£3.99 puri, plain or chilli and garlic naan, green salad and papad.

Gulab jamun 3 vegan doughnuts with sweet syrup £3.50 and paan £1.

Juices £3.50 such as green, passion or red, fresh coconut water. Soft drinks £1.80. Tea and coffee £1.99.

Most items can be prepared hot, medium, mild, or without onion or garlic. Take-away Indian sweet shop too. Also in Harrow at 5/8 Dominion Parade, Station Road HA1 2T, and Hayes at 1-3 Uxbridge Road UB4 0JN.

At the entrance there is a juice bar and take-away food. High chairs. Wifi. Card minimum spending £5.

Sarashwathy Bavans
Vegetarian South Indian & Sri Lankan restaurant and caterer

- 549 High Road HA0 2DJ
- 020 8902 1515, 07748 636 264
- M-Su 11.00-24.00
- Wembley Park
- sarashwathy.com

Amazing value and with a huge menu. The chefs are from Chennai and if you've been to India you will recognise how authentic it is right down to the stainless steel thali dishes and complimentary tumblers of water. Very bright inside and lots of Indian diners.

Top value are the Madras thali £7.95 with 15 items and Punjab thali £8.95 with 12 items. Business lunch Mon-Thursday mini thali £4.50.

A la carte starters 75p-£5.75. 25 dosas £3.95-£4.95 or £19.95 for a 6-foot family dosa. Lots of uttapam £3.25-£5.95, the special one has onion, chilli, tomato, capsicum, corn, pineapple, coriander and mushroom. Curries £1.75-£4.95. Sri Lankan kottu roti £4.95. Five Indo-Chinese dishes £4.95-£5.50 such as garlic gobi Manchurian, special noodles, mushroom Manchurian gravy. Rice from £1.95 up to £5.50 for a special biryani. Main dishes £2.95-£5.50.

On the separate dessert menu everything contains milk, but from the main menu vegans can have fruit salad.

Fresh juices £1.95-£2.95. Soft drinks £1.25-£1.50. Tea and coffee £1-£1.50.

Children welcome. High chairs. £10 minimum charge on cards. Free delivery within 3 miles, minimum £25 cash only. Mobile catering for 50+ people £6.50 per person plus set up fee £50. Their mobile outside catering dosa unit will make fresh dosas, idli, vadai etc at your home or garden.

Saravanaa Bhavan Wembley
Vegetarian South Indian restaurant

- 22 & 22A Ealing Road HA0 4TL
- 020 8900 8526
- M-Su 10.00-22.00
- Wembley Central
- saravanabhavan.co.uk
  facebook.com/saravanaawembley

Restaurant with a sweet shop at the front, though all sweets are made with butter. Part of a UK and international chain, with branches in East Ham, Harrow, Ilford, Southall, Croydon and Tooting. Lots of Chinese dishes.

Restaurant with a sweet all made with butter, shop at the front, part of a UK and international chain, with branches in East Ham, Harrow, Ilford, Southall, Croydon and Tooting. Lots of Chinese dishes.

Starters £3.45-£5.75 include chilli mushrooms; and spring rolls. Main courses include of course dosas £3.95 to £5.95 for a tailor-made one with your choice of three fillings. Uttapam £4.75-£5.25. Curry £5.45-£5.75. Chinese mains £5.45-£6.25.

Juices £3.50. Soft drinks £1.50-£2. Tea or coffee £1.75-£2.25. No alcohol and you can't bring it in. Children welcome, high chairs.

Suraj Sweet Mart
Vegetarian Indian sweet shop

- 🍴 44a Ealing Road HA0 4TL (corner of Chaplin Road)
- ☎ 020 8900 1339
- 🕐 M-Su 9.00-19.00
- ⊖ Wembley Central
- ↖ Facebook Suraj Sweet Mart

Very busy little place with a long table by the window but no seats.

On the counter curry and rice small £1.25, medium £1.50 , large £2.50. Biryani and curry small £1.25, medium £1.75, large £2.50. Vegetable curry small £1.25, medium £2, large £3.75.

Snacks such as samosas, bhajias, veg cutlets. 3 small samosas £1. Dry snacks mostly vegan, some of them are salt-free. Other items sold by weight. Soft drinks 65p.

Pizza Express, Wembley
Italian restaurant

- 🍴 London Designer Outlet, Empire Way, Wembley HA9 0FD
- ☎ 020 8795 4910
- 🕐 M-Su 11.30-22.30
- ⊖ Wembley Stadium BR
- ↖ pizzaexpress.com

Handy for Wemley Stadium and Wembley Arena. Garden dining. Baby facilities. Disabled toilet. Wifi.

Also nearby are Zizzi and Wagamama.

Sarashwathy Bavans

Ambala

Ashutosh

Shayona

Ambala
Indian sweet shop

- 6 Glenmore Parade, off Ealing Rd, HA0 4BP
- 020 020 8903 9740
- M-Su 09.00-21.00
- Alperton

Indian sweets and savouries. Same items as at Drummond Street (Euston, Central London).

Holland & Barrett
Health food shop

- 488 High Street, Wembley HA9 7BH
- 020 8903 7802
- M-Sa 9.00-18.00, Su 11.00-17.00
- Wembley Central,

Fridge and freezer.

- Unit 51, London Designer Outlet, Wembley Park Boulevard HA9 0FD
- 020 3774 2686
- M-Sa 10.00-20.00, Su 11.00-17.00
- Wembley Stadium,

Fridge and freezer.

NORTH WEMBLEY & SUDBURY

Ashutosh
Indian fusion vegetarian restaurant

- 205 Watford Road HA1 3UA (at Sudbury Court Drive)
- 020 3535 7555, 020 8908 0893
- M-Tu 18.30-21.30; W closed; Th, Su 18.00-22.00, F-Sa 18.00-22.30
- South Kenton
- ashutoshcatering.com
  facebook.com/
  ashutoshvegetarianrestaurant

Lovely restaurant to the north-west of Wembley Central, seating up to 50 guests. Lots of vegan Indian and Guarati items.

As well as South Indian, Punjabi and Gujarati dishes, there are Indo-Mexican dishes such as tacos, Indo-Italian andIndo-Chinese

Tiffin take-away. Can open lunchtime for group and party bookings.

Uber Eats. Wedding and corporate catering.

Jalsa
Vegetarian Indian take-away & shop

- 28 Watford Rd (south end) HA0 3EP
- 020 8908 4148
- M closed, Tu-Th 10.00-19.00, F 10.00-19.00, Sa 09.00-19.00, Su 09.00-18.00
- Sudbury & Harrow Road BR
- jalsafoods.com
  facebook.com/Jalsafood

Fast food snacks £2 such as mung dal or pea kachori, samosa, potato wada. Chaat £3 such as pani or bhel or sev puri

One table and two chairs. Huge catering menu for events such as vegan birthday parties, even Lebansese dishes such as falafel, hummus, baba ghanoush.

NEASDEN TEMPLE

Shayona
Vegetarian Indian restaurant

- 54-62 Meadow Garth Neasden NW10 8HD
- 020 8965 3365
- M-F 12.00-22.00, Sa 11.00-22.00 (last order 21.30
- Neasden
- shayonarestaurants.com

Beautiful restaurant with bright colours, vibrant wall paintings, chandeliers and Indian artefacts, in the grounds of the huge Swaminarayan Mandir temple. Gujarati thalis, Mumbai street food, Punjabi curries, South Indian dosas and uttapam, and East African dishes like masala mojo. Food is saatvic, without onion and garlic. Two car parks.

A la carte and thali buffet M-F till 4pm Starters £3.45-£7.50, or have a mixed platter for £5.95 or £6.95. Dosas and uttapam £5.95-£7.45. Evenings and all weekend there is a bigger menu with the same starters, dosas £7.45, curries £6.45-£7.45, biryani, Indian breads and rice.

Soft drinks £3.50 or litre jug £8.75, litre jug of juice £9.50, cans £2, coffee and tea £2.25.

Lounge with projector and separate entrance for events, corporate meetings and celebrations.

MIDDLESEX

Eastcote, Greenford, Ruislip, Uxbridge

Crispy Dosa, Greenford

Vegetarian South Indian restaurant & take-away

- 1280 Greenford Rd UB6 0HH (near Horsenden Lane N)
- 020 8869 0111
- M closed, Tu-F. Su 11.00-23.00, Sa 14.00-23.00
- Sudbury Hill, Greenford
- crispydosavegetarianrestaurant.co.uk

Good old-fashioned sit-down meals, and free home delivery. Just Eat.

Village Pizza, Eastcote

Omnivorous Italian restaurant

- 214 Field End Road, Eastcote HA5 1RD
- 020 8426 2026
- M-Th, Sa 11.00-02.00; F, Su 11.00-03.00
- Eastcote
- villagepizzauk.com
  villagepizzaeastcote.co.uk (Just Eat)

Separate vegan menu on the website or Just-Eat of pizzas made with vegan style chicken, tikka or Mexican chicken, pepperoni, garlic sausage, spicy kidney beans.

Revital Health Centre, Ruislip

Health food shop

- 78 High Street, Ruislip HA4 7AA (near Ickenham Rd)
- 01895 630869
- M-Sa 9.00-17.30, Su 11.00-16.00
- Ruislip
- revital.co.uk

Health foods. Bodycare and natural beauty including Dr Hauschka. Mother and baby products. Supplements. Herbal and ayurvedic. Healthnotes touch-screen information kiosk

You can book a free appointment with their nutritionist. Professional treatments include aromatherapy, Indian head massage, Reiki, kinesiology or facial rejuvenation. To book call 01895-833045 or 07702 322699.

.

Other branches: Chelsea, Hampstead, Putney, Richmond, Willesden, Wigmore Street.

Holland & Barrett, Eastcote
Health food shop

- 151 Field End Road, Eastcote HA5 1QL
- 020 8866 0919
- M-Sa 09.00-18.30, Su 10.30-16.30
- Eastcote

No fridge or freezer.

Holland & Barrett, Greenford
Health food shop

- 24 The Broadway UB6 9PT
- 020 3275 1011
- M-Sa 08.00-18.30, Su 10.00-18.00
- Greenford

Fridge and freezer.

Holland & Barrett, Ruislip
Health food shop

- 93 High Street, Ruislip HA4 8JB
- 01895 713701
- M-Sa 9.00-18.00, Su 10.30-16.30
- Ruislip

Fridge and freezer with take-away pasties etc.

Holland & Barrett, Uxbridge
Health food shop

- 17-19 Pantile Walk, The Pavillions shopping centre, Uxbridge UB8 1LT
- 01895 237841
- M-Sa 9.00-18.00, Su 10.30-16.30
- Uxbridge

Fridge and freezer.

- 205 Intu Uxbridge, The Chimes Shopping Centre, High Street, Uxbridge UB8 1GB
- 01895 713629
- M-Sa 9.30-19.00 (Th 20.00), Su 11.00-17.00
- Uxbridge

Fridge and freezer.

VEGAN WEST LONDON © Copyright

1st edition by Alex Bourke
EAN 978-1-902259-19-2
Published January 2020
by Vegetarian Guides Ltd
www.veganlondon.guide

2 Hilborough Court, Livermere Road, London E8 4LG, UK
Tel: 020-3239 8433 (24 hrs)
International: +44-20-3239 8433

Distributed in UK by Bertrams, Gardners, Marigold
In USA/Canada by Book Publishing Company, TN. www.bookpubco.com
Updates to this guide at: vegetarianguides.co.uk/updates
Link and earn 10% commisssion: vegetarianguides.co.uk/affiliate

In the same series:
VEGAN CENTRAL LONDON
VEGAN EAST LONDON
VEGAN NORTH LONDON
VEGAN SOUTH LONDON
VEGAN LONDON comprehensive edition

Printed by Buxton Press, England

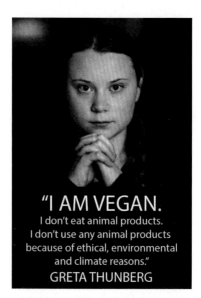

"I AM VEGAN.
I don't eat animal products.
I don't use any animal products
because of ethical, environmental
and climate reasons."
GRETA THUNBERG

THE KNOWLEDGE

Accommodation

Alcoholic Drinks

Eating Out With Your Dog

Festivals

Going Vegan

Health Practitioners

Local Groups

Pet Food

Shoes & Clothing

P.S. Vegan London Loves...

ACCOMMODATION

Vegan house shares

Facebook London Vegan Flatshares

Facebook Vegan Room Rent London

vegcom.org.uk

Short term accommodation

vegvisits.com

lsevacations.co.uk

Hotels

My Chelsea boutique hotel in Chelsea, Sloane Zone (West London) has a vegan raw food restaurant Tanya's

myhotels.com/my-hotel-chelsea

Temple Lodge is a vegetarian hotel in Hammersmith, West London, see the entry there. It is in the same building as The Gate vegetarian restaurant. It's handy for the M4 motorway and Heathrow airport.

templelodgeclub.com

La Suite West boutique hotel in Bayswater, West London, is on the north side of Hyde Park. It has an in-house vegan restaurant, Cafe Forty One.

lasuitewest.com

Hostels

The Birds pub in Leytonstone, at the end of East London, offers vegan food and has a hostel upstairs.

thebirds.pub

The Bird's Nest pub in Deptford, South London, has vegan food, and upstairs is a Japanese-style capsule hostel.

thebirdsnestpub.co.uk

Vegan London Where To Stay

Directory of accommodation offering vegan food, or run by vegans or vegetarians. Includes links to vegan owned Airbnb places in London.

veganlondon.co.uk/where-to-stay.html

ALCOHOLIC DRINKS

Alcoholic drinks are almost always made with entirely vegan ingredients, with the exception of Irish Cream liqueurs which contain actual cream, and Advocaat, which contains egg yolk. However, the way in which many of them are cleared of sediment (fined) can involve animal products like isinglass, egg shells, egg white, blood and gelatine. So if you're strict about your vegan lifestyle, you may want to avoid buying from breweries and wine producers that do this, and instead choose un-fined drinks, or support more modern, animal-free methods.

Spirits

Whisky and **brandy** are always totally vegan, as are almost all lagers and cloudy ciders. Wine and beer are the drinks most likely to be made using animal products.

Wine

It's a closely-guarded industry secret that a bottle of **wine** can contain all kinds of nasties. Grapes are a delicate fruit, and an arsenal of toxic chemicals is employed to blast the voracious bugs and fungi that infest them. There are over 50 pesticides in use by the wine industry, which puts vineyard workers, our environment, and you, the drinker, at risk. However, the good news is that there's an increasing demand for organic wine, and it is now easy to find in off-licences, supermarkets and other shops.

Although gelatine is less often used as a 'fining' (clarifying) agent, the fish extract isinglass is still added to many wines, regardless of whether they're organic, and it's very unlikely to be listed on the label. Many vegetarian wines are cleared with

beaten egg white. Organic producers can use the eggs of free-range organic chickens.

So if you want to be sure that your wine is both free from toxic chemicals and cleared with clay rather than animal products, you can get it from a health food shop, a large supermarket, or a specific vegetarian wine supplier. It used to be very difficult to find vegan wines in supermarkets, though this has changed dramatically in recent years, with almost all own-brand bottles and quite a few other brands having allergy warnings and vegan status listed in small print on the back label. A quick browse is all that's needed.

Beer and Cider

Beer and **cider** production, like wine, often involves animal products in the fining (clearing) process to help remove impurities and improve the appearance of the final product. EU and UK legislation does not require brewers to list ingredients in any drinks with an alcoholic content of more than 1.2% volume - so usually you don't know by the label if it is vegetarian or vegan. Fortunately, many cask and keg beers and ciders are animal-free and use either bentonite (a type of clay) or pea extract, or are left longer to settle. Unlike wines, popular beers and ciders are generally branded clearly and it is nearly always possible to find some in a pub or supermarket.

Bottle-conditioned **real ales** are almost always vegan because they are not filtered. Yeast needs to be in the bottle in order for it to continue fermenting. The same applies to cloudy ciders. **Lagers** are brewed in a different way to beer, and are usually (though not always) chill-filtered.

As a general rule, most cask-conditioned ales on tap in pubs, and even some bottled ales, are fined with isinglass.

All **German beers** and lagers and most Dutch, Czech and Belgian ones are vegan, as are some British brands that are available in almost every supermarket, such as Badger and Shepherd Neame. We haven't included a longer list as it would go out of date soon after publication, however you can find a link to a more comprehensive list on the Vegetarian Guides website.

Pubs

The **Sam Smiths** pub chain sells a variety of beers from their own breweries at affordable prices, and 90% are certified with the Vegan Society, though there's no guarantee of vegan food on the menu. The **Brewdog** chain of pubs clearly label their vegan beers, and their branch in Dalston (East London) has only vegan beers and food.

For another 100% vegan pub including all drinks and food, and even the furniture, visit **The Spread Eagle** in Homerton, East London. Or **Karamel** in Wood Green, North London.

Many wholefood shops in this book sell wine. Chains that clearly label their vegan wines include Planet Organic and Co-op.

Online Vegan Booze Directory
barnivore.com

Vegan Alcohol Mail Order
vinceremos.co.uk
vintageroots.co.uk

MAZE COURIER SERVICES

Half delivery man, half personal assistant, our couriers are on hand to facilitate your vegan lifestyle any time of day or night

- LONG DISTANCE RESTAURANT TAKEAWAYS
- PERSONAL OR OUTSOURCED SHOPPING SERVICES
- REMOTE BUFFET / VIDEO-CALL SERVICE FROM ANY SHOP, RESTAURANT, MARKET OR OTHER LOCATION OF YOUR CHOICE
- RECOMMENDATIONS
- SOURCING ADVICE
- MISCELLANEOUS ERRAND SERVICES
- 24/7
- £7.00 PER DROP*

WhatsApp: **+44 7738 492 536**
FaceTime: **+44 7738 492 536**
Messenger: **m.me/maze1x7**
Skype: **Maze Courier Services**

* Plus the cost of any goods purchased on your behalf
* Within London zones 1 to 9
* Max load 21 kg.
* For this purpose a "drop" means an errand involving one collection point and one destination, but if any two collection or delivery points in a chain of errands are within walking distance, they'll be considered part of the same drop
* See website (www.mazecourierservices.com/services) for restrictions on certain types of goods

Maze Courier Services

86-90 Paul Street, London EC2A 4NE Tel: +447738 492 536 Email: maze_cs@icloud.com

TIPS

783

EATING OUT WITH YOUR DOG

Top vegan travel writer **Caitlin Galer-Unti** *and* **Benito**, *her poodle sidekick, present their favourite dog- and vegan-friendly spots in London.*

After a long stroll along the Thames riverside path or a muddy romp through Regent's Park with your dog by your side, nothing's better than sitting down for a well-deserved vegan pizza and a vegan beer, or a bowl of water in Fido's case. Fortunately, an increasing number of places in London are welcoming our dogs, especially vegetarian and vegan restaurants, though it's always worth calling ahead to check.

To help you out, Benito (my poodle sidekick) and I have put together a list of our favourite dog- and vegan-friendly spots in London.

PickyWops

Pizza and pups, what more could you want? Originally a tiny 100% vegan pizzeria in Fulham, Picky Wops has now relocated to be the in-house restaurant at vegan pub The Queen's Head in Brixton, south London, and welcomes dogs. The staff members are definite dog lovers, who welcome canines with open arms—literally! When Benito and I visited, I left Benito in the safe hands of a friend while I went to the toilet…when I came back the whole staff had gathered around, fussing over him and making sure he didn't miss me. In addition to veggies, non-dairy cheese and vegan meats, you can choose from a variety of different bases, from turmeric to burned wheat or kamut.

▸ pickywops.com

Copperhouse Chocolate

At this chocolate themed vegan cafe in Islington, north London, on many days you're more likely to see a dog than a human curled up in one of their armchairs. One neighbourhood dog even has an armchair he's more or less claimed as his own! They specialise in all things chocolate, from specialty hot chocolate made with cocoa beans which they grind onsite, to their sweet and savoury goods. You'll find that everything here includes chocolate, even avocado toast is topped with chilli flakes and cacao nibs! Alas this means none of the food is suitable for sharing with canines, but your dog will love sharing the sofa or an armchair.

▸ jazandjuls.co.uk

Essential Vegan Café

This Shoreditch, east London, café run by Brazilian chef Vanessa serves impressive cakes and is extremely dog-friendly. (I'm particularly enamoured with their white chocolate caramel cake. Vanessa is a dog lover and has her own dog, and so she goes to great lengths to make sure dogs are well-received. In addition to fussing over him, she even gave Benito a vegan sweet potato treat the day we came in, thus ensuring a lifelong friendship.

essentialvegan.uk

Mildreds

With branches in Soho (central London), Kings Cross (north), Camden (north) and Dalston (east), this trendy vegetarian eatery is also dog-friendly! Perfect if you want to grab a cocktail and one of Mildred's famous burgers in Soho but you don't want to leave your dog home alone. Just beware that the Soho branch is small and can get very crowded during peak times. Of course, staff vary by location, but generally the restaurants seem staffed by dog lovers, and Benito has received lots of strokes in every branch he's visited.

mildreds.co.uk

Wulf & Lamb

Another vegan restaurant with an owner who's a true dog lover, this Sloane Square vegan spot is a haven for Chelsea dogs. (See Sloane Zone, west London) There have been at least a few dogs in every time I've gone, and the owner often comes over to say hi to them. Choose from burgers, vegan mac & cheese and a big selection of vegan pastries.

wulfandlamb.com

Café Van Gogh

Moving south of the river, between Kennington and Brixton (near Oval station) Cafe Van Gogh (see Vauxhall, south London) is a non-profit vegan café. They not only make you and your dog feel welcome, but they go above and beyond! Last time we visited, Benito feasted on a whole carrot while our group ate our Sunday lunch. The menu changes frequently and usually includes seasonal ingredients.

cafevangogh.co.uk

Lele's

This bright vegan café in Lower Clapton, Hackney, east London, is dog friendly. Valentina the owner loves dogs and even named one of her brunch dishes after her own rescue dog ZZ (scrambled tofu on toast with grilled tomatoes and avocado).

leleslondon.com

Love Shack

This vegan, plastic-free café in Bethnal Green, east London is dog-friendly and boasts a beautiful fenced-in garden area complete with hammocks. Sometimes the resident dog even makes an appearance. The proprietors love dogs so much that they even run special discounts for those who escort their four-legged friends to the café! Grab a stack of vegan pancakes and a matcha latte and enjoy the canine-friendly ambience.

ᐟ loveshackldn.com

Take your dog out & about with you

Can't bear to leave your dog at home while you shop? Many of London's vegan markets are dog friendly such as Soho Vegan Market, along with London's vegan shops Vx, Green Bay, Harmless and Hetu. You can even get your hair cut at vegan salon The Rabbit Hole in West Kensington, west London, with your dog in tow!

London is a prime spot for dogs, with its many green spaces and an increasing number of dog-friendly restaurants. As a general rule, I've found most all-vegan restaurants are dog-friendly, but always

call and check first, and many vegetarian eateries are too. You'll also find plenty of independent coffee shops, pubs, farmers' markets, bookshops and charity shops welcome dogs with open arms.

If you're eager to take your four-legged pal along to a restaurant that's not listed here, phone ahead and ask if they're dog-friendly. I've also put together a dog- and vegan-friendly map of London for you! You can download my free map of more dog-friendly and vegan-friendly restaurants and cafes in London here:

ᐟ theveganword.com/dog-friendly-vegan-london-map

Caitlin Galer-Unti *is a vegan food and travel writer based in London and Barcelona, who blogs at theveganword.com. She has published two vegan travel guidebooks,* The Essential Vegan Travel Guide *which will help you plan your travels anywhere in the world, and* The Barcelona Vegan Guide, *available as paperback or ebook on Amazon. You can find her travel adventures, tips and food commentary on her blog and every month in* Vegetarian Living *magazine. Caitlin has lived in London on and off since 2008, but her dog Benito is a recent transplant from Barcelona, having moved to London in 2017.*

VEGAN FESTIVALS

New to veganism, or an old hand looking for new products? Check out these fabulous events.

Vegan Life Live

Huge weekend event early in the year at Alexandra Palace at the top of north London. In 2020 it's on 14-15 March.

veganlifelive.com

London Vegfest

Britain's biggest vegan show. A whole weekend every autumn at Olympia, with over 300 stalls. 20 rooms of free talks and entertainment. And a new event for 1-2 February 2020 at Olympia called Plant Powered Expo.

london.vegfest.co.uk

Animal Aid Christmas Festival

The first or second Sunday of December. Vegetarian Guides has a stall there.

animalaid.org.uk/events

Vevolution

One day weekend event a few times a year with keynote talks by leading vegan creators, thinkers and entrepreneurs who are shaping the future in London and beyond. Food and stalls. Excellent for new vegans and the vegan-curious.

vevoloution.co

Vegan Nights

Huge Thursday evening party several times a year in Brick Lane, East London, featuring around 40 food stalls and bars, DJs and hundreds of vegans and their mates dancing and partying their butts off indoors and out. In summer they also do Vegan Days at the weekend.

vegannights.uk

Vegan Campout

An absolute bargain of a holiday with thousands of vegans camping for a long weekend in August every year, featuring famous vegan speakers, workshops, catering and loads of fun and new friends.

vegancampout.co.uk

Calendar of vegan events

Covers the whole world, so seach on "London, UK"

vegevents.com

Animal Aid's UK events calendar

animalaid.org.uk/events

GOING VEGAN

These national organisations provide free information and support for new vegans and those catering for them.

They also get the truth about animal foods into mass media, responding to stories, informing the public about the real living conditions of sol-called farm animals, and explaining vegan alternatives.

Some offer fabulous merchandise such as books and clothing. They all welcome donations to enable them to continue their work.

Animal Aid

All animal issues. Particularly good for young people.

animalaid.org.uk
govegan.org.uk

Go Vegan World

goveganworld.com

PETA

People for the Ethical Treatment of Animals. All animal issues, worldwide.

peta.org.uk

Plant Based News

plantbasednews.org

ProVeg UK

Their mission is to globally reduce animal consumption by 50% by 2040 by motivating people to live a more plant-based lifestyle.

proveg.com/uk

Veganuary

Vegan starter kit, try it for a month. It's not just for January New Year resolutions.

veganuary.com

For what's vegan in restaurants and cafe chains, whose menus are constantly improving, check out this fantastic guide

veganuary.com/eating-out

The Vegan Society

Promoting veganism since 1944 when their founder Donald Watson invented the word. The Vegan Society trademark helps you be confident of vegan products from non-vegan manufacturers like Heinz, and that cosmetics are not tested on animals *and* contain no animal ingredients.

vegansociety.com

Viva!

Originally Vegetarians International Voice for Animals, they are in fact fully vegan. Campaigning for all food animals. The experts at helping teenagers and younger children who've decided to go vegan, and their parents.

viva.org.;uk

HEALTH PRACTITIONERS

Plant Based Health Professionals

In 2017 London haematologist Shireen Kassam M.D., PhD founded Plant-Based Health Professionals UK to promote plant-based nutrition and lifestyle interventions for prevention and treatment of chronic disease, optimal health and well-being, to both health professionals and the general public.

The website includes a directory of UK vegan doctors, dietitians, nutritionists and allied health professionals.

In November 2019 PBHP, together with the University of Winchester, launched the first university-based course on plant-based nutrition in the UK. This is a fully online, 6-week distance learning course.

plantbasedhealthprofessionals.com

Reverse Diabetes & Heart Disease

Free and low-cost cooking classes in Camden on Monday evenings taught by London chef Farrah Rainfly, who reversed her own diabetes type 2 and other serious health issues by changing to a healthy vegan lifestyle following the vegan doctor-led Food For Life programme of PCRM, the Physicians Committee for Responsible Medicine. She is now a certified Foods For Life instructor.

lifeafterhummus.com

Hypnotherapy

Brian Jacobs, clinical hypnotherapist and trainer. Smoking cessation, weight loss, stress mamagement, anxiety and phobias, motivation and confidence.

hypnoticsolutions.co.uk

Nutritional Therapists

Theresa Webb

kitchenbuddies.eu

Yvonne Bishop-Weston

foodsforlife.co.uk

Psychotherapy

Gian Montagna

gianmontagna.net

Silvia Milton

silviamilton.com

Read and Watch All About It

nutritionfacts.org

pcrm.org

What the Health on Netflix

The Game Changers on Netflix

Forks Over Knives on Netflix

TIPS

Nutritional Therapy with Theresa

Theresa Webb Nutritional Therapist BA. Dip. Nut

Treatment for following conditions:

- Digestive disorders: IBS, Colitis, Candida, Thrush
- Skin: Eczema
- Fertility (male and female)
- Pre and post-natal nutrition
- Mental: Concentration and focus, depression,
- Fatigue
- Cardiovascular: High blood pressure
- Urinary: Cystitis
- [Endocrine] Hormonal balance: PMT
- Female health: menstrual cycles, fibroids, hyperthyroidism, hypothyroidism
- Muscular aches
- Joint discomfort
- Kidney Stones
- Weight Control, weight regulation, weight loss and gain
- Recommendations for Cancer Support

Theresa's mission is to make better physical and mental health attainable to anyone, no matter what their original reasons for seeking support, or their budget. This takes place through a Naturopathic Medicine approach: dietary and lifestyle changes, improving fitness and in certain circumstances, decreasing medication (through GP referral only).

Private home visits and consultations

Rates: 1.5-2 hr Consultation £70.00. 1 hr Follow up sessions £35.00.

Theresa is also the Founder of **Kitchen Buddy** which provides ethical small function catering, culinary workshops and menu development and consultancy. Nutrition and Eating well programme with a fun, hands-on approach to making fast food with a difference. Theresa is passionate about vegan health, with a focus on raw living foods, wheat and gluten-free, no-added sugar ingredients.

Outlets: London's Borough Market

Practical Tuition: Treatment of disorders and conditions through KB classes and workshops aimed at individuals and groups . Offers private home visits.

Theresa is [also] the founder, workshop leader and Catering and Consultancy Manager at Kitchen Buddy.

www.kitchenbuddies.eu

LOCAL GROUPS

London Vegan Meetup

Almost 10,000 members and growing. Lots of events every month including restaurant meals, Geekstravaganza board games all day in a restaurant or pub, See You Last Tuesday (C.U.L.T.) at Tibits restaurant in Mayfair (Central London), Vegan Book Club at Tibits Mayfair, Brixton Vegan Walkabout on a Saturday afternoon, London Vegan Drinks at Karamel vegan pub and restaurant in Wood Green on the first Saturday evening of the month, Second Sunday of the month lunch at Karamel, baking group, or organise your own event. Some of these free events attract over 100 people, so you're sure to make new friends.

> www.meetup.com/londonvegan
> Facebook London Vegan Meetup

London Vegans

Last Wednesday evening of every month except December in Bloomsbury, with a guest speaker, a book stall, and hot food from Shambhu's. See the end of the Bloomsbury chapter in Central London.

> www.londonvegans.org.uk

There are also lots of local London groups like Vegans of East London, try searching on Facebook.

Vegan Events Calendar

This covers the whole world and is very useful if you search on "London, UK."

> www.vegevents.co.uk

Vegan Pet Food

not so fishy - by vegan vet Prof Andrew Knight

A fearless predator of the oceans?

Imagine drifting along in a turquoise sea, lulled by waves gently lapping at the white sands of the exotic location your boss has finally flown you to, in humble appreciation of your years of skilled and valued service. The sun is warm, the sky blue, and the breeze gently flutters the palm leaves shading the cocktail by your deckchair. All is as it should be.

Suddenly, your peace is shattered by an almighty splash. A furry, ginger blur zooms past you, frothy bubbles rising from its wake. Squinting against the bright light, you are just able to make out a pair of soggy ear tips and a keenly quivering tail, rapidly receding into the blue. "Aha," you declare, "it's just a local house-cat, seeking to fulfil the natural feline diet of fish!"

You settle back to cast your gaze once more into the infinite depths of the azure sky and reflect that you know a thing or two about cats. The feline predilection for fish is well established, particularly tuna. Soon after rising each day, you know that coastal cats naturally swim 10 to 20 miles out into the ocean to hunt bluefin tuna weighing up to ¾ of a ton, which they engage in underwater battles to the death. You know

they garnish their meals with smaller species such as salmon, prawns and whitebait. Thankfully, attacks on sunburnt floating primates have not yet been recorded.

'Ridiculous!' did I hear you scoff? Think again! Millions of cat and dog guardians worldwide consider it entirely natural to feed their companions canned fish and prawns, body parts from cows, sheep, pigs, turkeys, ducks, chickens, and milk. Perhaps you might even be one of them. Yet contrary to sea and sun-induced hallucinations, cats in their natural environments hunt and kill a variety of small mammals, birds and large insects. They have not yet been recorded pursuing deep sea tuna, nor terrorizing herds of cows, sheep or pigs.

Meat-based pet food

Despite the biological evidence, millions of people cling to the belief that it is somehow natural to feed their feline or canine companions commercial diets comprised of assorted body parts from a variety of animals they would never naturally eat. To these are added abattoir products condemned as unfit for human consumption, such as '4-D' meat (from animals that are disabled, diseased, dying or dead on arrival at the abattoir), cleverly disguised using names like 'meat derivatives' or 'by-products.'

Brands from countries such as the US also contain rendered dog and cat carcasses sourced from animal shelters. Similarly, toxic flea collars are not always removed. Unsurprisingly, a 1998 US Food and Drug Administration study detected the euthanizing solution sodium pentobarbital, which is specifically designed to kill dogs, cats and other animals, in 43 randomly-selected varieties of dry dog food.

To enhance palatability, dry food is sprayed with a combination of refined animal fat, lard, used restaurant grease and other oils considered too rancid or inedible for human consumption, containing high levels of unhealthy free radicals and trans fatty acids. These oils provide the distinctive smell that wafts from a newly-opened packet of kibble.

Additional hazards include bacterial, protozoal, fungal, viral and prion contaminants, along with their assorted endotoxins and mycotoxins; hormone and antibiotic residues, particularly in brands from countries such as the US, where more of these chemicals are administered to livestock; and potentially dangerous preservatives, some of which have been banned in various countries.

Vegan diets: a healthy alternative

Properly formulated vegan diets can provide a healthy alternative for both cats and dogs, eliminating the numerous hazards inherent to meat-based pet food. They supply all required nutrients using only vegetable, mineral and synthetic sources. Each species requires particular dietary nutrients, after all, rather than specific ingredients.

A growing number of manufacturers now supply vegan companion animal diets, both complete diets and dietary supplements. The former offer convenience, while the latter provide a cheaper alternative for those wishing to add nutritional supplements to home-made diets. Recipes are available in books such as *Vegetarian Cats & Dogs* (Peden, 1999) and *Obligate Carnivore* (Gillen, 2003), and from suppliers.

But is it healthy?

In 2006 the first study of the health of a population of long-term vegetarian cats (most, in fact, were vegan), was published in the *Journal of the American Veterinary Medical Association,* one of the world's leading veterinary journals. Most were clinically healthy, barring minor deficiencies in three cats who were fed partly on table scraps. Similarly, a 1994 study of a population of vegan and vegetarian dogs found the vast majority to be in good to excellent health, particularly lifetime vegans or vegetarians. Based on numerous additional reported cases, nutritionally-sound vegan or vegetarian companion animal diets may be associated with the following health benefits: increased overall health and vitality, decreased incidences of cancer, infections, hypothyroidism (an important hormonal disease), ectoparasites (fleas, ticks, lice and mites), improved coat condition, allergy control, weight control, arthritis regression, diabetes regression and cataract resolution.

Health issues

Correct use of a complete and balanced nutritional supplement or complete diet is essential to prevent the nutritional diseases that will otherwise eventually occur, if certain dietary nutrients are deficient.

Changing to a vegan diet may result in urinary alkalinisation, which can increase the risk of urinary stones and blockages, especially in male cats. These can be life-threatening. Hence, regular monitoring of the urine acidity of both sexes of cats and dogs is essential, weekly during any dietary transition, and monthly after stabilisation.

Urine can be collected from dogs using containers such as foil baking trays, and from cats using non-absorbent plastic cat litter available from veterinarians. pH (acidity) test strips are also available from veterinarians, although pH meters provide the most accurate results. The pH of cat and dog urine is normally 6.0 – 7.5, where 7.0 is neutral, and lower numbers indicate acidity. A variety of dietary additives listed at www.VegePets.info can correct alkalinisation, should it occur.

Conclusions

Perhaps one day you'll be the first to spot a house-cat chasing tuna whilst floating along on that tropical island vacation your boss surely owes you. Perhaps you'll be the first to acquire hard evidence that it's natural for cats and dogs to eat fish, or any of the other incongruous and potentially hazardous ingredients in meat-based pet foods. Until then, however, you might want to consider a nutritionally-sound vegan alternative. This would maximise the chances of good health and longevity for not only your cat or dog, but also, of course, our frequently mistreated, so-called 'food' animals! Tips on transitioning to vegan diets and a comprehensive list of brands and suppliers are available at www.VegePets.info.

Originally published in Lifescape magazine

Illustrations © Copyright Marc Vyvyan-Jones

Prof Andrew Knight is a European Veterinary Specialist in Welfare Science, Ethics & Law. He is Professor of Animal Welfare and Ethics, and Founding Director of Winchester University's Centre for Animal Welfare.

He authors the informational site **www.VegePets.info**

SHOES AND CLOTHING

Why vegan shoes?

It's horrifying to realise that we are still wearing animals on our feet as shoes and around our waists as belts. Whilst few today wear fur, it can come as a shock to realise that leather is just fur with the hair scraped off. The skin is a large part of the value of an animal, and without it the meat industry would not be viable. For these reasons, vegans at some point stop buying leather, though many continue to wear items they already have until they wear out, or give them to charity shops to avoid another person buying new ones.

What's the alternative?

Materials such as lorica are as good as or better than. They breathe like leather, letting perspiration out, but don't let water in - great if you step in a deep puddle.

Where to buy

Many vegans get shoes and boots mail order from specialist manufacturers, catalogues and websites. Such companies are becoming common in Britain, USA, Germany and Italy, and normally will ship internationally. They also sell belts, jackets, bags, wallets and T-shirts. There are also a few dedicated leather-free shoe shops set up by vegan entrepreneurs to provide an ethical alternative to high street shops, with the same personal service and opportunity to try things on. London vegans can visit **The Third Estate** in Brecknock Road, North London, and **Vegetarian Shoes** in Brighton. Combine a shoe shopping expedition with a trip to veggie cafes, and remember to check first they aren't closed that day if making a special trip. Vegan shoe companies also run stalls at vegan festivals.

You can find vegan sandals made by international clothing brands in pretty much every outdoors gear shop. Crocs make waterproof clogs in a huge range of colours. Recently some of the biggest high street chain stores such as Marks & Spencer have launched their own ranges of vegan shoes, bags and accessories.

Not just leather

We presumably don't need to explain what's wrong with fur, or leather which is just cow fur with the hairs scraped off, or suede which is pig fur with the hairs scraped off. Vegans avoid buying wool, which is the fur of sheep, because it is wrong to think that the sheep don't mind having it removed. Shearing is a violent process, in which the timid sheep are usually left with cuts and bruises. A lot of wool comes from Australia, a hot country where many sheep die from dehydration and heat exhaustion. Like dairy cows, sheep are slaughtered at a relatively young age. Wool and mutton, leather and beef, they're all the same, bloody, animal slave industry.

It's not a case of giving up things, but replacing them with better, kinder alternatives. It's a lot easier than you might think. You can give your animal skins to a charity shop, if you don't want to throw them away. If you can't afford to buy replacements, wear them until they fall apart and then buy something kinder next time. And you avoid embarrassment when cocky meat-eaters accuse you of hypocrisy.

P.S. VEGAN LONDON LOVES...

Happy Dogs & Cats

Vicky Alhadeff helps you solve animal behaviour problems and training needs.

happydogsandcats.co.uk

Jeannie's Animal Kingdom

London based vegan artist and animal rights activist Jeannie Ford can paint a beautiful portrait of your companion animal. Makes a fantastic present. Check out her Facebook page for examples of her work.

facebook.com/
JEANNIESANIMALKINGDOM

London Savate

Former world savate kickboxing champion James Southwood is your vegan sensei.

londonsavate.co.uk

Vegetarian for Life

The advocacy charity for older vegetarians and vegans. They can help with nutritional advice, their catering guide, Code of Good Practice, UK list of care homes and caterers following the Code, recipe service.

vegetarianforlife.org.uk

Vegan Caterers

giancarloroncato.co.uk
facebook.com/pg/PomoBasilico
shambhus.co.uk

And many restaurants and cafes in this book will cater your event.

Vegan Jobs

veganjobs.com/uk
Facebook Vegan Chefs London

London Vegan Bloggers

Clare Every posts mouthwatering photos of the food at new vegan openings.

thelittlelondonvegan.com

Sean O'Callaghan is the unstoppable man who takes London veganism where it has never gone before. Founded London Vegan Potluck, London's first vegan street market and UK Vegan Beer Fest.

fatgayvegan.com

Caitlin Galer-Unti, vegan travel writer.

theveganword.com

King Cook Daily, chef extraordinaire.

instagram.com/kingcookdaily

Miranda Larbi, championing vegans, BME, women and Meghan Markle in Metro.

twitter.com/mirandalarbi

Updates to this book

See new openings at

Facebook Vegetarian London